A HANDBOOK TO
Literature

A HANDBOOK TO
Literature

by C. Hugh Holman

Based on the Original by

William Flint Thrall

and

Addison Hibbard

THIRD EDITION

The Odyssey Press
A Division of
The Bobbs-Merrill Company, Inc., Publishers
Indianapolis · New York

PREFACE

For the second time I have had the privilege of preparing a new edition of *A Handbook to Literature,* which the late Professor William Flint Thrall and the late Dean Addison Hibbard first published in 1936. I have tried to be faithful to the idea of that original volume and to do for this greatly changed world of scholarship and criticism what I believe these two scholars would do if they were living to address themselves to the present-day reader and student. While the Third Edition is, I hope, a work thoroughly in harmony with the intentions of Professor Thrall and Dean Hibbard, it is a book quite different in several respects from the original. It contains no single article unchanged from the 1936 edition; it is geared to the present-day literary student, who is much more critical than historical in his interests; and it is greatly expanded in size. The 1936 edition contained 750 entries, only a few of which have been completely dropped in the 1960 edition or in this one. The Revised and Enlarged Edition of 1960 contained over 1025 entries. This Third Edition contains over 1360 entries. The more than 600 articles which I have added to the original *Handbook* reflect the growing sophistication and professionalism in the study of literature, a growth that has resulted in a host of new terms—or revived old ones—now being in regular critical usage. They reflect, too, a broadening audience for the *Handbook,* one different in some respects from the one made up largely of literary historians to whom the original edition was addressed.

In making this revision, I found still to be true what I said in the Preface to the 1960 edition: " . . . that I was working with a basic plan and a fundamental structure so firmly and solidly made that their adaptation to the demands of literary students in our time was a relatively simple task." Yet I feel that there is so much of the present edition that represents my own judgments and my own approaches that it is no longer fair to the eminent scholars who did the original work to attribute to them without qualification material as different as this edition is from the 1936 edition. Hence the change of the title page, a change through which I assume responsibility for the judgments on which this edition rests, while recognizing the fact that *A Handbook to Literature* in its Third Edition is still an

Preface

adaptation and enlargement of the work of Professor Thrall and Dean Hibbard.

I have received aid from many sources. Teachers using the *Handbook* have noted omissions and have generously communicated them to the publishers and to me; many of these omissions have been remedied, but not all, since the author's ideal for the book is not always the same as that of the individual user. Far too many people have helped with constructive suggestions for me to acknowledge them here. But the ultimate decision to include or exclude a topic has been mine, as all errors of fact and judgment are mine.

My debts are many and beyond my ability to recall. When I think on my sources I am reminded of Washington Irving's statement: "My brain is filled, therefore, with all kinds of odds and ends. In travelling, these heterogeneous matters have become shaken up in my mind, as the articles are apt to be in an ill-packed travelling trunk; so that when I attempt to draw forth a fact, I cannot determine whether I have read, heard, or dreamt it." And certainly Marcel Proust spoke truly when he called a book "a great cemetery in which, for the most part, the names upon the tombs are effaced."

Into the making of such a work as this, all one's study, reading, and conversations go, but I would in this place single out certain groups to whom I am especially indebted. To my own teachers, both undergraduate and graduate, I owe much for what is in this book. To my students at the University of North Carolina this edition owes perhaps as much as it owes to any single source, for over the years they have shown me what they needed and their critical intelligence has shaped and sharpened my efforts to satisfy those needs. To my colleagues on the English faculty of the University my debts are great. In the immediate preparation of this Third Edition, I have been particularly aided by Professor J. O. Bailey.

Mrs. Frances W. Hellweg, through her faith in the *Handbook*, her continued support of it and of me in my work on it, has been both an inspiring and indispensable element in the book's success. Mr. Ernest Strauss brought to the editing of the manuscript his considerable knowledge of literature, his thorough knowledge of publishing, his enthusiasm for the book, and a persistent care and informed attention that almost defies belief. Never was an author more fortunate in his editor.

For the assistance, encouragement, and patience of my wife in this, as in all things, only my debt exceeds my gratitude.

C. Hugh Holman

CONTENTS

TO THE USER
OF THIS HANDBOOK

In the Handbook proper an attempt is made to include in alphabetical order comparatively brief explanations of the words and phrases peculiar to the study of English and American literature and which a reader or a student may wish to have defined, explained, or illustrated. The listings are not exhaustive or the comments complete; those terms which may cause the reader or the student difficulty are listed, and about them the basic things which the student or reader of writings in English may need to know are given.

A single alphabetical listing is made, with cross references at the proper places in the listing. Whenever it has been possible in the practical limits of the book, the essential information on a given term appears under that term in its alphabetical place in the Handbook. In the body of an article, a term used in a sense which is defined in its proper place in the handbook is printed in SMALL CAPITAL LETTERS; the term being defined and sometimes its synonyms are printed in *italic letters*. If other articles in the Handbook will enrich the student's understanding of a particular entry, the statement "See AN APPROPRIATE ARTICLE" is made at the end of the entry. For example, the entry on **Complication** uses the terms PLOT, RESOLUTION, DRAMATIC STRUCTURE, RISING ACTION, ACT, and TRAGEDY, all of which are defined in the Handbook; therefore, each of them appears in SMALL CAPITAL LETTERS, a fact indicating that entries on them may be consulted if one of them is not clear to the user of the Handbook. On the other hand, the entry concludes with the statement, "See DRAMATIC STRUCTURE, ACT," which means that these entries contain supplementary material which will enrich the user's understanding of *complication*. The word *complication* is itself italicized since it is the term being defined.

A HANDBOOK TO
Literature

HANDBOOK TO
Literature

A

Abbey Theatre: The name generally associated with the DRAMA of THE IRISH LITERARY REVIVAL. The company was an outgrowth of an earlier group, the Irish Literary Theatre, founded in 1899, which became the Irish National Theatre Society in 1902. In 1904, on a subsidy from Mrs. A. E. F. Horniman, the company moved to the Abbey Theatre in Dublin, from which it took its name. It continued, producing plays of a markedly national emphasis, until the theater burned in 1951. W. B. Yeats was director of the *Abbey Theatre* until his death in 1939. Among the major playwrights of the company were Yeats, Lady Gregory, J. M. Synge, Sean O'Casey, James Stevens, and Lord Dunsany. See CELTIC RENAISSANCE.

Abecedarius: An ACROSTIC the initial letters of whose successive lines form the alphabet. Strictly speaking, each word in a line should begin with the same letter, although this difficult task is seldom attempted. See ACROSTIC.

Abridgment: A shortened version of a work, but one which attempts to present the essential elements of the longer work. See ABSTRACT, EPITOME, SYNOPSIS, PRÉCIS.

Abstract: A severe ABRIDGMENT which makes a brief summary of the principal ideas or arguments advanced in a much longer work. *Abstracts* of scholarly articles and dissertations are widely produced today.

Abstract Poetry: A term used by Dame Edith Sitwell to describe poetry analogous in its use of sounds to abstract painting in its use of colors and shapes. In abstract painting the meaning results from the arrangement of colors and shapes without the representation of objects; in *abstract poetry*, words are chosen not for their customary

3

meanings but for the effect produced by tonal qualities, RHYMES, and RHYTHMS. See ABSTRACT TERMS.

Abstract Terms: Terms which represent ideas or generalities as opposed to CONCRETE TERMS, which represent specific objects or entities. *Abstract terms* describes a quality related to but not always the same as that described by GENERAL TERMS, in that *abstract* implies the formulation of an idea by the process of abstraction, in which the mind selects characteristics common to the members of a group and builds a conception which describes not one but all things of that same kind or marked by that same quality, whereas GENERAL broadly means generic. For example, "beauty" is an *abstract term,* "girl," a GENERAL TERM, and "Helen of Troy" a concrete, specific term. Abstract words may be described as words which do not have observable referents to which one may compare their meanings; note, for example, the special use of the term in ABSTRACT POETRY, where this meaning is intended. *Abstract terms* tend to describe ideas, concepts, attitudes, attributes, qualities isolated from their embodiment in a specific object. Their appeal is usually nonsensory. Although they sometimes carry a heavy freight of undefined emotion—for example, "honor," "peace," "patriotism" (see CONNOTATION)—they are more usually lacking in the heightened emotional response evoked by CONCRETE TERMS. *Abstract terms* are particularly the language of philosophy and science; whereas the language of literature tends more to that which can express its meanings through IMAGE and METAPHOR. See CONCRETE TERMS.

Absurd, Theater of the: A kind of DRAMA that presents a view of the absurdity of the human condition by the abandoning of usual or rational devices and the use of nonrealistic form. It expounds no thesis or ideology and views its task as essentially metaphysical. Conceived in perplexity and spiritual anguish, the *theater of the absurd* portrays not a series of connected incidents telling a story but a pattern of images presenting man as a bewildered being in an incomprehensible universe. The first true example of the *theater of the absurd* was Eugène Ionesco's *The Bald Soprano* (1950). The most widely acclaimed play of the school is Samuel Beckett's *Waiting for Godot* (1953). Other playwrights in the school, which flourished in Europe and America in the 1950's and 1960's, include Jean Genet, Arthur Adamov, Edward Albee, Arthur Kopit, and Harold Pinter.

Academic Drama: Plays written and performed in schools and colleges in the ELIZABETHAN AGE. See SCHOOL PLAYS.

Academies: Associations of literary, artistic, or scientific men brought together for the advancement of culture and learning within their special fields of interests. The term is derived from "the olive grove of Academe" where Plato taught at Athens. One general purpose of the literary academies has been, to quote the expressed purpose of *l'Académie française* (originated *ca.*1629), "to labor with all care and diligence to give certain rules to our language and to render it pure, eloquent, and capable of treating the arts and sciences." A secondary objective has often been that of immortalizing great writers, though the success with which great writers have been recognized by such organizations is a moot point. In addition to the French Academy and the Royal Society of London for Improving Natural Knowledge, the following ought to be cited: The Royal Academy of Arts founded in 1768 (England); the *Real Academia Española* founded in 1713 (Spain); and the AMERICAN ACADEMY OF ARTS AND LETTERS founded in 1904. More like the original academy of Plato was the famous "Platonic Academy" led by Marsilio Ficino, at Florence, Italy, in the late fifteenth century, which disseminated the doctrines of Neo-Platonism.

Acatalectic: Metrically complete; applied to a line that carries out fully the basic metrical pattern of the poem. See CATALEXIS.

Accent: In traditional English METRICS, the emphasis given a syllable in pronunciation. Perhaps no aspect of PROSODY has been the subject of greater uncertainty than that dealing with the nature of *accent;* it is considered to be a matter of force, of timbre, of duration, of loudness, of pitch, and of various combinations of these. In common usage, however, it is used to describe some aspect of emphasis, as opposed to duration or QUANTITY. The distinction is sometimes made between *accent* as the normal emphasis upon a syllable and STRESS as the emphasis upon a word required by the METER.

In VERSIFICATION *accent* usually implies contrast; that is, a patterned succession of opposites, in this case, accented and unaccented syllables. In traditional terminology ICTUS is the name applied to the STRESS itself, ARSIS the name applied to the stressed syllable, and THESIS the name applied to the unstressed syllable. It should be noted, however, that the Greek usage, predating this Latin usage, applied THESIS to the stressed and ARSIS to the unstressed syllables.

There are three basic types of *accent* in English: WORD ACCENT, or the normal placement of STRESS upon the syllables of a word; RHETORICAL ACCENT, in which the placement of STRESS is determined by the meaning of the sentence; and METRICAL ACCENT, in which the placement of STRESS is determined by the metrical pattern of the line. If the METRICAL ACCENT does violence to the WORD ACCENT the resulting alteration in pronunciation is called WRENCHED ACCENT, a phenomenon common in the folk BALLAD. See QUANTITY, METRICS, SCANSION, STRESS.

Accentual-Syllabic Verse: VERSE that depends both on the number of syllables to the line and on the pattern of accented and unaccented syllables in establishing its RHYTHM. The basic METERS in English POETRY are *accentual-syllabic*. See METER, FOOT.

Accismus: A form of IRONY, a pretended refusal that is insincere or hypocritical. Caesar's refusal of the crown, as it is reported by Casca in Shakespeare's *Julius Caesar* (Act I, Scene ii), is an example of *accismus,* as is Richard's disavowal of his kingly qualities in Shakespeare's *Richard III* (Act III, Scene vii).

Acrostic: A composition, usually verse though sometimes prose, arranged in such a way that it spells names or phrases or sentences when certain letters are selected according to an orderly sequence. It was used by early Greek and Latin writers as well as by the monks of the Middle Ages. Though creditable verse has appeared in this form, *acrostics* are likely to be tricks of versifying. An example of a *true acrostic-telestich* (see below) presented through a RIDDLE follows: 1. By Apollo was my first made. 2. A shoemaker's tool. 3. An Italian patriot. 4. A tropical fruit. Answer: *Lamb* and *Elia* as shown in the wording:

1.	L	yr	E
2.	A	w	L
3.	M	azzin	I
4.	B	anan	A

An *acrostic* in which the initial letters form the word is called a *true acrostic;* one in which the final letters form the word is called a TELESTICH; one in which the middle letters form the word is called a MESOSTICH; one in which the first letter of the first line, the second letter of the second line, the third letter of the third line, etc., form the word is called a *cross acrostic*, of which Poe's "A Valentine" is an example. An *acrostic* in which the initial letters form the alphabet is called an ABECEDARIUS. Perhaps the best known of all *acrostics* is the word *cabal*, formed from the first letters of the names of the unpopular ministry of Charles II, composed of Clifford, Ashley, Buckingham, Arlington, and Lauderdale.

Act: A major division of a DRAMA. The major parts of the Greek plays were distinguished by the appearance of the CHORUS, and they generally fell, as Aristotle implies, into five parts. The Latin tragedies of Seneca were divided into five *acts*, and when, in the ELIZABETHAN AGE, English dramatists began using *act* divisions they followed their Roman models, as did other modern European dramatists. In varying degrees the five-*act* structure corresponded to the five main divisions of dramatic action: EXPOSITION, COMPLICATION, CLIMAX, FALLING ACTION, and CATASTROPHE. Freytag wrote of the "*act* of introduction," the "*act* of the ascent," the "*act* of the climax," the "*act* of the descent," and the "*act* of the catastrophe"; but such a correspondence, especially in Elizabethan plays, is by no means always apparent. The five-*act* structure was followed until the late nineteenth century when, under the influence of Ibsen, the fourth and fifth *acts* were combined. In the twentieth century, the standard form for serious drama has been three *acts*, for MUSICAL COMEDY and COMIC OPERA usually two; but great variation is used, with serious plays frequently divided into EPISODES or SCENES, without *act*-division. Late in the nineteenth century a shorter form, the ONE-ACT PLAY, developed. See DRAMATIC STRUCTURE.

Adage: A proverb or wise saying made familiar by long use. Example: "No bees, no honey" (Erasmus, *Adagia*). See PROVERB.

Adaptation: The re-writing of a work from its original form to fit it for another medium; also the new form of such a rewritten work. A novel may be "adapted" for the stage or motion pictures or television; a play may be rewritten as a novel; the new form of such a modification is called an "*adaptation*." The term implies an attempt to retain the characters, actions, and as much as possible of the language and tone of the original, and thus *adaptation* differs significantly from the reworking of a SOURCE.

Adonic Verse: A verse form associated with Greek and Latin PROS-ODY and denoting that METER which consists of a DACTYL and a SPONDEE, as $\_ \cup \cup \mid \_\_$, or TROCHEE, as $\_ \cup \cup \mid \_ \cup$, probably so called after the Adonia, the festival of Adonis.

Aesthetic Distance: A term used by critics to describe the effect produced when an emotion or an experience, whether autobiographical or not, is so objectified by the proper use of FORM that it can be understood as being objectively realized and independent of the immediate personal experience of its maker. The term is also used to describe the reader's awareness that art and reality are separate. In this sense it is sometimes called "psychic distance." It is closely related to Keats' NEGATIVE CAPABILITY and T. S. Eliot's OBJECTIVE CORRELATIVE. See OBJECTIVITY.

Aestheticism: A late nineteenth-century literary movement that rested on the credo of "Art for art's sake." Its roots reached back to the poetry of John Keats and to Théophile Gautier's preface to *Mademoiselle de Maupin* (1836), and it had a close kinship to the reverence for beauty of the Pre-Raphaelites. Its dominant figures were Oscar Wilde, who insisted on the separation of art and morality, and Wilde's master, Walter Pater. The English PARNASSIANS—Ernest Dowson, Lionel Johnson, Andrew Lang, and Edmund Gosse—were a part of the movement but were primarily concerned with questions of form rather than sharp separations of art from moral issues. Tennyson angrily paraphrased "art for art's sake" as meaning:

> The filthiest of all paintings painted well
> Is mightier than the purest painted ill!

Aet., Aetat.: Abbreviations for the Latin phrase *aetatis suae*, of his, her, their age. The term is used to designate the year of a man's life at which an event occurs, a picture is made, or a work composed. A picture of Henry David Thoreau bearing the legend "*Aet. 35*," would be one made during Thoreau's thirty-fifth year, that is, between the ages of 34 and 35.

Affective Fallacy: A term used in contemporary criticism to describe the error of judging a work of art in terms of its results, especially its emotional effect. It was introduced by W. K. Wimsatt, Jr., and M. C. Beardsley (see *The Verbal Icon*, by Wimsatt) to describe the "confusion between the poem and its *result* (what it *is* and what it *does*)." It is a converse error to the INTENTIONAL FALLACY. Notable examples of the *affective fallacy* are Aristotle's CATHARSIS and Longinus' "transport."

Afro-American Literature: Frequently called today BLACK LITERA-TURE, both terms refer to writings by American Negroes. The formal study of such writing, long a neglected area of American literary scholarship, is an increasingly important aspect of the serious study of writing in America. This heightened interest in the work of Americans of African ancestry has come about for two primary reasons: the rapid emergence in the last half century of black people as a significant portion of American culture and the development in the same period of a body of Negro writing of impressive scope and quality.

To all practical purposes, *Afro-American literature* began in the eighteenth century with the poetry of two Negro slaves, Jupiter Hammon and Phillis Wheatley. The first half of the nineteenth century saw further efforts by slave poets, among them George Moses Horton, but it was particularly marked by a flood of auto-biographical records of the slaves' terrible experiences, known as SLAVE NARRATIVES, of which the most famous was that by Frederick Douglass. There was also a flood of polemical pamphlets and fiery sermons by Negroes, and in 1853 William Wells Brown, an escaped slave, published the first novel by an American Negro, *Clotel, or, the President's Daughter*. As the century closed Charles W. Chesnutt began publishing the novels which established him as an important literary figure.

In the twentieth century a host of skillful Negro writers have produced work of high quality in almost every field. There have been poets such as Paul Laurence Dunbar, James Weldon Johnson, Langston Hughes, Arna Bontemps, Countee Cullen, and Gwendolyn Brooks, who was in 1949 the first American Negro to receive the Pulitzer Prize. The century has been particularly rich in Negro novelists, including such writers as W. E. B. DuBois, Walter White, Jean Toomer, Claude McKay, Zora Neale Hurston, Ann Petry, Rich-ard Wright, Ralph Ellison, and James Baldwin. There have been a number of black playwrights, among them Hall Johnson, Wallace Thurman, Langston Hughes, Lorraine Hansberry, Ossie Davis, and LeRoi Jones.

These American Negroes have written with passion and convic-tion of the place they and their race have occupied and endured in a predominantly white society. By so doing they have broadened the range, enriched the sympathy, and deepened the quality of American literary expression. Their contributions, notable most obviously for their power, are major forces changing the earlier American literary monolith of the white middle class.

Age of Johnson in English Literature: The interval between 1750 and 1798 was a transitional age in English literature. The NEO-CLASSICISM which dominated the first half of the century was giving way in many different ways to the impulse toward ROMANTICISM, although the period was still predominantly neo-classical. The NOVEL which had come into being in the decade before 1750 continued to flourish, with sentimental attitudes and GOTHIC horrors becoming a significant part of its content. Little was accomplished in DRAMA except for the creation of "laughing" COMEDY by Sheridan and Goldsmith, in reaction against SENTIMENTAL COMEDY. The chief poets were Burns, Gray, Cowper, Johnson, and Crabbe—a list which indicates how thoroughly the pendulum was swinging away from Pope and Dryden. Yet it was Dr. Samuel Johnson, poet, lexicographer, essayist, novelist, journalist, and neo-classic critic who was the major literary figure, as his friend Boswell's biography of him (1791) was the greatest work of the age, challenged for such an honor, perhaps, only by Gibbon's monumental history, *The Decline and Fall of the Roman Empire* (1776). An interest in the past, particularly in the middle ages, in the primitive, and in the literature of the folk was developing and was feeding with increasing strength the growing tide of ROMANTICISM. See NEO-CLASSIC PERIOD, *Outline of Literary History*.

Age of Reason: A term often applied to the NEO-CLASSIC PERIOD in English literature and sometimes to the REVOLUTIONARY AND EARLY NATIONAL PERIOD IN AMERICAN LITERATURE, because these periods emphasized self-knowledge, self-control, rationalism, discipline, the rule of law, order, and decorum in public and private life and in art. See NEO-CLASSIC PERIOD, REVOLUTIONARY AND EARLY NATIONAL PERIOD IN AMERICAN LITERATURE.

Age of the Romantic Triumph in England, 1798–1832:   Although a major Romantic poet, Robert Burns, had died in 1796, William Blake's *Songs of Innocence* had appeared in 1789, and adumbrations of ROMANTICISM had been apparent in English writing throughout much of the eighteenth century, the publication of *Lyrical Ballads* by Wordsworth and Coleridge in 1798 is often recognized as marking the beginning of a period of more than three decades in which ROMANTICISM triumphed in British letters, a period that is often said to have ended in 1832, with the death of Sir Walter Scott. During these thirty-four years, the poetic careers of Wordsworth, Coleridge, Byron, Shelley, and Keats flowered; Scott created the HISTORICAL NOVEL and made it a force in international literature; Wordsworth and Coleridge articulated a revolutionary theory of Romantic poetry; Jane Austen wrote her NOVELS OF MANNERS; and Lamb, DeQuincey, and Hazlitt raised the PERSONAL ESSAY to a high level of accomplishment. ROMANTICISM did not die with Sir Walter Scott, but the decade of the thirties saw it begin a process of modification as a result of the varied forces of the Victorian world which played upon it. See ROMANTICISM, ROMANTIC PERIOD IN ENGLISH LITERATURE, and *Outline of Literary History*.

Agon: Literally a contest of any kind. In Greek TRAGEDY it was a prolonged dispute, often a formal debate in which the CHORUS divided and took sides with the disputants. In the OLD COMEDY in Greece this debate, called epirrhematic *agon,* involved an elaborate and stylized series of exchanges between the CHORUS and the debaters, and addresses to the audience.

Agrarians: A term applied to a group of Southern American writers who published in Nashville, Tennessee, between 1922 and 1925, *The Fugitive,* a LITTLE MAGAZINE of poetry and some criticism championing agrarian REGIONALISM but attacking "the old high-caste Brahmins of the Old South." Most of its contributors were associated with Vanderbilt University; among them were John Crowe Ransom, Allen Tate, Donald Davidson, Robert Penn Warren, and Merrill Moore. In the 1930's they championed an agrarian economy as opposed to that of industrial capitalism and issued a collective manifesto, *I'll Take My Stand.* They were active in the publication between 1933 and 1937 of *The American Review,* a socioeconomic magazine that also analyzed contemporary literature. They found an effective literary organ in *The Southern Review* (1935–1942), under the editorship of Cleanth Brooks and Robert Penn Warren. In addition to their poetry and novels, the *Agrarians* have been prominent among the founders of the NEW CRITICISM.

Alazon

Alazon: The braggart in Greek COMEDY. He takes many forms: the quack doctor, the religious fanatic, the swaggering soldier, the pedantic scholar—anyone who is pretentious through his sense of self-importance and who is held up to ridicule because of it. From Plautus' *Miles Gloriosus* he enters English literature where he is a STOCK CHARACTER in ELIZABETHAN DRAMA. He has been widely used in other literary forms, particularly the novel. James Fenimore Cooper's Dr. Obed Battius, in *The Prairie,* is a good example of a later mutation of this character. See MILES GLORIOSUS.

Alba: A Provençal lament over the parting of lovers at the break of day, the name coming from *alba* the Provençal word for "dawn." It has no fixed metrical form, but each STANZA usually ends with "*alba.*" The medieval *albas* were inspired in large part by Ovid. With the TROUBADOURS the *albas* grew to a distinct literary form. On occasion they were religious, being addressed to the Virgin. See AUBADE.

Alcaics: Verses written according to the manner of the ODES of Alcaeus, usually a four-STANZA poem, each STANZA composed of four lines, the first two being HENDECASYLLABIC, the third being nine syllables, and the fourth DECASYLLABIC. Since the pattern is a classical one based on quantitative DACTYLS and TROCHEES, exact English *Alcaics* are practically impossible. The most notable English attempt is in Tennyson's "Milton," which begins: "O mighty-mouthed inventor of harmonies."

Alexandrine: A VERSE with six IAMBIC feet (IAMBIC HEXAMETER). The form, that of HEROIC VERSE in France, received its name possibly from the fact that it was much used in Old French romances of the twelfth and thirteenth centuries describing the adventures of Alexander the Great, or possibly from the name of Alexandre Paris, a French poet who used this meter. Its appearance in English has been credited to Wyatt and Surrey. Perhaps the most conspicuous instance of its successful use in English is by Spenser, who, in his SPENSERIAN STANZA, after eight PENTAMETER lines employed a HEXAMETER (*Alexandrine*) in the ninth. Both the line and its occasional bad effect are described in Pope's couplet:

> A needless Alexandrine ends the song,
> That, like a wounded snake, drags its slow length along.

12

Allegory: A form of extended METAPHOR in which objects, persons, and actions in a narrative, either in prose or verse, are equated with meanings that lie outside the narrative itself. Thus it represents one thing in the guise of another—an abstraction in that of a concrete IMAGE. The characters are usually PERSONIFICATIONS of abstract qualities, the action and the setting representative of the relationships among these abstractions. *Allegory* attempts to evoke a dual interest, one in the events, characters, and setting presented, and the other in the ideas they are intended to convey or the significance they bear. The characters, events, and setting may be historical, fictitious, or fabulous; the test is that these materials be so employed that they represent meanings independent of the action in the surface story. Such meaning may be religious, moral, political, personal, or satiric. Thus Spenser's *The Faerie Queene* is on one level a chivalric ROMANCE, but it embodies moral, religious, social, and political meanings. Bunyan's *Pilgrim's Progress* describes the efforts of a Christian to achieve a godly life by triumphing over inner obstacles to his faith, these obstacles being represented by outward objects such as the Slough of Despond and Vanity Fair.

It is important that one distinguish between *allegory* and SYM-BOLISM, which attempts to suggest other levels of meaning without making a structure of ideas a formative influence on the work, as it is in *allegory*.

Among the kinds of *allegory*, in addition to those suggested above, are PARABLE, FABLE, APOLOGUE, EXEMPLUM, and BEAST EPIC. See also ANAGOGE, FOUR SENSES OF INTERPRETATION.

Alliteration: The repetition of initial identical consonant sounds or any vowel sounds in successive or closely associated words or syllables. A good example of consonantal *alliteration* is Coleridge's lines:

> The fair breeze blew, the white foam flew,
> The furrow followed free.

Vowel *alliteration* is shown in the sentence: "Apt alliteration's artful aid is often an occasional ornament in prose." *Alliteration* of sounds within words appears in Tennyson's lines:

> The moan of doves in immemorial elms,
> And murmuring of innumerable bees.

OLD ENGLISH VERSIFICATION rested in large measure on *alliteration*, as did much Middle English poetry. In modern times *alliteration* has usually been a secondary ornament in both verse and prose, although poets as unlike as Whitman, Swinburne, and W. H. Auden have made extensive and skillful use of it. In our time it has become the stock in trade of the sports writer and the advertising copy writer, in whose hands it often produces ludicrous effects.

Alliterative Romance: A METRICAL ROMANCE written in ALLITERA-TIVE VERSE, especially one produced during the revival of interest in alliterative poetry in the fourteenth century, e.g., *William of Palerne* (unrhymed long lines similar to the alliterative verse of the Old English period), *Sir Gawain and the Green Knight* (in stanzas of varying numbers of long lines followed by five short rhymed lines), and the "alliterative" *Morte Arthure.* See MEDIEVAL ROMANCE.

Alliterative Verse: A term used to characterize verse-forms, usually Germanic in origin, in which metrical structure generally is based on repetition of certain initial letters or sounds within the lines. See OLD ENGLISH VERSIFICATION.

Allonym: The name of an actual person other than the author which is signed by the author to a work. The term is also applied to the work so signed. Compare with PSEUDONYM, which is a fictitious name assumed by the author.

Allusion: A figure of speech making casual reference to a famous historical or literary figure or event. Biblical *allusions* are common in English literature, such as Shakespeare's "A Daniel come to judgment," in *The Merchant of Venice.* Complex literary *allusion* is characteristic of much modern poetry; a good example is T. S. Eliot's *The Waste Land* and the author's notes to that poem.

Almanac: In medieval times an *almanac* was a permanent table showing the movements of the heavenly bodies, from which calculations for any year could be made. Later, *almanacs* or calendars for short spans of years and, finally, for single years were prepared. A further step in the evolution of the form came with the inclusion of useful information, especially for farmers. This use of the *almanac* as a storehouse of general information led ultimately to such modern works as the annual *World Almanac,* a compendium of historical and statistical data not limited to the single year. As early as the six-teenth century, forecasts, first of the weather and later of such

Ambiguity

events as plagues and wars, were important features of *almanacs*. The *almanac* figures but slightly in literature. Spenser's *Shepheardes Calender* (1579) takes its title from a French "Kalendar of Shepards" and consists of twelve poems, under the titles of the twelve months, with some attention paid to the seasonal implications. By the latter part of the seventeenth century *almanacs* contained efforts at humor, consisting usually of coarse jokes. This feature was elaborated somewhat later, with some refinements such as MAXIMS and pithy sayings, as in Franklin's *Poor Richard's Almanac* (1732–1758), itself partly inspired by the English comic almanac, *Poor Robin*. In Germany in the eighteenth and nineteenth centuries *almanacs* included printed poetry of a high order. The Davy Crockett *almanacs*, issued in America between 1835 and 1856, recorded many frontier TALL TALES based mainly on oral tradition and helped to preserve a significant aspect of American culture.

Ambages: A form of CIRCUMLOCUTION in which the truth is spoken in a way that tends to deceive or mislead. The RIDDLE:

> Brothers and sisters have I none,
> But this man's father is my father's son,

is an example in which the relationship of "this man" to the speaker (i.e., son to father) is concealed in an accurate statement.

Ambiguity: The expression of an idea in language that gives more than one meaning and leaves uncertainty as to the intended significance of the statement. The chief causes of unintentional *ambiguity* are undue brevity and compression of statement, "cloudy" reference of pronoun, faulty or inverted sequence, and the use of a word with two or more meanings.

However, in literature of the highest order may be found another aspect of *ambiguity* which results from the fact that language functions in art on other levels than that of DENOTATION, where *ambiguity* is a cardinal sin. In literature words demonstrate an astounding capacity for suggesting two or more equally suitable senses in a given context, for conveying a core meaning and accompanying it with overtones of great richness and complexity, and for operating with two or more meanings at the same time. One of the attributes of the finest poets is their ability to tap what I. A. Richards has called the "resourcefulness of language" and to supercharge words with great pressures of meaning. The kind of *ambiguity* which results from this capacity of words to stimulate simultaneously several different streams of thought all of which make sense is a genuine characteristic of the richness and concentration that makes great poetry.

William Empson, in *The Seven Types of Ambiguity,* in 1931 extended the meaning of the term to include these aspects of language. Although there have been those who feel that another word than *ambiguity* should be used for these characteristics of language functioning with artistic complexity (among those suggested have been MULTIPLE MEANINGS and PLURISIGNATION), Empson's "seven types" of linguistic complexity "which adds some nuance to the direct statement of prose" have proved to be effective tools for the examination of literature. These "types of *ambiguity*" are (1) details of language which are effective in several ways at once; (2) alternative meanings that are ultimately resolved into the one meaning of the author; (3) two seemingly unconnected meanings that are given in one word; (4) alternative meanings that act together to clarify a complicated state of mind in the author; (5) a simile that refers imperfectly to two incompatible things and by this "fortunate confusion" shows the author discovering his idea as he writes; (6) a statement that is so contradictory or irrelevant that the reader is made to invent his own interpretation; and (7) a statement so fundamentally contradictory that it reveals a basic division in the author's mind.

Ambivalence: The existence of mutually conflicting feelings or attitudes. The term is often used to describe the contradictory attitudes an author takes toward characters or societies and also to describe a confusion of attitude or response called forth by a work. Although it is sometimes used by contemporary critics as a synonym for AMBIGUITY, it can properly be used only for the sixth and seventh of Empson's types of AMBIGUITY.

American Academy of Arts and Letters: An organization brought into being in 1904 to recognize distinguished accomplishment in literature, art, or music. The American Social Science Association in 1898 realized the need for a society devoted entirely to the interests of letters and the fine arts, and organized the National Institute of Arts and Letters with membership limited to 250. Six years later a smaller society composed of the most distinguished members of the Institute, the American Academy of Arts and Letters, was organized with a membership limited to fifty. Only members of the Institute may be elected to the Academy. The seven men first elected to membership were: William Dean Howells, Augustus Saint-Gaudens, Edmund Clarence Stedman, John LaFarge, Samuel Langhorne Clemens, John Hay, and Edward MacDowell. Annually the National Institute awards its gold medal for distinguished work in literature and the arts; every five years is conferred the William Dean Howells medal for the best American fiction; and annually another gold medal is awarded for good diction on the stage.

American Indian Literature: The writings and oral traditions of the aboriginal tribes of America. See AMERIND LITERATURE.

American Language: A term used to designate certain idioms and forms peculiar to English speech in America. These differences arise in several ways: some forms originate in America independent of English speech ("gerrymander" is an example); some expressions which were once native to England have been brought here and have lived after they had died out in England ("fall" for "autumn"); and certain English forms have taken on modified meanings in America (as we use "store" for "shop"). Besides these matters of vocabulary, H. L. Mencken points out six respects in which American expression differs from English: syntax, intonation, slang, idiom, grammar, and pronunciation.

Although for many years the sensitiveness of Americans made them deny the existence of anything like an *American language,* its existence has been recognized and its nature applauded for over a half century. It is a unique language of American literary art, impressively present in the work of writers like Mark Twain, Ring Lardner, Ernest Hemingway, and J. D. Salinger. Scholars have given it serious attention; it is the subject of two major dictionaries, *A Dictionary of American English on Historical Principles,* edited by Sir William Craigie and J. R. Hulbert, and *A Dictionary of Americanisms,* edited by M. M. Mathews; and a group of scholars, led by Hans Kurath, compiled a mammoth *Linguistic Atlas of the United States.* Significant earlier studies were G. P. Krapp's *The English Language in America* and H. L. Mencken's *The American Language* and its *Supplements.*

American Literature, Periods of: Any division of the literary history of a nation is an arbitrary oversimplification. In the case of America, where the national record long predates the development of a self-sufficient literature, the problem is complicated further by the fact that most divisions into early periods are based upon political and social history and most divisions into later periods upon the dominance of literary types or movements. Almost all historians of *American literature* have made their own systems of period division. In this handbook *American literature* is treated in a chronological pattern set against the dominant English movements in the *Outline of Literary History,* and the characteristics of its own periods are treated in the following articles:

COLONIAL PERIOD IN AMERICAN LITERATURE, 1607–1765
REVOLUTIONARY AND EARLY NATIONAL PERIOD IN AMERICAN
  LITERATURE, 1765–1830
ROMANTIC PERIOD IN AMERICAN LITERATURE, 1830–1865
REALISTIC PERIOD IN AMERICAN LITERATURE, 1865–1900
NATURALISTIC AND SYMBOLISTIC PERIOD IN AMERICAN LITERATURE,
  1900–1930
PERIOD OF CRITICISM AND CONFORMITY IN AMERICAN LITERA-
  TURE, 1930—

If read in this sequence, these articles will give a brief history of American writing by periods.

Amerind Literature: The writing and oral traditions of the Indian tribes of America. The term is a combination of syllables from *American* and *Indian.* Originally transmitted almost entirely by word of mouth, the literature was at first such as could easily be memorized: the rituals of annual festivals, tribal traditions, narrative accounts of gods and heroes. Since much of this literature grew up about the rhythmic accents of the ceremonial drum, it took on a regularity of metric pattern which gave it the quality of poetry; another part, perhaps less associated with ceremonials, was more simply natural in its recounting of events and took the form of prose. A characteristic quality of this Amerind language is its building of many ideas into one term. ("Hither-whiteness-comes-walking" being, according to Mary Austin, the Algonquin parallel for "dawn.") Most of this literature known to us today is confined to a few types: the EPIC, the folk-tale, the DRAMA, ritualistic and ceremonial exercises, and NARRATIVES of adventure. A useful collection is *The Winged Serpent: An Anthology of American Indian Prose and Poetry,* edited by Margot Astrov.

The PORTMANTEAU WORD *Amerind* is today less widely used than the longer term, *American Indian.*

Amphibology (or **Amphiboly**):   A term applied to statements capable of two different meanings, a kind of AMBIGUITY. In literature, *amphibology* is usually intentional when it occurs. The witches' prophecies in *Macbeth* and Fedallah's deceptive assurances to Captain Ahab in *Moby-Dick* are well-known examples.

Amphibrach: A metrical FOOT consisting of three syllables, the first and last unaccented, the second accented.

Example: *ăr ráng mĕnt.*

Amphigory or **Amphigouri:**   Verse that sounds well but contains little or no sense or meaning; either NONSENSE VERSE, like Edward Lear's, or nonsensical PARODY, like Swinburne's self-mockery in "Nephelidia," which begins: "From the depth of the dreamy decline of the dawn through a notable nimbus of nebulous moonshine."

Amphimacher: A metrical FOOT consisting of three syllables, the first and last accented, the second unaccented. Example: *át tĭ túde.*

Amplification: A figure of speech in which bare expressions, likely to be ignored or misunderstood by a hearer or reader because of their bluntness, are emphasized through restatement with additional detail. The device is used in music, oratory, and poetry quite commonly. The chief danger accompanying the use of *amplification* is that prolix writers will so elaborate a statement as to rob it even of its original meaning. Holofernes, in Shakespeare's *Love's Labour's Lost,* affords a perfect example of the evils of over-amplification:

He draweth out the thread of his verbosity finer than the staple of his argument. I abhor such fanatical phantasimes, such insociable and pointdevise companions; such rackers of orthography, as to speak dout, fine, when he should say doubt; det, when he should pronounce debt,— d,e,b,t, not d,e,t; he clepeth a calf, cauf; half, hauf; neighbour *vocatur* nebour; neigh, abbreviated ne. This is abhominable, which he would call abominable,—it insinuateth me of insanie; *anne intelligis, domine?* To make frantic, lunatic.

Ana: Miscellaneous sayings, anecdotes, gossip, and scraps of information about a particular person, place, or event; or a book which

Anachronism

records such sayings and anecdotes. Englishmen in the seventeenth century were much devoted to this type of writing. *The Table Talk of John Selden* (1689) is a typical collection of such curiosities. The term also exists as a suffix, as in Goldsmith*iana,* where it denotes a collection of information about Goldsmith.

Anachronism: False assignment of an event, a person, a scene, language—in fact anything—to a time when that event or thing or person was not in existence. Shakespeare is guilty of sundry *anachronisms* such as his placing cannon in *King John,* a play dealing with a time many years before cannon came into use in England. The *anachronism,* however, is usually a greater sin to the realist than to the romanticist. Humorists sometimes use *anachronisms* as comic devices. Mark Twain's *A Connecticut Yankee in King Arthur's Court* rests on a sustained, satirically humorous *anachronism.*

Anacoluthon: The failure, accidental or deliberate, to complete a sentence according to the structural plan on which it was started. Used accidentally, anacoluthic writing is, of course, a vice; used deliberately for emotional or rhetorical effect it is a recognized FIGURE OF SPEECH, effective especially in oratory. The term is also applied to units of composition larger than the sentence when there is within the unit an obvious incoherency among the parts. Browning is very much given to this sort of construction, as the following stanza from *A Toccata of Galuppi's* shows:

Ay, because the sea's the street there; and 'tis arched by . . . what you call
. . . Shylock's bridge with houses on it, where they kept the carnival:
I was never out of England—it's as if I saw it all.

Anacreontic Poetry: Verse in the mood and manner of the lyrics of the Greek poet Anacreon; that is, poems characterized by an erotic, amatory, or Bacchanalian spirit. The characteristic *Anacreontic* STANZA consists of four lines rhyming *abab,* each line composed of three trochaic feet with one long syllable added at the end of the line: $\_ \cup \mid \_ \cup \mid \_ \cup \mid \_.$ English imitations, of which there have been many, are usually written in TROCHAIC TETRAMETER.

Anacrusis: A term denoting one or more extra unaccented syllables at the beginning of a VERSE before the regular RHYTHM of the line makes its appearance. Literally an upward or back beat. The third VERSE of the following STANZA by Shelley is an example:

What thou art we know not;
What is most like thee?
From rainbow clouds there flow not
Drops so bright to see
As from thy presence showers a rain of melody.

Anadiplosis: A kind of REPETITION in which the last word or phrase of one sentence or line is repeated at the beginning of the next. These lines from Bartholomew Griffin's *Fidessa* illustrate the term:

> For I have loved long, I crave reward
> Reward me not unkindly: think on kindness,
> Kindness becommeth those of high regard
> Regard with clemency a poor man's blindness.

Anagnorisis: In drama, the DISCOVERY OF RECOGNITION that leads to the PERIPETY or reversal.

Anagoge (or **Anagogy**):   In Biblical and allegorical interpretation, the mystical or spiritual meaning of words or passages. For example, when certain passages in Virgil were interpreted in the Middle Ages as foretelling the coming of Christ they were being given anagogical interpretations. It is the highest of the FOUR SENSES OF INTERPRETATION, the others being the literal, the allegorical, and the moral. Thus, Jerusalem is literally a city in Palestine, allegorically the Church, morally the believing soul, and anagogically the heavenly City of God. These levels of meaning are regularly applied to Dante's *Divine Comedy*.

Anagram: A word or phrase made by transposing the letters of another word or phrase, as "cask" is an *anagram* of "sack." *Anagrams* have usually been employed simply as an exercise of one's ingenuity, but writers sometimes use them to conceal proper names or veiled messages. It is said, too, that some of the astronomers of the seventeenth century used *anagrams* to conceal certain of their discoveries until it was convenient to announce their findings. *Anagrams* have been used frequently as a means of coining pseudonyms, as "Calvinus" became "Alcuinus," "Bryan Waller Procter" became "Barry Cornwall, poet," and "Arouet, l.j." (*le jeune*), with *u* being a variant of *v* and *j* a variant of *i*, is said to have given the name "Voltaire" to the world. *Erewhon* (no where) is an instance of an *anagram* as a book title. A variety of the *anagram,* the PALINDROME, is an arrangement of letters which gives the same meaning whether read forward or backward and is illustrated in the remark by which Adam is alleged to have introduced himself to his wife upon her first appearance before him: "Madam, I'm Adam."

Analecta (**Analects**):   Literary gleanings, fragments, or passages from the writings of an author or authors; also the title for a collection of choice extracts, e.g., *Analects of Confucius*.

Analogue: Something that is analogous to or like another given thing. An *analogue* may mean a cognate or word in one language corresponding with one in another, as the English word "mother" is an *analogue* of the Latin word *mater*. In literary history two versions of the same story may be called *analogues,* especially if no direct relationship can be established between the works though a remote one is probable. Thus the story of the pound of flesh in *Gesta Romanorum* may be called an *analogue* of the similar plot in *The Merchant of Venice*.

Analogy: A comparison of two things, alike in certain respects; particularly a method of EXPOSITION by which one unfamiliar object or idea is explained by comparing it with more familiar objects or ideas. In ARGUMENTATION and logic *analogy* is also frequently used to establish contentions, it being argued, for instance, that since A works certain results, B, which is like A in vital respects, will also accomplish the same results. *Analogy,* however, is often a treacherous weapon since few *different* objects or ideas are essentially the *same* to more than a superficial observer or thinker.

Analytical Criticism: A term applied to criticism which views the work of art as an autonomous whole and believes that its meaning, nature, and significance can be discovered by applying rigorous and logical systems of analysis to its several parts and their organization. The work of the NEW CRITICS is often called *analytical criticism.* See NEW CRITICS; CRITICISM, TYPES OF.

Analyzed Rhyme: A complex kind of RHYME that must be analyzed to be fully comprehended. An example would be a QUATRAIN in which the vowel sounds of words in the rhyming position in the first and third lines are the same (ASSONANCE) and the consonant sounds of words in the rhyming position in the second and fourth lines are the same (CONSONANCE). There is no true RHYME in the

Anatomy

STANZA, since no two words contain both ASSONANCE and CONSONANCE.

Anapest: A metrical FOOT in VERSE, consisting of three syllables, with two unaccented syllables followed by an accented one (⌣ ⌣ ⁄). The following lines from Shelley's *The Cloud* are anapestic:

> Like a child from the womb, like a ghost from the tomb,
> I arise and unbuild it again.

Anaphora: One of the devices of REPETITION, in which the same expression (word or words) is repeated at the beginning of two or more lines, clauses, or sentences. It is one of the most obvious of the devices used in the poetry of Walt Whitman.

Anastrophe: Inversion of the usual, normal, or logical order of the parts of a sentence. *Anastrophe* is deliberate rather than accidental and is used to secure RHYTHM or to gain EMPHASIS or EUPHONY.

> Not fierce Othello in so loud a strain
> Roar'd for the handkerchief that caus'd his pain.
> —Pope

Anathema: A formal and solemn denunciation or imprecation, particularly as pronounced by the Greek or Roman Catholic Church against an individual, an institution, or a doctrine. The form conventionally reads: *Si quis dixerit*, etc., *anathema sit*, "If any one should say (so and so) let him be anathema." One of its most notable appearances in English literature is in Sterne's *Tristram Shandy* (Vol. III, Ch. XI, pp. 171–177 in the Odyssey edition).

Anatomy: Used as early as Aristotle in the sense of logical dissection or analysis, this term, which meant "dissection" in a medical sense, came into common use in England late in the sixteenth century in the meaning thus explained by Robert Burton in his *Anatomy of Melancholy* (1621): "What it is, with all the kinds, causes, symptoms, prognostickes, and severall cures of it." There are several pieces in English literature preceding Burton in which the medical sense of *anatomy* is still less evident, such as Thomas Nash's *Anatomy of Absurdity,* and John Lyly's *Euphues, the Anatomy of Wit.* The *anatomies* anticipated to some degree the characteristics of the essay

23

and philosophical and scientific treatises of the seventeenth century. The term is also used by Northrop Frye, in his *Anatomy of Criticism*, to designate the kind of narrative prose work organized around ideas and dealing with intellectual themes and attitudes by piling up masses of erudition around the theme, after the manner of Menippean satire. Sterne's *Tristram Shandy* is an example, as are the whaling chapters in Melville's *Moby-Dick*.

Ancients and Moderns, Quarrel of the: The phrase is used in literary history to designate the complicated controversy which took place in France and England in the late seventeenth and early eighteenth centuries over the relative merits of classical and contemporary thinkers, writers, and artists. Some of the forces which stimulated the dispute were the RENAISSANCE, which produced a reverence for classical writers; the growth of the new science in the seventeenth century; and the interest in the doctrine of progress.

The dispute in France centered about the vigorous advocacy of the moderns by Charles Perrault, Fontenelle, Thomas Corneille, P. Perrault, and others. These moderns were opposed by Boileau, Racine, La Fontaine, La Bruyère, and others. Perrault in *Parallèles des anciens et des modernes* (1688–1697) and Fontenelle in his *Digression sur les anciens et les modernes* (1688) held that in art and poetry the efforts of the moderns showed superior taste and greater polish of form as compared with those of the ancients. Thus the superiority of classical thought and art was vigorously challenged (see HUMANISM, CLASSICISM).

In England, the "battle of the books" began with the publication of Sir William Temple's *An Essay upon the Ancient and Modern Learning* (1690). Temple rejected the doctrine of progress and criticized the Royal Society, upheld the claims of the ancients, and could not see that they were inferior to the moderns in knowledge or genius. Temple was answered in 1694 by William Wotton in *Reflections upon Ancient and Modern Learning*, in which he gave the palm to the moderns in most branches of learning. The scientific as opposed to the literary aspects of the quarrel were particularly stressed in England, the English moderns generally being willing to admit the superiority of the ancients in such fields as poetry, oratory, and art.

An episode arose over the *Letters of Phalaris*, which Temple listed as a praiseworthy ancient work. Charles Boyle presently republished these letters and attacked Dr. Richard Bentley for an alleged slight.

When Wotton published a second edition of his essay (1697), Bentley included in it an appendix which not only criticized Boyle's edition, but presented evidence, later elaborated in his famous *Dissertation* (1699), for believing that the Phalaris letters were spurious. Bentley employed the methods of the new science in the field of classical literature itself, and his study went far toward initiating modern historical scholarship. Jonathan Swift, in the "digressions" of the *Tale of a Tub* (written *ca*.1696) and in his famous *Battle of the Books* (written *ca*.1697, pub. 1704)—the most important literary document produced by the controversy in England —undertook the defense of his patron Temple, though Swift's satire is not altogether one-sided.

Anecdote: A short NARRATIVE detailing particulars of an interesting EPISODE or event. In careful usage the term most frequently refers to a narrated incident in the life of an important person and should lay claim to an element of truth. Though *anecdotes* are often used by writers as the basis for short stories, an *anecdote* definitely differs from a SHORT STORY in that it lacks complicated PLOT and relates a single EPISODE. At one time the term connoted secret and private details of a man's career given forth in the spirit of gossip, though now it is used generally to cover any brief narrative. Anecdotic literature has a long heritage extending from ancient times and comprising books as different as the *Deipnosophistae* of Athenaeus, the *Lives* of Plutarch, the *Anecdotes* of Percy, and the *Anecdota* of Procopius. The term still retains something of its original sense of an unpublished item.

Anglicism: A peculiarity of expression or IDIOM characteristic of the English language and distinguishing it from other languages. The term is also given to foreign expressions when taken over into English and forced to conform to English usage and syntax. Any form of expression peculiar to the English. In the United States it is used also to refer to a word or expression used particularly in England but not in common use in the United States.

Anglo-Catholic Revival: A movement in the second third of the nineteenth century in England, centered primarily at Oxford University. The revival moved from reform of the Established Church to espousal of the Catholic Church. See OXFORD MOVEMENT.

Anglo-French: The French language as it was used in England from 1100–1350. See ANGLO-NORMAN (LANGUAGE).

Anglo-Irish Literature: Literature produced in English by Irish writers, especially those living in Ireland and actuated by a conscious intent to utilize Celtic materials, often employing an English style flavored by Irish idioms, called "Hibernian English" or "Anglo-Irish." See CELTIC RENAISSANCE.

Anglo-Latin: A term applied to the learned literature produced in Latin by Englishmen or others dwelling in England during the MIDDLE ENGLISH PERIOD. It is largely in prose and includes CHRONICLES, serious treatises on theology, philosophy, law, history, and science, though SATIRE (like Walter Map's *De Nugis Curialium*) and LIGHT VERSE (like the GOLIARDIC SONGS) were also written, as well as hymns and prayers and religious plays. See ANGLO-NORMAN PERIOD and MIDDLE ENGLISH PERIOD.

Anglo-Norman (Language): The term *Anglo-Norman* (also ANGLO-FRENCH) is applied to the French language as it was used in England in the period following the Norman Conquest (*ca.*1100–1350) and also to the literature written in *Anglo-Norman*. The relations of France and England were so close during this period that it is difficult to be certain in all cases whether a given writer or work is to be classed as *Anglo-Norman* or merely as French. Although the terms *Anglo-Norman* and ANGLO-FRENCH are commonly used interchangeably, some writers make distinctions between them. Thus ANGLO-FRENCH is sometimes used to designate French that shows the definite influence of English idioms. *Anglo-Norman* is often restricted to the early period of Norman times (1066 and immediately following) and is sometimes used to denote pieces written in England by persons of Norman descent using the Norman dialect of French. A third term *Franco-Norman* is also used in this sense. See ANGLO-NORMAN PERIOD.

Anglo-Norman Period: The period in English literature between 1100 and 1350, so-called because of the dominance of Norman-French culture, art, and language. The period is also often called the Early MIDDLE ENGLISH PERIOD and is frequently dated from the triumph of William the Conqueror at the Battle of Hastings in 1066, although it was early in the twelfth century before the impact of Norman culture was marked on the English or before the Norman conquerors began to think of themslves as inhabitants of the British Isles.

In Europe this was the age of the great crusades and the period of the dominance of French literature. In England, under Henry I, Stephen, and the Plantagenet Kings Henry II, Richard the Lion-Hearted, and John, the conquered Saxon natives and the Norman lords were establishing the working pattern of government that reached its epitomizing statement in the *Magna Charta* of 1215. Throughout the period the characteristics that are usually associated with England were developing. Feudalism was established. Parliament came into being, with a movement toward definite limits on the power of the monarchy. Oxford and Cambridge rose as strong universities. The Old English language, for a period after the Conquest the tongue of conquered slaves, not only survived in the period but blended with the French dialect of the Norman victors. Gradually it emerged as the language of England, a fact that King John's successor, Henry III, recognized when in 1258 he used English as well as French in a proclamation. By 1300 English was becoming again the language of the upper clasɔes and was beginning to displace French in schools and legal pleadings. Henry III was succeeded in 1272 by the first of the three Edwards, who ruled England for over a hundred years (until 1377).

Latin was the language used for learned works, French for courtly literature, and English chiefly for popular works—religious plays, METRICAL ROMANCES, and popular BALLADS. On the continent Dante, the *Chanson de Roland,* and Boccaccio flourished. In England and France the body of legend and artful invention that gave England its national hero, Arthur, was coming into being in French, Latin, and English through the work of writers like Chrétien de Troyes, Wace, Geoffrey of Monmouth, Walter Map, and Layamon. (See ARTHURIAN LEGEND.)

Writings in native English were few. The last entry in the *Anglo-Saxon Chronicles* was made at Petersborough in 1154. About 1170 a long didactic poem in FOURTEENERS, the *Poema Morale,* appeared. Early in the twelfth century English METRICAL ROMANCES using English themes began to appear, the first being *King Horn.* Such ROMANCES flourished throughout the period. The DRAMA made its first major forward leaps in this period. The first recorded MIRACLE PLAY in England, *The Play of St. Catherine,* was performed at Dunstable about 1100. By 1300 the MYSTERY PLAYS were moving outside the churches and into the hands of the town guilds. The establishment of the Feast of Corpus Christi in 1311 led to the great extension of the CYCLIC DRAMAS and to the use of movable stages or PAGEANTS. The Chester CYCLE was composed around 1328.

Native English poetry, both in the older alliterative tradition and in the newer French forms, continued to develop. About 1250 came "The Owl and the Nightingale," the most famous English DÉBAT poem; about the same time lyric verse was getting under way with poems like "The Cuckoo Song"("Sumer is i-cumen in"). About 1300 came the heavily didactic *Cursor Mundi,* and around 1340 the popular *The Pricke of Conscience,* describing the misery of earth and glory of heaven and often ascribed to Richard Rolle of Hampole.

But significant as these works are in the developing strength of native English writing, the period between 1100 and 1350 is predominantly the age of the Latin CHRONICLE and of the glories of French and ANGLO-NORMAN writings. Throughout the period, but particularly in the twelfth century, a veritable cultural renaissance was occurring which expressed itself in England primarily through imaginative literature written in ANGLO-NORMAN. In general it follows the lines of the contemporary literature of France itself and embraces ROMANCES, tales, historical works, political poems and SATIRES, LEGENDS and SAINTS' LIVES, didactic works, LYRICS and DÉBATS, as well as religious DRAMA. The rich culture of the court of Henry II proved a fertile field for these works, and the problem of deciding which shall be classed as ANGLO-NORMAN and which French today defies solution. By 1350, however, the French qualities of grace, harmony, humor, and chivalric idealism together with its many lyric forms, worldly subjects, and syllabic meters had been absorbed into the mainstream of English writing; and in folk BALLAD, in CYCLE PLAY, in both alliterative VERSE and accentual poem, England was ready for a new flowering of native literary art. See *The Outline of Literary History,* under "Anglo-Norman Period."

Anglo-Saxon: A Teutonic tribal group resident in England in post-Roman times. In the fifth and sixth centuries the Angles and Saxons from the neighborhood of what is now known as Schleswig-Holstein, together with the Jutes, invaded and conquered Britain. From the Angles came the name England (Angle-land). After Alfred (ninth century), king of the West Saxons, conquered the Danish-English people of the Anglian territory, the official name for his subjects was, in Latin, *Angli et Saxones* (the English themselves were in-

(*Under the Volcano*), Nathanael West (*The Day of the Locust*), and Henry Miller. The major *anti-realists* at present are Samuel Beckett, Jorge Luis Borges, John Hawkes, and Joseph Heller. They are producing works that dispose of plot and reduce man to a minimal self in vivid states of anxiety, such as Beckett's *Molloy;* vivid vignettes presenting a fully-imagined new order of reality radically different from ours, such as Borges' brief tales; works that distort real experience in the manner of dreams, such as John Hawkes' nightmare NOVELS, *The Cannibal* and *The Lime Twig;* and portrayals of an insane kind of order, such as Joseph Heller's *Catch-22.* See ABSURD, THEATER OF THE, and SURREALISM.

Antispast: In PROSODY a FOOT consisting of four syllables, with the ACCENTS falling on the two middle syllables, or a VERSE pattern in which an IAMBIC FOOT is followed by a TROCHAIC FOOT, as in bĕyǒnd go̍ing.

Antistrophe: One of the three stanzaic forms of the Greek choral ODE, the others being STROPHE and EPODE. It is identical in METER with the STROPHE, which precedes it. As the chorus sang the STROPHE they moved from right to left; while singing the *antistrophe* they retraced these steps exactly, moving back to the original position. In RHETORIC, the term describes the reciprocal conversion of the same words in succeeding phrases or clauses, as, "the master of the servant, the servant of the master." See ODE.

Antithesis: A FIGURE OF SPEECH characterized by strongly contrasting words, clauses, sentences, or ideas. A balancing of one term against another for impressiveness and emphasis. An attractive device when used within reason, antithetical expression with writers who make a mannerism of it becomes a vice. Pope, in the *Rape of the Lock* for example, relies on this figure so frequently that its significance, which lies in the quality of surprise afforded by the sudden contrast, is likely to be lost in the regularity of its recurrence. "Man proposes, God disposes" is an example of *antithesis,* as is the second line of the following characteristic Pope couplet:

> The hungry judges soon the sentence sign,
> *And wretches hang that jury-men may dine.*

True antithetical structure demands that there be not only an op-

position of idea, but that the opposition in different parts be manifested through similar grammatical structure—the noun "wretches"
being opposed by the noun "jury-men" and the verb "hang" by the
verb "dine" in the above example.

Antonomasia: A FIGURE OF SPEECH in which a proper name is substituted for a general class or idea of which it is a representative,
as in "Some mute inglorious Milton here may rest," where "Milton"
is used for "poet." *Antonomasia* also is used to describe the substitution of an EPITHET for a proper name, as in using "The Iron Duke"
to stand for Wellington, or "The Prince of Peace" for Christ.

Aphorism: A concise statement of a principle or precept given in
pointed words. The term was first used by Hippocrates, whose
Aphorisms were tersely worded medical precepts, synthesized from
experience. It was later applied to statements of general principle
briefly given in a variety of practical fields, such as law, politics,
and art. *Aphorism* implies specific authorship and compact, telling
expression. The opening sentence of Hippocrates' *Aphorisms* is a
justly famous example: "Life is short, art is long, opportunity fleeting,
experimenting dangerous, reasoning difficult."

Apocalyptic: A term applied to literature which predicts the ultimate destiny of the world, usually through a kind of SYMBOLISM
that is obscure, strange, or difficult. *Apocalyptic* writing has also
the character of imminent catastrophe, is likely to be grandiose or
unrestrained and wild, and often suggests a terrible final judgment.
The term is taken from *The Apocalypse,* the final book of the New
Testament, commonly called *The Revelation of St. John,* a work
which describes through complex SYMBOLISM the ultimate end of
the world. *Apocalyptic* writing, prophecying the end of the world,
was common in Jewish and Christian writing between 200 B.C. and
A.D. 150. The "prophetic books" of the poet William Blake are
considered *apocalyptic,* as is some of the poetry of William Butler
Yeats. American fiction is frequently said to have an *apocalyptic*
tradition which includes the work of Charles Brockden Brown,
Edgar Allan Poe, Nathaniel Hawthorne, and William Faulkner.

Apocopated Rhyme: RHYME in which the end of one rhyming word
is cut off. A convention frequently used in modern poetry, it was
also a feature of the BALLAD, as in these lines:

Fly around, my pretty little Miss,
Fly around, I say,
Fly around, my pretty little Miss,
You'll drive me almost crazy.

Apocrypha: Writings that have been attributed to authors but have not been generally accepted in the CANON of their works are called *apocryphal*. Thus there are Shakespeare *apocrypha* and Chaucer *apocrypha*. *Apocrypha* commonly means "spurious" or "doubtful," because "apocrypha," which originally meant hidden or secret things, became the term used to denote Biblical books not regarded as inspired, and hence excluded from the sacred CANON. Saint Jerome (A.D. 331–420) is said to be the first writer to apply the term to the uncanonical books now known as the *Apocrypha*. *Apocryphal* books connected with both the Old and the New Testaments circulated in great numbers in the early Middle Ages. Almost all literary types found in the Bible are represented by *apocryphal* compositions. Examples of Old Testament *apocrypha* include: The Book of Enoch (vision), Life of Adam and Eve (legend), The Wisdom of Solomon (wisdom book), The Testament of Abraham (testament), and the Psalter of Solomon (hymns). New Testament types include: Acts of Matthew (apostolic "acts"), Third Epistle to the Corinthians (epistle), Apocalypse of Peter (vision), and Gospel of Peter (gospel). These books abound in miracles, accounts of the boyhood of Jesus, reported wise sayings of sacred character, and martyrdoms. The influence of *apocryphal* literature, blended with authentic Biblical influence, was exerted on such medieval literary types as saints' legends, visions, sermons, and even ROMANCES. Certain books accepted by the medieval church but rejected by Protestants became *apocryphal* in the sixteenth century, such as Ecclesiasticus, Baruch, and Maccabees, though they were often printed in Protestant Bibles as useful for edification but not authoritative in determining doctrine.

Apollonian: A term used, along with DIONYSIAN, by Friedrich Nietzsche, in *The Birth of Tragedy*, to designate contrasting elements in Greek TRAGEDY. Apollo, the god of youth and light, stood for reason, culture, and moral rectitude. Dionysus, the god of wine, stood for the irrational and undisciplined. These contrasting terms connote much the same thing as CLASSICISM and ROMANTICISM, and are very similar to Matthew Arnold's HELLENISM and HEBRAISM.

Apologue

Apologue: A fictitious NARRATIVE about animals or inanimate objects, which, by acting like human beings, reflect the weaknesses and follies of mankind. A more bookish term for FABLE. See FABLE.

Apology: Two special uses of the word may be noted. It often appears in literature, especially in literary titles, in its older sense of "defense," as in Stevenson's *Apology for Idlers* and Sidney's *Apologie for Poetrie*. The Latin form *apologia* is also used in this sense, as in Cardinal Newman's *Apologia pro Vita Sua*. No admission of wrong-doing or expression of regret is involved. *Apology* is also an old spelling for APOLOGUE, a FABLE.

Apophasis: A rhetorical FIGURE in which one makes an assertion while he seems or pretends to suppress or deny it. "Were I not aware of your high reputation for honesty, I should say that I believe you connived at the fraud yourself."

Aposiopesis: The intentional failure to complete a sentence. As a FIGURE OF SPEECH the form is frequently used to convey an impression of extreme exasperation or to imply a threat, as, "If you do that, why, I'll ——." *Aposiopesis* differs from ANACOLUTHON in that the latter completes a sentence in irregular structural arrangement; the former leaves the sentence incomplete.

Apostrophe: A FIGURE OF SPEECH in which someone (usually, but not always absent), some abstract quality, or a nonexistent personage is directly addressed as though present. Characteristic instances of *apostrophe* are found in the invocations to the muses in poetry—

> And chiefly Thou, O Spirit, that dost prefer
> Before all temples the upright heart and pure,
> Instruct me, for Thou know'st;

Or, to quote Milton again:

> Hail holy Light, offspring of Heav'n firstborn!

The form is frequently used in patriotic oratory, the speaker addressing some glorious leader of the past and invoking his aid in the present. Since *apostrophe* is chiefly associated with deep emotional expression, the form is readily adopted by humorists for purposes of PARODY and SATIRE.

Apothegm: A sharply pointed and often startling MAXIM, more particularly centered and practical than an APHORISM, although like it in other respects. A famous example is Johnson's "Patriotism is the last refuge of a scoundrel." See APHORISM.

Apprenticeship Novel: A NOVEL which recounts the youth and young manhood of a sensitive PROTAGONIST who is attempting to learn the nature of the world, discover its meaning and pattern, and acquire a philosophy of life and "the art of living." Goethe's *Wilhelm Meister* is the archetypal *apprenticeship novel;* noted examples in English are Samuel Butler's *The Way of All Flesh,* James Joyce's *A Portrait of the Artist as a Young Man,* Somerset Maugham's *Of Human Bondage,* and Thomas Wolfe's *Look Homeward, Angel.* The *apprenticeship novel* is sometimes called a BILDUNGSROMAN. It is also often called an *Erziehungsroman,* or "education novel." An *apprenticeship novel* that deals with the development of an artist or writer is called a KÜNSTLERROMAN.

A Priori Judgment: Deductive reasoning, based upon an hypothesis or theory rather than experiment or experience. In making *a priori judgments* conclusions are reached by reasoning from assumed principles which are considered to be self-evident. In the philosophy of Kant, for example, the term is applied to anything which is considered as antecedently necessary to make experience in general intelligible. The term, when used in literary CRITICISM, is usually pejorative, implying arbitrary judgments based on preconceived postulates. See AXIOM.

Apron Stage: The *apron* is the portion of a STAGE which extends in front of the PROSCENIUM arch. If all or most of the STAGE is in front of any devices which could give it a frame, the STAGE is called an *apron stage.* The ELIZABETHAN STAGE, which was a raised platform surrounded on three sides by the audience, is the outstanding example in the history of the British theater.

Ara: A lengthy and formal CURSE or IMPRECATION or MALEDICTION. Psalm 109 is a classic example.

Arabesque: A style of decorative design favored by the Moors as a means of giving play to their aesthetic creativity without violating the Mohammedan prohibition against reproducing natural forms. It employs intricate patterns of interlaced lines from stylized flowers, foliage, fruits, and animal outlines in geometrical or calligraphic designs. The term was applied by Edgar Allan Poe to his stories in which the material was selected for its strangeness and its appeal to the faculty of wonder. Poe probably got the term from Sir Walter Scott's essay "On the Supernatural in Fictional Composition" (1827), where he uses it as a rough synonym for GROTESQUE. Poe distinguished between the GROTESQUE, which had an element of horror, and the *Arabesque*, which had an element of wonder, in his *Tales of the Grotesque and Arabesque* (1840).

Arcadian: Arcadia, a picturesque plateau region in Greece, the reputed home of PASTORAL poetry, was pictured by PASTORAL poets as a land of ideal rural peace and contentment. *Arcadian* suggests an idealized rural simplicity and contentment such as shepherds in conventional PASTORAL poetry exhibited. It is sometimes used as synonymous with BUCOLIC or PASTORAL. Sir Philip Sidney, following Italian precedent, uses *Arcadia* as the title of his PASTORAL ROMANCE. See ECLOGUE, PASTORAL, IDYLL.

Archaism: Obsolete DICTION, phrasing, IDIOM, or syntax. Used intentionally, an archaic STYLE can be useful in recreating the atmosphere of the past, as in Spenser's *The Faerie Queene;* unless carefully controlled, however, *archaisms* result in an artificial and affected STYLE so absurd as to defeat the purpose of the writer.

Archetype: A term brought into literary criticism from the depth psychology of Carl Jung, who holds that behind each individual's "unconscious"—the blocked-off residue of his past—lies the "collective unconscious" of the human race—the blocked-off memory of our racial past, even of our prehuman experiences. This unconscious racial memory makes powerfully effective for us a group of "primordial images" shaped by the repeated experience of our ancestors and expressed in MYTHS, religions, dreams, fantasies, and powerfully in literature. T. S. Eliot says, "The pre-logical mentality persists in civilized man, but becomes available only to or through the poet." The "primordial image" which taps this "pre-logical mentality" is called the *archetype*.

The literary CRITIC applies the term to an IMAGE, a descriptive detail, a PLOT pattern, or a CHARACTER type that occurs frequently in literature, MYTH, religion, or FOLKLORE and is, therefore, believed to evoke profound emotions in the reader because it awakens a primordial image in his unconscious memory and thus calls into play illogical but strong responses. The *archetypal* critic studies the poem, play, or novel in terms of the images or patterns it has in common with other poems, plays, or novels, and thus by extension as a portion of the total human experience. In this sense the *archetype* is, as Northrop Frye defines it, "a symbol, usually an image, which recurs often enough in literature to be recognizable as an element of one's literary experience as a whole." (For an extensive treatment, see Maud Bodkin's *Archetypal Patterns in Poetry*.)

In earlier senses, the term refers to the original model or pattern from which something develops. In this sense it is a near synonym of PROTOTYPE. It is also used to refer to a no longer extant manuscript from which others were copied.

Architectonics: A critical term which expresses collectively those structural qualities of proportion, UNITY, EMPHASIS, and scale which make a piece of writing proceed logically and smoothly from beginning to end with no waste effort, no faulty omissions. The requirements of *architectonics*, a term borrowed from architecture, are felt to have been fulfilled when a piece of literature impresses a reader as a building, carefully planned and constructed, impresses the spectator. Currently the term is used to describe the successful achieving of organic UNITY, of "the companionship of the whole," in which the parts are not only perfectly articulated but are combined into an integrated whole, so that the work has meaning not through its parts but through its totality.

Arena Stage: A STAGE on which the actors are surrounded by the audience and make exits and entrances through the aisles. Sometimes, especially in England, the STAGE is against a wall, with the audience on three sides. The *arena stage* is often called THEATER IN THE ROUND. It differs from the APRON STAGE primarily in that the APRON STAGE is a traditional stage extending in front of any framing devices, whereas the ARENA STAGE is an area entered by actors through the audience which surrounds it.

Areopagus: The "hill of Ares (Mars)," the seat of the highest judicial court in ancient Athens. By association the name has come to represent any court of final authority. In this sense Milton used the term in his *Areopagitica*, addressed to the British parliament on the question of censorship and the licensing of books.

"The Areopagus" is the name used for what some literary historians believe was a sort of literary club existing in London shortly before 1580, supposed to be analogous with the *Pléiade* group in France. Whether there was a formal club or not is doubtful, but certain writers, including Gabriel Harvey, Sir Philip Sidney, Edmund Spenser, and Sir Edward Dyer engaged in a "movement" to reform English versification on the principles of classical PROSODY. In their best work, however, Sidney and Spenser abandoned these experiments in classical measures in favor of Italian, French, and native English forms.

Argument: A prose statement summarizing the plot or stating the meaning of a long poem or occasionally of a play. The best known English examples are Milton's *Arguments* to each of the books of *Paradise Lost* and Coleridge's MARGINALIA to *The Rime of the Ancient Mariner*. The term is sometimes used by the NEW CRITICS to describe the paraphrasable idea of a poem.

Argumentation: One of the four chief "forms of discourse," the others being EXPOSITION, NARRATION, and DESCRIPTION. Its purpose is to convince a reader or hearer by establishing the truth or falsity of a proposition. It is often combined with EXPOSITION. It differs from EXPOSITION technically in its aim, EXPOSITION being content with simply making an explanation.

Arianism: A Christian heresy expounded by Arius, a priest in Alexandria, in the fourth century. Arius believed that God is ultimately single, unknowable, and alone; that Christ was created by God and is not, therefore, equal to him; and that in the incarnation Christ assumed a body but not a human soul and was, therefore, neither fully human nor divine. *Arianism* was condemned by the First Council of Nicaea (325), but in the confusion of beliefs and allegiances that followed, the Arians for a time triumphed; but by 379 *Arianism* was outlawed in the Roman Empire. *Arianism* has remained a doctrinal interpretation that has from time to time proved attractive. Milton is accused of tending toward it in his interpretation of the relationship of God and Christ in *Paradise Lost,* although he has also been vigorously—and usually effectively—defended against the charge.

Aristotelian Criticism: Literally, criticism by Aristotle, as in the *Poetics*, or CRITICISM which follows the method of analysis used by Aristotle in the *Poetics*, although the exact nature of the Aristotelian method has been a subject of much debate (see CRITICISM, HISTORICAL SKETCH). In present-day critical parlance, however, the term *Aristotelian criticism* is frequently used as a contrast to the term PLATONIC CRITICISM, particularly by the NEW CRITICS. In this sense, the term implies a judicial, logical, formal criticism that is centered in the work rather than in its historical, moral, or religious context, and finds its values either within the work itself or inseparably linked to the work; the term is roughly synonymous with *intrinsic*. See CRITICISM, TYPES OF; PLATONIC CRITICISM; AUTOTELIC.

Arminianism: An anti-Calvinistic theology, founded by Jacobus Arminius in Holland in the early seventeenth century. It opposes the Calvinistic doctrines of election, reprobation, and absolute predestination, asserting that the human will can forfeit divine grace after receiving it and denying that predestination is absolute. It was a strong element in the theological arguments in England and America in the seventeenth and eighteenth centuries. In America Jonathan Edwards was its most powerful attacker. See CALVINISM.

Arsis: In METRICS, the term is usually applied today to a stressed syllable. In Greek usage, however, *arsis* was the name of the unstressed syllable. See ACCENT, THESIS.

Art Ballad: A term occasionally used to distinguish the modern or literary BALLAD of known authorship from the early BALLADS of unknown authorship. Some successful *art ballads* are *La Belle Dame sans Merci* by Keats, *Rosabelle* by Scott, and *Sister Helen* by Rossetti. Possibly the most famous poem imitating the BALLAD manner is *The Rime of the Ancient Mariner* by Coleridge.

Art Epic: A term sometimes employed to distinguish such an EPIC as Milton's *Paradise Lost* or Virgil's *Aeneid* from so-called FOLK EPICS such as *Beowulf*, the *Nibelungenlied*, and the *Iliad* and *Odyssey*. The FOLK EPIC is so named because it deals with tradition closely associated with the people or "folk" for whom it was written and whose credulity it commanded. The *art epic* is supposed to be more sophisticated, more highly idealized, and more consciously moral in purpose than is the FOLK EPIC, which it imitates. The author takes greater liberties with the popular materials he is treating and expects less credulity. The events he narrates are in a more remote past. The present-day tendency to discredit the theories of epic origins advanced by the romantic critics of the eighteenth century is breaking down the distinction between the two kinds, as the FOLK EPICS are now viewed as the work of single poets who worked according to traditional artistic technique. See EPIC.

Article: A type of ESSAY that is impersonal and largely factual. In an *article* the author writes as an authority on a subject and presents his argument and information in a systematic fashion. The term is applied to informative pieces for such widely varying places of publication as newspapers, magazines, learned and scholarly journals, and encyclopedias. The longer entries in this volume are *articles*. See ESSAY.

Art Lyric: The *art lyric* is characterized by a minuteness of subject, great delicacy of touch, careful perfection in phrasing, artificiality of sentiment, and formality. For its subject this kind of LYRIC avoids the passionate outbursts of a Burns, harking back, rather, to the sort of thing Horace and Petrarch wrote about—the tilt of a lady's eyebrow, the glow of a cheek. With Herrick, Lovelace, Jonson, and Herbert, RENAISSANCE English writers made much of the manner, polishing and perfecting their songs to gem-like brightness; with Shelley and Keats the *art lyric* began to carry ABSTRACT ideas. In brief, it may be said that the *art lyric* differs from the ordinary LYRIC in the degree to which the poet's self-conscious struggle for perfection of FORM dominates the spontaneity of his emotion. Certain French lyric forms, the TRIOLET, BALLADE, RONDEAU, and RONDEL, are instances of this highly polished manner of the *art lyric*.

Arthurian Legend: Probably the LEGEND of Arthur grew out of the deeds of some historical person. He was probably not a king, and it is very doubtful that his name was Arthur. He was presumably a Welsh or Roman military leader of the Celts in Wales against the Germanic invaders who overran Britain in the fifth century. The deeds of this Welsh hero gradually grew into a vast body of romantic story. He provided a glorious past for the Britons to look back upon. When Arthur developed into an important king, he yielded his position as a personal hero to a group of great knights who surrounded him. These knights of the Round Table came to be representative of all that was best in the age of chivalry, and the stories of their deeds make up the most popular group ("Matter of Britain") of the great CYCLES of MEDIEVAL ROMANCE.

There is no mention of Arthur in contemporary accounts of the Germanic invasion, but a Roman citizen named Gildas who lived in Wales mentions in his *De Excidio et Conquestu Britanniae* (written between 500 and 550) the Battle of Mt. Badon, with which later accounts connect Arthur, and a valiant Roman leader of a Welsh rally, named Ambrosius Aurelianus. About 800, Nennius, a Welsh chronicler, in his *Historia Britonum* uses the name Arthur in referring to a leader against the Saxons. About a century later an addition to Nennius' history called *Mirabilia* gives further evidences of Arthur's development as a hero, including an allusion to a boar-hunt of Arthur's which is told in detail in the later Welsh story of Kilhwch and Olwen (in the *Mabinogion*). There are other references to Arthur in the annals of the tenth and eleventh centuries, and William of Malmesbury in his *Gesta Regum Anglorum* (1125) treats Arthur as an historical figure and identifies him with the Arthur whom the Welsh "rave wildly about" in their "idle tales." A typical British Celt at this time believed that Arthur was not really dead but would return.

About 1136 Geoffrey of Monmouth, in his *Historia Regum Britanniae,* professedly based upon an old Welsh book, added a wealth of matter to the Arthurian legend—how much of it he invented cannot now be determined—such as the stories of Arthur's supernatural birth, his weird "Passing" to Avalon to be healed of his wounds, and the abduction of Guinevere by Modred. Geoffrey probably was attempting to create for the Norman kings in England a glorious historical background. He traces the history of the Britons from Brut, a descendant of Aeneas, to Arthur. Soon after Geoffrey additions to the story were made by the French poet Wace in his *Roman de Brut,* and a little later appear the famous ROMANCES of Chrétien de Troyes, in Old French, in which Arthurian themes are given their first highly literary treatment. About 1205 the English poet Layamon added some details in his *Brut*. By this time Arthurian legend had taken its place as one of the great themes of MEDIEVAL ROMANCE.

The great popularity of Arthurian tradition reached its climax in medieval English literature in Malory's *Le Morte Darthur* (printed 1485), a book destined to transmit Arthurian stories to many later English writers, notably Tennyson. Spenser used an Arthurian background for his romantic EPIC *The Faerie Queene* (1590), and Milton contemplated a national EPIC on Arthur. Interest in Arthur decreased in the eighteenth century, but Arthurian topics were particularly popular in the nineteenth century, the best known treatment appearing in Tennyson's *Idylls of the King.* Tennyson's version, as well as E. A. Robinson's *Merlin, Lancelot,* and *Tristram,* show how different generations have modified the Arthurian stories to make them express contemporary modes of thought and individual artistic ends. Arthurian themes received powerful and sympathetic musical treatment in an opera by Dryden with music by Purcell, *King Arthur,* and in Richard Wagner's operas, *Lohengrin, Tristan,* and *Parsifal.* The burlesquing treatment of chivalry in Mark Twain's *A Connecticut Yankee in King Arthur's Court* is in contrast to the usual romantic idealization, as is T. W. White's trilogy of novels published under the collective title, *The Once and Future King,* which is a powerful tribute to the continuing strength of the Arthurian legend, and which was the basis of an enormously popular musical drama, *Camelot.* See MEDIEVAL RO-MANCE, CHRONICLE.

Artificial Comedy: A term sometimes used (as by Lamb) for COM-EDY reflecting an artificial society, like the COMEDY OF MANNERS.

Artificiality: In CRITICISM a term used to characterize a work that is consciously and deliberately mannered, elaborate, or conventional. *Artificiality* describes a quality which the critic senses as being studied and self-conscious; what is specifically meant by the term varies greatly from critic to critic. There is little question, however, that the style of John Lyly is artificial and that the style of Burns is not; about writers like Donne and Hemingway, however, debate can and does rage.

Aside: A dramatic CONVENTION by which an actor directly and audibly addresses the audience but is not supposed to be heard by the other actors on the stage. In RENAISSANCE DRAMA the device was widely used to allow the inner feelings of the character to be made known to the audience. In the nineteenth century the CONVENTION was used for melodramatic and comic effect. Eugene O'Neill's *Strange Interlude* (1928) was a serious, successful, and extended application of the *aside* to the modern theater. See SOLILOQUY.

Assonance: Resemblance or similarity in sound between vowels followed by different consonants in two or more stressed syllables. *Assonance* differs from RHYME in that RHYME is a similarity of vowel and consonant. "Lake" and "fake" demonstrate RHYME; "lake" and "fate" *assonance*.

Assonance is a common substitution for END-RHYME in the popular BALLAD, as in these lines from "The Twa Corbies":

> —In behint yon auld fail dyke,
> I wot there lies a new-slain Knight.

Such substitution of *assonance* for END-RHYME is also characteristic of Emily Dickinson's verse, and is used extensively by many contemporary poets.

As an enriching ornament within the line, *assonance* is of great use to the poet. Poe and Swinburne used it extensively for musical effect. Gerard Manley Hopkins introduced modern poets to its wide use. The skill with which Dylan Thomas manipulates *assonance* is one of his high achievements. Note its complex employment in the first STANZA of Thomas' "Ballad of the Long-Legged Bait":

> The bows glided down, and the coast
> Blackened with birds took a last look
> At his thrashing hair and whale-blue eye;
> The trodden town rang its cobbles for luck.

Assonance is involved in "bows" (pronounced "boughs") and "down"; "blackened," "last," "thrashing," "hair," "whale," and "rang"; "took" and "look"; and "trodden" and "cobbles." (In passing one might also note the pattern of ALLITERATION in this stanza and that the RHYMING of "look" with "luck" is an example of CONSONANCE.) See RHYME.

Asyndeton: A form of condensed expression in which words or short phrases, usually joined by conjunctions, are presented in series, separated only by commas. Perhaps the most famous example is Caesar's *"Veni, vidi, vici."*

Atmosphere: The prevailing TONE or MOOD of a literary work, particularly—but not exclusively—when that MOOD is established in part by SETTING or landscape. It is, however, not simply SETTING but rather the emotional aura which the work bears and which establishes the reader's expectations and attitudes. Examples are the somber mood established by the description of the prison door in the opening chapter of Hawthorne's *The Scarlet Letter*, the brooding sense of fatality engendered by the description of Egdon Heath at the beginning of Hardy's *The Return of the Native*, the sense of "something rotten in the state of Denmark" established by the scene on the battlements at the opening of *Hamlet*, or the more mechanical but still effective opening stanza of Poe's "The Raven."

Attic: Writing characterized by a clear, simple, polished, and witty STYLE. Attica, a province of Greece today, was formerly one of the ancient Greek states. With Athens as its capital city, Attica arose to such fame for its culture and art as to survive in the term *Attic*, an adjective denoting grace and culture and the classic in art. Joseph Addison is a favorite example of an English author who may be said to have written *Attic* prose.

Attic Salt: *Salt* in this sense means WIT. *Attic salt* is writing distinguished by its classic refinement, its intellectual sharpness, and its elegant but stinging WIT. See ATTIC.

Aubade: A LYRIC about dawn or a morning serenade, a song of lovers parting at dawn. A French form originally, it differs from the Provençal ALBA in usually being joyous, whereas the ALBA is a lament. Shakespeare's "Hark! Hark! the Lark" and Browning's "The Year's at the Spring" are good English examples. See ALBA.

Aube: A morning SONG by a lady in a COURTLY LOVE triangle, expressing regret that the approach of dawn heralds the parting of the lovers. The *aube* was a highly conventionalized LYRIC sung by the Provençal TROUBADOURS. See ALBA, AUBADE.

Augustan: Specifically refers to the age of the Emperor Augustus of Rome (ruled 27 B.C. to A.D. 14), but since the time of Augustus was notable for the perfection of letters and learning, the term has, by analogy, been applied to other epochs in world history when literary culture was high. As Virgil and Horace made the *Augustan* age of Rome, so Addison and Steele, Swift, and Pope are said to have made the *Augustan* age of English letters. In a narrow sense the term *English Augustan Age* applies only to the reign of Queen Anne (1702–1714); in a broader sense it is sometimes given the dates of Pope—1688–1744. The writers of the age were self-consciously

"Augustan," aware of the parallels of their writing to Latin literature, given to comparing London to Rome, and, in the case of Pope, addressing George II satirically as "Augustus." See Neo-Classic Period, and *The Outline of Literary History*, where the period 1700–1750 is designated "The Augustan Age."

Augustinianism: The doctrines of St. Augustine of Hippo (354–430), author of *Confessions*, the first extended and completely honest self-analysis in literary history, and of the monumental *De Civitate Dei* (*The City of God*), as well as a vast amount of other writing. He strongly defended the orthodox view of God and man against the heresies of Pelagius, who held that there is no original sin, that the human will is absolutely free, and that the grace of God is universal but not indispensable. In opposing Pelagianism, St. Augustine exalted the glory of God, stressed original sin, and asserted the necessity of divine grace. His is essentially the view of man which, in the Renaissance and in America, became known as Calvinism. See Calvinism.

Autobiography: The story of a person's life written by himself. Although a common loose use of the term includes under autobiographical writings memoirs, diaries, journals, and letters, distinctions among these forms need to be made. Diaries, journals, and letters are not extended, organized narratives prepared for the public eye; *autobiographies* and memoirs are. But whereas memoirs deal at least in part with public events and noted personages other than the author himself, an *autobiography* is a connected narrative of the author's life, with some stress laid upon introspection. Notable great *autobiographies*—and works which tend to clarify the distinction made above—are St. Augustine's *Confessions*, Benvenuto Cellini's *Autobiography*, Franklin's *Autobiography*, and *The Education of Henry Adams*. Simulated *autobiography* is a device often used in the novel, as in Defoe's *Moll Flanders*, and novels can on occasion be *autobiography* in the guise of fiction, as in those of Thomas Wolfe and in Joyce's *A Portrait of the Artist as a Young Man*. See biography.

Autotelic: A term applied to a work that is nondidactic; that is, one whose end-purpose or intention is within itself and not dependent upon the achievement of objectives outside the work. The term is used by the NEW CRITICS to indicate a poem that speaks its own truth in its own terms rather than referring for its value to some external truth. See BELIEF, THE PROBLEM OF.

Avant-Garde: A military METAPHOR drawn from the French (vanguard, or van of an army) and applied to new writing that shows striking (and usually very self-conscious) innovations in STYLE, FORM, and subject matter. The military origin of the term is appropriate, for in every age the *avant-garde* (by whatever name it is known) makes a frontal and often an organized attack on the established FORMS and literary traditions of its time. See ANTI-NOVEL, ANTI-REALISTIC NOVEL, SURREALISM.

Awakening, The Great: A phrase applied to a great revival of emotional religion in America which took place about 1735–1750, the movement being at its height about 1740–1745 under the leadership of Jonathan Edwards. It arose as an effort to reform religion and morals. Religion, under the "PURITAN hierarchy" led by the Mathers, had become rather formal and cold, and the clergy somewhat arrogant. The revival meetings began as early as 1720 in New Jersey. In 1734 Edwards held his first great revival at Northampton, Mass. In 1738 the famous English evangelist George Whitefield began his meetings in Georgia and in 1739–1740 made a spectacular evangelistic tour of the colonies, reaching New England in 1740. Whitefield's meetings were marked by great emotional manifestations, such as trances, shoutings, tearing of garments, faintings. In 1740–1742 Edwards conducted a long "revival" at Northampton, preached in other cities, published many sermons, including *Sinners in the Hands of an Angry God* (1741). The conservatives, or "Old Lights," representing the stricter Calvinists, led by the faculties of Harvard and Yale, protested against the emotional excesses of the movement; they were answered by Edwards in his *Treatise on the Religious Affections* (1746). Yet Edwards himself opposed the more extreme exhibitions of emotionalism and by 1750 a reaction against the movement was underway. See CALVINISM, DEISM, PURITANISM.

Axiom: A MAXIM or APHORISM whose truth is held to be self-evident. In logic an AXIOM is a premise accepted as true without the need of demonstration and used in building an argument. See A PRIORI JUDGMENT, MAXIM.

B

Bacchius: In METRICS, a three-syllable FOOT, with the first syllable unaccented and the last two accented but with the heavier STRESS on the first accented syllable: Examples: *ă bŏ́ve bŏ́ard, ă bŏ́ut fáce.*

Background: A term borrowed from painting, where it signifies those parts against which the principal objects are portrayed. In literature the term is rather loosely used to specify either the SETTING of a piece of writing or the TRADITION and point of view from which an author presents his ideas. Thus one might speak either (1) of the Russian *background* (SETTING) of *Anna Karenina* or (2) of the *background* of education, philosophy, and convictions from which Tolstoy wrote the novel.

Baconian Theory: The theory that the plays of William Shakespeare were written by Francis Bacon. It grew out of an eighteenth-century English suggestion that Shakespeare, an unschooled countryman, could not have written the plays attributed to him. In the nineteenth century the idea that the plays were by Bacon developed in England and America, with the American Delia Bacon being a particularly influential advocate of Baconian authorship. Other authors for the plays than Bacon have been suggested, among them the Earl of Oxford, Sir Walter Raleigh, and Christopher Marlowe (who, according to this theory, was not murdered in 1593). The evidence offered in support of any or all of these theories is fragmentary and inconclusive at best, at its worst it is absurd; and our steadily growing scholarly knowledge of Shakespeare and his world increasingly discredits these theories without silencing their advocates.

Balance: In RHETORIC refers to that structure in which parts of a sentence—as words, phrases, or clauses—are set off against each other in position so as to emphasize a contrast in meaning. Macaulay's sentence, "The memory of other authors is kept alive by their works; but the memory of Johnson keeps many of his works alive," is an example. As a critical term *balance* is often used to characterize nicety of proportion among the various elements of a given piece of writing. A story, for example, wherein SETTING, CHARACTERIZATION, and PLOT are carefully planned, with no element securing undue emphasis, might be said to have fine *balance*.

Ballad: A form of verse to be sung or recited and characterized by its presentation of a dramatic or exciting EPISODE in simple narrative form. F. B. Gummere describes the *ballad* as "a poem meant for singing, quite impersonal in material, probably connected in its origins with the communal dance, but submitted to a process of oral tradition among people who are free from literary influences and fairly homogeneous in character." Though the *ballad* is a FORM still much written, the so-called "popular *ballad*" in most literatures belongs to the early periods before written literature was highly developed. They still appear, however, in isolated sections and among illiterate and semi-literate peoples. In America the folk of the southern Appalachian mountains have maintained a *ballad* tradition, as have the cowboys of the western plains, and people associated with labor movements, particularly when marked by violence. In Australia the "bush" *ballad* is still vigorous and popular. In the West Indies the "Calypso" singers produce something close to the *ballad* with their impromptu songs. Debate still rages as to whether the *ballad* originates with an individual composer or as a group or communal activity. Whatever the origin, the folk *ballad* is, in almost every country, one of the earliest forms of literature. Certain common characteristics of these early *ballads* should be noted: the supernatural is likely to play an important part in events, physical courage and love are frequent themes, the incidents are usually such as happen to common people (as opposed to the nobility) and often have to do with domestic episodes; slight attention is paid to CHARACTERIZATION or DESCRIPTION, transitions are abrupt, action is largely developed through DIALOGUE, tragic situations are presented with the utmost simplicity, INCREMENTAL REPETITION is common, IMAGINATION though not so common as in the ART BALLAD nevertheless appears in brief flashes, a single EPISODE of a highly dramatic nature is presented, and often the *ballad* is brought to a close with some sort of summary STANZA. The greatest impetus to the study of *ballad* literature was given by the publication in 1765 of Bishop Percy's *Reliques of Ancient English Poetry*. The standard modern collection still is *The English and Scottish Popular Ballads* edited by Francis James Child. The tradition of composing story-songs about current events and personages has been common for a long time. Hardly an event of national interest escapes being made the subject of a so-called *ballad*. Casey Jones, the railroad engineer; Floyd Collins, the cave explorer; the astronauts—all have been the subjects of *ballads*. Popular songs, particularly those engendered by the youthful protest movements, have revived the *ballad* form; for example, "Hang Down Your Head, Tom Dooley," or the *ballads* of Bob Dylan or Joan Baez. Strictly speaking, however, these are not *ballads* in the traditional sense, and that form probably belongs to a period in the history of Western civilization which is past. See ART BALLAD, BALLAD STANZA.

Ballad-Opera: A sort of burlesque OPERA which flourished on the English stage for several years following the appearance of John Gay's *The Beggar's Opera* (1728), the best known example of the type. Modeled on Italian OPERA, which it burlesqued, it told its story in SONGS set to old tunes and appropriated various elements from FARCE and COMEDY. See OPERA, COMIC OPERA.

Ballad Stanza: The STANZAIC form of the folk or popular BALLAD. Usually it consists of four lines, rhyming *abcb*, with the first and third lines carrying four accented syllables and the second and fourth carrying three. There is great variation in the number of unstressed syllables. The RHYME is often approximate, with ASSONANCE and CONSONANCE frequently appearing. A REFRAIN is not uncommon. This stanza from "The Unquiet Grave" is typical:

> "The wind doth blow today, my love,
>   And a few small drops of rain;
> I never had but one true-love,
>   In cold grave she was lain.

Ballade: One of the most popular of the artificial French verse forms. The *ballade* should not, however, be confused with the *ballad*. The *ballade* form has been rather liberally interpreted. Early usage most frequently demanded three STANZAS and an ENVOY, though the number of lines to the STANZA and of syllables to the line varied. Typical earmarks of the *ballade* have been: (1) the REFRAIN (uniform as to wording) carrying the MOTIF of the POEM and recurring regularly at the end of each STANZA and of the ENVOY; (2) the ENVOY, by nature a peroration of climactic importance and likely to be addressed to a high member of the court or to the poet's patron; and (3) the use of only three (or at the most four) RHYMES in the entire poem, occurring at the same position in each STANZA

and with no rhyme-word repeated except in the REFRAIN. STANZAS
of varied length have been used in the *ballade,* but the most common one is an eight-line STANZA rhyming *ababbcbc,* with *bcbc* for
the ENVOY. A good example of early use of English *ballade* form is
Chaucer's "Balade de bon conseyl," while one of the best-known
modern *ballades* is Rossetti's rendering of François Villon's "Ballade
of Dead Ladies."

Banality: A quality of statements that lack effectiveness and seem
tasteless or offensive because they express what has been too often
thought by too many in METAPHORS and CLICHÉS so conventional
that they lose the ability to communicate. *Banal* is perhaps best
defined by citing some of its common synonyms: hackneyed, commonplace, stale, STEREOTYPED, trite. See CLICHÉ.

Barbarism: A mistake in the form of a word, or a word which results from such a mistake. Strictly speaking, a *barbarism* results
from the violation of an accepted rule of derivation or inflection,
as *hern* for *hers, goodest* for *best, shooted* for *shot.* Originally it
referred to the mixing of foreign words and phrases in Latin or
Greek. See SOLECISM.

Bard: In modern use, simply a "poet." Historically the term refers
to poets who recited verses glorifying the deeds of heroes and
leaders, to the accompaniment of a musical instrument such as the
harp. *Bard* technically refers to the early poets of the Celts, as
TROUVÈRE refers to those of Normandy, SKALD to those of Scandi-
navia, and TROUBADOUR to those of Provence. See WELSH LITERA-
TURE.

Baroque: A term of uncertain origin applied first to the architec-
tural style which succeeded the classic style of the RENAISSANCE
and flourished, in varied forms in different parts of Europe, from
the late sixteenth century until well into the eighteenth century. The
baroque style is a blending of "picturesque" elements (the unexpected, the wild, the fantastic, the accidental) with the more ordered,
formal style of the "high RENAISSANCE." The *baroque* stressed movement, energy, and realistic treatment. Although the *baroque* is bold
and startling, even fantastic, its "discords and suspensions" are consciously and logically employed. The change to the *baroque* was

a radical effort to adapt the traditional modes and forms of expression to the uses of a self-conscious modernism. In its considered efforts to avoid the effects of repose, tranquillity, and complacency, it sought to startle by the use of the unusual and unexpected. This led sometimes to grotesqueness, obscurity, and contortion. The term in its older or "popular" sense implied the highly fantastic, the whimsical, the bizarre, the DECADENT.

The realization that the *baroque* arose naturally from existing conditions and is a serious and sincere STYLE, resting upon a sober intellectual basis and designed to express the newer attitudes of its period, has had the effect not only of causing the *baroque* to be regarded with more sympathy and seriousness than formerly, but also of extending the use of the term to literature as well as to painting and sculpture. The student of literature may encounter the term (in its older English sense) applied unfavorably to a writer's literary STYLE; or he may read of the *baroque* period or "age of *baroque*" (late sixteenth, seventeenth, and early eighteenth centuries); or he may find it applied descriptively and respectfully to certain stylistic features of the *baroque* period. Thus the broken rhythms of Donne's verse and the verbal subtleties of the English METAPHYSICAL poets have been called *baroque* elements. Richard Crashaw is said to have expressed the *baroque* spirit supremely in verse. See ROCOCO, CONCEIT, METAPHYSICAL POETRY.

Basic English: A simplified form of English for non-English speaking peoples, consisting of a vocabulary of 850 words, of which 600 are nouns, 150 adjectives, and 100 "operators" (verbs, adverbs, prepositions, and conjunctions). It was set up by C. K. Ogden, acting on a suggestion in the works of Jeremy Bentham. In America its strongest advocate has been I. A. Richards. The New Testament and certain of Plato's works have been "translated" into *Basic English*.

Bathos: The effect resulting from an unsuccessful effort to achieve dignity or pathos or elevation of style; an unintentional ANTICLIMAX, dropping from the sublime to the ridiculous. The term gained currency from Pope's use of it in a "Martinus Scriblerus" paper in which he ironically defended the commonplace effects of the English POETASTERS on the ground that depth (*bathos*) was a literary virtue of the moderns, as contrasted with the height (*hypsos*) of the ancients. An example of *bathos* given by Pope is:

Advance the fringed curtains of thy eyes,
And tell me who comes yonder.

Here the author (Temple) fails because of the (unintentional) ANTI-
CLIMAX resulting from the effort to treat poetically a commonplace,
prosaic idea. The PATHETIC FALLACY is sometimes responsible for
a "bathetic" effect. If a NOVEL or a play or a cinema tries to make
the reader or spectator weep and succeeds only in making him
laugh, the result is *bathos*. The term is sometimes, though not accurately, applied to the deliberate use of ANTICLIMAX for satiric or
humorous effect.

Battle of the Books, The: A quarrel between adherents of classical
and of modern writing in the late seventeenth and early eighteenth
centuries. See ANCIENTS AND MODERNS, QUARREL OF THE.

Beast Epic: A medieval literary FORM consisting of a series of
linked stories grouped about animal characters and often presenting
satirical comment on contemporary life of church or court by means
of human qualities attributed to beast characters. Some scholars believe that the stories developed from popular tradition and were
later given literary form by monastic scholars and TROUVÈRES who
molded the material at hand; others find the origin in the writing of
Latin scholastics. The oldest example known seems to be that of
Paulus Diaconus, a cleric at the court of Charlemagne, who wrote
about 782–786. Whether the form first developed in Germany or
France is a question for scholarly debate, though there is no doubt
that in the twelfth and thirteenth centuries the *beast epics* were very
popular in North France, West Germany, and Flanders. The various
forms of the *beast epic* have one EPISODE generally treated as the
nucleus for the story, such as the healing of the sick lion by the fox's
prescription that he wrap himself in the wolf's skin. Some of the
other animals common to the form, besides Reynard the Fox, the
lion, and the wolf, are the cock (Chanticleer), the cat, the hare, the
camel, the ant, the bear, the badger, and the stag. The best known
of the *beast epics*—and the most influential—is the *Roman de Renard,*
a poem of 30,000 lines comprising twenty-seven sets or "branches"
of stories.

Beast Fable: A short TALE in which the principal actors are animals. See FABLE, BEAST EPIC.

Bestiary

Beat Generation: A term applied to a group of American poets and novelists of the 1950's and 1960's who were in romantic rebellion against the culture and the value systems of present-day America, and expressed their revolt through literary works of loose STRUCTURE and slang DICTION asserting the essentially valueless nature of existence. Their leaders were the poet Allen Ginsberg and the novelist Jack Kerouac.

Beginning Rhyme: RHYME that occurs in the first syllable or syllables of VERSES.

Belief, The Problem of: The question of the degree to which the aesthetic value of a literary work for a given reader is necessary or properly affected by the acceptability to that reader of its doctrine or philosophic or religious assumptions. Although the question is certainly as old as Plato, it has assumed an unusual relevance in present-day CRITICISM because the traditional answer—that doctrinal acceptability is one of the necessary conditions for aesthetic value—has been brought into serious question by a group of critics, notably those usually designated NEW CRITICS. See AUTOTELIC.

Belles-Lettres: Literature, more especially that body of writing, comprising DRAMA, POETRY, FICTION, CRITICISM, and ESSAYS, which lives because of inherent imaginative and artistic rather than scientific, philosophical, or intellectual qualities. Lewis Carroll's *Alice in Wonderland,* for example, belongs definitely to the province of *belles-lettres,* while the mathematical works of the same man, Charles Lutwidge Dodgson, do not. Now sometimes used to characterize light or artificial writing.

Benthamism: The philosophy of Jeremy Bentham. It holds that the ultimate goal of man should be to achieve the greatest happiness for the greatest number. See UTILITARIANISM.

Bestiary: A type of literature, popular during the medieval period, in which the habits of beasts, birds, and reptiles were made the text for allegorical and mystical Christian teachings. These *bestiaries* often ascribed human attributes to animals and were designed to moralize and to expound church doctrine. The natural history employed is fabulous rather than scientific and has helped to make popular in literature such abnormalities as the phoenix, the siren, and the unicorn. Many of the qualities literature familiarly attributes to animals owe their origin to the *bestiaries*. The development of the type is first attributed to Physiologus, a Greek sermonizer of about A.D. 150, but it was rapidly taken over by Christian preachers and homilists throughout Europe. The *bestiary* in one form or another has appeared in various world literatures: Anglo-Saxon, Arabic, Armenian, English, Ethiopic, French, German, Icelandic, Provençal, and Spanish.

Bible: Derived from a Greek term meaning "little books," *Bible* is now applied to the collection of writings known as the Holy Scriptures, the sacred writings of the Christian religion. Of the two chief parts, the Old Testament consists of the sacred writings of the ancient Hebrews, and the New Testament of writings of the early Christian period. The Jewish Scriptures include three collections— The Law, The Prophets, and Writings—written in ancient Hebrew at various dates in the pre-Christian era. The New Testament books were written in the Greek DIALECT employed in Mediterranean countries about the time of Christ. An important Greek form of the Hebrew Bible is the Septuagint, dating from the Alexandrian period (third century B.C.). Latin versions were made in very early times, both of the Old and New Testament books, including many of the APOCHRYPHA, the most important being that made by St. Jerome about A.D. 400, known as the Vulgate—the Bible of the Middle Ages. See next three topics and DEAD SEA SCROLLS.

Bible as Literature: The high literary value of many parts of the Bible has been almost universally recognized. Many English authors, including Milton, Wordsworth, Scott, and Carlyle, have paid tribute to Biblical literature, Coleridge even rating the style of Isaiah and the Epistle to the Hebrews as far superior to that of Homer or Virgil or Milton. The literary qualities of the Bible are accounted for partly by the themes treated, partly by the poetic character of the Hebrew tongue, and partly by the literary skill exhibited by Biblical writers and translators. The themes of Biblical literature are among the greatest that literature can treat: God, man, the physical universe, and their interrelations. Such problems as human morality, man's relation to the unseen world, and ultimate human destinies are treated with a simplicity, sincerity, intensity, and vigor seldom matched in world literature. The character of the Hebrew language, abounding in words and phrases of CONCRETE sensuous appeal and lacking the store of ABSTRACT words characteristic of the Greek, imparted an emotional and imaginative richness to He-brew writings of a sort which lends itself readily to translation (the idea of pride, for example, is expressed by "puffed up"). The Bible is partly in prose and partly in verse, the principles of Hebrew verse being ACCENT and PARALLELISM rather than METER. The literary types found in the Bible have been variously classified. A few examples may be given: the short story, Ruth, Jonah, Esther; biographical narrative, the story of Abraham in Genesis; love LYRIC, Song of Solo-mon; the battle ODE, the song of Deborah (Judges, 5); EPIGRAM, in Proverbs and elsewhere; devotional LYRIC, Psalms; dramatic philo-sophical poem, Job; ELEGY, lament of David for Saul and Jonathan (II Samuel, 1: 19–27); LETTERS, the epistles of Paul.

Bible, English Translations of: From Caedmon (seventh century) to Wycliffe (fourteenth century) there were TRANSLATIONS and PARA-PHRASES in OLD ENGLISH and in MIDDLE ENGLISH of various parts of the BIBLE, all based upon the Latin Vulgate edition. The parts most frequently translated were the Gospels, the Psalms, and the Pentateuch. The Caedmonian poetic paraphrases (seventh century) are extant, but Bede's prose translation of a portion of the gospel of St. John (seventh century) is not. From the ninth century come GLOSSES of the Book of Psalms and prose translations by King Alfred. The West Saxon Gospels and the GLOSSES in the Lindisfarne Gospels date from the tenth century, while Ælfric's incomplete translations of the Old Testament date from the late tenth and early eleventh cen-turies. The subordinate position occupied by the English language for some time after the eleventh century perhaps accounts for the lack of translations in MIDDLE ENGLISH times until the fourteenth century, when there was renewed activity in preparing English versions and commentaries, notably by Richard Rolle of Hampole. In about 1382 came the first edition of the Wycliffe Bible, largely the work of Wycliffe himself. A revision of this work, chiefly the work of John Purvey, 1388, though interdicted by the Church from 1408 to 1534, circulated freely in manuscript form for the next 150 years.

Printed English Bibles first appeared in the sixteenth century, products of the new learning of the HUMANISTS and the zeal of the Protestant Reformation. They were mainly based upon Greek and Hebrew manuscripts, or recent translations of such manuscripts. Some important English translations are: (1) William Tyndale—the

New Testament (1525–26), the Pentateuch (1530), Jonah (1531). Tyndale is credited with the creation of much of the picturesque phraseology which characterizes later English translations. (2) Miles Coverdale, first complete printed English Bible (1535), based upon Tyndale and a Swiss-German translation. (3) "Matthew's" Bible (1537), probably done by John Rogers, based upon Tyndale and Coverdale, is important as a source for later translations. (4) Taverner's Bible (1539), based on "Matthew's" Bible, but revealing a tendency to greater use of native English words. (5) The Great Bible (1539), sometimes called Cranmer's Bible, because Cranmer sponsored it and wrote a preface for the second edition (1540)—a very large volume designed to be chained to its position in the churches for the use of the public. Coverdale superintended its preparation. It is based largely on "Matthew's" Bible. (6) The Geneva Bible (1560), the joint work of English Protestant exiles in Geneva, including Coverdale and William Whittington, who had published in 1557 in Geneva an English New Testament which was the first version in English divided into the familiar chapters and verses. It became the great Bible of the PURITANS and ran through sixty editions between 1560 and 1611. (7) Bishops' Bible (1568), prepared by eight bishops and others and issued to combat the Calvinistic, anti-episcopal tendencies of the Geneva Bible. (8) The Rheims-Douai Bible (1582), a Catholic translation based upon the Vulgate, issued to counteract the Puritan Geneva Bible and the Episcopal Bishops' Bible. The Old Testament section was not actually printed till 1609.

By far the most important and influential of English Bibles is the "Authorized" or King James Version (1611). It is a revision of the Bishops' Bible and was sponsored by King James I. The translators, about fifty of the leading Biblical scholars of the time, including PURITANS, made use of Greek and Hebrew texts. This version is the most widely read English Bible, and it exerted a profound influence upon the literature of the English and American peoples through the seventeenth, eighteenth, and nineteenth centuries.

The Revised Version (1885) and the standard American edition of the Revised Version (1901), the joint work of English and American scholars, were modern versions which aimed chiefly at scholarly accuracy.

A group of American Biblical scholars produced in 1946 an extensive revision of the King James Version of the New Testament, bringing to bear upon it the wealth of textual discovery and scholarship which we now have, and in 1952 they added the Old Testament. This translation, known as the Revised Standard Version, although generally considered inferior to the King James Version from a literary point of view, has attained wide usage because of its accuracy and clarity. A number of renderings into contemporary and idiomatic English have been made in this century of the whole or parts of the Bible. Notable among them are the translations into American idiom by James Moffatt and by Edgar Goodspeed and the translations into British idiom by J. B. Phillips and by Father Ronald Knox.

The most important recent translation is *The New English Bible*, prepared by a joint committee of the Protestant churches of the British Isles, who were joined by observers representing the Roman Catholic Church. This version is a totally new translation, utilizing all known manuscripts, including recent discoveries such as the DEAD SEA SCROLLS. It aims at—and generally achieves—accuracy, clarity, and graceful dignity. *The New Testament* appeared in 1961, *The Old Testament* and the APOCRYPHA in 1970.

Another new version that seems certain to have wide use and a long life is *The New American Bible*, translated by the Catholic Biblical Association of America. This completely new translation began to be published in parts in 1952, at which time it was known as the Confraternity version. The entire Bible, with the earlier translations revised, was published as *The New American Bible* in 1970. The aim of the translators was to make as exact a version as possible, resting on modern textual scholarship and resisting modification for the sake of literary quality.

Bible, Influence on Literature: The influence of the BIBLE upon English literature is so subtly pervasive that it can merely be suggested, not closely traced. Much of its influence has been indirect —through its effect upon language and upon the mental and moral interests of the English and American people. The English Bibles of the sixteenth century brought the common people a new world by the revival of ancient Hebrew literature. The picturesque imagery and phraseology were an enriching element in the lives of the people, and profoundly affected not only their conduct but their language and literary tastes.

Great authors commonly show a familiarity with the Bible, and few great English and American writers of the seventeenth, eighteenth, nineteenth, and twentieth centuries can be read with satisfaction by one ignorant of Biblical literature. The Authorized Version

Bibliography

of the Bible has affected subsequent English literature in the use of Scriptural themes (Milton's *Paradise Lost,* Bunyan's *Pilgrim's Progress,* Byron's *Cain*), of Scriptural phraseology, allusions, or modified quotations (as "selling birthright" for a "mess of pottage"); incorporation, conscious or unconscious, of Biblical phraseology into common speech ("highways and hedges," "thorn in the flesh," "a soft answer"). The Bible is thought to have been highly influential in substituting pure English words for Latin words (Tyndale's vocabulary is 97 per cent English, that of the Authorized Version, 93 per cent). The style of many writers has been directly affected by study of the Bible, as has Bunyan's, Lincoln's, and Hemingway's. Whitman's prosodic methods as well as his vocabulary demonstrate a great debt to the Hebrew poets and prophets. Novelists of twentieth-century America are increasingly turning to the Bible for themes and plots; among the many examples are Hemingway's *The Sun Also Rises,* Faulkner's *Light in August* and *A Fable,* and Steinbeck's *The Grapes of Wrath* and *East of Eden.*

Bibliography: Used in several senses. The term may be applied to a SUBJECT BIBLIOGRAPHY; this is a list of books or other printed (or manuscript) material on any chosen topic. A SUBJECT BIBLIOGRAPHY may aim at comprehensiveness, even completeness; or it may be selective, intended to list only such works as are most important, or most easily available, or most closely related to a book or article to which it may be attached. *Bibliographies* following a serious essay, for example, may be merely a list of sources used by the writer of the essay, or they may be meant to point out to the reader sources of additional information on the subject. In a related use, the word designates a list of works of a particular country, author, or printer ("national" and "trade" *bibliography*). *Bibliographies* of these kinds are sometimes called ENUMERATIVE BIBLIOGRAPHIES. The process of making such lists either by students or by professional bibliographers is also referred to as *bibliography.*

In the historical sense, as used by book collectors, bibliophiles, and scholars, *bibliography* means the history of book production, history of writing, printing, binding, illustrating, and publishing. It involves a consideration of the details of book-making. *Bibliography* in this sense is sometimes used by scholars in TEXTUAL CRITICISM—the employing of bibliographical evidence to help settle such questions as that of the order of publication and the relative value of different editions of a book; whether certain parts of a book were originally intended to be a part of it or were added afterwards; whether a later edition was printed from an earlier one; and other problems of a similar kind, which often have an important literary bearing. This sort of bibliographical work has been much stressed in the twentieth century, especially by members of the London Bibliographical Society, one striking result being the discovery of the forged dates on certain QUARTOS of Shakespeare's plays, actually printed in 1619 but assigned earlier dates on the title pages.

Another use of the term *bibliography* is to denote the methods of work of student and author: reading, research, taking of notes, compilation of *bibliography*, preparation of manuscript for the press, publication, etc. These last two uses of the word are of especial interest to advanced students who take university courses in *bibliography*.

"A *bibliography* of *bibliographies*" means a list of lists of works dealing with a given subject or subjects. An "annotated *bibliography*" is one in which some or all of the items listed are followed by brief descriptive or critical comment.

Bildungsroman: A NOVEL that deals with the development of a young person as he grows up. Dickens's *David Copperfield* and Samuel Butler's *The Way of All Flesh* are standard examples. See APPRENTICESHIP NOVEL.

Billingsgate: Coarse, vulgar, violent, abusive language. The term is derived from the fact that the fishwives in Billingsgate fish market in London achieved a certain distinction from the scurrility of their language.

Biography: A written account of a person's life, a life history. *Biography* derives its impetus from the commemorative instinct, the didactic or moralizing instinct, and, perhaps most important of all, the instinct of curiosity. LETTERS, MEMOIRS, DIARIES, JOURNALS, and AUTOBIOGRAPHY, though they spring from these same desires of men, must be distinguished from *biography* proper. MEMOIRS, DIARIES, JOURNALS, and AUTOBIOGRAPHY are closely related to each other in that each is recollection written down by the subject himself. LETTERS are likely to be colored by various prejudices and purposes. The subject himself may or may not have been spontaneous in his correspondence. The editor may or may not be completely honest in his printing of the letters. Nearer the *biography* than any of these

Biography

forms—and yet not an exact parallel—is the "life and times" book. In this kind of writing the author is concerned with two points: the life of his central figure and the period in which this figure lived. The writer may do a very fascinating book, one both interesting and instructive, but pure *biography*, in the more modern sense, does not look two ways; it centers its whole attention on the character and career of its subject.

In England the word *biography*, as a term denoting a form of writing, first came into use with Dryden, who, in 1683, defined it as "the history of particular men's lives." Today the term carries with it certain definite demands. It must be a history, but an accurate history; one which paints not only one aspect of the man but all important aspects. It must be the life of a "particular" man focused clearly on that man with more casual reference to the background of the social and political institutions of his time. It must present the facts accurately and must make some effort to interpret these facts in such a way as to present character and habits of mind. It must emphasize personality, and this personality must be the central thesis of the book. If the biographer looks at the times, it must be only with the purpose of presenting a well-constructed and unified impression of the personality of his subject; if he introduces LETTERS and ANECDOTES (as he surely will) it will be only such anecdotes and letters as reflect this central conception of personality. *Biography* today, then, may be defined as the accurate presentation of the life history from birth to death of an individual, this presentation being secured through an honest effort to interpret the facts of the life in such a way as to offer a unified impression of the character, mind, and personality of the subject.

Just how this modern attitude differs from past conceptions may best be appreciated after a brief survey of the history of the *biography* as a literary type. English biography perhaps begins with the ancient runic inscriptions which celebrated the lives of heroes and recorded the exploits of deceased and legendary warriors. It is an element in such early Anglo-Saxon verse as *Beowulf* and the *Widsith* fragment. And in these early manifestations we find what was, probably, the first conception of *biography*—the commemorative instinct, the "cenotaph-urge." These accounts were written to glorify.

This desire to commemorate greatness was, later on, united with a second purpose—the encouragement of morality. This purpose accounts for HAGIOGRAPHY, records of saints. Great men and women were commemorated for their virtue, their vices being conveniently overlooked. The lives of the saints occupied the attention of scholars in the monasteries. One list of early English historical material reports 1,277 writings, almost all of which were devoted to the glorification of one or another Irish or British saint. Even Bede (who died in 735) was little more than a hagiographer. It was not until Bishop Asser wrote his *Life of Alfred the Great* (893) that anything appears which closely resembles *biography*.

With Monk Eadmer of the twelfth century, English *biography* reached another milestone. Eadmer, in his *Vita Anselmi*, somehow managed to humanize his subject beyond the capacity of former biographers. He introduced LETTERS into his narrative to make his points; he reported ANECDOTES and conversation. He wrote what may be the first pure *biography* in England. The fourteenth- and fifteenth-century *biography* gradually became somewhat less serious, less commemorative, less didactic.

For the purposes of this brief survey, however, this summary need not pause again until the middle of the sixteenth century when William Roper (1496–1578), More's son-in-law, wrote what is now most often referred to as the first English *biography,* his *Life of Sir Thomas More,* and George Cavendish (1500–1561) wrote his *Life of Wolsey.* With these two books, English *biography* had arrived as a recognized form of literature. The didactic purpose was still obvious, the commemorative spirit was still present. But both books make a greater effort to avoid prejudice than had before manifested itself in English *biography*. Both books resorted to EPISODE and ANECDOTE and fairly vivid DIALOGUE. Both books devoted their space to the life of one man, the *Wolsey* beginning with the birth of the subject and ending with the death. Both books made an avowed declaration to follow the truth.

The seventeenth century was, in general, a time of brevities. The character sketch, the ANA, flourished. The CHARACTER was the contemporary enthusiasm. John Aubrey wrote his frank, gossipy *Minutes for Lives* as brief estimates of his contemporaries. Thomas Fuller wrote his *Worthies*. DIARIES, LETTERS, and MEMOIRS were plentiful—the *Memoirs of Lady Fanshawe* and the *Memoirs of Colonel Hutchinson* serve as examples. The first worthwhile AUTO-BIOGRAPHY, perhaps, is that of Lord Herbert. But were it not for Izaak Walton's *Lives* the century would be almost a complete loss so far as *biography* is concerned. Walton, who wrote his *Lives* from 1640 to 1678, has been considered by some the first English professional biographer since he attempted the form deliberately and sustained it over a long period. Opposed to Walton and his biographical manner was Thomas Sprat, whose *Life of Cowley* appeared in 1668. It is to him that the Victorian demand for "decency" in *biography* seems largely due, for Sprat wrote a life that was a cold and dignified thing, formal and proper, emasculated and virtuous. "The tradition of 'discreet' biography," writes one critic, "owes its wretched origin to him."

If *biography* almost stood still during the seventeenth century, the eighteenth saw it march forward to the greatest accomplishment it has enjoyed. Boswell's *Life of Johnson* stands, probably for all time, at the head of any list of *biographies*. Two lesser luminaries were Roger North and William Mason—North (*Lives of the Norths*), who insisted that panegyric be avoided and wrote brightly and colloquially, and Mason (*Life and Writings of Gray*), who carried further the use of letters and pretty largely left his reader to deduce the sort of man his subject was by a simple placing before the reader of a wide range of illustrative material. Dr. Johnson himself dignified *biography* by developing a philosophy for the writing of the form and by his insistence that to a real biographer truth was much more important than respect for a dead man or his relatives. In his *Lives of the Poets* he himself practiced his doctrines. The writing of the supreme English *biography* was, however, reserved for Johnson's biographer—James Boswell. What is important is the new twist which Boswell gave to biographic method. He used most of the methods developed by earlier writers, but he wrought of them a new combination. Humor of a sort was here; here was introduced a great wealth of petty detail from which the reader might make for himself his deductive analysis; here, too, were the ANECDOTE and ANA of the seventeenth century; and here were intimacy and personal comment. To Boswell was given the privilege of making *biography* actual, real, convincing. In the work of James Boswell *biography* painted a living, breathing human being.

The Boswell tradition was in a fair way of being accepted when Victorianism, with its studiousness, its two-volume "life and letters" *biography*, its "authorized" biographers more or less controlled by the family and relatives of the hero, blurred the picture. True enough, in the nineteenth century, there had been Tom Moore's *Life of Sheridan* and *Letters and Journals of Lord Byron;* as well as Lockhart's *Life of Scott*. But on the whole the freedom which Boswell had brought to this writing was restricted and confined by the Victorians. Religious orthodoxy, piety, and moral judgments were in the saddle. Tennyson spoke for the epoch when he thundered, "What business has the public to know about Byron's wildnesses? He has given them fine work and they ought to be satisfied."

The growing scientific attitude had become operative on *biography* by the early years of the twentieth century, and it brought with it not only a rejection of the polite reticence of the Victorian biographer but also a direct attack upon the admiration of famous men. Lytton Strachey, in *Eminent Victorians* (1918) and *Queen Victoria* (1921), wrote lives that were brief, ironic, artistically shaped and (his critics declare) too often inaccurate. Coupled with Strachey's method have been the assumptions of the depth psychologists, particularly of Freud, and our century has seen a host of biographical studies which are virtually attempts to read the hidden emotional life and even the unconscious experiences and motives of the subject. Van Wyck Brooks' studies of Mark Twain and of Henry James as the products of frustration are particularly significant for the American literary student, although Gamaliel Bradford's "psychographs" may have more enduring value as *biography*. Philip Guedalla in England and Carl Sandburg, Douglas Southall Freeman, and Leon Edel in America have made the twentieth century not only a period in which *biography* has been popular and widely read and written but also one in which at its best it has achieved high distinction.

Black Humor: The use of the morbid and the absurd for darkly comic purposes in modern FICTION and DRAMA. The term refers as much to the TONE of anger and bitterness as it does to the grotesque and morbid situations, which often deal with suffering, anxiety, and death. *Black humor* is a substantial element in the ANTI-NOVEL and the THEATER OF THE ABSURD. Joseph Heller's *Catch-22* is an almost archetypal example.

Black Letter: A heavy type face with angular outlines and thick, ornamental serifs. It is also called "Gothic," "church text," and "Old English." It was widely used in the early centuries of printing. The term is used descriptively to imply an early work, as in "*black letter* book," where the kind of type is indicative of the age of the work.

Black Literature: A currently fashionable term for literary materials produced by American Negro authors. See AFRO-AMERICAN LITERATURE.

Blank Verse

Blank Verse: *Blank verse* consists of unrhymed lines of ten syllables each, the second, fourth, sixth, eighth, and tenth syllables bearing the ACCENTS (IAMBIC PENTAMETER). This form has generally been accepted as that best adapted to dramatic VERSE in English and is commonly used for long POEMS whether dramatic, philosophic, or narrative. It appears easy to write, but good *blank verse* probably demands more artistry and genius than any other verse form. The freedom gained through lack of RHYME is offset by the demands for variety to be secured through its privileges. This variety may be obtained by the skillful poet through a number of means: the shifting of the CAESURA, or pause, from place to place within the line; the shifting of the STRESS among syllables; the use of the RUN-ON LINE, which permits thought-grouping in large or small blocks (these thought-groups being variously termed verse "paragraphs" or verse STANZAS); variation in tonal qualities by changing DICTION from passage to passage; and, finally, the adaptation of the form to reproduction of differences in the speech of characters in dramatic and narrative verse and to differences of emotional expression.

Blank verse appears to have first found general favor in England as a medium for dramatic expression, but with Milton it was turned to EPIC use and since then has been employed in the writing of IDYLLS and LYRICS. The distinction of the first use of *blank verse* in English, though the claims are not quite clear, is usually given to Surrey, who used it in his translation of parts of the *Aeneid* (made prior to 1547). The earliest dramatic use of *blank verse* in English was in Sackville and Norton's *Gorboduc*, 1561; the earliest use in DIDACTIC POETRY was in Gascoigne's *Steel Glass*, 1576; but it was only with Marlowe (prior to 1593) that the form first reached the hands of a master capable of using its range of possibilities and passing it on for Shakespeare and Milton to develop to its ultimate perfection. In more recent times some critics have manifested a willingness to extend the meaning of the term to include almost any metrical unrhymed form, and not to restrict its use to VERSES predominantly of ten syllables and five accents, but such loose usage is probably unwise.

Bleed: A term used in printing to describe the trimming of the edges of a sheet or a page in such a way that some of the type or illustration is cut off. If an illustration is so printed that it comes to the very edge of the page, leaving no margin, it is said that the illustration *"bleeds* off." A page so printed or trimmed is called a *"bleed* page."

Block-Books: Books printed from engraved blocks of wood. Books were so produced in Flanders and Germany in the early part of the fifteenth century. The printing was on only one side of the sheet, and in binding the sheets together to make a book, the sheets were often glued together to form pages printed on both sides.

Bloomsbury Group: A group of writers many of whom lived in Bloomsbury, a residential district near central London. These writers, of whom Virginia Woolf was the unofficial leader, began meeting early in the twentieth century, and became a powerful force in British literary and intellectual life in the 1920's and 1930's. Their philosophy was derived from G. E. Moore's *Principia Ethica,* which asserts that "the pleasures of human intercourse and the enjoyment of beautiful objects" are the rational ends of social progress. Among the members of this informal and highly sophisticated group were John Maynard Keynes, Lytton Strachey, Clive Bell, Roger Fry, E. M. Forster, Duncan Grant, and David Garnett.

Blues: An AFRO-AMERICAN FOLK-SONG developed by the Negroes of the southern United States. A *blues* is characteristically short (three-line STANZA), melancholy in TONE, marked by frequent REPETITION, and sung slowly in a minor key. Probably each *blues* was originally the composition of one person, but so readily are *blues* appropriated and changed that in practice they are a branch of FOLK LITERATURE. The following is an example:

> Gwine lay my head right on de railroad track,
> Gwine lay my head right on de railroad track,
> 'Cause my baby, she won't take me back.

Bluestockings: A term applied to women of pronounced intellectual interests. It gained currency after 1750 as a result of its application (for reasons not now easy to establish beyond dispute) to a group of women of literary and intellectual tastes who held in London assemblies or "conversations" to which "literary and ingenious men" were invited. It was the English equivalent of the French *salon.* There was no formal organization and the personnel of the group changed from time to time, so that no "membership" list can be given with assurance or completeness. Among the women *bluestockings* were Mrs. Elizabeth Montagu (the "Queen of the Blues"), Hannah More, Fanny Burney, and Mrs. Hester Chapone. Horace Walpole was one of the male "members," and Dr. Samuel Johnson, Edmund Burke, and David Garrick were at times frequent visitors. The activities of the group were directed toward encouraging an interest in literature and fostering the recognition of literary genius (see PRIMITIVISM), and hence helped remove the odium which had attached to earlier "learned ladies." It is used today as a term of opprobrium to describe pretentiously intellectual and pedantic females.

Blurb: A term applied in the American book trade to the descriptive matter printed on the jackets of new books, usually extravagant in its claims. The term was invented by Gelett Burgess in 1914.

Bombast: Ranting, insincere, extravagant language. Grandiloquence. Elizabethan TRAGEDY, especially early SENECAN plays, contains much bombastic style, marked by extravagant IMAGERY. An example from Shakespeare's *Hamlet* (Act II, Sc. 2) is:

> Roasted in wrath and fire,
> And thus o'er-sized with coagulate gore,
> With eyes like carbuncles, the hellish Pyrrhus
> Old grandsire Priam seeks.

Bon Mot: A witty REPARTEE or statement. A clever saying.

Book Sizes: To understand the terms, QUARTO, OCTAVO, and the rest, used in describing *book sizes,* it is first of all necessary to know the principle determining these sizes. This principle is best understood by imagining before one a sheet of paper, "foolscap" size, 17 inches by 13½ inches.

When this paper is folded along 1–2, 3–4, and 5–6, the resulting folds mark off the sizes of book pages cut from the large foolscap sheet. Thus 1–2–7–8 represents one of two leaves cut from the original foolscap and is, therefore, a FOLIO (Latin for *leaf*) sheet or page; 2–3–4–7 represents one fourth of the original sheet and, therefore, gives us a QUARTO page; 2–3–5–6 constitutes one eighth of the original and gives us an OCTAVO page. A book size, then, is determined by the number of book leaves cut from a single large sheet. To determine the number of pages cut from the original

Book Sizes

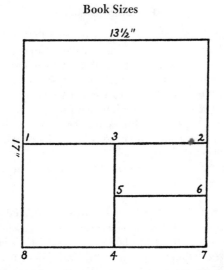

sheet count the number of pages to a SIGNATURE; this may often be done by noting the occurrence of the SIGNATURE marks (themselves sometimes called SIGNATURES) which appear at regular intervals at the foot of a page. These symbols are usually numerals or letters and may be found regularly in early printed books and sometimes in recently printed ones. They indicate the beginning of new SIGNA-TURES. *The number of leaves (not pages) in a single SIGNATURE shows the number of leaves cut from the original sheet and is, there-fore, the indication of the book size.* When there are two leaves to the SIGNATURE, the book is a FOLIO; when there are four leaves, it is a QUARTO; and so on. The table below shows the principle as it manifests itself in the more frequently used book sizes.

No. of Folds	No. of Leaves	Pages to Signature	Name
1	2	4	FOLIO
2	4	8	QUARTO(4to)
3	8	16	OCTAVO(8vo)
	12	24	DUODECIMO(12mo)
4	16	32	sixteenmo(16mo)
5	32	64	thirty-twomo(32mo)
6	64	128	sixty-fourmo(64mo)

This would all be very simple but for the fact that in modern print-ing there is a variety of sizes of original stock. In addition to the "foolscap 8vo" in our example, we may have Post 8vo, Demy 8vo, Crown 8vo, Royal 8vo, etc., the terms Demy, Crown, and the others referring to varying sizes of original sheets which, in turn, give varying sizes of book pages even when the number of leaves cut from the sheets is the same. So complicated has the whole question of *book sizes* become that expert bibliographers urge more attention to the position of the watermark on the page (a guide to book measurements too complicated to discuss here) and even then frequently give up the question in despair. Publishers arbitrarily use 12mo, OCTAVO, etc., for books of certain sizes regardless of the number of pages to the signature.

Boulevard Drama: A term applied to sophisticated COMEDY and MELODRAMA popular in the French theater in the nineteenth century. It centered around the Opera house (1861–1874), where the operettas of Jacques Offenbach, frequently with books by Meilhac and Ludovic Halévy, were performed. The COMEDIES and FARCES of Eugène Labiche, with their extravagance and violent behavior, presented dramatic pictures of the irreverance, prankishness, and material practicality of the French Second Empire. In present-day usage, the term is sometimes applied to brittle, sophisticated COMEDY aimed at a popular audience.

Bourgeois Drama: A term applied to plays in which the life of the common folk and the middle class rather than that of the courtly or the rich is depicted. Such widely differing kinds of plays as Heywood's *Interludes, Gammer Gurton's Needle,* Dekker's *Shoemaker's Holiday* (REALISTIC COMEDY), and Lillo's *The London Merchant* (DOMESTIC TRAGEDY) are embraced in the term, which in its broadest sense refers to the development of a middle-class subject matter for the theater.

Bourgeois Literature: Literature produced primarily to appeal to the middle-class reader. Compare BOURGEOIS DRAMA, where *bourgeois* does not denote the class of readers but the social sphere of the action of the play.

Bourgeois Tragedy: Plays with somber and often pathetic PLOTS dealing with the life of middle-class PROTAGONISTS. The term is a synonym for DOMESTIC TRAGEDY, and embraces plays as different as O'Neill's *Beyond the Horizon,* Lillo's *The London Merchant,* and Arthur Miller's *The Death of a Salesman.* See DOMESTIC TRAGEDY.

Bouts-rimés: A kind of literary game in which players are given lists of rhyming words and are expected to write impromptu VERSES with the RHYMES in the order given. The game has been popular in France since the seventeenth century; it was a popular pastime of the BLUESTOCKINGS in England; and clubs devoted to it sprang up in Scotland in the nineteenth century. It bears some similarity to the CLERIHEW and the LIMERICK.

Bowdlerize: To expurgate a book or piece of writing by omitting offensive, indecorous passages. *Bowdlerize* derives from Thomas Bowdler, an English physician, who published (in 1818) an expurgated edition of Shakespeare.

Box Set: A STAGE set that realistically represents a room with a ceiling and three walls, the FOURTH WALL being imagined as existing between the audience and the actors.

Brachycatalectic: A line of VERSE that lacks two syllables of a FOOT. See CATALEXIS.

Braggadocio: A vain, pretentious, noisy, and boasting braggart who is actually a craven coward. Although the name comes from such a character in Spenser's *The Faerie Queene,* the *Braggadocio* is really a STOCK CHARACTER with a long history stretching back to Greek and Roman comedy. See MILES GLORIOSUS, ALAZON.

Brahmins: Members of the highest caste among the Hindus. The name is applied to the highly cultured and socially exclusive families of New England, particularly in the nineteenth century. In his novel *Elsie Venner,* Oliver Wendell Holmes uses the term to characterize "the harmless, inoffensive, untitled aristocracy," particularly of Boston and its environs, which became "a caste by the repetition of the same influences generation after generation." The term is customarily used in a derisive sense. John P. Marquand's character George Apley in *The Late George Apley* is a typical *Brahmin* of relatively late vintage.

Breton Lay: Both the relatively brief form of the medieval French ROMANCES, professed to have been sung by Breton minstrels on Celtic themes, and English medieval POEMS written in imitation of such French works. See BRETON ROMANCE and LAY.

Breton Romance: A medieval French METRICAL ROMANCE, emphasizing love very strongly as the central force in the PLOT. *Breton romances* drew on the traditions of COURTLY LOVE and frequently dealt with legends such as the Tristan and Iseult stories or the Arthurian materials. "The Franklin's Tale," in Chaucer's *Canterbury Tales,* is in a short form of the *Breton romance* called the BRETON LAY.

Breve: The name of the symbol (◡) used to indicate a short syllable in the SCANSION of QUANTITATIVE VERSE and an unstressed syllable in ACCENTUAL-SYLLABIC VERSE.

Brief: A condensed statement, a résumé, of the main arguments or ideas presented in a speech or piece of writing. In legal practice, a formal summary of laws and authorities bearing on the main points of a case; in church history, a papal letter less formal than a bull.

British Museum: Of importance to students of literature since it houses probably the most important library in the world. The collection, founded in 1753 through a bequest from Sir Hans Sloane, now embraces over 6,000,000 printed volumes, 10,000 INCUNABULA, and 75,000 manuscripts. It is located in Great Russell Street, in Bloomsbury, London. The *British Museum* is particularly wealthy in its collection of manuscripts including, besides the famous Harleian and Cottonian MSS., a series of documents from the third century to the present. Particularly noteworthy are its collections comprising English historical chronicles, Anglo-Saxon materials, charters, Arthurian romances, the Burney Collection of classical MSS., Greek papyri, Irish, French, and Italian MSS., and the genealogical records of English families. From time to time it has been given by bequest special libraries such as Archbishop Cranmer's Collection, the Thomas Collection, the C. M. Cracherode Collection, and the Sir Joseph Banks Collection. Other important features are its assortment of items from American, Chinese and Oriental, Hebrew, and Slavonic literatures. According to the British copyright law the Museum receives copies of every publication seeking copyright pro-

Brook Farm

tection. The result is an astonishing grouping together in one place of the learning and literatures of the world.

Broadside Ballad: Soon after the development of printing in England BALLADS were prepared for circulation on FOLIO sheets, printed on one side only, two pages to the sheet, and two columns to the page. Because of their manner of publication these were called *broadsides.* These BALLADS ranged from reproductions of old popular BALLADS of literary distinction to semi-illiterate screeds with little poetic quality. These *broadsides* had great variety of subject matter: accidents, dying speeches of criminals, miraculous events, religious and political harangues. They were often satirical in nature and frequently personal in their invective. In the sixteenth century, the heyday of their popularity, they served, as one critic states, as a "people's yellow journal."

Brochure: Originally the term referred to a small work or PAMPHLET with its pages stitched or wired, not bound. It now refers to any relatively brief work regardless of the type of binding.

Broken Rhyme: A term describing the breaking of a word at the end of a VERSE in order to produce a RHYME. Although the effect is apt to be comic, it is also used by serious poets, notably Gerard Manley Hopkins. The opening lines of his "The Windhover" illustrate *broken rhyme:*

I caught this morning morning's minion, king-
    dom of daylight's dauphin, dapple-dawn-drawn Falcon, in his riding
  Of the rolling level underneath him steady air, and striding
High there, how he rung upon the rein of a wimpling wing.

Brook Farm: A UTOPIAN experiment in communal living, sponsored by the Transcendental Club of Boston. The farm, located at West Roxbury, Massachusetts, then nine miles from Boston, was taken over in 1841 by a joint stock company, headed by George Ripley. The full name of the organization was "The Brook Farm Institute of Agriculture and Education." The basic reasons for the scheme were efforts to provide for the residents opportunity for cultural pursuits and leisure at little cost, the farm being supposed, through the rotation of labor of the members, to support the residents who, in most of their time, were to be free to attend lectures, read, write, and discuss intellectual problems. The project was influenced by the doctrines of François Fourier and Robert Owen. While many transcendentalists were interested in the enterprise, it was not the outgrowth of a general activity on their part. Hawthorne (see *The Blithedale Romance*) was there for a short period as were other prominent leaders, but such people as Emerson, Alcott, and Thoreau never actively took part. Dissension among the members, the discovery that the soil was not fertile enough to yield the necessary return, and the burning of a new and uninsured central "phalanstery" (which was the term applied to a dwelling at such a community) were some of the reasons which in 1846 brought about the end of the project. See TRANSCENDENTALISM.

Bucolic: A term used to characterize PASTORAL writing concerned with shepherds and rural life. The treatment is usually rather formal and fanciful. In the plural, *bucolics,* the term refers collectively to the PASTORAL literature of such writers as Theocritus and Virgil. In the present loose usage the expression connotes simply POETRY with a rustic background and is not necessarily restricted to VERSE with the conventional PASTORAL elements. See PASTORAL.

Burden: The CHORUS or REFRAIN of a SONG or a LYRIC, usually coming at the end of each STANZA.

Burlesque: A form of comedy characterized by ridiculous exaggeration. This distortion is secured in a variety of ways: the sublime may be made absurd, honest emotions may be turned to SENTIMENTALITY, a serious subject may be treated frivolously or a frivolous subject seriously. Perhaps the essential quality which makes for *burlesque* is the discrepancy between subject-matter and STYLE. That is, a STYLE ordinarily dignified may be used for nonsensical matter, or a STYLE very nonsensical may be used to ridicule a weighty subject. *Burlesque,* as a form of art, manifests itself in sculpture, painting, and even architecture, as well as in literature. It has an ancient lineage in world literature: an author of uncertain identity used it in the *Battle of the Frogs and Mice,* to TRAVESTY Homer. Aristophanes made *burlesque* popular, and in France, under Louis XIV, nothing was sacred to the satirist. Chaucer in *Sir Thopas* burlesqued MEDIEVAL ROMANCE as did Cervantes in *Don Quixote.* One of the best known uses of *burlesque* in DRAMA is Gay's *The Beggar's Opera.* In recent use the term—already broad—has been broadened to include musical plays light in nature though not essentially *burlesque* in tone or manner. A distinction between *burlesque* and PARODY is commonly made, in which *burlesque* is a TRAVESTY of a literary FORM and PARODY a TRAVESTY of a particular work. See TRAVESTY, PARODY.

Burletta: A term used in the late eighteenth century for a variety of musical dramatic forms, somewhat like the BALLAD-OPERA, the EXTRAVAGANZA, and the PANTOMIME. One of its sponsors (George Colman, the younger) asserted that the proper use of the word was for "a DRAMA in RHYME, entirely musical—a short comick piece consisting of recitative and singing, wholly accompanied, more or less, by the orchestra."

Burns Stanza: A variant form of the TAIL-RHYME STANZA, named for Robert Burns, who used it frequently. It consists of six VERSES, rhyming *aaabab,* with the lines ending with *a* RHYMES being TETRAMETER and those with *b* RHYMES being DIMETER or TRIMETER. The following STANZA from Burns's "Lines to John Lapraik" illustrates the *Burns stanza:*

> Your critic-folk may cock their nose
> And say, "How can you e'er propose,
> You wha ken hardly verse frae prose,
>   To mak a sang?"
> But, by your leave, my learned foes,
>   Ye're may be wrang.

Buskin: A boot, thick-soled and reaching halfway to the knee, worn by Greek tragedians with the purpose of increasing their stature, even as comedians wore SOCKS for the opposite purpose. By association *buskin* has come to mean TRAGEDY. Milton used "the buskin'd stage" and "Jonson's learned SOCK" to characterize TRAGEDY and COMEDY respectively.

C

Cabal: A word formed from the first letters of the names of Charles II's unpopular ministry, Clifford, Ashley, Buckingham, Arlington, and Lauderdale; hence an ACROSTIC.

Cacophony: The opposite of EUPHONY; a harsh, unpleasant combination of sounds or tones. Though most specifically a term used in the CRITICISM of POETRY, the word is also employed to indicate any disagreeable sound effect in other forms of writing. *Cacophony* may be an unconscious flaw in the poet's music, resulting in harshness of sound or difficulty of articulation, or it may be used consciously for effect, as Browning and Eliot often use it. See EUPHONY.

Cadence: Measured, rhythmical movement either in prose or verse. The recurrence of EMPHASIS or ACCENT often accompanied by rising and falling modulations of the voice. *Cadence* is related to RHYTHM, but exists usually in larger and looser units of syllables than the formal, metrical movement of regular VERSES. Properly used, *cadence* can be made one of the most subtle and pleasing of stylistic qualities. See FREE VERSE.

Cæsura: A pause or break in the metrical or rhythmical progress of a line of VERSE. Originally, in classical literature, the *cæsura* characteristically divided a FOOT between two words. Usually the *cæsura* has been placed near the middle of a VERSE. Some poets, however, have sought diversity of rhythmical effect by placing the *cæsura* anywhere from near the beginning of a line to near the end. Examples of variously placed *cæsuras* are shown in these lines by Milton:

> Sleepst thou, Companion dear, ‖ what sleep can close
> Thy eye-lids? ‖ and remembrest what Decree
> Of yesterday, ‖ so late hath past the lips
> Of Heav'ns Almightie. ‖ Thou to me thy thoughts
> Wast wont, etc.

Viewed in another sense, the *cæsura* is an instrument of prose *rhythm* which cuts across and, by varying, enriches the regularity of accentual VERSE. The interplay of prose sense and VERSE demand can be observed in the selection given above. Metricists who follow closely the classical distinctions use *cæsura* to indicate a pause within a FOOT and DIERESIS to indicate a pause that coincides with the end of the FOOT. This distinction is seldom made in English METRICS, where *cæsura* is employed as the generic term.

Calendar: Any of various systems of demarcating the segments of time, as days, weeks, months, and years; or a table that lists such arbitrary divisions. The term is occasionally used in literature when some temporal structure is given a work, as in Spenser's *Shepheardes Calender,* which consists of twelve poems entitled for the twelve months. See ALMANAC.

Calligraphy: The art of beautiful writing. In literature the significance of the term springs from the development of the art during the Middle Ages when the monks gave much attention to copying ancient manuscripts.

Calvinism: The great religious conflict of medieval times was between AUGUSTINIANISM, which would exalt the glory of God at the expense of the dignity of man (stressing original sin and the necessity of divine grace), and PELAGIANISM, which asserted man's original innocence and his ability to develop moral and spiritual power through his own efforts. ARMINIANISM was a compromise between these positions, insisting upon the part both God and man must play in human redemption. *Calvinism* was a RENAISSANCE representative of the Augustinian point of view.

Some understanding of the teachings of *Calvinism*—the charter of which is John Calvin's famous *Institutes of the Christian Religion* (1536)—is important to the student of literature. The essential doctrines of the system are frequently summed up in the famous Five Points: (1) total depravity, man's natural inability to exercise free will, since he inherited corruption from Adam's fall; (2) unconditional election, which manifests itself through God's election of those to be saved, despite their inability to perform saving works; (3) prevenient and irresistible grace, made available in advance but only to the elect; (4) the perseverance of saints, the predetermined elect inevitably persevering in the path of holiness; and (5) limited atonement, man's corruption being partially atoned for by Christ, this atonement being provided the elect through the Holy Spirit, giving them the power to attempt to obey God's will as it is revealed in the Bible.

This system developed both zeal and intolerance on the part of the elect. It fostered education, however, which in early New England was regarded as a religious duty, and thereby profoundly affected the development of American culture. To this attitude of the *Calvinistic* PURITANS may be traced much of the inspiration for such things as: the founding of many colleges and universities, the creation of a system of public schools, and the great activity of early printing presses in America—as well as the development of religious sects. Historically, especially in Europe, it is probably true that the political effects of *Calvinism* have been in the main calculated to encourage freedom and popular government.

In New England the COVENANT THEOLOGY early softened and

modified *Calvinism,* but the term Puritan in America usually refers, at least in a philosophical sense, to a belief in the doctrines of *Calvinism.* See Augustinianism, Arianism, Arminianism, Covenant theology, Pelagianism.

Calypso: A type of music which originated in the West Indies, particularly Trinidad. It is a ballad-like improvisation in African rhythms. The singers, who compose as they sing, frequently deal with current topics, often in a satiric manner.

Canon: (1) A standard of judgment; a criterion; (2) the authorised or accepted list of books belonging in the Christian Bible. Apocryphal books are uncanonical. The term is often extended to mean the accepted list of books of any author, such as Shakespeare. Thus *Macbeth* belongs without doubt in the *canon* of Shakespeare's work, while *Sir John Oldcastle,* though printed as Shakespeare's soon after his death, is not canonical, because the evidence of Shakespeare's authorship is unconvincing. A similar use of the word is illustrated in the phrase "the Saints' *Canon,*" the list of Saints actually authorized or "canonized" by the Church. See Apocrypha.

Canso: A Provençal love song, usually in stanzas, sung by the troubadours. Compare with the variant form canzo, which is peculiar to northern France.

Cant: Insincere, specious language calculated to give the impression of piety or religious fervor. In critical writing the term is used to signify the language and phraseology characteristic of a profession or art, as "the pedagogue's *cant,*" "the artist's *cant.*" In this sense of a special language, the term indicates any technical or special vocabulary or dialect, as "thieves' *cant,*" "beggars' *cant.*" More loosely still, the word signifies any insincere, superficial display of language, planned to convey an impression of conviction, but devoid of genuine emotion or feeling; that is, language used chiefly for display or effect. See Jargon.

Canto: A section or division of a long poem. Derived from the Latin *cantus* (song) the word originally signified a section of a narrative poem of such length as to be sung by a minstrel in one singing. Byron's *Childe Harold's Pilgrimage* is divided into *cantos.*

Carol

Canzo: A love song, sung by the TROUVÈRES. Compare with CANSO.

Canzone: A lyrical POEM, a SONG or BALLAD. In several ways the *canzone* is similar to the MADRIGAL. The *canzone* is a short poem consisting of equal STANZAS and an ENVOY of fewer lines than the STANZA. It is impossible to be specific about the VERSE FORM since different writers have wrought wide variations in structure. The number of lines to the STANZA ranges from seven to twenty, and the ENVOY from three to ten. Petrarch's *canzoni* usually consisted of five or six STANZAS and the ENVOY. In general it may be said that the *canzone* form is not unlike the CHANT ROYAL though its conventions are less fixed. The *canzone* is generally conceded to have first developed in Provence during the Middle Ages and Giraud de Borneil is credited with having first evolved the pattern which has proved very popular in Italy. Others than Petrarch who have written *canzoni* are Dante, Tasso, Leopardi, Chiabrera, and Marchetti. Frequent subjects used were love, nature, and the wide range of emotional reactions to life, particularly if sad, which poets commonly present. The term and the aspects of the medieval form it designates are used by contemporary poets on occasion for POEMS of considerable complexity of STRUCTURE.

Caricature: Descriptive writing which seizes upon certain individual qualities of a person and through exaggeration or distortion produces a BURLESQUE, ridiculous effect. *Caricature* more frequently is associated with drawing (cartoons) than with writing, since for writing the related types—SATIRE, BURLESQUE, and PARODY—are more generally used. *Caricature,* unlike the highest SATIRE, is likely to treat *personal* qualities, though, like SATIRE, it lends itself to the ridicule of political, religious, and social foibles.

Carmen Figuratum: A POEM so written that the form of the printed words suggests the subject matter; the device is not common in English poetry, and is usually considered a form of false WIT. Examples are Herbert's "Easter Wings," the humorous "long and sad tail of the Mouse," in *Alice in Wonderland,* and several poems of Dylan Thomas, notably "Vision and Prayer."

Carol (*Carole*):   In medieval times in France a *carole* was a dance. The term later was applied to the song which accompanied the dance. The leader sang the STANZAS, the other dancers singing the REFRAIN. The *carole* became very popular, and in the twelfth and thirteenth centuries spread through other European countries and was instrumental in extending the influence of the French LYRIC. Later, *carol* was used to mean any joyous song, then HYMNS of religious joy, and finally Christmas HYMNS in particular. Some *carols*, such as "Joseph was an old man," were definitely popular, belonging to the culture of the folk, while later ones, such as Charles Wesley's "Hark, the Herald Angels Sing," are the product of more conscious and sophisticated literary effort. The Christmas HYMN is called a *noël* in France.

Caroline: Applied to whatever belonged to or was typical of the age of Charles I of England (1625–1642), but more particularly to the spirit of the court of Charles. Thus *Caroline* literature might mean all the literature of the time, both Cavalier and PURITAN, or it might be used more specifically to suggest that of the royalist group, such as the CAVALIER LYRISTS. *Caroline* literature was in some senses a decadent carry-over from the ELIZABETHAN and JACOBEAN periods. Melancholy not only characterized the work of the META-PHYSICAL POETS but permeated the writings of both the conflicting groups, PURITAN and Cavalier. DRAMA was decadent; ROMANTICISM was in decline; CLASSICISM was advancing; the scientific spirit was growing in spite of the absorption of the people in violent religious controversies. It was in *Caroline* times that the PURITAN migration to America was heaviest. The *Caroline* Age was the last segment of the RENAISSANCE in England, if the COMMONWEALTH is considered an interregnum between the RENAISSANCE and the NEO-CLASSIC PERIOD. See RENAISSANCE for a sketch of the literature; see BAROQUE, JACOBEAN, CAVALIER LYRISTS; see also "The Caroline Age" in *The Outline of Literary History.*

Carpe Diem: "Seize the day." The phrase was used by Horace and has come to be applied generally to literature, especially to lyric POEMS, which exemplify the spirit of "Let us eat and drink, for tomorrow we shall die." The theme was a very common one in sixteenth- and seventeenth-century English love poetry; lover-poets continually were exhorting their mistresses to yield to love while they still had their youth and beauty, as in Robert Herrick's famous

> Gather ye rosebuds while ye may,
> Old Time is still a-flying;
> And this same flower that smiles today,
> Tomorrow will be dying.

Catalexis: Incompleteness of the last FOOT at the end of a VERSE; truncation at the close of a line of POETRY by omission of one or two final syllables; the opposite of ANACRUSIS. *Catalexis* is one of the many ways in which the poet secures variety of metrical effects. The term ACATALECTIC is used to designate particular lines where *catalexis* is *not* employed. In the following lines by Thomas Hood, written in DACTYLIC DIMETER, the second and fourth are *catalectic* because the second FOOT of each lacks the two unaccented syllables which would normally complete the DACTYL. The first and third lines, in which the unaccented syllables are *not* cut off and which therefore are metrically complete, are ACATALECTIC.

> One more unfortunate,
> Weary of breath,
> Rashly importunate,
> Gone to her death!

Catalexis is also applied to the truncation of an initial unstressed syllable; the resulting line is called HEADLESS. *Catalexis* of two syllables, as in the lines by Hood, is sometimes called BRACHYCATALEXIS.

Catalog: A list of people, things, or attributes. *Catalogs,* sometimes extended to great length, are characteristic of many primitive literatures. The EPIC uses the *catalog* of HEROES, of ships, of armor, and such. The Bible has many *catalogs,* the most notable example being the genealogy of Jesus in Matthew, Chapter 1. In the RENAISSANCE, one of the conventions of the SONNET and the LYRIC was the *catalog* of the physical charms of the beloved. In modern POETRY the *catalog* has been used very extensively by Walt Whitman, Carl Sandburg, and Vachel Lindsay. For an impressively extended *catalog,* see Whitman's *Song of Myself,* Section 15.

Catastasis: In DRAMA, the heightening; the third of the four parts into which the ancients divided a play. See DRAMATIC STRUCTURE. In RHETORIC it is the narrative part of the introduction of a speech.

Catastrophe: The conclusion of a play, particularly a TRAGEDY; the last of the four parts into which the ancients divided a play. It is the final stage in the FALLING ACTION, ending the dramatic CONFLICT, winding up the PLOT and consisting of the actions that result from the CLIMAX. Since it usually is used in connection with a TRAGEDY and involves the death of the hero, it is sometimes used by extension to designate an unhappy ending (or event) in nondramatic FICTION and even in life. In the strict sense of DRAMATIC STRUCTURE, however, every DRAMA has a *catastrophe;* see the line in *King Lear* which reads: "Pat, he comes, like the catastrophe of the old comedy." Today, however, DÉNOUEMENT is more commonly used than *catastrophe* in this sense. See DRAMATIC STRUCTURE, DÉNOUEMENT.

Catch: In music a round for at least three voices, in which each singer begins a line or a phrase behind the preceding one. It was a popular musical form in the seventeenth and eighteenth centuries and still occurs predominantly in children's songs today. In METRICS the term *catch* is applied to an extra unstressed syllable at the beginning of a line that would normally begin with a stressed syllable: it is, thus, a form of ANACRUSIS. *Catch* was also applied in the seventeenth and eighteenth centuries to the intermingling of strong and weak voices in SONGS where the strong voices interject a bawdy twist. Jonathan Swift wrote such verses.

Catch-Word: A word so often repeated that it is identified with a person or object. In printing, *catch-word* has two meanings. The current usage of the term is as the name for a word printed at the top of a column or a page to indicate the first or last word on that page. The words printed in boldface at the top of the page in this book are *catch-words.* Early printers frequently printed at the bottom of each page under the last word on the last line of that page the first word on the next page. This word was called a *catch-word.*

Catharsis (or **Katharsis**): In the *Poetics* Aristotle, in defining TRAGEDY, speaks of its "through pity and fear effecting the proper purgation [*catharsis*] of these emotions," but he fails to explain what he means by "proper purgation." That a physiological METAPHOR has been used to describe the effect produced upon the emotions of the spectator by the witnessing of the tragic action is clear, but the implications of that METAPHOR—and indeed its accurate translation into concept—have been much debated in the history of CRITICISM. Two widely differing interpretations are customary today: one is that the spectator, by vicariously participating in the actions of the hero, learns through the effects upon him of fear and pity that the evil emotions or "mistakes" of the hero are destructive and thereby learns to avoid them in his own life (this is a didactic interpretation); the other is that the spectator's emotional conflicts are temporarily resolved and his inner agitations stilled by having an opportunity vicariously to expend fear and pity upon the tragic hero. This is a psychological interpretation that has undergone great subtlety of elaboration and qualification in recent years. R. B. Sharpe, in *Irony in the Drama,* suggests that the hero of a TRAGEDY comes before its conclusion to represent to the spectator "what Jung calls a symbol and Fraser a scapegoat—that is, a human figure upon whom we are able to load our emotions, from our loftiest to our lowest, our hopes, and our sins, through such a deep and complete emotional identification that he can carry them away with him into heaven or the wilderness and so free us of the burden and the tension of keeping them for ourselves. This empathic identification is . . . catharsis." See TRAGEDY.

Causerie: An INFORMAL ESSAY, usually on a literary topic, and frequently in a series. The term is applied to such ESSAYS because of their similarity to *Causeries du lundi* by Charles Augustin Sainte-Beuve. In the strictest sense it probably should be restricted to the kind of combined biographical and critical treatments for which Sainte-Beuve was noted. Edmund Wilson today writes literary ESSAYS that might be called *causeries.*

Cavalier Lyric: A light-hearted poem characteristic of the CAVALIER LYRISTS; gay in tone; graceful, melodious, and polished in manner; artfully showing Latin classical influences; sometimes licentious and cynical or epigrammatic and witty. At times it breathed the careless braggadocio of the military swashbuckler, at times the aristocratic ease of the peaceful courtier. Many of the poems were OCCASIONAL in character, as Suckling's charming if doggerel-like "Ballad upon a Wedding" or Lovelace's pensive "To Althea from Prison." The themes were love, war, chivalry, and loyalty to the king. The term *Cavalier Lyric* is also applied to a poem of a later age but that illustrates the spirit of the times of the CAVALIER LYRISTS, such as Browning's "Boot, Saddle, to Horse and Away."

Cavalier Lyrists: The followers of Charles I (1625–1649) were called Cavaliers, as opposed to the supporters of Parliament, who were called ROUNDHEADS. The *Cavalier Lyrists* were a group of these Cavaliers who composed gay and light-hearted poems, especially Thomas Carew, Richard Lovelace, and Sir John Suckling. These men were soldiers and courtiers first and the authors of

CAVALIER LYRICS only incidentally. Robert Herrick, although he was a country parson and not a courtier, is often classed with the *Cavalier Lyrists*, because many of his poems included in *Hesperides* are in the vein of the Cavaliers. See CAVALIER LYRIC.

Celtic Literature: Literature produced by a people speaking any one of the Celtic DIALECTS. Linguistically, the Celts are divided into two main groups. The "Brythonic" Celts include the Ancient Britons, the Welsh, the Cornish (Cornwall), and the Bretons (Brittany); while the Goidelic (Gaelic) Celts include the Irish, the Manx (Isle of Man), and the Scottish Gaels. At one time the Celts, an important branch of the Indo-European family, dominated Central and Western Europe. The Continental Celts (including the Bretons, who came from Britain) have left no literatures. The Celts of Great Britain and Ireland, however, have produced much literature of interest to students of English and American literature. See IRISH LITERATURE, WELSH LITERATURE, SCOTTISH LITERATURE, CELTIC RENAISSANCE.

Celtic Renaissance (or **Irish Renaissance**): A general term for a movement of the late nineteenth and early twentieth centuries which aimed at the preservation of the Gaelic language (the GAELIC MOVEMENT), the reconstruction of early Celtic history and literature, and the stimulation of a new literature authentically Celtic (esp. Irish) in spirit. From before the middle of the nineteenth century there had been a growing interest in Celtic, especially Irish, antiquities, and much work was done in the collection and study, and later in printing and translation, of manuscripts embodying the history and literature of ancient Ireland. There also developed the practice of collecting and printing folk-tales preserved in oral tradition. In the 1890's came the GAELIC MOVEMENT, which stressed the use of the Gaelic language itself. More fruitful was the contemporaneous Anglo-Irish movement, which stimulated the production of a new literature in English (or "Anglo-Irish") by Irish writers on Irish themes and in the Irish spirit. Standish O'Grady's imaginative treatment of Irish history (1880) provided impetus to the movement, and themes drawn from ancient Irish tradition were exploited in verse and drama. Fortunately, genuine poetic geniuses were at hand to further the project, such as W. B. Yeats, George W. Russell ("A.E."), George Moore, J. M. Synge, and (later) James Stephens, Lord Dunsany, and Padraic Colum. From the beginning

Celtic Revival

Lady Gregory was an enthusiastic worker—as collector, popularizer, essayist, and playwright. A striking phase of the renaissance was its dramatic manifestation. In 1899 under the leadership of Yeats, Moore, Edward Martyn, Lady Gregory, and others the Irish Literary Theater was founded in Dublin. Yeats and Martyn wrote for it some plays employing Irish folk-materials. Later Yeats joined another group more devoted to the exploitation of native elements, The Irish National Theatre Society, to which he attracted J. M. Synge, the most gifted playwright of the movement, whose *Playboy of the Western World* (1907) and *Deirdre of the Sorrows* (1910) attracted wide recognition. This group worked in the famed ABBEY THEATRE. Later exemplars of dramatic activity were Lord Dunsany and Sean O'Casey. The *Celtic Renaissance* produced little of importance in Wales. In Scotland it is perhaps best represented by the work of "Fiona MacLeod" (William Sharp).

Celtic Revival: A term sometimes used for the GAELIC MOVEMENT, the CELTIC RENAISSANCE, or the IRISH LITERARY MOVEMENT, as well as for the eighteenth-century movement described below.

Celtic Revival, The (Eighteenth Century): A literary movement of the last half of the eighteenth century which stressed the use of the historical, literary, and mythological traditions of the ancient Celts, particularly the Welsh. Through confusion Norse mythology was included in "Celtic." *The Celtic Revival* was a part of the ROMANTIC MOVEMENT, in that it stressed the primitive, the remote, the strange and mysterious, and aided the revolt against pseudo-classicism by substituting a new mythology for classical myths and figures. Specifically it was characterized by an intense interest in the druids and early Welsh bards, numerous translations and imitations of early Celtic poetry appearing in the wake of the discovery of some genuine examples of early Welsh verse. The most influential and gifted poet in the group was Thomas Gray, whose "The Bard" (1757) and "The Progress of Poesy" (1757) reflect early phases of the movement. The most spectacular figure in the group of "Celticists" was James Macpherson, whose long poems, *Fingal* (1762) and *Temora* (1763)—chiefly his own invention but partly English renderings of genuine Gaelic pieces preserved in the Scottish Highlands—he published as TRANSLATIONS of the poems of a great Celtic poet of primitive times, Ossian. Both Gray's and Macpherson's work influenced a host of minor poets, who were especially numerous

Center for Editors of American Authors

and active in the last two decades of the century. There was also a considerable reflection of the movement in the DRAMA, e.g., Home's *The Fatal Discovery* (acted 1769).

Center for Editors of American Authors: A committee of scholars representing the American Literature Section of the Modern Language Association of America for the production of definitive EDITIONS of nineteenth-century American authors. It has operated under a series of grants from the National Endowment for the Humanities. The Center establishes editorial procedures, maintains an overview of the work of editors, and approves for publication the texts of the authors. It has enunciated rigorous and highly sophisticated principles for textual editing, and after verification that these principles have been meticulously followed in the preparation of a volume, it awards the volume the right to display the Center's seal of approval. At present work is in progress on carefully prepared editions of the works of Stephen Crane, Emerson, Howells, Irving, Mark Twain, Melville, Simms, Thoreau, and Whitman.

Cento: A literary patchwork, usually in verse, made up of scraps from one or many authors. An example is a fifth-century life of Christ by the Empress Eudoxia, which is in verse with every line drawn from Homer.

Chain Verse: POETRY in which the STANZAS are linked through some pattern of repetition. The last line of one STANZA may be the first of the next producing a linked group of STANZAS that may be considered a *chain*. This linkage may be secured by the repetition of RHYME. The VILLANELLE, a nineteen line POEM in TERCETS followed by a QUATRAIN and having only two RHYMES and frequent repetition of lines, is a complex example of *chain verse*.

Chanson: A song. Originally composed of two-line STANZAS of equal length (COUPLETS), each STANZA ending in a REFRAIN, the *chanson* is now more broadly interpreted to include almost any POEM intended to be sung, and written in a simple style.

Chanson de geste: A "song of great deeds." A term applied to the early French EPIC. The earliest and best existing example, the *Chanson de Roland*, dates from *ca.* 1100. The early *chansons de geste* are written in ten-syllable lines marked by ASSONANCE and

88

grouped in STANZAS of varying length. CYCLES developed, such as that of Charlemagne (*geste du roi*); that of William of Orange, which reflects the efforts of Christian heroes against the invading Saracens; and that dealing with the strife among the rebellious Northern barons. The stories generally reflect chivalric ideals with little use of love as the theme. The form flourished for several centuries, a total of about eighty examples being extant. These epic tales supplied material ("Matter of France") for MEDIEVAL ROMANCE, including English ROMANCES. See MEDIEVAL ROMANCE.

Chant: Loosely used to mean a SONG, but more particularly the term signifies the intoning of words to a monotonous musical measure of few notes. The words of the *chants* in the English Church are drawn from such Biblical sources as the Psalms. CADENCE is an important element, and usually one note (the "reciting note") is used for a series of successive words or syllables. DIRGES are often chanted. Repetition of a few varying musical phrases is a characteristic, and the intonation of the voice plays an important role. *Chants* are generally considered less melodious than SONGS.

Chant royal: One of the more complex, and therefore less used, FRENCH VERSE FORMS. The tradition for this VERSE FORM demands a dignified, heroic subject such as can best be expressed in rich DICTION and courtly formalities of speech. The *chant royal* consists of sixty lines arranged in five STANZAS of eleven VERSES each and an ENVOY of five VERSES, the ENVOY ordinarily starting with an INVOCATION in the manner of the BALLADE. The RHYME SCHEME usually followed is ababccddede for the STANZA and ddede (as in the last five lines of the STANZA) for the ENVOY. The italicized *e* above indicates the recurrence of a complete line as a REFRAIN at the end of each STANZA and at the close of the ENVOY. All STANZAS must be the same in all details and no RHYME-word may appear twice.

Chantey (Shanty): A sailors' SONG marked by strong RHYTHM and, in the good old days of sail, used to accompany certain forms of hard labor (such as weighing anchor) performed by seamen working in a group. The leader of the singing was referred to as the "chantey man," his responsibility being to sing a line or two introductory to a REFRAIN joined in by the whole group.

Chapbook

Chapbook: Literally "cheap" book; a small book or PAMPHLET, usually a single SIGNATURE of sixteen or thirty-two pages, poorly printed and crudely illustrated, which was sold to the common people in England and America through the eighteenth century by peddlers or "chapmen." *Chapbooks* dealt with all sorts of topics and incidents: travel tales, murder cases, prodigies, strange occurrences, witchcraft, biographies, religious legends and tracts, stories of all sorts. They are of interest to the literary historian because they reflect contemporary attitudes toward themes and situations treated in literature. The term has been revived in this century as the name for miscellaneous small books and PAMPHLETS.

Character: Most often used to refer to a person in a story, *character* is also a term applied to a literary form which flourished in England and France in the seventeenth and eighteenth centuries. It is a brief descriptive SKETCH of a personage who typifies some definite quality. The person is described not as an individualized personality but as an example of some vice or virtue or type, such as a busybody, a superstitious fellow, a fop, a country bumpkin, a garrulous old man, a happy milkmaid, etc. Similar treatments of institutions and inanimate things, such as "the *character* of a coffee house," also employed the term, and late in the seventeenth century, by a natural extension of the tradition, *character* was applied to longer compositions, sometimes historical, as Viscount Halifax's *Character of Charles II*. The vogue of *character*-writing followed the publication in 1592 of a Latin translation of Theophrastus, an ancient Greek writer of similar sketches. Though the *character* may have influenced Ben Jonson in his treatment of the man of HUMOURS in COMEDY, the first English writer to cultivate the form as such was Bishop Joseph Hall in his *Characters of Virtues and Vices* (1608). Two of his successors were Sir Thomas Overbury (1614) and John Earle (1628). Later, under the influence of the French writer La Bruyère, *characters* became more individualized and were combined with the ESSAY, as in the PERIODICAL ESSAYS of Addison and Steele. Subjects of *characters* were given fanciful proper names, often Latin or Greek, such as "Croesus." See ESSAY.

Characterization: In the LYRIC, the ESSAY, and the AUTOBIOGRAPHY, the author reveals aspects of his own character; in the BIOGRAPHY and the HISTORY, he presents the characters of actual persons other than himself; and in FICTION (the DRAMA, the NOVEL,

the SHORT STORY, and the NARRATIVE POEM), he reveals the characters of imaginary persons. The creation of images of these imaginary
persons so credible that they exist for the reader as real within the
limits of the FICTION is called *characterization*. The ability to
characterize the people of his imagination successfully is one of the
primary attributes of a good novelist, dramatist, or short-story
writer.

There are three fundamental methods of *characterization* in
FICTION: (1) the explicit presentation by the author of the
character through direct EXPOSITION, either in an introductory block
or more often piece-meal throughout the work, illustrated by action;
(2) the presentation of the character in action, with little or no
explicit comment by the author, in the expectation that the reader
will be able to deduce the attributes of the actor from the actions;
and (3) the representation from within a character, without comment on the character by the author, of the impact of actions and
emotions upon his inner self, with the expectation that the reader
will come to a clear understanding of the attributes of the character.

It is difficult to distinguish among these methods of *characterization* without discussing them in terms of narrative POINT OF VIEW.
Usually the explicit method results when the story is told by a first-
person NARRATOR, such as Dickens' David Copperfield or Sterne's
Tristram Shandy, or by an OMNISCIENT AUTHOR, such as Fielding
in *Tom Jones* or Thackeray in *Vanity Fair*. The success of the
explicit method of *characterization* rests at least in part upon the
personality of the NARRATOR or OMNISCIENT AUTHOR. The presentation of characters through actions is essentially the dramatic method.
It is the traditional way of establishing character in the DRAMA; so
much so, in fact, that only by changing some of the DRAMATIC
CONVENTIONS, as in the use of a CHORUS, or EXPRESSIONISM, or in
plays like O'Neill's *Strange Interlude,* can other methods of
characterization than this be used in the theater. We know Hamlet
through what he says and does; the riddle of what Shakespeare intended his true character to be is eternally unanswerable. The
NOVEL and the SHORT STORY in this century have frequently
adopted the dramatic technique by making objective presentations
of characters in action without authorial comment, to such an
extent that the SELF-EFFACING AUTHOR is today a fictional commonplace. Writers of the REALISTIC NOVEL, such as Bennett, Galsworthy,
and Howells, usually employ this method of character presentation. The presentation of the impact upon the PROTAGONIST's inner

self of external events and emotions begins with the novels of Henry James, whose *The Ambassadors* is an excellent example, and continues into the STREAM OF CONSCIOUSNESS NOVEL where, through INTERIOR MONOLOGUES, the subconscious or unconscious mind of the character is revealed, as in Joyce's *Ulysses* or Faulkner's *The Sound and the Fury.*

But regardless of the method by which a character is presented, the author may concentrate upon a dominant trait to the exclusion of the other aspects of the character's personality or he may attempt to present a fully rounded personality. If the presentation of a single dominant trait is carried to an extreme, not a believable character but a CARICATURE will result. If this method is handled with skill, it can produce two-dimensional characters that are striking and interesting but lack depth. Mr. Micawber in *David Copperfield* comes close to being such a two-dimensional character through the emphasis that Dickens puts upon a very small group of characteristics. Sometimes such characters are given descriptive names, such as Mr. Deuceace, the gambler in *Vanity Fair.* On the other hand the author may present us with so convincing a congeries of personality traits that a complex rather than a simple character emerges; such a character is three-dimensional or, in E. M. Forster's term, "round." As a rule, the major characters in a FICTION need such three-dimensional treatment, while minor characters are often handled two-dimensionally.

Furthermore, a character may be either STATIC or DYNAMIC. A STATIC CHARACTER is one who changes little if at all in the progress of the narrative. Things happen *to* such a character without things happening *within* him. The pattern of action reveals the character rather than showing the character changing in response to the actions. Sometimes a STATIC CHARACTER gives the appearance of changing simply because our picture of him is revealed bit by bit; this is true of Uncle Toby in *Tristram Shandy,* who does not change, although our view of him steadily changes. A DYNAMIC CHARACTER, on the other hand, is one who is modified by the actions through which he passes, and one of the objectives of the work in which he appears is to reveal the consequences of these actions upon him. Most great DRAMAS and NOVELS have DYNAMIC CHARACTERS as PROTAGONISTS. SHORT STORIES are more likely to reveal STATIC CHARACTERS through action than to show changes in characters resulting from actions.

Ultimately every successful character represents a fusion of the universal and the particular and becomes an example of the CONCRETE UNIVERSAL. It is in this dramatic particularization of the typical and universal that one of the essences of the dramatic and of *characterization* is to be found. Our minds may delight in abstractions and ideas, but it is our emotions that ultimately give the aesthetic and dramatic response, and they respond to the personal, the particular, the CONCRETE. This is why a NOVEL speaks to us more permanently than an ALLEGORY, why Hamlet has an authority forever lacking the "Indecisive Man" in a seventeenth-century CHARACTER. See POINT OF VIEW, NOVEL, SHORT STORY, DRAMA, PLOT, CONCRETE UNIVERSAL.

Chartism: A political movement in England just before the middle of the nineteenth century, the object of which was to secure more social recognition and improved material conditions for the lower classes. The Chartists advocated universal suffrage, vote by ballot, annual parliaments, and other reforms. This platform is given in the *People's Charter* (1838). Carlyle's *Chartism* (1839) is an attack upon the movement. The chartist agitation is favorably reflected in some of Kingsley's novels. See INDUSTRIAL REVOLUTION.

Chiasmus: A type of rhetorical BALANCE in which the second part is syntactically balanced against the first but with the parts reversed, as in Coleridge's line, "Flowers are lovely, love is flower-like," or Pope's "Works without show, and without pomp presides."

Chivalric Romance: MEDIEVAL ROMANCE reflecting the customs and ideals of CHIVALRY. See MEDIEVAL ROMANCE, ARTHURIAN LEGEND, COURTLY LOVE, CHIVALRY IN ENGLISH LITERATURE.

Chivalry in English Literature: The system of manners and morals known as *chivalry,* chiefly a fruit of the feudal system of the Middle Ages, because it had been presented in MEDIEVAL ROMANCE in a highly idealized form amounting almost to a religious system for the upper classes, has furnished much color, atmosphere, and inspiration for later literature. The medieval knight, seen in the light of literary idealization (as a matter of fact the typical medieval knight had many unlovely characteristics), has been portrayed not only by the many writers of MEDIEVAL ROMANCE, but by later poets like Chaucer, with his "parfit, gentle knight" and Spenser, who fills *The Faerie Queene* with a procession of courteous and heroic Guyons, Scudamores, and Calidores. Knights whose high oaths bind them to fidelity to God and king, truth to their lady-loves, and ready service for all ladies in distress or other victims of unjust tyrants, cruel giants, or fiendish monsters, have become commonplaces of romantic literature.

They impart a vigor and glow to the action of such HISTORICAL NOVELS as Scott's *Ivanhoe* and find an unreal but earnestly sympathetic treatment in the *Idylls of the King* of Tennyson. Tennyson's poem *Guinevere,* indeed, includes the following poetic statement of the ideals of knighthood (King Arthur is speaking):

> I made them lay their hands in mine and swear
> To reverence the King, as if he were
> Their conscience, and their conscience as their King,
> To break the heathen and uphold the Christ,
> To ride abroad redressing human wrongs,
> To speak no slander, no, nor listen to it,
> To honor his own word as if his God's,
> To lead sweet lives in purest chastity,
> To love one maiden only, cleave to her,
> And worship her by years of noble deeds,
> Until they won her.

A more faithful picture may be found in the pages of Malory's *Le Morte Darthur,* where the glamour of knighthood, with all the effort to idealize Lancelot and Arthur and find in the "good old days" a perfect pattern for later times, is not allowed to obscure some of the less pleasing realities of medieval knighthood. So glorious a thing as *chivalry* has not, of course, gone unnoticed by the satirists. The early seventeenth century not only produced the immortal *Don Quixote* in Spain but Beaumont and Fletcher's dramatic BURLESQUE *The Knight of the Burning Pestle* in England, while modern America has brought forth not only its broadly comic *A Connecticut Yankee in King Arthur's Court* (Mark Twain) but its more subtly mocking *Galahad* (John Erskine). See ARTHURIAN LEGEND.

Choriambus: In METRICS a FOOT in which two accented syllables flank two unaccented syllables: ⌣ ⌣ ⌣ ⌣. This FOOT is sometimes used in a VERSE form called *choriambics,* in which the line begins with a TROCHEE, three *choriambics* follow, and it closes with an IAMBUS. Swinburne used the form, as did Rupert Brooke, whose line: "Í have / ténd ĕd ănd lovéd / yéar ŭp ŏn yéar, / Í ĭn the sól / ĭ túde" illustrates the *choriambic* line.

Chorus: In ancient Greece, the groups of dancers and singers who participated in religious festivals and dramatic performances. Also the songs sung by the *chorus*. At first the choral songs made up the bulk of the play, the spoken MONOLOGUE and DIALOGUE being interpolated. Later, however, the *chorus* became subordinate, offering inter-act comments. Finally, it became a mere LYRIC used to take up the time between ACTS. In Elizabethan drama the role of the *chorus* was often taken by a single actor, who recited PROLOGUE and EPILOGUE and gave inter-act comments which linked the ACTS and foreshadowed coming events. So in Sackville and Norton's *Gorboduc,* the "first" English TRAGEDY, the *chorus* consists of a few STANZAS accompanied by a DUMB SHOW, the latter foreshadowing the coming action. In Kyd's *Spanish Tragedy* the part of the *chorus* is played by a ghost and the figure Revenge, the ghost urging Revenge to inspire the actors to hasten the vengeance demanded by the action. Shakespeare sometimes employed the *chorus,* as in *Pericles,* where the old poet Gower, accompanied by a DUMB SHOW, provides PROLOGUE and inter-act comment, and in *King Henry the Fifth,* where the *chorus* comments on the action, explains change of scene, and PROLOGUE-like begs for a sympathetic attitude on the part of the spectators. Sometimes, within the play proper, one of the characters, like the Fool in *King Lear,* is said to play a *"chorus*-like" role when he comments on the action.

Although not commonly used, the *chorus* is still employed occasionally by the modern playwright, notably T. S. Eliot in *Murder in the Cathedral.* Sometimes a *chorus*-character—one whose role in the DRAMA is to comment on the action—is used; such a character is Seth Beckwith in O'Neill's *Mourning Becomes Electra.* Novelists, too, have used the *chorus,* sometimes as a group of characters who comment on action, sometimes as a single character. Both Scott and Hardy often used *choruses* of rustic characters. The group of good wives in the first scene of Hawthorne's *The Scarlet Letter* serves the function of a *chorus.* The CONFIDANTE of the Henry James novel is a *chorus*-character.

In music, a *chorus* may be a composition in at least four parts written for a large group of singers, and the term is also applied to the singers of such choral compositions. It is also applied to a REFRAIN repeated after each STANZA of a POEM or a SONG.

Chrestomathy: A collection of choice passages to be used in the study of a language or a literature and, thus, a kind of ANTHOLOGY.

Usually when the term is used today, it signifies a volume of selected passages or stories by a single author; *chrestomathy* was given currency today by its use in this sense by H. L. Mencken.

Christianity, Established in England: There were Christians in Roman Britain as early as the third century, and probably there was an organized church as early as A.D. 314, when the bishops of London and York are said to have attended a church council in Gaul. After the lapse into barbarism which followed the Germanic invasions of the fifth century, *Christianity* was reintroduced directly from Rome by St. Augustine, who landed in Kent in A.D. 597. It flourished in southeastern England under Ethelbert, spread northward, and gained a foothold in Northumbria under Edwin (d. 633), who had married a Kentish princess. Another group of missionaries soon came into Northumbria from the celebrated Celtic monastery of Iona, an island off the west coast of Scotland. Iona had been established in A.D. 563 by St. Columba, a missionary from Ireland, where a form of *Christianity* reflecting the monastic ideals of Bishop Martin of Tours (flourished *ca*.371–*ca*.400) had been introduced from Gaul in the fourth or early fifth century. The Celtic and Roman churches differed in certain doctrines and customs (such as the date for Easter, the form of baptism, and style of tonsure for priests). The resulting disputes were settled in favor of the Roman party at the Synod of Whitby in 664.

The establishment of *Christianity* in England had far-reaching effects upon literature, for the Church was for centuries the chief fosterer of learning. The pagan literature which survived from early Germanic times passed through the medium of Christian authors and copyists, who gave a Christian coloring to the writings that they did not wholly reject. For centuries most writings owed both their inspiration and direction to Christian zeal and to the learning fostered by the Church. The Christianization in the thirteenth century of the great body of Arthurian romances is an outstanding example of the dominance of *Christianity* over medieval literary activity.

Chronicle: A name given to certain forms of historical writing. *Chronicles* differ from ANNALS in their more comprehensive character—their concern with larger aspects of history. Though there were PROTOTYPES in Hebrew, Greek, Latin, and French, it is the medieval *chronicles* in English and their RENAISSANCE successors that are of chief interest to the student of English literature. The

Chronicle Play

Anglo-Saxon Chronicle, begun under King Alfred late in the ninth century and carried on by various writers in a number of monasteries in succeeding centuries, has been called the "first great book in English prose." The record begins with 60 B.C. and closes with 1154 ("Peterborough" version). Alfred and his helpers revised older minor *chronicles* and records and wrote first-hand accounts of their own times. The work as a whole is a sort of historical miscellany, sometimes sketchy in detail and detached in attitude, at other times spirited, partisan, and detailed. An important Old English poem preserved through its inclusion in the *Anglo-Saxon Chronicle* is the spirited *Battle of Brunanburh.* A famous Latin prose *chronicle* is Geoffrey of Monmouth's *History of the Kings of Britain* (*ca.*1136), which not only records legendary British history but also romantic accounts of King Arthur. The earliest important verse *chronicle* in Middle English is Layamon's *Brut* (*ca.*1205), based upon Wace's French poetic version of Geoffrey. It is a long poem composed in an imaginative, often dramatic, vein, and exhibits a picturesque STYLE sometimes reminiscent of Old English poetry.

Later Middle English *chronicles* include those of Robert of Gloucester (late thirteenth century), Robert Manning of Brunne (1338), Andrew of Wyntoun (*Original Chronicle of Scotland,* early fifteenth century), John Hardyng (late fifteenth century), and John Capgrave (fifteenth century). With the rise of the Tudor dynasty came a wave of patriotic nationalism, one result of which was the production in the sixteenth century of many *chronicles*—some in Latin prose, some in English verse; some mere abstracts, some very voluminous; some new compositions, some retellings of older ones. Some of the more important *chronicles* of Elizabeth's time, besides the famous *Mirror for Magistrates,* are Richard Grafton's (1563), John Stowe's (1565, 1580, 1592), and Ralph Holinshed's (1578). Not only are portions of this mass of *chronicle*-writing themselves of genuine literary value, full of lively anecdote and description, but some of them were important as SOURCES for Shakespeare and other dramatists. See CHRONICLE PLAY.

Chronicle Play: A type of DRAMA flourishing in the latter part of Elizabeth's reign, which drew its English historical materials from the sixteenth-century CHRONICLES, such as Holinshed's, and which stressed the nationalistic spirit of the times. It enjoyed increasing popularity with the outburst of patriotic feeling which resulted from the defeat of the Spanish Armada (1588) and served as a medium for teaching English history to the uneducated portions of the London populace. The STRUCTURE of the earlier *chronicle* plays was very loose, UNITY consisting mainly in the inclusion of the events of a single king's reign. The number of characters was large. Much use was made of pageantry (coronations, funerals) and other spectacular elements, such as battles on the stage. The serious action was often relieved by comic scenes or sub-plots, as in Shakespeare's famous Falstaff plays (*Henry IV*, 1, 2; *Henry V*). The tendency to merge with ROMANTIC COMEDIES appeared as early as Greene's *James IV* (*ca*.1590); in Shakespeare's *Cymbeline* (*ca*.1610) the CHRONICLE material is completely subordinated to the demands of ROMANTIC COMEDY. The relation of the *chronicle play* to TRAGEDY is important, Shakespeare's *Richard III* (*ca*.1593) being an early example of the tendency of the *chronicle play* to develop into TRAGEDY of character, a movement which culminates in such plays as *King Lear* (1605) and *Macbeth* (1605). The term HISTORY PLAY is sometimes applied to a restricted group of *chronicle plays* like Shakespeare's *Henry V*, which are unified but are neither COMEDY nor TRAGEDY. The earliest true *chronicle play* is perhaps *The Famous Victories of Henry V* (*ca*.1586). Peele's *Edward I* (1590–91) and Marlowe's *Edward II* (1592) are among the best pre-Shakespearean *chronicle plays*.

Chronique Scandaleuse: A type of writing presenting intrigues, love affairs, and petty gossip, and usually associated with life at court. As a rule these writings give the impression of having been written by an eyewitness. The personal element is important, and scandal is the food upon which such CHRONICLES thrive. *The History of Louis XI* (1460–1483) of France, a *chronique scandaleuse* credited to Jean de Troyes, is an example. This same interest in gossip about the intimate, personal life of the great and of the near-great survives today in the tabloids and in the stories, for instance, which are told of the life of moving-picture stars and other popular entertainers.

Chronological Primitivism: The belief that, on the whole, the life and actions of man were more admirable and desirable at an earlier stage of his history than at present. See PRIMITIVISM.

Ciceronian Style: A highly ornamental STYLE, modeled after Cicero, the Roman orator, who was noted for his prose RHYTHMS,

his cadenced periodic sentences, and his use of BALANCE and AN-
TITHESIS. The *Ciceronian style* is particularly rich in its use of
FIGURES OF SPEECH. It was very popular with the writers of the
English RENAISSANCE, and Doctor Samuel Johnson in the eighteenth
century and Thomas Babington Macaulay in the nineteenth are outstanding practitioners of *Ciceronian style*. It should be compared
with the SENECAN STYLE.

"Ciceronians": A group of Latin stylists in the RENAISSANCE who
would not use any Latin word that could not be found in Cicero's
writings. See PURIST.

Circumlocution: Roundabout or evasive speech or writing, in
which many words are used where a few would have served. It is a
form of PERIPHRASIS.

Classic (noun): In the singular, *classic* is usually applied to a
piece of literature which by common consent has achieved a recognized position in literary history for its superior qualities; also an
author of similar standing. Thus, *Paradise Lost* is a *classic* in English
literature. The plural is used in the same sense, as in the phrase
"the study of English *classics*"; it is also used collectively to designate the literary productions of Greece and Rome, as in the statement, "A study of the *classics* is an excellent preparation for the
study of modern literature."

Classic, Classical (adjectives): Used in senses parallel with those
given under CLASSIC (noun); hence, of recognized excellence or
belonging to established tradition, as a *classical* piece of music or
such as bids fair to win such recognition, as "a *classic* pronounce-
ment"; used specifically to designate the literature or culture of
Greece and Rome or later literature which partakes of its qualities.
"*Classical* literature" may mean Greek and Roman literature, or it
may mean literature that has gained a lasting recognition, or it
may mean literature that exhibits the qualities of CLASSICISM. When
it is used to describe the attributes of a literary work it usually
implies OBJECTIVITY in the choice and handling of the THEME,
simplicity of STYLE, clarity, restraint, and formal STRUCTURE.

Classical Tragedy: This term may refer to the TRAGEDY of the
ancient Greeks and Romans, as Sophocles' *Antigone;* or to tragedies

based upon Greek or Roman subjects, as Shakespeare's *Coriolanus;* or to modern tragedies modeled upon Greek or Roman TRAGEDY or written under the influence of the critical doctrines of CLASSICISM. The earliest extant English TRAGEDY, Sackville and Norton's *Gorboduc* (acted 1562), is sometimes called *classical* because it is written in the manner of the SENECAN TRAGEDIES. Ben Jonson's tragedies *Catiline* and *Sejanus* not only are based upon Roman themes but are *classical* in their conscious effort to apply most of the "rules" of tragic composition derived from Aristotle and Horace. In the Restoration period John Dryden, under the influence of the French *classical tragedies* of Racine, advocated CLASSICAL rules and applied them in part to his *All for Love,* which contrasts with Shakespeare's romantic treatment of the same story in *Antony and Cleopatra.* Joseph Addison's *Cato* has been referred to as "the triumph of *classical tragedy.*" See CLASSICISM, TRAGEDY, SENECAN TRAGEDY, UNITIES, ROMANTIC TRAGEDY.

Classicism: As a critical term, a body of doctrine thought to be derived from or to reflect the qualities of ancient Greek and Roman culture, particularly in literature, philosophy, art, or CRITICISM. It is commonly opposed to ROMANTICISM and REALISM, although these terms overlap in their "characteristics" and are not mutually exclusive. It is dangerous to classify writers or types as perfect exponents of *classicism.* Ben Jonson, for example, was a self-proclaimed advocate of *classicism* as a critic and dramatist, yet his CLASSICAL TRAGEDIES contain non-classical elements, such as COMIC RELIEF. Likewise some of the "romanticists" of the eighteenth century cultivated CLASSICAL qualities, just as such a "neo-classicist" as Pope exhibited some "romantic" traits.

Classicism does, however, stand for certain definite ideas and attitudes, mainly drawn from the critical utterances of the Greeks and Romans or developed through an imitation of ancient art and literature. They include restraint; restricted scope; dominance of reason; sense of FORM; UNITY of design and aim; clarity; simplicity; BALANCE; attention to structure and logical organization; chasteness in STYLE; severity of outline; moderation; self-control; intellectualism; DECORUM; respect for tradition; IMITATION; conservatism; "good sense."

The Greeks were notable for their clarity of thought, an attribute that found expression in lucid, direct, simple expression, and that placed a premium on communication *among* men rather than self-expression *by* a man. UNITY was a dominating idea in the minds of the Greeks, and they naturally constructed buildings and works of art around central ideas, and expended great effort in making the structures symmetrical, logical, balanced, harmonious, and well-proportioned. They had a marked sense of appropriateness or DECORUM and in structure, STYLE, and subject worked with what was fitting and dignified. Restraint of the passions, emphasis upon the common or generic attributes of men and states, and a dispassionate objectivity made them the natural foes of enthusiasm, of uniquely personal states and emotions, and of excessive subjectivity. Although not all Greek or Roman writers displayed all these characteristics, some complex of these qualities is what is usually implied when we use the term *classicism*.

In English literature *classicism* has been an important force, often an "issue," since RENAISSANCE times. The humanists became conscious advocates of CLASSICAL doctrine, and even such an essentially romantic artist as Spenser fell strongly under its influence, not only drawing freely upon CLASSICAL materials but definitely espousing CLASSICAL doctrines and endeavoring to "imitate" such CLASSICAL masters as Virgil and Homer. Sir Philip Sidney, though he wrote PASTORAL ROMANCES, speaks mainly as a classicist in his critical essay, *The Defence of Poesie*. Ben Jonson stands as the stoutest RENAISSANCE advocate of *classicism*, both in dramatic CRITICISM and in his influence upon English poetry. Milton has been said to show a perfect balance of ROMANTICISM and *classicism*. The CLASSICAL attitude, largely under French inspiration, triumphed in the RESTORATION and AUGUSTAN AGES, and John Dryden, Joseph Addison, and Alexander Pope, together with Doctor Samuel Johnson of the next generation, stand as exemplars of the CLASSICAL (or NEO-CLASSIC) spirit in literature and criticism. Though nineteenth-century literature was largely romantic (or in its later phases realistic), the vitality of the CLASSICAL attitude is shown by the critical writings of such men as Francis Jeffrey, Matthew Arnold, and Walter Pater. In the twentieth century there has been a strong revival of CLASSICAL attitudes in the literary practice and the critical principles of men like T. E. Hulme, T. S. Eliot, and Ezra Pound, and much of our most distinguished and sophisticated poetry and criticism is today redolent of *classicism*. See HUMANISM, NEO-CLASSICISM, CLASSICAL, ROMANTICISM, REALISM, NEW CRITICISM.

Clerihew

Clerihew: A form of LIGHT VERSE which in two COUPLETS of irregular METER touches off a well-known person whose name forms one of the RHYMES. It was invented by Edmund Clerihew Bentley, who, while in school listening to a chemistry lecture, wrote:

> Sir Humphrey Davy
> Abominated gravy.
> He lived in the odium
> Of having discovered sodium.

Cliché: From the French word for a stereotype plate; a block for printing. Hence any expression so often used that its freshness and clarity have worn off is called a *cliché,* a stereotyped form. Some examples are: "bigger and better," "loomed on the horizon," "the light fantastic," "stood like a sentinel," "sadder but wiser."

Climax: In rhetoric a term used to indicate the arrangement of words, phrases, and clauses in sentences in such a way as to form a rising order of importance in the ideas expressed. Such an arrangement is called climactic and the item of greatest importance is called the *climax.* Originally the term meant such an arrangement of succeeding clauses that the last important word in one is repeated as the first important word in the next, each succeeding clause rising in intensity or importance.

In larger pieces of composition—the ESSAY, the SHORT STORY, the DRAMA, or the NOVEL—the *climax* is the point of highest interest, the point at which the reader makes his greatest emotional response. The term used in this sense is an index of emotional response in the reader or the spectator. However, in DRAMATIC STRUCTURE *climax* is a term used to designate the turning point in the action, the place at which the RISING ACTION reverses and becomes the FALLING ACTION. In Freytag's five-part view of DRAMATIC STRUCTURE, the *climax* is the third part or third ACT. Both narrative FICTION and DRAMA have tended to move the *climax,* both in the sense of turning action and in that of highest response, nearer the end of the work and thus have produced structures less symmetrical than those that follow FREYTAG'S PYRAMID. In speaking of DRAMATIC STRUCTURE, the term *climax* is synonymous with CRISIS. However, CRISIS is used exclusively in the sense of STRUCTURE, whereas *climax* is used as a synonym for CRISIS *and* as a description of the intensity of interest in the reader or spectator. In this latter sense *climax* sometimes occurs at other points than at the CRISIS. See CRISIS, DRAMATIC STRUCTURE.

Cloak and Sword Romance: The term comes from the Spanish *comedia de capa y espada,* a dramatic type of which the ingredients were gallant cavaliers, lovely ladies, elegance, adventure, and intrigue. In English it refers to swashbuckling PLAYS or NOVELS characterized by much action and presenting gallant heroes in love with fair ladies, a glamorous color thrown over all. Settings and characters are often, though not necessarily, Spanish, Italian, or French, the manners are courtly and gracious, the plot full of intrigue resulting most commonly in duels.

Dumas' *The Three Musketeers* and many currently popular television plays are good examples. *Cloak and sword romances* were very popular in America in the period between 1890 and 1915.

Closed Couplet: Two successive VERSES rhyming *aa* and containing within the two lines a complete, independent statement. It is "closed" in the sense that its meaning is complete within the two VERSES and does not depend on what goes before or follows for its grammatical structure or thought. An example from Pope is:

> One prospect lost, another still we gain;
> And not a vanity is giv'n in vain . . . .

Closet Drama: A PLAY (usually in VERSE) designed to be read rather than acted. Notable examples are Milton's *Samson Agonistes,* Shelley's *The Cenci,* Browning's *Pippa Passes,* and the ONE-ACT PLAYS that W. D. Howells wrote for the *Atlantic Monthly.* Giving the term a broader meaning, some writers include in it such dramatic poems as Swinburne's *Atalanta in Calydon* and other products of the effort to write a literary DRAMA by imitating the style of an earlier age, such as Greek DRAMA. Such poetic DRAMAS as Tennyson's *Becket* and Browning's *Strafford* are not infrequently called *closet dramas* because, though meant to be acted, they are more successful as literature than acted DRAMA. In English literature the nineteenth century was noted for the production of *closet drama,* perhaps because the actual stage was so monopolized by BURLESQUE, MELODRAMA, OPERETTA, and such light forms that literary men were stimulated either to attempt to provide more worthy DRAMAS for the contemporary stage or at least to preserve the TRADITION of literary DRAMA by imitating earlier masterpieces. See DRAMATIC POETRY, POETIC DRAMA, PASTICHE.

Cockney School: A derogatory title applied by *Blackwood's Magazine* to a group of nineteenth-century writers including Hazlitt,

Leigh Hunt, Keats, and Shelley, because of their alleged poor taste in such matters as DICTION and RHYME. Some offending RHYMES were *name* and *time, vista* and *sister,* words which, the suggestion was, could rhyme only to a cockney ear. One sentence from the denouncement printed in *Blackwood's Magazine* must serve as illustrative of the whole spirit of his attack: "They [the writers above] are by far the vilest vermin that ever dared to creep upon the hem of the majestic garment of the English muse." The attack reflected the Tory view that men of "low" or "cockney" birth and breeding would inevitably have cockney politics and write cockney VERSE. The famous attack on Keats (August, 1818) associates his "bad" VERSE with his radical political friends and his "lowly" beginnings as an apothecary's apprentice.

Coda: A concluding portion of a literary or dramatic work. The *coda* usually restates or summarizes or integrates the preceding themes or movements. The term is also applied to a tail-piece to a SONNET, giving sixteen or more lines.

Codex: A manuscript BOOK, particularly of Biblical or CLASSICAL writing. There are over 1200 Biblical manuscripts that date from the fourth to the sixteenth centuries that exist as *codices.* Originally manuscripts were written on rolls of papyrus or parchment, but as early as the first century A.D. manuscripts were being assembled into book form or *codices.*

Coherence: A fundamental principle of composition demanding that the parts of any piece of writing be so arranged and bear such a relationship one to the other that the meaning of the whole may be immediately clear and intelligible. Words, phrases, clauses, within the sentence; and sentences, paragraphs, and chapters in larger pieces of writing are the units which, by their progressive and logical arrangement, make for *coherence* or, contrariwise, by an illogical arrangement, result in incoherence.

Coincidence: The coinciding of events in such a way that the movement of a PLOT or fate of a CHARACTER is determined or significantly altered without there being a causal relationship among them or any intentional planning or mutual motivation behind them. If two CHARACTERS by accident are in the same place with results that are important to one or both of them, it is called *coincidence.* In

CLASSICAL TRAGEDY such occurrences were considered the working out of Fate, and the same concept of human lives being drastically affected by seemingly accidental events is used in NOVELS and DRAMAS that are deterministic, such as Thomas Hardy's NOVELS and Eugene O'Neill's DRAMAS. In COMEDY and particularly in FARCE *coincidence* is very common. It is also used widely today in the THEATER OF THE ABSURD, the ANTI-NOVEL, and the ANTI-REALISTIC NOVEL, where the occurrence of fortuitous conjunctions of CHARACTERS with grave consequences reflects the "motiveless malignity" of a hostile or indifferent universe.

Coined Words: Words consciously and arbitrarily manufactured "out of whole cloth," as opposed to those which enter the language as a result of one of the more natural processes of language development. Many words which were originally *coined words* (such as *telephone, airplane,* and *Kodak*) have become accepted terms. Constantly occurring examples of such words are those fabricated by commercial firms for advertising purposes: "Nabisco" (National Biscuit Company), "Socony" (Standard Oil Company of New York). Often frowned upon as a literary practice, word coining is nevertheless constantly affecting our language. It is characteristic of writers as various in method as "Lewis Carroll," James Joyce, and Brigid Brophy.

Collaboration: The association of two or more people in the composition of a literary work. Beaumont and Fletcher afford one of the most famous instances of *collaboration* in the field of English literature.

Collate: To compare in detail two texts, versions, EDITIONS, or IMPRESSIONS in order to determine and record the points of agreement and disagreement; also to verify the order of the sheets or SIGNATURES of a book before binding.

Colloquialism: An expression used in informal conversation but not accepted as good usage in formal speech or writing. A *colloquialism* lies between the upper speech level of dignified, formal, or "literary" language and the lower level of slang. It may differ from more formal language in pronunciation, grammar, vocabulary, imagery, or connotative quality. As in the case of slang, a colloquial expression eventually may be accepted as "standard" usage. See SLANG, PROVINCIALISM, DIALECTS.

Colloquy

Colloquy: A conversation or DIALOGUE, especially when it is in the nature of a formal discussion or a conference; used in this sense occasionally in literary titles, as Erasmus' *Colloquies*. See DIALOGUE.

Colonial Period in American Literature, 1607–1765: From the founding of the colony at Jamestown, which began the colonial period in America, until the Stamp Act in 1765 finally forced the colonists into a widespread consciousness of themselves as separate from their mother land, the writing produced in America was generally utilitarian, polemical, or religious. Three major figures emerged in this period: Edward Taylor, whose religious METAPHYSICAL POETRY, written at the close of the seventeenth and the beginning of the eighteenth centuries, did not see publication until 1937; Jonathan Edwards, whose religious and philosophical treatises have not been surpassed by an American; and Benjamin Franklin, whose Addisonian rephrasings of the teachings of the Enlightenment are the stylistic epitome of the period.

That BELLES-LETTRES should not have come is hardly surprising. Whether PURITANS of the North or ROYALISTS of the South, the colonists were uniformly engaged throughout the period in possessing the land, cultivating it, making it safe and fruitful. Wilderness, Indians, and disease were common foes that demanded the strict attention of the early colonists. Wealth, government, progress, political rights absorbed a major portion of the attention of the Americans of the later colonial period.

The seventeenth century was the age of travel and personal records, DIARIES, historical and descriptive accounts, sermons, and a little VERSE—largely instructive, like Wigglesworth's *The Day of Doom*, or religious, like the *Bay Psalm Book* and the numerous funeral elegies. Only Anne Bradstreet, "The Tenth Muse Lately Sprung Up in America," raised a thin and faltering but true poetic voice.

In the eighteenth century, the dangers of early colonization were over, but the colonial attitude persisted. Religious controversy was prevalent. Newspapers and ALMANACS flourished. Jonathan Edwards both in the pulpit and in his writing demonstrated his greatness as a thinker and a didactic writer. Benjamin Franklin created what was perhaps the first fully realized and widely popular American fictional character in Richard Saunders of *Poor Richard's Almanac*. William Byrd wrote with CAVALIER grace and urbanity of his life and neighbors in Virginia and North Carolina. But little important

VERSE and no native DRAMA emerged. As the period in which Americans had thought and acted like colonials of the British crown drew to a close in the 1760's, a vast amount of writing had been done in America, some of it of a high quality, but very little that did not self-consciously take English authors as models and even less that could merit the term *belletristic*. See the section on "The Colonial Period in American Literature," in *The Outline of Literary History*.

Colophon: A publisher's symbol or device formerly placed at the end of a book but now more generally used on the title page or elsewhere near the beginning. The function of *colophons* is to identify the publisher. *Colophons* at different times and with different publishers have incorporated one or more of these items: title and author of book, the printer, the date and place of manufacture. The earliest known use of *colophons* was in the fifteenth century, at which time they were likely to be complete paragraphs wherein the author addressed the reader in a spirit of reverence—now that he had completed his work. Sir Thomas Malory, for example, closed his *Le Morte Darthur* with the statement that it "was ended in the ix yere of the reygne of Kyng Edward the fourth," and asks that his readers "praye for me whyle I am on lyue that God sende me good delyuerance, and whan I am deed I praye you all praye for my soule." The term is also applied to any device, including the words "The End" or "Finis," that marks the conclusion of any printed work.

Column: One of two or more vertical sections of printed material which lie side by side on a page. In a more literary sense, a feature ARTICLE that appears periodically in a newspaper or a magazine and is written by a single author. Its subject may be comic, literary, religious, instructive, polemical, or gossipy. Although it is sometimes very serious in TONE and solemn in STYLE, as the columns of Walter Lippmann were, it is the closest approximation that we have today to the eighteenth-century PERIODICAL ESSAY.

Comedy: As compared with TRAGEDY, *comedy* is a lighter form of DRAMA which aims primarily to amuse and which ends happily. It differs from FARCE and BURLESQUE by having a more sustained PLOT, more weighty and subtle DIALOGUE, more natural CHARACTERS, and less boisterous behavior. The border-line, however, between *comedy* and other dramatic forms cannot be sharply defined, as there is much overlapping of technique, and different "kinds" are frequently com-

Comedy

bined. Even the difference between *comedy* and TRAGEDY tends to disappear in their more idealistic forms. HIGH COMEDY and LOW COMEDY may be further apart from each other in nature than are TRAGEDY and some serious *comedy*. Psychologists have shown the close relation between laughter and tears; and *comedy* and TRAGEDY alike sprang, both in ancient Greece and in medieval Europe, from diverging treatments of ceremonial performances.

Since *comedy* strives to provoke smiles and laughter, both WIT and HUMOR are utilized. In general the comic effect arises from a recognition of some incongruity of speech, action, or character revelation. The incongruity may be merely verbal as in the case of a play on words, exaggerated assertion, etc.; or physical, as when stilts are used to make a man's legs seem disproportionately long; or satirical, as when the effect depends upon the beholder's ability to perceive the incongruity between fact and pretense exhibited by a braggart. The range of appeal here is wide, varying from the crudest effects of LOW COMEDY to the most subtle and idealistic reactions aroused by some HIGH COMEDY. The "kinds" of *comedy* and, in part, the relation between *comedy* and TRAGEDY are thus accounted for.

Viewed in another sense *comedy* may be considered to deal with man in his human state, restrained and often made ridiculous by his limitations, his faults, his bodily functions, and his animal nature. In contrast, TRAGEDY may be considered to deal with man in his ideal or god-like state. *Comedy* has always viewed man more realistically than TRAGEDY, and drawn its laughter or its SATIRE from the spectacle of human weakness or failure. Hence its tendency to juxtapose appearance and reality, to deflate pretense, and to mock excess. The judgment made by *comedy* is almost always critical.

English *comedy* developed from native dramatic forms growing out of the religious DRAMA, the MORALITY PLAYS and INTERLUDES, and possibly folk games and plays and the performances of wandering entertainers, such as dancers and jugglers. In the RENAISSANCE the rediscovery of Latin *comedy* and the effort to apply the rules of classical CRITICISM to DRAMA profoundly affected the course of English *comedy*. Foreign influences also have at times been important, as the French influence on Restoration *comedy* or the Italian influence upon Jacobean PASTORAL DRAMA. The more ambitious *comedy* of the earlier Elizabethans was ROMANTIC, while the *comedy* of the seventeenth century, both Jacobean and Restoration, was prevailingly REALISTIC (though the Fletcherian TRAGI-COMEDY flourished early in the century). SENTIMENTAL COMEDY was dominant in the

eighteenth century, but was opposed late in the period by a revival
of the realistic COMEDY OF MANNERS. In the early nineteenth century
such light forms as BURLESQUE and OPERETTA were popular, serious
comedy again appearing late in the century. Some of the more prom-
inent authors of English *comedy* are: John Lyly, Robert Greene,
George Peele, William Shakespeare, Ben Jonson, George Chapman,
Thomas Middleton, Thomas Heywood, John Fletcher, Philip Massinger (Elizabethans and Jacobeans); Sir George Etheredge, William
Congreve, and Thomas Shadwell (Restoration); Richard Steele,
Richard B. Sheridan, Oliver Goldsmith (eighteenth century); T. W.
Robertson (mid-nineteenth century); H. A. Jones, Oscar Wilde,
A. W. Pinero, G. B. Shaw, J. M. Barrie, Philip Barry, S. N. Behrman
(late nineteenth and twentieth centuries).

Attention may be called to a special use of the word *comedy* in
medieval times, when it was applied to non-dramatic literary compositions marked by a happy ending and by a less exalted style than
was found in TRAGEDY. Dante's *Divine Comedy*, for example, was
so named by its author because of its "prosperous, pleasant, and desirable" conclusion, and because it was written in the vernacular
(Italian) "in which women and children speak." The nomenclature
employed in describing different kinds of *comedy* is somewhat confused, and it is impossible in this handbook to include all the terms
employed by the many writers on the subject. An effort has been
made to include the most important ones, however. See HIGH
COMEDY, LOW COMEDY, REALISTIC COMEDY, ROMANTIC COMEDY,
COURT COMEDY, TRAGI-COMEDY, SENTIMENTAL COMEDY, COMEDY OF
MANNERS, COMEDY OF MORALS, INTERLUDE, TRAGEDY, DRAMA, WIT
AND HUMOR.

Comedy of Humours: A term applied to the special type of REALIS-
TIC COMEDY which was developed in the closing years of the sixteenth century by Ben Jonson and George Chapman and which derives its comic interest largely from the exhibition of "humourous"
characters; that is, persons whose conduct is controlled by some
one characteristic or whim or HUMOUR. Some single HUMOUR or
exaggerated trait of character gave each important figure in the action a definite bias of disposition and supplied the chief motive for
his actions. Thus in Jonson's *Every Man in His Humour* (acted
1598), which made this type of play popular, all the words and acts
of Kitely are controlled by an overpowering suspicion that his wife
is unfaithful; George Downright, a country squire, must be "frank"

above all things; the country gull in town determines his every decision by his desire to "catch on" to the manners of the city gallant. In his "Induction" to *Every Man out of His Humour* (1599) Jonson explains his character-formula thus:

> Some one peculiar quality
> Doth so possess a man, that it doth draw
> All his affects, his spirits, and his powers,
> In their confluctions, all to run one way.

The *comedy of humours* owes something to earlier vernacular COMEDY, but more to a desire to imitate the classical COMEDY of Plautus and Terence and to combat the vogue of ROMANTIC COMEDY. Its satiric purpose and realistic method are emphasized and lead later into more serious character studies, as in Jonson's *The Alchemist*. It affected Shakespeare's art to some degree—the "humourous" man appearing now and again in his plays (Leontes in *The Winter's Tale* is a good example)—and it is perhaps worth mentioning that most of Shakespeare's tragic heroes are such because they allow some one trait of character (ambition, jealousy, contemplation, etc.) to be overdeveloped and thus to destroy the balance necessary to a poised, well-rounded, and effective personality. The *comedy of humours* was closely related to the contemporary COMEDY OF MANNERS and exerted an important influence upon the COMEDY of the Restoration period. See COMEDY OF MANNERS.

Comedy of Intrigue: A COMEDY in which the manipulation of the action by one or more CHARACTERS to their own ends is of more importance than are the CHARACTERS themselves. Another name for COMEDY OF SITUATION.

Comedy of Manners: A term most commonly used to designate the REALISTIC, often satirical, COMEDY of the Restoration period, as practiced by Congreve and others. It is also used for the revival, in modified form, of this COMEDY a hundred years later by Goldsmith and Sheridan, as well as for a revival late in the nineteenth century. Likewise the REALISTIC COMEDY of Elizabethan and Jacobean times is sometimes called *comedy of manners*. In the stricter sense of the term, the type is concerned with the manners and conventions of an artificial, highly sophisticated society. The fashions, manners, and outlook on life of this social group are reflected. The CHARACTERS are more likely to be types than individualized personalities.

Comedy of Morals

PLOT, though often involving a clever handling of situation and intrigue, is less important than ATMOSPHERE, DIALOGUE, and SATIRE. The DIALOGUE is witty and finished, often brilliant. The appeal is intellectual but not imaginative or idealistic. SATIRE is directed in the main against the follies and deficiencies of typical characters, such as fops, would-be wits, jealous husbands, coxcombs, and others who fail somehow to conform to the conventional attitudes and manners of the elegant society of the time. This SATIRE is directed against the aberrations of social behavior rather than of human conduct in its larger aspects. A distinguishing characteristic of the *comedy of manners* is its emphasis upon an illicit love duel, involving at least one pair of witty and often amoral lovers. This prevalence of the immoral "love game" is partly explained by the manners of the time and social groups concerned, and partly by the special satirical purpose of the comedy itself. In its SATIRE, REALISM, and employment of "humours" the *comedy of manners* was indebted to Elizabethan and Jacobean COMEDY. It owed something, of course, to the French *comedy of manners* as practiced by Molière.

The reaction against the questionable morality of the plays and a growing sentimentalism brought about the downfall of this type of COMEDY near the close of the seventeenth century, and it was largely supplanted through most of the eighteenth century by SENTIMENTAL COMEDY. Purged of its objectionable features, however, the *comedy of manners* was revived by Goldsmith and Sheridan late in the eighteenth century, and in a somewhat new garb by Oscar Wilde late in the nineteenth century. The *comedy of manners* has been popular in the twentieth century in the works of playwrights like Noel Coward, Somerset Maugham, and Philip Barry.

A few typical *comedies of manners* are: Wycherley, *The Plain Dealer* (1674); Etheredge, *The Man of Mode* (1676); Congreve, *The Way of the World* (1700); Goldsmith, *She Stoops to Conquer* (1773); Sheridan, *The Rivals* (1775) and *The School for Scandal* (1777); Wilde, *The Importance of Being Earnest* (1895); Maugham, *The Circle* (1921); Coward, *Private Lives* (1931); Barry, *The Philadelphia Story* (1939). See HIGH COMEDY, REALISTIC COMEDY, COMEDY OF HUMOURS.

Comedy of Morals: A term applied to COMEDY which uses ridicule to correct abuses, hence a form of dramatic SATIRE, aimed at the moral state of a people or a special class of people. Molière's *Tartuffe* (1664) is often considered a *comedy of morals*.

111

Comedy of Situation: A COMEDY which depends for its interest chiefly upon ingenuity of PLOT rather than upon character interest; COMEDY OF INTRIGUE. Background, too, is relatively unimportant. There is much reliance upon ridiculous and incongruous situations, a heaping up of mistakes, PLOTS within PLOTS, disguises, mistaken identity, unexpected meetings, etc. A capital example is Shakespeare's *The Comedy of Errors,* a play in which the possibilities for confusion are multiplied by the use of twin brothers who have twins as servants. In each case the twins look so much alike that at times they doubt their own identity. A COMEDY of this sort sometimes approaches FARCE. Ben Jonson's *Epicœne* and Middleton's *A Trick to Catch the Old One* are later Elizabethan *comedies of situation* or intrigue. A modern example is Shaw's *You Never Can Tell.* The phrase *comedy of situation* is sometimes used also to refer merely to an incident, such as Falstaff's description of his fight with the robbers in Shakespeare's *King Henry IV,* Part I. See FARCE-COMEDY.

Comic Opera: An OPERETTA, or comedy OPERA, stressing spectacle and music but employing spoken DIALOGUE. An early example is Sheridan's *The Duenna* (1775). The best-known *comic operas* are those of Gilbert and Sullivan produced in London, chiefly at the Savoy (constructed for the purpose) in the 1870's and 1880's, e.g., *The Mikado* (1885). See BALLAD-OPERA.

Comic Relief: A humorous scene, incident, or speech in the course of a serious FICTION or DRAMA. Such comic intrusions are usually introduced by the author to provide relief from emotional intensity and, by contrast, to heighten the seriousness of the story. When properly employed, they can enrich and deepen the tragic implications of the action; notable examples are the drunken porter scene in *Macbeth* (see De Quincey's essay, "On the Knocking at the Gate in Macbeth"), the gravedigger scene in *Hamlet,* and Mercutio's role in *Romeo and Juliet.* Although not a portion of Aristotle's formula for a TRAGEDY, *comic relief* has been almost universally employed by English playwrights.

Commedia Dell'arte: Improvised COMEDY; a form of Italian LOW COMEDY dating from very early times, in which the actors, who usually performed conventional or STOCK parts, such as the "pantaloon" (Venetian merchant), improvised their DIALOGUE, though a PLOT or SCENARIO was provided them. A "harlequin" interrupted the action at times with low buffoonery. A parallel or later form of the *commedia dell'arte* was the masked comedy, in which conventional figures (usually in masks) each spoke his particular dialect (as the Pulcinella, the rogue from Naples). There is some evidence that the *commedia dell'arte* colored English LOW COMEDY from early times, but its chief influence on the English stage came in the eighteenth century in connection with the development of such spectacle forms as the PANTOMIME.

Common Measure: A STANZA form, also called COMMON METER, defined below.

Common Meter: A STANZA form consisting of four lines, the first and third being IAMBIC TETRAMETER (eight syllables, ˘ ˊ ˘ ˊ ˘ ˊ ˘ ˊ) and the second and fourth IAMBIC TRIMETER (six syllables, ˘ ˊ ˘ ˊ ˘ ˊ). An example from the Marquis of Montrose is:

> He either fears his fate too much,
>   Or his deserts are small,
> That dares not put it to the touch
>   To gain or lose it all.

It is distinguished from the BALLAD STANZA principally by its metrical regularity. Often it is called COMMON MEASURE and is designated by the abbreviation *C.M.*

Commonplace Book: A classified collection of quotations or arguments prepared for reference purposes. Thus, a reader interested in moral philosophy might collect thoughts and quotations under such heads, as truth, virtue, or friendship. *Commonplace books* were utilized by authors of ESSAYS, theological arguments, and other serious treatises. The *Commonplace Book* of John Milton is still in existence. The term is also sometimes applied to private collections of favorite pieces of literature such as the poetical miscellanies of Elizabethan times. R. W. Stallman's *The Critic's Notebook* is an excellent *commonplace book* of the NEW CRITICISM.

Commonwealth Interregnum: The period between the execution of Charles I in 1649 and the restoration of the monarchy under Charles II in 1660, during which England was ruled by Parliament under the control of the PURITAN leader, Oliver Cromwell, whose death in 1658 marked the beginning of the end of the Commonwealth.

John Milton was Latin Secretary in the Commonwealth government. Although the theaters were closed in 1642, dramatic performances continued more or less openly, but only Davenant's *The Siege of Rhodes* (1656), a spectacle play heralding the HEROIC DRAMA of the RESTORATION, was a significant new DRAMA. It was an age of major prose works: Milton's political pamphlets, Hobbes' *Leviathan* (1651), Jeremy Taylor's *Holy Dying* and *Holy Living* (1650, 1651), Walton's *The Compleat Angler* (1653), and works by Sir Thomas Browne and Thomas Fuller. The age delighted in translations of the contemporary French prose romances, and in 1654 Roger Boyle published *Parthenissa,* in the style of Mlle. de Scudéry, a precursor of the NOVEL. In poetry Vaughan, Waller, Cowley, Davenant, and Marvell flourished; the metaphysical strain continued; and two attempts at the EPIC were made, Davenant's *Gondibert* (1650) and Cowley's *Davideis* (1656), but both are incomplete. By the end of the *Commonwealth Interregnum,* John Dryden's poetic career was under way. He and Marvell, both of whose best work was to come later, shared with Milton the honor of being the best poets of a troubled time, although they wrote little poetry during it.

Companion Poems: Poems by the same author designed to complement each other. Each of the poems is complete by itself, but each is enriched and broadened in feeling or meaning when viewed with its *companion poem.* Robert Browning was fond of *companion poems;* his "Home-Thoughts, From Abroad" and "Home-Thoughts, From the Sea" are *companion poems,* as are his "Meeting at Night" and "Parting at Morning," and his "Fra Lippo Lippi" and "Andrea del Sarto," where sharply contrasting views about art are presented.

Compendium: A brief composition that condenses the subject matter of a longer work, or a work that treats in brief form the important features of a whole field of knowledge. A *compendium* is a brief, systematic presentation of essential facts. It differs from an ABRIDGMENT in that it does not attempt to present the general characteristics of the work or works from which its data are drawn. Indeed, it most often is used to present a concise and well-organized summary of data on a specific subject drawn from many sources no single one of which is imitated in TONE or organization.

Compensation: In METRICS a means of supplying omissions in a line; a form of SUBSTITUTION. Such omissions are usually unstressed syllables; the customary means of compensating for their absence is the pause, which has the effect of a *rest* in music. It is illustrated in Tennyson's lines:

> Break, break, break,
> On thy cold grey stones, O Sea!

Each of these lines has three stressed syllables; and metrically they are approximately equivalent, despite the fact that there are only three syllables in the first but seven in the second. The pronounced pauses following each word of the first line compensate for the unstressed syllables that have been omitted. See SUBSTITUTION.

Complaint: A LYRIC poem, frequent in the Middle Ages and the RENAISSANCE, in which the poet (1) laments the unresponsiveness of his mistress, as in Surrey's "A Complaint by Night of the Lover Not Beloved"; (2) bemoans his unhappy lot and seeks to remedy it, as in "The Complaint of Chaucer to His Empty Purse"; or (3) regrets the sorry state of the world, as in Spenser's *Complaints.* In a *complaint,* which usually takes the form of a MONOLOGUE, the poet commonly explains his sad mood, describes the causes of it, discusses possible remedies, or appeals to some lady or divinity for help from his distress.

Complication: That part of a dramatic or narrative PLOT in which the entanglement of affairs caused by the conflict of opposing forces is developed. It is the tying of the knot to be untied in the RESOLUTION. In the five-part idea of DRAMATIC STRUCTURE it is synonymous with RISING ACTION. The second ACT of a five-act TRAGEDY is often called "the act of *complication.*" See DRAMATIC STRUCTURE, ACT.

Comstockery: The overzealous and prudish censorship of literature and the other arts because of their supposed immorality. The term is derived from Anthony Comstock, a nineteenth- and early twentieth-century American social reformer, crusader against vice, and relentless censor of suspect books and pictures.

Concatenation: A name sometimes applied to CHAIN VERSE.

Conceit: Originally the term was almost synonymous with "idea" or "conception," and implied something made or conceived in the

Concrete Terms

mind. Its later specialized uses in describing a type of poetic META-
PHOR still retain the essential sense of the original meaning, in that
conceit implies intellectual ingenuity whether applied to the Petrarchan conventions of the ELIZABETHAN PERIOD or the elaborate
and witty analogies of the writers of METAPHYSICAL VERSE.

The term is used to designate an ingenious and fanciful notion or
conception, usually expressed through an elaborate ANALOGY, and
pointing to a striking parallel between two seemingly dissimilar
things. A *conceit* may be a brief METAPHOR but it also may form the
framework of an entire poem. In English there are two basic kinds
of *conceits:* the PETRARCHAN CONCEIT, most often found in love
poems and SONNETS, in which the subject of the poem is compared
extensively and elaborately to some object, a rose, a ship, a garden,
etc.; and the METAPHYSICAL CONCEIT, in which complex, startling,
and highly intellectual analogies are made.

In the eighteenth and nineteenth centuries, the term was used in
a derogatory sense, the *conceit* being considered strained, arbitrary,
and false. Dr. Johnson was particularly devastating on the META-
PHYSICAL CONCEIT. Today the term is more nearly neutral, being
used to describe the unhappy over-reaches of poets as well as their
striking and effective comparisons. In contemporary verse the *conceit* is again a respected vehicle for the expression of witty perceptions and telling analogies. It is used with great effect by Emily
Dickinson, T. S. Eliot, Allen Tate, and John Crowe Ransom. See
METAPHYSICAL CONCEIT, PETRARCHAN CONCEIT, CONTROLLING IMAGE,
METAPHYSICAL VERSE, BAROQUE, GONGORISM, MARINISM.

Concrete Terms: The converse of ABSTRACT TERMS; although *concrete terms* are close to specific terms or particular terms, the phrase
carries with it significantly the sense of describing something that
has actual existence and can be palpably known or experienced. A
concrete noun evokes an IMAGE of something with an objective
existence; a *concrete* illustration brings what is abstract into the
range of personal, usually sensory, experience. As ABSTRACT TERMS
form the language of philosophy and science by reducing the particular instance to the general case or quality, so *concrete terms,*
with their emphasis on the sensory and the tangible and their address to the emotional response, form the basic language of the
literary arts. As Arthur Quiller-Couch said of Shakespeare, so may
we say to some degree of all literary artists: "He chooses the con-

crete word, in phrase after phrase forcing you to touch and see."
See ABSTRACT TERMS, CONCRETE UNIVERSAL, ALLEGORY.

Concrete Universal: A critical term used to designate the idea that a work of art expresses the universal through the concrete and the particular. The quarrel between the universal and the particular in literature is at least as old as Aristotle, who declared POETRY to be more universal than history. The writers in periods of CLASSICISM and NEO-CLASSICISM tend to stress the universal aspects; the writers in periods of ROMANTICISM and REALISM the particular aspects. Yet if literature is "knowledge brought to the heart" it must talk ultimately of universals and express them in concrete and particular instances. See UNIVERSALITY, ARCHETYPE, ALLEGORY, ABSTRACT TERMS, CONCRETE TERMS.

Condensation: An abbreviated form of a longer work, but one which attempts to retain the salient characteristics, including STYLE, of the longer work. Condensation is very much like ABRIDGMENT in basic meaning; however, it is usually applied to a shortened version of a work of FICTION, whereas the application of ABRIDGMENT is broader.

Confession: A form of AUTOBIOGRAPHY that deals with customarily hidden or highly private matters. The *confession* usually has a theoretical or intellectual focus in which religion, politics, art, or some such interest plays a strong role. One of the distinctive aspects of the *confession* is the way in which it gives an intellectualized account of intensely personal and introverted experiences. It is what the author has learned about such matters that makes his inner life a fitting subject for a book. St. Augustine established the form with his *Confessions* in the fifth century. Sir Thomas Browne's *Religio Medici* and John Bunyan's *Grace Abounding* were seventeenth-century English *confessions*. Jean Jacques Rousseau gave it a modern form and popularity with his *Confessions* in the eighteenth century. Thomas De Quincey's *Confessions of an English Opium Eater* and Alfred de Musset's *Confessions d'un enfant du siècle* are nineteenth-century examples.

The term *confession* is often applied to fictional works that place an emphasis on the introspective view of a character in the process of developing attitudes toward life or religion or art. In this sense the

Confidant

APPRENTICESHIP NOVEL, the BILDUNGSROMAN, and the KÜNSTLER-ROMAN are all *confessions.*

Confidant (feminine, **Confidante**):   A character in a NOVEL or a DRAMA who takes little part in the action but is a close friend of the PROTAGONIST and who receives the confidences and intimate thoughts of the PROTAGONIST. The use of the *confidant* enables a dramatist to reveal the thoughts and intentions of the PROTAGONIST without the use of asides or SOLILOQUIES or the POINT OF VIEW of an OMNISCIENT AUTHOR. Well-known *confidants* are Horatio in *Hamlet,* Dr. Watson in the Sherlock Holmes stories, and Maria Gostrey in James' *The Ambassadors.* James referred to Maria Gostrey and similar *confidantes* who function primarily as a means of allowing the viewpoint characters to comment on their own experience as *ficelles.* See CHORUS.

Conflict: The struggle which grows out of the interplay of the two opposing forces in a PLOT. It is *conflict* which provides the elements of interest and suspense in any form of FICTION, whether it be a DRAMA, a NOVEL, or a SHORT STORY. At least one of the opposing forces is usually a person, or, if an animal or an inanimate object, is treated as though it were a person. This person, usually the PRO-TAGONIST, may be involved in *conflicts* of four different kinds: (1) he may struggle against the forces of nature, as in Jack London's "To Build a Fire"; (2) he may struggle against another person, usually the ANTAGONIST, as in Stevenson's *Treasure Island* and most MELO-DRAMA; (3) he may struggle against society as a force, as in the novels of Dickens and George Eliot; or (4) two elements within him may struggle for mastery, as in the RESTORATION HEROIC DRAMA or in *Macbeth.* A fifth possible kind of *conflict* is often cited, the struggle against Fate or destiny; however, except where the gods themselves actively appear, such a struggle is realized through the action of one or more of the four basic *conflicts.* Seldom do we find a simple, single *conflict* in a PLOT, but rather a complex one partaking of two or even all the elements given above. For example, the basic *conflict* in *Hamlet* may be interpreted to be a struggle within Hamlet himself, but it is certainly also a struggle against his uncle as ANTAG-ONIST, and, if the Freudian interpretations of motive are accepted, even a struggle against nature. Dreiser's *Sister Carrie* records a girl's struggle against society, as represented by the city, and yet it is a struggle against her animal nature and even partly with herself. Even

118

Conte

so seemingly simple a story as London's "To Build a Fire," in which the PROTAGONIST battles the cold unsuccessfully, is also the record of an inner *conflict*. The term *conflict* not only implies the struggle of a PROTAGONIST against someone or something, it also implies the existence of some MOTIVATION for the *conflict* or some goal to be achieved by it. *Conflict* is the raw material out of which PLOT is constructed. In the terminology associated with Greek DRAMA, the *conflict*, in the form of an extended debate, was called the AGON. Our terms PROTAGONIST and ANTAGONIST are derived from the roles these characters play in the *conflict*. See PLOT, MOTIVATION, PROTAGONIST, ANTAGONIST, DRAMATIC STRUCTURE.

Connecticut Wits: A group of eighteenth-century American poets associated with Hartford, Connecticut, and often called the HARTFORD WITS, under which heading they are discussed.

Connotation: The cluster of implications that words or phrases may carry with them, as distinguished from their denotative meanings. *Connotations* may be (1) private and personal, the result of individual experience, (2) group (national, linguistic, racial), or (3) general or universal, held by all or most men. The scientist and the philosopher attempt to hold words to their denotative meaning; the literary artist relies upon *connotation* to carry his deepest meanings. See DENOTATION, AMBIGUITY, CONCRETE TERMS, ABSTRACT TERMS.

Consonance: The use at the ends of VERSES of words in which the final consonants in the stressed syllables agree but the vowels that precede them differ, as "add-read," "bill-ball," and "born-burn." Contemporary poets frequently use *consonance*. In this stanza by Emily Dickinson

> A quietness distilled,
> As twilight long begun,
> Or Nature, spending with herself
> Sequestered afternoon,

the linking of "begun" and "afternoon" is an example of *consonance*. It is also sometimes called HALF RHYME and SLANT RHYME. See ASSONANCE.

Conte: The French word for TALE, *conte* is used in several and sometimes conflicting senses. In its original sense it referred to a short TALE of adventure. It came in the nineteenth century, particularly in France, to be used for SHORT STORIES of tightly constructed PLOT and great concision, such as those by Guy de Maupassant. In this sense it is used to designate a work shorter and more concise than a NOUVELLE. However, in England the term is sometimes used for a work longer than a SHORT STORY and shorter than a NOVEL. This English usage is flatly contradictory to the modern French usage. In most cases the reader must use both the nation and the period to which *conte* is assigned to determine whether it refers to a TALE of marvelous adventures, a tightly knit SHORT STORY, or a NOVELLA.

Contemporary Period in English Literature: The contemporary period in English literature may be considered to begin with the first World War in 1914, to be marked by the strenuousness of that experience and by the flowering of talent and experiment that came during the boom of the twenties and then fell away during the ordeal of economic depression in the 1930's. The second World War, making England an embattled fortress, had catastrophic effects on all of English life. It was followed by a period of desperate readjustment, a period whose literature was marked by a groping uncertainty. In very recent times, this uncertainty has given way to the anger and the protest against their elders of the "Angry Young Men," such as John Wain, Colin Wilson, Kingsley Amis, and John Osborne.

In the early years of the period the novelists of the EDWARDIAN AGE continued as major figures, with Galsworthy, Wells, Bennett, Forster, and Conrad dominating the scene, and to be joined before the 'teens were over by Somerset Maugham. A new fiction, centering itself in the experimental examination of the inner self was coming into being in the works of writers like Dorothy Richardson and Virginia Woolf. It reached its peak in the publication in 1922 of James Joyce's *Ulysses,* a book perhaps as influential as any prose work by a British writer in this century. In their highly differing ways D. H. Lawrence, Aldous Huxley, and Evelyn Waugh protested against the nature of modern society; and the maliciously witty NOVEL, as Huxley and Waugh wrote it in the twenties and thirties, was typical of the attitude of the age and is probably as truly representative of the English NOVEL in the contemporary period as is the NOVEL exploring the private self through the STREAM OF CONSCIOUSNESS. In the thirties and forties, Joyce Cary and Graham Green produced a more traditional fiction of great effectiveness, and Henry Green made comedy of the everyday life of man. Today in writers like Elizabeth Bowen, Angus Wilson, and Ivy Compton-Burnett the English novel continues its urbane and sharply witty way, while the "Angry Young Men" write fictional accounts of their deep dissatisfaction. Throughout the period English writers have practiced the SHORT STORY with distinction; notable examples being Katherine Mansfield and Somerset Maugham, working in the tradition of Chekhov.

The theater saw the social plays of Galsworthy, Jones, and Pinero, the play of ideas of Shaw, and the COMEDY OF MANNERS of Maugham—all well established in the EDWARDIAN AGE—continue and be joined by Noel Coward's COMEDY, the proletarian DRAMA of Sean O'Casey, the serious verse plays of T. S. Eliot and Christopher Fry, and the high craftsmanship of Terence Rattigan. John Osborne, of the "Angry Young Men," has more recently had marked success.

Perhaps the greatest changes in literature, however, came in poetry and criticism. In 1914 Bridges was poet laureate; he was succeeded in 1930 by John Masefield. Masefield died in 1967, and Cecil Day-Lewis was appointed poet laureate. Wilfred Owen was one of the most powerful poetic voices of the early years of the contemporary period, but his career ended with an untimely death in the first World War. Through the period Yeats continued poetic creation, steadily modifying his style and subjects to his late form. At the time of his death in 1939 he probably shared with T. S. Eliot the distinction of being the most influential poet in the British Isles. Yet Eliot's *The Waste Land*, although its author was American, was the most important single poetic publication in England in the period. In the work of Yeats and Eliot, of W. H. Auden, of Stephen Spender, of C. Day-Lewis, of Edith Sitwell, and of Gerard Manley Hopkins, whose poems were posthumously published in 1918, a new poetry came emphatically into being. The death at thirty-nine of Dylan Thomas in 1953 silenced a powerful lyric voice, which had already produced fine poetry and gave promise of doing even finer work. T. S. Eliot and I. A. Richards, along with T. E. Hulme, Herbert Read, F. R. Leavis, Cyril Connolly, and others, have created an informed, essentially anti-Romantic, analytical criticism, centering its attention on the work of art itself.

England in the twentieth century has watched her political and military supremacy gradually dissipate, and since the second World War she has found herself greatly reduced in the international scene and torn by internal economic and political troubles. Her writers

Contrast

during these turbulent and unhappy years have turned inward for their subject matter and have expressed bitter and often despairing cynicism. Her major literary figures in the present age, as they were in the EDWARDIAN AGE, have often been non-English. Her chief poets have been Irish, American, and Welsh; her most influential novelists, Polish and Irish; her principal dramatists, Irish and American. Yet in the very young and the very talented writers now at work may be seen a promise of new strength and new assurance. See *Outline of Literary History*.

Contrast: A rhetorical device by which one element (idea or object) is thrown into opposition to another for the sake of emphasis or clearness. The effect of the device is to make both contrasted ideas clearer than either would have been if described by itself. The principle of *contrast*, however, is useful for other purposes than to make definitions or to secure clearness. Skillfully used by an artist, *contrast* may become, like colors to the painter or chords to the musician, a means of arousing emotional impressions of deep artistic significance.

Controlling Image: An IMAGE or METAPHOR which runs throughout and determines the form or nature of a literary work. The *controlling image* of the following poem by Edward Taylor is the making of cloth:

> Make me, O Lord, thy Spinning Wheele compleat;
>   Thy Holy Worde my Distaff make for mee.
> Make mine Affections thy Swift Flyers neate,
>   And make my Soule thy holy Spoole to bee.
>   My Conversation make to be thy Reele,
>   And reele the yarn thereon spun of thy Wheele.
>
> Make me thy Loome then, knit therein this Twine:
>   And make thy Holy Spirit, Lord, winde quills:
> Then weave the Web thyselfe. The yarn is fine.
>   Thine Ordinances make my Fulling Mills.
>   Then dy the same in Heavenly Colours Choice,
>   All pinkt with Varnish't Flowers of Paradise.
>
> Then cloath therewith mine Understanding, Will,
>   Affections, Judgment, Conscience, Memory;
> My Words and Actions, that their shine may fill
>   My wayes with glory and thee glorify.
>   Then mine apparell shall display before yee
>   That I am Cloathed in Holy robes for glory.

See FUNDAMENTAL IMAGE, CONCEIT, METAPHYSICAL CONCEIT, IMAGE.

Copyright

Convention: A literary *convention* is any device or style or subject matter which has become, in its time and by reason of its habitual use, a recognized means of literary expression, an accepted element in technique. The use of ALLITERATIVE VERSE among the Anglo-Saxons and of the HEROIC COUPLET in the time of Dryden or Pope are *conventions* in this sense. The personified virtues of the MORALITY PLAYS, the braggart soldier of the Elizabethan stage, and the fainting heroine of sentimental fiction are examples of conventional STOCK CHARACTERS. Features which later become *conventions* usually arise from freshness of appeal, acquire a pleasing familiarity at the hands of good writers, and eventually, through excessive or unskillful use, become distasteful and fall into disuse. Sometimes, however, discarded *conventions* are revived when apparently dead, as when the French poet Villon revived successfully the BALLADE. Poetic IMAGERY tends to become conventional, as when a "code" of EPITHETS, adjectives, METAPHORS, and SIMILES came to be regarded by the Augustans as "poetic." Not infrequently *conventions* depart so far from the realities and probabilities of life that literature could not employ them if custom had not made them acceptable, as in the case of the SOLILOQUY in drama. In real life men do not talk to themselves in long, rhetorical MONOLOGUES in which they analyze their thoughts and motives. Yet the device has become so conventional in DRAMA that Shakespeare could rely upon it as a medium for some of his finest effects, and a modern playwright such as Eugene O'Neill can have his characters speak their thoughts in the presence of other characters who are supposed to hear nothing, an illustration of how an impossibility in real life can become accepted in literature because of its conventional character. For an illuminating discussion of some aspects of the subject see J. L. Lowes, *Convention and Revolt in Poetry.* See TRADITION, STOCK CHARACTERS, MOTIF, DRAMATIC CONVENTIONS.

Copy: Material, either in manuscript or printed, which is to be set in type or duplicated by some other printing process. The term is used without an article and in the singular, as "When can you supply *copy* for the printer?" *Copy* which has been set and which bears printers' and editors' markings is called foul *copy.*

Copyright: The exclusive legal right to publish or reproduce for sale works of literature or art. Such rights are protected for the author or publisher by an Act of March 4, 1909, in the United States, and by the Copyright Act of 1911 in England. International *copyright* was established in 1891 but it is generally considered inadequate. In America a *copyright* is for twenty-eight years, renewable once, making a maximum period of protection of fifty-six years. An effort to modify the American copyright law has been under way for some time, and the expiration of copyright on works published after 1906 has been suspended awaiting action on the proposed changes. In England the *copyright* protects a work for fifty years after the author's death, regardless of the date of initial publication of the work. Secondary rights—rights to serialize, adapt for motion pictures, stage, or television—create a complicated problem. Detailed information on British *copyright* can be found in Appendix II of the *Oxford Companion to English Literature*. See PIRATED EDITIONS.

Copy Text: That particular text of a work used by a textual scholar as the basic text against which to compare various EDITIONS, IMPRESSIONS, and ISSUES in his effort to arrive at the closest possible approximation of the author's original intent. If the author's manuscript exists, it is usually used as the *copy text;* if no manuscript exists, the first printed EDITION set directly from the author's manuscript is usually the *copy text,* although cases where works have undergone major revision by the author between EDITIONS present complex problems.

Coronach: A song of lamentation; a funeral DIRGE. A Gaelic word reflecting a custom in Ireland (where "keening" is the more commonly used term) and in the Scottish Highlands. The word means a "wailing together," and judging from Sir Walter Scott's presentation a typical *coronach* was sung by the Celtic women. In one of his novels he says, "Their wives and daughters came, clapping their hands, and crying the coronach, and shrieking." In *The Lady of the Lake* (Stanza xvi of Canto III) appears a *coronach* of Scott's own composition:

> He is gone on the mountain,
> He is lost to the forest,
> Like a summer-dried fountain,
> When our need was the sorest, ...

Corpus Christi Plays: Medieval religious plays based upon the Bible and performed by town guilds on movable wagons, or "pag-

eants," as a part of the procession on Corpus Christi day. See
MYSTERY PLAYS.

Counterplayers: The characters in a DRAMA who plot against the
HERO or heroine, e.g., Claudius, Polonius, Laertes, and their associates in *Hamlet*. See ANTAGONIST.

Counterpoint Rhythm: A term used by Gerard Manley Hopkins to
describe the superimposing of a new RHYTHM upon a different one
that is already established. As Hopkins sees it, we hear the new
RHYTHM but still remember the old one, so that two RHYTHMS are
running concurrently in our minds. Milton was, Hopkins asserted,
the great master of *counterpoint rhythm* and the CHORUSES of *Samson Agonistes* were excellent examples of it. The following CHORUS
lines, which follow speeches in regular IAMBIC PENTAMETER, are
examples (the mind is hearing the RHYTHM of IAMBIC PENTAMETER
behind them):

> Just are the ways of God,
> And justifiable to Men;
> Unless there be who think not God at all.

It should be noted, however, that Karl Shapiro feels that such a
CHORUS in *Samson Agonistes*, "Flows by the count of ear and no
more scans . . . than Hebrew." Certainly *counterpoint rhythm* is
sufficiently subjective to defy precise analysis.

Coup de Théâtre: A surprising and usually unmotivated turn in a
DRAMA, which produces a sensational effect; by extension any piece
of claptrap or anything designed solely for effect.

Couplet: Two lines of VERSE with similar END-RHYMES. Formally,
the *couplet* is a two-line STANZA with both grammatical structure
and idea complete within itself, but the form has gone through
numerous adaptations, the most famous of which is HEROIC VERSE.
In French literature *couplet* is sometimes used in the sense of
STANZA. It is customary but not essential that the length of each
line be the same. *Couplets* are usually written in octosyllabic and
decasyllabic lines. See CLOSED COUPLET, HEROIC VERSE.

Court Comedy: COMEDY written to be performed at the royal
court. *Love's Labour's Lost* is a *court comedy* belonging to Shake-

speare's early period. Some years before Shakespeare came to London, the Elizabethan *court comedy* had been developed to a high degree of effectiveness by John Lyly in such plays as *Endimion* and *Alexander and Campaspe*. Characteristics include: artificial PLOT; little action; much use of mythology; pageantry; elaborate costuming and scenery; prominence of music, especially SONGS; lightness of TONE; CHARACTERS numerous and often balanced (arranged in contrasting pairs); artificial STRUCTURE; STYLE marked by WIT, grace, verbal cleverness, quaint IMAGERY, PUNS; prose DIALOGUE; pages prominent, being witty and saucy; eccentric characters such as braggarts, witches, and alchemists often employed; much farcical action; allegorical meanings sometimes embodied in the characters and action. Though some of these traits of the Lylian *court comedy* dropped out later, *court comedy* in the seventeenth century retained many of them and was always operatic in tone and spectacular in presentation. See MASQUE.

Courtesy Books: A class of books which flourished in late RENAISSANCE times and dealt with the training of the "courtly" person. Often in DIALOGUE form, the *courtesy book* discussed such questions as the qualities of a gentleman or court lady, what constituted a gentleman, the etiquette of COURTLY LOVE, the education of the future courtier or prince, and the duties of the courtier as a state counsellor. The *courtesy book* originated in Italy, the most famous example being Castiglione's *Il Cortegiano*, "The Courtier" (1528), which exerted great influence on English writers, especially after its translation into English by Sir Thomas Hoby in 1561. The earliest English *courtesy book* is Sir Thomas Elyot's *Book Named the Governour* (1531).

Somewhat similar to the *courtesy books,* but not to be confused with them, were the numerous etiquette books written not to explain the character of the noble or royal person but to deal with the problems of conduct confronting the well-bred citizen as well as the "gentleman." One of the best is *Galateo* by the Italian Della Casa. Early English examples of this type are *The Babees Book* and *The Boke of Curtasye* (1450).

Many books of the seventeenth century carried on the tradition such as: Henry Peacham's *Compleat Gentleman,* 1622 (courtly); Richard Brathwait's *The English Gentleman,* 1630 (PURITAN); and Francis Osborne's *Advice to a Son,* 1658 (a precursor of Lord Chesterfield's *Letters*). By extension the term *courtesy book* can be applied to a poem like Spenser's *The Faerie Queene,* since one of the objects of the work is to portray the moral virtues. A similar extension has applied the term to Franklin's *Autobiography,* since that work was written to instruct his son in the ways of the world.

Courtly Love: A philosophy of love and a code of love-making which flourished in chivalric times, first in France and later in other countries, especially in England. The exact origins of the system cannot be traced, but fashions set by the Provençal TROUBADOURS and ideas drawn from the Orient and especially from Ovid were probably the chief sources. The conditions of feudal society and the veneration of the Virgin Mary, both of which tended to give a new dignity and independence to woman, also affected it. The method of debate or SOLILOQUY by which the doctrines of *courtly love* are given expression in literature was probably indebted to current scholastic philosophy.

According to the system, falling in love is accompanied by great emotional disturbances; the lover is bewildered, helpless, tortured by mental and physical pain, and exhibits certain "symptoms," such as pallor, trembling, loss of appetite, sleeplessness, sighing, weeping, etc. He agonizes over his condition and indulges in endless self-questioning and reflections on the nature of love and his own wretched state. His condition improves when he is accepted, and he is inspired by his love to great deeds. He and his lady pledge each other to secrecy, and they must remain faithful in spite of all obstacles. Andreas Capellanus wrote a treatise late in the twelfth century in which he summarized prevailing notions of *courtly love* through imaginary conversations and through his thirty-one "rules." According to the strictest code, true love was held to be impossible in the married state. Hence some authorities distinguish between true *courtly love* as it is illustrated in the story of Lancelot and Guinevere in Chrétien's "The Knight of the Cart," and Ovidian love. Basically, *courtly love* was illicit and sensual, but a sort of Platonic idealism soon appeared and is found in the usual literary presentation.

Courtly love ideas abound in medieval ROMANCE and are perhaps not unconnected with the Petrarchan and Platonic love doctrines as found, for example, in Elizabethan SONNET-SEQUENCES. The system of *courtly love* largely controls the behavior of the characters in Chaucer's *Troilus and Criseyde.* C. S. Lewis has made a detailed study of *courtly love* in *The Allegory of Love.* See COURTS OF LOVE.

"Courtly Makers": A phrase applied to the court poets in the reign of Henry VIII who introduced the "new poetry" from Italy and France into England. *"Maker"* was used in the sixteenth century, both in Scotland and England, for poet, the use of the term arising from the concept of the poet as a creator (the word *poet* itself comes from a Greek word meaning *maker* or *do-er*). The *"courtly makers"* were given credit by the Elizabethans for "reforming" or polishing the "rude and homely manner" of earlier English poetry. Their work was imitative and experimental, based upon forms and fashions developed by the Italians. They were most successful in poetic TRANSLATIONS or PARAPHRASES and in SONGS, even Henry VIII himself being credited with the authorship of both words and music of several graceful songs. The introduction of the SONNET into English is due to the efforts of the two most important poets of the group, Sir Thomas Wyatt and the Earl of Surrey. BLANK VERSE was introduced by the Earl of Surrey. Other *"courtly makers"* were William Cornish, Lord Vaux, Lord Rochford (George Boleyn), Sir Anthony St. Leger, Lord Morley (Henry Parker), Sir Francis Bryan, Sir Thomas Chaloner, John Heywood, Robert Fairfax, and Robert Cooper. Most of the work of these men has probably perished, as their ideas of "gentlemanly" conduct did not lead them to publish their work, poetry being cultivated as an incidental grace. Manuscript collections were made for private libraries, however, one of which, now commonly known as *Tottel's Miscellany*, was published in 1557 and exerted a powerful influence on Elizabethan poetry. In fact, the chief importance of the *"courtly makers"* lies in the pioneer character of their work, as their efforts were brought to a perfect flowering by the poetic generations which followed them. Sometimes the term *"courtly maker"* is applied to any court poet.

Courts of Love: Tribunals for settling questions involved in the system of COURTLY LOVE. The judge, a court lady or Venus herself, would hear debate on such questions as: "Can a lover love two ladies at once?" "Are lovers or married couples more affectionate?" Though it was once believed that such courts were actually held in high society in chivalric times, modern scholarship is inclined to regard the *courts of love* as mere literary conventions. The term *court of love* is also sometimes extended to include allegorical and processional pageants such as the Masque of Cupid passage in Spenser's *The Faerie Queene* (Book III, Cantos xi–xii). The phrase, too, is sometimes used loosely as a synonym for COURTLY LOVE.

Critical Realism

Covenant Theology: A modification of the doctrines of CALVINISM made in the seventeenth century and particularly important in New England. It substitutes for divine decrees as a basis for election the idea of a contractual relationship between God and man. In the *Covenant theology* it is held that God promised Adam and his posterity eternal life in exchange for absolute obedience. When Adam broke this covenant, he incurred punishment as a legal responsibility for himself and his posterity. However, God made another covenant with Abraham, promising man the ability to struggle toward perfection. During THE GREAT AWAKENING Jonathan Edwards attacked the *Covenant theology* and urged a return to CALVINISM. See CALVINISM; AWAKENING, THE GREAT.

Cowleyan Ode: A form of the IRREGULAR ODE used by Abraham Cowley in the seventeenth century. See ODE, IRREGULAR ODE.

Crisis: In a FICTION or a DRAMA the point at which the opposing forces that create the CONFLICT interlock in the decisive action on which the PLOT will turn. *Crisis* is applied to the EPISODE or incident wherein the situation in which the PROTAGONIST finds himself is sure either to improve or grow worse. Since *crisis* is essentially a structural element of PLOT rather than an index of the emotional response which an event may produce in a reader or spectator, as CLIMAX is, the *crisis* and the CLIMAX do not always occur together. (See CLIMAX on this point.) The actual turning point in the action may result in events which produce climactic effects without themselves being of compelling interest. See CLIMAX, PLOT, CONFLICT, DRAMATIC STRUCTURE.

Critic: One who estimates and passes judgment on the value and quality of literary works. The term is used for a great variety of persons ranging from the writers of brief REVIEWS and notices in the popular press to expounders of the aesthetic principles that define the nature and function of art. A *critic* may employ any of many different types of CRITICISM and support any of many different theories of art. See CRITICISM, HISTORICAL SKETCH; and CRITICISM, TYPES OF.

Critical Realism: A term applied to realistic FICTION in the late nineteenth and early twentieth centuries, particularly in America. The MUCKRAKERS belong to the school of *critical realism*. Vernon L.

Parrington gave the term currency in his posthumously published (1930) third volume of *Main Currents in American Thought,* which he called *The Beginnings of Critical Realism in America,* where he uses it to refer to the tendency of writers and intellectuals in the period between 1875 and 1920 to apply the methods of realistic FICTION to the criticism of society and the examination of social issues.

Criticism, Historical Sketch: *Classical Criticism.*—The first important critical treatise, the *Poetics* of Aristotle (fourth century B.C.), has proved to be the most influential. This Greek philosopher defined POETRY as an idealized representation of human action, and TRAGEDY as a serious, dramatic representation or IMITATION of some magnitude, arousing pity and fear wherewith to accomplish a CATHARSIS of such emotions; tragedies should have UNITY and completeness of PLOT, with beginning, middle, and end. The *Poetics* also treats the element of CHARACTER in TRAGEDY and the relation of TRAGEDY to EPIC poetry. Aristotle's treatise on the Homeric EPIC has not survived. The great attention given by the ancients to RHETORIC is also important critically, though developed largely because of the interest in oratory. The great influence of the *Poetics* began in the RENAISSANCE.

Another important Greek document is the treatise of Longinus, *On the Sublime* (date uncertain, perhaps third century after Christ). Very different from the *Poetics* of Aristotle in content and spirit, this work acclaims sublimity, height, and imagination in a style that is itself enthusiastic and eloquent. Longinus finds the sources of the Sublime in great conceptions, noble passions, and elevated diction.

The foremost Latin critic was Horace, whose *Art of Poetry,* written as an informal EPISTLE in VERSE, has exercised considerable power. It discusses types of POETRY and of CHARACTER, stresses the importance of Greek models, emphasizes the importance of DECORUM, and advises the poet to write both for entertainment and instruction. Many of Horace's phrases have entered the language of criticism, such as *ut pictura poesis,* "poetry is like painting"; *labor limae,* "the labor of the file" (i.e., revision); and *aut prodesse aut delectare,* "either to profit or to please." The influence of Horace's criticism was especially great in England in the sixteenth and seventeenth centuries. Quintilian's *Institutes of Oratory* is, after Horace's epistle, perhaps the most important Latin critical treatise. Other ancient critics include Plato, Dionysius of Halicarnassus, Plutarch, and Lucian among the Greeks; and Cicero, the Senecas, Petronius, and Macrobius among the Latin writers. The art of RHETORIC constituted an integral part of this literary criticism.

The Middle Ages.—There was little interest in criticism in the Middle Ages. Much of what there was dealt perfunctorily with Latin VERSIFICATION, RHETORIC, and grammar. The ecclesiastical theologians who dominated intellectual life regarded literature as a servant of theology and philosophy, and there was consequently a reduced interest in imaginative literature as such. Classical literature was generally neglected or little known, and there was not much contemporary literature of a sort to arouse critical interest. The rhetoricians dealt in great detail with technical matters of vital interest to the creative writer: the use and nature of FIGURATIVE LANGUAGE; organization; beginnings; endings; development (amplification, condensation); STYLE—especially the adaptation of STYLE to type of composition; ornamentation, etc. The very great influence of such teachings upon the early work of Chaucer has been demonstrated in detail.

St. Augustine (d. 430) condemned poets because they pictured the gods as vicious. His teachings contributed to the general distrust of literature on moral and religious grounds which persisted through the Middle Ages into modern times. However, St. Augustine's attack on imaginative writing produced replies which anticipate later critical attitudes and arguments: the literary and the moral points of view should not be confused; the ancients should be followed, etc. Isidore of Seville (sixth and seventh centuries) listed the types and kinds of literature (based on Biblical forms). But it was not until the end of the medieval period that a really great critic appeared in the Italian poet Dante, whose *De Vulgari Eloquentia* (early fourteenth century) discusses the problems of vernacular literature. Dante reflects classical ideas on DECORUM, IMITATION, and the nature of the poet. He discusses diction, sentence-structure, STYLE, VERSIFICATION, and dialects. Petrarch and Boccaccio, great Italian scholars and writers of the fourteenth century, produced critical works which belong in part to the medieval period and in part to the RENAISSANCE which they helped to usher in. Boccaccio's famous defense of poetry in Books XIV and XV of his *Genealogia Deorum Gentilium* is particularly important to students of later criticism.

The Renaissance: Italy and France.—The RENAISSANCE reacted against the theological interpretation of poetry and attempted to justify it as an independent art, along lines suggested by humanistic ideals. In Italy, Vida, Robortelli, Daniello, Minturno, Giraldi Cinthio, J. C. Scaliger, Castelvetro, and others were concerned with such topics as: POETRY as a form of philosophy and an imitation of life; the doctrine of VERISIMILITUDE; pleasurable instruction as the object of POETRY; the theory of DRAMA, especially TRAGEDY—the tragic hero and the UNITIES were much debated—and the theory of the EPIC poem. The causes for the growth of CLASSICISM have been assigned to HUMANISM, Aristotelianism, and RATIONALISM—with PLATONISM, medievalism, and nationalism acting as ROMANTIC forces. These tendencies toward CLASSICISM actuated Italian criticism of the sixteenth century and French criticism of the seventeenth. The first French critical works were rhetorical and metrical, the most important being Sibilet's *Art of Poetry* (1548); but the first highly significant French criticism centered around the *Pléiade*, a group interested in refining the French language and literature by borrowings and imitations of the classics, Ronsard being its most famous writer and Du Bellay being the author of its manifesto, his epochal *Defence and Illustration of the French Language* (1549). Among the prominent seventeenth-century French critics were Malherbe, who reacted strongly against the *Pléiade*, Chapelain, Corneille, Saint-Évremond, d'Aubignac, Rapin, Le Bossu, and Boileau, whose influence was especially powerful. These writers illustrate the course of French criticism in the direction of CLASSICISM, a rational crystallizing of poetic theory, and a codification of the principles of literary STRUCTURE.

The English Renaissance.—In Renaissance England the earliest critical utterances were directed toward matters of RHETORIC and diction, as in the "prefaces" of the printer Caxton (late fifteenth century) and the rhetorics of Leonard Cox (*ca.*1530) and Thomas Wilson (1553). As early as Sir Thomas Elyot's *Book Named the Governour* (1531) the claims of English as a vehicle for literature were being urged against the extreme humanist opposition to the vernacular as crude and not permanent. The actual development of a native literature was accompanied by discussions of how best to build up the English vocabulary, the extreme humanists and INK-HORNISTS, who favored the introduction of heavy Latin and Greek words, being opposed by those who stressed native words (see PURISTS). Much attention was given to the requirements of DECORUM and IMITATION. The first technical treatise on English VERSIFICATION was Gascoigne's *Certain Notes of Instruction* (1575). VERSE FORMS already developed in English, including RHYME, were perfected in the face of the critical impulse to insist upon such CLASSICAL FORMS as the unrhymed HEXAMETER. Practice ran ahead of theory in this matter, as may be seen by comparing the actual practices of Sidney and Campion with their serious critical condemnation of RHYME. Campion's essay, *Observations in the Art of English Poesie* (1602), was effectively answered by Samuel Daniel in his *A Defence of Rime*. Similarly, Shakespearean ROMANTIC TRAGEDY developed in spite of the prevailing critical insistence upon the UNITIES.

But perhaps the most vital critical issue centered about the effort to justify literature in the face of the PURITAN attack based upon moral grounds, a movement which attacked the DRAMA in particular, as in Stephen Gosson's *The School of Abuse* (1579). Many of these critical questions were treated in Sidney's *Defence of Poesie* (pub. 1595), the most significant piece of criticism of the period. Sidney stressed the high function of the poet, exalted POETRY above philosophy and history, answered the objections to poetic art, examined the types of POETRY, and assigned praise and blame among the writers of the preceding generation on the basis of their conformity to CLASSICAL principles as expressed by the Italian critics. Important critical expressions came from Francis Bacon (*Advancement of Learning*, 1605) and Ben Jonson (*Timber: or Discoveries*). In Jonson, a man of vast learning and uncommon common sense, we may see the definite tendency toward the NEO-CLASSICISM that was to become the center of English criticism for more than a century.

The Restoration: Dryden.—The next master was John Dryden, with his numerous prefaces and essays, the greatest of which is the *Essay of Dramatick Poesie* (1668). This treatise, written in DIA-LOGUE form with ease and vigor, fairly presents the claims of "ANCIENTS AND MODERNS," of French and English dramatists; RHYME, TRAGI-COMEDY, and the UNITIES receive consideration; the influence of Corneille is apparent; and much applied criticism keeps the essay from being entirely theoretical. In his *Preface to the Fables* (1700) Dryden gives a noteworthy estimate of the genius of Chaucer. Other Restoration critics include: Sir Robert Howard, Thomas Rymer, the Earls of Mulgrave and Roscommon, and Sir William Temple. The foreign influence was predominantly French.

The Eighteenth Century: Pope, Addison, Johnson.—Alexander Pope was not merely the first poet of his generation, but also its most significant critic, what with the prefaces to his translation of

Homer and his edition of Shakespeare, and his *Essay on Criticism* (1711), by far the leading piece of VERSE CRITICISM in the language. In this work Pope set forth the NEO-CLASSIC principles of following nature and the ancients, outlined the causes of bad criticism, described the good critic, and concluded with a short history of CRITICISM. Addison's critical papers in the *Spectator* (1711–1712) on TRAGEDY, WIT, BALLADS, *Paradise Lost,* and the pleasures of the imagination were designed for a popular audience, but they exerted a strong influence upon formal CRITICISM and aesthetic theory. The neo-classical critics in general devoted themselves to such topics as reason, correctness, WIT, TASTE, GENRES, rules, IMITATION, the CLASSICS, the function of the imagination, the status of emotion, and the dangers of enthusiasm. Gradually the sway of authority was weakened; the historical point of view gained in general acceptance; TEXTUAL CRITICISM became more scientific. But Samuel Johnson remained the defender of the older order; his large body of critical expression may be gleaned from his periodical essays, the preface to his edition of Shakespeare, and his *Lives of the Poets.* The personality of Doctor Johnson stimulated orthodoxy as much as did his writings.

Early Romantic Tendencies.—Joseph Warton (*Essay on the Genius and Writings of Pope,* 1756, 1782) refused Pope the highest rank among poets because of insufficient emotion and imagination; Thomas Warton (*Observations on The Faerie Queene of Spenser,* 1754) emphasized the emotional quality of the great Elizabethan poet; Young (*Conjectures on Original Composition,* 1759) spoke in favor of independence and against the imitation of other writers; Hurd (*Letters on Chivalry and Romance,* 1762) justified Gothic manners and design, Spenser's poetry, and the Italian poets; and attacked some of the main tenets of the AUGUSTANS. Other eighteenth-century critics of note were John Hughes, John Dennis, Henry Fielding, Edmund Burke, Goldsmith, Lord Kames, Hugh Blair, and Sir Joshua Reynolds.

Romanticism: Wordsworth, Coleridge, Shelley, Lamb.—The volume of poems by Wordsworth and Coleridge entitled *Lyrical Ballads* (1798) is frequently cited as formally ushering in the ROMANTIC MOVEMENT. For the second edition (1800) Wordsworth wrote a preface that acted as a manifesto for the new school and set forth his own critical creed. It was his object to "choose incidents and situations from common life," to use "language really used by men." Wordsworth was reacting from what he considered the artificial poetic practice of the preceding era; he condemned the use of PERSONIFICATION and "POETIC DICTION." There could be "no essential difference between the language of prose and metrical composition." Wordsworth defined the poet as a "man speaking to men" and POETRY as "the breath and finer spirit of all knowledge," "the spontaneous overflow of powerful feelings" which takes its origin from emotion "recollected in tranquillity." Though not ideally equipped for the role of critic, Wordsworth here produced a document, free from inherited critical JARGON and replete with illustrious passages.

Coleridge became one of the great critics. The *Biographia Literaria* (1817) is both autobiographical and critical. Therein he explained the division of labor in the *Lyrical Ballads:* his own endeavors "should be directed to persons and characters supernatural, or at least romantic; yet so as to transfer from our inward nature a human interest and a semblance of truth sufficient to procure for these shadows of imagination that willing suspension of disbelief for the moment, which constitutes poetic faith"; while Wordsworth was "to propose to himself as his object, to give the charm of novelty to things of every day, and to excite a feeling analogous to the supernatural, by awakening the mind's attention to the lethargy of custom, and directing it to the loveliness and the wonders of the world before us; an inexhaustible treasure, but for which, in consequence of the film of familiarity and selfish solicitude, we have eyes, yet see not, ears that hear not, and hearts that neither feel nor understand." These two fundamental romantic points of view were applied to *The Rime of the Ancient Mariner* of Coleridge and *Lucy Gray* of Wordsworth. Coleridge disagreed, however, with Wordsworth's statements about the principles of METER and POETIC DICTION: rustic life is not favorable to the formation of a human diction; POETRY is essentially ideal and generic; the language of Milton is as much that of real life as is that of the cottager; art strives to give pleasure through beauty. Coleridge subtly expounded the nature of beauty and the conditions for its existence. His discussion of the IMAGINATION and the FANCY has had wide influence. The English ROMANTICISM of Coleridge and others found considerable support and some sources in the philosophy, aesthetics, and literature of German ROMANTICISM.

Other critics of importance in the first half of the nineteenth century were Lamb, Hazlitt, and Leigh Hunt. Lamb's criticism was charming and enthusiastic but eccentric, capricious, and unorganized; it showed good taste, great originality of thought as well as keenness of phrase; and it stimulated the appreciation of earlier English literature. Hazlitt is remarkable for many happy phrases, sound judgment, and an infectious spirit. Hunt is a most catholic and readable critic. The poet Shelley's *Defence of Poetry* (1821) is an abstract *apologia* reminiscent of RENAISSANCE treatises. Other critics of this period are: William Blake, Cardinal Newman, Carlyle, De Quincey, Landor, Henry Hallam, and Macaulay. The review journals, the Whig *Edinburgh Review* (ed. Francis Jeffrey) and the Tory *Quarterly Review* (ed. William Gifford), voiced fundamentally conservative opinions and dominated periodical criticism.

The Nineteenth Century: Arnold, Pater; Realism.—Matthew Arnold was the leading critic of the last half of the nineteenth century. He thought of poetry as a "criticism of life" and of CRITICISM itself as the effort to "know the best that is known and thought in the world and by in its turn making this known, to create a current of true and fresh ideas." CRITICISM should seek absolute truth. Form, order, and measure constituted the CLASSICAL qualities which Arnold admired. He sought to judge literature by high standards; he used specimens (or "touchstones") of great POETRY as well as his own sensitive TASTE in forming judgments. "The grand style," he said, "arises in poetry, when a noble nature, poetically gifted, treats with simplicity or with severity a serious subject." The greatness of a poet "lies in his powerful and beautiful application of ideas to life." Arnold was primarily interested in the true and the great; he subordinated the historical method. Three of his better known critical essays are *The Function of Criticism* (1865), *The Study of Poetry* (1888), and *On Translating Homer* (1861).

In the later nineteenth century we find the tenets of ROMANTICISM still in the field and the principles of REALISM and of IMPRESSIONISM gaining ground. The expansion of natural science helped the progress of realistic and naturalistic criticism (see NATURALISM), which was a reaction against both CLASSICISM and ROMANTICISM. HISTORICAL CRITICISM, the attempt to understand a work in the light of "the man and the *milieu*," had been in process of development for at least two centuries and at last was crystallized in the writings of the Frenchmen Sainte-Beuve and Taine. IMPRESSIONISM grew out of ROMANTICISM and obtained an eloquent advocate in Walter Pater. Victorian critics discussed such topics as the function and nature of art and literature, the role of morality, the place of the IMAGINATION, the problems of STYLE, the province of the NOVEL, and the theory of the comic. Though there were no real schools of critics, the tendency of criticism was away from the application of standards toward the use of impressionistic methods. The German influence yielded ground to the French. Significant contributions were made by Thackeray on the English humorists; John Stuart Mill on the nature of poetry; Walter Bagehot on pure, ornate, and grotesque art in poetry; Pater on STYLE and on hedonism in art; George Meredith on the comic spirit; Leslie Stephen on the eighteenth century; and Swinburne on the Elizabethan and Jacobean dramatists.

M. H. Abrams, in *The Mirror and The Lamp*, has pointed out that all critical theories, whatever their language, discriminate four elements in "the total situation of a work of art," and he discriminates both the kinds of criticism and the history of critical theory and practice in terms of the dominance of one of these elements. They are: the *work*, that is, the thing made by the maker, the poem produced by the poet, the artifact created by the artificer; the *artist*, the maker, the poet, the artificer; the *universe*, that is, the "nature" that is imitated, if art is viewed as IMITATION, the materials of the real world or the world of ideal entities out of which the work may be thought to take its subject; and the *audience*, the readers, spectators, or listeners to whom the work is addressed. If the critic views art basically in terms of the *universe*, in terms of what is imitated, he is using the MIMETIC THEORY. If the critic views art basically in terms of its effect on the *audience*, he is using the PRAGMATIC THEORY. If the critic views art basically in terms of the *artist*, that is, views it as expressive of the maker, he is using the EXPRESSIVE THEORY. If the critic views art basically in its own terms, seeing the *work* as a self-contained entity, he is using an OBJECTIVE THEORY.

A backward glance over the history of criticism in the light of these theories is revealing. The MIMETIC THEORY is characteristic of the criticism of the CLASSICAL age, with Aristotle as its great expounder. Horace, however, introduced the idea of instruction with pleasure—*utile et dulce*—and thereby put the effect upon the audience in the center of his view of art. From Horace through most of the eighteenth century, the PRAGMATIC THEORY was dominant, although the NEO-CLASSIC critics revived a serious interest in IMITATION. Indeed, as M. H. Abrams asserts, "the pragmatic view, broadly conceived, has been the principal aesthetic attitude of the Western world." At the same time, it is true that criticism through the eighteenth century was securely confident of the imitative nature

137

of art. With the beginnings of ROMANTICISM came the EXPRESSIVE THEORY, in a sense the most characteristic of the ROMANTIC attitudes. When Wordsworth calls poetry "the spontaneous overflow of powerful feeling," the *artist* has moved to the center. Now the poet's IMAGINATION is a new force in the world and a source of unique knowledge, and expression is the true function of art. Beginning in the nineteenth century and becoming dominant in the twentieth has been the "poem *per se* . . . written solely for the poem's sake," as Poe expressed it. Here FORM and STRUCTURE, patterns of IMAGERY and SYMBOLS, become the center of the critic's concern, for he looks at the work of art as a separate cosmos. However, increasing interest in psychology has kept the contemporary critic also aware of the fact that the *audience* functions in the work of art, and views of the MYTH current today tend to bring the *artist* back to a central position and at the same time to value in terms of the *audience* the truth he speaks through his ARCHETYPAL patterns and IMAGES from his racial unconscious.

These views of criticism will help us chart the history of the craft in America in the nineteenth century and in England and America in the twentieth.

American Criticism in the Nineteenth Century.—Criticism in America, besides reflecting, sometimes tardily, European attitudes, has been concerned with questions peculiar to a literature growing out of a transplanted culture. To what extent is American literature derivative and imitative? How can American literature develop a purely American spirit? What is this spirit? What of the effect of PURITAN ethical conceptions upon American literature? How has the frontier affected it?

Early nineteenth-century criticism, as evidenced by the earlier numbers of the *North American Review* (estab. 1815), was conservative and NEO-CLASSIC. Pope and the Scottish school reigned. Later, the ROMANTIC attitude triumphed, and Byron, Scott, Wordsworth, and eventually Shelley, Keats, Coleridge, Carlyle, and Tennyson were exalted. The earlier writer-critics were in the main ROMANTIC: Poe, Lowell, and Emerson. Poe, however, stressed workmanship, technique, STRUCTURE, the divorce of art and morality; was highly rational; and enunciated independent theories of the LYRIC and the SHORT STORY. Emerson believed art should serve moral ends; asserted that all American literature was derivative but should not be; and assumed the ROMANTIC attitude toward nature and individualism. Lowell is first IMPRESSIONISTIC and ROMANTIC;

at times professedly REALISTIC; and eventually CLASSICAL and ethical, after his revolt against SENTIMENTALISM.

After the Civil War a strong critical movement toward REALISM developed, and it had two powerful critical spokesmen, William Dean Howells and Henry James. Interested almost exclusively in FICTION and particularly in the NOVEL, they advanced a theory that the fidelity of the *work* to the *universe,* with universe defined in a materialistic or psychological-social sense, was the object of art. REALISM was defined by Howells as "neither more nor less than the truthful treatment of material." Yet there were aspects of the PRAGMATIC THEORY here, for he saw a moral obligation resting on the *artist* in terms of the *effects* of his works on the *audience.* At the close of the century, under the influence of the French, particularly Zola, a group of American novelists were advancing a theory of art that was frankly MIMETIC; this is the application of scientific method, even of scientific law, to enhance the seriousness and increase the depth of the portraying of the actual by the artist. The theory is NATURALISM, and Frank Norris was its most vocal expounder as the century ended. However, Henry James, in critical essays already written and in the prefaces which he prepared for the collected edition of his NOVELS in the first decade of the twentieth century, was to make the most significant formulation of critical principles about the NOVEL, centering in craftsmanship, that an American has produced. James and Poe emerge from nineteenth-century America as the most powerful and original American critics of the age.

Twentieth-century Criticism.—In England and America the first decade of the twentieth century saw a continuation of the concern with REALISM and NATURALISM, but little serious critical examination of them. IMPRESSIONISM and "appreciation," led in England by Walter Pater and his followers and in America by James Huneker, ruled the day. In the second decade, a group of Americans, under the leadership of Van Wyck Brooks, attacked the cultural failures of America and began the search for a "usable past," a search which was to occupy men like Randolph Bourne, Lewis Mumford, and Bernard De Voto down to the 1950's and which saw in 1927–1930 in Vernon L. Parrington's *Main Currents in American Thought* one of the major documents in critical scholarship in the century. At the same time, in England two young Americans, Ezra Pound and T. S. Eliot, were learning from T. E. Hulme to distrust ROMANTIC expressionism and to turn to formalism and objectivity. In the 1920's the impact of the new psychologies was deeply felt in England, particularly in

the work of I. A. Richards, whose reaction against IMPRESSIONISM
expressed itself in efforts to make an exact science of the examination
of how literature produced psychological states in its reader. He
was followed by Herbert Read and William Empson. And in
America Freudian psychology was applied to literary problems by
a variety of critics, but the strong movement was the NEW HUMAN-
ISM, which, under the leadership of Irving Babbitt and Paul Elmer
More, formulated a critical position resting on the traditional moral
and critical standards of the humanists.

In the 1930's, as a partial aftermath of the financial collapse,
came a wave of critics espousing Marxist and near-Marxist ideas—
a specialized form of PRAGMATIC THEORY—both in England and
America. The major English Marxist was Christopher Caudwell;
while no Americans approached him in excellence, critics like Gran-
ville Hicks and V. F. Calverton strongly espoused the reading of
literature in the light of radical social views. During the 1930's in
America, reacting both against the NEW HUMANISTS and the Marxist critics came a group, drawn largely from the AGRARIANS, who
vigorously embraced an OBJECTIVE THEORY of art. Led by John
Crowe Ransom, who gave them a name and something resembling
a credo in his book *The New Criticism,* these essentially conservative and anti-romantic writers—Allen Tate, Robert Penn Warren,
Donald Davidson, Yvor Winters, and later Cleanth Brooks, started
from the position of T. S. Eliot and Ezra Pound and quickly formed
themselves into a powerful force in the formal criticism of literature. At the same time a similar group, though much less organized,
were practicing a stringent and aesthetically centered criticism in
England, among them being Eliot himself, F. R. Leavis, and Cyril
Connolly. Both in England and America, the theories of Carl Jung
about the racial unconscious (see ARCHETYPE) have been operative
and have received vigorous expression by writers like Maud Bodkin and Eliot in England and Susanne Langer and Francis Fergusson
in America. Centered around Chicago and often called "The Chicago
Critics," a group of neo-Aristotelian critics, led by Ronald Crane,
Richard McKeon, and Elder Olson, have formulated a kind of formal
criticism based on Aristotle's principles. From this group has come
Wayne Booth's *The Rhetoric of Fiction,* the major critical effort to
come to grips with FICTION since Henry James. The twentieth
century is often called an age of criticism and in the richness and
complexity of its systems, the rigor of its application, and the enthusiasm of its espousal of the cause of the literary arts it can wear

Criticism, Types of

that title with honor. Today these many movements are fusing into a healthy eclecticism, and readers and writers alike are benefited by it.

Criticism, Types of: *Criticism* is a term which has been applied since the seventeenth century to the description, justification, analysis, or judgment of works of art. There are many ways in which *criticism* may be classified. Some of the more common classifications are given here, as supplementary to M. H. Abrams' discrimination among the major critical theories as MIMETIC, PRAGMATIC, EXPRESSIVE, and OBJECTIVE (see CRITICISM, HISTORICAL SKETCH, beginning at "The Nineteenth Century"). One common dichotomy for *criticism* is ARISTOTELIAN VS. PLATONIC. In this sense, ARISTOTELIAN implies a judicial, logical, formal *criticism* that tends to find the values of a work either within the work itself or inseparably linked to the work; and PLATONIC implies a moralistic, utilitarian view of art, where the values of a work are to be found in the usefulness of art for other and nonartistic purposes. Such a view of PLATONIC CRITICISM is narrow and in part inaccurate, but those who hold it point to the exclusion of the poet from Plato's Republic. Essentially what is meant by the ARISTOTELIAN–PLATONIC dichotomy is an intrinsic-extrinsic separation.

A separation between *relativistic criticism* and *absolutist criticism* is also often made, in which the *relativistic* critic employs any or all systems which will aid him in reaching and elucidating the nature of a work of art, whereas the *absolutist* critic holds that there is one proper critical procedure or set of principles and no others should be applied to the critical task.

There is also an obvious division between THEORETICAL CRITICISM, which attempts to arrive at the general principles of art and to formulate inclusive and enduring aesthetic and critical tenets, and PRACTICAL CRITICISM (sometimes called "applied" criticism), which brings these principles or standards to bear upon particular works of art.

Criticism may also be classified according to the purpose which it is intended to serve. The principal purposes which critics have had are: (1) to justify one's own work or to explain it and its underlying principles to an uncomprehending audience (Dryden, Wordsworth, Henry James); (2) to justify imaginative art in a world that tends to find its value questionable (Sidney, Shelley, the NEW CRITICISM); (3) to prescribe rules for writers and to legislate taste for the audience (Pope, Boileau, the Marxists); (4) to interpret works to

141

readers who might otherwise fail to understand or appreciate them (Edmund Wilson, Matthew Arnold); (5) to judge works by clearly defined standards of evaluation (Samuel Johnson, T. S. Eliot); (6) to discover and to apply the principles which describe the foundations of good art (Coleridge, Addison, I. A. Richards).

Criticism is also often divided into the following types in literary and critical histories: (1) IMPRESSIONISTIC, which emphasizes how the work of art affects the critic; (2) HISTORICAL, which examines the work against its historical surroundings and the facts of its author's life and times; (3) TEXTUAL, which attempts by all scholarly means to reconstruct the original manuscript or textual version of the work; (4) FORMAL, which examines the work in terms of the characteristics of the type or GENRE to which it belongs; (5) JUDICIAL, which judges the work by a definable set of standards; (6) ANALYTICAL, which attempts to get at the nature of the work as an object in itself through the detailed analysis of its parts and their organization; (7) MORAL, which evaluates the work in relation to human life; and (8) MYTHIC, which explores the nature and significance of the ARCHETYPES and archetypal patterns in the work.

These widely differing classification systems for *criticism* are not mutually exclusive, and there are certainly others. These will serve, however, to indicate to the student that the critic has employed a great variety of strategies in getting at the work of art and communicating what he finds there.

Critique: An ESSAY or ARTICLE which makes a critical examination of a work of art, usually literary, with a view to determining its nature and assessing its value according to some established standards. A *critique* is far more serious and judicious than a REVIEW.

Crown of Sonnets: Seven SONNETS interlinked by having the last line of the first form the first line of the second, the last line of the second form the first line of the third, etc., with the last line of the last SONNET repeating the first line of the first. Donne's "La Corona" is an example.

Cruelty, Theater of: A concept of DRAMA, originated by Antonin Artaud in the 1930's in which the theater becomes a ceremonial act of magic purgation. Artaud hoped to raise the theater to a level of religious ceremony. In so doing he subordinated words to action, gesture, and sound in an effort to overwhelm the spectator and liberate his instinctual preoccupations with crime, cruelty, and eroticism. It is called the *theater of the cruel* because it utilizes all means of shock to make the spectator aware of—and even participate in—the fundamental cruelty of life. Artaud delivered several manifestoes and projected plays based on Blue Beard and the Marquis de Sade, but he did not complete them. His theories, however, and the *theater of cruelty* appear importantly in the work of several contemporary playwrights, among them Peter Brook, Jean-Louis Barrault, Roger Blin, and Jean Genet. The most widely successful example of the *theater of cruelty* is Peter Weiss' *The Persecution and Assassination of Jean-Paul Marat as Performed by Inmates of the Asylum of Charenton under the Direction of the Marquis de Sade,* commonly known as *Marat/Sade.* See ABSURD, THEATER OF THE.

Cubist Poetry: POETRY that attempts to do in VERSE what the cubist painters do on canvas; that is, take the elements of an experience, totally fragment them (creating what Picasso calls "destructions") and then so re-arrange them that a new and meaningful synthesis is made (Picasso's "sum of destructions"). The poetry of e. e. cummings, Kenneth Rexroth, and some of that of Archibald MacLeish fits this category.

Cultural Primitivism: The belief that nature (what exists undisturbed by man's artifice) is preferable and fundamentally better than any aspect of man's culture (any area of human activity where, by art or craft, man has modified or ordered nature). It is a belief that distrusts artifice, logic, social and political organizations, rules, and conventions. See PRIMITIVISM, CHRONOLOGICAL PRIMITIVISM.

Curse: An INVOCATION which calls upon a supernatural being to visit evil upon someone. In this sense it is a MALEDICTION, or, if a formal and solemn imprecation, an ANATHEMA. The term *curse* is also used for the effects that result from the INVOCATION of great evil, as in a phrase such as "the curse of the Pyncheons," in Hawthorne's *The House of the Seven Gables,* where the *curse* put upon the Pyncheon family by Matthew Maule darkens the history of succeeding generations. See ANATHEMA, MALEDICTION, ARA.

Curtain: In the physical sense, a piece of heavy cloth or some other material that screens the STAGE from the audience and by being raised or opened and lowered or closed marks the beginning and end of an ACT or a SCENE. The *curtain* came into use in this sense in the early seventeenth century along with the development of the PROSCENIUM ARCH. By extension from this sense, *curtain* is used for a line, speech, or situation at the very end of an ACT or SCENE, just before the *curtain* falls. The ending of portions of a DRAMA are sometimes called *curtains,* as in the expression "quick *curtain*" for a sudden conclusion to a SCENE, or "strong *curtain*" for a dramatically powerful conclusion, or "*curtain* speech" for the final speech of an ACT or a PLAY. The term "*curtain* speech" also applies to a talk given in front of the *curtain* after the conclusion of a theatrical performance.

Curtain Raiser: A short play—either one-act or a SKIT—presented before the principal dramatic production on a program. By analogy, the term *curtain raiser* is applied to any preliminary event.

Curtal Sonnet: A term used by Gerard Manley Hopkins for a SONNET that has been curtailed or shortened and whose last line is very short. The OCTAVE is shortened to a SESTET and rhymes *abcabc.* The SESTET is shortened to a QUATRAIN and rhymes either *dbcd* or *dcbd.* A short line rhyming *c* ends the POEM. Hopkins' "Pied Beauty" is a famous example of a *curtal sonnet.*

Cycle: A word, originally meaning circle, which came to be applied to a collection of POEMS or ROMANCES centering about some outstanding event or character. Cyclic NARRATIVES are commonly accumulations of TRADITION given literary form by a succession of authors rather than by a single writer. "Cyclic" was first applied to a series of EPIC poems intended to supplement Homer's account of the Trojan War and written by a group of late Greek poets known as the Cyclic Poets. Other examples of cyclic NARRATIVE are the Charlemagne EPICS and Arthurian ROMANCES, like the "*Cycle* of Lancelot," etc. The MEDIEVAL religious DRAMA presents a cyclic treatment of Biblical themes.

Cyclic Drama: The great CYCLES of medieval religious DRAMA. See MYSTERY PLAY.

Cynicism: Doubt of the generally accepted standards or of the innate goodness of human action. In literature the term is used from time to time to characterize groups of writers or movements distinguished by dissatisfaction with contemporary conditions. Originally the expression came into being with a group of ancient Greek philosophers, led by Antisthenes and including such others as Diogenes and Crates. The major tenets of the cynics were belief in the moral responsibility of the individual for his own acts and the dominance of the will in its right to control human action. Reason, mind, will, individualism were, then, of greater importance than the social or political conduct so likely to be worshiped by the multitudes. It is this exaltation of the individual over society which makes most unthinking people contemptuous of the cynical attitude. Any highly individualistic writer, scornful of the commonly accepted social standards and ideals, is, for this reason, called cynical. Almost every literature has had its schools of cynics. It is important to remember that *cynicism* is not necessarily a weakness or a vice, and that the cynics have done much for civilization. Samuel Butler's *Way of All Flesh* and W. Somerset Maugham's *Of Human Bondage* are examples of the cynical NOVEL. The THEATER OF THE ABSURD, the THEATER OF CRUELTY, and many ANTI-REALISTIC NOVELS of today reflect *cynicism*.

D

Dactyl: A metrical FOOT consisting of one accented syllable followed by two unaccented syllables, as in the word *mánnĭkĭn*. See METER and VERSIFICATION.

Dadaism: A movement of young writers and artists in Paris during and just after World War I, which attempted to suppress the logical relationship between idea and statement, argued for absolute freedom, held meetings at bars and in theaters, and delivered itself of numerous nonsensical and seminonsensical "manifestoes." It was founded in Zurich in 1916 by Tristan Tzara (who then went to Paris) with the admittedly destructive intent of perverting and demolishing the tenets of art, philosophy, and logic and replacing them with conscious madness as a protest against the insanity of the war. Similar movements sprang up in Germany, Holland, Italy, Russia, and Spain. About 1924 the movement developed into SURREALISM. In certain respects it seems to have been a forerunner of the ANTI-REALISTIC NOVEL and the THEATER OF THE ABSURD.

Dandyism

Dandyism: A literary STYLE used by the English and French DECA-DENT writers of the last quarter of the nineteenth century. The term is derived from *dandy*, a word descriptive of one who gives an overly fastidious and exaggerated attention to dress and personal appearance. *Dandyism* as a literary STYLE is marked by excessively refined emotion and PRECIOSITY of language. The work of Oscar Wilde often displays *dandyism*.

Dark Ages: A phrase sometimes loosely used as a synonym for the medieval period of European history. Its use is vigorously objected to by most modern students of the Middle Ages, since the phrase reflects the old, discredited view that the period in question was characterized by intellectual darkness, an idea that arose from lack of information about medieval life. The studies of modern scholars have made it certain that *dark ages* is a phrase that completely misrepresents the medieval period, which, as a matter of fact, was characterized by intellectual, artistic, and even scientific activity which led to high cultural attainments. Most present-day writers, therefore, avoid the phrase altogether. Some who do use it restrict it to the earlier part of the Middle Ages (fifth to eleventh centuries).

Dead Metaphor: A FIGURE OF SPEECH so long and so often used that it is now taken in its denotative sense only, without the conscious comparison or ANALOGY to a physical object which it once conveyed. For example, in the sentence "The keystone of his system is the belief in an omnipotent God," "keystone"—literally an actual stone in an arch—functions as a *dead metaphor*. Many of our ABSTRACT TERMS are *dead metaphors*. See METAPHOR.

Dead Sea Scrolls: Documents written between the first century B.C. and the middle of the first century A.D. and discovered in 1947 and later in caves near the Dead Sea, on the border of Jordan and Israel. The principal finds were in caves on or near the site of the Qumran community, a group of people who lived an ascetic religious life much like the Essenes. The scrolls, stored in jars, contain portions of every book of the Bible except Esther; these manuscripts are almost a thousand years older than any previously known versions of the Bible, and they have been of paramount interest and concern to all students and translators of the Bible. Also found at Qumran were original books of the Qumran sect and groups of devotional poems.

Decadents

To all literary students concerned in any way with the Biblical texts, the discovery of the *Dead Sea Scrolls* has been an event of incalculable importance.

Débat: A type of literary composition, usually in VERSE, highly popular in the Middle Ages, in which two persons or objects, frequently allegorical, debate some specific topic and then refer it to a judge. Possibly the *débat* reflects the influence of the "pastoral contest" in Theocritus and Virgil. It was particularly popular in France, where the subjects ranged over most human interests, such as theology, morality, politics, COURTLY LOVE, and social questions. In England the *débat* tended to be religious and moralistic. The best English example is *The Owl and the Nightingale* (*ca.*12th century), whose interpretation has caused much scholarly debate.

Decadence: A term used in literary history and criticism to denote the decline or deterioration which commonly marks the end of a great period. *Decadent* qualities include self-consciousness, a restless curiosity, an oversubtilizing refinement, and often moral perversity. The term, however, is relative and does not always suggest the same qualities to the same writers, and no two periods of *decadence* can be just alike. In English dramatic history the period following Shakespeare was marked by such *decadent* qualities as a relaxing of critical standards, a breaking down of types (COMEDY and TRAGEDY merging), a lowered moral tone, sensationalism, overemphasis upon some single interest (like PLOT-construction or "prettiness" of STYLE), a decreased seriousness of purpose, and a loss of poetic power. The "silver age" of Latin literature (reign of Trajan), including such writers as Tacitus, Juvenal and Martial (satirists), Lucan, and the Plinys, is called *decadent* in relation to the preceding "golden age" of Augustus made illustrious by Virgil, Horace, Ovid, and Livy. In the last half of the nineteenth and the early years of the twentieth centuries *decadence* found a special expression in the work of a group known as the DECADENTS. In general today the term is used to describe a period or a work of art in which a declining seriousness of purpose or loss of adequate subject matter is combined with an increasing skill and even virtuosity of technique and form to produce an overly intense sensationalism or effect.

Decadents: A group of late nineteenth- and early twentieth-century writers, principally in France but also in England and

Decasyllabic

America, who held that art was superior to nature, that the finest beauty was that of dying or decaying things, and who, both in their lives and their art, attacked the accepted moral, ethical, and social standards of their time. In France the group included Verlaine, Rimbaud, Baudelaire, Huysmans, and Villiers de l'Isle-Adam. In England the *decadents* included Oscar Wilde, Ernest Dowson, Aubrey Beardsley, and Frank Harris. In America it is best represented by Edgar Saltus, although there are *decadent* qualities in Stephen Crane. See DANDYISM.

Decasyllabic: A line of VERSE composed of ten syllables. IAMBIC PENTAMETER and TROCHAIC PENTAMETER are *decasyllabic* lines.

Decorum: A critical term describing that which is proper to a character, subject, or setting in a literary work. According to classical standards, the UNITY and harmony of a composition could be maintained by the observance of DRAMATIC PROPRIETY. The STYLE should be appropriate to the speaker, the occasion, and the subject matter. So RENAISSANCE authors were careful to have kings speak in a "high" STYLE (such as majestic blank verse), old men in a "grave" STYLE, clowns in prose, and shepherds in a "rustic" STYLE. Puttenham (1589) cites as an example of the lack of *decorum* the case of the English translator of Virgil who said that Aeneas was fain to "trudge" out of Troy (a beggar might "trudge," but not a great hero). Beginning in the RENAISSANCE the type to which a character belonged was regarded as an important element in determining his qualities; age, rank, and social status were often held as fundamental in the art of CHARACTERIZATION. But on the use of *decorum* in the *Iliad* Pope said: "The *speeches* are to be considered as they flow from the characters, being perfect or defective as they agree or disagree with the manners of those who utter them. As there is more variety of characters in *The Iliad*, so there is of speeches, than in any other poem," and "Homer is in nothing more excellent than in that distinction of characters which he maintains through his whole poem. What Andromache here says can be spoken properly by none but Andromache." *Decorum* has often been considered the controlling critical idea of the NEO-CLASSIC AGE in England.

Definition: A brief EXPOSITION of a term designed to explain its meaning. Formal *definitions* consist of two elements: (1) the general class (*genus*) to which the object belongs, and (2) the specific

Deism

ways (*differentiae*) in which the object differs from other objects within the same general class. For instance, in the first sentence above "brief exposition" lists the general class to which *definition* belongs and "designed to explain its meaning" shows the way in which *definition* differs from other expositions which may be intended, for instance, to make clear the location of a site, the operation of a machine or any one of the various other functions which expositions in general may perform. The following examples should help to make this clear:

Term defined	General class to which it belongs	Specific ways in which it differs from other objects in the same general class
A canoe is a	boat	pointed at both ends and propelled by paddling.
A radio is an	instrument	for receiving or transmitting wireless messages.

Rarely are single-sentence *definitions* satisfactory in themselves. But the principle above stated guides in forming longer expositions in which both the second and third elements of the *definition* may be extended almost indefinitely.

Deism: The religion of those believing in a God who rules the world by established laws but not believing in the divinity of Christ or the inspiration of the Bible; "natural" religion, based on reason and a study of nature, as opposed to "revealed" religion. The scientific movement which grew out of the new knowledge of the world and the universe following upon the discoveries and theories of Columbus, Copernicus, Galileo, Francis Bacon, and later the members of the Royal Society, furthered the development of a rationalistic point of view which more and more tended to rely upon reason instead of upon revelation in the consideration of man's relation to God and the Universe. *Deism* was a product of this general point of view. It absorbed also something from the theological movements of ARIANISM (opposition to the doctrine of the Trinity) and ARMINIANISM (which stressed moral conduct as a sign of religion and opposed the doctrine of election; see CALVINISM). The somewhat prevalent notion that the deists believed in an "absentee" God, who, having created the world and set in motion machinery for its operation, took no further interest either in the world or in man is not applicable to all eighteenth-century deists, some of whom even believed in God's pardoning of the sins of a repentant individual.

Denotation

The following statements perhaps fairly represent the point of view of the English deists: 1. The Bible is not the inspired word of God; it is good so far as it reflects "natural" religion and bad so far as it contains "additions" made by superstitious or designing persons. 2. Certain Christian theological doctrines are the product of superstition or the invention of priests and must be rejected; e.g., the deity of Christ, the doctrine of the Trinity, and theory of the atonement for sins. 3. God is perfect, is the creator and governor of the Universe, and works not capriciously but through unchangeable laws (hence "miracles" are to be rejected as impossible). 4. Human beings are free agents, whose minds work as they themselves choose; even God cannot control man's thoughts. 5. Since man is a rational creature, like God, he is capable of understanding the laws of the universe; and as God is perfect, so can man become perfect through the process of education. Man may learn of God through a study of nature, which shows design and must therefore be an expression of God. 6. Practical religion for the individual consists in achieving virtue through the rational guidance of conduct (as exemplified in the scheme for developing the moral virtues recorded by Franklin in his *Autobiography*).

The effects of deistic thinking upon literature were very great and cannot be briefly traced. The *deism* of Pope's *Essay on Man* (partly inspired by Bolingbroke) illustrates the effect on the "classical" school, while the doctrine of man's perfection in Shelley's poetry and much of the Wordsworthian worship of nature are examples of deistic influences on the "romantic" school. The poet James Thomson was an acknowledged deist. Gibbon's *Decline and Fall of the Roman Empire* (1776–1788) excited much controversy because of its deistic treatment of Christianity. Tom Paine's *Age of Reason* is more deistic than atheistic. In America *deism* affected the work of many writers of the Revolutionary period, notably Franklin and Jefferson.

Denotation: The specific, exact meaning of a word, independent of its emotional coloration or associations. See CONNOTATION.

Dénouement: The final unraveling of the PLOT in DRAMA or FICTION; the solution of the mystery; the explanation or outcome. *Dénouement* implies an ingenious untying of the knot of an intrigue, involving not only a satisfactory outcome of the main situation but an explanation of all the secrets and misunderstandings connected

Detective Story

with the plot COMPLICATION. In DRAMA *dénouement* may be applied
to both TRAGEDY and COMEDY, though the common term for a tragic
dénouement is CATASTROPHE. The final scene of Shakespeare's
Cymbeline is a striking example of how clever and involved a
damatic *dénouement* may be: exposure of villain, clearing up of
mistaken identities and disguises, reuniting of father and children,
of husband and wife, etc., etc. By some writers *dénouement* is used
as a synonym for FALLING ACTION. See also CATASTROPHE, DRAMATIC
STRUCTURE, SHORT STORY.

Description: That one of the four chief types of composition (see
ARGUMENTATION, EXPOSITION, and NARRATION) which has as its
purpose the picturing of a scene or setting. Though often used apart
for its own sake (as in Poe's *Landor's Cottage*) it more frequently is
subordinated to one of the other types of writing; especially to
NARRATION, with which it most frequently goes hand in hand. Descriptive writing is most successful when its details are carefully
selected according to some purpose and to a definite point of view,
when its IMAGES are concrete and clear, and when it makes discreet
use of words of color, sound, and motion.

Detective Story: A NOVEL or SHORT STORY in which a crime, usually
a murder—the identity of the perpetrator unknown—is solved by a
detective through a logical assembling and interpretation of palpable
evidence, known as clues. This definition is the accepted one for the
true *detective story*, although in practice much variation occurs. If
the variations are too great, however—such as the absence of the
detective, or a knowledge from the beginning of the identity of the
criminal, or the absence of a process of reasoning logically from clues
—the story falls into the looser category of MYSTERY STORY. The
specific form *detective story* had its origin in "The Murders in the
Rue Morgue," by Edgar Allan Poe (1841). In this tale, "The Purloined Letter," "The Mystery of Marie Rogêt," and "Thou Art the
Man," Poe is said to have established every one of the basic conventions of the *detective story*. The form has been remarkably popular in
England and America, as a form of light entertainment for the intellectual. Generally, American *detective stories* have had greater
sensationalism and action than the English ones, which have usually
placed a premium on tightness of plotting and grace of STYLE. The
greatest of *detective story* writers was Sir Arthur Conan Doyle,
whose Sherlock Holmes stories seem to have established a character,

151

a room, a habit, a few gestures, and a group of phrases in the enduring heritage of English-speaking readers. "S. S. Van Dine" (Willard Huntington Wright) carried ingenuity of plotting to a very high level in America in the 1920's in his Philo Vance stories, a course in which he was ably followed by the authors of the Ellery Queen novels. The introduction of brutal REALISM coupled with a poetic but highly idiomatic STYLE in the *detective stories* of Dashiell Hammett in the 1930's has resulted in distinguished work by the Americans Raymond Chandler and Ross MacDonald. In England the continuing ingenuity of Agatha Christie and John Dickson Carr (also "Carter Dickson") and the skill and grace of Dorothy Sayers and the New Zealander Ngaio Marsh are contributions to the form. All of these practitioners have made it a point of honor to observe the fundamental rule of the *detective story* (and the rule which most clearly distinguishes it from the MYSTERY STORY): that the clues out of which a logical solution to the problem can be made be fairly presented to the reader at the same time that the detective receives them and that the detective deduce the answer to the riddle from a logical reading of these clues. See MYSTERY STORY.

Determinism: The belief that all acts of the will are the result of causes which determine them. When used as a term to describe a doctrine in a literary work, *determinism* has a wide range of philosophical possibilities. The possible determining forces are many. In CLASSICAL literature it may be fate. In writing produced by Christians of Calvinistic leanings it may be the predestined will of God (see CALVINISM). In naturalistic literature it may be the action of scientific law (see NATURALISM). In Marxist writing, it may be the inevitable operation of economic forces (see MARXISM). In all these cases the CHARACTERS illustrate *determinism* because their actions are controlled from without rather than being the products of free will.

Deus ex Machina: The employment of some unexpected and improbable incident in a STORY or PLAY in order to make things turn out right. In the ancient Greek theater when gods appeared in plays they were lowered to the STAGE from the "machine" or stage structure above. The abrupt but timely appearance of a god in this fashion, when used to extricate the mortal characters of the DRAMA from a situation so perplexing that the solution seemed beyond mortal powers, was referred to in Latin as the *deus ex machina*

("god from the machine"). The term is now employed to characterize any device whereby an author solves a difficult situation
by a forced invention. A villain may fail to kill a hero because he
has forgotten to load his revolver. A long-lost brother, given up
for dead, suddenly appears on the scene provided with a fortune
he has won in foreign parts, just in time to save the family from
disgrace or a sister from an unwelcome marriage. The employment
of the *deus ex machina* is commonly recognized as evidence of
deficient skill in PLOT-making or an uncritical willingness to disregard
the probabilities. Though it is sometimes employed by good authors,
it is found most frequently in MELODRAMA. See PLOT, COUP DE
THÉÂTRE.

Deuteragonist: The actor taking the part second in importance to
the PROTAGONIST in a Greek DRAMA. Historically Aeschylus added a
second actor to the traditional religious ceremonials, thus making
DRAMA possible; this second actor was called the *deuteragonist*. By
analogy, the term is sometimes applied to a CHARACTER who serves
as a FOIL to the leading CHARACTER.

Devil's Advocate: One who, at the examination of the claims of
a person to canonization as a saint, argues the claim of Satan to his
soul by marshalling all his sins and all other evidence against canonization. By extension the term *Devil's advocate* has come to be
applied to anyone who presents an unpopular or apparently erro-
neous side in order to bring out the whole truth, or who opposes a
case with which he does not really disagree in order to test or
strengthen its validity.

Dial, The: A periodical published in Boston from 1840 to 1844
as the mouthpiece of the New England transcendentalists. Margaret
Fuller was its first editor (1840–42) and Emerson its second
(1842–44). Among the most famous contributors to *The Dial*
were Alcott, Emerson, Margaret Fuller, Lowell, Thoreau, and Jones
Very.

In 1860 another organ of TRANSCENDENTALISM named *The Dial*
appeared briefly in Cincinnati, edited by Moncure Conway and
with contributions by Emerson, Alcott, and Howells. From 1880
to 1929, a distinguished literary monthly (and between 1892 and
1916, a fortnightly) was published under the name *The Dial*, first
in Chicago and after 1916 in New York. Until 1916 it was a con-

servative literary review. From 1916 to 1920, under the editorship of Conrad Aiken, Randolph Bourne, and Van Wyck Brooks, it was a radical journal of opinion and criticism, publishing writers like Dewey, Veblen, Laski, and Beard. After 1920 it became the most distinguished literary monthly in America, noted for its reproductions of modern graphic art and a powerful advocate of modern artistic movements. It published writers like Thomas Mann, T. S. Eliot, and James Stephens. Marianne Moore was editor from 1926 until it ceased publication in 1929.

Dialects: When the speech of two groups or of two persons representing two groups both speaking the same "language" exhibits very marked differences, the groups or persons are said to speak different *dialects* of the language. If the differences are very slight, they may be said to represent "subdialects" rather than *dialects.* If the differences are so great that the two groups or persons cannot understand each other, especially if they come from separate political units or countries, they are said to speak different languages. Yet the gradations are so narrow that no scientific method has been devised which will make it possible in all cases to distinguish between a language and a *dialect.* The chief cause of the development of *dialects* is isolation or separation due to lack of ease of communication. Natural barriers such as mountain ranges and social barriers caused by hostile relations tend to keep groups from frequent contact with each other with a resultant development of habitual differences in speech habits, leading toward the formation of *dialects* or even languages. Likewise among neighboring groups the *dialect* of one group commonly becomes dominant, as did West Saxon in early England.

When the Teutonic tribes which form the basis of the English "race" (Angles, Saxons, etc.) came to England from the Continent in the fifth century, they spoke separate *dialects* of West Germanic. In Old English times (fifth to eleventh centuries) there were four main *dialects:* (1) Northumbrian (north of the Humber River) and (2) Mercian (between the Thames and the Humber), both being branches or subdialects of the original Anglian *dialect;* (3) the Kentish (southeastern England), based upon the language of the Jutes, and (4) the Saxon (southern England). The early literature produced in the Northern districts (seventh to ninth centuries) is preserved chiefly in Southern (West Saxon) versions of the tenth and eleventh centuries. In Middle English times the old *dialects* appear under different names and with new subdialects. Northumbrian is called Northern; Saxon and Kentish are called Southern; the Northern English spoken in Scotland becomes Lowland Scottish; Mercian becomes Midland, and is broken into two main subdialects, West Midland and East Midland. The latter was destined to become the immediate parent of modern English. Middle English literature, therefore, exists in a variety of *dialects,* more or less clearly differentiated. Layamon's *Brut* and *The Owl and the Nightingale,* for example, are in the Southern *dialect; Cursor Mundi* and *Sir Tristrem* are in Northern; the *Ormulum* is early Midland, while *Havelok the Dane, Piers Plowman,* and the poetry of Chaucer are in later Midland. The Middle English *dialects* differed in vocabulary, sounds, and inflections, so that Northerners and Southerners had difficulty in understanding each other. A few examples of the differences may be given: In Northern, "they sing" would be "they singes"; in Midland, "they singen"; in Southern, "they singeth." Northern "kirk" is Southern "church." The present participle in Northern ended in *-ande;* in Southern, in *-inde* or *-inge;* in Midland, in *-ende* or *-inge.* Though the literary language in modern times has been standardized, it must not be supposed that *dialects* ro longer exist, especially in oral speech. Skeat lists nine modern *dialects* in Scotland; in England proper he finds three groups of Northern, ten groups of Midland, five groups of Eastern, two groups of Western, and ten groups of Southern.

Dialects, American: American *dialects* are less marked than English *dialects,* although some dialectal differences are easily discernible. However, only in areas where a local *patois,* such as Cajun in Louisiana or Gullah on the South Carolina coast, is spoken do Americans have serious difficulty in understanding one another. Three broad dialectal areas are generally recognized in the United States, although their speeches are sometimes given differing names. These areas are: New England and eastern New York, the speech of which is usually called "Eastern"; the area south of Pennsylvania and the Ohio River, extending westward beyond the Mississippi River into Texas, the speech of which is usually called "Southern"; and the broad area which extends from New Jersey on the Atlantic coast, through Pennsylvania and western New York into the middle west and the southwest and then over all the Pacific Coast, an area which comprises more than three-fourths of the American population; the speech of this area is usually called "General American" and some-

Dialogue

times "Western." Modern methods of transportation and mass communication are steadily leveling American speech and eradicating dialectal differences which once existed. At one time a great number of subdialects were recognized and exploited in LOCAL COLOR writings; most of these have today merged into the speech patterns of "General American." As a result of the work on the *Linguistic Atlas of the United States* (see AMERICAN LANGUAGE), much more accurate records of remaining regional and local differences of speech were made, although at the time when they were being lost. Dialectal differences in America are matters of vocabulary, of grammatic habit, and of pronunciation.

Dialogue: Conversation of two or more people as reproduced in writing. Most common in FICTION, particularly in DRAMAS, NOVELS, and SHORT STORIES, *dialogue* is sometimes used in general expository and philosophical writing. An analysis of *dialogue* as it has been employed by great writers shows that it embodies certain literary and stylistic values: (1) It advances the action in a definite way and is not used as mere ornamentation. (2) It is consistent with the character of the speakers, their social positions and special interests. It varies in TONE and expression according to the nationalities, DIALECTS, occupations, and social levels of the speakers. (3) It gives the *impression* of naturalness without being an actual, *verbatim* record of what may have been said, since FICTION, as someone has explained, is concerned with "the semblance of reality," not with reality itself. (4) It presents the interplay of ideas and personalities among the people conversing; it sets forth a conversational give and take—not simply a series of remarks of alternating speakers. (5) It varies in DICTION, RHYTHM, phrasing, sentence length, etc., according to the various speakers participating. The best writers of *dialogue* know that rarely do two or more people of exactly the same cultural and character background meet and converse, and the *dialogue* they write notes these differences. (6) It serves, at the hands of some writers, to give relief from, and lightness of effect to, passages which are essentially serious or expository in nature.

It should be noted, however, that in the Elizabethan DRAMA the CONVENTION of using BLANK VERSE and high RHETORIC for noble or elevated characters and prose for underlings and comic characters modifies these rules, as did the doctrine of DECORUM in the seventeenth and eighteenth centuries. Furthermore, plays of WIT, such as those by Oscar Wilde, and plays of idea, such as those by G. B.

Shaw, unhesitatingly take liberties with the idea of appropriateness to station and character in *dialogue*.

The *dialogue* is also a specialized literary composition in which two or more characters debate or reason about an idea or a proposition. There are many notable examples in the world's literature, the best known being the *Dialogues* of Plato. Others include Lucian's *Dialogues of the Dead*, Dryden's *Essay of Dramatick Poesie*, and Landor's *Imaginary Conversations*.

Diary: A day-by-day CHRONICLE of events, a JOURNAL. Usually a personal and more or less intimate record of events and thoughts kept by an individual. Not avowedly intended for publication—though it is difficult to insist on this point since many diarists have certainly kept a possible audience in mind—most *diaries,* when published, have appeared posthumously. The most famous *diary* in English is that of Samuel Pepys, which details events between January 1, 1660, and May 29, 1669. Other important English *diaries* are those of John Evelyn, Bulstrode Whitelock, George Fox, Jonathan Swift, John Wesley, and Fanny Burney. Noted American diarists include Samuel Sewall, Sarah K. Knight, and William Byrd. The *diary* has, in late years, become a conscious literary form used by travelers, statesmen, politicians, etc., as a convenient method of presenting the run of daily events in which they have had a hand. See AUTOBIOGRAPHY, BIOGRAPHY.

Diatribe: Writing or discourse characterized by bitter INVECTIVE, abusive argument. A harangue. Originally it was a treatment in DIALOGUE of a limited philosophical proposition in a simple, lively, conversational tone. Popular with the Stoic and Cynic philosophers, it became noted for the abusiveness of the speakers, a fact which led to its present-day meaning.

Dibrach: A term applied in Greek and Latin PROSODY to a FOOT consisting of two short or unstressed syllables. It is another name for the PYRRHIC.

Diction: The use of words in oral or written discourse. A simple list of words makes up a vocabulary; the accurate, careful *use* of these words in discourse makes good *diction*. The qualities of proper *diction* as illustrated by the work of standard authors are: (1) the apt selection of the word for the particular meaning to be conveyed,

(2) the use of legitimate words accepted as good usage (excluding all SOLECISMS, BARBARISMS, and improprieties), and (3) the use of words which are clear-cut and specific. The manner in which words are combined constitutes STYLE rather than *diction* since *diction* refers only to the selection of words employed in the discourse.

There are at least four levels of usage for words: the formal, the informal, the colloquial, and SLANG. Formal refers to the level of usage common in serious books and formal discourse; informal refers to the level of usage found in the relaxed but polite conversation of cultivated people; colloquial refers to the everyday usage of a group and it may include terms and constructions accepted in that group but not universally acceptable; and SLANG refers to a group of newly COINED WORDS which are not acceptable for formal usage as yet.

It should be noted that the accepted *diction* of one age is often unacceptable to another. See POETIC DICTION.

Dictionaries: At different times during their five hundred years of development, English *dictionaries* have emphasized different elements and have passed through an evolution as great as any of our literary forms or tools. In their modern form *dictionaries* arrange their words alphabetically, give explanations of the meanings, the derivations, the pronunciations, illustrative quotations and idioms, synonyms, and antonyms. Sometimes, however, the "dictionary" is restricted to word-lists of a special significance as *dictionaries* of law, of medicine, of art, etc.

English LEXICOGRAPHY began with attempts to define Latin words by giving English equivalents. The *Promptorium Parvulorum* (1440) of Galfridus Grammaticus, a Dominican monk of Norfolk, printed by Pynson in 1499 was an early example. Which publication deserves to be called the first English *dictionary* is difficult to say because the evolution was so gradual that the conception of what constituted a good word-book differed from year to year. Vizetelly gives credit to Richard Huloet's *Abecedarium* (1552) as the first *dictionary;* some believe the first person to succeed in defining all words in good usage in the English language was Nathaniel Bailey, whose major work was not published until 1721; *The Dictionary of Syr T. Eliot, Knyght* (1538) appears to have been the work first to establish the term *"dictionary."*

The early word-books started off listing simply the "hard words" which people might not be expected to know; the classification was sometimes alphabetical, sometimes by subject matter. Later, the

Dictionaries

lexicographers looked upon themselves as literary guardians of national speech and listed only such words as were dignified enough to be of "good usage"; the function of these compilers was to standardize, to "fix" the national language. Illustrative of this point of view were the collections of such scholarly academies as those of Italy and France; and, indeed, Dr. Samuel Johnson, a whole academy in himself, first held and later abandoned this same sort of ideal. Archbishop Trench, a British scholar, declared roundly in 1857 that a proper *dictionary* was really an "inventory of language" including colloquial uses as well as literary uses, and Trench's insistence on the philological attitude for the lexicographer probably did much to develop the modern word-book.

A list of some of the titles important in the evolution of the *dictionary* includes:

John Florio (1598), *A Worlde of Wordes.*
Robert Cawdrey (1604) (who used English words only), *A Table Alphabeticall Contyning and Teaching the True Writing and Understanding of Hard Usuall English Wordes.*
Randle Cotgrave (1611), *A Bundle of Words.*
John Bullokar (1616), *An English Expositor.*
Henry Cockeram (1623), *The English Dictionarie* (in which "idiote" was defined as "an unlearned asse").
Thomas Blount (1656), *Glossographia.*
Edward Phillips (1658), *A New World in Words.*
Nathaniel Bailey (1721), *Universal Etymological English Dictionary.*
Samuel Johnson (1755), *Dictionary of the English Language* (in which 50,000 words were explained. The most ambitious volume published up to that time. The personal element injected into definitions gives us such famous explanations as that for *oats:* "a grain which in England is generally given to horses, but in Scotland supports the people," and, further, that *Whig* was "the name of a faction" while *Tory* signified "one who adhered to the antient constitution of the state and the apostolical hierarchy of the Church of England, opposed to a Whig").
Thomas Sheridan (1780), *Complete Dictionary of the English Language* (which gave special emphasis to the pronunciation of the words).
Samuel Johnson (1798?) *A School Dictionary.* The first American *dictionary*. This Johnson was not related to the earlier Dr. Samuel. This first American *dictionary* simplified some of the English spellings and began the use of phonetic marks as aids to pronunciation.
Noah Webster (1828), *American Dictionary;* the most famous name in American lexicography.
Joseph Emerson Worcester (1846), *Universal and Critical Dictionary of the English Language.*

In 1884 was begun in England the great work *A New English*

Didactic Poetry

Dictionary on Historical Principles, edited by James A. H. Murray, Henry Bradley, and W. A. Craigie. It is more commonly called the *New English Dictionary* or the *Oxford English Dictionary,* and it is often referred to as the *OED* or *O.E.D.* It was completed in 1928. Though issued in "parts" the full work is now printed in ten large volumes or twenty "half-volumes." It is easily the greatest of all English *dictionaries* in the fullness of its illustrative examples and in its elaborate analysis of the meanings and etymologies. The citations are drawn from English writings ranging in date from the years 1200 to 1928. It is particularly valuable for its dated quotations of actual sentences showing the meanings of a word at various periods. It contains 240,165 "main words," of which 177,970 are in current use. With the addition of subordinate words, combinations, and a small number of foreign words, the total number of words entered for definition runs to 414,825. See LEXICOGRAPHY.

Didactic Poetry: POETRY which is intended primarily to teach a lesson. The distinction between *didactic poetry* and nondidactic poetry is difficult to make and always involves a subjective judgment of the author's purpose on the part of the critic or reader. For example, Bryant's "To a Waterfowl" is obviously concerned with an ethical or religious idea, yet it is not generally considered *didactic,* perhaps because most readers sense that the idea of a protective Providence is dramatically appropriate to the physical and emotional situation being presented—that the poet is communicating his feeling about the idea rather than communicating the idea itself. On the other hand, Pope's *Essay on Criticism* is an emphatic instance of *didactic poetry.* See DIDACTICISM.

Didacticism: Instructiveness in a literary work one of the purposes of which appears to be to give guidance, particularly in moral, ethical, or religious matters. Since all literary art exists in order to communicate something—an idea, a teaching, a precept, an emotion, an attitude, a fact, an autobiographical incident, a sensation—the ultimate question of *didacticism* in a literary work appears to be one of the intent of the author or his ostensible purpose. If, of Horace's dual functions of the artist, he elects instruction as his primary goal, he is didactic in intent or we may say that the purpose of the work he produces is didactic. Another way of stating the problem is to say that if the thing to be communicated takes precedence as an act of communication over the artistic qualities of the FORM through which

160

it is communicated the work is didactic. Viewed in still another way, a work is didactic if it would have as its ultimate effect a meaning or a result outside itself. In a sense those who divide CRITICISM into PLATONIC and ARISTOTELIAN are dividing the purposes of literary art into didactic and nondidactic. From this definition it is obvious that *didacticism* is an acceptable aspect of literature, at least up to a certain point, despite the fact that the term usually carries a derogatory meaning in CRITICISM. The objection to *didacticism* results from a feeling that, if carried too far or borne too self-righteously, it will subvert the object of literature to lesser and ignoble purposes. Among those who make didactic demands of literature today are the practitioners of MORAL CRITICISM, the Marxists, those who measure literature by sociological standards, and those who insist that literature be "relevant." The most bitter foes of *didacticism* today are probably the NEW CRITICS, who do not declare poetry to be meaningless but who declare its significant meaning to be intrinsic. See AUTOTELIC; BELIEF, THE PROBLEM OF; ARISTOTELIAN CRITICISM; PLATONIC CRITICISM; NEW CRITICISM; CRITICISM, TYPES OF; CRITICISM, HISTORICAL SKETCH; PARAPHRASE, HERESY OF.

Dieresis: A term sometimes used in METRICS to designate the situation where the pause in a VERSE falls at the end of a FOOT; usually called CAESURA. See CAESURA.

Digest: A systematic arrangement of condensed materials on some specific subject, so that it becomes a summation of the body of information on that subject. By extension, the term *digest* is often applied to a JOURNAL which publishes CONDENSATIONS or ABRIDGMENTS of material previously published elsewhere, such as *The Reader's Digest*.

Digression: The insertion of material unrelated or distantly related to the specific subject under discussion in a given work. In a work with a firm PLOT, a *digression* is a serious violation of UNITY. In the FAMILIAR ESSAY it is a standard device, and it was not infrequently used in the EPIC. The device was particularly popular in seventeenth- and eighteenth-century English writing, notable examples being the *digressions* in Swift's *Tale of a Tub* and Sterne's "Digression on Digressions" in *Tristram Shandy*. If a *digression* is lengthy and formal it is sometimes called an EXCURSUS.

Dilettante: One who follows an art for the love of it rather than as a serious profession. In literature, as with the other arts, the term has taken on a derogatory meaning, however, and is usually employed to indicate one who reads and talks books and writers from hearsay and a careless reading, perhaps of REVIEWS, as apposed to the student who makes a careful and critical study of a writer, period, movement, or book. Originally a *dilettante* meant an amateur; now it usually means a dabbler.

Dime Novel: A cheaply printed, paperbound TALE of adventure or detection, priced to sell for about ten cents; an American equivalent of the British PENNY DREADFUL. They were SHORT NOVELS, dealing with the American Revolution, the Civil War, the frontier, lurid crime and spectacular detection, and sometimes exemplary actions of moral instruction for the young. The first *dime novel* was *Malaeska: the Indian Wife of the White Hunter,* by Anne Stephens, published by the firm of Beadle and Adams, in 1860. It sold over 300,000 copies in one year. During the Civil War *dime novels* were popular with the troops, and after the war they continued to be popular until the 1890's, when boys' stories, such as the Frank Merriwell and the Rover Boys series, and the PULP MAGAZINES began to replace them. At the height of their popularity, they were written—or at least ostensibly written—by men like Ned Buntline, Colonel Prentiss Ingraham, and W. F. "Buffalo Bill" Cody about their own adventures in the wars and on the frontier. The two most popular series were the "Deadwood Dick" stories of the frontier by Edward L. Wheeler and the "Nick Carter" detective stories by various writers. The firm of Street and Smith published more than a thousand Nick Carter *dime novels.* Present-day equivalents of the *dime novel* are some of the cheaper and more sensational "paperback originals." One of the popular series of these paperbacks today is, significantly, the Nick Carter books. See PENNY DREADFUL.

Dimeter: A VERSE consisting of two FEET. See SCANSION.

Dionysian: A term used, along with APOLLONIAN, by Friedrich Nietzsche, to designate the element in Greek TRAGEDY associated with Dionysus, the god of wine. It refers to states of the ecstatic, orgiastic, or irrational. Nietzsche associates it with creative and imaginative power, as opposed to the critical and rational qualities represented by APOLLONIAN. See APOLLONIAN.

Dissociation of Sensibility

Dirge: A wailing SONG sung at a funeral or in commemoration of death. A short LYRIC of lamentation. See CORONACH, ELEGY, MONODY, PASTORAL ELEGY, THRENODY.

Discovery: In a TRAGEDY, the revelation of a fact previously unknown to the character, a knowledge of which now results in the turning of the action. See DRAMATIC STRUCTURE.

Disguisings: In medieval times (and in some places into the twentieth century) a species of game or spectacle with a procession of masked figures. *Disguisings* were usually of a popular or folk character. See MASQUE.

Dissertation: A formal, involved EXPOSITION written to clarify some scholarly problem. *Dissertation* is sometimes used interchangeably with THESIS but the usual practice, at least in college and university circles, is to reserve *dissertation* for the more elaborate ESSAYS and papers written "in partial fulfillment of the requirements for the doctor's degree" and to limit the use of THESIS to smaller problems, less perplexing, less involved, submitted for the bachelor's or master's degree. Of course these words as employed in academic circles are part of the CANT of college language since both THESIS and *dissertation* are commonly used off college campuses simply to signify careful, thoughtful discussions, in writing or speech, on almost any serious problem. In literature the term has been used lightly, as in Lamb's "A Dissertation on Roast Pig" and formally as in Bolingbroke's *Dissertation on Parties* or in Newton's *dissertations;* here the term implies learned formality.

Dissociation of Sensibility: A term given wide currency by T. S. Eliot to describe a disjunction of thought and feeling in the writers of the seventeenth, eighteenth, and nineteenth centuries. Earlier writers, and particularly John Donne, had had "direct sensuous apprehension of thought." To them a thought was an experience and thus affected their sensibility. For these writers mind and feeling functioned together and thus they possessed "a mechanism of sensibility which could devour any kind of experience." In the seventeenth century, says Eliot in "The Metaphysical Poets," a *dissociation of sensibility* set in, fostered by Milton and Dryden, who performed a part of the total poetic function so well that the rest of it appeared not to exist, and in their imitators did not exist. In the eighteenth and nineteenth centuries, as language grew in refinement and subtlety, feeling tended to become cruder. The result was poets who thought but who did not feel their thoughts and fuse thought and feeling in their poetry, or, in other words, poets who suffered from a *dissociation of sensibility*.

Dissonance: Harsh and inharmonious sounds, a marked breaking of the music of a VERSE of POETRY, which may be intentional, as it often is in Browning, but if unintentional is a major poetic flaw. The term is also sometimes applied to RHYMES that are almost true RHYMES but fail by a slight margin to be perfect because of variations in vowel sounds too slight to earn them the name of ASSONANCE; a form of HALF-RHYME or SLANT RHYME.

Distance: The degree of dispassionateness with which reader or audience can view the people, places, and events in a literary work. See AESTHETIC DISTANCE, OBJECTIVE CORRELATIVE, OBJECTIVITY, PSYCHIC DISTANCE.

Distich: A COUPLET. Any two consecutive lines in similar FORM and rhyming. An EPIGRAM or MAXIM completely expressed in couplet form, as in Pope's COUPLET:

> Hope springs eternal in the human breast;
> Man never is, but always to be, blest.

See -STICH.

Distributed Stress: A term used to describe a situation in METRICS where each of two syllables takes, or shares, the STRESS. Also called HOVERING STRESS or RESOLVED STRESS. The following lines from Walt Whitman's "Tears" shows *distributed stress* in "swift steps" and "night storm":

Ŏ stórm, ĕmbódied, rísĭng, cáreerĭng wĭth swíft stéps ălóng the beách!

Ŏ wíld ănd dísmăl níght stórm, wĭth wínd—Ŏ bélchĭng ănd désperăte!

See HOVERING STRESS.

Dithyramb: Literary expression characterized by wild, excited, passionate language. Its LYRIC power relates it most nearly to VERSE

Doggerel

though its unordered sequence and development, its seemingly improvised quality, give it often the form of prose. Dithyrambic VERSE was probably originally meant to be accompanied by music and was historically associated with Greek ceremonial worship of Dionysus. It formed the original for the choral element in Greek VERSE, later developing into the finer quality which we know in Greek TRAGEDY. Rather rare in English, dithyrambic verse is most closely related to the ODE; it finds its best expression in Dryden's *Alexander's Feast*.

Ditty: A SONG, a REFRAIN. The term is somewhat vaguely and loosely used for almost any short, popular, simple melody. It implies something familiar and is perhaps most often applied to SONGS of the sailor. The term is also used, in the sense of THEME, to refer to any short, apt saying or idea which runs through a composition.

Divine Afflatus, The: A phrase used to mean poetic inspiration, particularly the exalted state immediately preceding creative composition, when the poet is felt to be receiving his inspiration directly from a divine source. The doctrine of divine inspiration for poets was advocated by Plato. Although the phrase and doctrine have been used in a serious and sincere sense by such a poet as Shelley, the term is often used now in a contemptuous sense, to imply a pretentious overvaluation in a poet or a bombastic spirit in an orator, whose fervid style or manner is not justified by the actual substance of the poem or oration.

Doctrinaire: An adjective applied to one whose attitude is controlled by a preconceived theory or group of theories and who is inclined to disregard other points of view as well as practical considerations. His view is likely to be theoretical, narrow, and one-sided, as compared with practical and broad-minded. Criticism like Dr. Samuel Johnson's may be *doctrinaire* because controlled by a definite code of critical doctrines. Literature itself may be called *doctrinaire* when written, like some of Carlyle's books, to demonstrate such a doctrine as "hero-worship" or the "gospel of work"; or like a novel of William Godwin's, to preach a social doctrine. Politically, the word was applied to the constitutional royalists in France after 1815. See DIDACTICISM.

Doggerel: Jerky, rude composition in VERSE. Any poorly executed attempt at POETRY. Characteristics of *doggerel* verse are monotony of RHYME and RHYTHM, cheap sentiment, and trivial, trite subject matter. Some *doggerel* does, however, because of certain humorous and BURLESQUE qualities it attains, become amusing and earn a place on one of the lower shelves of literature. Doctor Johnson's parody on Percy's "Hermit of Warkworth" is an example:

> As with my hat upon my head
> I walk'd along the Strand,
> I there did meet another man
> With his hat in his hand.

Domestic Tragedy: TRAGEDY dealing with the domestic life of commonplace people. The English stage at various periods has produced tragedies based not upon the lives of historical personages of high rank (see TRAGEDY) but upon the lives of everyday contemporary folk. Running contrary to the prevailing critical conceptions of the proper sphere of TRAGEDY, *domestic tragedy* was long in winning critical recognition. In Elizabethan times were produced such powerful *domestic tragedies* as the anonymous *Arden of Feversham* (late sixteenth century), Thomas Heywood's *A Woman Killed With Kindness* (acted 1603), and the anonymous *Yorkshire Tragedy* (1608). This early Elizabethan *domestic tragedy* specialized in murder stories taken from contemporary bourgeois life. In the eighteenth century *domestic tragedy* reappeared, tinged this time with the SENTIMENTALISM of the age, as in George Lillo's *The London Merchant* (1731) and Edward Moore's *The Gamester* (1753), in which the tragic hero is a gambler who, falsely accused of murder, takes poison and dies just after hearing that a large amount of money has been left to him. The eighteenth-century *domestic tragedy* was crowded out by other forms, though the idea was taken over by foreign playwrights and later in the nineteenth century reintroduced from abroad, especially under the influence of Ibsen, since whose time the old conception of TRAGEDY as possible only with heroes of high rank has given way to plays which present fate at work among the lowly. John Masefield's *Tragedy of Nan* (1909) may be noted as an early twentieth-century example of the form. O'Neill's *Desire Under the Elms*, Arthur Miller's *The Death of a Salesman*, and Williams' *Cat on a Hot Tin Roof* are all examples of *domestic tragedy*.

Doric: The *Doric* DIALECT in ancient Greece was thought of as lacking in refinement, and *Doric* architecture was marked by simplicity and strength rather than by beauty of detail. So a rustic or "broad" DIALECT may be referred to as *Doric,* and such simple idyllic pieces of literature as Tennyson's *Dora* or Wordsworth's *Michael* may be said to exhibit *Doric* qualities. It is often applied to PASTORALS. Perhaps the best single synonym is "simple." See ATTIC, with which *Doric* was and is in conscious contrast.

Double Entendre: A statement that is deliberately ambiguous, one of whose possible meanings is risqué or suggestive of some impropriety. *Double entendre* is not good French—the proper French phrase for "double meaning" is *double entente*—but it has been used since Dryden as an English term applied to ambiguities where one of the meanings is indecent. It should not be italicized in normal usage.

Double Rhyme: FEMININE RHYME, that is, RHYME in which the similar stressed syllables are followed by identical unstressed syllables. "Stream" and "beam" are RHYMES; "streaming" and "beaming" are *double rhymes.*

Drama: Aristotle called *drama* "imitated human action." But since his meaning of IMITATION is in doubt, this phrase is not as simple or clear as it seems. Professor J. M. Manly saw three necessary elements in *drama:* (1) a STORY (2) told in action (3) by actors who impersonate the CHARACTERS of the STORY. This admits such forms as PANTOMIME. Yet many writers insist that DIALOGUE must be present.

Origins: Greek and Roman Drama.—Drama arose from religious ceremonial. Greek COMEDY developed from those phases of the DIONYSIAN rites which dealt with the theme of fertility; Greek TRAGEDY came from the DIONYSIAN rites dealing with life and death; and MEDIEVAL DRAMA arose out of rites commemorating the birth and the resurrection of Christ. These three origins seem independent of each other. The word COMEDY is based upon a word meaning "revel," and early Greek COMEDY preserved in the actors' costumes evidences of the ancient phallic ceremonies. Comedy developed away from this primitive display of sex interest in the direction of greater DECORUM and seriousness, though the "Old Comedy" was gross in character. SATIRE became an element of COMEDY as early as the sixth century B.C. Menander (342–291 B.C.) is a representative of the "New Comedy"—a more conventionalized form which was imitated by the great Roman writers of COMEDY, Plautus and Terence, through

Drama

whose plays classical COMEDY was transmitted to the Elizabethan dramatists.

The word TRAGEDY seems to mean a "goat-song," and may reflect DIONYSIAN death and resurrection ceremonies in which the goat was the sacrificial animal. The DITHYRAMBIC chant used in these festivals is perhaps the starting point of TRAGEDY. From this chant the ceremonial song developed. The song then became a primitive duologue between a leader and a CHORUS, developed narrative elements, and reached a stage in which it told some story. Two leaders appeared instead of one, and the chorus sank into the background. The great Greek authors of TRAGEDIES were Aeschylus (525–456 B.C.), Sophocles (496–406 B.C.), and Euripides (480–406 B.C.). Modeled on these were the Latin CLOSET-DRAMAS of Seneca (4? B.C.–A.D. 65) which exercised a profound influence upon Renaissance TRAGEDY (see SENECAN TRAGEDY).

Rebirth of Drama in Middle Ages.—The decline of Rome witnessed the disappearance of acted classical DRAMA. The MIME survived for an uncertain period and perhaps aided in preserving the tradition of acting through wandering entertainers (see JONGLEUR, MINSTREL). Likewise, dramatic ceremonies and customs, some of them perhaps related to the ancient DIONYSIAN rites themselves, played an uncertain part in keeping alive in medieval times a sort of substratum of dramatic consciousness. Scholars are virtually agreed, however, that the great institution of MEDIEVAL DRAMA in Western Europe, leading as it did to modern *drama,* was a new form which developed, about the ninth and following centuries, from the ritual of the Christian Church (see MEDIEVAL DRAMA). The dramatic forms resulting from this development, MYSTERY or CYCLIC PLAYS, MIRACLE PLAYS, MORALITIES, flourishing especially in the fourteenth and fifteenth centuries, lived on into the RENAISSANCE.

Renaissance English Drama.—The new interests of the RENAISSANCE included TRANSLATIONS and IMITATIONS of classical DRAMA, partly through the medium of SCHOOL PLAYS, partly through the work of university-trained professionals engaged in supplying *dramas* for the public stage or the court or such institutions as the INNS OF COURT, and partly through the influence of classical dramatic CRITICISM, much of which reached England through Italian scholars. Thus a revived knowledge of ancient *drama* united with the native dramatic traditions developed from medieval forms and technique to produce in the later years of the sixteenth century the many-

sided phenomenon known as ELIZABETHAN DRAMA, with its spectacular and patriotic CHRONICLE PLAYS, its TRAGEDIES OF BLOOD, its
light-hearted COURT COMEDIES, its dreamy ROMANTIC COMEDIES, its
PASTORAL PLAYS, satirical plays, and realistic presentations of
London life. These *dramas* were written by an illustrious group of
able dramatists, led by Shakespeare. All English *drama* shared the
DECADENT tendencies of JACOBEAN and CAROLINE times and in
1642 the PURITANS officially closed the theaters.

Restoration and Eighteenth-century Drama.—The efforts of Ben
Jonson in Elizabethan times to curb romantic tendencies and to
insist upon the observance of CLASSICAL rules of *drama* bore late
fruit when in RESTORATION times, under the added influence of
French *drama* and theory, English *drama* was officially revived
under court auspices. NEO-CLASSIC tendencies held sway. The
HEROIC PLAY and the new COMEDY OF MANNERS flourished, followed
in the eighteenth century first by the SENTIMENTAL COMEDY and
DOMESTIC TRAGEDIES and in the latter part of the century by a
chastened COMEDY OF MANNERS under Goldsmith and Sheridan.

Nineteenth-century Drama.—MELODRAMA and spectacle reigned
through the early nineteenth century, efforts to produce an actable
literary *drama* proving futile. The late nineteenth century witnessed
an important revival of serious *drama*, with, however, a tendency
away from the established TRADITIONS of poetic TRAGEDY and
COMEDY in favor of shorter plays stressing ideas or problems or
situations and depending much upon DIALOGUE.

American Drama.—In America theatrical performances occurred
very early in the eighteenth century in Boston, New York, and
Charleston, S. C., though no *drama* was written by an American till
about the middle of the century, at which time important groups of
professional actors also appeared. The early *drama* was imitative
and dependent upon English originals or models. The Revolutionary
War produced some political plays. The first native TRAGEDY was
Thomas Godfrey's *Prince of Parthia* (acted 1767), and the first
COMEDY professionally produced was Royall Tyler's *The Contrast*
(1787). The early nineteenth century witnessed a growing interest
in the theater, William Dunlap and John Howard Payne (author of
"Home, Sweet Home") being prolific playwrights. Increased use was
made of American themes. In the middle of the century George
Henry Boker produced notable ROMANTIC TRAGEDIES, and literary
drama received some attention. American dramatic art advanced
in the period following the Civil War with such writers as Bronson

Howard, though it was restricted greatly by the triumph of commercial theatrical management. The early twentieth century produced several dramatists of note (William Vaughn Moody, Percy MacKaye, Josephine Peabody) and witnessed the growth of the LITTLE THEATER MOVEMENT.

Twentieth-century Drama.—There has been a healthy rebirth of dramatic interest and experimentation in the twentieth century both in Great Britain and in the United States. In the Irish Theatre, under the leadership of people like Lady Gregory and Douglas Hyde, a vital *drama* has emerged, with original and powerful plays from men like W. B. Yeats, J. M. Synge, Padraic Colum, and Sean O'Casey (see CELTIC RENAISSANCE). Meanwhile, in England the influence of Ibsen (also important on the Irish playwrights) made itself strongly felt in the PROBLEM PLAYS and DOMESTIC TRAGEDIES of Henry Arthur Jones and Arthur Wing Pinero, in the witty and highly intellectual *drama* of G. B. Shaw, and in the REALISM of W. S. Houghton and John Galsworthy. Somerset Maugham, Noel Coward, and James Barrie have been active producers of COMEDY; John Masefield gave expression to the tragic vision in a long series of plays. T. S. Eliot and Christopher Fry revived and enriched verse *drama*. Also important is John Osborne, the leader of England's "Angry Young Men" (*Look Back in Anger*).

The twentieth century saw the development of a serious American *drama*. Early in the century REALISM, which had had its first American dramatic representation in J. A. Herne's *Margaret Fleming* in 1890, was followed, sometimes afar off, by Percy MacKaye and William Vaughn Moody. But it remained for the great craftsmanship, serious experimentation, and imagination of Eugene O'Neill to give a truly American expression to the tragic view of experience. Thornton Wilder, Philip Barry, Lillian Hellman, Sidney Howard, Robert Sherwood, Tennessee Williams, and Arthur Miller have given America a serious *drama* for the first time in its history. Barry, S. N. Behrman, George Kaufman, and John van Druten have practiced the comic craft with skill. Maxwell Anderson revived the verse play successfully, and Rodgers and Hammerstein gave the musical comedy unexpected depth and beauty in *Oklahoma!* and other "musicals."

Details of dramatic history are given throughout the *Outline of Literary History*. See also COMEDY, CONFLICT, CHARACTERIZATION, DRAMATIC STRUCTURE, PLOT, and TRAGEDY.

Dramatic Irony

Dramatic Conventions: Although the DRAMA is, as Aristotle asserted, an IMITATION of life, the stage and the printed page present physical difficulties for the making of such IMITATIONS. The various devices which have been employed as substitutions for reality in the DRAMA and which the audience must accept as real although it knows them to be false are called *dramatic conventions*. One approaching a DRAMA must, in the first place, accept the fact of impersonation or representation. The actors on the stage must be taken as the persons of the story (though this acceptance by no means precludes a degree of detachment sufficient to enable the spectator to appraise the art of the actor). The stage must be regarded as the actual SCENE or geographical SETTING of the action. The intervals between ACTS or SCENES must be expanded imaginatively to correspond with the needs of the story. Moreover, one must accept special CONVENTIONS, not inherent in DRAMA as such but no less integral because of their traditional use, such as the SOLILOQUY, the ASIDES, the fact that ordinary people are made spontaneously to speak in highly poetic language and that actors always speak louder than would be natural, actually pitching their voices to reach the most distant auditor rather than the persons in the group on the stage. Similarly one must be prepared at times to accept costuming that is conventional or symbolic rather than realistic.

In the ELIZABETHAN THEATER, the spectator had imaginatively to picture the platform as in turn a number of different places; in the modern theater, he must accept the idea of the invisible FOURTH WALL through which he views interior actions. All means of getting inside the minds of characters—and they are many—are CONVENTIONS (even if only within the single play; see O'Neill's *Strange Interlude*) that are successful exactly to the extent that the audience is willing to believe them. Even the CURTAIN which opens and closes the DRAMA is in its way as pure a CONVENTION as the CHORUS of a Greek TRAGEDY. See CONVENTION.

Dramatic Irony: The words or acts of a character in a play may carry a meaning unperceived by himself but understood by the audience. Usually the character's own interests are involved in a way he cannot understand. The IRONY resides in the contrast between the meaning intended by the speaker and the added significance seen by others. The term is occasionally applied also to non-dramatic NARRATIVE, and is sometimes extended to include any situation (such as mistaken identity) in which some of the actors on the stage or some of the characters in a story are "blind" to facts known to the spectator or reader. So understood, *dramatic irony* is responsible for much of the interest in FICTION and DRAMA, because the reader or spectator enjoys being in on the secret. For an example see TRAGIC IRONY.

Dramatic Monologue: A LYRIC poem which reveals "a soul in action" through the conversation of one character in a dramatic situation. The character is speaking to an identifiable but silent listener at a dramatic moment in the speaker's life. The circumstances surrounding the conversation, one side of which we "hear" as the *dramatic monologue,* are made clear by implication in the poem, and a deep insight into the character of the speaker is given. Although a quite old form, the *dramatic monologue* was brought to a very high level by Robert Browning, who is often credited with its creation. Tennyson used the form on occasion, and contemporary poets have found it congenial, as witness the work of Robert Frost, E. A. Robinson, Carl Sandburg, Allen Tate, and T. S. Eliot, whose "Love Song of J. Alfred Prufrock" is a distinguished twentieth-century example of a *dramatic monologue.* See SOLILOQUY.

Dramatic Poetry: A term that, logically, should be restricted to POETRY which employs dramatic FORM or some element or elements of dramatic technique as a means of achieving poetic ends. The DRAMATIC MONOLOGUE is an example. The dramatic quality may result from the use of DIALOGUE, MONOLOGUE, vigorous DICTION, BLANK VERSE, or the stressing of tense situation and emotional CONFLICT. Because of the presence of dramatic elements in the poems to be included in the volume, Browning used the phrase "Dramatic Lyrics" as the subtitle of *Bells and Pomegranates,* No. III (1842). However, the phrase *dramatic poetry* is used to include compositions which, like Shakespeare's *The Tempest,* may be more properly classed as POETIC DRAMA, or which, like Browning's *Pippa Passes,* are more commonly called CLOSET DRAMAS (see CLOSET DRAMA).

Dramatic Propriety: The principle that a statement or an action within any dramatic situation is to be judged not in terms of its correspondence to standards external to the dramatic situation but in terms of its appropriateness to the specific context within which it occurs. Cleanth Brooks argues, for example, that the statement

"Beauty is truth, truth beauty" in Keats' "Ode on a Grecian Urn" is a dramatic statement appropriate to the urn which utters it and has, therefore, "precisely the same status" as "Ripeness is all" in *King Lear.* We properly ask not whether it is an abstract truth but whether it is in character for the speaker and proper to the dramatic context. Many of the NEW CRITICS argue that every POEM implies a speaker and is, therefore, a little DRAMA. For them the principle of *dramatic propriety* becomes of cardinal importance.

Dramatic Structure: The ancients compared the PLOT of a DRAMA to the tying and untying of a knot. The principle of dramatic CON-FLICT, though not mentioned as such in Aristotle's definition of DRAMA, is implied in this figure. The technical STRUCTURE of a serious play is determined by the necessities of developing this dramatic CONFLICT. Thus a well-built TRAGEDY will commonly show the following divisions, each of which represents a phase of the dramatic CONFLICT: introduction, RISING ACTION, CLIMAX or CRISIS (turning point), FALLING ACTION, and CATASTROPHE. The relation of these parts is sometimes represented graphically by the figure of a pyramid, called FREYTAG'S PYRAMID, the rising slope suggesting the RISING ACTION or tying of the knot, the falling slope the FALLING ACTION or resolution, the apex representing the CLIMAX.

The *introduction* (or EXPOSITION) creates the tone, gives the setting, introduces some of the characters, and supplies other facts necessary to the understanding of the play, such as events in the story supposed to have taken place before the part of the action included in the play, since a play, like an EPIC, is likely to plunge *in medias res,* "into the middle of things." In *Hamlet,* the bleak midnight scene on the castle platform, with the appearance of the ghost, sets the keynote of the TRAGEDY, while the conversation of the watchers, especially the words of Horatio, supply antecedent facts, such as the quarrel between the dead King Hamlet and the King of Norway. The ancients called this part the PROTASIS.

The RISING ACTION, or COMPLICATION, is set in motion by the EX-CITING FORCE (in *Hamlet* the ghost's revelation to Hamlet of the murder) and continues through successive stages of CONFLICT between the HERO and the COUNTERPLAYERS up to the CLIMAX or turning point (in *Hamlet* the hesitating failure of the hero to kill Claudius at prayer). The ancients called this part the EPITASIS.

The downward or FALLING ACTION stresses the activity of the forces opposing the HERO and while some suspense must be maintained, the trend of the action must lead logically to the disaster with which the TRAGEDY is to close. The FALLING ACTION, called by the ancients the CATASTASIS, is often set in movement by a single event called the TRAGIC FORCE, closely related to the CLIMAX and bearing the same relation to the FALLING ACTION as the EXCITING FORCE does to the RISING ACTION. In *Macbeth* the TRAGIC FORCE is the escape of Fleance following the murder of Banquo. In *Hamlet* it is the "blind" stabbing of Polonius, which sends Hamlet away from the court just as he appears about to succeed in his plans. The latter part of the FALLING ACTION is sometimes marked by an event which delays the CATASTROPHE and seems to offer a way of escape for the hero (the apparent reconciliation of Hamlet and Laertes). This is called the "moment of final suspense" and aids in maintaining interest. The FALLING ACTION is usually shorter than the RISING ACTION and often is attended by some lowering of interest (as in the case of the long conversation between Malcolm and MacDuff in *Macbeth*), since new forces must be introduced and an apparently inevitable end made to seem uncertain. RELIEF SCENES are often resorted to in the FALLING ACTION, partly to mark the passage of time, partly to provide emotional relaxation for the audience. The famous scene of the grave diggers in *Hamlet* is an example of how a RELIEF SCENE may be justified through its inherent dramatic qualities and through its relations to the serious action (see COMIC RELIEF).

The CATASTROPHE, marking the tragic failure, usually the death, of the HERO (and often of his opponents as well) comes as a natural outgrowth of the action. It satisfies not by a gratification of the emotional sympathies of the spectator but by its logical conformity and by a final presentation of the nobility of the succumbing HERO. A "glimpse of restored order" often follows the CATASTROPHE proper in a Shakespearean TRAGEDY, as when Hamlet gives his dying vote to Fortinbras as the new king.

This five-part *dramatic structure* was believed by Freytag to be reflected in a five-act structure for TRAGEDY. However, the imposing of a rigorous five-act structure upon Elizabethan TRAGEDY is questionable, since relatively few plays fall readily into the pattern of an ACT of EXPOSITION, an ACT of RISING ACTION, an ACT of CLIMAX, an ACT of FALLING ACTION, and an ACT of CATASTROPHE. It should be noted too that this structure based upon the analogy of the tying and untying of a knot is applicable to COMEDY, the NOVEL, and the SHORT STORY, with the adjustment of the use of the broader term DÉNOUEMENT for CATASTROPHE in works that are not tragic, despite the fact that technically CATASTROPHE and DÉNOUEMENT are synonymous. (See ACT, CATASTROPHE, and DÉNOUEMENT.)

During the nineteenth century conventional structure gave way to a newer technique. First, COMEDY, under the influence of French bourgeois COMEDY, the "well-made play" of Eugène Scribe and others, developed a set of technical CONVENTIONS all its own; and as a result of the movement led by Ibsen, serious DRAMA cast off the restrictions of five-act TRAGEDY and freed itself from conventional formality. By the end of the century the traditional five-act structure was to be found only in poetic or consciously archaic TRAGEDY, whose connection with the stage was artificial and generally unsuccessful. However the fundamental elements of structure given here remained demonstrably present, though in modified form, in these newer types of plays. If at first glance it seems that Ibsen opens one of his DOMESTIC TRAGEDIES at or just before the TRAGIC FORCE, the EXPOSITION, the EXCITING FORCE, and the RISING ACTION which brought about the situation with which he opens are still present and are communicated to the audience by implication and FLASH-BACK. The fundamental *dramatic structure* seems timeless and impervious to basic change. See TRAGEDY, CONFLICT, ACT, CATAS-TROPHE, CLIMAX, CRISIS, PLOT.

Dramatis Personae: The CHARACTERS in a DRAMA, a NOVEL, or a POEM. The term is also applied to a listing of the CHARACTERS in the program of a play, at the beginning of the printed version of a play, or sometimes at the beginning of a NOVEL. Such a list often contains brief characterizations of the persons of the work and notations about their relationships. By extension, the term *dramatis personae* is sometimes applied to the participants in any event.

Drame: A form of play between TRAGEDY and COMEDY developed by the French in the eighteenth century and later introduced into England, where it is often called a "drama." It is a serious play, of which the modern PROBLEM PLAY is an example.

Drawing Room Comedy: A form of the COMEDY OF MANNERS that deals with people of substance and position in high society, hence a DRAMA concerned with life in polite society. It is called a *drawing room comedy* because it is usually a WELL-MADE PLAY with its action centered in a drawing room. See COMEDY OF MANNERS.

Dream Allegory (or **Vision**): The dream was a conventional narrative frame that was widely used in the Middle Ages and is still employed on occasion. The NARRATOR falls asleep and while sleeping dreams a dream which is the actual STORY told in the dream frame. In the Middle Ages the device was used for ALLEGORY. Among the major *dream allegories* are *The Romance of the Rose*, Dante's *Divine Comedy*, Chaucer's *The Book of the Duchess* and *The House of Fame*, *The Pearl*, and *The Vision of Piers Plowman*. The *dream allegory* forms the narrative frame for Bunyan's *Pilgrim's Progress* and Edward Bellamy's *Looking Backward*. See ALLEGORY, FRAME-STORY.

Droll: A short dramatic piece (also known as "drollery" or "droll humor") cultivated on the COMMONWEALTH stage in England as a substitute for full-length or serious plays not permitted by the government. A *droll* was likely to be a "short, racy, comic" SCENE selected from some popular play (as a Launcelot Gobbo scene from *The Merchant of Venice*) and completed by dancing somewhat in the manner of the earlier JIG.

Dumb Show: A pantomimic performance used as a part of a play. The term is applied particularly to such specimens of silent acting as appeared in Elizabethan DRAMA. The *dumb show* provided a spectacular element and was often accompanied by music. Sometimes it employed allegorical figures like those in the MORALITY PLAY and the MASQUE. Sometimes it foreshadowed coming events in the action and sometimes it provided comment like that of the CHORUS. Sometimes it appeared as PROLOGUE or between ACTS and sometimes it was an integral part of the action, being performed by the CHARACTERS of the play proper. Whatever its origin, it seems to have appeared first in the third quarter of the sixteenth century in the Senecan plays (see SENECAN TRAGEDY). It continued in use well into the seventeenth century. More than fifty extant Elizabethan plays contain *dumb shows*. The one appearing in Shakespeare's *Hamlet* (Act III, Scene ii) is unusual in that it is preliminary to a show which is itself a "play within a play." Other well-known Elizabethan plays containing *dumb shows* are Sackville and Norton's *Gorboduc* (1562), Robert Greene's *James the Fourth* (1591), John Marston's *Malcontent* (1604), John Webster's *Duchess of Malfi* (1614), and Thomas Middleton's *The Changeling* (1623). See DISGUISINGS, MASQUE, PAGEANT, PANTOMIME.

Duodecimo: A BOOK SIZE, designating a book whose SIGNATURES result from sheets folded to twelve leaves or twenty-four pages. Its abbreviation is 12mo. See BOOK SIZES.

Duple Meter: In METRICS a line consisting of two syllables.

Dynamic Character: A CHARACTER in a FICTION or DRAMA who develops or changes as a result of the actions of the PLOT. See CHARACTERIZATION.

E

Early Tudor Age, 1500–1557: During the early years of the sixteenth century, the ideals of the RENAISSANCE were rapidly replacing those of the Middle Ages. The Reformation of the English church and the revival of learning known as HUMANISM were making major modifications in English life and thought. In literature it was a time of experimentation and of extensive formal borrowings from French and Italian writings. Wyatt and Surrey imported and "Englished" the SONNET, and Surrey first used BLANK VERSE, while Barclay and Skelton continued the older satiric tradition. Sir Thomas Elyot and Sir Thomas More were the major prose writers, and the translators and the chroniclers were adding substantially both to English knowledge and to English prose STYLE. The late MEDIEVAL DRAMA was still dominant, with the MYSTERY PLAYS, MORALITIES, and INTERLUDES in great vogue, although SCHOOL PLAYS were beginning to introduce new elements into the DRAMA, notably in *Ralph Roister Doister,* the first "regular" English COMEDY. Perhaps the most important single book, from a literary point of view, was *Tottel's Miscellany* (1557), a collection of the "new poetry" which paved the way for Elizabethan poets. See RENAISSANCE and *Outline of Literary History.*

Early Victorian Age, 1832–1870: The period between the death of Sir Walter Scott and 1870 was a time of the gradual lessening of the Romantic impulse and the steady growth of REALISM in English letters. It bears to ROMANTICISM much the same relation that the AGE OF JOHNSON bears to the NEO-CLASSIC PERIOD—it is an age in which the seeds of the new movement were being sown but which was still predominantly of the old. In poetry, the voices of the major

Romantics had been stilled by death, except for that of Wordsworth, and a new poetry more keenly aware of social issues and more marked by doubts and uncertainties resulting from the pains of the INDUSTRIAL REVOLUTION and the advances in scientific thought appeared. The chief writers of this poetry were Tennyson, Browning, Arnold, and the young Swinburne. In the NOVEL Dickens, Thackeray, the Brontë sisters, and Trollope flourished. In the essay Carlyle, Newman, Ruskin, Arnold, and De Quincey did outstanding work. See ROMANTIC PERIOD IN ENGLISH LITERATURE, VICTORIAN, and *Outline of Literary History*.

Echo Verse: A line or more often a POEM in which the closing syllables of one line are repeated, as by an echo, in the following line—and usually making up that line—with a different meaning and thus forming a reply or a comment. Barnaby Barnes' lines,

> Echo! What shall I do to my Nymph when I go to behold her?
> Hold her!

form an example. The device is as old as the *Greek Anthology*. It flourished in the sixteenth and seventeenth centuries, most often as a device in PASTORAL POETRY and DRAMA.

Eclogue: Literally, *eclogue* in Greek meant "selection" and was applied to various kinds of poems. From its application to Virgil's PASTORAL poems, however, *eclogue* came to have its present restricted meaning of a formal PASTORAL poem following the traditional technique derived from the IDYLLS of Theocritus (third century B.C.). Conventional *eclogue* types include: (1) the singing match: two shepherds have a singing contest on a wager or for a prize, a third shepherd acting as judge; (2) the rustic DIALOGUE: two "rude swains" engage in banter, perhaps over a mistress, perhaps over their flocks; (3) the DIRGE or lament for a dead shepherd (see PASTORAL ELEGY); (4) the love-lay: a shepherd may sing a song of courtship or a shepherd or shepherdess may complain of disappointment in love; (5) the EULOGY. In RENAISSANCE times, following Mantuan's Latin *eclogues* (fifteenth century) the *eclogue* was used for veiled SATIRE, particularly SATIRE against the corruptions of the clergy, against political factions, and against those responsible for the neglect of POETRY. The earliest and most famous collection of conventional *eclogues* in English literature is Spenser's *The Shepheardes Calender* (1579), made up of one *eclogue* for each

178

month. By the eighteenth century a distinction was made between *eclogue* and PASTORAL, the term *eclogue* being used to describe the FORM and PASTORAL the content. Hence *eclogue* came to mean a DRAMATIC POEM, with little action or characterization, in which sentiments are expressed in DIALOGUE or SOLILOQUY, and *eclogues* laid in towns became possible. See PASTORAL.

Edinburgh Review: A quarterly JOURNAL of CRITICISM founded in 1802 by Francis Jeffrey, Sydney Smith, and Henry Brougham. The founders determined on a vigorous, outspoken policy which not only made a successful publication (10,000 circulation after ten years), but also stirred up the whole English-reading world. Among the contributors to the *Review* were some of the most brilliant writers of the time, the list including in addition to the editors such men as Walter Scott, Henry Hallam, and Francis Horner. The motto of the publication—*Judex damnatur, cum nocens absolvitur,* "the judge is condemned when the guilty man is acquitted"—indicates clearly the rigorous policy of the founders, who were predominantly Whig in attitude. After seven years of being browbeaten, the Tories started a rival journal, the QUARTERLY REVIEW (1809). The two publications rode literary and political prejudices hard and enlivened British CRITICISM.

One of the abhorrences of the *Edinburgh Review* was the "lakers" (LAKE SCHOOL of writers), more particularly Southey and Wordsworth. An article by Henry Brougham called *Hours of Idleness* (reviewing an early volume by Byron) provoked Byron's famous satire, *English Bards and Scotch Reviewers.* Later contributors included Macaulay, Carlyle, Hazlitt, and Arnold. *The Edinburgh Review* ceased publication in 1929.

Edition: The entire number of bound copies of a book printed at any time or times from a single type setting or from plates or other modes of reproduction made from a single type setting. The copies made from one continuous operation at one time are called a PRINTING or an IMPRESSION. Thus there may be several PRINTINGS or IMPRESSIONS in an *edition.* As applied to old books, however, *edition* and IMPRESSION are practically synonymous, because of the practice of distributing type after a printing. The term ISSUE is applied to a distinct set of copies of an *edition* which are distinguishable from other copies of that *edition* by variations in printed matter. The term *edition* is also applied to a set of copies differing in some way other than in printed matter from others of the same text, as "the illustrated *edition*," "the ten-volume *edition*," or a special form of an author's work, as "the Centennial *Edition* of Emerson," or an especially edited work, as "Merritt Hughes' *edition* of *Paradise Lost*." In describing books the terms *edition*, PRINTING, IMPRESSION, and ISSUE need to be used with care and precision.

Editorial: A short ESSAY, expository or argumentative in character, used in newspapers or MAGAZINES. The purpose of the *editorial* is usually to discuss current news events, and the subjects treated may range from matters of purely local importance through county, state, national, and international affairs. The usual *editorial* form falls naturally into three divisions: a statement of the event or situation to be discussed, a clarification of this situation through elaboration of the points concerned, and an expression of the opinion of the editorial office as to the significance, justice, or purpose inherent in the situation. Some publications print as *editorials* pleasant little ESSAYS on insignificant or minor situations, frankly publishing such bits for the charm of their STYLE or the grace of their HUMOR.

Edwardian Age: The period in English literature between the death of Victoria in 1901 and the beginning of the first World War in 1914, so-called after King Edward VII, who ruled from 1901–1910. It was a period marked by a strong reaction in thought, conduct, and art to the stiff propriety and conservatism of the Victorian age. The regular mental posture of the Edwardians was critical and questioning. There was a growing distrust of authority in religion, morality, and art, a basic doubt of the conventional "virtues," and a deep-felt need to examine critically all existing institutions. These attitudes expressed themselves in literature that was brilliant and elegant, although not always deep or enduring.

The CELTIC RENAISSANCE in Ireland awakened the dramatic talents of Lady Gregory, Douglas Hyde, Lennox Robinson, J. M. Synge, and W. B. Yeats; the intellectual DRAMA of G. B. Shaw continued the Ibsen influence; James Barrie and Lord Dunsany kept romance and whimsy alive on the stage. In England John Galsworthy was producing social plays, such as *The Silver Box*, *Strife*, and *Justice*.

In poetry it was an age of endings and beginnings. Victorianism lingered on in the verses of the LAUREATE, Alfred Austin (succeeded in 1913 by Robert Bridges), and in the work of men like Noyes and

Effect

Kipling. George William Russell ("A.E.") and W. B. Yeats were beginning poetic careers; Masefield's first volumes appeared; and Hardy's *The Dynasts* made its ambitious appearance.

But it was predominantly an age of prose. REALISM and NATURAL-ISM advanced steadily. In the NOVELS of Arnold Bennett were detailed pictures of the grim commonplace; in those of Galsworthy the beginnings of the SAGA of the middle classes. H. G. Wells launched his novelistic criticisms of society; and Kipling recorded the march of empire. But the greatest writers of prose in the British Isles in the *Edwardian Age* were James Joyce, whose *Dubliners* appeared in 1914, and Joseph Conrad, who during the *Edwardian Age* published distinguished work, including *Youth* and *Nostromo*.

Other works of distinction or promise included Butler's *The Way of All Flesh*, Hudson's *Green Mansions*, Stephens' *Crock of Gold*, and Barrie's *The Admirable Crichton*.

The degree to which English writing was moving away from its older orientations is demonstrated by the fact that in the *Edwardian Age* the best dramatist was an Irishman, Shaw; the best poet an Irishman, Yeats; the best novelist an expatriated Pole, Conrad; and the figure with greatest promise for the future an Irishman, Joyce.

Effect: Totality of impression or emotional impact upon the reader. "The tale of *effect*" was a term used to describe GOTHIC and horror stories of the type published in *Blackwood's Magazine* in the first half of the nineteenth century. Poe considered the primary objective of the SHORT STORY to be the achieving of a unified *effect*. The *effect* striven for may be one of horror, mystery, beauty, or whatever the writer's mood dictates, but once the *effect* is hit upon, everything in the story—PLOT, CHARACTERIZATION, SETTING—must work toward this controlling purpose. One of the paragraphs in Poe's criticism of Hawthorne's *Twice-Told Tales* stands out as the best explanation of this principle of *effect*:

> A skillful literary artist has constructed a tale. If wise, he has not fashioned his thoughts to accommodate his incidents; but having conceived, with deliberate care, a certain unique or single *effect* to be wrought out, he then invents such incidents—he then combines such events as may best aid him in establishing his preconceived effect. If his very initial sentence tend not to the outbringing of this effect, then he has failed in his first step. In the whole composition there should be no word written, of which the tendency, direct or indirect, is not to the one preëstablished design. And by such means, with such care

and skill, a picture is at length painted which leaves in the mind of him who contemplates it with a kindred art, a sense of the fullest satisfaction. . . .

Eiron: A basic comic CHARACTER in Greek DRAMA. The *eiron* is a swindler, a trickster, a hypocrite, or a picaresque rogue. He pretends to ignorance in order to hide his knowledge and to trick others into ludicrous actions. He is the opposite of the ALAZON, who pretends to more knowledge than he has. The term is sometimes applied to figures in TRAGEDY who deceive through feigned ignorance; Hamlet is an example. See ALAZON.

Elaboration: A rhetorical method for developing a THEME or picture in such a way as to give the reader a completed impression. This may be done in various ways, such as: repetition of the statement or idea, a change of words and phrases, or supplying additional details. Over*elaboration*, however, immediately becomes a fault since it results in diffuseness, wordiness, and stupidity. *Elaboration* is also used as a critical term characterizing a literary, rhetorical STYLE which is ornate. See AMPLIFICATION.

Electra Complex: In psychoanalysis, an obsessive attachment of a daughter to her father and, thus, the female counterpart of the OEDIPUS COMPLEX. The term is often used in CRITICISM of a psychological bent to describe PLOT situations. It gets its name from Electra, in Greek mythology and DRAMA, a daughter of Agamemnon and Clytemnestra, who with her brother Orestes avenged the death of their father Agamemnon by killing their mother and her lover, Aegisthus. See OEDIPUS COMPLEX.

Elegiac: In classical PROSODY, a METER used in the DISTICH employed for lamenting or commemorating the dead; it consists of a VERSE of DACTYLIC HEXAMETER followed by one of PENTAMETER. The ancient poets used *elegiacs* not only for THRENODIES but also for SONGS of war and love. The *elegiac* meter has been popular in Germany but rarely used in England and America. Coleridge's DISTICH will serve as an example:

> In the hexameter rises the fountain's silvery column,
> In the pentameter aye falling in melody back.

In English CRITICISM, the term *elegiac* is used as an adjective to describe POETRY expressing sorrow or lamentation (as in *elegiac* strains) or belonging to or partaking of an ELEGY.

Elegiac Stanza: The IAMBIC PENTAMETER QUATRAIN, rhyming *abab*. The *elegiac stanza* takes its name from Thomas Gray's *Elegy Written in a Country Churchyard,* which is composed in such *stanzas.* Although the IAMBIC PENTAMETER QUATRAIN, rhyming *abab,* was a STANZA of long standing before Gray used it, in the last half of the eighteenth and the nineteenth centuries, it was almost always used for the writing of VERSE expressing sorrow or lamentation.

Elegy: A sustained and formal POEM setting forth the poet's meditations upon death or another solemn THEME. The meditation often is occasioned by the death of a particular person, but it may be a generalized observation or the expression of a solemn MOOD. A classical FORM, common to both Latin and Greek literatures, the *elegy* originally signified almost any type of serious, subjective meditation on the part of the poet whether this reflective element was concerned with death, love, or war, or merely the presentation of information. In classic writing the *elegy* was more distinguishable by its use of ELEGIAC METER than by its subject matter. The Elizabethans used the term for love poems, particularly COMPLAINTS. Notable English *elegies* include the OLD ENGLISH poem "The Wanderer," *The Pearl,* Chaucer's *The Book of the Duchess,* Donne's *Elegies,* Gray's *Elegy Written in a Country Churchyard,* Tennyson's *In Memoriam,* and Whitman's *When Lilacs Last in the Dooryard Bloom'd.* These poems indicate the variety of method, MOOD, and subject which is included under the term *elegy.* A specialized form of *elegy,* popular with English poets, is the PASTORAL ELEGY, of which Milton's *Lycidas* is an outstanding example. See PASTORAL ELEGY.

Elements: In ancient and medieval cosmologies, the fundamental constituents or *elements* of the universe were earth, air, fire, and water. Each was considered to have certain basic characteristics: earth was cold and dry; air was hot and moist; fire was hot and dry; and water was cold and moist. The HUMOURS of the body were closely allied to the four *elements.* The term *elements* is also applied to the bread and wine in the Eucharist. See HUMOURS.

Elision: The omission of a part of a word for ease of pronunciation, for EUPHONY, or to secure a desired rhythmic effect. *Elision* is most often accomplished by the omission of a final vowel preceding an initial vowel as "th'orient" for "the orient," but it also occurs between syllables of a single word as "ne'er" for "never."

Elizabethan Age: The name given in English literature to the segment of the RENAISSANCE which occurred during the reign of Elizabeth I (1558–1603). The meaning of the term is sometimes extended to include the JACOBEAN PERIOD (1603–1625). An age of great nationalistic expansion, commercial growth, and religious controversy, it saw the development of English DRAMA to its highest level, a great outburst of LYRIC song, and a new interest in CRITICISM. Sidney, Spenser, Marlowe, and Shakespeare flourished; and Bacon, Jonson, and Donne first stepped forward. It has justly been called the "Golden Age of English Literature." For details of its literary history, see "The Elizabethan Age" in *The Outline of Literary History;* for a sketch of its literature see RENAISSANCE.

Elizabethan Drama: This phrase is commonly used for the body of RENAISSANCE English DRAMA produced in the century preceding the closing of the theaters in 1642, although it is sometimes employed in a narrower sense to designate the DRAMA of the later years of Elizabeth's reign and the few years following it. Thus, Shakespeare is an Elizabethan dramatist, although more than one third of his active career lies in the reign of James I. Modern English DRAMA not only came into being in Elizabethan times but developed so rapidly and brilliantly that the Elizabethan era is the golden age of English DRAMA.

Lack of adequate records makes it impossible to trace the steps by which *Elizabethan drama* developed, though the chief elements which contributed to it can be listed. From MEDIEVAL DRAMA came the TRADITION of acting and certain CONVENTIONS approved by the populace, including some buffoonery. From the MORALITY PLAYS and the INTERLUDES came comic elements. With this medieval heritage was combined the classical TRADITION of DRAMA, partly drawn from a study of the Roman dramatists, Seneca (TRAGEDY) and Plautus and Terence (COMEDY), and partly from humanistic CRITICISM based on Aristotle. This classical influence appeared first in the SCHOOL PLAYS. Later it affected the DRAMA written under the auspices of the royal court and of the INNS OF COURT. Eventually it influenced the plays of the university-trained playwrights connected with the public stage. The modern theater arose with *Elizabethan drama* (see PUBLIC THEATERS, PRIVATE THEATERS). For types of *Elizabethan drama* and names of dramatists see *Outline of Literary History* and TRAGEDY, ROMANTIC TRAGEDY, CLASSICAL TRAGEDY, TRAGEDY OF BLOOD, COMEDY, COMEDY OF HUMOURS, COURT COMEDY, REALISTIC COMEDY, CHRONICLE PLAY, and MASQUE.

Elizabethan Literature: Literature produced in England during the ELIZABETHAN AGE; that is, 1558–1603, although the meaning is often extended to include the JACOBEAN PERIOD, and sometimes given as wide a scope as 1550–1660. See ELIZABETHAN AGE.

Elizabethan Miscellanies: Poetical ANTHOLOGIES made in the ELIZABETHAN AGE. See MISCELLANIES, POETICAL.

Elizabethan Theaters: Public and private playhouses that developed and flourished in the ELIZABETHAN AGE. See PUBLIC THEATERS, PRIVATE THEATERS.

Ellipsis: A FIGURE OF SPEECH characterized by the omission of one or more words which, while essential to the grammatic structure of the sentence, are easily supplied by the reader. The effect of *ellipsis* is rhetorical; it makes for EMPHASIS of statement. The device often traps the unwary user into difficulties, since carelessness will result in impossible constructions. The safe rule is to be sure that the words to be supplied occur in the proper grammatic form not too remote from the place the *ellipsis* occurs. In the following quotation from Pope the brackets indicate *ellipses:*

> Where wigs [strive] with wigs, [where] with sword-knots
> sword-knots strive,
> [Where] Beaus banish beaus, and [where] coaches coaches drive.

Emblem Books: An "emblem" consisted of a motto expressing some moral idea and accompanied by a picture and a short POEM illustrating the idea. The poem was always short—SONNETS, EPIGRAMS, MADRIGALS, and various STANZA forms being employed. The picture (originally itself the "emblem") was symbolic. A collection of emblems was known as an *emblem book.* Emblems and *emblem books,* which owed their popularity partly to the newly developed art of engraving, were very popular in all Western European languages in the fifteenth, sixteenth, and seventeenth centuries. Examples of emblems: The motto *Divesque miserque,* "both rich and poor," illustrated by a picture of King Midas sitting at a table where everything was gold and by a verse or "posie" explaining how Midas, though rich, could not eat his gold; *Parler peu et venir au poinct,* "speak little and come to the point," illustrated by a quatrain and a picture of a man shooting at a target with a cross-bow. Several of Spenser's poems, such as *The Shepheardes Calender* and *Muiopotmos,* show the influence of emblems. Shakespeare seems to have made much use of emblem literature, as in the casket scene in *The Merchant of Venice.* Francis Quarles is the author of an interesting seventeenth-century *emblem book.*

Emendation: A change made in a literary text by an editor for the purpose of removing error or supplying a supposed intended reading which has been obscured or lost through textual inaccuracy or tampering.

Emotional Element in Literature: Although generalizations about the nature, intent, and language of literature are at best unsatisfactory efforts to bind together a congeries of contrasting and often conflicting elements, men have usually agreed in distinguishing among scientific, philosophical, and artistic expressions. It is true that the term *literature* is sometimes applied to graceful and effective DESCRIPTIONS, EXPOSITIONS, and ARGUMENTS whose purpose is to explain, instruct, or persuade; in a stricter sense, however, *literature* is properly reserved for expressions in which the aesthetic aim is equal to or outweighs the scientific or philosophical. This is, of course, a way of asserting that the grace, beauty, and symmetry of art are more than ornaments or sugar-coating for the pill of fact or concept. In a basic sense, the scientist appeals to our sense of fact; the philosopher to our intellectual being, our powers of logic and conceptualizing; and the artist to our emotional being, our inner selves. On the simplest level of language, science employs words for their DENOTATIONS, giving them verifiable but GENERAL referents in the world of things; philosophy deals with ABSTRACT TERMS, being concerned with the conceptualizing of experience; art deals with CONCRETE TERMS, tangible, particular, specific. These CONCRETE TERMS are frequently IMAGES that evoke immediate emotional responses from the reader. (See ABSTRACT TERMS; CONCRETE TERMS; BELIEF, THE PROBLEM OF; CRITICISM, TYPES OF.)

In I. A. Richards' distinction, art uses "emotive language"—

language employed for the effects it produces in emotion and attitude—as contrasted with science which uses "referential language"—language used for the sake of the reference it produces. To insist upon this emotional quality of literature is not to deny it other kinds of meaning and value, but it is to insist that literature conveys these other meanings and values in the uniquely emotive language of art. (See CONCRETE UNIVERSAL.)

Contemporary criticism has interested itself deeply in the emotional aspect of literature, with the assertion that there is an aspect of knowledge which can be conveyed by no other means than through the language and FORM of art. (See OBJECTIVE CORRELATIVE.)

Empathy: The act of identifying ourselves with an object and participating in its physical and emotional sensations, even to the point of making our own physical responses, as, standing before a statue of a discus-thrower, one flexes his muscles to hurl the discus. *Empathy* may be expended upon an inanimate object, an animal, or a person. It may be active, in that it results in the creative process, or it may be passive, in that it results from reading and appreciation. It is to be contrasted with "sympathy" through which we have a fellow-feeling for someone; for *empathy* implies an "involuntary projection of ourselves" into something or someone else. Some modern critics see in *empathy* the key to the nature and meaning of art (see EMOTIONAL ELEMENT IN LITERATURE). The term is a translation of Hermann Lotze's word *Einfühlung*—"feeling into"—and it entered our critical vocabulary in this century.

Emphasis: A principle of RHETORIC dictating that important elements be given important positions and adequate development whether in the sentence, the paragraph, or the whole composition. The more important positions are, naturally, at the beginning and end. But *emphasis* may also be secured (1) by repetition of important ideas, (2) by the development of important ideas through supplying plenty of specific detail, (3) by simply giving more space to the more important phases of the composition, (4) by contrasting one element with another since such contrasts focus the reader's attention on the point in question, (5) by careful selection of details so chosen that subjects related to the main idea are included and all irrelevant material excluded, (6) by climactic arrangement, (7) by mechanical devices such as capitalization, italics, symbols, and different colors of ink.

Empiricism

Empiricism: In philosophy, the practice of drawing rules of practice not from theory but from experience. Hence an empirical method is sometimes equivalent to an "experimental" method. In medicine, however, an "empiric" usually means a quack. The term is sometimes borrowed by literary critics and used in a derogatory sense, an *empiric* judgment being an untrained one. The empirical method, in the sense of the experimental, is important in literary theories of NATURALISM.

Enallage: The intentional substitution of one grammatical form for another, as past for present tense, singular for plural, noun for verb. It is a very common figure of speech, as in "toe the line" or "boot the ball." A famous example is Shakespeare's "But me no buts" (*Richard II*).

Enclosed Rhyme: A term applied to the RHYME pattern of the *In Memoriam* STANZA: *abba*.

Encomium: In Greek literature a POEM or speech in praise of a living person before a select group. Today any speech or writing that is of a laudatory nature. See PANEGYRIC, EULOGY.

End-Rhyme: RHYME that occurs at the ends of the VERSES in a POEM. The most common place for RHYME in English POETRY. See RHYME.

End-stopped Lines: Lines of VERSE in which both the grammatical structure and the sense reach completion at the end of the line. The absence of ENJAMBEMENT, or RUN-ON LINES. As in Pope's

> All are but parts of one stupendous whole,
> Whose body Nature is, and God the soul.

English Language: The *English language* developed from the West Germanic dialects spoken by the Angles, Saxons, and other Teutonic tribes which participated in the invasion and occupation of England in the fifth and sixth centuries, a movement which resulted in the obliteration of the earlier Celtic and Roman cultures in the island. The word *English* applied to the language reflects the fact that Anglo-Saxon literature first flourished in the North and was written in the Anglian dialects (hence *Englisc*, "English") spoken in Northumbria and Mercia. Later, under King Alfred, the

West Saxon region became the cultural center. The word *Englisc* was still employed as its name, however, and the earlier Anglian literature was copied in the West Saxon dialect, now commonly referred to as OLD ENGLISH, or "Anglo-Saxon." As a language West Saxon was very different from modern English. It had grammatical gender, declensions, conjugations, tense-forms, and case-endings. The word "stone," for example, had six forms (singular: *stān, stānes, stāne;* plural: *stānas, stāna, stānum*) representing five cases (nominative, genitive, dative, accusative, instrumental). Pronouns and verbs likewise possessed inflectional systems. In addition, the four great DIALECTS of the OLD ENGLISH PERIOD (Northumbrian, Mercian, West Saxon, Kentish) differed among themselves in grammar, pronunciation, and vocabulary. The first writing was in RUNES, which were displaced later by the Roman alphabet used by the Christian missionaries. Specimens of OLD ENGLISH have survived from as early as the eighth century, but most of the existing manuscripts are in West Saxon of the tenth and eleventh centuries. Though a few Latin and fewer Celtic words were added to the vocabulary in OLD ENGLISH times, most of the words were Teutonic, consisting of words used by the Angles and Saxons, augmented by the introduction of Danish and Norse words as the result of later invasions.

The changes which have made modern English look like a different language from OLD ENGLISH are the result of the operation of certain natural tendencies in language development, such as the progressive simplification of the grammar; and the accidents of history, such as the NORMAN CONQUEST and the growth of London as a cultural center. The greatest change took place in the earlier part of the period known as MIDDLE ENGLISH (*ca.*1100–*ca.*1500) or a little earlier. The leveling of inflections and other simplifying forces, already under way in late OLD ENGLISH times, were accelerated by the results of the NORMAN CONQUEST, which dethroned English as the literary language, in favor of the French language spoken by the newcomers (see ANGLO-FRENCH and ANGLO-NORMAN). Left to the everyday use of the native elements of the population, English changed rapidly in the direction of modern English. By late MIDDLE ENGLISH times (fourteenth century) the process of simplification had gone so far that in Chaucer's time almost all the old inflections either were lost or were weakened to a final -*e*, often unpronounced. The introduction of French words in the MIDDLE ENGLISH period proved a source of enrichment to the English vocabulary. In the fourteenth and fifteenth centuries a significant step toward the development of a standardized, uniform language came with the new prominence given the London DIALECT (largely East Midland), which thus became the basis for Modern English. This development came chiefly from the growing importance of London commercially and politically, the influence of the writings of Chaucer and his followers, the adoption of English instead of French in the courts and schools (fourteenth century), and the employment of this DIALECT by Caxton, the first English printer (late fifteenth century).

Modern English (ca.1500 on) has been marked by an enormous expansion in vocabulary, the new words being drawn from many sources, chiefly Latin and French. Since French is itself based upon Latin, English has acquired many doublets, such as "strict" and "strait," permitting further developments in shades of meaning. An examination of a dictionary will show the vast preponderance of foreign words over native English words, though the latter include the more frequently used words of everyday intercourse, such as "man," "wife," "child," "go," "hold," "day," "bed," "sorrow," "hand." The stylistic effect of English prose writing is greatly affected by the nature of the vocabulary used, particularly as between native English words and those derived from Latin, either directly or through French. The native words in general give an effect of simplicity and strength, while the Latin or Romance words impart smoothness and make possible fine distinctions in meaning. Modern English has also drawn freely upon many other sources for new words. Greek, for example, has been resorted to for scientific terms, new words being formed from Greek root-meanings, and Greek prefixes and suffixes. In grammar, the simplification process has been retarded in modern times by such conservative forces as grammars, DICTIONARIES, printers, and school teachers. Likewise spelling and pronunciation have become fixed in somewhat chaotic and archaic forms by the influence of the same standardizing tendencies, as well as the mass communications media.

Today only a quarter of the words in common usage in English are of OLD ENGLISH derivation, yet the ones which determine the nature of the language—articles, pronouns, and connecting words—are of OLD ENGLISH origin. What inflectional endings remain for pronouns, adjectives, and adverbs are OLD ENGLISH, as are our verb forms. We have retained the Germanic word order, the Germanic tendency to associate ACCENT and loudness and to stress the first syllable of nouns. We have borrowed three-fourths of our words but have always fitted them into an English frame. The result is that English remains basically a Teutonic tongue, which perpetually renews itself at the fountain of the world's languages. See OLD ENGLISH, MIDDLE ENGLISH, ANGLO-NORMAN, DIALECTS, AMERICAN ENGLISH.

English Literature, Periods of: The division of a nation's literary history into periods offers a convenient method for studying authors and movements, as well as the literature itself, in their proper perspectives. Hence most literary histories and anthologies are arranged by periods. In the case of English literature, there are almost as many arrangements as there are books on the subject. This lack of uniformity arises chiefly from two facts. In the first place, periods merge into one another because the supplanting of one literary attitude by another is a gradual process. Thus the earlier Romanticists are contemporary with the later neo-classicists, just as the neo-classical attitude existed in the very heyday of Elizabethan Romanticism. Dates given in any scheme of literary periods, therefore, must be regarded as approximate and suggestive only, even when they reflect some very definite fact, as 1660 (the Restoration of the Stuarts) and 1798 (the publication of *Lyrical Ballads*). In the second place, the names of periods may be chosen on very different principles. One plan is to name a period from its greatest or its most representative author: Age of Chaucer, Age of Spenser, etc. Another is to coin a descriptive adjective from the name of the ruler: Elizabethan Period, Jacobean Period, Victorian Period. Or pure chronology or names of centuries may be preferred: Fifteenth-century Literature, Eighteenth-century Literature, etc. Or descriptive titles designed to indicate prevailing critical or philosophical attitudes or dominant fashions or "schools" of literature may be used: Neo-classicism, Romanticism, Age of Reason. Logically, some single principle should control in any given scheme, but such consistency is not always found. The table on the following page gives the scheme used in this book.

Historical sketches of the periods listed in this table are given in the Handbook, and briefer descriptions of the subdivisions of periods (here called uniformly *ages*) are also given in the Handbook. *The Outline of Literary History* follows this table and gives details of general and literary history.

PERIODS OF ENGLISH LITERATURE

428–1100	Old English Period
1100–1350	Anglo-Norman Period
1350–1500	Middle English Period
1500–1660	The Renaissance Period
1500–1557	Early Tudor Age
1558–1603	Elizabethan Age
1603–1625	Jacobean Age
1625–1649	Caroline Age
1649–1660	The Commonwealth Interregnum
1660–1798	The Neo-Classical Period
1660–1700	The Restoration Age
1700–1750	The Augustan Age
1750–1798	The Age of Johnson
1798–1870	The Romantic Period
1798–1832	The Age of the Romantic Triumph
1832–1870	The Early Victorian Age
1870–1914	The Realistic Period
1870–1901	The Late Victorian Age
1901–1914	The Edwardian Age
1914–1972	The Contemporary Period

English Sonnet: The name applied to the SONNET which consists of three QUATRAINS followed by a COUPLET, rhyming *abab cdcd efef gg*. It is often called the SHAKESPEAREAN SONNET. See SONNET.

Enjambement: The device of continuing the sense and grammatical construction of a VERSE or a COUPLET on into the next.

Enjambement occurs with the presence of the RUN-ON LINE and offers contrast to the END-STOPPED LINE. The first and second lines from Milton given below, carried over to the second and third for completion, are illustrations of *enjambement:*

> Or if Sion hill
> Delight thee more, and Siloa's brook, that flow'd
> Fast by the oracle of God.

Enlightenment, The: A philosophical movement of the eighteenth century, particularly in France but effectively over much of Europe and America. *The Enlightenment* celebrated reason, the scientific method, and man's ability to perfect himself and his society. It was the outgrowth of a number of seventeenth-century intellectual attainments and currents: the discoveries of Sir Isaac Newton, the rationalism of Descartes and Pierre Bayle, and the empiricism of

Francis Bacon and John Locke. The major champions of its beliefs were the *philosophes*, who made a critical examination of previously accepted institutions and beliefs from the viewpoint of reason and with a confident faith in natural laws and universal order. The *philosophes* agreed on faith in man's rationality and the existence of discoverable and universally valid principles governing man, nature, and society. They opposed intolerance, restraint, spiritual authority, and revealed religion. They were deists (see DEISM) and political theorists who considered the state a proper instrument of progress. *The Encyclopedie* of Denis Diderot epitomized the doctrines of *The Enlightenment*. Among the leading French figures in *The Enlightenment* were Montesquieu, Voltaire, Buffon, Turgot, and the *Physiocrats*. In England Addison, Steele, Swift, Pope, Edward Gibbon, Hume, Adam Smith, and Jeremy Bentham responded to elements of *Enlightenment* thought; as did Moses Mendelssohn, Lessing, Herder, and Kant in Germany. In America Benjamin Franklin, Tom Paine, and Thomas Jefferson were profoundly influenced by the principles of *The Enlightenment*. *The Enlightenment* was the intellectual ferment out of which the French Revolution came, and it gave philosophical shape to the American Revolution and the two basic documents of the United States, *The Declaration of Independence* and *The Constitution*. See AGE OF JOHNSON, AGE OF REASON, and DEISM.

Enthymeme: A SYLLOGISM informally stated and omitting one of the two premises—either the major or the minor. The omitted premise is to be understood. Example: "Children should be seen and not heard. Be quiet, John." Here the obvious minor premise—that John is a child—is left to the ingenuity of the reader.

Enumerative Bibliography: A list of works of a particular country, author, printer, or type. See BIBLIOGRAPHY.

Envoy (*envoi*): A conventionalized STANZA appearing at the close of certain kinds of poems; particularly associated with the French BALLADE form. The *envoy* (1) is usually addressed to a prince, a judge, a patron, or other person of importance; (2) repeats the REFRAIN line used throughout the BALLADE; (3) consists normally of four lines (though not necessarily so limited); (4) usually employs the *bcbc* RHYME-scheme. See BALLADE.

Epanodos

Epanodos: The REPETITION of the same word or phrase at the beginning and middle or at the middle and end of a sentence, as in *Ezekiel*, 35:6—"I will prepare thee unto blood, and blood shall pursue thee: sith thou hast not hated blood, even blood shall pursue thee." The term is also used for the reiteration of two or more things so as to make distinctions among them, as in "Mary and Elizabeth both spoke; Mary quietly but Elizabeth in harsh and angry tones." *Epanodos* is sometimes applied to the progressive REPETITION of words or phrases, such as these in Touchstone's speech in *As You Like It* (III, 2): "Why, if thou never wast at court, thou never saw'st good manners; if thou never saw'st good manners, then thy manners must be wicked; and wickedness is sin, and sin is damnation. Thou art in a parlous state, shepherd." *Epanodos* is also applied to the return to the main subject after a DIGRESSION.

Epic: A long narrative POEM in elevated STYLE presenting characters of high position in a series of adventures which form an organic whole through their relation to a central figure of heroic proportions and through their development of EPISODES important to the history of a nation or race. The origin of *epics* is a matter of great scholarly dispute. According to one theory, the first *epics* took shape from the scattered work of various unknown poets, and through accretion these early EPISODES were gradually molded into a unified whole and an ordered sequence. Though held vigorously by some, this theory has generally given place to one which holds that the materials of the *epic* may have accumulated in this fashion but that the *epic poem* itself is the product of a single genius who gives it STRUCTURE and expression. *Epics* without certain authorship are called FOLK EPICS, whether the scholar believes in a folk or a single authorship theory of origins, however.

Epics, both FOLK and ART EPICS, share a group of common characteristics: (1) the HERO is a figure of imposing stature, of national or international importance, and of great historical or legendary significance; (2) the SETTING is vast in scope, covering great nations, the world, or the universe; (3) the action consists of deeds of great valor or requiring superhuman courage; (4) supernatural forces— gods, angels, and demons—interest themselves in the action and intervene from time to time; (5) a STYLE of sustained elevation and grand simplicity is used; and (6) the *epic* poet recounts the deeds of his heroes with objectivity. To these general characteristics (some

Epic Simile

of which are omitted from particular *epics*), should be added a list of common devices or CONVENTIONS employed by most *epic* poets: the poet opens by stating his theme, invokes a Muse to inspire and instruct him, and opens his narrative *in medias res*—in the middle of things—giving the necessary EXPOSITION in later portions of the *epic;* he includes CATALOGS of warriors, ships, armies; he gives extended formal speeches by the main characters; and he makes frequent use of the EPIC SIMILE.

A few of the more important FOLK EPICS are: *The Iliad* and *The Odyssey* (by Homer), the Old English *Beowulf,* the East Indian *Mahabharata,* the Spanish *Cid,* the Finnish *Kalevala,* the French *Song of Roland,* and the German *Nibelungenlied.* Some of the best known ART EPICS are: Virgil's *Aeneid,* Dante's *Divine Comedy* (although it lacks many of the distinctive characteristics of the *epic*), Tasso's *Jerusalem Delivered,* Milton's *Paradise Lost.* American poets in the late eighteenth and early nineteenth centuries struggled to produce a good *epic* poem on the American adventure, but without success. Longfellow's *Hiawatha* is an attempt at an Indian *epic.* Whitman's *Leaves of Grass,* considered as the autobiography of a generic American, is sometimes called an American *epic,* as are Stephen Vincent Benét's *John Brown's Body,* Ezra Pound's *Cantos,* and Harte Crane's *The Bridge.*

In the Middle Ages there was a great mass of literature verging on the *epic* in form and purpose though not answering strictly to the conventional *epic* formula. These poems are variously referred to as *epic* and as ROMANCE. Spenser's *The Faerie Queene* is the supreme example.

Epic Formula: The CONVENTIONS of STRUCTURE employed by most EPIC poets, such as the statement of THEME, the INVOCATION to the Muse, beginning *in medias res,* CATALOGS of warriors, extended formal speeches, and similar structural devices. See EPIC.

Epic Simile: An elaborated comparison. The *epic simile* differs from an ordinary SIMILE in being more involved, more ornate, and a conscious imitation of the Homeric manner. The secondary object or VEHICLE is developed into an independent aesthetic object, an IMAGE which for the moment excludes the primary object or TENOR with which it is compared. The following *epic simile* is from *Paradise Lost:*

195

Epicurean

Angel Forms, who lay entranced
Thick as autumnal leaves that strow the brooks
In Vallombrosa, where the Etrurian shades
High over-arched embower; or scattered sedge
Afloat, when with fierce winds Orion armed
Hath vexed the Red-Sea coast, whose waves o'erthrew
Busiris and his Memphian chivalry,
While with perfidious hatred they pursued
The sojourners of Goshen, who beheld
From the safe shore their floating carcases
And broken chariot-wheels.

Epicurean: A philosophical position similar to that of the Greek philosopher Epicurus, who saw philosophy as the art of making life happy, with pleasure the highest goal of man and pain and emotional disturbance the greatest evils. But Epicurus was not a simple hedonist (see HEDONISM); for him pleasure came not primarily from sensual delights but from serenity. Thus intellectual processes were, he held, superior to bodily pleasures. He rejected the belief in an afterlife and the influence of the gods in human affairs, strongly asserted human freedom, and accepted the atomic theory of Democritus. In his social code Epicurus emphasized honesty, prudence, and justice, but as means through which one encounters the least trouble from society. The *Epicurean*, therefore, seeks not wine, women, and song but serenity of spirit. The term *Epicurean* is often but erroneously considered synonymous with hedonistic.

Epigone: A less distinguished follower or imitator of a work, an author, or a literary movement. The term comes from the Epigonoi, who were the sons of the Seven against Thebes and who imitated their fathers by themselves unsuccessfully attacking Thebes. Thus *Thyrsis*, by Matthew Arnold, might be called an *epigone* of the great English PASTORAL ELEGY tradition, or the HISTORICAL NOVELS of G. P. R. James might be called *epigones* of Sir Walter Scott's Waverley Novels.

Epigram: Any pithy, pointed, concise saying. An *epigram* is often antithetical, as "Man proposes but God disposes," or La Rochefoucauld's "Only those deserving of scorn are apprehensive of it." This use of the word is derived from certain qualities of a type of POEM known as an *epigram*. Originally (in ancient Greece) an

Epilogue

epigram meant an inscription, especially an EPITAPH. Then it came to mean a short poem summing up as though in such an inscription what is to be made permanently memorable. Hence the *epigram* was characterized by compression, pointedness, clarity, BALANCE, and polish. Examples of the ancient *epigram* may be found in the *Greek Anthology* and in the work of the Roman poet Martial (A.D. 40–104), whose work supplied models for Ben Jonson, the greatest writer of *epigrams* in English. Martial had used the *epigram* for various themes and purposes: EULOGY, friendship, compliment, EPITAPHS, philosophic reflection, JEUX D'ESPRIT, and SATIRE. Although numerous *epigrams* were written by sixteenth-century English writers, notably John Heywood, they did not conform closely to the classical type, reflecting various forms of medieval HUMOR and SATIRE. With the revolt against Elizabethan ROMANTICISM just before 1600, the classical *epigram* was cultivated, chiefly as a vehicle for SATIRE. Many collections were published between 1596 and 1616, including a famous one of Sir John Harington (1615). Jonson wrote not only satirical *epigrams* but EPISTLES, VERSES of compliment, EPITAPHS, and reflective VERSES. An *epigram* of this period was typically a short poem consisting of two parts, an introduction stating the occasion or setting the tone, and a conclusion which sharply and tersely gives the main point. In the eighteenth century the spirit though not the form of the *epigram* continued. Many of Pope's couplets are *epigrams* when separated from their context. Coleridge, too, indulged in the *epigram* on occasion, but Walter Savage Landor was its greatest and most persistent user after Jonson.

Epilogue: A concluding statement; an appendix to a composition. Sometimes used in the sense of a PERORATION to a speech, but more generally applied to the final remarks of an actor addressed to the audience at the close of the play. Opposed to PROLOGUE, a speech used to introduce the play. Puck, in *A Midsummer Night's Dream,* recites an *epilogue* which is characteristic of RENAISSANCE plays in that it bespeaks the good will of the audience and courteous treatment by critics. As the use of *epilogues* became more general, poets of reputation were often paid to contribute *epilogues* to plays much as PREFACES written by prominent authors are now sometimes paid for by publishers. *Epilogues* were a part of major dramatic efforts in the late seventeenth and eighteenth centuries, disappearing from common use about the middle of the nineteenth. They are now rarely employed.

197

Epiphany

Epiphany: Literally a manifestation or showing-forth, usually of some divine being. The Christian festival of *Epiphany* commemorates the manifestation of Christ to the Gentiles in the form of the Magi. It is celebrated on "Twelfth Night," January 6. *Epiphany* has been given wide currency as a critical term by James Joyce, who used it to designate an event in which the essential nature of something— a person, a situation, an object—was suddenly perceived. It is thus an intuitive grasp of reality achieved in a quick flash of recognition in which something, usually simple and commonplace, is seen in a new light, and, as Joyce says, "its soul, its whatness leaps to us from the vestment of its appearance." This sudden insight is the *epiphany*. But the term is also used for a literary composition which presents such *epiphanes*, so that we say that the stories that make up Joyce's *Dubliners* are *epiphanies*.

Episode: An incident presented as one continuous action. Though having a UNITY within itself, the *episode* in any composition is usually accompanied by other *episodes* so woven together according to the conscious artistic purpose of the writer as to create a SHORT STORY, DRAMA, or NOVEL. Originally, in Greek DRAMA, an *episode* referred to that part of a TRAGEDY which was presented between two CHORUSES. More narrowly the term is sometimes used to characterize an incident injected into a piece of FICTION simply to illuminate character or to create background where it bears no definite relation to the PLOT and in no way advances the action.

Episodic Structure: A term applied to writing which consists of little more than a series of incidents. Simple NARRATIVE as opposed to NARRATIVE with PLOT. The *episodes* succeed each other, in this type of writing, with no very logical arrangement (except perhaps that of chronology) and without COMPLICATION or a close interrelationship. Travel books naturally fall into *episodic structure*. The term is applied also to long narratives which may contain complicated PLOTS, like the Italian ROMANTIC EPIC, if the action is made leisurely by the use of numerous *episodes* employed for the purpose of developing character or PLOT. The METRICAL ROMANCE and the PICARESQUE NOVEL are said to have *episodic structure*, since the events that occur in them have no causal relationship and are together because they happened in chronological order to a single character. As a rule, a work with *episodic structure* has little or no central PLOT.

Epistolary Novel

Epistle: Theoretically an *epistle* is any LETTER, but in practice the term is limited to formal compositions written by an individual or a group to a distant individual or group. The most familiar use of the term, of course, is to characterize certain of the books of the New Testament. The *epistle* differs from the common LETTER in that it is a conscious literary form rather than a spontaneous, chatty, private composition. Ordinarily the *epistle* is associated with the scriptural writing of the past, but this is by no means a necessary restriction since the term may be used to indicate formal LETTERS having to do with public matters and with philosophy as well as with religious problems. It is regularly applied to the formal LETTERS of dedication that appear in books. Pope used it to describe formal LETTERS in verse.

Epistolary Novel: A NOVEL in which the narrative is carried forward by LETTERS written by one or more of the characters. It has the merit of giving the author an opportunity to present the feelings and reactions of characters without himself intruding into the action of the NOVEL; it further gives a sense of immediacy to the action, since the LETTERS are usually written in the thick of the action. The *epistolary novel* also enables the author to present multiple points of view on the same event through the use of several correspondents' *epistolary* records of the occurrence. It is also a device for creating VERISIMILITUDE, the author merely serving as "editor" for the correspondence of "actual" persons. Obvious disadvantages are the fact that the correspondents in an *epistolary novel* become incredible and indefatigable scribblers under the most surprising circumstances and the fact that the enforced objectivity of the "editor" shuts the author off from comment on the actions of his characters.

Samuel Richardson's *Pamela* (1740) is frequently considered the first English *epistolary novel*, although the use of LETTERS to tell stories and to give racy gossip and sage instruction goes back in England at least as far as Nicholas Breton's *A Poste with a Packet of Mad Letters* (1602) and includes such sentimental analyses of the feminine heart as Aphra Behn's *Love Letters Between a Nobleman and His Sister* (1682). Richardson's *Clarissa Harlowe* (1748) is certainly the greatest, as it is the most extended, of *epistolary novels*. The form was popular in the eighteenth century, particularly for the SENTIMENTAL NOVEL. Other notable examples are Smollett's *Humphry Clinker* (1771) and Fanny Burney's *Evelina*

(1778). The epistolary method has not often been successfully used in the nineteenth and twentieth centuries, although the use of LETTERS within NOVELS has been common. See NOVEL.

Epistrophe: A rhetorical term applied to the REPETITION of the closing word or phrase at the end of several clauses, sentences, or VERSES, as in Sidney's "And all the night he did nothing but weep Philoclea, sigh Philoclea, and cry out Philoclea" (The New *Arcadia*).

Epitaph: Inscription used to mark burial places. Commemorative VERSES or lines appearing on tombs or written as if intended for such use. Since the days of early Egyptian records *epitaphs* have had a long and interesting history, and while they have changed as to purpose and form, they show less development than most literary types. The information usually incorporated in such memorials includes the name of the deceased, the dates of birth and death, age, profession (if a dignified one), together with some pious motto or INVOCATION. Many prominent writers—notably Johnson, Milton, and Pope—have left *epitaphs* which they wrote in tribute to the dead. Early *epitaphs* were usually serious and dignified—since they chiefly appeared on the tombs of the great—but more recently they have, either consciously or unconsciously, taken on humorous qualities. One of the most famous inscriptions is that marking Shakespeare's burial place:

> Good frend, for Jesus sake forbeare
> To digg the dust encloased here;
> Bleste be ye man y^t spares thes stones,
> And curst be he y^t moves my bones,—

But this is as much a CURSE as an *epitaph*. "O rare Ben Jonson"—which may be a serious PUN on ORGRE (pray for)—and "*Exit* Burbage" are two examples of effective *epitaphs*. A famous French inscription is from Père Lachaise in Paris:

> Ci-gît ma femme: ah! que c'est bien
> Pour son repos, et pour le mien!

The *epitaph* "On the Countess Dowager of Pembroke," formerly attributed to Ben Jonson, though now credited to William Browne, deserves quotation:

> Underneath this sable hearse
> Lies the subject of all verse:
> Sidney's sister, Pembroke's mother.

Epithet

> Death, ere thou hast slain another,
> Fair and learned and good as she,
> Time shall throw a dart at thee.

Epitasis: A term used by the ancients to designate the RISING ACTION of a DRAMA. See DRAMATIC STRUCTURE.

Epithalamium (Epithalamion): A bridal SONG; a SONG or POEM written to celebrate a wedding. Many ancient poets (the Greek Pindar, Sappho, and Theocritus and the Roman Catullus) as well as modern poets (like the French Ronsard and the English Spenser) have cultivated the form. Perhaps Spenser's *Epithalamion* (1595), written to celebrate his own marriage, is the finest of the English marriage hymns. The successive STANZAS in this poem treat such topics as: invocation to the Muses to help praise his bride; bride is awakened by music; decking of the bridal path with flowers; nymphs adorn the bride; the assembling of the guests; description of the beauty of the bride, physical and spiritual; the bride at the altar; the marriage-feast; welcoming the night; asking the blessing of Diana and Juno and the stars.

Epithet: Strictly an adjective or adjective phrase used to point out a characteristic of a person or thing, as Goldsmith's "noisy mansions" (for schoolhouses), but sometimes applied to a noun or noun phrase used for a similar purpose, as Shakespeare's "The trumpet of the dawn" (for the cock). Many considerations enter into the success of an *epithet*, such as its aptness (indeed, *epithet* is actually used sometimes rather loosely to mean any apt phrase), its freshness, its pictorial quality, its connotative value (what it suggests rather than says), and its musical value. In literature rememberable *epithets* are very often figurative, as Keats' "snarling trumpets" and Milton's "laboring clouds."

The so-called HOMERIC EPITHET, often a compound adjective, as "all-seeing" Jove, "swift-footed" Achilles, "blue-eyed" Athena, "rosy-fingered" dawn, depends upon aptness combined with familiarity rather than upon freshness or variety. It is almost a part of a name. Since *epithets* often play a prominent part in the calling-of-names which characterizes INVECTIVE or personal SATIRE, some persons have the mistaken notion that an *epithet* is always uncomplimentary. A TRANSFERRED EPITHET is an adjective used to limit grammatically a noun which it does not logically modify, though

Epitome

the relation is so close that the meaning is left clear, as Shakespeare's "dusty death," or Milton's "blind mouths." This subtly suggestive device, often involving the PATHETIC FALLACY, is used effectively by the poets. The following phrases contain examples of *epithets:* glimmering landscape, murmuring brook, dazzling immortality, pure-eyed Faith, dusty answer, prostituted muse, dark-skirted wilderness, circumambient foam, care-charmer sleep, sweet silent thought, meek-eyed peace.

Epitome: A summary or ABRIDGMENT. A condensed statement of the content of a book. A "miniature representation" of a subject. Thus Magna Charta has been called the *epitome* of the rights of Englishmen, and Ruskin referred to St. Mark's as an *epitome* of the changes of Venetian architecture through a period of nine centuries.

Epode: One of the three STANZA forms employed in the PINDARIC ODE. The others are STROPHE and ANTISTROPHE. See ODE.

Eponym: The name of a person who is so commonly associated with some widely recognized attribute that the name comes to stand for the attribute, as Helen for beauty, Croesus for wealth, Machiavelli for duplicity, or Caesar for dictator.

Epyllion: A NARRATIVE POEM usually presenting an EPISODE from the heroic past and resembling an EPIC in THEME, TONE, and method but much briefer in length and more limited in scope. Matthew Arnold's *Sohrab and Rustum* is an *epyllion* and so are Tennyson's *Idylls of the King*.

Equivalence: In METRICS, a kind of SUBSTITUTION, in which a FOOT equal to the one expected but different from it is used in a VERSE. In QUANTITATIVE VERSE, one long syllable was considered the *equivalent* of two short syllables and thus a SPONDEE (two long syllables) could be substituted for an ANAPEST (two shorts and a long). See SUBSTITUTION, COMPENSATION.

Equivocation: The use of a word in two distinct meanings, with the intention to deceive. See EQUIVOQUE.

Equivoque: A kind of PUN in which the same word or phrase is so used that it has two different and incongruous meanings. If the

equivoque is used with the intention to deceive the result is called
EQUIVOCATION.

Erastianism: The doctrine that the civil authority has dominance
over the church in all matters. It is attributed to Thomas Erastus,
a sixteenth-century Swiss theologian, who insisted that the civil
authority and not the church should act in all punitive measures,
but who did not intend to give the state authority in ecclesiastical
matters, although the doctrine named for him came to mean such
civil dominance over spiritual matters. *Erastianism* became an issue
in England during the OXFORD MOVEMENT controversies. The Public
Worship Act of 1874 attempted to "put down Ritualism" as it had
developed under the OXFORD MOVEMENT. The Act was vigorously
and successfully resisted by Pusey and his followers as an instance
of *Erastianism*.

Erotic Literature: Amorous writing. The classification of literature
as *erotic* is based on the subject matter—love—rather than the
literary form employed. Consequently *erotic literature* embraces
almost any form of writing—the LYRIC, the DRAMA, SHORT STORY,
NOVEL, even EPIGRAMS and ELEGIES, the LYRIC proving perhaps
the most popular vehicle. The lines which distinguish *erotic literature*
from any writing based on the love theme are hard to draw. The
classification is broad enough to include the range of writing about
love from the mildly sentimental to the actually pornographic. The
presentation of love in literature called *erotic* must, however, approach the fleshly quality to be placed in this category.

Escape Literature: Writing whose clear intention is to amuse and
beguile the reader by offering him a strange world or exciting adventures or puzzling mysteries. It aims at no higher purpose than
amusement. Adventure stories, DETECTIVE STORIES, TALES of fantasy,
and many humorous stories are frankly *escape literature*, and they
exist for no other purpose than to translate the reader for a time
from the care-ridden actual world to an entrancing world of the
imagination. Longfellow, in "The Day is Done," defined the effect
of *escape literature* well:

> Come, read to me some poem,
>   Some simple and heartfelt lay,
> That shall soothe this restless feeling,
>   And banish the thoughts of day.

> . . . . .

Esemplastic

And the night shall be filled with music.
And the cares that infest the day
Shall fold their tents, like the Arabs,
And as silently steal away.

Esemplastic: A term applied by Samuel Taylor Coleridge to the quality in the IMAGINATION that enables it to shape disparate things into a unified whole. The word literally means "moulding into a unity."

Esperanto: An artificial speech constructed from roots common to the chief European languages and designed for universal use. *Esperanto* was devised by Dr. L. L. Zamenhof, a Russian, and took its name from Zamenhof's pseudonym, "Dr. Esperanto," used in signing his first pamphlet on the subject in 1887. The grammar is so simple as to be clear after a few minutes' study, the spelling is strictly phonetic, the language is euphonious and adaptable, and pronunciation is simple since the ACCENT always falls on the penult. Since 1887, *Esperanto* has grown in popularity, although it gives little promise today of becoming a truly universal tongue.

Essay: A moderately brief prose discussion of a restricted topic. Because of the wide application of the term, no satisfactory definition can be arrived at; nor can a wholly acceptable "classification" of *essay* types be made. Among the terms that have been used in attempting classifications of the *essay* are: moralizing, critical, character, anecdotal, letter, narrative, aphoristic, descriptive, reflective, biographical, historical, periodical, didactic, editorial, whimsical, psychological, outdoor, nature, cosmical, and personal. Such a list is incomplete; obviously classifying the *essay* has eluded human skill. A basic and very useful division can, however, be made: FORMAL and INFORMAL ESSAYS. The INFORMAL ESSAY, sometimes called the "true" *essay*, includes moderately brief aphoristic *essays* like Bacon's, PERIODICAL ESSAYS like Addison's, and PERSONAL ESSAYS like Lamb's. Qualities which make an *essay* INFORMAL include: the personal element (self-revelation, individual tastes and experiences, confidential manner), humor, graceful STYLE, rambling STRUCTURE, unconventionality or novelty of THEME, freshness of FORM, freedom from stiffness and affectation, incomplete or tentative treatment of topic. Qualities of the FORMAL ESSAY include: sober seriousness of purpose, dignity, logical organization, length. The term may include both short discussions, expository or argumentative, such as the serious magazine ARTICLE, and longer treatises, like the chapters in Carlyle's *Heroes and Hero-Worship*. However, a sharp distinction between even FORMAL and INFORMAL ESSAYS cannot be maintained at all times. In the following sketch the INFORMAL ESSAY will be given chief consideration, since it lies more completely in the realm of literature.

Montaigne: Beginnings.—When the French philosopher Montaigne retired from active life, he collected pithy sayings—MAXIMS, APHORISMS, ADAGES, APOTHEGMS, PROVERBS—along with ANECDOTES and quotations from his readings in the classics. A collection of such wise sayings upon a single topic was known in France as a *leçon morale*. Montaigne developed the habit of recording also the results of a searching self-analysis and became attracted by the idea that he was himself representative of man in general. He published his first collection of such writings in two volumes in 1580 under the title *Essais*—the first use of the word for short prose discussions. The word means "attempts," and by its use Montaigne meant to indicate that his discussions were tentative compared with ordinary philosophical writings. By adding the personal element to the aphoristic *leçon morale* Montaigne created the modern *essay*. "Myself," he said, "am the groundwork of my book." The new edition which included the third volume (1588) gave even greater emphasis to the personal element. Mainly philosophical and ethical, the *essays* cover a wide range of topics: "Of Idleness," "Of Liars," "Of Ready and Slow Speech," "Of Smells and Odors," "Of Cannibals," "Of Sleeping," "Upon Some Verses of Virgil," etc.

The Essay in England: Bacon and the Seventeenth Century.— When Francis Bacon published in 1597 his first collection of aphoristic *essays*, he borrowed his title, *Essays*, from Montaigne's book —and became the first English "essayist." The ten *essays* first published were short and consisted chiefly of a collection of MAXIMS on a given subject. The book was very popular, and enlarged editions were issued in 1612 and 1625. The later *essays* are longer, more personal, and developed by a wealth of illustration, quotation, and FIGURES OF SPEECH. Bacon's STYLE achieved a compactness, clarity, imaginative richness, phrasal power, and sentence-rhythm which have made his *essays* a part of the world's literature. The "aphoristic" quality of his STYLE is seen in such typical quotations as these: "The errors of young men are the ruin of business," and "He that hath a wife and children hath given hostages to fortune." Bacon's *essays* are highly practical and utilitarian. Like the Renaissance COURTESY BOOKS they had for their chief purpose the giving of useful advice to those who wished to get on in practical life, especially as men of affairs.

After Bacon the seventeenth century contributed little to the development of the INFORMAL ESSAY. Owen Felltham's *Resolves* (1620) shows the application of Bacon's method to religious topics. Sir William Cornwallis' *Essays* (1600, 1610, 1616) reflects the method of Montaigne. Better essayists appeared after the Restoration. Sir William Temple, the statesman, and Abraham Cowley, the poet, wrote PERSONAL ESSAYS while living in retirement, Cowley's being particularly happy efforts. Though the INFORMAL ESSAY, strictly defined, received little attention in this century, there was much prose writing closely related to the INFORMAL and FORMAL ESSAY. The chapters of Sir Thomas Browne's *Religio Medici* (1642) in their STYLE and in their tendency toward self-revelation and moralizing are suggestive of the INFORMAL ESSAY, as are the miscellaneous sketches in Ben Jonson's *Timber, or Discoveries Made upon Men and Matter* (1640). Dryden's *Essay of Dramatick Poesie* (1668) is an example of a critical *essay* in conventional DIALOGUE form. The numerous PREFACES and books on literary CRITICISM from the late sixteenth and early seventeenth centuries are also forerunners of the later critical *essay*. Milton's *Areopagitica*, in form an argumentative address, is a masterly example of a FORMAL ESSAY. Related to *essay* writing are such long prose treatises as Robert Burton's *Anatomy of Melancholy* (1621), Locke's *Essay Concerning Human Understanding* (1690), and Izaak Walton's *Compleat Angler* (1653). The LETTER or formal EPISTLE as a vehicle for writing much like the INFORMAL ESSAY appeared in James Howell's *Epistolae–Ho–elianae, Familiar Letters* (1650). The seventeenth century also saw the development in English of the CHARACTER, a brief character sketch of a quality or type-personality destined to become popular and exert an appreciable influence upon the PERIODICAL ESSAY of the eighteenth century, partly, to be sure, through the work of a French writer of CHARACTERS, La Bruyère, who had combined the CHARACTER with the *essay*. The EPIGRAM, as written by Ben Jonson, in its depiction of moral and social types, sometimes became a sort of counterpart of the CHARACTER and may have influenced *essay* writers.

The Periodical Essay: Eighteenth Century.—The second great step in the history of the INFORMAL ESSAY came with the creation by Steele and Addison in the early years of the eighteenth century of the PERIODICAL ESSAY, a new form which achieved great popularity and attracted the best writers of the time. In 1691 had appeared Dunton's *Athenian Gazette,* a new type of PERIODICAL, small in format and designed to entertain as well as instruct. A feature of Daniel Defoe's *A Weekly Review of Affairs in France* (1704) had been a department called "Advice from the Scandalous Club," gossipy in character. From this germ Richard Steele developed the new *essay* in his *Tatler* (1709–1711). The purpose of the papers was "to recommend truth, innocence, honor, virtue, as the chief ornaments of life." Joseph Addison soon joined Steele and the two later launched the informal daily *Spectator* (1711–1712; 1714). The new *essay* was affected not only by its periodical form, which pre-scribed the length, but by the general spirit of the times. RENAISSANCE individualism was giving way to a centering of interest in society, and the moral reaction from the excesses of the RESTORATION AGE made timely the effort of the essayists to reform the manners of the age, refine its tastes, and provide topics for discussion at the popular coffee houses of London.

As compared with earlier *essays,* the PERIODICAL ESSAY is briefer, less aphoristic, less intimate and introspective, less individualistic, less "learned," and is more informal in STYLE and tone, making more use of HUMOR and SATIRE, and embracing a wider range of topics. The appeal is to the middle classes as well as to the cultivated few, but the city reader seems always to have been in the authors' minds. Addison referred to two types of *Spectator* papers: "serious essays" on such well-worn topics as death, marriage, education, and friend-ship; and "occasional papers," dealing with the "folly, extravagance, and caprice of the present age." The latter class especially aided in fixing as a tradition of the INFORMAL ESSAY that delightful informality, whimsicality, HUMOR, and grace which appears in scores of *essays* on such topics as women's fashions, dueling, witchcraft, coffee houses, and family portraits. The type developed much machinery such as fictitious characters, clubs, and imaginary correspondents.

The popularity of the form led to many imitations, such as the *Guardian,* the *Female Tatler,* the *Whisperer,* and men like Swift, Pope, and Berkeley contributed *essays* to some of them. The novelist Fielding incorporated *essays* in his *Tom Jones.* Later in the century Dr. Samuel Johnson (in the *Rambler,* 1750–1752, and the *Idler* papers, 1758–1760), Lord Chesterfield, Horace Walpole, and Oliver Goldsmith appeared as accomplished informal essayists. Gold-smith's *Letters from a Citizen of the World* (1760–1761) are noted examples of the form. After Goldsmith the *essay* declined as a literary form.

The Personal Essay: Nineteenth Century.—A revival of interest in the writing of both FORMAL and INFORMAL ESSAYS accompanied the ROMANTIC MOVEMENT. The informal type responded to the romantic impulses of the time. The production of the PERSONAL ESSAY was stimulated by the development of a new type of periodical: *Blackwood's Magazine* (1817) and the *London Magazine* (1820), which provided a market for the *essays* of Lamb, Hazlitt, Hunt, De Quincey, and others. Lamb's *Essays of Elia* (begun in 1820) exhibited an intimate STYLE, an autobiographical interest, a light and easy HUMOR and sentiment, an urbanity and unerring literary TASTE. Even the novelists took up *essay* writing (Dickens, *Sketches by Boz,* 1836; Thackeray, *Roundabout Papers,* 1860–1863). Freed from the space restrictions of the *Tatler* type and encouraged by a reading public eager for "original" work, these writers modified the Addisonian *essay* by making it more personal, longer, and more varied in theme, and by freeing it from the stereotyped features of the earlier form. Late in the century a worthy successor to Lamb appeared in Robert Louis Stevenson, for whose whimsical humor, nimble imagination, accomplished STYLE, and buoyant personality, the PERSONAL ESSAY formed an ideal medium of expression (*Virginibus Puerisque,* 1881; *Memories and Portraits,* 1887). More recent writers of the informal *essay* in England are A. C. Benson, G. K. Chesterton, and E. V. Lucas.

The Formal Essay: Nineteenth Century.—The FORMAL ESSAY of the early nineteenth century was largely the result of the appearance of the critical magazine, especially the *Edinburgh Review* (1802), the *Quarterly Review* (1809), and the *Westminster Review* (1824). Book reviews in the form of long critical *essays* were written by Francis Jeffrey, T. B. Macaulay, Thomas De Quincey, Sir Walter Scott, Thomas Carlyle, and later by George Eliot, Matthew Arnold, and many others. The manner of the FORMAL ESSAY appears also in the works of many other prose writers of the century. The separate chapters in the books of such men as Thomas Carlyle, John Ruskin, Walter Pater, Charles Kingsley, Leslie Stephen, Walter Bagehot, T. H. Huxley, Matthew Arnold, and Cardinal Newman are essay-like treatments of phases of the historical, biographical, scientific, educational, religious, and ethical topics concerned.

The Essay in America.—Though there is some reflection of *essay*

Essay

literature in such early American writers as Cotton Mather, Jonathan Edwards, Benjamin Franklin, Thomas Jefferson, Alexander Hamilton, and such "itinerant" Americans as Tom Paine and J. H. St. John de Crèvecœur, the first really great literary essayist in America is Washington Irving, whose *Sketch-Book* (1820) contains *essays* of the Addisonian type. Some of H. D. Thoreau's works (e.g., *Walden*) exhibited characteristics of the INFORMAL ESSAY, and Oliver Wendell Holmes in *The Autocrat of the Breakfast Table* (1857) was a successful writer of informal, humorous *essays*. Ralph Waldo Emerson, reminiscent of Bacon in his aphoristic style, fired with transcendental idealism, became perhaps the best known of all American essayists. James Russell Lowell (*Among My Books*, 1870, 1876) is another notable writer of *essays*, as is Edgar Allan Poe, who produced important critical *essays*. Later able essayists, formal or informal, include G. W. Curtis, C. D. Warner, W. D. Howells, Mark Twain, and John Burroughs. More recent names are those of Agnes Repplier, S. M. Crothers, Katherine Fullerton Gerould, Dallas Lore Sharp, Henry Van Dyke, William Beebe, Christopher Morley, James Thurber, E. B. White, and the writers for the *New Yorker*.

Summary.—The FORMAL ESSAY, instead of crystallizing into a set literary type, has tended to become diversified in form, spirit, and length, according to the theme and serious purpose of its author. At one extreme it is represented by the brief, serious magazine ARTICLE and at the other by scientific or philosophical treatises which are books rather than *essays*. The technique of the FORMAL ESSAY is now practically identical with that of all factual or theoretical prose writing in which literary effect is secondary to serious purpose. Its tradition has doubtless tended to add clarity to English prose STYLE by its insistence upon unity, structure, and perspicacity.

The INFORMAL ESSAY, on the other hand, beginning in aphoristic and moralistic writing, modified by the injection of the personal element, broadened and lightened by a free treatment of human manners, modified and partly controlled in STYLE and length by the limitations of periodical publication, has developed into a recognizable literary GENRE, the first purpose of which is to entertain, and the manner of which is sprightly, light, novel, or humorous. As such the form has aided in giving something of a Gallic grace to other forms of prose composition, notably letterwriting. But valuable though its contributions to prose writing have been and respected as it is today as a literary GENRE, the INFORMAL

ESSAY has had few skillful or serious practitioners in the twentieth century. Perhaps our frenzied age is ill-suited to its sane, calm grace.

Etiquette Books (**Renaissance**): Books of instruction in manners, conduct, and the art of governing for young princes and noblemen. See COURTESY BOOKS.

Eulogy: A formal, dignified speech or writing, highly praising a person or a thing. See ENCOMIUM.

Euphemism: A FIGURE OF SPEECH in which an indirect statement is substituted for a direct one in an effort to avoid bluntness. With the advance of REALISM in recent years strained *euphemisms* are seldom found in literature, since such expressions are taken by discriminating readers as evidence of a tendency to be insincere or even sentimental. Small-town journalistic style, however, still abounds with such locutions as "passed on" for "died." Euphemistic terms have been much used by many writers in an effort to mention a disagreeable idea in an agreeable manner.

Euphony: A STYLE in which combinations of words pleasant to the ear predominate. Harsh, grating, cacophonous sounds violate *euphony* and make for unpleasantness in reading. Careful writers avoid such pitfalls as the juxtaposition of harsh consonants, a series of unaccented syllables, unconscious rhyming or repetition of similar sounds, jerky RHYTHM, and excessive ALLITERATION.

Euphuism: An affected STYLE of speech and writing which flourished late in the sixteenth century in England, especially in court circles. It took its name from *Euphues* (1578, 1580) by John Lyly. The chief characteristics of *euphuism* are: balanced construction, often antithetical and combined with ALLITERATION; excessive use of the RHETORICAL QUESTION; a heaping up of SIMILES, illustrations, and examples, especially those drawn from mythology and "unnatural natural history" about the fabulous habits and qualities of animals and plants. Following are some typical passages from *Euphues:* "Be sober but not too sullen; be valiant but not too venturous"; "For as the finest ruby staineth the color of the rest that be in place, or as the sun dimmeth the moon, so this gallant girl more fair than fortunate and yet more fortunate than faithful," etc.; "Do we

Exegesis

not commonly see that in painted pots is hidden the deadliest poison? that in the greenest grass is the greatest serpent? in the clearest water the ugliest toad?" "Being incensed against the one as most pernicious and enflamed with the other as most precious."

Lyly did not invent *euphuism;* rather he combined and popularized elements which others had developed. Important forerunners of Lyly in England were Lord Berners, in his translation of Froissart's *Chronicle* (1523, 1525); Sir Thomas North's translation (1557) of *The Dial of Princes* by Guevara (whose Spanish itself was highly colored); and George Pettie in his *A Petite Palace of Pettie his Pleasure* (1576). One of Pettie's sentences, for example, reads: "Nay, there was never bloody tiger that did so terribly tear the little lamb, as this tyrant did furiously fare with the fair Philomela."

The chief vogue of *euphuism* was in the 1580's, though it was employed much later. The court ladies cultivated it for social conversation, and such writers as Robert Greene and Thomas Lodge used it in their novels (as *Menaphon* and *Rosalynde*). Sir Philip Sidney reacted against it and was followed by many others. Shakespeare both employed it and ridiculed it in *Love's Labour's Lost.* Though the extravagance and artificiality of *euphuism* make it seem ludicrous to a modern reader, it is to be remembered that it actually played a powerful and beneficial role in the development of English PROSE. It established the idea that PROSE (formerly heavy and Latinized) might be written with IMAGINATION and FANCY, while its emphasis on short clauses and sentences and on balanced construction aided in imparting clearness to prose STYLE. These virtues of clearness and lightness and pleasant ornamentation remained as a permanent contribution after a better TASTE had eliminated the vices of extravagant artificiality. In a justly famous scene between Falstaff and Prince Hal, Shakespeare mocks the euphuistic style (*Henry IV*, Pt. I, Act II, Sc. 4).

Exciting Force: In a DRAMA the force which starts the CONFLICT of opposing interests and sets in motion the RISING ACTION of the play. Example: the witches' prophecy to Macbeth, which stirs him to schemes for making himself king. See DRAMATIC STRUCTURE.

Excursus: A formal, lengthy DIGRESSION. See DIGRESSION.

Exegesis: An explanation and interpretation of a difficult text. It is usually applied to the detailed study of the Bible. When it is used in reference to a literary text, it usually implies a close analysis and is equivalent to explication. See EXPLICATION DE TEXTE.

Exemplum: A moralized TALE. Just as modern preachers often make use of "illustrations," so medieval preachers made extensive use of TALES, ANECDOTES, and INCIDENTS, both historical and legendary, to point morals or illustrate doctrines. Often highly artificial and to a modern reader incredible, these "examples" seem to have appealed very strongly to medieval congregations, because of their concreteness, their narrative and human interest, as well as their moral implications. Collections of *exempla,* classified according to subject, were prepared for the use of preachers. An important book of the sort was Jacques de Vitry's *Exempla* (early thirteenth century). At times sermons degenerated into mere series of ANECDOTES, sometimes even humorous in character. Dante in thirteenth-century Italy and Wycliffe in fourteenth-century England protested against this tendency, and Wycliffe as an element in his reform program omitted *exempla* from his own sermons.

The influence of *exempla* and example-books on medieval literature was great, as may be illustrated from several of Chaucer's poems. The *Nun's Priest's Tale,* for example, itself cast into sermon form, uses *exempla,* as when Chanticleer tells Pertelot ANECDOTES to prove that dreams have a meaning. The *Pardoner's Tale* is itself an *exemplum* to show how Avarice leads to an evil end.

Existential Criticism: A contemporary school of CRITICISM, led by Jean-Paul Sartre, which denies the legitimacy of the traditional critical questions, and examines a literary work in terms of the ways in which it explores the *existential* questions and in terms of its existential impact on the reader. See EXISTENTIALISM.

Existentialism: A term applied to a group of attitudes current in philosophical, religious, and artistic thought during and after World War II, which emphasizes existence rather than essence and sees the inadequacy of the human reason to explain the enigma of the universe as the basic philosophical question. The term is so broadly and loosely used that an exact definition is not possible. In its modern expression it had its beginning in the writings of the nineteenth-century Danish theologian, Søren Kierkegaard. The German philosopher Martin Heidegger is important in its formulation, and

Existentialism

the French novelist-philosopher Jean-Paul Sartre has done most to give it its present form and popularity. *Existentialism* has found art and literature to be unusually effective methods of expression; in the NOVELS of Franz Kafka, Dostoyevski, Camus, and Simone de Beauvoir, and in the plays and NOVELS of Sartre, it has found its most persuasive media.

Basically the existentialist assumes that existence precedes essence, that the significant fact is that we and things in general exist, but that these things have no meaning for us except as we through acting upon them can create meaning. Sartre claims that the fundamental truth of *existentialism* is in Descartes' formula, "I think; therefore, I exist." The existential philosophy is concerned with the personal "commitment" of this unique existing individual in the "human situation." It attempts to codify the irrational aspect of man's nature, to objectify non-being or nothingness and see it as a universal source of fear, to distrust concepts, and to emphasize experiential concreteness. The existentialist's point of departure is the immediate sense of awareness that man has of his situation. A part of this awareness is the sense man has of meaninglessness in the outer world; this meaninglessness produces in him a discomfort, an anxiety, a loneliness in the face of man's limitations and a desire to invest experience with meaning by acting upon the world, although efforts to act in a meaningless, "absurd" world lead to anguish, greater loneliness, and despair. Man is totally free, but he is also wholly responsible for what he makes of himself. This freedom and responsibility are the sources for his most intense anxiety. Such a philosophical attitude can result in nihilism and hopelessness, as, indeed, it has with many of the literary existentialists.

On the other hand, the existential view can assert the possibility of improvement. Most pessimistic systems find the source of their despair in the fixed imperfection of human nature or of the human context; the existentialist, however, denies all absolute principles and holds that human nature is fixed only in that we have agreed to recognize certain human attributes; it is, therefore, subject to change if men can agree on other attributes or even to change by a single man if he acts authentically in contradiction to the accepted principles. Hence, for the existentialist, the possibilities of altering human nature and society are unlimited, but, at the same time, man can hope for aid in making such alterations only from within himself.

213

Exordium

In contradistinction to this essentially atheistic *existentialism,* there has also developed a sizable body of Christian existential thought, represented by men like Karl Jaspers, Jacques Maritain, Nicolas Berdyaev, Martin Buber, and Paul Tillich.

Exordium: In CLASSIC RHETORIC the first of the seven parts of an ORATION (see ORATION). By extension, *exordium* is now applied to the introductory portion of a composition or a discourse. Edgar Allan Poe, for example, opens his section of critical notices in *Graham's Magazine* for January, 1842, with an *"Exordium"* in which he sets forth his critical principles.

Expletive: An interjection to lend emphasis to a sentence or, in VERSE especially, the use of a superfluous word (some form of the verb "to do," for example) to make for RHYTHM. Profanity is, of course, another form of *expletive* use. Careless speech is full of superfluous words which are *expletive* in nature. A common colloquial *expletive* is "you know" added frequently to a statement, as "I went home, you know, at ten o'clock."

Explication de texte: A method which originated in the teaching of literature in France; it involves the painstaking analysis of the meanings, relationships, and AMBIGUITIES of the words, IMAGES, and small units that make up a literary work. It is now one of the tools of the NEW CRITICS. See ANALYTICAL CRITICISM, AMBIGUITY, NEW CRITICISM, EXEGESIS.

Exposition: One of the four chief types of composition, the others being ARGUMENTATION, DESCRIPTION, and NARRATION. Its purpose is to explain the nature of an object, an idea, or a THEME. *Exposition* may exist apart from the other types of composition, but frequently two or more of the types are blended, DESCRIPTION aiding *exposition,* ARGUMENT being supported by *exposition,* NARRATION reinforcing by example an *exposition.* The following are some of the methods used in *exposition* (they may be used singly or in various combinations): identification, definition, classification, illustration, comparison and contrast, and analysis.

In DRAMATIC STRUCTURE the *exposition* is the introductory material, which creates the tone, gives the SETTING, introduces the characters, and supplies other facts necessary to an understanding of the play. See DRAMATIC STRUCTURE.

Expressionism: A movement affecting painting, the DRAMA, the NOVEL, and POETRY, which followed and went beyond IMPRESSIONISM in its efforts to "objectify inner experience." Fundamentally it means the willing yielding up of the REALISTIC and NATURALISTIC methods, of VERISIMILITUDE, in order to use objects in art not as representational but as transmitters of the impressions and moods of a character or of the author or artist. In painting, for instance, "childhood" might be shown not through a conventional representational picture of children at play or at school but by seemingly unarticulated and exaggerated physical details that suggest "childhood" or convey the impression which the artist has of the concept "child."

As an organized literary movement *expressionism* was strongest in the theater in the 1920's, and its entry into other literary forms was probably through the stage. *Expressionism* had its origin in the German theater in the early years of the century. It was a response to several different forces: the growing size and mechanism of society with its tendency to depress the value of the arts made the artists seek new ways of making art forms valuable instruments for man; at the same time the depth psychologists, notably Freud, laid bare the phantasms in the depths of the human mind and offered the artist a challenge accurately to record them; meanwhile MARXISM had instructed even the non-Marxist artist that the individual was being lost in a mass society; to these pressures came the example of the dramas of Strindberg, whose plays *The Dance of Death* (1901) and *A Dream Play* (1902) employ extensive nonrealistic devices. The German dramatists Wedekind, Georg Kaiser, and Ernst Toller and the Czech dramatist Karel Capek (the author of the nightmarish FANTASY of the future, *R. U. R.*) were the major figures in the European expressionistic drama, which flourished in the 1920's. It was marked by unreal atmosphere, a nightmarish quality of action, distortion and oversimplification, the deemphasis of the individual (characters were likely to be called the "Father" or the "Bank Clerk"), anti-realistic stage SETTINGS, and staccato, telegraphic DIALOGUE. The expressionistic DRAMA was strongly influential on Pirandello and Lorca. For American students it is most important in its impact on Eugene O'Neill, whose *Emperor Jones* attempts to project by symbolic scenes and sound-effects the racial memories of a modern Negro. Elmer Rice's *The Adding Machine*, which uses moving stages and other nonrealistic devices to express the mechanical world seen by one cog in it named Mr. Zero, is an almost equally noted example. Elements of *expressionism* can be seen in the plays of Thornton Wilder, Arthur Miller, and Tennessee Williams.

In the NOVEL the presentation of the objective outer world as it expresses itself in the impressions or moods of a character is a device widely used. The most famous extended example is Joyce's *Finnegans Wake*, although the expressionistic intent and method is often apparent in works using the STREAM OF CONSCIOUSNESS technique, as witness the "Circe" episode in Joyce's *Ulysses*. Probably the most complete transfer of the quality of expressionistic DRAMA to the NOVEL, however, is to be found in the works of Franz Kafka. The ANTI-REALISTIC NOVEL is also a GENRE in the expressionistic tradition.

The revolt against REALISM, the distortion of the objects of the outer world, and the violent dislocation of time sequence and spatial logic in an effort accurately but not representationally to show the world as it appears to a troubled mind can be found in contemporary poetry, particularly that of Robinson Jeffers and T. S. Eliot, whose "The Hollow Men" is an excellent example and whose *The Waste Land* is the poetic classic of the movement. See IMPRESSIONISM, REALISM.

Expressive Theory of Criticism: A term, used by M. H. Abrams, that designates a theory of art which holds the object of the artist to be the expression of his emotions, impressions, or beliefs; an essential doctrine of the ROMANTIC critics. See CRITICISM, HISTORICAL SKETCH.

Extravaganza: A fantastic, extravagant, or irregular composition. It is most commonly applied to dramatic compositions such as those of J. R. Planché, the creator of the dramatic *extravaganza*. Planché himself defined it as a "whimsical treatment of a poetical subject as distinguished from the broad caricature of a tragedy or serious opera, which was correctly described as burlesque." The subject was often a FAIRY TALE. The presentation was elaborate, and included dancing and music. An example is Planché's *Sleeping Beauty* (acted 1840). A later use of *extravaganza*, still current, is to designate any extraordinarily spectacular theatrical production. The term *extravaganza* is also applied to fantastic musical compositions, especially musical CARICATURES. In literature the term is occasionally used to characterize such rollicking or unrestrained work as Butler's *Hudibras,* a CARICATURE of the PURITANS.

Eye-Rhyme: RHYME that appears correct from the spelling, but is HALF-RHYME or SLANT-RHYME from the pronunciation, as "watch" and "match" or "love" and "move."

F

Fable: A brief TALE, either in prose or VERSE, told to point a moral. The characters are most frequently animals, but they need not be so restricted since people and inanimate objects as well are sometimes the central figures. The subject matter of *fables* has to do with supernatural and unusual incidents and often draws its origin from FOLKLORE sources. By far the most famous *fables* are those accredited to Aesop, a Greek slave living about 600 B.C.; but almost equally popular are those of La Fontaine, a Frenchman writing in the seventeenth century, because of their distinctive HUMOR and WIT, their wisdom and sprightly SATIRE. Other important fabulists are Gay (England), Lessing (Germany), Krylov (Russia). A *fable* in which the characters are animals is called a BEAST FABLE, a form that has been popular in almost every period of literary history, usually as a satiric device to point out the follies of mankind. The BEAST FABLE continues to be vigorous in such diverse works as Kipling's *Jungle Books* and *Just So Stories,* Joel Chandler Harris' Uncle Remus stories, and George Orwell's *Animal Farm.* Many critics, particularly in the NEO-CLASSIC PERIOD, have used *fable* as a term for the PLOT of a FICTION or a DRAMA. See BEAST EPIC, BESTIARY, ALLEGORY.

Fabliau: A humorous TALE popular in medieval French literature. The *fabliaux* gained their wide diffusion largely through the popularity of the JONGLEUR, who spread the *fabliaux* throughout France. The conventional form was eight-syllable VERSE. These *fabliaux* consisted of stories of various types, but one point was uppermost —their humorous, sly SATIRE on human beings. These stories, which were often bawdy, dealt familiarly with the clergy, ridiculed womanhood, and were pitched in a key which made them readily and boisterously understandable to the uneducated. The form was also present in English literature of the MIDDLE ENGLISH PERIOD, Chaucer especially leaving examples of *fabliaux,* in the tales of the Miller, Reeve, Friar, Summoner, Merchant, Shipman, and Manciple. Although *fabliaux* often had ostensible "morals" appended to them, they lack the serious intention of the FABLE, and they differ from the FABLE too in always having human beings as characters and in always maintaining a REALISTIC TONE and manner.

Fairy Tale: A STORY relating mysterious pranks and adventures of supernatural spirits who manifested themselves in the form of diminutive human beings. These spirits possessed certain qualities which are constantly drawn upon for TALES of their adventures: supernatural wisdom and foresight, a mischievous temperament, the power to regulate the affairs of man for good or evil, the capacity to change themselves into any shape at any time. *Fairy tales* as such—though they had existed in varying forms before—became popular toward the close of the seventeenth century. Almost every nation has its own fairy literature, though the FOLKLORE element embodied in *fairy tales* prompts the growth of related TALES among different nations. Some of the great source-collections are the *Contes de ma Mère l'Oye* of Perrault (French), and those of the Grimm brothers in German and of Keightley and Croker in English. Hans Christian Andersen, of Denmark, is probably the most famous writer of original *fairy tales.* English writers of original *fairy tales* include Ruskin, Kingsley, and Wilde.

Falling Action: The second "half" or RESOLUTION of a dramatic PLOT. It follows the CLIMAX, beginning often with a TRAGIC FORCE, exhibits the failing fortunes of the hero (in TRAGEDY) and the successful efforts of the COUNTERPLAYERS, and culminates in the CATASTROPHE. See DRAMATIC STRUCTURE.

Falling Rhythm: In METRICS a FOOT in which the first syllable is accented, as in a TROCHEE or a DACTYL. Coleridge's VERSES on the poetic feet illustrate it:

> Trochee is in falling duble,
> Dactyl is falling, like—Tripoli.

Familiar Essay: A term applied to the more personal, intimate type of INFORMAL ESSAY. It deals lightly, often humorously, with personal experiences, opinions, and prejudices, stressing especially the unusual or novel in attitude and having to do with the varied aspects of everyday life. Goldsmith, Lamb, and Stevenson were particularly successful in the form. See ESSAY.

Fancy: A critical term now used almost exclusively in the Coleridgean opposition of IMAGINATION AND FANCY, in which *fancy* is "mechanic," logical, "the aggregative and associative power," as opposed to the "organic" and "creative" IMAGINATION. See IMAGINATION AND FANCY.

Fantastic Poets: A term applied by Milton to the school of metaphysical poets (see METAPHYSICAL VERSE).

Fantasy: Though sometimes used as an equivalent of FANCY and even of IMAGINATION (see IMAGINATION AND FANCY), *fantasy* is usually employed to designate a conscious breaking free from reality. The term is applied to a work which takes place in a non-existent and unreal world, such as fairyland, or concerns incredible and unreal characters, as in Maeterlinck's *The Blue Bird*, or employs physical and scientific principles not yet discovered or contrary to present experience, as in SCIENCE FICTION and UTOPIAN fiction. *Fantasy* may be employed merely for the whimsical delight of author or reader, or it may be the means used by the author for serious comment on reality. The most sustained example of *fantasy*, combining both intentions, in recent literature are the novels of James Branch Cabell laid in the mythical kingdom of Poictesme. The Brontë children created a *fantasy* world which they called Gondal and which they equipped with a geography, history, and even newspapers. Austin Tappan Wright's *Islandia* is an enormous fictional record of an imaginary world. J. R. R. Tolkien's three novels with the collective title *The Fellowship of the Ring* is currently proving the still strong appeal of *fantasy*.

Farce: The word developed from Late Latin *farsus*, connected with a verb meaning "to stuff." Thus an expansion or amplification in the church liturgy was called a *farse*. Later, in France, *farce* meant any sort of extemporaneous addition in a play, especially comic jokes or "gags," the clownish actors speaking "more than was set down" for them. In the late seventeenth century *farce* was used in England to mean any short humorous play, as distinguished from regular five-act COMEDY. The development in these plays of certain elements of LOW COMEDY is responsible for the usual modern meaning of

Farce-Comedy

farce: a dramatic piece intended to excite laughter and depending less on PLOT and character than on exaggerated, improbable situations, the HUMOR arising from gross incongruities, coarse WIT, or horseplay. *Farce* merges into COMEDY, and the same play (e.g., Shakespeare's *The Taming of the Shrew*) may be called by some a *farce,* by others a COMEDY. James Townley's *High Life Below Stairs* (1759), with the production of which Garrick was connected, has been termed the "best farce" of the eighteenth century. In the American theater, Brandon Thomas' *Charley's Aunt* (1892), dealing with the extravagant events resulting from a female impersonation, is the best known American *farce,* although *farce* is the stock-in-trade of motion-picture and television comedians. See FARCE-COMEDY.

Farce-Comedy: A term sometimes applied to comedies which rely for their interest chiefly on farcical devices (see FARCE, LOW COMEDY), but which contain some truly comic elements which elevate them above most FARCE. Shakespeare's *The Taming of the Shrew* and *The Merry Wives of Windsor* are called *farce-comedies* by some authorities. One writer distinguishes between the *farce-comedy* of Aristophanes (loose STRUCTURE, variety of appeal, operatic quality) and that of Plautus (careful STRUCTURE, intricate INTRIGUE, broad HUMOR).

Fatalism: The attitude of mind which accepts whatever happens as having been immutably decreed to happen. Strictly speaking, *fatalism* removes ethical concerns from human actions, for fate indifferently assigns man to the predetermined course of events. The Greeks held to the idea of the allotment, by the Moirai, to each individual at birth of a certain quantity of misfortune which he must endure. The Romans saw their gods, the Parcae, spinning man's destiny. In Islamic belief everything is ruled by an inexorable fate, called Kismet. It is important to distinguish between fate and chance. If fate is conceived as acting, then any event, however independent of the actions or merits of an individual, is the result of an impersonal force absolutely predetermining it and everything else that happens. On the other hand, if chance is believed to be operative, then the event is accidental rather than a part of a design, the working of COINCIDENCE rather than of fate.

Federalist Age in American Literature: The portion of American literary history between the formation of the national government and the "Second Revolution" of Jacksonian Democracy, so-called because of the dominance of the Federalist Party in American political life and thought. The period extends from 1790 to 1830. Internationally, the Age saw the emergence of the United States as a world force through the War of 1812. Internally it was an "Era of Good Feeling," with the sectional and social issues which were to plague the nation in mid-century just beginning to be felt. It was an age of rapid literary development. In 1790 the United States could boast of few distinguished writers of any kind and almost none of belletristic excellence; at its close America was clearly ready for the artistic burgeoning forth that marked the period from 1830 to the Civil War. POETRY moved from the imitative neoclassicism of Barlow and Dwight, through the limited romanticism of Freneau, to the first notable American achievements in verse in the work of Bryant. The NOVEL, first practiced in America in 1789, saw good work by Charles Brockden Brown and H. H. Brackenridge and the establishment of a distinctively American romance with the Leatherstocking Tales of James Fenimore Cooper. Irving in his burlesque *Knickerbocker's History of New York* and in his ESSAYS and TALES found an international audience. The *North American Review*, founded in 1815, was a thriving quarterly. In the decade 1800–1810, Hawthorne, Simms, Whittier, Longfellow, Poe, and Holmes were born; and 1819 was an *annus mirabilis*, being the birth year of Lowell, Melville, and Whitman. By 1830 the neo-classic, restrained, aristocratic Federalist that America had been had given way to a romantic, exuberant, democratic young giant that was flexing its muscles and was beginning effectively to express itself in art as well as action. See *Outline of Literary History* and REVOLUTIONARY AND EARLY NATIONAL PERIOD IN AMERICAN LITERATURE.

Feminine Ending: An extra-metrical syllable, bearing no STRESS, added to the end of a line in IAMBIC or ANAPESTIC METER. This variation gives a sense of movement and an irregularity to the METER which make for grace and lightness. The form is perhaps most commonly used in BLANK VERSE. The second line in this Shakespeare quotation is an illustration:

> O! I could play the woman with mine eyes
> And braggart with my tongue. But gentle heav*ens*,
> Cut short all intermission.

Feminine Rhyme

Feminine Rhyme: A RHYME of two syllables, one stressed and one unstressed, as *waken* and *forsaken, audition* and *rendition.* It is also called DOUBLE RHYME. In Chaucer, the *feminine rhyme* was very common because of the frequent recurrence of the final *-e* in Middle English. The term "feminine" is a courtesy—either to the form or to womanhood—since it is employed to connote the lightness and grace which result from the use of this type of RHYME. The following example is by Bret Harte:

> Above the pines the moon was slowly *drifting,*
>   The river sang below;
> The dim Sierras, far beyond, *uplifting*
>   Their minarets of snow.

Festschrift (plural, *Festschriften*):   From the German words for celebration and writing. A volume of miscellaneous learned ESSAYS by several hands, written by his students, colleagues, or admirers, and presented to a distinguished scholar on some special occasion, such as his retirement or seventieth birthday.

Feudalism: The system of social and political organization that prevailed in Western Europe during a large part of the medieval period. It developed from the anarchy which followed the fall of Charlemagne's empire in the ninth century. In feudal theory every landholder was merely the tenant of some greater landlord. Thus, the barons or powerful prelates were the tenants of the king; the lesser lords, knights, and churchmen were tenants of the barons and prelates; while the serfs and "villeins" were tenants of the lesser nobles. In practice—as the whole system was based upon force—the relations were more complicated: even kings sometimes owed allegiance to a great churchman or baron. Furthermore, there were interlocking fealties, by which one lord might owe allegiance to two kings, so that his allegiance to one might be set aside if that one attacked the other. As rent the various groups paid to their immediate superiors "service," which might consist of visible property or of military aid. Socially, there were two sharply defined classes: the workers (villeins or free renters; serfs or bondmen); and the "prayers and fighters" (knights, upper clergy, lords). *Feudalism* broke down in the fifteenth century. The ideals of chivalry (see CHIVALRY IN ENGLISH LITERATURE) grew out of *feudalism* and powerfully affected the character of much medieval and even REN-

AISSANCE literature, notably the ROMANCES and ROMANTIC EPICS. The feudal social order is pictured in Chaucer's *Canterbury Tales* and its evils set forth in the *Vision of Piers Plowman* (fourteenth century).

Fiction: NARRATIVE writing drawn from the IMAGINATION of the author rather than from history or fact. The term is most frequently associated with NOVELS and SHORT STORIES, though DRAMA and NARRATIVE POETRY are also FORMS of *fiction*, and FABLES, PARABLES, FAIRY TALES, and FOLKLORE contain fictional elements. Sometimes authors weave fictional episodes about historical characters, epochs, and settings and thus make "historical *fiction*.'" Sometimes authors use imaginative elaborations of incidents and qualities of a real person in a BIOGRAPHY, resulting in a type of writing popular in recent years, the "fictional BIOGRAPHY." Sometimes the actual events of the author's life are presented under the guise of imaginative creations, resulting in "autobiographical *fiction*." Sometimes actual persons and events are presented under the guise of *fiction*, resulting in the ROMAN À CLEF. The chief function of *fiction* is to entertain, to be "interesting" in Henry James' phrase; but it often serves also to instruct, to edify, to persuade, or to arouse. It is one of the major devices by which man communicates his vision of the nature of reality in CONCRETE TERMS.

Since *fiction* is a subject matter rather than a type of literature, one interested in any of the particular forms which *fiction* assumes should turn to the articles on specific types, such as NOVEL, SHORT STORY, DRAMA, NARRATIVE POEM, FABLE, for details of the history and STRUCTURE of these types.

Figurative Language: Intentional departure from the normal order, construction, or meaning of words in order to gain strength and freshness of expression, to create a pictorial effect, to describe by ANALOGY, or to discover and illustrate similarities in otherwise dissimilar things. *Figurative language* is writing that embodies one or more of the various FIGURES OF SPEECH, the most common of which are: ANTITHESIS, APOSTROPHE, CLIMAX, HYPERBOLE, IRONY, METAPHOR, METONYMY, PERSONIFICATION, REPETITION, SIMILE, SYNECDOCHE. These figures are often divided into two classes: TROPES, literally meaning "turns," in which the words in the figure undergo a decided change in meaning, and RHETORICAL FIGURES in which the words retain their literal meaning but their rhetorical pattern is changed. An APOSTROPHE, for example, is a "figure of thought," and a METAPHOR is a TROPE. See IMAGERY, METAPHOR, TROPE, FIGURES OF SPEECH.

Figures of Speech: The various uses of language which depart from customary construction, order, or significance in order to achieve special effects or meanings. *Figures of speech* are of two major kinds: RHETORICAL FIGURES, which are departures from customary or standard uses of language to achieve special effects without a change in the radical meaning of the words; and TROPES, in which basic change in the meaning of words occur. *"Figures of speech"* is a term sometimes used as synonymous with RHETORICAL FIGURES, and "figures of thought" as synonymous with TROPES; but "figures of speech" and "figures of thought" in this distinction have undergone so many changes and direct reversals of meaning from the classical rhetoricians to the present that their use in this way almost always results in confusion. It is, therefore, best to use *figures of speech* as the generic term and to use RHETORICAL FIGURES and TROPES as the subgenera. See FIGURATIVE LANGUAGE, RHETORICAL FIGURE, and TROPE.

Filidh (pl. *fili*):   Early Irish professional poets. See IRISH LITERATURE.

Fin de siècle: "End of the century," a phrase often applied to the last ten years of the nineteenth century. The 1890's were a transitional period, one in which writers and artists were consciously abandoning old ideas and conventions and attempting to discover and set up new techniques and artistic objectives. One writer (Holbrook Jackson) has noted three main characteristics of the decade in art and literature: DECADENCE, exemplified in Oscar Wilde and Aubrey Beardsley; REALISM or "sense of fact," represented by Gissing, Shaw, and George Moore, with their reaction against the sentimental; and radical or revolutionary social aspirations, marked by numerous new "movements" (including the "new woman," who dared ride a bicycle and seek political suffrage) and by a general sense of emancipation from the traditional social and moral order. When the term *fin de siècle* is used about a literary work, it usually is in the sense of DECADENCE or PRECIOSITY. See EDWARDIAN AGE.

Final Suspense, Moment of: A term used to indicate the ray of hope sometimes appearing just before the CATASTROPHE of a TRAGEDY. Thus Macbeth's continued faith that he cannot be hurt by any man born of woman keeps the reader or spectator in some suspense as to the apparently inevitable tragic ending. See DRAMATIC STRUCTURE.

Five Points of Calvinism: The basic tenets of John Calvin's doctrines: (1) total depravity of man, (2) unconditional election, (3) prevenient and irresistible grace, (4) perseverance of the saints, and (5) limited atonement. See CALVINISM for more detailed treatment.

Fixed Poetic Forms: A name sometimes given to definitely prescribed patterns of VERSE and STANZA. Although forms like the SONNET, the SPENSERIAN STANZA, and RHYME ROYAL are "fixed" forms in this general sense, the term usually refers to a specific group of stanzaic patterns that originated in France. See FRENCH FORMS.

Flashback: A device by which the writer of a FICTION or a DRAMA presents SCENES or INCIDENTS that occurred prior to the opening SCENE of the work. It is a method of presenting EXPOSITION dramatically. Various devices may be used, among them recollections of the characters, narration by the characters, dream sequences, and reveries. Notable examples in the theater occur in Elmer Rice's *Dream Girl* and Arthur Miller's *Death of a Salesman.* Maugham used the *flashback* skillfully and effectively in *Cakes and Ale,* and it is employed consistently in the novels of John P. Marquand. See EXPOSITION.

Flat Character: A term used by E. M. Forster to describe a CHARACTER constructed around a single idea or quality, like the HUMOURS CHARACTERS of the seventeenth-century STAGE. A *flat character* never surprises the reader, is immediately recognizable, and can usually be represented by a single sentence, as "I never will desert Mr. Micawber," which, Forster asserts, *is* Mrs. Micawber and is *all* she is. The term usually is employed in contrast to ROUND CHARACTER. See CHARACTERIZATION and ROUND CHARACTER.

Fleshly School of Poetry, The: A critical ESSAY in the *Contemporary Review,* October, 1871, signed "Thomas Maitland," a pseudonym for Robert W. Buchanan. The critic took to task Swinburne, Morris, and Rossetti, though most of the article is couched as a review of Rossetti's poems and Rossetti himself draws most of the fire. Buchanan accused the three of being in league to praise each other's work and refers to them as the "Mutual Admiration School." The following passage makes clear the general tone of Buchanan's criticism:

> The fleshly gentlemen have bound themselves by solemn league and covenant to extol fleshliness as the distinct and supreme end of poetic and pictorial art, to aver that poetic expression is greater than poetic thought, and by inference that the body is greater than the soul, and sound superior to sense; and that the poet, properly to develop his poetic faculty, must be an intellectual hermaphrodite. . . .

Rossetti replied with "The Stealthy School of Criticism," published in *The Athenaeum* (December 16, 1871).

Flyting: An extended and vigorous verbal exchange. In OLD ENGLISH POETRY it was a boasting match between warriors before combat. Similar boasting matches are found in Greek, Arabic, Celtic, Italian, and Provençal literature. It is typical of the Cycles of Charlemagne. However, it has been from the sixteenth century to the present a marked characteristic of Scottish writing, where it is an exchange of personal abuse or ridicule in VERSE between two CHARACTERS in a POEM or between two poets. In a *flyting* the poets attack each other in scurrilous VERSE, filled with vigorous and vulgar invective and profanity. *The Flyting of Dunbar and Kennedie* is an example from sixteenth-century Scotland.

Foil: A *foil* is literally a sheet of bright metal that is placed under a piece of jewelry to increase its brilliance. In literature, by extension, the term is applied to any person or sometimes thing that through strong contrast underscores or enhances the distinctive characteristics of another. Thus Laertes by his willingness to act in haste serves as a *foil* to Hamlet, as also do the Players and does Fortinbras.

Folio: A standard size sheet of paper folded in half. The term is also used to describe a volume made up of *folio* sheets—that is, whose SIGNATURES result from sheets folded to two leaves or four pages. It is the largest regular BOOK SIZE. Shakespeare's plays were first assembled in a *folio* edition in 1623, and the term *folio* is used to designate any of the early collections of Shakespeare's works. Hence it takes on a special meaning, referring in this case to content rather than BOOK SIZE.

Folk Ballad: An anonymous BALLAD transmitted by oral tradition and usually existing in many variant forms. In America the term *folk ballad* is often associated with the FOLK SONGS of the people of the Appalachian mountains, of the cowboys of the western plains, and of the labor movement. The term *folk ballad* is frequently, though inappropriately, used today by popular singers to designate a kind of contemporary song, usually accompanied by a guitar, which simulates *folk ballads*. See BALLAD and FOLK SONG.

Folk Drama: In its stricter and older sense, as usually employed by folklorists, the term means dramatic activities of the folk—the unsophisticated treatment of folk themes by the folk themselves, particularly activities connected with popular festivals and religious rites (for the development of ancient Greek DRAMA from such forms, see DRAMA). Medieval *folk drama* took such forms as the sword dance, the St. George play, and the mummers' play. The MEDIEVAL religious DRAMA, though based upon Scriptural materials and a religion with a fully developed theology, is by some regarded as a form of *folk drama,* and the "folk" character of such twentieth-century plays as Marc Connelly's *Green Pastures* is commonly recognized. The religious DRAMA of the Middle Ages (see MEDIEVAL DRAMA), however, is usually treated as a special form, not as *folk drama.*

Another sense in which the term *folk drama* is being employed, especially in America, includes plays which, while written by sophisticated and consciously artistic playwrights, reflect the customs, language, attitudes, and environmental difficulties of the folk. These plays are commonly performed, not by the folk themselves, but by amateur or professional actors. They tend to be realistic, close to the soil, and sympathetically human. The plays of J. M. Synge, Lady Gregory, and other authors of the CELTIC RENAISSANCE and the American plays by Paul Green and others published in the several volumes of *Carolina Folk-Plays* are examples. The latter reflect especially the life of the Negro and the Southern "mountain folk."

Folk Epic: An EPIC by an unknown author or authors or of doubtful attribution or assumed to be the product of communal composition. See EPIC, ART EPIC.

Folklore: A term first used by W. J. Thomas in the middle of the nineteenth century as a substitute for "popular antiquities." The existence of varied conceptions of the term makes definition difficult. The one adopted by the Folklore Society of London about 1890 is: "The comparison and identification of the survivals of archaic beliefs, customs, and traditions in modern ages." Alexander H. Krappe, in *The Science of Folk-lore* (1930) affirms that *folklore* "limits itself to a study of the unrecorded traditions of the people as they appear in popular fiction, custom and belief, magic and ritual," and he regards it as the function of *folklore* to reconstruct the "spiritual history of man" from a study of the ways and sayings of the folk as contrasted with sophisticated thinkers and writers. Although concerned primarily with the psychology of early man or with that of the less cultured classes of society, some of the forms of *folklore* (e.g., superstitions and proverbial sayings) belong also to the life of modern man, literate as well as illiterate, and may, therefore, be transmitted by written record as well as by word of mouth. *Folklore* includes MYTHS, LEGENDS, STORIES, RIDDLES, PROVERBS, NURSERY RHYMES, charms, spells, omens, superstitions of all sorts, popular BALLADS, cowboy SONGS, plant lore, animal lore, and customs dealing with marriage, death, and amusements. The relations of *folklore* to sophisticated literature are important, but not always easy to trace. A folk tale may be retold by an author writing for a highly cultivated audience, and later in a changed form again be taken over by the folk. Folk customs are associated with the development of dramatic activity, because of the custom of performing plays at folk festivals.

Literature is full of elements taken over from *folklore,* and some knowledge of the formulas and CONVENTIONS of *folklore* is often an aid to the understanding of great literature. The acceptance of the rather childish love-test in *King Lear* may rest upon the fact that the MOTIF was an already familiar one in *folklore.* The effects of such works as Coleridge's *Christabel* or Keats' *Eve of St. Agnes* depend upon the recognition of popular superstitions, while some familiarity with fairy lore is necessary if one is to catch in full the quality of James Stephens' *The Crock of Gold.* The fine MEDIEVAL ROMANCE of *Sir Gawain and the Green Knight,* written for a cultivated audience, centers round the folk-formula of the challenging of a mortal by a supernatural being to a beheading contest: the binding force of the covenant between Gawain and the Green Knight is explained by primitive attitudes rather than by rational rules of conduct. Shakespeare's *Hamlet* is a retelling of an old popular tale of the "exile-and-return" formula, and has its origins, as Francis Fergusson has pointed out, in a series of religious rituals.

Foot

The study of *folklore* in America, particularly that of the cow-boy, the mountaineer, and the Negro, has received increasing attention in the twentieth century.

Folk Song: A SONG of unknown authorship preserved and transmitted by oral tradition. It is generally believed to be the expression of a whole singing community. *Folk songs* are very old and appear in all cultures, although they flourish best in illiterate communities. Today there is a self-conscious effort by popular singers and composers to simulate the effects of *folk songs* in their BALLADS and protest SONGS. See BALLAD and FOLK BALLAD.

Foot: In PROSODY the unit of RHYTHM in a VERSE, whether QUANTITATIVE or ACCENTUAL-SYLLABIC. The concept of *foot* and the names by which the various *feet* are known in English PROSODY are borrowings from CLASSICAL PROSODY, which has only QUANTITATIVE VERSE. The result has been substantial confusion. Most English prosodists consider the fundamental character of regular English VERSE (as opposed to OLD ENGLISH VERSE or experimental VERSE) to be a RHYTHM consisting of units of one accented syllable and one or more unaccented syllables, arranged in various patterns. These units are called *feet*. The VERSE usually consists of definite numbers of specific *feet*. The most common English *feet* are:

IAMBUS: ˘ ´ , as in "return"

TROCHEE: ´ ˘ , as in "double"

ANAPEST: ˘ ˘ ´ , as in "contravene"

DACTYL: ´ ˘ ˘ , as in "merrily"

SPONDEE: ´ ´ , as in "football"

The PYRRHIC: ˘ ˘ , as in "the séa/son óf/mists", is usually included although some prosodists deny it a place in English VERSE, believing that an accented syllable must always be present in a *foot*.

Other *feet* than these are sometimes used in English VERSE, most of them being of CLASSICAL origin and occurring sporadically in English and frequently appearing to result from, or at last to be describable as, SUBSTITUTION when they do occur. Among them are:

AMPHIBRACH: ˘ ´ ˘ , as in "arrangement"

AMPHIMACHER: ´ ˘ ´ , as in "altitude"

ANTIBACCHIUS: ´ ´ ˘ , as in "high mountain"

BACCHIUS: ˘ ´ ´ , as in "above board"

CHORIAMBUS: ´ ˘ ˘ ´ , as in "year upon year"

PAEON: ´ ˘ ˘ ˘, as in "vegetable," although the accent may occupy any one of the four possible positions.

See METER, SCANSION.

Forgeries, Literary: The plagiarist tries to get the world to accept as his own what someone else has written. The literary forger tries to make the world accept as the genuine writing of another what he has himself composed. His motive may be to supply authority for some religious or political doctrine or scheme, or it may be to cater to some prevailing literary demand (as when spurious BALLADS were composed in the eighteenth century in response to the romantic interest in old BALLADS), or it may be, as Bacon would say, "for the love of the lie itself." *Literary forgeries* seem to be numerous in all countries and in all ages. A book of nearly 300 pages by J. A. Farrer gives accounts of many famous *literary forgeries,* yet, as Andrew Lang says, several additional volumes would be needed to make the account of known forgeries complete. It is possible here to call attention to but a few cases.

The Greek statesman, Solon, inserted forged verses in the revered *Iliad* to further his political purposes. A forged "diary" of a supposed soldier in the Trojan War, Dares the Phrygian, actually composed by some Roman about the fourth century after Christ, had the effect of turning the sympathy of European peoples from the Greeks to the Trojans and of supplying an account of the war which for over a thousand years was accepted as more "authentic" than Homer's. In addition it supplied the kernel for what developed into one of the most famous love stories of all time, that of Troilus and Cressida. A famous Italian scholar, Carlo Sigonio, about 1582 composed what pretended to be the lost *Consolatio* of Cicero. The imitation was so clever and the genuineness of the document so effectively argued by

Sigonio himself that although there was always some doubt, it was not till 200 years later that the facts were discovered.

In English literary history an example is afforded by the tragic story of Thomas Chatterton (1752–1770), the "boy poet," who wrote "faked" POEMS and prose pieces supposed to have been written by a fifteenth-century priest. Chatterton was only twelve years old when he began his forgeries, but his imitation of medieval English was so clever and his actual poetic gifts were so high that his efforts attracted wide attention before his suicide at the age of eighteen. About the same time came another famous case of an effort to supply the current romantic interest in the medieval and the primitive with supposedly ancient pieces of literature, James Macpherson's "Ossianic" poems (1760–1765). Macpherson seems to have made some use of genuine Celtic tradition but in the main to have composed himself the epic *Fingal* which he claimed had been written in the third century by Ossian, son of Fingal. Macpherson's public was sharply divided between those who accepted this "discovery" as genuine and those who, like Doctor Johnson, denounced him as an imposter. The episode is referred to as the OSSIANIC CONTROVERSY.

Just as it is not easy for editors and publishers to detect all plagiarized writing presented to them, so it is difficult for them to avoid being exploited by literary forgers, who sometimes mix the authentic and the spurious so cleverly that not only the editors and publishers, but the general public and the professional critics are deceived. And this is as true of the twentieth century as of the eighteenth. See PLAGIARISM.

Form: A term used in CRITICISM to designate the organization of the elements of a work of art in relation to its total EFFECT. VERSE *form* refers to the organization of rhythmic units in a line. STANZA *form* refers to the organization of the VERSES. The *form* of the IMAGES refers to the interrelationships existing among the IMAGES in a work. The *form* of the ideas refers to the organization or structure of thought in the work.

In a common division, critics distinguish between *form* and content, *form* being the pattern or STRUCTURE or organization which is employed to give expression to the content. A similar distinction is often made between "conventional" *form* and organic *form*. This is the difference between what Coleridge called "mechanic" *form* and *form* that "is innate; it shapes, as it develops, itself from within, and the fullness of its development is one and the same with the perfection of its outward form." Another way of expressing this difference is to think of "conventional" *form* as representing an ideal pattern or shape which precedes the content and meaning of the work and of organic *form* as representing a pattern or shape that develops as it is because of the content and meaning of the work. "Conventional" *form* presupposes certain characteristics of organization or pattern which must be present in the work and which are used as tests for the ultimate merit of the work as art—the chief one usually being UNITY. Organic *form* asserts that each poem has, as Herbert Read has said, "its own inherent laws, originating with its very invention and fusing in one vital unity both structure and content."

Form is also used to designate the common attributes that distinguish one GENRE from another. In this sense *form* becomes an ABSTRACT TERM describing not one work but the commonly held qualities of many. This abstract *form* in NEO-CLASSIC periods tends to become a legislative device, a congeries of "rules" to be followed. See STRUCTURE, GENRE.

Formal Criticism: CRITICISM which examines a work of art in terms of the characteristics of the type or GENRE to which it belongs. See CRITICISM, TYPES OF; FORM.

Formal Essay: A serious, dignified, logically organized ESSAY, written to inform or persuade. See ESSAY.

Formula: A hackneyed sequence of events typical of a number of instances in some popular form of writing. "Low budget" motion pictures with similar PLOTS are said to follow a *formula*. In dramatic series in television a *formula* is almost always present and easily recognizable. Many DETECTIVE STORIES and WESTERN STORIES are written to *formula*, in that the same ingredients show up in much the same relationships in their PLOTS. The number of PLOTS is limited, however, and the implicit criticism of triteness in the term *formula* is probably as much a condemnation of inartistic execution as it is of stereotyped PLOT.

Foul Copy: Manuscript that has already been used for typesetting by a printer. It bears printer's marks, editor's queries, and frequently spike holes, ink stains, and fingerprints, and occasionally authors' blasphemies against editors.

Foul Proof: Marked printer's proof, from which corrections have been made. See FOUL COPY.

Four Senses of Interpretation: The levels frequently used in interpreting Scriptural and allegorical materials; they are the literal, the allegorical, the moral or tropological, and the spiritual or anagogical. See ANAGOGE.

"Fourteeners":   A VERSE FORM consisting of fourteen syllables arranged in IAMBIC feet. George Chapman, for instance, has a translation of the *Iliad* in this meter, but in recent years the form has fallen into disuse. See "POULTER'S MEASURE."

Fourth Wall: The invisible wall of a room through which the audience witnesses the action occurring on a STAGE designed as a room with four walls and a ceiling, the *fourth wall* being imagined to be just behind the CURTAIN. One of the most striking uses of the *fourth wall* was in William Gillette's play *Sherlock Holmes*. In one scene, when Holmes is sealed in a room, he taps the walls and continues tapping the *fourth wall* while the sound effects of the tapping continue without interruption. See BOX SET.

Framework-story: A STORY within a narrative setting or *framework*, a STORY within a STORY. This is a CONVENTION frequently used in classical and modern writing. Perhaps the best known examples are found in the *Arabian Nights*, the *Decameron*, and the *Canterbury Tales*. Chaucer, for example, introduced in his Prologue a group of people making a pilgrimage. We are told something about each of his characters, how they meet at the Tabard Inn, and how they proceed on their journey. This general setting may be thought of as the *framework;* the stories which the various pilgrims tell along the way are stories within the general *framework*, or *framework-stories*. The extent to which the *framework* becomes an actual PLOT within which other PLOTS are inserted varies greatly. In the *Decameron* the tellers of the tales assemble and talk, and there is no PLOT in the *framework*. In the *Canterbury Tales* there is a PLOT in the *framework*, although a very limited one. In a work like *Moby-Dick*, in which the NARRATOR participates in an action within which the story of Ahab's quest for the whale occurs, both *framework* and *framework-story* are inextricably interwoven.

Franco-Norman: A term applied to material written in England shortly after the Norman Conquest by Normans or persons of Norman descent using the Norman DIALECT of French. See ANGLO-NORMAN (LANGUAGE).

Free Verse: POETRY that is based on the irregular rhythmic CADENCE of the recurrence, with variations, of phrases, images, and syntactical patterns rather than the conventional use of METER. RHYME may or may not be present in *free verse*, but when it is, it is used with great freedom. In conventional VERSE the unit is the FOOT, or the line; in *free verse* the units are larger, sometimes being paragraphs or STROPHES. If the *free verse* unit is the line, as it is in Whitman, the line is determined by qualities of RHYTHM and thought rather than FEET or syllabic count.

Such use of CADENCE as a basis for POETRY is very old. The poetry of the Bible, particularly in the King James Version, which attempts to approximate the Hebrew CADENCES, rests on CADENCE and PARALLELISM. *The Psalms* and *The Song of Solomon* are noted examples of *free verse*. Milton sometimes substituted rhythmically constructed VERSE paragraphs for metrically regular lines, notably in the CHORUSES of *Samson Agonistes,* as this example shows:

> But patience is more oft the exercise
> Of Saints, the trial of thir fortitude,
> Making them each his own Deliver,
> And Victor over all
> That tyranny or fortune can inflict.

Walt Whitman's *Leaves of Grass* was a major experiment in cadenced rather than metrical VERSIFICATION. The following lines are typical:

> All truths wait in all things,
> They neither hasten their own delivery nor resist it,
> They do not need the obstetric forceps of the surgeon.

Matthew Arnold sometimes used *free verse,* notably in "Dover Beach." But it was the French poets of the late nineteenth century —Rimbaud, Laforgue, Vielé-Griffin, and others—who, in their revolt against the tyranny of strict French VERSIFICATION, established the *vers libre* movement, from which the name *free verse* comes.

Freudianism

In the twentieth century *free verse* has had widespread usage by most poets, of whom Rilke, St.-John Perse, T. S. Eliot, Ezra Pound, Carl Sandburg, and William Carlos Williams are representative. Such a list indicates the great variety of subject matter, effect, and TONE that is possible in *free verse,* and shows that it is much less a rebellion against traditional English METRICS than a modification and extension of the resources of our language.

French Forms: (Sometimes referred to as the FIXED POETIC FORMS.) A name given to certain definitely prescribed VERSE patterns which originated in France largely during the time of the TROUBADOURS. The more usual *French forms* are: BALLADE, CHANT ROYAL, PANTOUM, RONDEAU, RONDEL, ROUNDEL, SESTINA, TRIOLET, and VILLANELLE. These are all explained in their proper places in this Handbook.

Freudianism: The psychological doctrines advanced by Sigmund Freud and his disciples. In Freud's system the great source of psychic energy is in the unconscious, which influences every action but through forces and means not subject to recall or understanding by normal processes. The mind has three major areas of activity: the id, which is in the unconscious and which is a reservoir of instinctual impulses, and works always for the gratification of its instincts (primarily sexual) through the pleasure principle; the superego, which is an internal censor bringing social pressures—reality—to bear upon the id; and the ego, which is the part of the id that is modified by contact with the social world. The ego, which is consciousness, must always mediate among the demands of social pressure or reality, the libidinal demands for satisfaction arising from the id, and the claims of the superego. A mature ego conforms to the reality principle, i.e., the denial of immediate pleasure to avoid painful consequences or to make gratification possible later. Furthermore, the ego has various defense mechanisms, in addition to repression and sublimation, with which to protect itself against the demands of the id.

Although Freud himself was most interested in the pathological aspects of psychoanalysis, the schema of the human mind which he unfolded has had incalculable influence on almost all literary forms and practically all writers in the twentieth century. The emphasis on the unconscious with its hidden springs of motivation, the drama of the eternal conflict of id, ego, and superego, and the PLOT situa-

235

tions inherent in relationships such as those in the OEDIPUS COMPLEX —all have been grist for the mills of the creative mind as well as instruments for the critical faculty. Biographers have tried to unlock the mysteries of creative personalities, as Marie Bonaparte did in *The Life and Works of Edgar Allan Poe*. Critics have seen character relationships in literary works in new lights, as Ernest Jones did in *Hamlet and Oedipus*. Imaginative overviews of literary history colored by psychoanalytical assumptions have been taken, as Leslie Fiedler did in *Love and Death in the American Novel*. Freud and his disciples, whether understood or misunderstood, used properly or improperly, have in their "depth psychology" proved a fructifying force in contemporary literature.

Freytag's Pyramid: A diagrammatic outline of the STRUCTURE of a five-act TRAGEDY, given by Gustav Freytag in *Technik des Dramas* (1863):

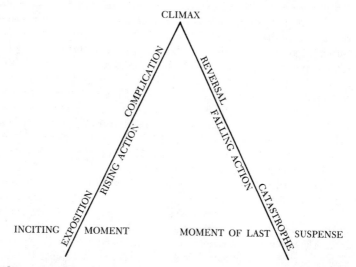

This pyramid has been widely accepted as a means of getting at the PLOT STRUCTURE of many kinds of fiction in addition to DRAMA. See appropriate entries for the terms on the pyramid, PLOT, and DRAMATIC STRUCTURE.

Frontier Literature: In America, writing done by and on the frontier or having as its subject the frontier and frontier life. Up to 1890, when the free lands had all been pretty generally claimed, one aspect of American history was the steady westward movement of the frontier. Cooper, for example, could write of the frontier as being in New York State; Brackenridge in *Modern Chivalry* saw the wilds of Pennsylvania as the outer edge of cultivation; Simms in his border romances could see Georgia and Alabama as untamed wildernesses. Mark Twain in *Roughing It* could picture a primitive West. The extent to which this westward moving frontier colored and shaped American thought and life and the extent to which its passing marked a sharp turn in the character of the American are matters of great debate among historians and literary scholars. But whatever one may think of Frederick Turner's much-praised and often-attacked thesis that the frontier has been the dominant influence in American history, there is little question that it has consistently found literary expression in a virile, humorous, often crude body of SONGS, TALES, and books which have been marked by a realistic view of life, a sanguine contemplation of violence, and an immense gusto. Much of the writing of this frontier was subliterary, confined to oral tradition and to newspapers, but it kept constantly alive in America a hearty HUMOR and a healthy REALISM, even in the face of the GENTEEL TRADITION. Important writers in the frontier tradition have been Timothy Flint, Augustus Baldwin Longstreet, Joseph Glover Baldwin, Artemus Ward, Caroline Kirkland, Joseph Kirkland, Bret Harte, Mark Twain, and Hamlin Garland. Whether the ultimate effect of the frontier on writers growing up in it was good or bad was a question that precipitated one of the most bitter critical controversies in American literary history, that between Van Wyck Brooks and Bernard De Voto over Brooks' thesis that the frontier was one of the stifling and frustrating influences that bridled Mark Twain's genius.

Fundamental Image: A central or controlling figure around which a work is organized. When the controlling figure is a METAPHOR, it is called a CONTROLLING IMAGE, a device often used in METAPHYSICAL VERSE. *Fundamental image* is used to designate the simpler, non-metaphorical use of some important aspect or feature of an object being described or discussed. This reduction of the complex whole to one main feature or unifying principle simplifies and focuses the description in such a way as to make for clearness. The famous description of the battle of Waterloo, in which Victor Hugo employed the outline of the letter A as illustrative of the position of the various armies, is a notable example of the clarifying value of the *fundamental image*. See CONTROLLING IMAGE.

Fustian: A coarse, thick, short-napped cotton cloth, usually dyed some dark color to resemble velveteen. By extension, it is used as a derogatory term for overblown, pretentious, empty speech or writing. Thomas Heywood, in *Faire Maid of the Exchange* (Act II, Sc. 3), speaks of "Some scurvy quaint collection of *fustian* phrases, and uplandish words."

G

Gaelic Movement: A movement begun late in the nineteenth century, especially as embodied in the Gaelic League, founded by Douglas Hyde in 1893, which aimed at the preservation of the Gaelic language. Celtic speech had been gradually giving way to English since the seventeenth century and had not been permitted in the new schools established in the middle of the nineteenth century. The *Gaelic Movement* attempted to foster the production of a new native Irish literature in Gaelic. Hyde himself wrote plays in Gaelic. Though the movement attracted wide attention and some controversy, it has not been notably successful in stopping the advance of English as a spoken language in Ireland, and on the literary side has been overshadowed by the IRISH LITERARY MOVEMENT, which encouraged the use of English in creating a new Irish literature exploiting Irish materials. See CELTIC RENAISSANCE.

Gallicism: A word or phrase or idiom characteristic of the French language, or a custom or turn of thought suggestive of the French people. Thus when an Englishman uses the phrase "reason for existence" or "stroke of policy," he is probably imitating the French idiomatic phrases *raison d'être* and *coup d'état*. The term is applied to any borrowing from the French language in which the borrower stops short of using the French word without disguise. Although *Gallicisms* have obviously enriched and enlivened the language, the danger is that they will be used as a form of affectation.

Gasconade: Since the natives of Gascony (in France) were considered inveterate boasters, *gasconade* came to be used to mean bravado or boastful talk. Vainglorious FICTION may be called *gas-conade*.

Gathering: A group of leaves in a book cut from a single printer's sheet after it has been folded. A FOLIO makes a *gathering* of two leaves or four pages, a QUARTO one of four leaves or eight pages (see BOOK SIZES). A *gathering* is often called a SIGNATURE, from the marking placed on its first page. Modern printers use *gathering* to mean the process by which SIGNATURES or *gatherings* are assembled to make a book; they rarely use it in the sense of SIGNATURE. See SIGNATURE.

General Terms: A *general term* refers to a group, a class, a type, whereas a SPECIFIC WORD refers to a member of that group, class, or type. Obviously the distinction between *general terms* and SPECIFIC WORDS is relative, not absolute. For example, "dog" is SPECIFIC if compared to "animal," but *general* if compared to "chihuahua," while "chihuahua" is SPECIFIC if compared to "dog," but *general* if compared to "Sancho," one particular chihuahua.

Genre: A term used in literary criticism to designate the distinct types or categories into which literary works are grouped according to FORM or technique or, sometimes, subject matter. The term comes from French, where it means "kind" or "type." In its customary application, it is used loosely, since the varieties of literary "kinds" and the principles on which they are made are numerous. The traditional *genres* include such "kinds" as TRAGEDY, COMEDY, EPIC, LYRIC, PASTORAL. Today a division of literature into *genres* would also include NOVEL, SHORT STORY, ESSAY, and, perhaps, RADIO or TELEVISION PLAY. The difficulty resulting from the loose use of the term is easily illustrated: NOVEL designates a *genre*, but so does PICARESQUE NOVEL; LYRIC designates a *genre*, but so does SONNET, as do both ELEGY and PASTORAL ELEGY.

Genre classification implies that there are groups of formal or technical characteristics existing among works of the same "kind" regardless of time or place of composition, author, or subject matter; and that these characteristics, when they define a particular group of works, are of basic significance in talking about literary art. Prior to the ROMANTIC AGE in England, there was a tendency to assume that literary "kinds" had an ideal existence and obeyed "laws of kind," these laws being criteria by which works could be judged.

Genteel Comedy

In the ROMANTIC AGE, *genre* distinctions were often looked upon merely as restatements of CONVENTIONS and were suspect. Today critics frequently regard *genre* distinctions as useful descriptive devices but rather arbitrary ones. See FORM.

In painting, the term *genre* is applied to works that depict ordinary, everyday life in realistic terms. By extension, the term is sometimes used in literary criticism to designate a poem that deals with commonplace or homely situations in subdued tones. By this usage, Whittier's "Snow-Bound" is often called "a *genre* study."

Genteel Comedy: A term employed by Addison to characterize such early eighteenth-century COMEDY as Cibber's *The Careless Husband*. This COMEDY was a sort of continuation of the Restoration COMEDY OF MANNERS, adapted to the polite, genteel manners of the age of Anne. Compared with Restoration COMEDY, the moral tone was higher, the motives of the characters more artificial, the WIT less brilliant, and the general ATMOSPHERE sentimentalized.

Genteel Tradition: A tradition of correctness and conventionality in American writing in the latter part of the nineteenth and the early part of the twentieth centuries. It was largely, although not exclusively, associated with New England. Both REALISM and NATURALISM were in differing ways reactions against the *Genteel Tradition*. Among its leading figures were R. H. Stoddard, Bayard Taylor, E. C. Stedman, T. B. Aldrich, and E. R. Sill. See BRAHMINS.

Georgian: Pertaining to the reigns of the four Georges (1714–1830). The romantic poets from Wordsworth to Keats have been called *"Georgians"* in this sense. A group of minor poets including Thomas Lovell Beddoes, W. M. Praed, and Thomas Hood are sometimes styled the "second *Georgian* school," as opposed to the earlier group. They are looked upon as representing a transition from the Romantic to the Victorian poets. From 1912 to 1922 there appeared five anthologies of modern verse entitled *Georgian Poetry*, *Georgian* here referring to the reign of George V (1910–1936). These volumes, according to their editor, E. H. Marsh, reflect a belief that English poetry was "once again putting on new strength and beauty" and beginning a new *"Georgian"* period. W. W. Gibson, Rupert Brooke, John Masefield, Walter de la Mare, and D. H. Lawrence are representative of the poets included. The term is, in fact, so varied in its applications as to be of questionable usefulness.

Georgic: A POEM about farming activities and the practical aspects of rustic life; so called from Virgil's *Georgics*.

Gest: An old word occasionally found in English, especially in literary titles from the medieval period, meaning a TALE of war or adventure, as the *Gest Historiale of the Destruction of Troy* (fourteenth century). The word is probably borrowed from the more common word in Old French, *geste*, as in the CHANSON DE GESTE. The corresponding Latin word appears in a somewhat similar sense in the title of the famous collection of STORIES written in Latin about 1250, the *Gesta Romanorum*, "deeds of the Romans."

Gestalt: A configuration of physical, biological, or psychological phenomena so constructed and interrelated that the whole possesses properties not derivable from its parts or their simple sum. As Herbert Read has suggested, such a theory is congenial to Coleridge's view of a work of art. The term comes from *Gestalt* psychology. Some literary critics, among them Herbert J. Muller, see in it a concept that allows concrete experience to precede logical analysis. The *Gestalt* critic sees all the elements of any work of art or literature as being variables with values that depend on their position in the "configuration" and on its total effect.

Ghost-writer: One who does journalistic writing which is published under the name of another. Businessmen, artists, athletes—in fact almost anyone who is much in the public eye but who is also either unskilled or uninterested in writing—often allow their names to be attached to articles and stories relating to their special fields and written by journalists employed for the purpose. *Ghost-writing* is more frequently employed in the preparation of newspaper and MAGAZINE ARTICLES than in the writing of books.

Gift-Books: Miscellaneous collections of literary materials—SHORT STORIES, ESSAYS, POETRY—published annually in book form for purchase as gifts. They were popular in England and America in the nineteenth century. Their value in American literary history has been great. See ANNUALS.

Gleeman: A musical entertainer among the Anglo-Saxons. *Gleemen* were usually traveling professionals who recited POETRY (especially STORIES) composed by others, though some of them were original poets. They were sometimes attached to kings' courts, but occupied a less dignified and permanent position than the SCOP. In the main, the SCOP composed and the *gleeman* sang or recited the SCOP's compositions, to the accompaniment of the harp or other instrument. Some writers, however, both medieval and modern, use the term loosely for any kind of medieval composer or reciter.

Gloss: An explanation. A hard word in a text might be explained by a marginal or interlinear word or phrase, usually in a more familiar language. Thus Greek manuscripts were "glossed" by Latin copyists and readers who gave the Latin word or phrase equivalent to the difficult one in Greek. Similar bilingual *glosses* were inserted in medieval manuscripts by scribes who would explain Latin words by native, vernacular words. Some of the earliest examples of written Irish, for example, are found in the margins and between the lines of Latin manuscripts written in the early Middle Ages. Extended explanatory and interpretative comment on medieval Scriptural texts were called *glosses*. They have been used extensively in interpreting medieval literature in recent years. Later the word came to have a still broader use in E. K.'s *"Gloss"* to Spenser's *The Shepheardes Calendar* (1579), which undertakes not only to explain the author's purpose and to comment on the degree of his success, but also to supply "notes" explaining difficult words and phrases and giving miscellaneous "learned" comments. The marginal *gloss* which Coleridge supplied in 1817 for his early *Rime of the Ancient Mariner* is little more than a summary of the story, slightly colored by the poet's effort to clarify the meaning.

The word is sometimes used in a bad sense, as when to *"gloss"* a passage means to misinterpret it and "to *gloss* over" is used in the sense of "explain away" or excuse. "Glossaries" developed from the habit of collecting *glosses* into lists.

Gnomic: Aphoristic, moralistic, sententious, from *gnome*, a pithy *Greek* poem that expressed a general truth wittily. The *"Gnomic* Poets" of ancient Greece (sixth century B.C.) arranged their wise sayings in series of MAXIMS; hence the term *gnomic* was applied to all poetry which dealt in a sententious way with ethical questions, such as the "wisdom" poetry of the Bible, the Latin *sententiae*, the Saemundian *Edda*, and the *gnomic* verses in Old English. Although more properly applied to a style of POETRY, as to some of the VERSE of Francis Quarles, the prose style of Bacon's early essays is also called *gnomic* when marked by the use of APHORISMS.

Goliardic Verse: Lilting Latin VERSE, usually satiric, composed by university students and wandering scholars in Germany, France, and England in the twelfth and thirteenth centuries. *Goliardic verse* celebrated wine, women, and song; was often licentious; and was marked by irreverent attacks on church and clergy. Its dominant theme was CARPE DIEM. Its name comes from a legendary bishop and "archpoet," Golias. Another of the Goliardic poets was Walter Map, to whom more verses have been attributed than he could possibly have written.

Gongorism: A highly affected style taking its name from Luis de Gongóra y Argote, a Spanish poet (1561–1627), whose writings exhibited in a high degree the various qualities characteristic of the stylistic extravagances of the time, such as the introduction of new words (NEOLOGISMS), innovations in grammar, BOMBAST, PUNS, PARADOXES, CONCEITS, and obscurity. It reflects both cultism (affected language) and conceptism (strained figures, obscure references). It has some of the qualities of EUPHUISM. See MARINISM, CONCEIT.

Gothic: Though the Goths were a single Germanic tribe of ancient and early medieval times, the meaning of *Gothic* was broadened to signify Teutonic or Germanic and, later, "medieval" in general. In architecture, *Gothic*, though it may mean any style not classic, is more specifically applied to the style which succeeded the Romanesque in Western Europe, flourishing from the twelfth to the sixteenth centuries. It is marked by the pointed arch and vault, a tendency to vertical effects (suggesting aspiration), stained windows (mystery), slender spires, flying buttresses, intricate traceries, and especially by wealth and variety of detail and flexibility of spirit. Applied to literature the term was used by the eighteenth-century NEO-CLASSICISTS as synonymous with "barbaric" to indicate anything which offended their CLASSIC tastes. Addison said that both in architecture and literature those who were unable to achieve the CLASSIC graces of simplicity and dignity and UNITY resorted to the use of foreign ornaments, "all the extravagances of an irregular fancy." The romanticists of the next generation, however, looked with favor upon the *Gothic;* to them it suggested whatever was medieval, natural, primitive, wild, free, authentic, romantic. Indeed, they praised such writers as Shakespeare and Spenser because of their *Gothic* elements—variety, richness, mystery, aspiration. Later vigorous celebrators of the *Gothic* were John Ruskin and Walter Pater. See GOTHIC NOVEL.

Gothic Novel: A form of NOVEL in which magic, mystery, and chivalry are the chief characteristics. Horrors abound: one may expect a suit of armor suddenly to come to life, while ghosts, clanking chains, and charnal houses impart an uncanny atmosphere of terror. Although anticipations of the *Gothic novel* appear in Smollett (esp. in *Ferdinand Count Fathom,* 1753), Horace Walpole was the real originator, his famous *Castle of Otranto* (1764) being the first. Its setting is in a medieval castle (hence the term "Gothic") which has long underground passages, trap doors, dark stairways, and mysterious rooms whose doors slam unexpectedly. William Beckford's *Vathek, an Arabian Tale* (1786) added the element of Oriental luxury and magnificence to the species. Mrs. Anne Radcliffe's five romances (1789–1797), especially *The Mysteries of Udolpho,* added to the popularity of the form. Her emphasis upon SETTING and STORY rather than upon character-delineation became conventional, as did the types of characters she employed. Succeeding writers who produced Gothic romances include: Matthew ("Monk") Lewis, William Godwin, and Mary Wollstonecraft Shelley, whose *Frankenstein* is a striking performance in the tradition. The form spread to practically every European literature, being especially popular in Germany. In America the type was cultivated early by Charles Brockden Brown. The *Gothic novels* are not only of interest in themselves but have exerted a significant influence upon other forms. This influence made itself felt in the poetry of the Romantic period, as in Coleridge's *Christabel* and *Kubla Khan,* Wordsworth's *Guilt and Sorrow,* Byron's *Giaour,* and Keats' *Eve of St. Agnes.* Some of the ROMANCES were dramatized, and some DRAMAS not based on RO-MANCES, like Byron's *Manfred* and Morton's *Speed the Plough,* have *Gothic* elements. The novels of Scott, Charlotte Brontë, and others, as well as the mystery and horror type of SHORT STORY exploited by Poe and his successors, contain materials and devices traceable to the *Gothic novel.* The term *Gothic novel* is today often applied to works which lack the Gothic setting or the medieval atmosphere but which attempt to create the same ATMOSPHERE of brooding and unknown terror which the true *Gothic novel* does, as Daphne du Maurier's *Rebecca* does. It is also applied to a host of currently popular TALES of "damsels in distress" in strange and terrifying locales—a type ridiculed as early as Jane Austen's *Northanger Abbey*.

"Graveyard School":   A phrase used to designate a group of eighteenth-century poets who wrote long POEMS on death and immortality. The "graveyard" poetry was related to early stages of the English romantic movement. The graveyard poets tried to get the atmosphere of "pleasing gloom" by realistic efforts to call up not only the horrors of death but the very "odor of the charnel house." An early exemplar or forerunner of the school was Thomas Parnell, whose *Night-Piece on Death* (1722) not only anticipates some of the sentiment of Gray's famous *Elegy Written in a Country Churchyard* (1751)—the most famous poem produced by the group— but whose "long palls, drawn hearses, cover'd steeds, and plumes of black" show an approach to the phraseology of Robert Blair's *The Grave* (1743), one of the most typical poems of the movement, and of the *Night-Thoughts* (1745) of Edward Young, an influential writer of melancholy verse. These last two writers, says W. L. Phelps, reflect "the joy of gloom, the fondness for bathing one's temples in the dank night air and the musical delight of the screech owl's shriek." While the *graveyard school* was philosophically contemplating immortality, the lasting effect of their POETRY, with the exception of a few pieces such as Gray's *Elegy*, has been one element in the GOTHIC aspect of ROMANTICISM. In America the poetry of the *graveyard school* was reflected in Philip Freneau's "The House of Night" (1779) and most notably in William Cullen Bryant's famous "Thanatopsis" (1817).

Great Awakening, The: A famed religious revival in America between 1735 and 1750. See AWAKENING, THE GREAT.

Grotesque: A term applied to a decorative art in sculpture, painting, and architecture, characterized by fantastic representations of human and animal forms often combined into formal distortions of the natural to the point of comic absurdity, ridiculous ugliness, or ludicrous CARICATURE. It was so named after the ancient paintings and decorations found in the underground chambers (*grotte*) of Roman ruins. By extension, *grotesque* is applied to anything having the qualities of *grotesque* art: bizarre, incongruous, ugly, unnatural, fantastic, abnormal.

In the twentieth century, *grotesque* has come to have special literary meanings. Critics use "the *grotesque*" to refer to special types of writing, to kinds of fictional CHARACTERS, and to subject matters. The interest in the *grotesque* is usually considered an outgrowth of contemporary interest in the irrational, distrust of any cosmic order, and frustration at man's lot in the universe. In this sense, *grotesque* is the merging of the comic and tragic, resulting from our loss of faith in the moral universe essential to TRAGEDY and in a rational social order essential to COMEDY. Where nineteenth-century critics like Walter Bagehot saw the *grotesque* as a deplorable variation from the normal, Thomas Mann sees it as the "most genuine style" for the modern world and the "only guise in which the sublime may appear" now. Flannery O'Connor seems to mean the same thing when she calls the *grotesque* character "man forced to meet the extremes of his own nature."

Although German writers have practiced the *grotesque* with distinction, notably Thomas Mann and Günter Grass, William Van O'Connor seems to have been correct when he called the *grotesque* an American GENRE. Sherwood Anderson called his *Winesburg, Ohio* "The Book of the Grotesque," and defined a *grotesque* character as a person who "took one of the [many] truths to himself, called it his truth, and tried to live by it." Such a person, Anderson asserted, "became a grotesque and the truth he embraced a falsehood." But the *grotesque* can have other origins and objectives than the psychological. Whenever in modern fiction CHARACTERS appear who are either physically or spiritually deformed and perform actions that are clearly intended by the author to be abnormal, the work can be called *grotesque*. It may be used for allegorical statement, as Flannery O'Connor uses it in her NOVELS and SHORT STORIES. It may exist for comic purposes, as it does in the work of Eudora Welty. It may be the expression of a deep moral seriousness, as it is in the NOVELS and SHORT STORIES of William Faulkner. It may make a comment on man as an animal, in works like Frank Norris' *McTeague* and *Vandover and the Brute*. It may be used for SATIRE, as Nathanael West uses it in his NOVELS. It may be a basis for social commentary, as it is in the works of Erskine Caldwell. Clearly, the *grotesque* is a mode of writing compatible with the spirit of this century and amenable to many kinds of uses.

Grub Street: Because struggling writers and literary "hacks" lived in Grub Street in London (now Milton Street), the phrase *Grub Street,* since the eighteenth century, has meant either the "tribe" of poor writers living there or the qualities which characterized such authors. *Grub Street* poets were bitterly attacked by Pope, and *Grub Street* has been used contemptuously by Doctor Johnson, Byron, and others to suggest "literary trash."

Grundy, Mrs.: A CHARACTER from Thomas Morton's play *Speed the Plough*, who does not actually appear in the play but of whose judgments everyone in the play is very much afraid. The question "What will *Mrs. Grundy* say?" points to her symbolic value as a strict upholder of social conventions and an intolerant advocate of pointless propriety.

H

Hagiography: The lives of the saints, particularly those devoted to the glorification of one or another Irish or British saint. Hence, by extension, a BIOGRAPHY which greatly overpraises the virtues of its subject. See BIOGRAPHY.

Haiku (sometimes written **Hokku**): A form of Japanese POETRY which states in three lines of five, seven, and five syllables a clear picture designed to arouse a distinct emotion and suggest a specific spiritual insight. Since the Second World War, a number of American writers have been interested in Japanese poetry. Earlier in the century it was a formative influence on the IMAGISTS. See SYLLABIC VERSE.

Half-Rhyme: Imperfect RHYME, the result usually of CONSONANCE, but occasionally of ASSONANCE. See RHYME, SLANT RHYME, ASSONANCE, CONSONANCE.

Hamartia: The "great error or frailty" through which the fortunes of the HERO of a TRAGEDY are reversed. Aristotle asserts that the PROTAGONIST of a TRAGEDY should be "a man who is not eminently good or just, yet whose misfortune is brought about not by vice or depravity, but by some error or frailty." This *hamartia*, often called the TRAGIC FLAW, may be caused by bad judgment, bad character, inherited weakness, or any of several other possible causes of error; it must, however, express itself through a definite action, or failure to perform a definite action. See TRAGEDY.

Harlequinade: A play in which a "harlequin" or buffoon stars. See COMMEDIA DELL' ARTE, PANTOMIME.

Hartford Wits: A group of Connecticut writers, many of whom were graduates of Yale, active about the period of the American Revolution. The three most prominent were Joel Barlow, Timothy Dwight, and John Trumbull; some others in the group were Richard Alsop, Theodore Dwight, and Lemuel Hopkins. Naturally conservative in politics and philosophy, these men were, as well, conservative in their literary models, following Addison and Pope, the two literary gods of their century. Some of the best-known works of these writers are Trumbull's *M'Fingal*, Dwight"s *Conquest of Canaan* (an epic poem of eleven books mingling Christian and Revolutionary history), and Barlow's *Columbiad*, planned as another American EPIC, a ten-book recitation of the glories of the future America as revealed to Columbus in prison. They are also known as the CONNECTICUT WITS.

Head Rhyme: ALLITERATION; repetition of the same sound at the beginning of two or more words. See ALLITERATION.

Headless Line: A line of VERSE from which an unstressed syllable has been dropped at the beginning. See CATALEXIS.

Hebraism: The attitude toward life which subordinates all other ideals to those of conduct, obedience, and ethical purpose. It is opposed to the Hellenistic conception of life which subordinates everything to the intellectual. The two terms, *Hebraism* and Hellenism, have each taken on a special and limited significance—neither of which is fully fair to the genius of the two peoples—as the result of critical discussion centering about the question of conduct and wisdom in living. In modern literature the most notable discussion of the two conflicting ideals is found in the fourth chapter of Matthew Arnold's *Culture and Anarchy*, where he says:

We may regard this energy driving at practice, this paramount sense of the obligation of duty, self-control, and work, this earnestness in going manfully with the best light we have, as one force. And we may regard the intelligence driving at those ideas which are, after all, the basis of right practice, the ardent sense for all the new and changing combinations of them which man's development brings with it, the indomitable impulse to know and adjust them perfectly, as another force. And these

Hendiadys

two forces we may regard as in some sense rivals,—rivals not by the necessity of their own nature, but as exhibited in man and his history,—and rivals dividing the empire of the world between them. And to give these forces names from the two races of men who have supplied the most signal and splendid manifestations of them, we may call them respectively the forces of Hebraism and Hellenism. Hebraism and Hellenism,—between these points of influence moves our world. . . . The final aim of both Hellenism and Hebraism, as of all great spiritual disciplines, is no doubt the same: man's perfection of salvation. . . . The governing idea of Hellenism is *spontaneity of consciousness:* that of Hebraism, *strictness of conscience.*

Hedge Club: An informal group of Transcendentalists living in or near Boston, headed by Frederick Henry Hedge. See TRANSCENDENTAL CLUB.

Hedonism: A philosophical doctrine that pleasure is the chief good of man. It takes two forms; in one, following the doctrines of the Cyrenaic school of philosophy, founded by Aristippus in the fifth century B.C., the chief good is held to be the gratification of the sensual instincts. In the other, following Epicurus, the absence of pain rather than the gratification of pleasurable impulses is held to be the source of happiness. Today *hedonism* is generally associated with a sensual gratification; its motto might be "Eat, drink, and be merry, for tomorrow we may die" (see CARPE DIEM), and it is held in contrast to the teachings of Epicurus. See EPICUREAN.

Hellenism: The Greek spirit, which manifests itself in the celebration of the intellect and of beauty. See HEBRAISM.

Hemistich: A half-line of VERSE. See -STICH.

Hendecasyllabic Verse: A VERSE of eleven syllables, frequent in Greek and Latin poetry and a standard line in Italian poetry. The form was originated by Catullus. Its English users have been few, chief among them being Tennyson.

Hendiadys: A FIGURE OF SPEECH in which an idea is expressed by giving its two components as though they were independent and connecting them with a coordinating conjunction rather than subordinating one part to the other. "Try and do better" instead of "Try to do better" is an example. The *hendiadys* was common in Greek and Latin writing, but it rarely occurs in formal English.

Heptameter: A line of VERSE consisting of seven FEET. See SCAN-
SION.

Hero or Heroine: The central character (masculine or feminine)
in a work of FICTION or a DRAMA. The terms are applied to the
characters who are the focal points of the readers' or the spectators'
interest, often without reference to the superiority of the moral
qualities of one character over another. Used as a technical term in
describing a work of FICTION, *hero* (or *heroine*) refers to a relationship of character to action; therefore, the more neutral term PRO-
TAGONIST is probably preferable. See PLOT, STRUCTURE, PROTAGO-
NIST.

Heroic Couplet: IAMBIC PENTAMETER lines rhymed in pairs. The
favorite METER of Chaucer—*The Legend of Good Women* is an
instance—this VERSE form did not come into its greatest popularity,
however, until the middle of the seventeenth century (with Waller
and Denham); after which time it was for several years the dominant mode for the POETIC DRAMA. The distinction of having made
first use of the *heroic couplet* in dramatic composition is variously
given to Orrery's *Henry V,* in which it was used throughout, and
Etherege's *The Comical Revenge,* in which it was employed for
most passages of dramatic action. Both of these plays date from
1664. Davenant had as early as 1656 made some use of the *heroic
couplet* in his *Siege of Rhodes.* It was with Dryden, however, that
the form became best known, Dryden using it in such plays as
Tyrannick Love, The Conquest of Granada, and *Aureng-Zebe.* With
Pope the *heroic couplet* became so important and fixed a form—
for various purposes—that its influence dominated English verse for
many years, until the Romanticists dispelled the tradition in their
demand for a new freedom. An example of the *heroic couplet* from
Pope is:

> But when to mischief mortals bend their will,
> How soon they find fit instruments of ill!

In the NEO-CLASSIC PERIOD, the *heroic couplet* was usually made
up of a rhymed pair of END-STOPPED LINES, the *couplet* forming a
short STANZA. The use of marked CAESURAS in the lines and a highly
symmetrical grammatical structure made the *heroic couplet* a form
well adapted to epigrammatic expression and to balanced sentences

marked by symmetry and ANTITHESIS. In the ROMANTIC AGE, poets
like Keats, in *Endymion*, retained rhymed pairs of IAMBIC PENTAM-
ETER lines but abandoned the other restrictions of the *heroic couplet*,
although Byron used and defended Pope's *couplets*.

Heroic Drama: A type of TRAGEDY and TRAGI-COMEDY that developed in England during the RESTORATION. It was characterized by
excessive spectacle, violent emotional conflicts in the main CHAR-
ACTERS, extravagant bombastic DIALOGUE, and EPIC personages as
chief characters. The heroic play usually had its setting in a distant
land such as Mexico, Morocco, or India. Its HERO is constantly torn
between his passion for some lady (more than likely a captive princess
or the daughter of his greatest enemy) and his honor or duty to his
country. If he is able to satisfy both the demands of love and duty,
the play ends happily for HERO and HEROINE and unhappily for the
VILLAIN and villainess. The HEROINE is always a paragon of virtue
and honor, often torn between her loyalty to her VILLAIN-father and
her love for the HERO. The VILLAIN is usually a tyrant and usurper
with an overweening passion for power or else with a base love
for some beautiful and virtuous lady. The villainess is the dark,
violently passionate rival of the HEROINE. The HERO's rival in love
is sometimes the VILLAIN and sometimes the HERO's best friend.
All are unreal, all speak in HYPERBOLE, all rant and rage. Since the
HEROIC COUPLET developed at the same time as the *heroic drama*, the
writers of heroic plays commonly, though not always, wrote in
HEROIC COUPLETS. The action of the play was grand, often revolving
around the conquest of some empire. The scenery used in producing
the heroic play was elaborate.

The influences that combined to produce the *heroic drama* were
the romantic plays of the Jacobeans, especially those of Beaumont
and Fletcher; the development of OPERA in England; and the French
court romances by de Scudéry and La Calprenède, some of which
were brought to England by the court of Charles II. Though elements of the heroic play appear in Davenant's *Siege of Rhodes*
(1656), the Earl of Orrery perhaps wrote the first full-fledged *heroic
drama, The General* (1664). Dryden, however, is the greatest ex-
ponent of the type, his *Conquest of Granada* typifying all that is
best and all that is worst in the species. Elkanah Settle, Nahum
Tate, Nathaniel Lee, Sir Robert Howard, John Crowne, and Thomas
Otway are other playwrights who cultivated the *heroic drama*.
Although the faults of the type were recognized early, the most

brilliant attack being the satirical play of George Villiers, Duke of Buckingham (and others), *The Rehearsal* (1671), the plays flourished until about 1680, and the extravagances that characterized them affected eighteenth-century TRAGEDY.

Heroic Verse: Poetry composed of IAMBIC PENTAMETER feet and rhymed in line-pairs. Also called HEROIC COUPLETS.

Hexameter: A line of six metrical FEET. As a CLASSICAL VERSE FORM in Latin or Greek POETRY, in which languages the *hexameter* was the conventional medium for EPIC and DIDACTIC POETRY, the term was definitely restricted to a set pattern: six feet, the first four of which were DACTYLS or SPONDEES, the fifth almost always a DACTYL (though sometimes a SPONDEE in which case the verse is called spondaic), the sixth a SPONDEE or TROCHEE. True *hexameters* are scarce in English poetry because of the rarity of actual SPONDEES in our language. However, poets writing in English, notably Longfellow in *Evangeline,* have variously modified the CLASSICAL form to adapt it to the exigencies of our language and have left us *hexameters* much less strictly patterned than the CLASSICAL. See ALEXANDRINE, ELEGIACS.

Hiatus: A pause or break between two vowel sounds not separated by a consonant. It is the opposite of ELISION, which prompts the sliding over of one of the vowels, whereas a *hiatus* occurs only when in a break between two words the final vowel of the first and the initial vowel of the second are each carefully enunciated. In logic *hiatus* signifies the omission of one of the logical steps in the process of reasoning.

High Comedy: Pure or serious COMEDY, as contrasted with LOW COMEDY. *High comedy* rests upon an appeal to the intellect and arouses "thoughtful" laughter by exhibiting the inconsistencies and incongruities of human nature and by displaying the follies of social manners. The purpose is not consciously didactic or ethical, though serious purpose is often implicit in the SATIRE which is not infrequently present in *high comedy*. Thoughtful amusement is aimed at. Emotion, especially SENTIMENTALITY, is avoided. If a man makes himself ridiculous by his vanity or ineffective by his stupid conduct or blind adherence to tradition, *high comedy* laughs at him. Some ability to perceive promptly the incongruity exhibited is demanded of the audience, so that *high comedy* has been said to be written for the few. As George Meredith suggests in his essay on *The Idea of Comedy,* care must be taken that the laughter provoked be not derisive but intellectual. An exhibition of poverty, for example, since it ridicules our unfortunate nature instead of our conventional life, is not truly comic. "But when poverty becomes ridiculous" by attempting "to make its rags conceal the bareness in a forlorn effort at decency," or foolishly tries to rival the ostentation of the rich, it becomes a fit theme for comic presentation. Although *high comedy* actually offers plenty of superficial laughter which the average playgoer or reader can enjoy, its higher enjoyment demands a certain intellectual acumen, poise, and philosophic detachment. "Life is a comedy to him who thinks." But the term *high comedy* is used in various senses. In NEO-CLASSIC times a criterion was its appeal to and reflection of the "higher" social class and its observance of DECORUM, as illustrated in Etherege and Congreve. In a broader sense it is applied to some of Shakespeare's plays, like *As You Like It,* and to modern comedies of G. B. Shaw. See COMEDY, COMEDY OF MANNERS, COMEDY OF HUMOURS, REALISTIC COMEDY, COMEDY OF MORALS.

Higher Criticism: A term applied to certain aspects of the intensive study of Biblical texts in the nineteenth century. The *higher criticism* seeks to determine the authorship, date, place of origin, circumstances of composition, author's purpose and intended meaning, and the historical credibility of the various books of the Bible. It is called the *higher criticism* in contrast to the much less common term "lower criticism," which refers to the establishment of the text itself. The *higher criticism* is important in literary study not only for its method but also for its impact on the religious issues of the nineteenth and twentieth centuries.

Historical Criticism: Criticism that examines a work and describes and evaluates it in terms of the social and historical context in which it was produced and the facts of its author's life and of its composition. The historical critic attempts to re-create through the historical process the meaning and the values which the work had for its own time; his objective is not to elucidate the meaning the work has for the present so much as it is to lead the reader in the present into a responsive awareness of the meaning the work had for its own age. The issues defined as the concern of the HIGHER CRITICISM (above) are all matters of concern for the historical critic. See CRITICISM, TYPES OF; and HIGHER CRITICISM.

Historical Fiction: FICTION whose time setting is in some period other than that in which it is written. See HISTORICAL NOVEL.

Historical Novel: A NOVEL which reconstructs a personage, a series of events, a movement, or the spirit of a past age and pays the debt of serious scholarship to the facts of the age being re-created. The classic formula for the *historical novel,* as evolved by Scott and given expression in his numerous prefaces and introductions to the Waverley Novels, calls for an age when two cultures are in conflict, one dying and the other being born; into this cultural conflict, fictional personages are introduced who participate in actual historical events and move among actual personages from history; these fictional characters undergo and give expression to the impact which the historical events had upon people living through them, with the result that a picture of a bygone age is given in personal and immediate terms. *Ivanhoe,* with its disinherited Saxon hero in a Norman world, is a striking example. *Historical novels* which take this task seriously have been called NOVELS OF MANNERS laid in the past.

The extent to which actual historical events of some magnitude must be present, the extent to which actual historic personages must be actors in the STORY, the time which must have elapsed between the events of the STORY and its writing are among the questions to which both historical novelists and critics of the form have given varying answers. There has been little dispute, however, over the responsibility of the historical novelist to give a truthful picture of the age he describes or over the fact that the *historical novel* is often centered in a social context. Two tendencies to depart from the "formula" should be noted: one is "the costume romance," in which history is exploited as a background for a series of adventurous or sexual exploits; the other is the "novel of character" laid in the past, in which the setting and the age are of secondary importance to the representation of a group of characters; *The Scarlet Letter* is a classic example of the latter.

Although writers have combined fiction and history since time began and although literary historians have found adumbrations of the *historical novel* in many forms and works, it required the development of a serious view of history before a serious *historical novel* could develop. This view came in the eighteenth century, and various writers began seriously to attempt works which would correspond to the ideals of the *historical novel,* but it remained for Sir Walter Scott in *Waverley* in 1814 to establish the form. Among his noted successors have been Thackeray, Alexander Dumas, Victor Hugo, Tolstoi, James Fenimore Cooper, Bulwer-Lytton, Charles Reade, Hervey Allen, and Kenneth Roberts. See NOVEL.

History Play: Strictly speaking, any DRAMA whose time setting is in some period other than that in which it is written. It is most widely used, however, as a synonym for CHRONICLE PLAY.

Holograph: A document or manuscript completely handwritten by the author himself. *Holographs* of important literary works not only have very high value for the bibliophile and the collector; they are frequently of inestimable worth in arriving at the author's intention.

Holy Grail: The cup from which Christ is said to have drunk at the Last Supper and which was used to catch his blood at the Crucifixion. It became the center of a tradition of Christian mysticism and eventually was linked with Arthurian ROMANCE as an object of search on the part of Arthur's knights. The *grail* as it appears in early Arthurian literature (Chrétien's *Perceval*) is perhaps of pagan origin, some sort of magic object not now to be traced with assurance. In the poems of Robert de Boron (*ca.*1200) it appears as a mystic symbol and is connected with Christian tradition (having been brought to England by Joseph of Arimathea). In the Vulgate Romances (see VULGATE), two great CYCLES are devoted to the *grail,* the first or "History" dealing with the Joseph tradition, the second or "Quest" dealing with the search for it by Arthurian knights. Perceval, the first hero of the quest, because he was not a pure knight, and Lancelot, because he was disqualified by his love for Guinevere, gave place to Galahad, the wholly pure knight, conceived as Lancelot's son and Perceval's kinsman. The pious quest for the *grail,* no less than the sinful love of Lancelot and Guinevere, helped bring about the eventual downfall of the Round Table fellowship. See ARTHURIAN LEGEND.

Homeric Epithet: An adjectival phrase so often repeated in connection with a person or thing that it almost becomes a part of the name, as "swift-footed Achilles." See EPITHET.

Homeric Simile: An unusually elaborate comparison, in the manner of Homer. See EPIC SIMILE.

Homily: A form of oral religious instruction given by an ordained minister with a church congregation as audience. The *homily* is sometimes distinguished from the sermon in that the sermon usually is on a theme drawn from a scriptural text and a *homily* usually gives practical moral counsel rather than discussion of doctrine. The distinction is by no means rigorously maintained. OLD ENGLISH literature contains *homilies* by Ælfric and Wulfstan.

Horatian Ode: Horace applied the term *ode* to comparatively informal POEMS written in a single stanzaic form, in contrast to the STROPHE, ANTISTROPHE, and EPODE of the PINDARIC ODE. The term *Horatian ode* is, therefore, often applied to such poems. Notable examples are Marvell's "Horatian Ode upon Cromwell's Return from Ireland," and Keats' "Ode on a Grecian Urn." See ODE.

Hornbook: A kind of primer common in England from the sixteenth to the eighteenth centuries. On a sheet of vellum or paper were printed the alphabet, combinations of consonants and vowels commonly used in making up syllables, the Lord's Prayer, and a list of Roman numerals. The sheet was mounted on wood and covered (for protection) by transparent horn (hence *hornbook*). Its most famous use in literature is in *The Gull's Hornbook* by Thomas Dekker, an amusing and satirical "primer" of instructions for the young innocent of early seventeenth-century London. The *hornbook* here supplies a framework for a social SATIRE.

Hovering Stress or Accent: A term designating the metrical effect that results from two adjacent syllables sharing the ICTUS, so that the STRESS appears to hover over both syllables. It is also called DISTRIBUTED STRESS and RESOLVED STRESS. It appears often in the work of Gerard Manley Hopkins and is sometimes considered a metrical device used by Whitman. See DISTRIBUTED STRESS for an example.

Hubris or Hybris: Overweening pride which results in the misfortune of the PROTAGONIST of a TRAGEDY. It is the particular form of HAMARTIA, or TRAGIC FLAW, which results from excessive pride, ambition, and overconfidence. *Hubris* leads the PROTAGONIST to break a moral law or ignore a divine warning with calamitous results. The excessive ambition of Macbeth is a standard example of *hubris* in English drama. See HAMARTIA, TRAGEDY.

Hudibrastic Verse: The OCTOSYLLABIC COUPLET as adapted by Samuel Butler in his satiric poem, *Hudibras*. In this long poem, published in three parts between 1663 and 1678, Butler satirized the PURITANS of England. *Hudibras* was conspicuous for its HUMOR, its BURLESQUE elements, its MOCK-EPIC FORM, and its wealth of satiric EPIGRAM. The meter is IAMBIC TETRAMETER rhyming in couplets, *aa—bb*, etc. It is filled with outrageous RHYMES that are often double and even triple. The term is used today to characterize VERSE following Butler's general manner and particularly his shocking RHYMES.

Humanism: Broadly, this term suggests any attitude which tends to exalt the human element or stress the importance of human interests, as opposed to the supernatural, divine elements—or as opposed to the grosser, animal elements. So a student of human affairs may be called a *humanist*, and the study of man as man, i.e., of the human race rather than of individual human beings, has been called *humanism*. In a more specific sense, *humanism* suggests a devotion to those studies supposed to promote human culture most effectively— in particular, those dealing with the life, thought, language, and literature of ancient Greece and Rome. In literary history the most important use of the term is to designate the revival of classical culture which accompanied the RENAISSANCE. The RENAISSANCE humanists found in the classics a justification to exalt human nature and build a new and highly idealistic gospel of progress upon it. Also they found it necessary to break sharply with medieval attitudes which had subordinated one aspect of human nature by exalting the supernatural and divine. The RENAISSANCE humanists agreed with the ancients in asserting the dignity of man and the importance of the present life, as against those medieval thinkers who considered the present life useful chiefly as a preparation for a future life.

RENAISSANCE *humanism* developed in the fourteenth and fifteenth centuries in Italy and was marked by a passion for rediscovering and studying ancient literature. It spread to other Continental countries and finally to England, where efforts to develop humanistic activities culminated successfully late in the fifteenth century with the introduction of the study of Greek at Oxford (see OXFORD REFORMERS). Early humanists in England applied themselves to mastering the Greek and Latin languages and to applying their new methods to theology, statecraft, education, criticism, and literature. Unlike some Continental humanists the English group, though they reacted against medieval asceticism and scholasticism and attacked abuses in the Church, retained their faith in Christianity. Indeed, they believed that the best of classical culture could be fused with Christianity—a fact which accounts for what seem to be incongruous mixtures of paganism and Christianity in much RENAISSANCE literature, notably the POETRY of Spenser and Milton. The efforts of such men as Dean John Colet and Erasmus to reform church conditions and theology through education and an appeal to reason were checked by the success of the more radical Lutheran movement. The "modern" character of this *humanism* may be indicated by recalling a few of its political and educational doctrines: political institutions are of human, not divine, origin and exist for human good, the monarch's "duties" being of greater concern than his "rights"; war is unchristian and inhumane and should be resorted to only when approved by the people themselves; the highest human happiness can come only through the virtuous life, which in turn can best be achieved through the control of reason, buttressed by education; women should be educated; nature should be employed as an educational tool; physical education is of the utmost importance; schoolmasters should be learned and gentle.

A later phase of humanistic activity was its interest in literary criticism, through which it affected powerfully the practice of RENAISSANCE authors. The validity of critical ideas drawn from Aristotle and Horace was asserted and the production of a vernacular literature which imitated the CLASSICS was advocated. Though this led to some unsuccessful efforts to restrict the English vocabulary and to repress native VERSE FORMS in favor of classical words and FORMS, in general humanistic criticism exerted a wholesome effect upon literature by lending it dignity (as in the EPIC and TRAGEDY) and grace (as in the Jonsonian LYRIC) and by stressing restraint and FORM. Its influence was especially great in the DRAMA, where it aided in establishing unified STRUCTURE. The texture of RENAISSANCE literature, too, was greatly enriched by the familiarity with the incidents, characters, motives, and IMAGERY of classical mythology, history, and literature. Sidney's *Defence of Poesie* is generally taken as the first major document in English criticism, and the establishment of the classical attitude (see CLASSICISM) through the influence of Jonson and (later) Dryden and Pope and others was itself

Humor

a fruit of RENAISSANCE *humanism*. A tracing of the effects of *humanism* upon the literature of the seventeenth and eighteenth centuries would largely coincide with the history of CLASSICISM and NEO-CLASSICISM. One of the phases of the reaction against ROMANTICISM in the nineteenth century was a revival of *humanism,* as exemplified in Matthew Arnold. See HUMANISM, THE NEW.

Humanism, The New: A philosophical-critical movement called *The New Humanism* took place in America between 1910 and 1930 inspired in large part by the humanist position of Matthew Arnold. Its leaders were Irving Babbitt, Paul Elmer More, Norman Foerster, and Robert Shafer. *The New Humanism* was in large part a reaction against certain forms of REALISM and particularly of NATURALISM, which the new humanists believed overstressed the animal elements in human nature. The movement was a protest against the philosophies and psychologies of "our professedly scientific time." No complete codification of the tenets of the new humanists can be made, but the following summary, based on Foerster's *American Criticism,* suggests their general attitudes: *The New Humanism* assumes (1) that assumptions are unavoidable, (2) that the essential quality of experience is not natural but ethical, (3) that there is a sharp dualism between man and nature, and (4) that man's will is free.

This reaction against the tenets of an age of science and artistic self-expression, however, failed to achieve a large following outside academic circles. The popular critic Stuart Sherman was active in it for a while, and the poet-critic T. S. Eliot was an interested observer. After 1930 it fell before attacks by two enemies, the sociological critics and the advocates of the NEW CRITICISM, a movement that effectively raised the New Humanists' standard of the validity of the art object in an age of science and yet one that began partially as a reaction against the strict morality and the intolerance of the contemporary in art which *New Humanism* had often displayed. See NEW CRITICISM; CRITICISM, HISTORICAL SKETCH.

Humor: A term used in English since the early eighteenth century to denote one of the two major types of writing (*humor* and WIT) whose purpose is the evoking of some kind of laughter. It is derived from the physiological theory of HUMOURS, and it was used to designate a person with a peculiar disposition which led to his readily perceiving the ridiculous, the ludicrous, and the comical and effectively giving expression to this perception. In the eighteenth century it was used to name a comical mode that was sympathetic, tolerant, and warmly aware of the depths of human nature, as opposed to the intellectual, satiric, intolerant quality associated with WIT. However, it is impossible to discuss *humor* separately from WIT, and the reader is referred to the article on WIT AND HUMOR.

Humours: In the old theory of physiology the four chief liquids of the human body, blood, phlegm, yellow bile, and black bile, were known as *humours*. They were closely allied with the FOUR ELEMENTS. Thus blood, like *air*, was hot and moist; yellow bile, like *fire*, was hot and dry; phlegm, like *water*, was cold and moist; black bile, like *earth*, was cold and dry. Both physical diseases and mental and moral dispositions ("temperaments") were caused by the condition of the *humours*. Disease resulted from the dominance of some element within a single *humour*, or from a lack of balance or proportion among the *humours* themselves. The *humours* gave off vapors which ascended to the brain. An individual's personal characteristics, physical, mental, and moral, were explained by his "temperament" or the state of his *humours*. The perfect temperament resulted when no one *humour* dominated. The sanguine man had a dominance of blood, was beneficent, joyful, amorous. The choleric man was easily angered, impatient, obstinate, vengeful. The phlegmatic man was dull, pale, cowardly. The melancholic man was gluttonous, backward, unenterprising, thoughtful, sentimental, affected. A disordered state of the *humours* produced, further, more exaggerated characteristics. These facts explain how the word *humour* in Elizabethan times came to mean "disposition," then "mood," or "characteristic peculiarity," later specialized to "folly," or "affectation." By 1600 it was common to use *humour* as a means of classifying characters. The influence on ELIZABETHAN literature of the doctrines based on *humours* was very great, and familiarity with them is an aid in understanding such characters as Horatio, Hamlet, and Jacques in Shakespeare. Many passages often taken as figurative may have had a literal meaning to the Elizabethans, as "my liver melts." See COMEDY OF HUMOURS.

Hymn: A LYRIC POEM expressing religious emotion and generally intended to be sung by a CHORUS. Church and theological doctrine, pious feeling, and religious aspiration characterize the ideas of these LYRICS, though originally the term referred to almost any song of praise whether of gods or famous men. The early Greek and Latin Christian churches developed many famous *hymn* writers, and the importance of *hymns* during the Dark and Middle Ages can hardly be exaggerated since they gave the great mass of people a new VERSE FORM as well as a means of emotional expression. The twelfth and thirteenth centuries saw the greatest development of Latin *hymns* (*Dies Irae,* etc.). The wide use of *hymns* helped to destroy certain literary CONVENTIONS of the past and exerted an important influence on the VERSIFICATION of English and German poetry as well as that of the romance languages. Some famous *hymn* writers of England were Wesley, Cowper, Watts, Toplady, Newman; of America, Whittier and Holmes. See ANTHEM, TROPE.

Hymnal Stanza: A four-line STANZA in IAMBIC TETRAMETER or IAMBIC TETRAMETER and TRIMETER, rhyming either *abcb* or *abab*. Often called COMMON MEASURE.

Hypallage: A FIGURE OF SPEECH in which an EPITHET is moved from the more natural to the less natural one of a group of nouns, as when Virgil writes of "the trumpet's Tuscan blare" when the normal order would be "the Tuscan trumpet's blare."

Hyperbaton: A FIGURE OF SPEECH in which the normal sentence order is transposed or rearranged in a major way, usually for rhetorical or poetic effect. These lines from Book II of Milton's *Paradise Lost* illustrate *hyperbaton:*

> Which when *Beëlzebub* perceiv'd, than whom
> *Satan* except, none higher sat, with grave
> Aspect he rose . . . .

Hyperbole: A FIGURE OF SPEECH in which conscious exaggeration is used without the intent of literal persuasion. It may be used to heighten effect or it may be used to produce comic effect. Macbeth is using *hyperbole* in the following lines:

> No; this my hand will rather
> The multitudinous seas incarnadine,
> Making the green one red.

Hypercatalectic or **Hypermetrical:** A line of POETRY with an extra syllable at its end. Many of Chaucer's lines are *hypercatalectic* when the terminal -*e*'s at the ends of lines are pronounced, such as these:

> Short was his gowne, with sleves longe and wyde.
> Wel koude he sitte on hors and faire ryde.

Hysteron Proteron: A FIGURE OF SPEECH in which what should logically come last comes first. Dogberry's speech in *Much Ado About Nothing* is an example: "Masters, it is proved already that you are little better than false knaves, and it will go near to be thought so shortly."

I

Iambus (Iamb): A metrical FOOT consisting of an unaccented syllable and an accented (˘ ´). The most common metrical measure in English verse. A line from Marlowe will serve as an illustration:

Cŏme líve | wĭth mé | ănd bé | mў lóve

Ictus: In VERSIFICATION, the ACCENT or STRESS that falls on a syllable; *ictus* does not refer to the stressed syllable but to the STRESS itself. See ACCENT.

Identical Rhyme: The use of the same word in two or more rhyming positions in a POEM, or the use of the same word sound, although the spelling may differ, in two or more rhyming positions in a POEM. See RHYME.

Idiom: A use of words, a grammatic construction peculiar to a given language, an expression which cannot be translated literally into a second language. "To carry out" may be taken as an example. Literally it means, of course, to carry something out (of a room perhaps), but idiomatically it means to see that something is done, as "to carry out a command." *Idioms* in a language usually arise from a peculiarity which is syntactical or structural or from the veiling of a meaning in a METAPHOR (as in the above instance).

Idyll (or Idyl): Not so much a definite poetic GENRE (like the SONNET, for instance) as a descriptive term which may be applied to one or another of the poetic GENRES which are short and possess marked descriptive, narrative, and PASTORAL qualities. In this popular sense, Whittier's "Maud Muller" might be called an *idyll*. PASTORAL and descriptive elements are usually the first requisites of the *idyll*, although the PASTORAL element is usually presented in a conscious literary manner. The point of view of the *idyll* is that of a civilized and artificial society glancing from a drawing-room window over green meadows and gamboling sheep, or of the week-end farm viewed through a picture window. Historically the term goes back to the *idylls* of Theocritus, who wrote short pieces depicting the simple, rustic life in Sicily to please the civilized Alexandrians. It has also been applied to long descriptive and narrative poems, particularly Tennyson's *Idylls of the King*. See PASTORAL, EPYLLION.

Image: Originally a sculptured, cast, or modeled representation of a person; even in its most sophisticated critical usage, this fundamental meaning is still present, in that an *image* is a literal and concrete representation of a sensory experience or of an object that can be known by one or more of the senses. It functions, as I. A. Richards has pointed out, by representing a sensation through the process of being a "relict" of an already known sensation. The *image* is one of the distinctive elements of the "language of art," the means by which experience in its richness and emotional complexity is communicated, as opposed to the simplifying and conceptualizing processes of science and philosophy. The *image* is, therefore, a portion of the essence of the meaning of the literary work, not ever properly a mere decoration.

Images may be either "tied" or "free," a "tied" *image* being one so employed that its meaning and associational value is the same or nearly the same for all readers; and a "free" *image* being one not so fixed by context that its possible meanings or associational values are limited; it is, therefore, capable of having various meanings or values for various people.

Images may also be either literal or figurative, a literal *image* being one that involves no necessary change or extension in the obvious meaning of the words, one in which the words call up a sensory representation of the literal object or sensation; and a figurative *image* being one that involves a "turn" on the literal meaning of the words. An example of a collection of literal *images* may be seen in Coleridge's "Kubla Khan":

Imagery

In Xanadu did Kubla Khan
A stately pleasure-dome decree:
Where Alph, the sacred river, ran
Through caverns measureless to man
Down to a sunless sea.

These *images* apparently represent a literal scene. The literal *image* is one of the basic properties of prose FICTION, as witness such different writers as Joseph Conrad and Ernest Hemingway, both of whose works are noted for the evocative power of their literal *images*. The opening lines of this Wordsworth sonnet show both kinds of *images*, literal and figurative:

It is a beauteous evening, calm and free;
The holy time is quiet as a Nun
Breathless with adoration; the broad sun
Is sinking down in its tranquillity.

The two middle lines are highly figurative, whereas the first and fourth lines are broadly literal, although there are figurative "turns" present by implication in "free" and "tranquillity."

The qualities usually found in *images* are particularity, concreteness, and an appeal to sensuous experience or memory. See IMAGERY, SYMBOL, METAPHOR, ABSTRACT TERMS, CONCRETE TERMS, FIGURATIVE LANGUAGE.

Imagery: A term used widely in contemporary criticism, *imagery* has a great variety of meanings. In its literal sense it means the collection of IMAGES within a literary work or a unit of a literary work. In a broader sense it is used as synonymous with TROPE or FIGURE OF SPEECH. Here the TROPE designates a special usage of words in which there is a change in their basic meanings. There are four major types of TROPES: IMAGES, which, in the strictest sense, are literal and sensory and properly should not be called TROPES at all; SYMBOLS, which combine a literal and sensuous quality with an abstract or suggestive aspect; SIMILE, which describes by expressed ANALOGY; and METAPHOR, which describes by implied ANALOGY. Not only do these four types of TROPES define the meaning of *imagery*, they also suggest the ranges of possible application that are to be found in the term.

Many contemporary critics are deeply concerned over the "structure of IMAGES," "the IMAGE-clusters," "IMAGE patterns," and "thematic *imagery*." Such patterns of *imagery*, often without the conscious knowledge of author or reader, are sometimes taken to be keys to the "deeper" meaning of a literary work or pointers to the unconscious motivations of its author. A few critics tend to see the "IMAGE pattern" as indeed being the basic meaning of the work and a sounder key to its values and interpretation than the explicit statements of the author or the more obvious events of PLOT or action. One of the notable contributions of the NEW CRITICS has been their awareness of the importance of the relationships among IMAGES to the nature and meaning of LYRIC poetry.

A study of the *imagery* of a literary work may center itself on the physical world which is presented through the language of the work; upon the rhetorical patterns and devices by which the TROPES in the work are achieved; upon the psychological state which produced the work and gave it its special and often hidden meaning; upon the ways in which the pattern of its IMAGES reinforces (or on occasion contradicts) the ostensible meaning of statement, PLOT, and action in the work; or upon how the IMAGES strike responsively upon resonant points in the racial unconscious producing the emotive power of ARCHETYPES and MYTH. See IMAGE, METAPHOR, FIGURATIVE LANGUAGE, NEW CRITICISM, ALLEGORY.

Imagination: The theories of POETRY advanced by the ROMANTIC critics of the early nineteenth century (Wordsworth, Coleridge, and others) led to many efforts to distinguish between *imagination* and FANCY, terms which had formerly been used as virtually synonymous. The word *imagination* had passed through three stages of meaning in England. In RENAISSANCE times it was opposed to reason and regarded as the means by which poetical and religious conceptions could be attained and appreciated. Thus Bacon cited it as one of the three faculties of the rational soul: "history has reference to the memory, POETRY to the *imagination,* and philosophy to the reason"; and Shakespeare says the poet is "of *imagination* all compact." In the NEO-CLASSIC PERIOD it was the faculty by which IMAGES were called up, especially visual IMAGES (see Addison's *The Pleasures of the Imagination*), and was related to the process by which "IMITATION of nature" takes place. Because of its tendency to transcend the testimony of the senses, the poet who might draw upon *imagination* must subject it to the check of reason, which should determine its form of presentation. Later in the eighteenth century the *imagination,* opposed to reason, was conceived as so vivid an imaging process that it affected the passions and formed "a world of beauty of its own," a poetical illusion which served not to affect conduct but to produce immediate pleasure.

The ROMANTIC critics conceived the *imagination* as a blending and unifying of the powers of the mind which enabled the poet to see inner relationships, such as the identity of truth and beauty. So Wordsworth says that poets

> Have each his own peculiar faculty,
> Heaven's gift, a sense that fits him to perceive
> Objects unseen before . . .
> An insight that in some sort he possesses, . . .
> Proceeding from a source of untaught things.

This conception of *imagination* necessitated a distinction between it and FANCY. Coleridge (*Biographia Literaria*) especially stressed, though he never fully explained, the difference. He called *imagination* the "shaping and modifying" power, FANCY the "aggregative and associative" power. The former "struggles to idealize and to unify," while the latter is merely "a mode of memory emancipated from the order of time and space." To illustrate the distinction Coleridge remarked that Milton had a highly imaginative mind, Cowley a very fanciful one. Leslie Stephen stated the distinction briefly, "FANCY deals with the superficial resemblances, and *imagination* with the deeper truths that underlie them."

While *imagination* is usually viewed as a "shaping" and ordering power, the function of which is to give art its special authority, the assumption is almost always present that the "new" creation shaped by the *imagination* is a new form of reality, not a FANTASY nor a fanciful projection. When Shakespeare writes

> As imagination bodies forth
> The forms of things unknown, the poet's pen
> Turns them to shapes and gives to airy nothing
> A local habitation and a name,

his reference is properly made to *imagination*, not to that power of inventing the novel and unreal by recombining the elements found in reality, which we commonly call FANCY and which expresses itself in FANTASY. See FANCY.

Imagists: The name applied to a group of poets prominent in America between 1909 and 1918. Their name came from the French title, *Des Imagistes,* given to the first anthology of their work (1914); this, in turn, having been borrowed from a critical term which had been applied to some French precursors of the movement. The most conspicuous figures of the *imagist* movement were Ezra Pound, "H.D.," John Gould Fletcher, Amy Lowell, Carl Sandburg, and William Carlos Williams. Imagism was a spirit of revolt against conventionalities rather than a goal set up as in itself a permanently lasting objective. According to Amy Lowell's *Tendencies in Modern American Poetry* (1917) the major objectives of the movement were: (1) to use the language of common speech, but to employ always the exact word—not the nearly-exact; (2) to avoid all CLICHÉ expressions; (3) to create new RHYTHMS as the expressions of a new mood; (4) to allow absolute freedom in the choice of subject; (5) to present an IMAGE (that is to be concrete, firm, definite in their pictures—harsh in outline); (6) to strive always for concentration which, they were convinced, was the very essence of poetry; (7) to suggest rather than to offer complete statements. The *Imagists* were influenced by Chinese poetry and particularly by the Japanese HAIKU, with its single sharp IMAGE.

Imitation: The concept of art as *imitation* has its origin with the CLASSICAL critics. Aristotle said at the beginning of his *Poetics* that all arts are modes of *imitation,* and he defines a TRAGEDY as an *imitation* of an action. Aristotle seems here (and elsewhere) to be defending art against Plato's charge that it is twice removed from truth or reality. On the other hand, the Greek and Roman schools of rhetoric used the *imitation* of literary models as an accepted form of composition. Both views of *imitation* have been persistently present in English literary history.

The concept of Aristotelian *imitation*—that art *imitates* "Nature" —was pervasively present in English critical thought until the end of the eighteenth century. This *imitation* of Nature came to be regarded as a realistic portrayal of life, a reproduction of natural objects and actions. Moreover, admiration of the success with which the greater CLASSIC writers had followed Nature bolstered the rhetorical theory of following in their footsteps. Critics in the RENAISSANCE and the NEO-CLASSIC PERIOD accepted *imitation* in this rhetorical sense of copying models in the various types of POETRY. They did not believe that *imitation* should replace genius, but an adherence to CLASSICAL models was considered a safe method of avoiding literary vices and attaining virtues. *Imitation* of this sort had several varieties: writing in the spirit of the masters and using merely their general principles; borrowing from the ancients with the necessity of accommodating the material to the poet's own age; the collection and use of special "beauties" in thought and expression from the works of the best poets; the exercise of PARAPHRASE and free TRANSLATION. *Imitation* as a copying of other writers was discussed and employed in all degrees of dependence, from the most dignified to the most servile.

In the ROMANTIC AGE, the MIMETIC THEORY OF ART was replaced by the EXPRESSIVE THEORY, and the meaning of Aristotle's term *imitation* underwent serious change as the concept of NATURE had been undergoing change. NATURE then became the creative principle of the universe, and Aristotelian *imitation* was considered to be "creating according to a true idea," and a work of art was "an idealized representation of human life—of character, emotion, action—under forms manifest to sense."

With the rise of REALISM and NATURALISM, a renewed emphasis on the accurate portrayal of the palpable actual returned, although the term *imitation* was not often used. Among contemporary critics there is some interest in the implications for the theory of *imitation* of the depth psychologies. See CRITICISM, HISTORICAL SKETCH; and CRITICISM, TYPES OF.

Imprecation: A CURSE; an INVOCATION of evil; a MALEDICTION.

Impression: The total number of copies of a book printed at one time or without removing the type or plates from the press, a PRINTING. See EDITION.

Impressionism: A highly personal manner of writing in which the author presents CHARACTERS or SCENES or MOODS as they appear to his individual temperament at a precise moment and from a particular vantage point rather than as they are in actuality. The term is borrowed from painting. About the middle of the nineteenth century the French painters Manet, Monet, Degas, Renoir, and others revolted from the conventional and academic conceptions of painting and held that it was more important to retain the impressions an object makes on the artist than meticulously to present the appearance of that object by precise detail and careful, realistic finish. Their especial concern was with the use of light on their canvases. They suggested the chief features of an object with a few strokes; they were more interested in ATMOSPHERE than in perspective or outline. "Instead of painting a tree," says Lewis Mumford, the impressionist "painted the effect of a tree." The movement had its counterpart in literature, writers accepting the same conviction that the personal attitudes and moods of the writer were legitimate elements in depicting character or setting or action. Briefly, the literary impressionist holds that the expression of such elements as these through the fleeting impression of a moment is more significant artistically than a photographic presentation of cold fact. The object of the impressionist, then, is not to present his material as it is to the objective observer but as it is *seen* or *felt* to be by himself in a single passing moment. He employs highly selective details, the "brush-strokes" of sense-data that can suggest the impression made upon him or upon some character in the story or poem. In poetry *impressionism* was an important aspect of the work of the IMAGISTS; in FICTION it is present in the works of writers like Dorothy Richardson and Virginia Woolf and in the "Camera Eye" sections of Dos Passos' *U.S.A. Impressionism* differs from EXPRESSIONISM significantly in avoiding conscious distortion and abstraction. See EXPRESSIONISM, IMAGISTS.

Impressionistic Criticism: A type of criticism that attempts to communicate what the critic sees and feels in the presence of a work of art. Anatole France called *impressionistic criticism* "the adventures of a sensitive soul among masterpieces." See CRITICISM, TYPES OF; CRITICISM, HISTORICAL SKETCH.

Imprimatur: An official approval or license to print a work; usually the sign of approval of the Roman Catholic Church. The term is also used ironically to refer to the approval of an autocratic critic or one who clearly considers himself a custodian of the public morality or TASTE. *Imprimatur* literally means, "Let it be printed."

Inciting Moment: The name used by Freytag for the event or force which sets in motion the RISING ACTION of a play. It is also called the EXCITING FORCE. See FREYTAG'S PYRAMID, DRAMATIC STRUCTURE.

Incremental Repetition: A form of iteration frequently found in the BALLAD. This kind of REPETITION is not that of a REFRAIN but the repeating of phrases and lines in such a way that their meaning is enhanced either by their appearing in changed contexts or by minor successive changes in the repeated portion of the BALLAD. A common form of *incremental repetition* occurs in the question and answer pattern in the BALLAD. These two STANZAS from "Child Waters" illustrate *incremental repetition:*

> There were four and twenty ladies
>   Were playing at the ball,
> And Ellen, she was the fairest lady,
>   Must bring his steed to the stall.
>
> There were four and twenty ladies
>   Was a playing at the chess,
> And Ellen, she was the fairest lady,
>   Must bring his horse to grass.

A very complex instance of *incremental repetition* occurs in the "Nevermore" at the end of each STANZA of Poe's "The Raven," where the meaning of the word changes greatly in the progress of the POEM.

Incunabulum: A term applied to any book printed in the last part of the fifteenth century (before 1501). Since the first printed books resembled in size, form, and appearance the medieval manuscript, which had been developed to a high degree of artistic perfection, *incunabula* are commonly large and ornate. As examples of early printing, *incunabula* are prized by modern collectors. From an historical and literary point of view they are interesting as reflecting the intellectual and literary interests of the late fifteenth century. The number of existing *incunabula* is large, including about 360 printed in England. Among famous English *incunabula* are Caxton's edition of Chaucer's *Canterbury Tales* and *Le Morte Darthur* of Malory.

Index Librorum Prohibitorum: A list of titles of works forbidden by church authority to be read by Roman Catholics, pending revision or deletion of some parts. Commonly called the "Index."

Induction: An old word for *introduction.* This term was sometimes used in the sixteenth century to denote a framework introduction (see FRAMEWORK-STORY). Thus Sackville's' "Induction" to a portion of *The Mirror for Magistrates* tells how the poet was led by Sorrow into a region of Hell where dwelt the shades of the historical figures whose tragic lives are the subject of the *Mirror.* In the book proper each "shade" relates his own sad tale; the *induction* supplies the FRAMEWORK much as the famous "Prologue" supplies the FRAMEWORK for the stories making up Chaucer's *Canterbury Tales.* In *The Taming of the Shrew* Shakespeare employs an *induction* in which a drunken tinker is persuaded that he is a lord, for whose amusement is performed a play—the play is *The Taming of the Shrew* itself.

Industrial Revolution: The social-political-economic struggle which characterized life in England for a hundred years or more but which was most intensified in the last quarter of the eighteenth and first quarter of the nineteenth centuries. Invention, scientific discovery, changing economic, political, and social ideas and ideals all contributed to the furor that was England during these years. By 1760 blast furnaces had begun to promote the manufacture of iron; the textile industry grew by leaps and bounds with the invention of the spinning jenny and the power loom (1785). The number of English looms increased in less than two decades from three thousand to one hundred thousand. James Watt made even greater strides possible through his perfection of the steam engine. Roads, canals, and railroads increased transportation facilities. Agriculture was all but deserted; by 1826 not a third of the former population was left on the farms. Hundreds of thousands of men wandered through the country, many dying, impoverished and diseased. The sweat shop was born; the master craftsman found his trade taken from him by the machine. Home work gave way to factory work. Industry and commerce flourished in cities which grew rapidly. The villages were all but deserted. A middle-class capitalistic group developed almost overnight, and progressed at the expense of men, women, and children whom they overworked in their mills.

The writers of the period concerned themselves with these contemporary problems. Crabbe in such pieces as *The Village* and *The Borough* set forth pictures of the conditions; Charles Kingsley in such novels as *Yeast* and *Alton Locke* and Mrs. Gaskell in *Mary Barton, a Tale of Manchester Life,* presented the struggles and unfairness of the times in FICTION. Dickens turned his attention to the relief of the poor. Ruskin and Carlyle sought to point the way to reform; Arnold in his *Essays* condemned a Philistine England which measured her greatness by her wealth and her numbers. Mill (*Principles of Political Economy*), Bentham (*Radical Reform*), Robert Owen (*New View of Society*), and Malthus (*Principles of Political Economy*) wrestled with the problems of the time from the point of view of the social sciences.

Informal Essay: As distinguished from the FORMAL ESSAY, the *informal essay* is less obviously serious in purpose, usually shorter, freer of STRUCTURE, easier of STYLE, and is written to please and entertain rather than to instruct. See ESSAY.

Inkhornists: A group in the RENAISSANCE PERIOD who favored the introduction of heavy Latin and Greek words into the standard English vocabulary. See PURIST and CRITICISM, HISTORICAL SKETCH.

In medias res: A term from Horace, literally meaning "in the midst of things." It is applied to the literary technique of opening a STORY in the middle of the action and then supplying information about the beginning of the action through FLASHBACKS and other devices for EXPOSITION. The term *in medias res* is usually applied to the EPIC, where such an opening is one of the CONVENTIONS.

Inns of Court: The four voluntary, unchartered societies or legal guilds in London which have the privilege of admitting persons to the bar. They take their names from the buildings they occupy— the Inner Temple, the Middle Temple, Lincoln's Inn, and Gray's Inn, buildings which they have occupied since the fourteenth century. Though the origin of these societies is lost in the medieval inns of law, it is clear that in late medieval times they became great law schools and so continued for centuries: today they are little more than lawyers' clubs, though they do exert considerable influence in guarding admissions to the bar. The *Inns of Court* were educational institutions and cultural centers in the sixteenth and seventeenth centuries. Their libraries as well as their spirit of fellowship fostered literary interests. Regular DRAMA, as well as MASQUES and INTERLUDES, were nurtured by the Inns. Shakespeare's *Comedy of Errors* was acted before the fellows of Gray's Inn during the Christmas season of 1594. The Inns, like the universities, saw much playwriting and amateur acting on the part of "gentlemen" who would scorn connection with the early PUBLIC THEATERS. Many English authors have received their education, in whole or in part, in the *Inns of Court.* Chaucer may have belonged to one; Sir Thomas More was a Lincoln's Inn product; George Gascoigne and Francis Bacon were admitted to law practice from Gray's Inn; Thomas Shadwell and Nicholas Rowe were members of the Inner Temple. A vivid description of life in the Inns appears in Thackeray's *Pendennis.*

Innuendo: An insinuation or indirect suggestion, often with harmful or sinister connotation.

Interior Monologue

Inscape: A term used by Gerard Manley Hopkins to refer to the "individually-distinctive" inner structure or nature of a thing; hence, the essence of a natural object, which, being perceived through a moment of illumination—an EPIPHANY—reveals the unity of all creation. *Inscape* is the inward quality of objects and events, as they are perceived by the joined observation and introspection of a poet, who in turn embodies them in unique poetic forms. See INSTRESS.

Instress: A term used by Gerard Manley Hopkins to refer to the force, ultimately divine, which creates the INSCAPE of an object or an event, and impresses that distinctive inner structure of the object on the mind of the beholder, so that he can perceive it and embody it in a work of art. See INSCAPE.

Intentional Fallacy: In contemporary criticism, a term used to describe the error of judging the success and the meaning of a work of art by the author's expressed or ostensible intention in producing it. The term was introduced by W. K. Wimsatt, Jr., and M. C. Beardsley (see *The Verbal Icon,* by Wimsatt) to insist that "the poem is not the critic's own and not the author's. . . . What is said about the poem [by the author] is subject to the same scrutiny as any statement in linguistics or in the general science of psychology or morals." The *intentional fallacy,* like the AFFECTIVE FALLACY, is an error in judgment when viewed from an OBJECTIVE THEORY OF ART, for holders of the OBJECTIVE THEORY tend—at least in their extreme statements—to see the work of art as AUTOTELIC. The degree to which biographical facts, data regarding linguistic change, and knowledge of the social and intellectual climate in which the work was produced become relevant factors, along with the author's statement of intention, are matters of sharp disagreement among contemporary critics. It should be noted that Wimsatt and Beardsley say, "The author must be admitted as a witness to the meaning of his work." It is merely that they would subject his testimony to rigorous scrutiny in the light of the work itself. See AFFECTIVE FALLACY, AUTOTELIC, HISTORICAL CRITICISM.

Interior Monologue: One of the techniques by which the STREAM OF CONSCIOUSNESS of a character in a NOVEL or a SHORT STORY is presented. It records the internal, emotional experience of the character on any one level or on combinations of several levels of consciousness, reaching downward to the nonverbalized level where

IMAGES must be used to represent nonverbalized sensations or emotions. It assumes the unrestricted and uncensored portrayal of the totality of interior experience on the level or levels being represented. It gives, therefore, the appearance of being illogical, associational, free of auctorial control. There are two distinct forms which an *interior monologue* may take: direct, in which the author seems not to exist and the interior self of the character is given directly, as though the reader were overhearing an articulation of the stream of thought and feeling flowing through the character's mind; and indirect, in which the author serves as selector, presenter, guide, and commentator. The Molly Bloom section at the close of Joyce's *Ulysses* is the best known example of a direct *interior monologue* in English; the novels of Virginia Woolf are excellent illustrations of the indirect *interior monologue*. It is generally agreed that Édouard Dujardin, in *Les Lauriers sont coupés* (1887) first used the *interior monologue* extensively. The term is often, although erroneously, used as a synonym for STREAM OF CONSCIOUSNESS. See STREAM OF CONSCIOUSNESS, IMPRESSIONISM.

Interlude: A kind of DRAMA that developed in late fifteenth- and early sixteenth-century England and that played an important part in the secularization of the DRAMA and in the development of REALISTIC COMEDY. The word may mean a play brief enough to be presented in the interval of a dramatic performance, entertainment, or feast (e.g., Medwall's *Fulgens and Lucres,* 1497), or it may mean a play or DIALOGUE between two persons. Some *interludes* imitate French FARCE and do not exhibit symbolic technique and didactic purpose, while others appear to have developed from the MORALITY PLAY, and still others from the Latin SCHOOL DRAMA: the two latter types are likely to be moralistic. Professor Tucker Brooke has stressed the aristocratic character of the *interlude* and says that the *interlude* was understood in Tudor times to mean a short play exhibited by professionals at the meals of the great and on other occasions where, later, MASQUES would have been fashionable. The essential qualities are brevity and WIT. Some writers regard such an episode as that of the sheep-stealing Mak in the Towneley *Second Shepherd's Play* as an *interlude.* The chief developers of the *interlude* were John Heywood and John Rastell, the first English dramatists, so far as known, to recognize that a play might be justified on the test of ability to amuse. Heywood's *interludes* were produced in the 1520's and 1530's, the most famous being *The Four P's* (the Palmer, the Pardoner, the 'Pothecary, and the Pedlar, who engage in a sort of lying contest managed as a satire against women), and *The Merry Play of John John the Husband, Tyb His Wife, and Sir John the Priest* (in which the priest and Tyb hoodwink the husband). Rastell's *interludes* include *The Nature of the Four Elements, The Field of the Cloth of Gold,* and *Gentilness and Nobility.* Homely details and realistic treatment are significant features of the *interludes,* which still followed the allegorical pattern of the MORALITY and yet represented the growth away from the abstract and toward the individual and particular.

Internal Rhyme: RHYME that occurs at some place after the first and before the last syllables in a VERSE. See RHYME, LEONINE RHYME.

Intrigue Comedy: A COMEDY in which the major interest is in PLOT complications resulting from scheming by a CHARACTER or CHARACTERS. See COMEDY OF SITUATION.

Introduction: The opening sentences or paragraphs of a piece of writing. All literary combinations have been said to have three parts: beginning, middle, end. On this basis the *introduction* is the beginning to the beginning. Sometimes the term is applied to an ESSAY printed at the beginning of a book—much like a preface—to explain the author's chief ideas, purposes, hopes, and disillusions regarding the book he has written. See INDUCTION, PROLEGOMENON.

Invective: Harsh, abusive language directed against a person or cause. Vituperative writing. The *Letters* of Junius and the open letter written by Stevenson in defense of Father Damien have qualities of *invective.*

Invention: Originality in thought, STYLE, DICTION, IMAGERY, or PLOT. In this present-day sense the term implies creative power of an independent sort. But the use of the term by early English critics often is colored by an older meaning of the term and by the implications of the theory of IMITATION, and the student will do well to remember that RENAISSANCE and NEO-CLASSIC critics in their use of the term may have in mind the older idea of the "discovery" of literary material as something to be IMITATED or represented. In Latin rhetoric *inventio* meant the "finding" of material and was applied, for example, to an orator's "working up" of his case before making a speech. According to the Aristotelian doctrine of IMITATION an author did not create his materials "out of nothing"; he found them in Nature. A critic writing under the control of these classical conceptions could not think of *invention* in its narrower, modern sense. Yet the idea of ORIGINALITY, of using "new" devices, and of avoiding the trite expression appears in the use of the term in England as early as RENAISSANCE times. As the term was used somewhat loosely for several centuries, it is not possible to give a single definition which will explain all the passages in which the term appears in writings of the sixteenth, seventeenth, and eighteenth centuries. In the ROMANTIC AGE and since, *invention,* in the sense of the discovery of an original or organizing principle, has been replaced by IMAGINATION.

Inversion: The placing of a sentence element out of its normal position either to gain EMPHASIS or to secure a so-called poetic effect. *Inversion* used with restraint and care is an effective rhetorical device, but used too frequently or grotesquely, it will result in artificiality. Probably the most offensive common use of *inversion* is the placing of the adjective after the noun in such expressions as "home beautiful."

The device is often happily employed in POETRY. Where the writer of prose might say: "I saw a vision of a damsel with a dulcimer" Coleridge writes:

> A damsel with a dulcimer
> In a vision once I saw.

It can also be a very effective rhetorical device for securing variety as well as EMPHASIS in prose. The PERIODIC SENTENCE, for example, is a standard and effective case of *inversion.*

Invocation: An address to a deity for aid. In classical literature CONVENTION demanded an opening address to the muses, an *invocation* bespeaking their assistance in the writing. EPICS, particularly, were likely to begin in this way. Milton, in *Paradise Lost,* accepts the tradition, but instead of invoking one of the muses of POETRY addresses the

> Heavenly Muse, that, on the secret top
> Of Oreb, or of Sinai, didst inspire
> That shepherd who first taught the chosen seed
> In the beginning how the heavens and earth
> Rose out of Chaos: ...

Irish Literature

Ionic: A CLASSICAL FOOT with two long and two short syllables. It is used by Horace in his *Odes*. When it is occasionally attempted in English, stressed syllables are used for the long ones and unstressed for the short.

Ipse dixit: Any dogmatic statement. Literally the Latin means: "He himself has said." Hence the term is used to characterize any edict or brief statement emphatically uttered, but unsupported by proof.

Irish Literary Movement, Irish Literary Revival, Irish Renaissance: Variant terms for the movement which encouraged the production of Anglo-Irish literature. See CELTIC RENAISSANCE.

Irish Literature: The early literature of Ireland is greater in bulk, earlier in date, and more striking in character than any other preserved vernacular Western European literature. It has furnished a storehouse of literary materials for later writers, especially those of the early ROMANTIC PERIOD and of the CELTIC RENAISSANCE. It is possible, too, that it supplies a clue to the origins of ARTHURIAN LEGEND. The development of this extensive native literature, as well as the remarkable flourishing of Latin learning in Ireland in the early Middle Ages, is due in part to the fact that the Teutonic invasions which destroyed Roman power in the fifth century failed to reach Ireland, which became a refuge for European scholars and for several centuries the chief center of Christian culture in Western Europe. The Irish clerics, too, seemed to be unusually tolerant of native pagan culture and therefore aided in preserving a great mass of native, often primitive, legendary and literary material of interest to the student of FOLKLORE.

Although poetry in Irish was written in very early times, definite metrical FORMS employing ALLITERATION and RHYME having been developed as early as the seventh century, the bulk of early Irish literature is in prose. The early Irish EPICS are distinguished from most other early EPIC literature by their use of prose instead of verse (though the Irish prose EPICS frequently include poetic PARAPHRASES or commentaries—"rhetorics"—scattered throughout the text). The basic stories of the chief EPIC CYCLE reflect a state of culture prevailing about the time of Christ. Verbally preserved from generation to generation for centuries, they seem to have been written down as early as the seventh and eighth centuries. These early copies of the

277

old stories were largely destroyed and scattered as a result of the Norse invasion (eighth and ninth centuries), the stories being imperfectly recovered and again recorded in manuscripts by the patriotic antiquarians of the tenth and later centuries. Two large manuscripts of the twelfth century containing these retellings of ancient story are still in existence, the *Book of the Dun Cow* (before 1106) and the *Book of Leinster* (before 1160).

The early SAGA literature is divided into three great CYCLES: the "mythological," based on early Celtic myths and historical legends concerning population groups or "invasions"; the Ulster Cycle, or "Red Branch," of which Cuchulain is the central heroic figure; and the Fenian Cycle, concerned with the exploits of Finn mac Cool and his famous companions. The Ulster Cycle was more aristocratic than the Fenian and is preserved in greater volume in the early manuscripts. The chief story is the *Táin bó Cualnge*, "The Cattle Raid of Cooley," the greatest of the early Irish EPICS. Other important stories of this cycle are *The Feast of Bricriu* (containing a beheading game like that in *Sir Gawain and the Green Knight*), *The Wooing of Etaine* (a fairy mistress story), and *The Exile of the Sons of Usnech* (the famous Deirdre story). The Fenian stories, perhaps later in origin than the Ulster tales, have shown greater vitality in oral tradition, many of them still being current among the Gaelic peasants of Ireland and Scotland. They were utilized by James Macpherson in the eighteenth century. See FORGERIES, LITERARY.

Early Irish professional poets (*fili*) or story-tellers were ranked partly by the extent of their repertory of tales, the highest class being able to recite no less than 350 separate stories. These stories were divided into numerous classes or types, such as cattle raids, wooings, battles, deaths, elopements, feasts, exiles, destructions, slaughters, adventures, voyages, and visions.

In addition to the SAGA literature there has been preserved (partly in Latin) a vast amount of historical, legal, and religious literature, the latter including a great many SAINTS' LIVES as well as HYMNS, martyrologies, and one of the earliest examples of medieval biographical writing, Adamnan's *Vita Sancti Columbae*, "The Life of Saint Columba" (before A.D. 700).

The traditional literary technique of the native Irish writers was much altered after the spread of English power and culture in Ireland in the seventeenth century, and the decline in the employment of the Irish language since that time has been accompanied by a lowering and lessening of literary activity. For "revivals" of Gaelic literature and culture see CELTIC RENAISSANCE, CELTIC REVIVAL, GAELIC MOVEMENT.

Irony: A broad term referring to the recognition of a reality different from the masking appearance. Verbal *irony* is a FIGURE OF SPEECH in which the actual intent is expressed in words which carry the opposite meaning. *Irony* is likely to be confused with SARCASM but it differs from SARCASM in that it is usually lighter, less harsh in its wording though in effect probably more cutting because of its indirectness. It bears, too, a close relationship to INNUENDO. The ability to recognize *irony* is one of the surest tests of intelligence and sophistication. Its presence is marked by a sort of grim HUMOR, and "unemotional detachment" on the part of the writer, a coolness in expression at a time when the writer's emotions are really heated. Characteristically it speaks words of praise to imply blame and words of blame to imply praise, though its inherent critical quality makes the first type much more common than the second. The great effectiveness of *irony* as a literary device is the impression it gives of great restraint. The writer of *irony* has his tongue in his cheek; for this reason *irony* is more easily detected in speech than in writing since the voice can, through its intonation, easily warn the listener of a double significance. One of the most famous ironic remarks in literature is Job's "No doubt but ye are the people, and wisdom shall die with you." Antony's insistence, in his oration over the dead Caesar, that "Brutus is an honorable man" bears the same ironic imprint. Goldsmith, Jane Austen, and Thackeray, in one NOVEL or another, make frequent use of this form; Jonathan Swift is an archironist—his "Modest Proposal" for saving a starving Ireland, by suggesting that the Irish sell their babies to the English landlords, is perhaps the most savagely sustained ironic writing in our literature. The novels of Thomas Hardy and Henry James are elaborate artistic expressions of the ironic spirit, for *irony* applies not only to statement but also to event, SITUATION, and STRUCTURE. In DRAMA, *irony* has a special meaning, referring to knowledge held by the audience but hidden from the relevant actors. TRAGIC IRONY is a form of DRAMATIC IRONY in which characters use words that mean one thing to them but have foreboding meaning to those who understand the situation better. In contemporary criticism, *irony* is used to describe a poet's "recognition of incongruities" and his controlled acceptance of them. Among the devices by which *irony* is achieved are HYPERBOLE, UNDERSTATEMENT, and SARCASM. See DRAMATIC IRONY.

Irregular Ode: An ODE that does not follow either the pattern of STROPHE, ANTISTROPHE, and EPODE of the PINDARIC ODE or the repetition of STANZAS of the HORATIAN ODE, but freely alters its stanzaic forms both in number and in length. It was introduced by Abraham Cowley in the seventeenth century. Wordsworth's "Ode on Intimations of Immortality" is a noted example. It is sometimes called the "pseudo-Pindaric ode." See ODE.

Issue: A distinct set of copies of an EDITION of a book. An *issue* is distinguishable from other copies or sets of copies of that EDITION by variations in the printed matter. A PRINTING may contain more than one *issue* if variations in the printed matter occur during the PRINTING.

Italian Sonnet: A SONNET divided into an OCTAVE always rhyming *abbaabba* and a SESTET usually rhyming in some arrangement of *cdecde*. See SONNET.

J

Jacobean Age: That portion of the RENAISSANCE PERIOD which fell during the reign of James I (1603–1625), so-called from the Latin form of James, *Jacobus*. Early Jacobean literature was in reality a rich flowering of ELIZABETHAN literature, while late Jacobean writing showed the attitudes characteristic of the CAROLINE AGE. During the *Jacobean Age* the breach between Puritan and Cavalier steadily widened, and there was a widespread growth of REALISM in art and CYNICISM in thought. It is the greatest period for the English DRAMA; Shakespeare wrote his greatest TRAGEDIES and his TRAGI-COMEDIES; Jonson flourished, producing CLASSICAL TRAGEDY, REALISTIC COMEDY, and MASQUES; and Beaumont and Fletcher, Webster, Chapman, Middleton, and Massinger were at their peaks. In poetry, Shakespeare published his *Sonnets,* Drayton his *Poems,* and Donne his META-PHYSICAL VERSE. In prose, it saw the publication of the King James translation of the Bible, Bacon's major work, Donne's sermons, Burton's *Anatomy of Melancholy,* the CHARACTER essays, and Dekker's realistic "NOVELS." See RENAISSANCE PERIOD and *Outline of Literary History*.

Jargon: Confused speech, resulting particularly from the mingling of several languages or dialects. The term is also used to refer to any strange language which sounds uncouth to us; in this sense outlandish speech. Sometimes *jargon* means simply nonsense or gibberish. *Jargon* also, like CANT, signifies the special language of a group or profession, as legal *jargon*, pedagogic *jargon*, thieves' *jargon*.

Jeremiad: A work that foretells destruction because of the evil of a group or a nation. It takes its name from the Hebrew prophet Jeremiah, who opens his prophecy with the Lord saying, "Out of the north an evil shall break forth upon all the inhabitants of the land . . . who have forsaken me, and have burned incense unto other gods, and worshiped the works of their own hands" (*Jeremiah,* 1:14, 16). The term is also used for literary expressions of great grief and complaint, similar to Jeremiah's *Lamentations,* an expression of his deep sorrow over the capture of Jerusalem.

Jest-books: A name applied to collections of humorous, witty, or satirical anecdotes and jokes, *jest-books* had some vogue in England and Germany and other European countries in the sixteenth and succeeding centuries. The "jests" in these miscellanies owe something to the Latin *facetia,* something to the medieval FABLIAU and EXEMPLUM, and borrow also from the EPIGRAM, the PROVERB, and ADAGE. They are usually short and often end with a "moral." Coarseness, ribaldry, REALISM, SATIRE, and CYNICISM often characterize the witty turns. The material in the *jest-books* probably is similar in character to the stock-in-trade of the medieval MINSTRELS, the printing press making possible the dissemination of such matter in book form. Women, friars, cuckolds, Welshmen, courtiers, tradesmen, foreigners, military officers, doctors, students, travelers, and many other classes are butts of the WIT or victims of practical jokes. The earliest English *jest-book* is *A Hundred Merry Tales* (*ca.*1526). Another famous one was *The Gests of Skoggan* (*ca.*1565), which illustrates a tendency of *jest-books* to be "biographical" in making the jokes cluster about a single man. So there were in the seventeenth and eighteenth centuries *jest-books* on Ben Jonson. One famous court jester, Archie Armstrong, published his own *jest-book, A Banquet of Jests and Merry Tales* (1630). It is divided into "Court Jests," "Camp Jests," "College Jests," "City Jests," and "Country Jests."

Jesuits: Members of the Society of Jesus, a Catholic religious order founded by Saint Ignatius Loyola in 1534. In contrast with the ascetic ideals of the medieval Catholic orders, the *Jesuits* were conceived as a band of spiritual soldiers living under strict military discipline who were expected to engage actively in affairs. The discipline was strict, the individual having no rights as such but vowing to serve God through the Society of Jesus. The members were bound by personal vows of poverty, chastity, and obedience. The head of the Order is called the "general," lives in Rome, and is subject to the Pope. The *Jesuits* became famous as schoolmasters and made effective efforts to raise the educational as well as spiritual standards of the clergy. Their activities as missionaries are well known; the letters of *Jesuit* missionaries in America give important pictures of early life in the colonies. They were very active in New France. Although political activities were technically forbidden, the objectives of the Order actually led the *Jesuits* into political intrigue and it is this fact that has led to much criticism of the Order, which is often accused of duplicity and casuistry, a charge perpetuated unjustly in the use of the term Jesuitical as a derogatory adjective. English poetry has been enriched by the poetic work of some *Jesuit* poets, notably Robert Southwell (1561–1595), whose *Saint Peter's Complaint* and his more brilliant short poems such as *The Burning Babe*, anticipate both the seriousness of Milton and the CONCEITS of Donne, and another *Jesuit* Gerard Manley Hopkins (1844–1899), whose *Poems*, posthumously published in 1918, demonstrated an intensity of feeling and a mastery of experimental poetic devices which have made him a master figure in modern poetry.

Jeu d'esprit: A witty playing with words, a clever sally. Much of Thomas Hood's verse, for example, may be said to be marked by a happy *jeu d'esprit*. The term is also applied to brief, clever pieces of writing, such as Benjamin Franklin's "bagatelles."

Jig: A non-literary farcical dramatic performance, the words being sung to the accompaniment of dancing. It was popular on the Elizabethan stage, often being used as an afterpiece. "He's for a *jig*, or a tale of bawdry," Hamlet says of Polonius. See DROLL.

Johnson's Circle: A name often applied to a literary group whose leader was Samuel Johnson, but better known as THE LITERARY CLUB. See LITERARY CLUB, THE.

Jongleur: A French term for a professional musical entertainer of medieval times, analogous to the Anglo-Saxon GLEEMAN and the later MINSTREL. Though primarily one who sang or recited the LYRICS, BALLADS, and stories of such original poets as the TROUBADOUR and the TROUVÈRE, the *jongleur* sometimes composed and sometimes supplied nonmusical forms of entertainment, such as juggling and tumbling. The dissemination of literary forms and materials from nation to nation in the Middle Ages is due partly to the activities of the *jongleur* and the MINSTREL.

Journal: A form of autobiographical writing, in which a day-by-day account of events and a record of personal impressions are kept. It is usually less intimate than a DIARY and more obviously chronological than an AUTOBIOGRAPHY. The term *journal* is also applied to any periodical publication that contains news or deals with matters of current interest in any particular sphere, as *The Journal of Southern History.*

Judicial Criticism: A kind of criticism that, in contradistinction to IMPRESSIONISTIC CRITICISM, attempts by the rigorous application of general standards and objective criteria to analyze, classify, define, and evaluate works of art. See CRITICISM, TYPES OF.

Jungian Criticism: Literary CRITICISM based on the psychology of Carl Jung, a Swiss psychiatrist and the founder of analytical psychology. His postulate of two dimensions in the unconscious: the personal, consisting of repressed events in the individual's life, and the archetypal, which is a part of the collective unconscious, has been widely employed by critics, particularly those interested in MYTH CRITICISM. See ARCHETYPE and MYTH.

K

Kabuki Plays: The most popular form of theatrical entertainment in Japan since the mid-seventeenth century. *Kabuki* is an eclectic theatrical form using stories, scenes, dances, and music, some of which are more than a thousand years old. It is a dance and musical theater, with elaborate stage settings. The actors are all men, some of whom are trained to impersonate women. They are skilled dancers and acrobats. The plays themselves seem of dubious literary value, being primarily important as vehicles for spectacle. They are of several kinds: EPIC plays, of the heroic period in Japanese history; "common-people's plays," tending toward naturalistic TRAGEDY; FARCES; and dance plays. All are marked by formalism and careful attention to theatricality. As Henry W. Wells has said, "The playwrights, if such they may be called, possessed an uncanny sense for the theatrical but a truly subversive view of dramatic literature." See NOH PLAYS.

Kailyard School: A name given to a group of Scottish writers whose work dealt idealistically with ordinary people in modern village life in Scotland. DIALECT was an important element in their writing. J. M. Barrie and "Ian Maclaren" are two of the best known members of the "school," which was popular toward the close of the nineteenth century. *Kailyard* is a Scottish term for a cabbage garden.

Kenning: A stereotyped figurative phrase used in OLD ENGLISH and other Germanic tongues as a synonym for a simple noun. *Kennings* are often picturesque metaphorical compounds. Specimen *kennings* from *Beowulf* are "the bent-necked wood," "the ringed prow," "the foamy-necked," "the sea-wood," and the "sea-farer," for *ship;* "the swan-road" and "the whale-road" for the *sea;* the "leavings of the file" for the *sword;* the "twilight-spoiler" for the *dragon;* the "storm of swords" for *battle;* and "peace-bringer among nations" for the *queen.*

Kind: A term widely used during the NEO-CLASSIC PERIOD for GENRE or literary type. Implicit in the use of the term is the assumption that literary GENRES have an objective, absolute existence analogous to the *"kinds"* of the natural world and that they obey "the laws of *kind."* See GENRE.

Kit-Cat Club: A club generally believed to have existed in London between 1703 and 1733, founded by members of the Whig Party and dedicated in part to the insuring of a Protestant succession to the throne. Among its members were Addison, Steele, Congreve, Vanbrugh, and Marlborough. It met at the "Cat and Fiddle" pastry-shop, kept by Christopher Cat, from whom it is generally assumed to have taken its name, although Addison in the *Spectator* (No. IX) says the name came from the pies served by Christopher Cat and called "kit-cats." In the summer it met in a room with a very low ceiling at the home of the publisher Jacob Tonson. When Sir Godfrey

Kneller painted the portraits of the members to hang in this room, he was forced to use small canvases, 36 by 28 inches, and this size was later called *kit-cat* size.

Knickerbocker Group: A name given to a group writing in and about New York during the first half of the nineteenth century. The name "Knickerbocker" was made famous by Washington Irving in his *Knickerbocker's History of New York*. The heyday of the group was the first third of the century, although it was represented in the *Knickerbocker Magazine* (1833–1865); the remnants of the Knickerbocker school were pilloried in Poe's *The Literati of New York City*. Journalism, editorship, the frontier, POETRY, NOVELS, SONGS, and, in the case of Bryant at least, translation from the classics, were the sorts of things which claimed the attention of these writers. The term "school" is, for them, a misnomer, since they consciously held few tenets in common and worked to no deliberate purpose as a group. Their association was one of geography and chance rather than of close organization. At the turn into the nineteenth century New York was forging ahead of Boston as a center of activity and of population, a fact which meant that naturally the city was becoming more important as a literary center. The more illustrious members of the school were: Washington Irving, James Fenimore Cooper, William Cullen Bryant, Joseph Rodman Drake, Fitzgreene Halleck, John Howard Payne, Samuel Woodworth, and George P. Morris.

Koran: A Moslem collection of scriptural writings. The text is believed to have been revealed to Mohammed from time to time over a period of years and, after many changes and much editing, took shape in an official transcription after Mohammed's death (A.D. 632). The book is the sacred scripture of millions of followers, and presents—in addition to matters of theology—moral teaching, liturgical directions, and advice as to religious conduct and ceremonials. The speaker is usually God.

Künstlerroman: A form of the APPRENTICESHIP NOVEL in which the PROTAGONIST is a writer or an artist and in which his struggles from childhood to maturity are both against an inhospitable environment and within himself toward an understanding of his creative mission. The most famous *Künstlerroman* is James Joyce's *A Portrait of the Artist as a Young Man*.

285

L

Lai: A SONG or short NARRATIVE POEM. See LAY.

Lake School: A name used to characterize Coleridge, Wordsworth, and Southey—three poets who at the beginning of the nineteenth century were living in the Lake District (Cumberland, Westmorland, and Lancashire). The name "lakers" is credited to the *Edinburgh Review,* which for several years adopted a very contemptuous attitude toward the poets. There was, properly, no "school" in the sense of the three all working for common objectives, but it is true that Coleridge and Wordsworth had certain convictions in common and on occasion worked together.

Lament: A poem expressing some great grief, usually more intense and more personal than that expressed in a COMPLAINT. *Deor's Lament,* an early Anglo-Saxon poem, for instance, presents the plaintive regret of the SCOP at his changed status after a rival had usurped his place in the esteem of a patron. The separate "tragedies" in such collections as the sixteenth-century *Mirror for Magistrates,* in which the ghosts of dead worthies tell the stories of their fall from fortune, were called *laments* in Renaissance times, an example being Sackville's "Lament" for the Duke of Buckingham. See COMPLAINT.

Lampoon: Writing which ridicules and satirizes the character or personal appearance of a person in a bitter, scurrilous manner. *Lampoons* were written in either VERSE or prose. Lampooning became a dangerous sport and fell into disuse with the development of the libel laws. See EPIGRAM.

Late Victorian Age, 1870–1901: The period between 1870 and the death of Queen Victoria saw the full flowering of the movement toward REALISM which had set in as early as the 1830's but which had been subordinated to the dominant ROMANTICISM of the first half of Victoria's reign. George Eliot and Thomas Hardy carried the realistic NOVEL to new heights. Spencer, Huxley, Newman, Arnold, and Morris, in the ESSAY, argued the meaning of the new science, the new religion, and the new society. The DRAMA, which had been sleeping for more than a century, awoke under the impact of Ibsen and the CELTIC RENAISSANCE. Stevenson, W. H. Hudson,

and Kipling revived romantic fiction. Oscar Wilde and the "decadents" wrote witty poetry and DRAMA. Walter Pater advanced the
doctrine of "Art for Art's sake." The tendency to look with critical
eyes on man, society, and God, to ask pragmatic questions, and to
seek utilitarian answers—a tendency which had begun in the second
quarter of the century—had become the dominant mode of thought
and of writing by the time that Queen Victoria died. See REALISTIC
PERIOD IN ENGLISH LITERATURE, VICTORIAN, and *Outline of Literary
History*.

Laureate: One honored by a crown of laurel; hence one especially
singled out because of distinctive achievement. The term has come
to be most frequently used in the British post of POET LAUREATE.
It is also applied to the recipient of other major honors, as Nobel
laureate. See POET LAUREATE.

Lay (*lai*): A SONG or short NARRATIVE POEM. The word has been
applied to several different poetic forms in French and English
literature. The earliest existing French *lais* were composed in the
twelfth century and were based upon earlier songs or verse-tales
sung by Breton minstrels on themes drawn from Celtic legend;
hence the term "Breton *lay*." Though some of the early French *lais*
were LYRIC, most of them were NARRATIVE, like those of Marie de
France, who wrote at the court of the English King Henry II about
A.D. 1175. A few of Marie's *lais* are related to ARTHURIAN LEGEND.
The prevailing VERSE of the early French *lais* was the eight-syllable
line rhyming in COUPLETS. Later French *lais* developed more complicated metrical forms.

The word *lay* was applied to English poems written in the fourteenth century in imitation of the French "Breton *lais*." Though a
few of them follow the short COUPLET form, more use the popular
TAIL-RHYME STANZA. Any short NARRATIVE POEM similar to the
French *lai* might be called a "Breton *lay*" by the English poets.
Actually themes from various sources were employed, including
classical, Oriental, and Celtic. Some of the best-known English Breton
lays are the *Lay of Launfal, Sir Orfeo, Sir Gowther*, and Chaucer's
Franklin's Tale.

Since the sixteenth century, *lay* has been used by English writers
as synonymous with *song*. In the early nineteenth century, *lay* sometimes meant a short historical BALLAD, as Scott's *Lay of the Last
Minstrel* and Macaulay's *Lays of Ancient Rome*. *Lais* as used by

Legend

François Villon for the title of the poems now known as *Petit Testament* (1456) is a different word, corresponding to modern French *legs,* "bequest."

Legend: A NARRATIVE or TRADITION handed down from the past. A *legend* is distinguished from a MYTH in that the *legend* has more of historical truth and perhaps less of the supernatural. *Legends* often indicate the lore of a people, and, in this way, serve as at least partial expressions of the racial or national spirit. Saints' *legends* are NARRATIVES of the lives of the early church heroes. *Legend* is also used for any brief explanatory comment accompanying paintings, charts, maps, or photographs.

Legitimate Theater: The presentation of regular plays, depending entirely on acting, on a STAGE before an audience, using living actors. Today it distinguishes what is commonly called "stage plays" from motion pictures, television, VAUDEVILLE, puppet shows, ballet, and MUSICAL COMEDY. The term derives from the PATENT THEATERS to which the presentation of DRAMA in the traditional sense was restricted from 1660 to 1843 in England.

Leitmotif: In literature an intentional and recurrent REPETITION of a word, a phrase, a situation, or an idea. Such REPETITION tends to unify a work through its power to remind the reader of its earlier occurrences. The phrases "A stone, a leaf, an unfound door" and "Ghost, come back again" in Thomas Wolfe's *Look Homeward, Angel* are examples of *leitmotives.* In a subtler way, "rain" in *A Farewell to Arms* functions as a *leitmotif.* See MOTIF.

Leonine Rhyme: A particular form of INTERNAL RHYME characterized by the rhyming of the syllable preceding the CAESURA with the last syllable of the line. Ordinarily *Leonine rhyme* is restricted to PENTAMETERS and HEXAMETERS, but less rigidly the term is applied to VERSES such as the "Stabat Mater" of the Church. The expression is said to be derived from the name of a writer of the Middle Ages, Leoninus, canon of St. Victor in Paris, who wrote ELEGIAC lines containing this variety of INTERNAL RHYME. An example of *Leonine rhyme* is italicized in the following:

> Ex rex Ed*vardus,* debacchans ut Leo*pardus.*

Also called INTERNAL RHYME. See RHYME.

Lexicography

Letter-press: Used to distinguish the reading matter, or the "text," of a book from the illustrative matter. This use of the term may have derived from the fact that, in the older processes of printing, the *letter-press* printed directly from type instead of from the plates, woodcuts, or blocks used for illustrations. The term is also employed to refer to the typography of a work, or to printing in a general sense. Among book manufacturers, *letter-press* refers to the process of printing by direct contact of the sheet to the inked raised surfaces of type, cuts, or those kinds of plates which duplicate raised type. *Letter-press* is then used in distinction to offset, gravure, and images printed by such methods as xerography or cathode-ray scanner-printing.

Letters: A general name sometimes given to literature (see BELLES-LETTRES). More specifically, of course, the classification refers to notes and EPISTLES exchanged between acquaintances, friends, or commercial firms. A great body of informal literature is preserved through collections of actual *letters*. The correspondence of such figures as Lord Byron, Jane and Thomas Carlyle, Lord Chesterfield, Charles Dickens, Edward FitzGerald, William Hazlitt, Charles Lamb, Mary Wortley Montagu, Thomas Gray, Horace Walpole, Sydney Smith, and Robert Louis Stevenson—to mention a few of the great letter writers—constitutes one of the pleasantest of byways in the whole realm of literature. *Letters*, in this sense, are distinguished from EPISTLES in that they present personal and natural relationships among friends, whereas EPISTLES are more usually formal documents prepared with a view to their being read by some public. See EPISTLE.

Lexicography: The art of making DICTIONARIES or LEXICONS. The most ancient DICTIONARY extant is said to be a Greek LEXICON called *Homeric Words,* prepared by Apollonius the Sophist in the reign of Augustus (27 B.C.–A.D. 14). The technique of making LEXICONS and DICTIONARIES developed slowly from the mere explanation of hard words by simpler ones in the same language to the preparation of elaborate lists, alphabetically arranged, with derivations, pronunciation, spellings, and illustrative quotations, and meanings, either in the same or other languages. For English *lexicography,* see DICTIONARIES, ENGLISH.

Lexicon: A word list or wordbook; a vocabulary; one of the standard terms for DICTIONARY, although it is usually applied only to dictionaries of Greek or Hebrew. See LEXICOGRAPHY.

Libretto: The text or book, containing the STORY, TALE, or PLOT of an OPERA or of any long musical composition—a cantata, for instance. It is the diminutive form of the Italian *libro,* a book.

Light Ending: In METRICS, a FEMININE ENDING.

Light Opera: A form of OPERA which lacks the dignity and seriousness of grand OPERA and usually stresses sentiment rather than passion. It is unlike COMIC OPERA in that spoken DIALOGUE is not commonly employed. An example is M. W. Balfe's *The Bohemian Girl* (1843).

Light Verse: Short LYRIC poems, gay and bantering in tone, sportive in mood, and often sophisticated in subject and formal in treatment. There are many varieties of *light verse:* PARODY, LIMERICK, OCCASIONAL VERSE, EPIGRAMS, VERS DE SOCIÉTÉ, CLERIHEWS, NONSENSE VERSE. Grace and ease of expression, fancifulness and will to delight, charming but mordant WIT, and frequently some serious or satiric intent are characteristic of a kind of POETRY that has been practiced with grace and honor by Aristophanes, Shakespeare, Goethe, Milton, Jonson, the CAVALIER LYRISTS, Swift, Pope, Dorothy Parker, Lewis Carroll, Edward Lear, W. S. Gilbert, T. S. Eliot, Phyllis McGinley, Christopher Morley, and Helen Bevington. Writers of *light verse* often employ difficult and challenging FORMS, delighting in particular in the FRENCH FORMS.

Limerick: A form of LIGHT VERSE, a particularly popular type of NONSENSE-VERSE. Its composition follows a definite pattern: five anapestic lines of which the first, second, and fifth, consisting of three *feet,* RHYME; and the third and fourth lines, consisting of two *feet,* RHYME. Sometimes a *limerick* is written in four lines, but when so composed, its third line bears an INTERNAL RHYME and might easily be considered two lines.

The origin of the *limerick* is not definitely known. Though originally a kind of epigrammatic SONG, passed around orally, *limericks* increased the range of their subject matter to encompass every possible theme, nothing being sacred to their HUMOR. They were chiefly concerned, however, with the manners, morals, and peculiarities of people. Their first recorded appearance in print was in 1820, when *Anecdotes and Adventures of Fifteen Young Ladies* and *The History of Sixteen Wonderful Old Women* were published, but they reached the peak of their vogue when Edward Lear published his *Book of Nonsense* in 1846. The following, taken from Lear's volume, illustrates the accepted *limerick* form:

> There was an old Man of the Dee,
> Who was sadly annoyed by a Flea;
>   When he said, "I will scratch it!"
>   They gave him a hatchet
> Which grieved that old Man of the Dee.

Linguistics: The scientific study of language. It is concerned with the description, comparison, or history of languages. *Linguistics* studies phonology (speech sounds), morphology (the history of word forms), semantics (the meaning of words), and syntax (the relationships among words in a sentence). Although once considered a division of PHILOLOGY, *linguistics* is today an independent and highly complex science. See PHILOLOGY.

Link Sonnet: An English SONNET in which the three QUATRAINS are linked by having the first RHYME of one QUATRAIN the second RHYME of the preceding QUATRAIN. The Spenserian SONNET, rhyming *abab bcbc cdcd ee,* is a *link sonnet*. See SONNET.

Linked Rhyme: A device borrowed from early Welsh poetry by Gerard Manley Hopkins. In *linked rhyme* the final syllable of one line is linked with the first consonant sound of the next line to make a RHYME with a sound already established in the STANZA. For example, in STANZA 31 of *The Wreck of the Deutschland* he is using the IDENTICAL RHYME "of them," and it is achieved for its third appearance in the STANZA in this way:

> Finger of a tender of, O of a feathery delicacy, the breast of the
>   Maiden could obey so . . .

The sound "of them" is achieved by linking the last two syllables "of the" with the beginning consonant sound "m" in the next line.

Litany: A ritualistic form of supplication commonly used in the Catholic Church. A solemn prayer. The form is sometimes adopted by writers for original poetic expression.

Literal: Accurate to the letter, without embellishment. Thus, in the first sense, the word is used, as in a "literal translation," to signify accuracy and thoroughness in presenting the exact meaning of the original—a TRANSLATION which is according to the usual meaning of the words and allows no freedom of expression or imagination to the translator. Quite different from PARAPHRASE. In the second sense, the term is frequently used to distinguish language which is matter of fact and CONCRETE from language which is given to much use of FIGURES OF SPEECH. *Literal* language is the opposite of FIGURATIVE.

Literary Ballad: A BALLAD composed by an author, as opposed to the FOLK BALLAD. See ART BALLAD.

Literary Club, The (Doctor Johnson's Circle): A club formed in London in 1764 at the suggestion of Sir Joshua Reynolds, famous painter, and with the cooperation of Dr. Samuel Johnson. Among the seven other charter members were Edmund Burke and Oliver Goldsmith. Famous men admitted to membership during Johnson's lifetime included Bishop Percy (ballad collector), David Garrick (actor), Edward Gibbon (historian), Adam Smith (economist), and James Boswell (Johnson's biographer). At first the members met at a weekly supper, and later at a fortnightly dinner during Parliament. At these meetings there was free and spirited discussion of books and writers, CLASSIC and contemporary, Doctor Johnson frequently dominating the conversation. Johnson became a sort of literary dictator and the Club itself was a formidable power: whole EDITIONS of a book were sold off in one day by its sanction. Though commonly thought of only in connection with late eighteenth-century literature, the Club has continued in existence, its later membership including fifteen prime ministers and such authors as Scott, Macaulay, Hallam, and Tennyson.

Litotes: A form of UNDERSTATEMENT in which a thing is affirmed by stating the negative of its opposite. To say "He was not unmindful" when one means that "He gave careful attention" is to employ *litotes*. Although a common device in ironic expression, *litotes* was also one of the characteristic FIGURES OF SPEECH of OLD ENGLISH POETRY.

Litterateur: A literary man, one who occupies himself with the writing or criticism or appreciation of literature. Although the term means one who is engaged in literary work or who has adopted literature as a profession, in practical usage it has a connotation of the DILETTANTE or of the "precious."

Little Magazine: A term used to designate literary JOURNALS of small circulation, very limited capital, and usually quite short lives, dedicated to the fostering of AVANT-GARDE aesthetic ideas and to publishing experimental POETRY and prose. Notable early examples were *The Yellow Book* (1894–1897) and *The Savoy* (1896) which gave expression to the English revolt against Victorian ideas, ideals, and materialism. Early American *little magazines* were *The Lark* (1895–1897) and *The Chap-Book* (1894–1898), but the most influential of all such American journals has been *Poetry: A Magazine of Verse,* founded by Harriet Monroe in Chicago in 1912 and still in existence.

A heyday of the *little magazine* came between World War One and the depression of the thirties. In England, in the United States, and particularly in Paris, a generation of artists in revolt against their culture and its standards found in the *little magazine* a sounding board for their ideas. *The Little Review* (1914–1929), *The Seven Arts* (1916–1917), *The Fugitive* (1922–1925), *The Dial* (after its move to New York in 1916 and to its end in 1929), *Hound and Horn* (1927–1934), *Secession* (1922–1924), *transition* (1927–1938), *Broom* (1921–1924), and *The Double Dealer* (1921–1925) were among the best of hundreds of such publications.

In the depression young writers tended to desert AVANT-GARDE aesthetic positions for radical social postures, and the *little magazines* were in large measure casualties. In the post-World-War-Two world, experimental writing and criticism found an effective sounding board in university circles, and the equivalent of the *little magazine* was frequently a joint student-faculty production operating under a grant from the parent institution.

Beginning in the late 1960's, however, a new *little magazine* movement has gotten vigorously underway, partly as a result of the UNDERGROUND PRESS and partly as the antiestablishmentarian new AVANT-GARDE. Its *little magazines* are too numerous to count and too new and untried to evaluate.

Thousands of pages of bad experimental POETRY, FICTION, and CRITICISM, have been published in the *little magazines,* but these debits are more than offset by the fact that James Joyce, T. S. Eliot, Sherwood Anderson, Ernest Hemingway, William Faulkner, Edgar

Lee Masters, Ezra Pound, Hart Crane, e. e. cummings, Edmund Wilson, the NEW CRITICS, Gertrude Stein, Thornton Wilder, John Crowe Ransom, and Allen Tate, among many others, found in the pages of the *little magazines* their first sympathetic publication media. Their present-day equivalents may now be publishing in the turbulent sea of today's *little magazines*.

Little Theater Movement: A term applied to a succession of efforts to encourage the writing and production of significant plays, as opposed to productions designed primarily for box-office success. The movement was originated by André Antoine in Paris in 1887 for the purpose of trying out certain dramatic experiments. There gathered about Antoine, himself a gifted actor, a group of young authors, whose plays he produced at the *Théâtre Libre* before a select audience of season ticket holders. His attempts to advance the cause of good DRAMA included also the introduction of foreign plays by such writers as Tolstoy, Ibsen, Hauptmann, Björnson, Strindberg, and Turgenev. His experiment aided in the development of French dramatists and influenced the founding of two other French *little theaters:* Lugné-Poë's *Théâtre de l'Œuvre* (1893) and Jacques Copeau's *Vieux Colombier* (1913). In Germany there was established in 1889 the *Freie Bühne*, followed by a rapid development of native talent: Hauptmann, Max Halbe, Otto Erich Hartleben, and others.

In England the movement began with the opening of the Independent Theatre (1891) under the management of Jacob Grein. Shaw, Jones, Pinero, Barrie, Galsworthy, and Barker were to some degree products of the movement. In Ireland the Irish Literary Theatre (1899) attempted to encourage Irish writers and the use of Irish themes. William Boyle, Lennox Robinson, J. M. Synge, Lady Gregory, and William Butler Yeats wrote for the Abbey players (see ABBEY THEATRE). The *little theater movement* began in America in 1906 and 1907 when three groups were organized in Chicago: The New Theatre, the Robertson Players, and the Hull House Theatre. In 1911–1912 came additional establishments: The Little Theatre of Maurice Browne (Chicago), Mrs. Lyman Gale's Toy Theatre (Boston), and the Festival Players of the Henry Street Settlement, the Provincetown Players, and the Washington Square Players (New York). Members of the Washington Square Players formed the Theatre Guild, which operated with spectacular success and was able by 1925 to build its own million-dollar playhouse. A splinter from the Guild formed the Group Theatre, which produced plays by writers like Paul Green and Clifford Odets. Despite these professional successes, however, the *little theater movement* in America remained essentially local and amateur, spread over thousands of groups in towns and cities across the nation. It sometimes had a strong university flavor, coming largely from the work of George P. Baker at Harvard and later at Yale and Frederich H. Koch at the University of North Carolina. The *little theater movement* established a flexible theater for serious writing and acting, brought the DRAMA to thousands who might never otherwise have seen it, and developed men of such talent as Eugene O'Neill, Paul Green, Philip Barry, Thornton Wilder, and R. E. Jones.

An outgrowth of the *little theater movement* came in 1936 with the establishment of the Federal Theatre Project, which annually employed over 13,000 theater workers and in its three years of existence produced more than 1200 plays. Its purpose was to supplement the commercial stage with serious and experimental DRAMA at low prices.

Liturgical Drama: A term sometimes applied to the early phase of MEDIEVAL religious DRAMA when the MYSTERY PLAYS were performed as part or extension of the liturgical service of the church. In their earliest form they were in Latin, and were operatic in character, the lines being chanted or sung rather than spoken. The name *liturgical drama* is also sometimes used for the MYSTERY PLAYS developed from the liturgy. See MYSTERY PLAY, MEDIEVAL DRAMA.

Local Color Writing: Writing which exploits the speech, dress, mannerisms, habits of thought, and topography peculiar to a certain region. Of course all FICTION has a LOCALE, but *local color writing* exists primarily for the portrayal of the people and life of a geographical setting. About 1880 this interest became dominant in American literature; what was called a "local color movement" developed. The various sectional divisions of America were "discovered." Bret Harte, Mark Twain, and Joaquin Miller wrote of the West; George Washington Cable, Lafcadio Hearn, Mary Noailles Murfree, and Joel Chandler Harris spoke for the South; Sarah Orne Jewett and Mary E. Wilkins Freeman interpreted New England.

Local color writing was marked by the attempt at accurate DIALECT reporting, a tendency toward the use of eccentrics as CHARACTERS, and the use of sentimentalized pathos or whimsical HUMOR in plotting. A subdivision of REALISM, *local color writing* lacked the basic seriousness of true REALISM; by and large it was content to be entertainingly informative about the surface peculiarities of special regions. It emphasized VERISIMILITUDE of detail without being concerned often enough about truth to the larger aspects of life or human nature. Although local color NOVELS were written, the bulk of the work done in the movement was in the SKETCH and the SHORT STORY, aimed at the newly developing mass-circulation MAGAZINE audience. See REGIONAL LITERATURE.

Locale: The physical SETTING within which the action of a NARRATIVE takes place. It implies geographical and scenic qualities rather than the less tangible aspects of SETTING. *Locale* is the actual context within which the action of the NARRATIVE occurs. See SETTING.

Locution: A term applied to a word or a group of words that constitutes a meaning group. It is also applied to a STYLE of speech or verbal expression, particularly when it involves some peculiarity of IDIOM or manner.

Logaoedic: In CLASSICAL PROSODY a VERSE composed of ANAPESTS and IAMBS or DACTYLS and TROCHEES. The term is also used to designate any mixed METER.

Lollards: The name applied to the followers of John Wycliffe, who inspired a popular religious reform movement in England late in the fourteenth century. Lollardism sprang from the clash of two ideals— that of worldly aims, upheld by the rulers of church and state, and that of self-sacrificing religion, separated from worldly interests, upheld by the humbler elements among the clergy and the laity. Wycliffe himself died in 1384 after sponsoring and aiding in the translation of parts of the Bible into English; but the movement continued to gain strength. In 1395 the *Lollards* presented a petition to Parliament demanding reform in the church. Though it was not successful, its terms are early expressions of the attitude which triumphed with the Reformation in the sixteenth century. It denounced the riches of the clergy, asked that war be declared unchristian, and expressed disbelief in such doctrines and practices as transubstantiation, image-worship, and pilgrimages. Though suppressed early in the fifteenth century, Lollardism lived on secretly and later flared up in time to furnish a strong native impetus to the Lutheran Reformation in England early in the sixteenth century. This survival of Lollardism helps explain the fact that the English Reformation movement in its early stages was a popular movement rather than a scholarly one. Some *Lollards* were burned as heretics. Early Lollardism is reflected in *Piers Plowman's Crede* (1394) (popular attitude). Chaucer's country parson, sympathetically described in the *Prologue* to the *Canterbury Tales,* was accused by the Host of being a "Loller." Lollardist attitudes find late expression in many of the pamphlets of the Reformation controversy.

Long Measure: A STANZA form consisting of four lines of IAMBIC TETRAMETER and rhyming either *abcb* or *abab*. Compare with BALLAD STANZA, COMMON MEASURE.

Loose Sentence: A sentence grammatically complete at some point (or points) before the end; the opposite of a PERIODIC SENTENCE. A complex *loose sentence* consists of an independent clause followed by a dependent clause. Most of the complex sentences we use are loose (the term implies no fault in structure), the PERIODIC SENTENCE being usually reserved for emphatic statements and to secure variety. The constant use of the PERIODIC SENTENCE would impose too great a strain on the reader's attention. *Loose sentences* with too many dependent clauses become "stringy."

Lost Generation: A term applied to the American writers, most of whom were born around 1900, who fought in the First World War, and who constituted a group reacting against the tendencies of the older writers in the 1920's. Although many of them spent much of their time in Paris, others lived and worked in New York, and some remained in the Middle West and the South. They were very active in the publication of LITTLE MAGAZINES. The term "Lost Generation" came from Gertrude Stein's remark to a mechanic in Hemingway's presence that "You are all a lost generation." Hemingway used it as a motto in his novel *The Sun Also Rises,* whose HERO, the emasculated Jake Barnes, is often considered the archetypal man of the generation. It was widely applied to such figures as F. Scott Fitzgerald, Hemingway, Hart Crane, Louis Bromfield, and Malcolm Cowley, as descriptive of the traditional values which had been lost to them as a result of the war and the nature of the modern world.

Low Comedy: The opposite of HIGH COMEDY, *low comedy* has been called "elemental comedy," in that it is lacking in seriousness of purpose or subtlety of manner and has little intellectual appeal. Some typical features of *low comedy* are: quarreling, fighting, noisy singing, boisterous conduct in general, boasting, BURLESQUE, trickery, buffoonery, clownishness, drunkenness, coarse jesting, servants' chatter (when unrelated to the serious action), scolding, and shrewishness. In English dramatic history *low comedy* appears first as an incidental expansion of the action, often originated by the actors themselves, who speak "more than is set down for them." Thus in MEDIEVAL religious DRAMA Noah's wife exhibits stubbornness and has to be taken into the ark by force and under loud protest, or Pilate or Herod engage in uncalled-for ranting. In the MORALITY PLAYS the elements of *low comedy* became much more pronounced, and the antics of the Vice and other boisterous horseplay were introduced to lend life to the plays. In ELIZABETHAN DRAMA such elements persisted, in spite of their violation of the law of DECORUM, because they were demanded by the public; but playwrights like Shakespeare frequently made them serve serious dramatic purposes (such as relief, marking passage of time, echoing main action). A few of the many examples of *low comedy* in Shakespeare are: the porter scene in *Macbeth,* Launcelot Gobbo and old Gobbo in *The Merchant of Venice*, the Audrey-William love-making scene in *As You Like It,* and the Trinculo-Stephano-Caliban scene in *The Tempest.* The famous Falstaff scenes in *King Henry the Fourth* are examples of how Shakespeare could lift *low comedy* into pure COMEDY by stressing the human and character elements and by infusing an intellectual content into what might otherwise be mere buffoonery. *Low comedy* is not a recognized special type of play, as is the COMEDY OF HUMOURS, for example, but may be found either alone or combined with various sorts of both COMEDY and TRAGEDY. See COMEDY, FARCE, VAUDEVILLE.

Lyric: A brief subjective POEM strongly marked by IMAGINATION, melody, and emotion, and creating for the reader a single, unified impression. The early Greeks distinguished between *lyric* and choric poetry by terming that poetry *lyric* which was the expression of the emotion of a single singer accompanied by a lyre, and "choric" those verses which were the expression of a group and were sung by a CHORUS. This distinction has now quite disappeared, though the conception of the *lyric* as the individual and personal emotion of

Lyric

the poet still holds and is, perhaps, the chief basis for discriminating between the *lyric* and other poetic forms. No longer primarily designed to be sung to an accompaniment, the *lyric* nevertheless is essentially melodic since the melody may be secured by a variety of RHYTHM patterns and may be expressed either in rhymed or unrhymed VERSES. Subjectivity, too, is an important element of a form which is the personal expression of personal emotion imaginatively phrased. It partakes, in certain high examples, of the quality of ecstasy. With a record of existence for thousands of years in every literature of the world, the *lyric* has naturally been different things to different people at different times. Strict definition is impossible.

The history of the *lyric* in English starts almost with the beginnings of our literature. In *Beowulf* certain passages have *lyric* qualities. *Deor's Lament* is essentially lyrical in purpose. Later the introduction of Latin HYMNS and the NORMAN CONQUEST brought in French and Italian elements. By about 1280 we have in "Sumer is icumen in" what would pass the strictest critic today as a lyrical expression. By 1310 a manuscript collection of POEMS was made which, in addition to South European FORMS, presented some forty English *lyrics*. Before 1400 Chaucer had written a fair body of *lyrics*, particularly modeled on French forms. The TROUBADOUR of France had done his work well and had so awakened interest in lyrical forms as to make them common to the various European literatures; and Petrarch had made current the SONNET. Thomas Wyatt and the Earl of Surrey popularized in England these Italian lyrical FORMS, particularly the SONNET, and by the time Tottel's *Miscellany* appeared (1557) the body of English *lyrics* was large and creditable. In ELIZABETHAN England the *lyric* burst into full bloom at the touch of such poets as Sidney, Spenser, Daniel, and Shakespeare. SONGS, MADRIGALS, airs, became numerous. Jonson and Herrick carried the tradition further. To seventeenth-century England Cowley introduced the IRREGULAR ODE (a *lyric* form), and later Dryden adopted the FORM. The romantic revival brought English literature some of its noblest poetry in the ODES of Gray, Collins, Wordsworth, and Coleridge. Burns raised the *lyric* to new power. Coleridge and Wordsworth made it the vehicle of ROMANTICISM. Scott, Byron, Shelley, and Keats molded the form to new perfection. Bryant, Emerson, Whittier, Longfellow, and Poe gave it expression in America. Victorian poets spoke through it frequently. Tennyson, Browning, Rossetti, William Morris, Swinburne—England's greatest poets of the period—were also some of our greatest lyricists. And in twentieth-century England and America the *lyric*—in its various types—is still the most frequently used poetic expression.

The *lyric* is perhaps the most broadly inclusive of all the various types of VERSE. In a sense it could be argued to be not so much a form as a manner of writing. Subjectivity, IMAGINATION, melody, emotion—these qualities have been fairly persistently adhered to by the poets. But as the *lyric* spirit has flourished, the manner has been confined in various ways with the result that we have, within the *lyric* type, numerous subclassifications. HYMNS, SONNETS, SONGS, BALLADS, ODES, ELEGIES, VERS DE SOCIÉTÉ, the whole host of FRENCH FORMS, BALLADE, RONDEL, RONDEAU—all these are varieties of lyrical expression classified according to differing qualities of FORM and subject matter and mood.

Lyrical Drama: A term used for a dramatic poem (see DRAMATIC POETRY) in which the form of DRAMA is used to express LYRIC themes (author's own emotions or ideas of life) instead of relying upon a story as the basis of the action.

M

Mabinogion: A term applied to a collection of old Welsh tales translated by Lady Charlotte Guest from the *Red Book of Hergest,* a Welsh manuscript written in the thirteenth or fourteenth century containing tales written centuries earlier. Only four of these tales, *Pwyll, Prince of Dyved; Branwen, Daughter of Llyr; Manawyddan, Son of Llyr;* and *Math, Son of Mathonwy* (the so-called four branches), are in the strictest sense of the word included in the term *mabinogion.* Although some modern authors follow Lady Charlotte Guest in explaining this word as meaning "a collection of tales for the young," later authorities explain *mabinogion* as the plural of *mabinogi,* "a collection of tales every young poet should know," a *mabinog* being a literary apprentice, a young man receiving instruction from a qualified BARD. For a classification of the contents of the *Mabinogion* and for the possible relation of the tales to Arthurian ROMANCES, see WELSH LITERATURE.

Macaronic Verse: A type of VERSE which mingles two or more languages. More especially it refers to poems incorporating modern

Magazine

words (given Latin or Greek endings) with Latin or Greek. The origin of this often nonsensical sort of VERSE is credited to Tisi degli Odassi, who interspersed Latin with Italian in *Carmen Maccaronicum* (1488). A Benedictine monk, Teofilo Folengo (1491–1544), wrote a famous MOCK HEROIC called *Liber Macaronicus* (1520). Verse of the sort was soon written in France and other European countries; the best example in English is said to be the *Polemo-Middinia,* credited to William Drummond of Hawthornden. The following, by "E.C.B.," will be a self-explanatory example to anyone who knows his Latin (or his Mother Goose):

> Cane carmen SIXPENCE, pera plena rye,
> De multis atris avibus coctis in a pie:
> Simul hæc apert'est, cantat omnis grex,
> Nonne permirabile, quod vidit ille rex?
> Dimidium rex esus, misit ad reginam
> Quod reliquit illa, sending back catinum.
> Rex fuit in aerario, multo nummo tumens;
> In culina Domina, bread and mel consumens;
> Ancell' in horticulo, hanging out the clothes,
> Quum descendens cornix rapuit her nose.

Macaronic verse was not always NONSENSE VERSE; its intent was frequently that of serious SATIRE. The term is sometimes, although incorrectly, applied to any VERSE which has two languages, such as William Dunbar's "Lament for the Makaris" (*ca.*1508) which uses a Latin REFRAIN, *"Timor mortis conturbat me."*

Macron: The name of the symbol ($^-$) used to indicate a long syllable in QUANTITATIVE VERSE.

Madrigal: A short LYRIC, usually dealing with love or a PASTORAL theme and designed for—or at least suitable for—a musical setting. In the ELIZABETHAN PERIOD the term was used to describe a kind of SONG sung without accompaniment by five or six voices with intricate interweaving of words and melody. The Italian *madrigal* usually consisted of six to thirteen lines based on three RHYMES. Today the term is used quite loosely. Shakespeare's "Take, O, take those lips away" from *Measure for Measure* is a *madrigal.*

Magazine: A term applied to any of several kinds of periodical miscellanies containing various kinds of material by several authors.

Magnum opus (pl. *Magna opera*): A great work, a masterpiece. Formerly the term was used in all seriousness, but nowadays it often carries with it a suggestion of IRONY or SARCASM.

Malapropism: An inappropriateness of speech resulting from the use of one word for another which has some similarity to it. The term is derived from a character, Mrs. Malaprop, in Sheridan's *The Rivals,* who was constantly giving vent to such expressions as the following: "as headstrong as an allegory on the banks of the Nile," "a progeny of learning," "illiterate him, I say, quite from your memory."

Malediction: A CURSE. The opposite of benediction since it invokes evil rather than good. The famous "Cursed be he that moves my bones" used as an EPITAPH for Shakespeare is an example.

Manichaeism: An Oriental religion founded in the third century (A.D.) by a Persian, Mani. *Manichaeism* sees God and Satan as coeval and engaged in an eternal struggle. The forces of light (good) do endless battle against the forces of darkness (evil). This cosmic struggle also takes place in each individual man. His body, like all material substance, is evil and belongs to Satan, but he is also infused with a modicum of godly light, and the struggle between the material (his body) and the godly (his light or spirit) continues as long as body and soul are united. The elect succeed in freeing the light from the evil of darkness. Through metempsychosis the unelect may progress upward toward election. Such beliefs led to a very ascetic way of life for the true believers. Mani borrowed from the Gnostics, various Oriental religions, including the Zoroastrian, and Christianity. His teachings were popular through the fifth century, but since the sixth century have been considered a major source for heresy in most religions.

Manners: When used in the sense of defining various literary GENRES, *manners* refers to prevailing modes of social conduct of a specific class at a definite period of time. It involves, in addition to the accepted rules of polite behavior for that class, its system of values and mores, as reflections of moral attitudes. See COMEDY OF MANNERS, NOVEL OF MANNERS.

Manuscript, Medieval: The art of manuscript-making was highly developed in the Middle Ages; the finer existing "illuminated" manuscripts and early printed books modeled on them show an artistry perhaps superior to that of the best examples of modern book-making. The Gutenberg Bible (1456), for example, has been called the finest printed book in existence. As no mechanical means such as printing existed for multiplying copies, each manuscript required for its manufacture an infinite amount of skilled labor. Parchment was first employed, the finest kind being vellum (made from calf-skin), though paper was employed in the later Middle Ages. The actual writing was done chiefly in the monasteries, first by ordinary monks and later by professional scribes. The process of making the book included (1) the copying of the text by the scribe on separate sheets, (2) the inspection by the corrector, (3) the insertion of the capital letters and rubrics and other colored decorative matter by the rubricator and illuminator, (4) the binding by a binder who arranged the sheets (usually by folding a group of four sheets once to make a "quire" of eight leaves, or sixteen pages) and completed the binding by the use of wooden boards, leather, and velvet. The result was a substantial "manuscript" in form much like a modern book of large size but far sturdier in construction. The illuminator did his work with great care. Favorite colors were gold and red and blue, though green and purple and yellow were frequently employed. In spite of losses by fire, war, robbery, and neglect, thousands of *medieval manuscripts* are still in existence and are carefully preserved in numerous public and private libraries. Early printed books (see INCUNABULUM) were modeled on the manuscript. In England, many *medieval manuscripts* are thought to have been destroyed as a result of the suppression of the monasteries during the Protestant Reformation.

Märchen: A German FAIRY TALE. It may be a simple folk TALE of the sort collected by Wilhelm and Jacob Grimm, known as the *Volksmärchen,* or it may be a short ALLEGORY laid in a fantastic realm of the sort written in the nineteenth century by Goethe, Novalis, Tieck, and E. T. A. Hoffmann, known as the *Kunstmärchen* (art tale).

Marginalia: Notes and comments written in the margins of a book by a reader as commentaries on the text. In some cases such *marginalia* have value in reconstructing the reader's life and mind, as such *marginalia* by Herman Melville have, or make valuable critical comments, as *marginalia* of Coleridge's do. The term is also sometimes used to characterize brief critical OBITER DICTA, as in Edgar Allan Poe's *Marginalia.*

Marinism: An affected poetic STYLE practiced by the Italian poet Giambattista Marino (1569–1625) and his followers. It is the manifestation of a general tendency toward a strained, flamboyant, or shocking STYLE during the later phases of the RENAISSANCE, in some respects analogous to the BAROQUE in art. Marino expressed this aspect of his creed thus:

> Astonishment's the poet's aim and aid:
> Who cannot startle best had stick to trade.
> (*Fletcher's translation*)

A typical conceit of Marino is his calling stars "blazing half-dimes of the celestial mint." Another aspect of *Marinism* was its "effeminate voluptuousness." Some English METAPHYSICAL poets were influenced by Marino: Lord Herbert of Cherbury, Thomas Stanley, Sir Edward Sherburne, and Richard Crashaw. See EUPHUISM, CONCEIT, GONGORISM, METAPHYSICAL VERSE, BAROQUE.

Marprelate Controversy: In the 1580's the Puritan opposition to the bishops of the established church in England, whose power was greatly strengthened by state support, expressed itself in outspoken pamphlets. Some of the authors of these tracts were severely punished—one executed—and in 1585 the censorship over such publications was made more rigid by a provision limiting printing rights to London and the two universities. In defiance of these regulations the Puritan party began issuing, in 1588, a series of violent attacks on the episcopacy, printed surreptitiously and signed by the pen name "Martin Marprelate." The attacks were answered with corresponding scurrility by the conservatives, including Robert Greene, John Lyly, and Thomas Nash. The authorship of the Marprelate pamphlets has never been definitely established, but whoever the author was or whoever the authors were, they and their opponents supplied interesting examples of spirited prose SATIRES. The controversy was suppressed by the death in prison of one alleged author and the execution in 1593 of two others.

Marxism: The social, economic, and political doctrines of Karl Marx, Friedrich Engels, and their disciples. *Marxism* assumes the independent reality of matter and its priority over mind (dialectical materialism). It teaches a theory of value based upon labor, the economic determination of all social actions and institutions, the class struggle as the basic pattern in history, the inevitable seizure of power through the revolution of the proletariat, the dictatorship of that proletariat, and the ultimate establishment of a classless society. In one sense *Marxism* is an interpretation of history and a prophecy of an evolutionary process in which revolution is not necessary. In another sense, that taken by the Communists, *Marxism* is a revolutionary program. The principal Marxist doctrines were set forth in *The Communist Manifesto,* by Marx and Engels (1848) and *Das Kapital,* by Marx (1867). The impact of *Marxism* on historical theory has been pervasive, and in this sense it has permeated much twentieth-century thought, even that of the anti-Marxist. *Marxism* has had notable influence on FICTION, particularly that of radical sociological leanings, and on sociologically inclined literary CRITICISM. It was a strong influence on the writing done in America in the 1930's, and to some extent on English writing of the same period. It has, of course, been a dominant influence on Russian writing of all kinds. The leading Marxist critic today is the Hungarian Georg Lukács.

Masculine Rhyme: RHYME that falls on the stressed and concluding syllables of the RHYME-words. See RHYME, FEMININE RHYME.

Masked Comedy: COMEDY in which masked figures spoke in distinctive regional DIALECTS. See COMMEDIA DELL'ARTE.

Masque: In England as well as in other European countries there existed in medieval times (partly as survivals or adaptations of ancient pagan seasonal ceremonies) species of games or spectacles characterized by a procession of masked figures. In these DISGUISINGS or MUMMINGS, which were usually of a popular or folk character, a procession of masquers would go through the streets, enter house after house, silently dance, play at dice with the citizens or with each other, and pass on. Adopted by the aristocracy, these games, modified by characteristics borrowed from civic pageants, chivalric customs, sword-dances, and the RELIGIOUS DRAMA, developed into elaborate spectacles, which evolved into the entertainments known as *masques.* Because of this gradual evolution of the FORM and the scanty records it is impossible to say when the *masque* actually came into existence. The famous EPIPHANY spectacle of 1512, given by and participated in by Henry VIII, is sometimes referred to as the first English *masque*.

The chief development of the *masque* came in the latter part of Elizabeth's reign and, especially, in the reigns of James I and Charles I, and reached its climax under such poets as Daniel, Beaumont, Middleton, and Ben Jonson. The greatest development was due to the poetic and dramatic genius of Jonson and Inigo Jones, famous court architect and deviser of stage machinery. The "essential" *masque*, as distinguished from the "literary" *masque* (e.g., *Comus*), makes an appeal to the eye and the ear, with a succession of rapidly changing scenes and tableaux crowded with beautiful figures. The gods of Olympus, the monsters of Tartarus, the heroes of history, the ladies of romance, the fauns, the satyrs, the fairies, the witches were presented to the eye, while musical instruments charmed the ear.

Masques became increasingly expensive, almost unbelievable amounts being expended in costumes, scenery, properties, and for professional musicians, dancers, and actors. In the *masque* proper, which was the arrival and dancing of masked figures, the actors were amateurs drawn from the court society—princes and princesses, even queens and kings, taking part. With the development by Jonson of the ANTIMASQUE, the dramatic and literary qualities increased. Mythological and PASTORAL elements were emphasized, Jonson maintaining (against Daniel and Jones) that the *masque* should be based upon some poetic idea and the action should be significant as well as spectacular, so that Milton's *Comus* (1634), one of the best known of all *masques*, represents a legitimate development of what was originally little but spectacle. The *masque* commonly was a feature of some celebration, such as a wedding or coronation, and served as a formal preliminary entertainment to a court ball, and was frequently employed at the entertainments in the INNS OF COURT. *Masques* exerted much influence upon the poetry and DRAMA of the RENAISSANCE. Spenser, for example, incorporates *masque*-like episodes in his *The Faerie Queene* (e.g., the procession of the Seven Deadly Sins in Book I, Canto iv, and the *masque* of Cupid in III, xii). The effect upon the popular DRAMA itself was probably great, since some dramatists wrote for both the court and the London stage. Peele's *Arraignment of Paris* is a PASTORAL play much like a *masque*. Many of Shakespeare's plays show the influence; the betrothal *masque* in *The Tempest* is an example. *As You Like It* has been called a mere "series of tableaux and groupings," *masque*-like in the lack of serious action, in the prominence of music, and in the spectacular appearance of Hymen as a DEUS EX MACHINA at the end. The glorious era of the *masque* ended with the triumph of the Puritan Revolution (1642). See ANTIMASQUE.

Maxim: A short, concise statement, usually drawn from experience and inculcating some practical advice; an ADAGE. "When in doubt, win the trick," a saying of Hoyle's, is an example of a *maxim* in bridge. See APHORISM, PROVERB.

Meaning: It is possible to distinguish four different aspects in the *meaning* of a statement. As given by I. A. Richards, they are (1) sense, the denotative "something" that the speaker or writer is trying to communicate, (2) feeling, the attitude the speaker or writer has toward this sense, (3) TONE, the attitude he has toward his audience, and (4) intention, the effect he consciously or unconsciously intends to produce through what he says or writes, how he feels about it, and the attitude he takes toward his audience. In another way, *meaning* can be seen as of two kinds: DENOTATION and CONNOTATION. For a literary work there are also four possible levels of *meaning:* the literal, the allegorical, the tropological or moral, and the anagogical or spiritual. See DENOTATION, CONNOTATION, FOUR SENSES OF INTERPRETATION.

Medieval Drama: A general term used to include all forms of DRAMA in the Middle Ages, though the religious DRAMA and its allied forms are usually meant by the phrase. The medieval religious DRAMA was an outgrowth of the liturgical services of the church. As early as the tenth century, perhaps in Northern France, TROPES or musical elaborations of the church services, particularly of the Easter Mass, developed into true DRAMA when the Latin lines telling the story of the Resurrection, instead of being sung antiphonally by the two parts of the choir, were sung or spoken by priests who impersonated the two angels and the three Marys in the scene at the tomb of Christ.

Such dramatic TROPES later became detached from the liturgical service, and *medieval drama* was born. That such performances appeared early in England is shown by the existence of the *Concordia Regularis* (*ca.*975), a complete set of instructions (stage directions) supplied to the Benedictine monks by the Bishop of Winchester. The conscious dramatic intent is shown in the first few lines of the

Concordia: "While the third lesson is being chanted, let four brethren vest themselves. Let one of these, vested in an alb, enter as though to take part in the service, and let him approach the sepulchre without attracting attention and sit there quietly with a palm in his hand . . . and let them all . . . stepping delicately as those who seek something, approach the sepulchre" (Chambers' translation). Dramatic TROPES developed around the Christmas and Easter services.

This use of the dramatic method for the purpose of making vivid religious rites and instruction must have struck a responsive chord in the medieval audience, and it was not long till further important developments, the stages of which cannot now be exactly traced, took place. The performances were transferred from the church to the outdoors; Latin gave way to native language; and eventually the performances became secularized when the town authorities, utilizing the trade guilds as dramatic companies, took charge of the production of the plays. Eventually great CYCLES of Scriptural plays developed in which the whole plan of salvation was dramatically set forth (see MYSTERY PLAY). Plays employing the same technique as the Scriptural plays but based upon the lives of saints, especially miracles performed by saints including the Virgin Mary (MIRACLE PLAYS, or SAINTS' PLAYS), also developed about A.D. 1100, though they seem not to have been numerous in England. Much later (*ca.*1400) the MORALITY PLAY (dramatization of a moral ALLEGORY) became popular and with the somewhat similar play known as INTERLUDE became an immediate precursor of ELIZABETHAN DRAMA. There was also a considerable body of FOLK DRAMA in the late Middle Ages, performed out of doors on such festival days as Hock Tuesday—Robin Hood plays, Sword-dance plays, MUMMINGS, and DISGUISINGS. Perhaps also there were plays based on MEDIEVAL ROMANCES.

The CYCLIC DRAMA (MYSTERY PLAYS) and the MORALITIES became so secularized as to bring on the disapproval of the church. The development of secular elements, especially the stressing of comic features such as the shrewish behavior of Noah's wife or the addition of comic scenes not demanded by the serious action, such as the sheep-stealing episode in the Towneley *Second Shepherd's Play,* led definitely toward Elizabethan COMEDY. Though it is difficult to analyze the full influence exerted by *medieval drama* upon later DRAMA, it is certain, as Felix E. Schelling remarks, that "it was in the ruins and débris of the MIRACLE PLAY and MORALITY that ELIZABETHAN DRAMA struck its deepest roots." For the method of performance of the medieval religious drama see MYSTERY PLAY. See DRAMA, MIRACLE PLAY, LITURGICAL DRAMA, TROPE, MORALITY PLAY, FOLK DRAMA, INTERLUDE.

Medieval Romance: *Medieval romances* are tales of adventure in which knights, kings, or distressed ladies, acting under the impulse of love, religious faith, or the mere desire for adventure, are the chief figures. The *medieval romance* appears in Old French literature of the twelfth century as a FORM which supplants the older CHANSON DE GESTE, an EPIC FORM. The EPIC reflects an heroic age whereas the *romance* reflects a chivalric age; the EPIC has weight and solidity, whereas the *romance* exhibits mystery and fantasy; the EPIC does not stress rank or social distinctions, important in the *romance;* the tragic seriousness of the EPIC is not matched in the lighter-hearted *romance;* the heroic figures of the EPIC are more consistently conceived than the heroes of *romance;* where the EPIC HERO aims at high achievement, the HERO of *romance* is usually satisfied with more or less aimless adventure; the EPIC observes narrative UNITY, whereas the STRUCTURE of the *romance* is loose; love is absent or of minor interest in the EPIC, whereas it is supreme in the *romances;* EPIC fighting is serious and well motivated, whereas fighting in the *romances* is spontaneous; the EPIC uses the dramatic method of having the characters speak for themselves, whereas the reader of a *romance* is kept conscious of a NARRATOR. The *romances* became extremely popular in Western Europe, occupying a place comparable with that of the NOVEL in modern literature. The earliest *romances* were in VERSE (hence the term METRICAL ROMANCES), but prose was also employed later. The materials for the early French *romances* were drawn chiefly from the Charlemagne material or CHANSONS DE GESTE ("Matter of France"), ancient history and literature ("Matter of Rome the Great"), and Celtic lore, especially Arthurian material ("Matter of Britain").

Romances were produced in English as early as the thirteenth century. They flourished in the fourteenth century, and continued to be produced in the fifteenth and sixteenth centuries, though the disfavor which they met at the hands of RENAISSANCE HUMANISTS caused them to lose standing, and RENAISSANCE versions as well as versions appearing in seventeenth- and eighteenth-century CHAPBOOKS are frequently degenerate forms, written to appeal chiefly to the middle and lower social classes. Middle English *romances* may be grouped on the basis of their subject-matter. The "Matter of England" includes stories based upon Germanic (including English) tradition and embraces *King Horn* (*ca.*1275), *Richard Lionheart* (1350), *Beves of Hampton* (*ca.*1300), *Havelock the Dane* (before 1300), *Guy of Warwick* (*ca.*1300), and *Athelston* (*ca.*1350). The "Matter of France" includes stories of Charlemagne and William of Orange, drawn from the CHANSONS DE GESTE. Important *romances* of the group are *Sir Ferumbras* (*ca.*1375), *Otuel* (*ca.*1300), *The Song of Roland* (fifteenth century), and *Huon of Bordeaux* (thirteenth century). The "Matter of Antiquity" includes various legends of Alexander the Great, legends of Thebes, and legends of Troy (including Chaucer's famous *Troilus and Criseyde*). The "Matter of Britain" includes the important Arthurian literature and is represented by such classics as the fourteenth-century METRICAL ROMANCE, *Sir Gawain and the Green Knight* and the fifteenth-century prose *Le Morte Darthur* of Malory. The Arthurian *romances* developing about the legend of King Arthur (see ARTHURIAN LEGEND) had eventually developed into great CYCLES of stories in Old French literature, some of the heroes of which, such as Tristram and Lancelot, did not belong to the original legend of Arthur. They were greatly elaborated in the bulky thirteenth-century French prose *romances* ("VULGATE Romances") which became sources for such English treatments of Arthurian themes as Malory's. A fifth group might include *romances* of miscellaneous origin, especially Oriental. Examples are *Amis and Amiloun* (before 1300), *Floris and Blanchefleur* (*ca.*1250), *Sir Isumbras* (1350–1400), and *Ipomedon* (twelfth century).

The MIDDLE ENGLISH *romances* are largely in verse, a few alliterative, others in COUPLETS or stanzaic forms borrowed from France. In comparison with French *romances* they usually show inferior artistry, less attention to psychological treatment (as COURTLY-LOVE characteristics), less sophistication, more credulity and use of the grotesque (like Richard's eating the lion's heart), and a higher moral tone.

Structurally, the *medieval romance* follows the loose pattern of the quest. Usually the PROTAGONIST sets out on a journey to accomplish some goal—rescue a maiden, meet a challenge, obey a kingly command, seek the HOLY GRAIL. On this journey, which forms the controlling outline of the PLOT, he encounters numerous adventures, many of them unrelated to his original quest except that they impede him or occur in a chronological sequence. Hence, except in the very best of these *romances*, the PLOTS are little better than threads on which the beads of EPISODES are strung in chronological rather than logical order. See ROMANCE, ARTHURIAN LEGEND, COURTLY LOVE, MIDDLE ENGLISH.

Meditative Poetry: A term applied to certain kinds of METAPHYSICAL POETRY of the sixteenth and seventeenth centuries, which yoke a practice of religious meditation of that period with RENAISSANCE poetic techniques. "The Practical Methode of Meditation" (1614), by the Jesuit Edward Dawson, describes the religious practice, which was probably strongly indebted to Ignatius Loyola's *Spiritual Exercises*. The aim of such meditation was to utilize all human faculties to apprehend the presence of God. Most *meditative poetry*, through its use of striking and often sensuous imagery, its records of studying religious topics until they are understood and deeply felt, and its technique for dramatizing the self in intense meditative experiences, becomes accounts of memorable moments of self-knowledge and of union with some transcendent reality. Louis L. Martz, while acknowledging that a precise definition of *meditative poetry* is probably impossible, suggests that it is poetry in which "the central meditative action consists of an interior drama, in which a man projects a self upon a mental stage, and there comes to understand that self in the light of a divine presence." Often such POEMS were written as a part of the author's preparation for religious ceremonies, such as the American poet Edward Taylor's *Preparatory Meditations before my Approach to the Lord's Supper*. Among notable writers of *meditative poetry* were Robert Southwell (1561–1595), John Donne (1572–1631), George Herbert (1593–1633), Richard Crashaw (*ca.*1612–1649), Henry Vaughan (1621–1692), and Thomas Traherne (1637–1674).

Meiosis: Intentional UNDERSTATEMENT for humorous or satiric effect and occasionally for emphasis. See UNDERSTATEMENT, LITOTES, IRONY.

Melic Poetry: POETRY written to be accompanied by the music of the lyre or flute. It was to this POETRY that the Alexandrians applied the term LYRIC, which is the designation under which it is generally known. *Melic poetry* was written in a variety of METERS and STANZA forms. It flourished in Greece between the seventh and the fifth centuries, B.C. Among its greatest POETS were Sappho, Anacreon, and Pindar.

Meliorism: A name applied to the belief that society has an innate tendency toward improvement and that that tendency can be furthered by conscious human effort. The belief was widely held in the late nineteenth century. Writers like George Eliot embraced it in the faith that by our frail and faulty efforts to aid the world, we move, though imperceptibly, toward a better world. At the conclusion of *Middlemarch* she expresses the idea very clearly: ". . . the growing good of the world is partly dependent on unhistoric acts; and that things are not so ill with you and me as they might have been, is half owing to the number who lived faithfully a hidden life, and rest in unvisited tombs." Thomas Hardy believed in an evolutionary *meliorism,* although his optimism about its operation or its rate was much smaller than George Eliot's. In his "Apology" in *Late Lyrics and Earlier,* he says, "Whether the human and kindred animal races survive till exhaustion or destruction of the globe . . . pain to all upon it, tongued or dumb, shall be kept down to a minimum by loving-kindness, operating through scientific knowledge, and actuated by the modicum of free will conjecturally possessed by organic life when the necessitating forces . . . happen to be in equilibrium, which may or may not be often."

Melodrama: A play based on a romantic PLOT and developed sensationally, with little regard for convincing MOTIVATION and with an excessive appeal to the emotions of the audience. The object is to keep the audience thrilled by the awakening, no matter how, of strong feelings of pity or horror or joy. POETIC JUSTICE is superficially secured, the characters (who are either very good or very bad) being rewarded or punished according to their deeds. Though typically a *melodrama* has a happy ending, TRAGEDIES which use much of the same technique are sometimes referred to as melodramatic. Likewise by a further extension of the term STORIES are sometimes said to be melodramatic in character.

The term literally means "a play with music," and at one time it was applied to the OPERA in a broad sense. *Melodrama* came into widespread use in England in the nineteenth century as a device to circumvent the Licensing Act, which restricted "legitimate" plays to the PATENT THEATERS but which allowed musical entertainments in other theaters. The use of SONGS, recitative, and incidental music disguised the dramatic nature of popular stage pieces, and they came to be known as *melodramas.* The first English *melodrama* is believed to have been Thomas Holcroft's *A Tale of Mystery,* produced in 1802. These *melodramas* usually exhibited the deplorable characteristics already listed, and finally the term by extension was applied to these characteristics independent of the presence or absence of music.

Memoirs: A form of autobiographical writing dealing with the recollections of prominent people or people who have been a part of or have witnessed significant events. *Memoirs* differ from AUTO-BIOGRAPHY proper in that they are usually concerned with personalities and actions other than those of the writer himself, whereas the AUTOBIOGRAPHY lays a heavier stress on the inner and private life of its subject.

Menippean Satire: A form of SATIRE originally developed by the Greek cynic Menippus and transmitted by his disciples Lucian and Varro. Varro in turn influenced Petronius and Apuleius. *Menippean satire* deals with mental attitudes rather than fully realized CHAR-ACTERS. It uses PLOT freely and loosely to present a view of the world in terms of sharply controlled intellectual patterns. In its shorter forms, *Menippean satire* is a DIALOGUE or a COLLOQUY, with its interest in the conflict of ideas. In longer works, the Menippean satirist piles up vast accumulations of fact and presents this erudition through some intellectual organizing principle. Robert Burton's *Anatomy of Melancholy* is an outstanding example of *Menippean satire*. Other works that may be so classified include *Gulliver's Travels*, by Swift; *Imaginary Conversations,* by Landor; Peacock's novels; *Alice in Wonderland,* by Lewis Carroll; *Noctes Ambrosianae,* by Christopher North; *Tristram Shandy,* by Laurence Sterne; and the whaling material in *Moby-Dick,* by Melville. A recent work that is an almost perfect example of *Menippean satire* is *Giles Goatboy,* by John Barth. The term ANATOMY is sometimes used to describe such works rather than *Menippean satire*. The current usage of *Menippean satire* to define a GENRE was made popular by Northrop Frye in his *Anatomy of Criticism.*

Mesostich: An ACROSTIC in which the middle letters form a word. See ACROSTIC.

Metaphor: An implied ANALOGY which imaginatively identifies one object with another and ascribes to the first one or more of the qualities of the second or invests the first with emotional or imaginative qualities associated with the second. It is one of the TROPES; that is, one of the principal devices by which poetic "turns" on the meaning of words are achieved. I. A. Richards' distinction between the TENOR and the VEHICLE of a *metaphor* has been widely accepted and is very useful. The TENOR is the idea being expressed or the subject of the comparison; the VEHICLE is the IMAGE by which this idea is conveyed or the subject communicated. When Shakespeare writes

> That time of year thou mayst in me behold
> When yellow leaves, or none, or few, do hang
> Upon those boughs which shake against the cold,
> Bare ruined choirs where late the sweet birds sang.

the TENOR is old age, the VEHICLE is the season of late fall or early winter, conveyed through a group of IMAGES unusually complex in their implications. The TENOR and VEHICLE taken together constitute the FIGURE OF SPEECH, the TROPE, the "turn" in meaning which the *metaphor* conveys. The purposes for using *metaphors* can vary widely. At one extreme, the VEHICLE may merely be a means of decorating the TENOR; at the other extreme, the TENOR may merely be an excuse for having the VEHICLE. ALLEGORY, for example, may be thought of as an elaborate and consistently constructed extended *metaphor* in which the TENOR is never expressed, although it is implied. In the simplest kinds of *metaphors* there is an obvious direct resemblance that exists objectively between the TENOR and the VEHICLE, and in some *metaphors,* particularly those which lend themselves to elaborate CONCEITS, the relationship between TENOR and VEHICLE is in the mind of the maker of the *metaphor,* rather than in specific qualities of VEHICLE or TENOR. The first kind tends to be sensuous and the second witty.

Aristotle praised the *metaphor* as "the greatest thing by far" for the poet, and saw it as the product of his insight which permitted him to find the similarities in seemingly dissimilar things. Modern criticism follows Aristotle in placing a similarly high premium on the poet's abilities in the making of *metaphors,* and ANALYTICAL CRITICISM tends to find almost as much rich suggestiveness in the differences between the things compared as it does in the recognition of surprising but unsuspected similarities. Cleanth Brooks uses the term "functional *metaphor*" to describe the way in which the *metaphor* is able to have "referential" and "emotive" characteristics and to go beyond them and become a direct means in itself of representing a truth incommunicable by any other means. Clearly when a *metaphor* performs this function, it is behaving as a SYMBOL.

Metaphors may be simple, that is, may occur in the single isolated comparison, or a large *metaphor* may function as the CONTROLLING IMAGE of a whole work (see Edward Taylor's poem quoted in the article on CONTROLLING IMAGE), or a series of VEHICLES may all be associated with a single TENOR, as in Hamlet's "To be or not to be" soliloquy. In this last kind of case, however, unless the IMAGES can harmoniously build the TENOR without impressing the reader with a sense of their incongruity, the danger of a MIXED FIGURE is grave.

The whole nature of our language is highly metaphorical. Most of our modern speech, which now seems prosaic enough, was once largely metaphorical. Our ABSTRACT TERMS are borrowed from physical objects. Natural objects and actions have passed over into abstractions because of some inherent metaphorical significance. Thus "transgression"—which today signifies a misdemeanor, an error, or mistake—formerly meant "to cross a line." The metaphorical significance has been lost—is said to be "dead"—and the former figure of speech now stands simply for an abstraction. (It is thus, in fact, that ABSTRACT TERMS possibly first came into language; early man was necessarily content simply to name the objects about him which he could see and feel and smell.) See IMAGE, TROPE, FIGURE OF SPEECH, CONTROLLING IMAGE, ALLEGORY, METAPHYSICAL CONCEIT.

Metaphysical Conceit: A highly ingenious kind of CONCEIT widely used by the metaphysical poets, who explored all areas of knowledge to find in the startlingly esoteric or the shockingly commonplace telling and unusual analogies for their ideas. The use of such unusual CONCEITS as CONTROLLING IMAGES in their poems is a hallmark of the writers of METAPHYSICAL POETRY. The *metaphysical conceit* often exploits verbal logic to the point of the GROTESQUE, and it sometimes achieves such extravagant turns on meaning that it becomes absurd, as when Richard Crashaw writes of Mary Magdalene's eyes as

> Two walking baths; two weeping motions,
> Portable and compendious oceans.

But when a *metaphysical conceit* strikes from our minds the same spark of recognition which the poet had, so that it gives us a perception of a real but previously unsuspected similarity that is enlightening, it speaks to both our minds and our emotions with force, as in Donne's "The Flea" or his comparison of the union of himself with his lover in the figure of a draftsman's compass in "A Valediction Forbidding Mourning" or in Taylor's "Huswifery" (quoted in the article on CONTROLLING IMAGE). See METAPHYSICAL POETRY, CONCEIT, CONTROLLING IMAGE, METAPHOR.

Metaphysical Poetry: Sometimes used in the broad sense of philosophical POETRY, VERSE dealing with metaphysics, POETRY "unified by a philosophical conception of the universe and of the role assigned to the human spirit in the great drama of existence" (H. J. C. Grierson). In this sense Lucretius and Dante wrote *metaphysical poetry*. Herbert Read sees it as the "emotional apprehension of thought," felt thought, to be contrasted with the LYRIC, and regards some of the poetry of Chapman and Wordsworth, as well as that of John Donne and his followers, as *metaphysical*.

Commonly, however, the term is used to designate the work of the seventeenth-century writers referred to as the "Metaphysical Poets." They formed a school in the sense of employing similar methods and of being actuated by a spirit of revolt against the romantic conventionalism of Elizabethan love poetry, in particular the PETRARCHAN CONCEIT. Their tendency toward psychological analysis of the emotions of love and religion, their penchant for the novel and the shocking, their use of the METAPHYSICAL CONCEIT, and the extremes to which they sometimes carried their techniques resulted frequently in obscurity, rough VERSE, and strained IMAGERY. These faults gave them a bad reputation in the NEO-CLASSIC PERIOD. However, there has been a twentieth-century revival of interest in their work and admiration for their accomplishments. Consequently the reader will find the word *metaphysical* used in both a derogatory and a complimentary sense.

The characteristics of the best *metaphysical poetry* are logical elements in a technique intended to express honestly, if unconventionally, the poet's sense of the complexities and contradictions of life. The poetry is intellectual, analytical, psychological, disillusioning, bold; absorbed in thoughts of death, physical love, religious devotion. The DICTION is simple as compared with that of the ELIZABETHAN or the NEO-CLASSIC PERIODS, and echoes the words and the cadences of common speech. The IMAGERY is drawn from the com-

Metaphysical Poetry

monplace or the remote, actual life or erudite sources, the figure itself often being elaborated with self-conscious ingenuity. The FORM is frequently that of an argument with the poet's lover, with God, or with himself. The metaphysical poets wrote of God and of theology, of the court and of the church, of love and of nature— often elaborately—but usually with a high regard for FORM and the more intricate subtleties of METER and RHYME. Yet the VERSE is often intentionally rough; Ben Jonson thought Donne "deserved hanging" for not observing ACCENT. The roughness may be explained in part by the dominance of thought over strict FORM, in part by the fact that ruggedness or irregularity of movement goes naturally with a sense of the seriousness and perplexity of life, with the realistic method, with the spirit of revolt, and with the sense of an argument expressed in speech rather than SONG

If the results of the metaphysical manner are not always happy, if the unexpected details and surprising figures are not always integrated imaginatively and emotionally, it must be remembered that these POETS were attempting a more difficult task than confronts the complacent writer of conventional VERSE. Their failures appear most strikingly in their fantastic METAPHYSICAL CONCEITS. When they succeed—as they often do—their poetry, arising out of their own sense of incongruity and confusion, is an effective "emotional apprehension of thought," hauntingly real to us in our perplexing world.

The term *metaphysical* was applied to Donne in derogation of his excessive use of philosophy by Dryden in 1693, but its present use to designate a special poetic manner originated with Samuel Johnson's description of *metaphysical poetry* in his "Life of Cowley."

No exact list of metaphysical poets can be drawn up. Donne was the acknowledged leader. Crashaw and Cowley have been called the most typically *metaphysical*. Some were Protestant religious mystics, like Herbert, Vaughan, and Traherne; some Catholic, like Crashaw; some were CAVALIER LYRISTS, like Carew and Lovelace; some were satirists, like Donne and Cleveland; one was an American clergyman, Edward Taylor. The new recognition that has come to the metaphysical poets has arisen from a realization of the seriousness of their art, an interest in their spirit of revolt, their REALISM, their intellectualism, and other affinities with modern interests, as well as from the fact that they produced some fine poetry. T. S. Eliot, John Crowe Ransom, and Allen Tate are modern poets affected by the metaphysical influence. See CONCEIT, META-PHYSICAL CONCEIT, CONTROLLING IMAGE, BAROQUE, MARINISM.

Meter: The recurrence in POETRY of a rhythmic pattern, or the RHYTHM established by the regular or almost regular occurrence of similar units of sound pattern. In POETRY there are four basic kinds of rhythmic patterns: (1) QUANTITATIVE, in which the RHYTHM is established through units containing regular successions of long syllables and short syllables; this is the CLASSICAL *meter;* (2) accentual, in which the occurrence of a syllable marked by STRESS OR ACCENT determines the basic unit regardless of the number of unstressed or unaccented syllables surrounding the stressed syllable; OLD ENGLISH VERSIFICATION employs this kind of *meter,* and so does SPRUNG RHYTHM; (3) syllabic, in which the number of syllables in a line is fixed, although the ACCENT varies; much Romance VERSIFICATION employs this *meter;* and (4) ACCENTUAL-SYLLABIC, in which both the number of syllables and the number of ACCENTS are fixed or nearly fixed; when the term *meter* is used in English it usually refers to ACCENTUAL-SYLLABIC RHYTHM.

The rhythmic unit within the line is called a FOOT. In English ACCENTUAL-SYLLABIC VERSE, the standard feet are: IAMBIC ($\smile\,\diagup$), TROCHAIC ($\diagup\,\smile$), ANAPESTIC ($\smile\,\smile\,\diagup$), DACTYLLIC ($\diagup\,\smile\,\smile$), SPONDAIC ($\diagup\,\diagup$), and PYRRHIC ($\smile\,\smile$), although others sometimes occur. The number of FEET in a line forms another means of describing the *meter.* The following are the standard English lines: MONOMETER, one foot; DIMETER, two feet; TRIMETER, three feet; TETRAMETER, four feet; PENTAMETER, five feet; HEXAMETER, six feet, also called the ALEXANDRINE; HEPTAMETER, seven feet, also called the "FOURTEENER" when the feet are IAMBIC. See ACCENT, SUBSTITUTION, CATALEXIS, OLD ENGLISH VERSIFICATION, QUANTITATIVE VERSE, FOOT, SCANSION.

Metonymy: A FIGURE OF SPEECH which is characterized by the substitution of a term naming an object closely associated with the word in mind for the word itself. In this way we commonly speak of the king as "the crown," an object closely associated with kingship thus being made to stand for "king." So, too, in the book of Genesis we read, "In the sweat of thy face shalt thou eat bread," a FIGURE OF SPEECH in which "sweat" represents that with which it is closely associated, "hard labor." See HYPALLAGE, SYNECDOCHE.

Middle English Period

Metrical Accent: The ACCENT demanded by the RHYTHM pattern of a VERSE of poetry. See ACCENT.

Metrical Romance: A romantic TALE in VERSE. The term is applied both to such medieval VERSE ROMANCES as *Sir Gawain and the Green Knight* and to the type of VERSE ROMANCES produced by Sir Walter Scott (*The Lady of the Lake, Marmion*) and Lord Byron (*The Bride of Abydos, The Giaour*). The latter kind reflects the tendencies of ROMANTICISM in its freedom of technique and its preference for remote settings (the past in Scott, the Near East in Byron) as well as in its sentimental qualities. See MEDIEVAL ROMANCE.

Metrics: The systematic examination of the patterns of RHYTHM in POETRY, and the formulation of principles describing their nature; another term for PROSODY.

Middle English: English as spoken and written in the period following the NORMAN CONQUEST and preceding the Modern English period beginning at the RENAISSANCE. The dates most commonly given are 1100 to 1500, though both are approximate dates, as the NORMAN CONQUEST came in 1066 and some writings earlier than 1500 (e.g., Malory's *Le Morte Darthur*) may properly be called "modern" English. For the changes in the language which mark *Middle English,* see ENGLISH LANGUAGE.

Middle English Period: The period in English literature between the replacement of French by MIDDLE ENGLISH as the language of court and art and the early appearances of definitely modern English writings, roughly the period between 1350 and 1500. The Age of Chaucer (1350–1400) was marked by political and religious unrest, the Black Death (1348–1350), Wat Tyler's Rebellion (1381), and the rise of the LOLLARDS. The fifteenth century was badly torn by the Wars of the Roses. There was a steadily increasing nationalistic spirit in England, and at the same time early traces of HUMANISM were appearing.

The great CYCLES of MYSTERY PLAYS flourished. Toward the end of the period the MORALITY came into existence, and the last years of the fifteenth century saw the arrival of the INTERLUDE, while the FOLK DRAMA was popular among the common people. In prose it was the period of Wycliffe's sermons and his translation of the Bible, of Mandeville's *Travels,* of the medieval CHRONICLES, of prose RO-

MANCES, and, supremely, of Malory's *Le Morte Darthur*. ROMANCES, both prose and metrical, continued to be popular, with *Sir Gawain and the Green Knight* as the finest example. The period between 1350 and 1400 was a rich poetic age: it saw the first truly major English poet, Chaucer, as well as poetry like *The Pearl, The Vision of Piers Plowman,* and Gower's *Confessio Amantis.* There was a revival of ALLITERATIVE VERSE, although the ACCENTUAL-SYLLABIC METERS of Chaucer and his school eventually carried the day. The fifteenth century was a weak poetic age; its POETRY consisted chiefly of Chaucerian imitations, and only Hoccleve, Skelton, and James I of Scotland gave it any distinction. The popular BALLAD flourished. With the establishment of the Tudor Kings on the English throne in 1485, however, England once more had internal peace, and it possessed a flexible language that was very close to modern English and had a powerful dramatic tradition. The glories of the RENAIS- SANCE were almost ready to burgeon forth. See MIDDLE ENGLISH PERIOD in *Outline of Literary History.*

Middle Rhyme: RHYME falling at the middle as well as the end of the line. See INTERNAL RHYME, for which *middle rhyme* is another name.

Miles gloriosus: The braggart soldier, a STOCK CHARACTER in COM- EDY. The type appeared in Greek COMEDY as the ALAZON, was stressed by the Roman playwrights (Terence's Thraso in *Eunuchus* and Plautus' *Miles Gloriosus*), and adopted by RENAISSANCE dra- matists. An early example is Ralph Roister Doister, central figure in the play named after him (the "first" English COMEDY). Examples in ELIZABETHAN DRAMA are Captain Bobadil in Jonson's *Everyman in his Humour,* Quintiliano in Chapman's *May Day,* and Shakespeare's Sir John Falstaff (*King Henry IV,* 1, 2), Don Adriano de Armado (*Love's Labour's Lost*), Parolles (*All's Well*), and Ancient Pistol (*King Henry V*). Although the treatments differ in different exam- ples, the *miles gloriosus* is likely to be cowardly, parasitical, bragging, and subject to being victimized easily by practical jokers.

Miltonic Sonnet: A variation made by Milton on the ITALIAN SON- NET, in which the RHYME scheme is retained but the "turn" between the OCTAVE and the SESTET is eliminated. See SONNET.

Mime: A form of popular COMEDY developed by the ancients (fifth century B.C. in Southern Italy). It portrayed the events of everyday life by means of dancing, imitative gestures, and witty DIALOGUE. It finally degenerated into sensual displays and the performers sank to a low social level. The Christian Church frowned upon the performances and they were largely driven from the public STAGE. They were kept alive, however, by wandering entertainers. In England, the exhibitions seem to have consisted generally of low forms of buffoonery. The *mime* aided in preserving the comic spirit in DRAMA, its influence possibly being apparent in the medieval MYSTERY PLAY and the Renaissance INTERLUDE—perhaps also the Renaissance "DUMB SHOW" and through it the modern PANTOMIME. Many elements of modern VAUDEVILLE are in direct line of descent from the *mime*. The *mime* is not regarded as a true link between ancient CLASSICAL DRAMA and modern DRAMA, though it aided in keeping alive the acting profession in the DARK AGES.

Mimesis: The Greek word for IMITATION, often used in criticism to indicate Aristotle's theory of IMITATION.

Mimetic Theory of Art: A theory of art which places a primary emphasis upon the actuality which is imitated in the art work. See CRITICISM, HISTORICAL SKETCH.

Minnesinger: "Singer of love," a medieval German LYRIC POET whose art was perhaps inspired by that of the TROUBADOUR. Though the German poets reflect the love system known as COURTLY LOVE, their poetry in general is more wholesome than that of the TROUBADOURS. They flourished in the twelfth and thirteenth centuries. Walther von der Vogelweide is regarded as the greatest of the class.

Minor Plot: A subordinate action or COMPLICATION running through a work of FICTION or DRAMA. See SUBPLOT.

Minstrel: A musical entertainer or traveling poet of the later Middle Ages who carried on the tradition of the earlier GLEEMAN and JONGLEUR. *Minstrels* flourished especially in the late thirteenth and the fourteenth centuries and played a prominent part in the cultural life of the time. The typical *minstrel* may be thought of as a gifted wandering entertainer, skilled with the harp and tabor, singing songs, reciting ROMANCES, and carrying news from town to town, castle to castle, country to country, delighting all classes of society, from kings and knights to priests, burgesses, and laborers. Love LYRICS, BALLADS, LEGENDS, and ROMANCES were so composed and disseminated. They were at once the actors, journalists, poets, and orchestras of their time. The *Lay of Havelok the Dane* is a good example of the "minstrel ROMANCE." Flourishing in Chaucer's day, minstrelsy declined in the fifteenth century and tended to disappear with the increase of literacy following the introduction of printing. In their enthusiasm for "primitive" or untutored poetic genius and for medievalism in general, the poets and novelists of the romantic school, such as Beattie and Scott, imparted an idealized meaning to *minstrel* as they did to BARD.

Miracle Play: Although this term is used by many authorities on English drama in a broad sense which includes the Scriptural CYCLIC DRAMA (see MYSTERY PLAY), it is restricted by others to its early sense of a non-Scriptural play based upon the legend of some saint or upon a miracle performed by some saint or sacred object (such as the sacramental bread). However common *miracle plays* in this stricter sense may have been in medieval England, very few have been preserved. It is known that a play of St. Catherine, probably in Latin or ANGLO-NORMAN, was performed at Dunstable about A.D. 1100. At this time *miracle plays* on St. Nicholas were being produced in France. A play called *Dux Moraud* (thirteenth or fourteenth century), in English, which exists in a fragmentary form, may have been a *miracle play*, possibly one in which the Virgin Mary supplied the DEUS EX MACHINA. Other, extant English plays that either are *miracle plays* or plays of very similar character are the *Play of the Sacrament* (late fifteenth century) and the *Conversion of St. Paul* and *Saint Mary Magdalene* (*ca.*1500). See MYSTERY PLAY.

Miscellanies, Poetical: The collection of poems by Wyatt, Surrey, and others published by Richard Tottel in 1557 as *Songs and Sonnets,* commonly known as *Tottel's Miscellany* (see COURTLY MAKERS), set a fashion that resulted in the publication of nearly twenty *poetical miscellanies* within the next half-century, usually under highly figurative or alliterative titles and varying greatly in quality and kind of VERSE printed. Some are posthumous publications of COMMONPLACE BOOKS such as the *Paradise of Dainty Devices* of Richard Edwards (1576), a very popular collection of poems of a serious character. Some *miscellanies* have a specialized character, like the *Handful of Pleasant Delights* (1584), a collection of BALLADS. Some of the later ones, like *England's Parnassus* (1600), are collections not of complete poems but of poetical quotations. One,

Mixed Figures

The Passionate Pilgrim (1599), was published as Shakespeare's, and does contain some of Shakespeare's VERSE. Frequently the *miscellany* was made up of poems selected from other *miscellanies* or from manuscript sources. Much of the VERSE is anonymous, some is falsely ascribed, and some indicates authorship by initials not now understandable. Much uncertainty and some intentional mystification are connected with the parts played by collectors or editors. New poems were frequently printed along with old ones, and old ones sometimes appear in variant forms. The *miscellanies* are important as reflecting the great poetical activity of the time, particularly of the years preceding the appearance of Spenser, Sidney, and other major figures. They reflect, too, the metrical experiments of this earlier period. The poems in *A Gorgeous Gallery of Gallant Inventions* (1584), for example, make free use of ALLITERATION and employ a wide variety of metrical forms. Such poet-dramatists as Shakespeare borrowed LYRICS from the earlier *miscellanies* and lived to see their own VERSE appear in the later ones. Aside from *Tottel's*, particularly important *miscellanies* are *The Phoenix Nest* (1593) and *England's Helicon* (1600). The former contains poems by Sidney, Spenser, Lodge, and others. The latter, the best of them all, is a storehouse of Elizabethan POETRY selected from many poets, great and small.

The practice of publishing *poetical miscellanies* thus begun in the sixteenth century, of course, has continued to the present time. Professor Arthur E. Case, in his *Bibliography of English Poetical Miscellanies, 1521–1750,* lists several hundred titles of various sorts of poetical collections.

Mise en scène: The stage setting of a play, including the use of scenery and properties, and the general arrangement of the piece. Modern DRAMA relies far more upon *mise en scène* for its effects than did earlier DRAMA. Indeed, the lack of scenery has been given as a partial explanation of the high literary quality of ELIZABETHAN DRAMA, the playwright being forced to rely upon his language for his descriptive effects; while the increased dependence upon scenery is said to be one of the reasons for the decreased attention to purely literary devices on the modern stage. By extension the term *mise en scène* is applied to the total surroundings of any event.

Mixed Figures: The mingling of one FIGURE OF SPEECH with another immediately following with which the first is incongruous.

A notable example is the sentence of Castlereagh: "And now, sir, I must embark into the feature on which this question chiefly hinges." Here, obviously, the sentence begins with a nautical figure ("embark") but closes with a mechanical figure ("hinges"). The effect is grotesque. Lloyd George is reported to have said, "I smell a rat. I see it floating in the air. I shall nip it in the bud." Mixed IMAGERY, however, is sometimes deliberately used by writers with great effectiveness, when the differing figures contribute cumulatively to a single referent which is increasingly illuminated as they pile up. It is important, however, that the cumulative effect of the various IMAGES not be one of incongruity. See METAPHOR, TENOR, VEHICLE.

Mock Drama: A term applied to plays one of whose purposes is to ridicule the customs, CONVENTIONS, and playwrights of the theater of their time. Henry Fielding, in *The Tragedy of Tragedies; or, The Life and Death of Tom Thumb the Great* (1731) held up to boisterous ridicule the CONVENTIONS of the HEROIC DRAMA, as the Duke of Buckingham's *The Rehearsal* (1671) had also done. Oscar Wilde, in *The Importance of Being Earnest* (1895), produced a PARODY of the WELL-MADE PLAY and the sentimental COMEDY popular in his time, and as well mocked his fellow playwrights for their failure to acknowledge the hypocrisy and self-deception of their age.

Mock Epic or **Mock Heroic:** Terms frequently used interchangeably to designate a literary FORM which burlesques the EPIC by treating a trivial subject in the "grand style," or which uses the EPIC FORMULAS to make ridiculous a trivial subject by ludicrously overstating it. Usually the characteristics of the classical EPIC are employed, particularly the INVOCATION to a deity; the formal statement of theme; the division into books and CANTOS; the grandiose speeches (challenges, defiances, boastings) of the HEROES; descriptions of warriors (especially their dress and equipment), battles, and games; the use of the EPIC or HOMERIC SIMILE; and the employment of supernatural machinery (gods directing or participating in the action). When the mock POEM is much shorter than a true EPIC some prefer to call it *mock heroic,* a term also applied to poems which mock ROMANCES rather than EPICS. Ordinary usage, however, employs the terms interchangeably. Chaucer's *Nun's Priest's Tale* is partly *mock heroic* in character as is Spenser's finely wrought *Muiopotmos,* "The Fate of the Butterfly," which imitates the opening of the *Aeneid* and employs elevated STYLE for trivial subject-matter. Swift's *Battle of the Books* is an example of a cuttingly satirical *mock epic* in prose. Pope's *The Rape of the Lock* is perhaps the finest *mock heroic* poem in English, satirizing in polished verse the trivialities of polite society in the eighteenth century. The cutting of a lady's lock by a gallant is the central act of heroic behavior, a card game is described in military terms, and such airy spirits as the sylphs hover over the scene to aid their favorite heroine.

Modern: A term applied to one of the main directions in writing in this century. It is not a chronological designation but one suggestive of a loosely defined congeries of characteristics. Much twentieth-century literature is not "*modern*" in the common sense of the term, as much that is contemporary is not. *Modern* refers to a group of characteristics, and not all of them appear in any one writer who merits the designation *modern*.

In a broad sense, *modern* is applied to writing marked by a strong and conscious break with traditional forms and techniques of expression. It employs a distinctive kind of IMAGINATION, one that insists on having its general frame of reference within itself. It thus practices the solipsism of which Allen Tate accused the modern mind: it believes that we create the world in the act of perceiving it. *Modern* implies a historical discontinuity, a sense of alienation, of loss, and of despair. It not only rejects history, but also the society of whose fabrication history is a record. It rejects traditional values and assumptions, and it rejects equally the RHETORIC by which they were communicated. It elevates the individual and his inner being over social man, and prefers the unconscious to the self-conscious. The psychologies of Freud and Jung have been seminal in the *modern* movement in literature (see FREUDIANISM and JUNGIAN CRITICISM). Its most interesting artistic strategies are its attempts to deal with the unconscious and the MYTHOPOEIC. It is basically anti-intellectual, celebrating passion and will over reason and systematic morality. In many respects it is a reaction against REALISM and NATURALISM and the scientific postulates on which they rest. Although by no means all *modern* writers have been philosophical existentialists, EXISTENTIALISM has created a schema within which much of the *modern* temper can see a reflection of its attitudes and assumptions (see EXISTENTIALISM). The *modern* revels in a dense and often unordered actuality as opposed to the practical and systematic, and in exploring that actuality as it exists in the mind of the writer it has been richly experimental with language and with FORM, with SYMBOL and with MYTH.

The *modern* has meant a decisive break with tradition in most of its manifestations, and what has been distinctively worthwhile in the literature of this century has come, in considerable part, from this *modern* temper. Merely to name some of the writers who belong in the *modern* tradition, although none of them partake of all of it, is to indicate the vitality, variety, and artistic success of *modern* writing: T. S. Eliot, Ezra Pound, Wallace Stevens, Ernest Hemingway, William Faulkner, W. B. Yeats, W. H. Auden, D. H. Lawrence, James Joyce, Henry Adams, André Gide, Marcel Proust, Albert Camus, Jean-Paul Sartre, Stéphane Mallarmé, Rainer Maria Rilke, Thomas Mann, Eugene O'Neill, Tennessee Williams, Arthur Rimbaud. And such a list could be continued for many pages.

Modulation: In music a change in key in the course of a passage. In POETRY a variation in the metrical pattern by the SUBSTITUTION of a FOOT that differs from the basic METER of the line or by the addition or deletion of unstressed syllables.

Monodrama: The term *monodrama* is used in three senses, all related to its basic meaning of a dramatic situation in which a single person speaks. At its simplest level a *monodrama* is a DRAMATIC MONOLOGUE, in Browning's sense of that term. It is more often applied to a series of extended DRAMATIC MONOLOGUES in various METERS and STANZA FORMS that tell a connected STORY. The standard example is Tennyson's *Maud,* which he called a *monodrama.* The term is also applied to theatrical presentations that feature only one actor.

Monody: A DIRGE or LAMENT in which a single mourner expresses individual grief, e.g., Arnold's *Thyrsis, A Monody.* See DIRGE, ELEGY, THRENODY.

Monologue: A composition, oral or written, presenting the discourse of one speaker only. A SOLILOQUY. Any speech or narrative presented wholly by one person. Sometimes loosely used to signify merely any lengthy speech. See DRAMATIC MONOLOGUE, INTERIOR MONOLOGUE, MONODRAMA.

Monometer: A line of VERSE consisting of only one FOOT. See SCANSION, METER.

Mood

Monorhyme: A POEM that uses only one RHYME.

Monostich: A POEM consisting of a single line.

Montage: A device, probably borrowed from motion pictures, used in IMPRESSIONISM to establish a SCENE or an ATMOSPHERE by a series of brief pictures or impressions following one another quickly without apparent logical order. The "Newsreels" in Dos Passos' *U.S.A.* are examples of *montages*. The device is sometimes used in the INTERIOR MONOLOGUE.

Mood: A state of mind in which one emotion or set of emotions has ascendancy. In a literary work the *mood* is the emotional or emotional-intellectual attitude which the author takes toward his subject or theme. It is relatively easy to distinguish between subject matter and *mood*. A group of POEMS on the subject of death may range from a *mood* of noble defiance in Donne's "Death, Be Not Proud," to PATHOS in Frost's "Out, Out—," to IRONY in Housman's "To an Athlete Dying Young," to joyous acceptance in Whitman's "When Lilacs Last in the Dooryard Bloom'd." Clearly the state of mind with which each author views the subject of death is different, and we would say, therefore, that the *moods* are different. The literary work should be a unified vehicle for the communication of this state of mind. As Willa Cather expressed it, "[T]he language, the stresses, the very structure of the sentences are imposed upon the writer by the special *mood* of the piece"—i.e., the *mood* as expression of the author's attitude becomes a control over the techniques of literary expression.

To distinguish between *mood* and TONE is more difficult, and some critics say it is impossible. Brooks and Warren, in *Understanding Poetry,* for instance, use TONE exclusively, assigning to it the qualities here presented as peculiar to *mood*. If a distinction is made between *mood* and TONE, it will be the fairly subtle one of *mood* being the emotional attitude of the author toward his subject and TONE the attitude of the author toward his audience. In cases where the author uses ostensible "authors" within the work, *mood* and TONE can be quite distinct, as in Washington Irving's use of Diedrich Knickerbocker. Byron, in Canto III of *Don Juan,* has "a poet" (presumably Southey) write a poem beginning "The isles of Greece, the isles of Greece!", which is solemn, brave, and freedom-loving in *mood;* yet the TONE of Byron (not the *mood* of the imaginary "poet") is mocking and satiric. There are obviously a great variety of *moods* and no accepted system of naming or classifying them. See TONE; EMOTIONAL ELEMENT IN LITERATURE.

Mora, Morae: Terms used to designate periods of duration in QUANTITATIVE VERSE, the *mora* being the duration of a short syllable and the *morae* being that of a long syllable. The symbol (⌣) which indicates a *mora* is called a BREVE, that (–) which indicates a *morae* is called a MACRON.

Moral Criticism: Criticism which evaluates a work of art in moral terms, judging it in terms of the ethical principles which, the critic feels, should govern human life. See CRITICISM, TYPES OF.

Morality Play ("Morality"): A kind of POETIC DRAMA which developed in the late Middle Ages (probably late fourteenth century) and which was distinguished from the religious DRAMA proper, such as the MYSTERY PLAY, by the fact that it was a dramatized ALLEGORY in which the abstract virtues and vices (like Mercy, Conscience, Perseverance, and Shame) appear in personified form, the good and the bad usually being engaged in a struggle for the soul of man. One student of the drama (A. H. Tolman) has distinguished two classes. The "full-scope" *morality* is one in which the theme is the saving of man's soul, and the central figure is man in the sense of humanity in general. The best-known example is *Everyman* (*ca.*1500). The "limited-scope" *morality* is one which deals with a single vice or moral problem or a situation applicable to a certain person. Thus Skelton's *Magnificence* has for its theme the dangers of uncontrolled expenditures and was possibly written as advice to Henry VIII. Later, pedagogical and political themes as well as theological became quite common. The limited-scope *morality* developed later than the full-scope and is perhaps superior dramatically because of its independence and greater concreteness and REALISM. *Morality plays* have also been classified by content or purpose, as religious (*Everyman*), doctrinal (John Bale's *King Johan*), didactic-pedagogical (*Wyt and Science*), political (Skelton's *Magnificence*). By the sixteenth century some of the *morality plays* had admitted so much realistic, farcical material that they had begun to establish a tradition of English COMEDY, and doubtless contributed much to the INTERLUDE. In fact, INTERLUDE and *morality* became more or less interchangeable in describing plays. Such comic figures as the Vice and the Devil were especially well-developed and were influential upon later COMEDY. Though morality themes were widely employed in RENAISSANCE drama of the sixteenth century, the *morality plays* as such lost their popularity in ELIZABETHAN times.

Mosaic: A term applied to a kind of RHYME in which more than one word is used to make one RHYME-sound, as rhyming "lewd ditties" with "nudities." *Mosaic* is also applied to compositions consisting exclusively of quotations from one or more authors. See CENTO.

Motif (**Motive**):   A simple element which serves as a basis for expanded NARRATIVE; or, less strictly, a conventional situation, device, interest, or incident employed in FOLKLORE, FICTION, or DRAMA. The carrying off of a mortal queen by a fairy lover is a *motif* about which full stories were built in MEDIEVAL ROMANCE. In the BALLAD called *The Elfin Knight* the "fairy music" *motif* appears when the sound of the knight's horn causes the maiden to fall in love with the unseen hero. In music and art the term is used in various other senses, as for a recurring melodic phrase, a prevailing idea or design, or a subject for detailed sculptural treatment. In literature, recurrent IMAGES, words, objects, phrases, or actions that tend to unify the work are called *motives*. See LEITMOTIF.

Motivation: The justification of the action of a CHARACTER in a PLOT by presenting a convincing and impelling cause for that action. The chief difference, perhaps, between amateurish, puerile FICTION and great works of imaginative power lies in the question of *motivation*. The STORY or DRAMA of action is sometimes content to unfold a series of thrilling, unnatural EPISODES, exciting in themselves, but growing out of no inherent purpose of the author other than his desire to excite his reader. Motivated action, however, is action justified by the make-up of the CHARACTER partaking in the activity. Hamlet is slow to resolve and refuses to kill Claudius when he finds him at prayer; Othello is intensely jealous and proud—and smothers Desdemona when he thinks her unfaithful; Falstaff is more of a wit than a HERO—and runs from the scene of the robbery. All this is *motivation* through character. *Motivation* usually consists of a combination of psychological traits and external events. If it is worked out satisfactorily, it leaves the reader with a recognition of those emotive and circumstantial forces which made the action inevitable.

Movement: A critical term denoting action or incident. Thus a play is spoken of as having, or not having, *movement,* implying that the dramatic action is strong or weak, rapid or slow. The term is also used to indicate a new development in literary activity or interest, as the OXFORD MOVEMENT, the FREE-VERSE movement.

"Muckrakers":   A term applied derisively to a group of American writers who between 1902 and 1911 worked actively to expose the dishonest methods and unscrupulous motives operative in big business and in city, state, and national government. A group of MAGAZINES—*The Arena, Everybody's, McClure's,* the *Independent, Collier's* and the *Cosmopolitan*—led the movement, publishing the writings of the leading *"muckrakers"*—Ida Tarbell, Lincoln Steffens, T. W. Lawson, Mark Sullivan, and Samuel H. Adams. Upton Sinclair's novel *The Jungle* and some of the novels of Winston Churchill and of D. G. Phillips are "muckraking" books. The term comes from a character in Bunyan's *Pilgrim's Progress,* who is so busy raking up muck that he does not see a celestial crown held over him. It was applied to this group of writers as a derogatory epithet by Theodore Roosevelt.

Multiple meanings: A term sometimes used by contemporary critics as a substitute for AMBIGUITY when that word is used to designate the capacity of words to stimulate several quite different streams of thought, all of which make sense. See AMBIGUITY, PLURISIGNATION.

Mummery: A simple dramatic performance usually presented by players masked or disguised. A farcical presentation, a sort of PANTOMIME. See MASQUE.

"Mummings":   Masked folk processions, dancing, and plays. See MASQUE.

Muses: Goddesses represented as presiding over song, the various departments of literature, and the liberal arts. They were nine in number and are generally considered the daughters of Zeus and Mnemosyne (memory). In literature, their traditional significance is that of inspiring and helping poets. In various periods of Greek history, the *muses* were given different names and attributes, but the conventionally accepted list and the realm of interest ascribed to each are as follows: Calliope (EPIC POETRY), Clio (history),

Erato (LYRICS and love POETRY), Euterpe (music), Melpomene (TRAGEDY), Polyhymnia (sacred POETRY), Terpsichore (choral dance and SONG), Thalia (COMEDY), and Urania (astronomy).

Musical Comedy: Closely related, especially in its earlier forms, to BURLESQUE and VAUDEVILLE, *musical comedy* developed in the early twentieth century in England and America into one of the most popular of all dramatic forms. Though much use is made of music, both vocal and orchestral, the DIALOGUE is spoken, not sung. The success of the form depends partly upon the acting, partly upon the success of the SONGS, and partly upon the spectacular staging. Satirical "hits" at current figures and interests are features. The comic effects are sometimes farcical (see FARCE) in character.

Mystery Play: A medieval religious play based upon Biblical history; a Scriptural play. *Mystery plays* originated in the liturgy of the Church and developed from LITURGICAL DRAMAS into the great CYCLIC PLAYS, performed outdoors and ultimately upon movable PAGEANTS. They were the most important forms of the MEDIEVAL DRAMA of Western Europe and flourished in England from the late Middle Ages until well into RENAISSANCE times. They seem to have developed about three nuclei: (1) Old Testament plays treating such events as the Creation, the fallen angels, the fall of man, the death of Abel, and the sacrifice of Isaac, and the Prophet plays, which prepared for (2) the New Testament plays dealing with the birth of Christ—the Annunciation, the birth, the visit of the wise men, the shepherds, and the visit to the temple; and (3) the Death and Resurrection plays—entry into Jerusalem, the betrayal by Judas, trial and crucifixion, lamentation of Mary, sepulchre scenes, the resurrection, appearances to disciples, Pentecost, and sometimes the Day of Judgment. So the whole scheme of salvation was presented. They were often known as CORPUS CHRISTI PLAYS because of the habit of performing the plays on PAGEANTS in connection with the Corpus Christi processional. The great CYCLES whose texts have been preserved to us are the York, the Chester, the Coventry, and the Wakefield (or "Towneley"). They differ in length and in the list of plays or scenes included as well as in literary and dramatic value, the Towneley plays being especially important in dramatic development.

After the plays left the Church and became "secularized," they were performed by trade guilds, sometimes on fixed stages or stations (the crowds moving from station to station), sometimes on movable PAGEANTS. A writer of the sixteenth century, Archdeacon Rogers, who witnessed a late production of the Chester cycle at Whitsuntide, has left the following oft-quoted description:

> Every company had its pageant, or part, which pageants were a high scaffold with two rooms, a higher and a lower, upon four wheels. In the lower they appareled themselves, and in the higher room they played, being all open on the top, that all beholders might hear and see them. The places where they played them was in every street. They began first at the Abbey gates, and when the first pageant was played it was wheeled to the high cross before the mayor, and so to every street; and so every street had a pageant playing before them at one time, till all the pageants for the day appointed were played: and when one pageant was near ended, word was brought from street to street, that so they might come in place thereof exceeding orderly, and all the streets have their pageants afore them all at one time playing together; to see which players there was great resort, and also scaffolds and stages made in the streets in those places where they determined to play their pageants.

The word *mystery* was first applied to these plays by an eighteenth-century editor (Robert Dodsley, 1744), on the analogy of the French *mystère*, a Scriptural play; medieval writers were more likely to refer to the plays as CORPUS CHRISTI PLAYS, "Whitsuntide plays," "PAGEANTS," etc., and possibly as MIRACLE PLAYS, the term preferred for them by many modern authorities. See MEDIEVAL DRAMA, MIRACLE PLAYS, LITURGICAL DRAMA, PAGEANT, DRAMA.

Mystery Story (or **Novel**): A term used to designate a work of prose FICTION in which the element of mystery or terror plays a controlling part. It is applied to such various types of FICTION as the DETECTIVE STORY, the GOTHIC NOVEL, the STORY of strange or frightening adventure, the "suspense" novel, the TALE of espionage, the TALE of crime, and the STORY in which the PROTAGONIST, usually a woman, is relentlessly pursued by some unknown but alarming menace. See DETECTIVE STORY, GOTHIC NOVEL.

Mysticism: The theory that a knowledge of God or immediate reality is attainable through the use of some human faculty that transcends intellect and does not use ordinary human perceptions or logical processes. *Mysticism* takes many different forms and does not yield itself readily to definition. Objective studies of *mysticism* are impossible, since one not himself a mystic must be content to receive as fact the autobiographical or artistic record of an experience that is, by its very nature, ineffable. There are two broad types of *mysticism;* in one God is seen as transcendent, outside the human soul, and union with Him is achieved through a series of steps or stages; in the other God is immanent, dwelling within the soul and to be discovered by penetrating deeper into the inner self. The terminology of *mysticism,* since it is forced to be figurative, is often difficult and obscure. A conventional statement of the Christian mystic's progress on the path to God is as follows: the soul undergoes a purification (the purgative way), which leads to a sense of illumination in the love of God (the illuminative way), and after a period the soul enters into a union with God (the unitive way), and progresses into a final ecstatic state of perfect knowledge of God (the spiritual marriage), during some period of which there comes a time of alienation and loss in which the soul cannot find God at all (the soul's dark night).

Aspects of *mysticism* and the mystical experience are common in English and American literature, although to call any single writer—with a few exceptions like Richard Rolle of Hampole and William Blake—a mystic is to invite a challenge. Clearly, however, there are mystical elements in the work of Richard Crashaw, George Herbert, John Bunyan, William Cowper, William Wordsworth, S. T. Coleridge, P. B. Shelley, Thomas Carlyle, the New England TRANSCENDENTALISTS, Walt Whitman, and W. V. Moody. To survey the works of so heterodox a group of writers is to realize that *mysticism* refers to a wide spectrum of experience and is a means of perceiving reality or absolute truth in many different forms and in many different patterns of religious belief.

Myth: Anonymous stories having their roots in the primitive folk-beliefs of races or nations and presenting supernatural episodes as a means of interpreting natural events in an effort to make concrete and particular a special perception of man or a cosmic view. *Myths* differ from LEGENDS in that they have less of historical background and more of the supernatural; they differ from the FABLE in that they are less concerned with moral didacticism and are the product of a racial group rather than the creation of an individual. Every country and literature has its mythology; the best known to English readers being the Greek, Roman, and Norse. But the mythology of all groups takes shape around certain common themes; they all attempt to explain the creation, divinity, and religion, to guess at the meaning of existence and death, to account for natural phenomena, and to chronicle the adventures of racial heroes.

They also have a startlingly similar group of MOTIFS, CHARACTERS, and actions, as a number of students of *myth* and religion, particularly Sir James Frazer, have pointed out. Although there was a time when *myth* was a virtual synonym for error, notably in the NEO-CLASSIC PERIOD, the tendency today is to see *myths* as dramatic or narrative embodiments of a people's perception of the deepest truths. Various modern writers have insisted on the necessity of *myth* as a material with which the artist works, and in varying ways and degrees have appropriated the old *myths* or created new ones as necessary substances to give order and a frame of meaning to their personal perceptions and images; notable among such "mythmakers" have been William Blake, W. B. Yeats, T. S. Eliot (particularly in *The Waste Land*), James Joyce, and Wallace Stevens.

Since the introduction of Jung's concept of the "racial unconscious" (see ARCHETYPE) and of Ernst Cassirer's theories of language and *myth*, contemporary critics have found in the *myth* a useful device for examining literature. There is a type of IMAGINATION, Philip Wheelwright insists, that can properly be called "the Archetypal Imagination, which sees the particular object as embodying and adumbrating suggestions of universality." The possessors of such IMAGINATION arrange their works in archetypal patterns, and present us with narratives which stir us as "something at once familiar and strange." They thus give concrete expression to something deep and primitive in us all. Thus those critics—and they are many— who approach literature as *myth* see in it vestiges of primordial ritual and ceremony, or the repository of racial memories, or a structure of unconsciously held value systems, or an expression of the general beliefs of a race, social class, or nation, or a unique embodiment of a cosmic view. One significant difference should be noted, however; *myth* in its traditional sense is an anonymous, non-literary, essentially religious formulation of the cosmic view of a people who approach its formulations not as representations of truth but as truth itself; *myth* in the sophisticated literary sense in which it is currently used is the intelligible and often self-conscious use of such primitive methods to express something deeply felt by the individual artist which will, he hopes, prove to have universal responses. The MYTHOPOEIC poet attempts to return to the role of the prophet-seer, by creating a *myth* which strikes resonant points in the minds of his readers and

speaks with something of the authority of the old *myths*. See
ARCHETYPE, JUNGIAN CRITICISM, MYTHOPOEIC.

Mythic Criticism: Criticism which explores the nature and significance of the ARCHETYPES and archetypal patterns in a work of art.
See MYTH; JUNGIAN CRITICISM; ARCHETYPE; CRITICISM, TYPES OF.

Mythopoeic: A term applied to writers who, suffering the lack of
an acceptable or widely believed body of mythic material to give
order to their imaginative restatements of experience, set about
consciously to make a mythic frame for their works. Notable
mythopoeic writers have been Blake, Yeats, Joyce, and Eliot.

N

Naïve Narrator or **Hero:** A disingenuous character who is the
ostensible author (often the oral NARRATOR) of a NARRATIVE whose
implications are much plainer to the reader than they are to the
NARRATOR himself. The *naïve narrator* can be a device for IRONY,
either gentle or savage, or it can be a device for PATHOS, as it
frequently is when a child narrates with open-eyed innocence events
whose implications are tragic or horrible. The *naïve narrator* is used
a great deal by Sherwood Anderson in short stories like "I'm a
Fool" and "The Egg"; Swift employs the device in "A Modest Proposal" with savage effectiveness; Mark Twain's *Adventures of Huckleberry Finn* and Ring Lardner's "Hair-Cut" are also well-known examples of the use of the *naïve narrator*.

Narration: That one of the four types of composition (see ARGU-
MENTATION, DESCRIPTION, and EXPOSITION) the purpose of which is
to recount an event or a series of events. *Narration* may exist, of
course, entirely by itself, but it is most likely to incorporate with
it considerable DESCRIPTION. There are two forms of *narration:
simple narrative*, which is content to recite an event or events and
is largely chronological in its arrangement of details—as in a newspaper account of a fire; and *narrative with plot*, which is less often
chronological and more often arranged according to a preconceived artistic principle determined by the nature of the PLOT and
the type of story intended (see PLOT). The chief purpose of *nar-*

ration is to interest and entertain, though, of course, it may be used to instruct and inform.

Narrative: An account in prose or VERSE of an actual or fictional event or a sequence of such events; anything that is narrated. See NARRATION.

Narrative Essay: An INFORMAL ESSAY in NARRATIVE form—ANECDOTE, INCIDENT, or ALLEGORY. It differs from a SHORT STORY not only in its simpler STRUCTURE, but especially in its ESSAY-like intent, the STORY being a means of developing an idea rather than being an end in itself. Addison's *Vision of Mirzah* is an example. See ESSAY.

Narrative Poem: A nondramatic POEM which tells a STORY or presents a NARRATIVE, whether simple or complex, long or short. EPICS, BALLADS, and METRICAL ROMANCES are among the many kinds of *narrative poems.*

Narrator: In the broadest sense, anyone who recounts a NARRATIVE, either in writing or orally. In FICTION the term is used in a more technical sense, as the ostensible author or teller of a STORY. In FICTION presented in the first person, the "I" who tells the story is the *narrator;* he may be in any of various relations to the events he describes, ranging from being their center (the PROTAGONIST) through various degrees of minor importance (MINOR CHARACTERS) to being merely a witness. In FICTION told from an OMNISCIENT-AUTHOR POINT OF VIEW, the author himself acts self-consciously as *narrator,* recounting the STORY and freely commenting on it. A *narrator* is always present, at least by implication, in any work of FICTION, except a STORY in which a SELF-EFFACING AUTHOR relates events with apparent OBJECTIVITY; yet even there the *narrator* exists in fact, although we and the author act as though he did not. See POINT OF VIEW and PANORAMIC METHOD.

National Book Awards: Cash awards given annually, in the spring, to the authors of books in several categories published during the preceding year and adjudged to be the best. Awards are made for fiction, poetry, nonfiction (since 1964 called "arts and letters"), and other categories, including recently children's literature and translation. The awards were founded in 1950 under the sponsorship of the American Book Publishers Council, the American Book-sellers Association, and the Book Manufacturers Institute. Their aim is to give industry-wide recognition to distinguished books. A list of the National Book Awards in the three chief categories is given in the APPENDIX.

Naturalism: A term sometimes applied to writing that demonstrates a deep interest in NATURE, such as Wordsworth and other Romantic writers had; and sometimes used to describe any form of extreme REALISM, although this usage is a very loose one. It should properly be reserved to designate a movement in the NOVEL in the late nine-teenth and early twentieth centuries in France, America, and England.

In its simplest sense *naturalism* is the application of the principles of scientific DETERMINISM to FICTION. It draws its name from its basic assumption that everything that is real exists in NATURE, NATURE being conceived as the world of objects, actions, and forces which yield the secrets of their causation and their being to objective scientific inquiry. The fundamental view of man which the naturalist takes is of an animal in the natural world, responding to environmental forces and internal stresses and drives, over none of which he has control and none of which he fully understands. It tends to differ from REALISM, not in its attempt to be accurate in the portrayal of its materials but in the selection and organization of those materials, selecting not the commonplace but the representa-tive and so arranging the materials that the structure of the novel reveals the pattern of ideas—in this case, scientific theory—which forms the author's view of the nature of experience. In this sense, *naturalism* shares with ROMANTICISM a belief that the actual is impor-tant not in itself but in what it can reveal about the nature of a larger reality; it differs sharply from ROMANTICISM, however, in finding that reality not in transcendent ideas or absolute ideals but in the scientific laws which can be perceived through the action of indi-vidual instances. This distinction may be illustrated in this way. Given a block of wood and a force pushing upon it, producing in it a certain acceleration: REALISM will tend to concentrate its attention on the accurate description of that particular block, that special force, and that definite acceleration; ROMANTICISM will tend to see in the entire operation an illustration or symbol or suggestion of a philosoph-ical truth and will so represent the block, the force, and the accelera-tion—often with complete fidelity to fact—that the idea or ideal that it bodies forth is the center of the interest; and *naturalism* will tend to see in the operation a clue or a key to the scientific law which undergirds it and to be interested in the relationship between the force, the block, and the produced acceleration, and will so represent the operation that Newton's second law of motion (even on occasion in its mathematical expression—$F \propto ma$) is demonstrated or proved by this representative instance of its universal occurrence in nature.

In this sense *naturalism* is the novelist's response to the revolution in thought that modern science has produced. From Newton it gains a sense of mechanistic determinism; from Darwin (the greatest single force operative upon it) it gains a sense of biological determinism and the inclusive METAPHOR of the lawless jungle which it has used perhaps more often than any other; from Marx it gains a view of history as a battleground of vast economic and social forces; from Freud it gains a view of the determinism of the inner and subconscious self; from Taine it gains a view of literature as a product of deterministic forces; from Comte it gains a view of social and environmental determinism. In the most influential statement ever made of the theory of *naturalism*, Émile Zola's *Le roman expérimental*, the ideal of the naturalist is stated as the selection of truthful instances subjected to laboratory conditions in a novel, where the hypotheses of the author about the nature and operation of the forces that work upon man can be put to the test. Zola's term *expérimental*, usually translated "Experimental," is more properly understood as "Empirical."

Although the fidelity to detail and the disavowal of the assumptions of the Romanticists give *naturalism* clear affinities with REALISM, so that it is often confused in its origins with that movement and Balzac and Flaubert are credited with being naturalists, the Goncourt Brothers and Zola are generally recognized as having begun the naturalistic novel and codified its theory. Strong elements of *naturalism* are to be seen in the work of George Eliot and of Thomas Hardy, but American novelists have been generally more receptive to its theories than the English have. Frank Norris (1870–1902) wrote naturalistic novels in conscious imitation of Zola and made an American critical defense of the school, *The Responsibilities of the Novelist*, in which he saw that its real enemy was REALISM and not ROMANTICISM. Stephen Crane (1871–1900) used the devices of IMPRESSIONISM in producing naturalistic novels. Jack London (1876–1916) wrote naturalistic novels with Nietzschean "supermen" (and "superdogs") as PROTAGONISTS. But the greatest American naturalist—after Zola perhaps the greatest of all—was Theodore Dreiser (1871–1945), whose *An American Tragedy* is an archetypal American example. James T. Farrell and James Jones, among others, have kept the school alive in America.

The novels produced in this school have tended to emphasize either a biological determinism, with an emphasis on the animal nature of man, particularly his heredity, portraying him as an animal engaged in the endless and brutal struggle for survival, or a socio-economic determinism, portraying man as the victim of environmental forces and the product of social and economic factors beyond his control or his full understanding. Occasionally, as in the novels of Thomas Hardy, man is seen as the victim of "destiny" or "fate." But whichever of these views is taken, the naturalist strives to be objective, even documentary, in his presentation of material; to be amoral in his view of the struggle in which the human animal finds himself, neither condemning nor praising man for actions which he cannot control; to be pessimistic in his view of human capabilities—life, he seems to feel, is a vicious trap, a cruel game; to be frank and almost clinically direct in his portrayal of man as an animal driven by fundamental urges—fear, hunger, and sex; to be deterministic in his portrayal of human actions, seeing them as explicable in cause-and-effect relationships; and to exercise a bias in the selection of characters and actions, frequently choosing primitive characters and simple, violent actions as best giving him "experimental conditions." No single naturalistic novel displays completely this catalog of qualities, but taken together they tend to define the directions and intentions of *naturalism*.

Naturalistic and Symbolistic Period in American Literature: The period between 1900 and 1930 in America was the age of the birth of contemporary attitudes and contemporary writing. It is sharply divided by World War I, the first part being a time dominated by NATURALISM, and the part after the War being marked by a growing international awareness, a sensitivity to European literary models, and a steadily developing SYMBOLISM in POETRY and FICTION. The first decade of the twentieth century saw the flourishing of the "muckraking" MAGAZINE exposé and the "muckraking" NOVEL. During this decade, Henry James, living in England, probably carried American REALISM to its greatest height in *The Ambassadors, The Wings of the Dove,* and *The Golden Bowl;* Mark Twain, although still alive, was no longer producing works comparable to those of the 1880's and his pessimism was growing more darkly marked; Howells, too, was still producing his NOVELS and his amiable critical ESSAYS but without the strength of his heyday. Frank Norris, Theodore Dreiser, and Jack London were producing crude but powerful examples of the naturalistic NOVEL. William Vaughn Moody was writing a socially conscious VERSE and extremely popular DRAMA; and Edwin Arlington Robinson had launched the career that was to flower into great distinction in the second and third decades of the century.

The second decade saw the virtual birth of modern American POETRY, with the founding of *Poetry* magazine in Chicago in 1912 by Harriet Monroe, the emergence of the IMAGISTS, the beginning of the careers of Frost, Pound, Eliot, Sandburg, and Masters. The realistic NOVEL continued in the work of Howells, Ellen Glasgow, Willa Cather, and Edith Wharton. As the decade ended, the plays of Eugene O'Neill gave promise of a theatrical revival to match the growing LITTLE THEATER MOVEMENT and the development of the FOLK DRAMA. Prior to the twentieth century American CRITICISM had been sporadic and uncertain, but the work of W. C. Brownell, James Huneker, and a group of young critics demanding a "usable past"—among them, Randolph Bourne and Van Wyck Brooks—joined with the developing artistic concern of the AVANT-GARDE groups and the LITTLE MAGAZINES to produce an increasingly sensitive body of critical work as the second decade of the century drew toward a close.

The First World War produced a major dislocation of a number of talented young men, most of them born between 1895 and 1902, who became volunteer ambulance and ammunition truck drivers in the French and Italian armies, came early in contact with European culture, and emerged from the War disillusioned with American "idealism" and with the crassness of American culture. This postwar generation, considering itself self-consciously as a "LOST GENERATION," set about a repudiation of American culture in three ways: one group, largely from the East, went back to Europe and there published LITTLE MAGAZINES, waited upon Gertrude Stein, took part in DADAISM, and formulated a polished and *symbolistic* style—among them were F. Scott Fitzgerald, Ernest Hemingway, Edmund Wilson, e. e. cummings, Malcolm Cowley, and Sherwood Anderson, and, on the English side of the channel, Ezra Pound and T. S. Eliot; another group, largely from the Middle West, came east and in Cambridge, New Haven, and Greenwich Village, produced a literature that was realistic, satiric, and critical, aimed at the standardized mediocrity of the American village—among them were Ring Lardner and Sinclair Lewis; and another group, largely Southern, repudiated the meaningless mechanism of capitalistic America by looking backward to a past that had had tradition and order—these were the poets and critics who published the *Fugitive* in Nashville and were AGRARIANS, and others who contributed to magazines like the *Double Dealer* in New Orleans. Out of this last group have come the contemporary Southern NOVEL and much of the NEW CRITICISM; the group includes John Crowe Ransom, Allen Tate, Robert Penn Warren, and William Faulkner.

All of these groups—expatriates, revolters against the village, and seekers of a tradition of order—sought for art forms and critical standards different from those of the traditional American writer, and they found them in the methods of the French *symbolists,* in the work of Joyce and Proust, in the complex intellectual POETRY of the seventeenth century "Metaphysicals," and in the kind of experimentation that the LITTLE MAGAZINES existed to foster. By the end of the period, a group of academic critics, the NEW HUMANISTS, were formulating a doctrine of life and art that repudiated the contemporary artist, and in the late fall of 1929 the collapse of the stockmarket, signaling the beginning of the depression, marked an effective end to a period in which most of the seeds of contemporary American writing had been sown. See *Outline of Literary History.*

Nature: Few terms are so important to the student of literature—or so difficult—as this one. Since conformity with *nature*—the resort to *nature* as a norm or standard for judging artistic expression—long permeated critical thinking (see MIMETIC THEORY OF ART), some knowledge of the "normative" meanings of the term is necessary to the understanding of much criticism and literature. Professor A. O. Lovejoy found as many as sixty different meanings for *"nature"* in its normative functions. Both neo-classicists and romanticists would "follow *Nature";* but the former drew from the term ideas of order, regularity, and universality, both in "external" *nature* and in human *nature,* while the latter found in *nature* the justification for their enthusiasm for irregularity ("wildness") in external *nature* and for individualism in human *nature.* Other contradictory senses may be noted: the term *nature* might mean, on the one hand, human *nature* (typical human behavior); or, on the other

Nature

hand, whatever is antithetical to human *nature* and man's works—what has not been "spoiled" by man.

The neo-classic view of *nature* as implying universal aesthetic validity led to a reverence for "rules" drawn from long-continued acceptance by human beings, such acceptance being taken as an evidence of their basis in what is universal in human *nature.* The rules were based upon proved models. Opposed to this was the romantic tendency to regard as "natural" the primitive, the unsophisticated, the naïve—a conception which justified the *disregard* of rules and precedents and the exaltation of the freedom of individual expression. Among some neo-classic writers the words "reason" and "nature" were closely allied in meaning, because both were related to the idea of "order" (John Dennis said that *nature* was order in the visible world, while reason was order in the invisible realm). The distinction between *nature* and WIT (in one of its senses) was not always clear, since both provided tests of excellence, though, properly, WIT was specific, while *nature* was generic, thought of as an ultimate, as indicated in the familiar lines from Pope's *Essay on Criticism:*

> True Wit is Nature to advantage dressed,
> What oft was thought, but ne'er so well expressed.

Nature in the sense of "external nature"—the objects of the natural world such as mountains, trees, rivers, flowers, and birds—has supplied a large part of the imaginative substance of literature, especially POETRY, from the earliest times. Some survey, therefore, of the attitudes toward external *nature* may be useful. Poets make the following different uses of external *nature:* (1) they express childlike delight in the open-air world; (2) they use *nature* as the background or setting to human action or emotion; (3) they see *nature* through historic coloring; (4) they make *nature* sympathize with their own feelings; (5) they dwell upon the infinite side of *nature;* (6) they give description of *nature* for its own sake; (7) they interpret *nature* with imaginative sympathy; (8) they use *nature* as a symbol of the spirit.

The greatest attention to *nature* in English literature came in the ROMANTIC PERIOD, when the revolt against the conventionalities of neo-classic fashions led to much theorizing about the relation of man to external *nature* and the production of a vast amount of POETRY putting the new theories into practice. To be sure, earlier

342

Nature

English literature had made much use of *nature*. The comparatively small amount of Anglo-Saxon literature remaining reflects both a simple love of *nature* and a power for picturesque description—as in the "Riddles" (see RIDDLE) and such poems as the *Wife's Complaint* and the *Husband's Message*—and especially a sense of mystery and awe in the presence of *nature*, as in *Beowulf*. Late medieval literature—Chaucer and the ROMANCES—was apt to present *nature* in idyllic, conventionalized forms, a pleasant garden or "bower" on a May morning. In the RENAISSANCE there was sometimes a genuine, subjective response to natural surroundings, as in some of Surrey's poems, though often the treatment was conventional in character, as in the PASTORALS and the SONNETS. Shakespeare, of course, though no theorist like Wordsworth, shows a wide knowledge of *nature* and an unsurpassed faculty for drawing upon subjects from *nature*, whether conventional or fresh, to give appropriate settings and to impart an air of reality to dramatic situations and human moods.

The eighteenth century brought the great conflict between NEO-CLASSICISM and ROMANTICISM, and nowhere were the issues sharper between the two schools than in their treatment of external *nature*. In their zeal to follow "correct" models, to restrain enthusiasm, and in their preference of city to rural life, the neo-classicists found little room for recording intimate observations of *nature*, though they did, of course, employ natural imagery, usually conventionalized, and use *nature* descriptions as settings and as a basis for philosophical reflections. For the wilder aspects of *nature* they expressed strong abhorrence. Winter was "the deformed wrong side of the year," while mountains were a positive blemish upon the landscape and the ocean was a dangerous, wearying waste of waters. The writers who adumbrated the coming change, such as Lady Winchilsea, John Dyer, James Thomson (especially *The Seasons*, 1726–1730), were giving voice to the new enthusiasm for *nature* while NEO-CLASSICISM was at its height, and the movement grew with Gray, Collins, Cowper, and others till readers a little later were ready to respond to the beauties of the homelier aspects of *nature* as sung by Robert Burns.

With Wordsworth came the climax of the nature cult in English poetry, *nature* now being recognized as closely akin to man, able to minister to his spiritual needs and to reveal God to him (see *Tintern Abbey* for a classic poetic statement of the progressive phases of Wordsworth's responses to *nature*). Coleridge, too, gave climactic expressions to the romantic enthusiasm for the wilder, disordered aspects of *nature* which the neo-classicists could not brook. Observe the sharp contrast between the following passages, the first from Pope, and the second from Coleridge:

> Here hills and vales, the woodland and its plain,
> Here earth and water seem to strive again;
> Not chaos-like together crushed and bruised,
> But, as the world, harmoniously confused:
> Where order in variety we see,
> And where, though all things differ, all agree.
> (Windsor Forest)

> But oh! that deep romantic chasm which slanted
> Down the green hill athwart a cedarn cover!
> A savage place! as holy and enchanted
> As e'er beneath a waning moon was haunted
> By woman wailing for her demon lover!
> (Kubla Khan)

The poetry of the other great romantic poets, Shelley, Keats, and Byron, is shot through with intimate, subjective presentations of *nature,* from the delicate and mysterious to the GROTESQUE and awesome. This attitude was not only reflected widely in American literature (Bryant, Lowell, Whittier, Emerson, Thoreau) but persisted in much of the verse of the Victorians, notably Tennyson.

The widespread acceptance of the Darwinian concepts of *nature* and of a natural struggle for existence has colored and modified the view of *nature,* and Wordsworth's gentle instructor in beauty can become "nature red in tooth and claw" in Tennyson's *In Memoriam,* although that is not his persistent attitude. With the development of NATURALISM a view of *nature* as a raw and primitive jungle within which the struggle for survival relentlessly continues came into being, with *nature* viewed as a scientific fact, devoid of meaning in philosophical terms. However, in its calmer moments, it still can minister to the human spirit, as can be seen in Hemingway's "Big Two-Hearted River" or the fishing scenes in *The Sun Also Rises* or in Faulkner's *The Bear. Nature* is for the contemporary writer what it has always been for the writer, not an objective fact, but the "world's body" through which he speaks in concrete terms his perceptions of himself and the world, and it is capable of having fluctuating meanings in the same author's work and at the same time of speaking with authority. Emerson's *nature,* in his essay *Nature,* exists for five uses: as commodity, beauty, language, discipline, and, finally, ideal symbol. These varying uses are found by one man writing from a pronounced point of view. The reader is, therefore, well warned that *nature,* like one of Humpty Dumpty's words in *Alice in Wonderland,* means exactly what its user intends it to mean, just that, and nothing more!

Negative Capability: A term used by Keats to describe the objective and impersonal aspect of Shakespeare. Shakespeare had "innate universality," Keats asserted. "A poet has no Identity . . . he is continually . . . filling some other Body." The term has since been applied widely to the qualities in an artists's work which enable him to avoid expressing in it the expression of his own personality. See AESTHETIC DISTANCE, OBJECTIVE CORRELATIVE.

Neo-Classicism: The term applied to the CLASSICISM which dominated English literature in the RESTORATION AGE and in the eighteenth century. It draws its name from the fact that it found in CLASSICAL literature and in contemporary French neo-classical writings models for its literary expressions and a group of attitudes toward life and art. It was, at least in part, the result of the reaction against the fires of enthusiasm which had blazed in the RENAISSANCE. Upon the RENAISSANCE idea of the limitless potentiality of man was imposed a view of man as limited, dualistic, imperfect; upon the intensity of his responses were imposed a reverence for order and a delight in reason and rules; upon the burgeoning of his IMAGINATION into new and strange worlds was imposed a distrust of innovation and INVENTION; upon his expanding individualism was imposed a view that saw him most significantly in his generic qualities and his group activities; upon the enthusiasms of religious MYSTICISM was imposed the restrained good sense of DEISM. From the French critics, from Horace, Virgil, and other writers of CLASSICAL literature came the artistic ideals of order, logic, restrained emotion, accuracy, "correctness," "good taste," and DECORUM. A sense of symmetry, a delight in design, and a view of art as centered in man, with man as its primary subject matter, and the belief that literature should be judged in terms of its service to man (see PRAGMATIC THEORY OF ART) resulted in the seeking of proportion, UNITY, harmony, and grace in literary expressions that aimed to delight, instruct, and correct man, primarily as a social animal. It was the great age of the ESSAY, of the LETTER, of SATIRE, of moral instruction, of PARODY, and of BURLESQUE. The play of mind upon life was regarded as more important than the play of feeling, with the result that a polite, urbane, witty, intellectual art developed.

Neo-Classic Period

A few of the concrete effects of neo-classic ideals upon literature may be mentioned. POETIC DICTION and IMAGERY tended to become conventional with details subordinated to design. The appeal to the intellect rather than to the emotions resulted in a fondness for WIT and the production of much SATIRE, both in prose and VERSE. The irregular or unpleasant aspects of external NATURE, such as mountains, ocean, winter, were less frequently utilized than the pleasanter phases as represented in stars, flowers, or a formal garden. A tendency to REALISM marked the presentation of life with the generic qualities and common attributes and actions of men being stressed. Literature exalted FORM—polish, clarity, brilliance. It avoided the obscure or the mysterious. It valued the CLASSICAL critical requirements of universality and DECORUM. It "imitated" (see IMITATION) the CLASSICS and cultivated CLASSICAL literary FORMS and types, such as SATIRE and the ODE. The earlier English authors whose works were produced in a "less cultivated" age either were ignored or were admired more for their genius than for their art. Didactic literature flourished. Though BLANK VERSE and the SPENSERIAN STANZA were cultivated, rhymed COUPLETS were the favorite form of verse. Although many of the attitudes and mannerisms of the neo-classicists were swept aside by the great tide of ROMANTICISM, the movement exerted a permanently wholesome effect upon literature in its clarifying and chastening effect upon English prose style and in its establishing in English literature the importance of certain classical graces, such as order, good form, unified structure, clearness, conciseness, and restraint. Poetic technique as developed by Pope, too, has become a permanent heritage. In the twentieth century there has been a strong neo-classical tendency in much of the best poetry and criticism, growing out of a reaction against ROMANTICISM and out of a growing distrust of the potentialities of man, together with a new respect for the place of intellect in life and art. Writers like T. E. Hulme, T. S. Eliot, and the NEW CRITICS are on many issues at one with *neo-classicism*.

Neo-Classic Period: The period in English literature between the return of the Stuarts to the English throne in 1660 and the full assertion of ROMANTICISM which came with the publication of *Lyrical Ballads* by Wordsworth and Coleridge in 1798. It falls into three relatively distinct segments: the RESTORATION AGE (1660–1700), the AUGUSTAN AGE (1700–1750), and the AGE OF JOHNSON (1750–1798).

Neo-Classic Period

In the RESTORATION AGE, England underwent a strong reaction against the Puritanism of the COMMONWEALTH INTERREGNUM; its already strong interest in scientific investigation and philosophical thought increased; and NEO-CLASSICISM, with particularly strong French influences, developed steadily. The HEROIC COUPLET became a major verse form; the ODE was a widely used poetic GENRE; and the poetic muse usually served didactic or satiric purposes. In prose, despite the tendency toward utilitarian goals, the "modern" STYLE was developing, notably in Dryden's work. In DRAMA, the reopening of the theaters and the establishment of the PATENT THEATERS led to the development of the HEROIC DRAMA in COUPLETS and the COMEDY OF MANNERS in prose. Milton, Bunyan, and Dryden were the principal writers of the period, with *Paradise Lost* and *Pilgrim's Progress,* although atypical of the spirit of license and revolt dominant in the age, perhaps its major achievements in literature. Dryden's accomplishments, although none of them reached the individual heights of Milton or Bunyan, were signally fine, and pointed forward toward the AUGUSTAN AGE. Otway, Wycherley, and Congreve enriched the stage, while the prose of Locke found its way into a permanent place in English thought.

In the AUGUSTAN AGE, NEO-CLASSICISM found its highest English expression. The classical ideals of taste, polish, "common sense," and reason (drawn from the ancients, from France, and from the RESTORATION AGE, and modified by current philosophical and scientific activities) were more important than emotion and IMAGINATION. DEISM was advancing steadily, and the same rule of reason resulted in a literature that was realistic, satirical, moral, correct, and affected strongly in its origins and its expressions by politics and intrigue. POETRY sparkled with the polished COUPLETS of Pope. It was concerned with truth, with the satiric, and the didactic. The MOCK EPIC and the verse ESSAY were common forms. In the work of James Thomson was to be found, in BLANK VERSE and in the SPENSERIAN STANZA, a growing concern with NATURE and science; and in the "GRAVEYARD SCHOOL" a sentimental melancholy.

On the stage the HEROIC DRAMA was no more, being replaced by the DOMESTIC TRAGEDY of writers like Lillo and imitations of CLASSICAL TRAGEDY such as Addison's *Cato.* SENTIMENTAL COMEDY replaced the less "moral" COMEDY OF MANNERS, in the work of men like Cibber and Steele. The Licensing Act of 1737 imposed a stifling political censorship on the English theater.

It was a great age of prose. The essay PERIODICAL was adumbrated in JOURNALS like Defoe's *Review,* and attained its epitome in *The Tatler* and *The Spectator*—journals that had a profound influence on English prose STYLE and were followed by a host of imitators. The prose SATIRES of Swift were among the glories of the age. The prose FICTION of Defoe, and the early NOVELS of Richardson, Fielding, and Smollett had all appeared before the mid-century mark.

The AGE OF JOHNSON was a period of transition that was still dominated by the critical energies and the prose vigor of a great representative of the passing tradition, Dr. Samuel Johnson. The developing interest in human freedom, the impact of German ROMANTICISM, the widening range of intellectual interests and human sympathies, the developing appreciation of external NATURE and the country life, the developing cult of the primitive—all joined with political events like the American and the French revolutions and religious occurrences like the rise of Methodism to establish the bedrock upon which English ROMANTICISM was to rest.

In poetry Gray, Cowper, Burns, and Crabbe flourished. An interest in folk literature and popular BALLADS developed. In the DRAMA Goldsmith and Sheridan returned laughter to the stage with the COMEDY OF MANNERS, although SENTIMENTAL COMEDY still flourished. Shakespeare was immensely popular on the stage; and the BURLESQUE, the PANTOMIME, and the MELODRAMA—forms that freed the DRAMA (although at a high price) from the sharp restrictions of the PATENT THEATERS—developed. In prose, the NOVEL advanced steadily. Sterne and Mackenzie developed the NOVEL OF SENSIBILITY; Walpole, Mrs. Radcliffe, and Clara Reeves the GOTHIC NOVEL. By the end of the century Brooke and Godwin were producing novels of political and philosophical purpose.

In the AGE OF JOHNSON the greatest literary figures were Johnson himself, as poet, critic, novelist, journalist, and lexicographer—an embodiment of the ideals of the *Neo-Classic Period*—and Robert Burns, as poet of the common people, the Scottish soil, and the Romantic soul—an adumbration of the coming ROMANTIC PERIOD. By 1798, Wordsworth, Coleridge, and Blake had already launched their careers; Johnson and Burns were dead; and Shelley, Byron, and Keats had been born. See the *Outline of Literary History,* AUGUSTAN AGE, RESTORATION AGE, and the AGE OF JOHNSON.

Neologism: A word newly introduced into a language, especially as a means of enhancing literary style. There was much conscious use of *neologisms,* especially from Greek and Latin, in RENAISSANCE times, partly as a result of a definite critical attitude toward the enrichment of the native English vocabulary. But the practice is not confined to any one period. Too often authors employ *neologisms* in a failing effort to give their style an atmosphere of freshness or erudition (see PEDANTRY), but the variety and flexibility and resourcefulness of the modern English vocabulary are largely the cumulative result of the successful use of *neologisms.* A vast number of *neologisms,* of course, employed by individual authors or by stylistic "schools" (see EUPHUISM, GONGORISM) have not gained permanent foothold in the vocabulary. See COINED WORDS.

Neo-Platonism: A system of belief which originated in Alexandria in the third century, composed of elements of PLATONISM mixed with Oriental beliefs and with some aspects of Christianity. Its leading representative was Plotinus. See PLATONISM.

New Comedy: Greek COMEDY of the fourth and third centuries, B.C. After the decline of Greece and the rise of Macedonia, the OLD COMEDY, of which Aristophanes was the greatest creator, was replaced by a COMEDY OF MANNERS, featuring STOCK CHARACTERS and conventional PLOTS. The place SETTING was usually a street, the CHARACTERS young lovers, courtesans, parsimonious elders, and scheming servants. The best writers of the *New Comedy* were Menander, Philemon, and Diphilus. The *New Comedy* had a powerful influence on the Roman COMEDIES of Plautus and Terence, and through them upon much of the COMEDY written since. See COMEDY.

New Criticism, The: In a strict sense, the term is applied to the criticism written by John Crowe Ransom, Allen Tate, R. P. Blackmur, Robert Penn Warren, and Cleanth Brooks, and it is derived from Ransom's book, *The New Criticism,* published in 1941, which discussed a movement in America in the 1930's which paralleled movements in England led by critics like T. S. Eliot, I. A. Richards, and William Empson. Generally the term is applied, however, to the whole body of contemporary criticism which centers its attention in the work of art as an object in itself; finds in it a special kind of language opposed to—or at least different from—the languages of science or philosophy; and examines it through a process of close analysis. The New Critics constitute the school in contemporary criticism which most completely employs the OBJECTIVE THEORY OF ART. The movement has varied sources; among them are I. A.

New Criticism

Richards' *The Principles of Literary Criticism* (1924), William Empson's *Seven Types of Ambiguity* (1930), the work of Remy de Gourmont, the anti-ROMANTICISM of T. E. Hulme, the French EX-PLICATION DE TEXTE, the psychological theories of the ARCHETYPE, the concepts of order and tradition of the Southern AGRARIANS, and the work of Ezra Pound and T. S. Eliot.

Not even the group to which the term can be applied in its strictest sense has formed a school subscribing to a fixed dogma; when to this group are added others like Yvor Winters and Kenneth Burke, it can be seen that the *New Criticism* is really a cluster of attitudes toward literature rather than an organized critical system. The primary concern of these critics has been to discover the intrinsic worth of literature, to demonstrate that worth to intelligent readers, and to defend that worth against the types of attack they believe to be inherent in contemporary thought. Indeed, the *New Criticism* is primarily a protest against the conventional and traditional ways of viewing life and art. The New Critics are protesting against the mechanistic and positivistic nature of the modern world; and their protest is framed in terms of a cultural tradition, a religious order, and sometimes an aristocratic social system. They are protesting against a view of life and knowledge that rests on fact and inference from fact alone; and their protest takes the form of an insistence on literature as a valid form of knowledge and as a communicator not of the truths of other languages but of the truths incommunicable in other terms than those of the language of literature itself. They are protesting against ROMANTICISM with its doctrines of self-expression, its EXPRESSIVE THEORY OF ART, and its philosophy of perfectibility; and their protest takes the form of the OBJECTIVE THEORY OF ART, of the impersonal artist, and of NEO-CLASSIC restraint. They are protesting against IMPRESSIONISM in criticism; and their protest takes the form of intense methodological concern and often of semantic analysis. They were originally protesting against the NEW HUMANISM of Babbitt and More; and their protest took the form of an insistence that the morality and value of a work of art is a function of its inner qualities and that literature cannot be evaluated in general terms or terms not directly related to the work itself. Their concern has been with the IMAGE, the SYM-BOL, the MEANING, and only infrequently with GENRE, with PLOT, or with CHARACTER. This aspect of the *New Criticism* has led to attacks by critics interested in GENRE or FORM who assert that the New Critics reduce literature to a linguistic or symbolic monism that makes the significant discrimination among types impossible. In actual practice, the *New Criticism* has most often been applied, and has worked best when applied, to the LYRIC; it has been less successful when applied to extended works of FICTION or DRAMA. See CRITICISM, TYPES OF; INTENTIONAL FALLACY; AFFECTIVE FALLACY; IMAGERY; EXPLICATION DE TEXTE; AUTOTELIC; ARCHETYPE; MYTH; OBJECTIVE THEORY OF ART.

Newgate: A prison of unsavory reputation in London, dating from the twelfth century to 1902, when it was demolished. Originally it was in the gate house of the principal west gate of the city. Until 1868 executions were held outside *Newgate* and attracted large crowds. The *Newgate Calendar* (begun 1773) was a biographical record of the most notorious criminals confined in the prison. NOVELS and TALES dealing with London crime and criminals are often referred to as *Newgate* NOVELS and TALES.

New Humanism, The: An American critical school in the first third of the twentieth century which emphasized the moral qualities of literature. See HUMANISM, THE NEW.

Nine Worthies, The: Late medieval and early RENAISSANCE literature reflects the widespread tradition or classification of the heroes known as the "nine worthies." Caxton lists them in his preface to Malory's *Le Morte Darthur* in the conventional three groups: Hector, Alexander, Julius Caesar (pre-Christian pagans); Joshua, David, Judas Maccabeus (pre-Christian Jews); Arthur, Charlemagne, Godfrey of Boulogne (Christians). They are personated in the burlesque play incorporated in Shakespeare's *Love's Labour's Lost*.

Nobel Prize: A large sum of money awarded annually to the person having produced during the year the most eminent piece of work in the field of idealistic literature. In actuality the recipient's total career seems to be more important than any single work by him. This award, granted through the Swedish Academy in Stockholm, was made possible by Alfred Bernhard Nobel (1833–1896), a Swedish chemist and engineer. Nobel willed the income from practically his entire estate for the establishment of such annual prizes and the endowment of research foundations, not only in the field of literature but also in physics, chemistry, medicine or physiology, and for the promotion of world peace. The amount of each prize varies with the income from the main fund, but is now about $90,000. Nationality does not enter into consideration at all in the awarding of the prizes, which was begun on December 10, 1901, the fifth anniversary of Nobel's death. A further stipulation of Nobel's will empowers the Swedish Academy, which awards the prize for literature, to withhold the grant for any one year; if no work during that year is deemed worthy of the recognition, the amount of the prize reverts to the main fund. The winners of the prize in literature are listed in the Appendix.

Nocturne: A poetic and often sentimental composition, expressing moods supposed to be especially appropriate to evening or night time. A SERENADE; a SONG.

Noh (or Nō) Plays: The most important form of Japanese DRAMA, *noh* literally meaning "highly skilled or accomplished." The *noh plays* are harmonious combinations of dance, POETRY, music, MIME, and acting. Their origins are in early religious ceremony; they began as religious ritual and have so continued. There are 240 *noh plays* in the standard repertory, all of them written between 1300 and 1600. *Noh plays* were originally a part of the ritual of the Japanese feudal aristocracy and they continue that tradition. They are short, one or two ACTS, and are usually presented at a religious festival in programs consisting of one each of the five types of *noh plays:* (1) a play of praise to a god, adorned with dancing, (2) a play about a warrior HERO from the EPIC period in Japanese history, (3) a "female-wig" or "woman" play, in which a male actor impersonates a woman, (4) a play of great violence, sensationalism, and often of ghosts and supernatural beings, and (5) a solemn play of warlike dancing, which ends with a grateful recognition of the occasion of the festival. These plays aim at creating a serene and elegant contemplation of aesthetic beauty and a sense of religious sublimity. They are performed on stylized sets, with lavish, symbolic costuming. Elevated speech is in VERSE and common speech in prose. Their performance techniques, settings, costuming, and acting styles represent an unbroken tradition stretching back to the fourteenth century. They thus constitute the oldest continuous aesthetic tradition in the world. See KABUKI PLAYS.

Nom de plume (**pen name**): A fictitious name adopted by a writer for professional use or to disguise his true identity. For example,

Sidney Porter assumed the pen name "O. Henry"; and Madame Amandine Aurore Lucie Dupin, *baronne* Dudevant, almost unknown by her real name, was famous as the French novelist, George Sand. See PSEUDONYM.

Nominalism: A philosophical doctrine first advanced by Roscellinus (twelfth century) and revived and popularized by William of Ockham (fourteenth century). It holds that abstract concepts, general terms, and universals have no objective referents but exist only as names. This doctrine, which leads toward materialism and empiricism in its insistence that only particular things exist, has been popular in the nineteenth and twentieth centuries.

Nonce word: In earlier forms of a language, a word for which there is a single recorded occurrence. There are a number of *nonce words* in Old English writing. In modern times, a *nonce word* is one invented by an author for a particular usage or special meaning. James Joyce made *nonce words* one of the chief elements of his later STYLE.

Nonsense Verse: A variety of LIGHT VERSE entertaining because of its strong rhythmic quality and lack of logic or consecutive development of thought. In addition to the marked RHYTHM, *nonsense verse* is often characterized by the presence of coined nonsense words, NONCE WORDS ("frabjous day") a mingling of words from various languages (MACARONIC VERSE), "tongue twisters," and a calling upon the printer for unbelievably freakish arrangement of type to portray Christmas trees, pipes, men falling downstairs—anything which occurs to the fancy of the versifier. LIMERICKS are a popular *nonsense verse* FORM. Edward Lear and Lewis Carroll have built large reputations through writing *nonsense verse*.

Norman Conquest: The conquest of England by the Normans following the victory of William I in 1066 at the Battle of Senlac (Hastings). It affected English literature and the English language drastically by the introduction of Norman-French cultural and racial characteristics and ideals and by the introduction of the French language. It was followed by three centuries of social, political, and linguistic readjustment, out of which modern England was to come. See ANGLO-NORMAN (LANGUAGE), ANGLO-NORMAN PERIOD, ENGLISH LANGUAGE, MIDDLE ENGLISH, MIDDLE ENGLISH PERIOD.

Nouvelle

Nouvelle: A SHORT NOVEL or NOVELETTE; a work of FICTION of intermediate length and complexity between the SHORT STORY and the NOVEL. Henry James used the French term *nouvelle* for SHORT NOVEL. See SHORT NOVEL.

Novel: The term *novel* is used in its broadest sense to designate any extended fictional prose NARRATIVE. In practice, however, its use is customarily restricted to NARRATIVES in which the representation of character occurs either in a static condition or in the process of development as the result of events or actions (see CHARACTERIZATION). Often the term implies that some organizing principle—PLOT or THEME or idea—should be present in a NARRATIVE that is called a *novel*. Almost without exception, *novel* refers to a prose work; although Chaucer's *Troilus and Criseyde* has frequently been called a *novel*. The term *novel* is an English transliteration of the Italian NOVELLA, a short, compact, broadly realistic TALE popular in the medieval period and perhaps best represented by the tales in the *Decameron*. In most European countries the word *roman* is used rather than *novel*, thus linking the *novel* with that body of legendary, imaginative, and poetic material associated with the older ROMANCE, of which, in one sense the *novel* is a modern extension. The conflict between the imaginative and poetic recreation of experience implied in *roman* and the realistic representation of the soiled world of common men and actions implied in *novel* has been present in the FORM from its beginning, and it accounted for a distinction often made in the eighteenth and nineteenth centuries between the ROMANCE and the *novel*, in which the ROMANCE was the tale of the long ago or the far away or the imaginatively improbable; whereas the *novel* was bound by the facts of the actual world and the laws of probability.

All *novels* are representations in fictional NARRATIVE of life or experience but the form is itself as protean as life and experience themselves have proved to be. Serious FICTION deals with man in significant action in his world. The world which appears to be a significant stage for such action varies greatly from author to author. An author's world may be only within the lowest recesses of the human unconscious; it may be the haunted deck of a whaling ship; it may be the fixed social structure of an aristocratic society; it may be the jungle of Africa or of a vast city; it may be the ideal structure of a Utopian dream. And man in his essential self can be viewed in an endlessly varying series of guises. Basically what we are saying here is that the subject matter of the *novel* defies cataloging or analysis; it may range from the puckish recollections of *Tristram Shandy* to the complex and seemingly total actuality of *War and Peace*.

In shaping this various material to the formal demands of FICTION, the novelists have displayed an equal variety. The *novel* may concentrate upon character, almost to the exclusion of incident or PLOT. It may be merely a series of incidents strung together like beads on a string, as the PICARESQUE NOVEL tends to be. It may be firmly plotted, with a structure as firm and sure as that of a TRAGEDY (see DRAMATIC STRUCTURE). It may attempt to present the details of life with a scientist's detached and objective completeness, as in NATURALISM; or it may try by IMAGE and linguistic and syntactic modification to reproduce the unconscious flow of the emotions, as in the STREAM-OF-CONSCIOUSNESS NOVEL. It may be episodic, loose in structure, epic in proportions—what is called "panoramic"—or it may be as tightly knit as a well-made play, bringing its material forward in dramatic orderliness—what is called "scenic."

But however diffuse and various the *novel* is as a form, it has always submitted itself to the dual test of artistic success and imitative accuracy or truth. It has, therefore, proved to be a continuing problem to the critic, while it has spoken with unique authority to the average reader of the past two centuries. Its best definition is ultimately the history of what it has been.

The English *novel* is essentially an eighteenth-century product. However, without the richness of literary activity which had preceded the eighteenth century, the *novel* could not have matured. The NARRATIVE interest developed in the stories of Charlemagne and Arthur, the various romantic CYCLES, the FABLIAUX; the descriptive values and appreciation of nature found in the PASTORALS; the historical interest of DIARIES and JOURNALS; the enthusiasm for character portrayal developed in sketches and BIOGRAPHIES; the use of suspense in TALES and MEDIEVAL ROMANCES—all these had to be familiar and understood before writers could evolve the *novel,* a form which draws certain elements from many of the literary types which preceded it.

The Roots of the English Novel.—But the matter is hardly as simple as this situation may suggest. CLASSICAL literature of Greece and Italy had its forms of the modern *novel*. In the second century B.C., Aristides wrote a series of TALES of his home town, Miletus, a collection which was called *Milesiaka* but which is not known to scholars today, though Edmund Gosse ventures to say that it "was probably the beginning of the modern novel." Six centuries later Heliodorus, a Syrian, wrote *Aethiopica*—a love story at least somewhat true to life. *Daphnis and Chloë* (Greek), attributed to Longus of the third century, can be, says the same critic, "strictly called a novel." In Latin there were various contributory works of which only two will be mentioned here, the *Golden Ass* of Apuleius, a translation from the Greek, and the *Satyricon* of Petronius which presented the life and customs of the time of Nero.

But the NOVELLA of Italy is one of the earlier literary forms to which the modern *novel* is deeply indebted both for its narrative form and for its name. The appearance of *Cento Novelle Antiche* just before the opening of the fourteenth century gave great vogue to the NOVELLA form. These NOVELLE were stories of scandalous love, of chivalry, of mythology and morals, of the type best known to modern English readers through the stories of Boccaccio's *Decameron* (*ca.*1348). Loose women, unscrupulous priests, rough peasants, and high-born nobles, formed the central figures of most of these tales. A few of the more famed collections of NOVELLE are: Sacchetti's *Trecente Novelle*, Fiorentino's *Il Pecorone*, Masuccio's *Novellino*, and Bandello's *Novelle*.

From Spain came at least two works which were major influences on the development of the *novel*: the *Lazarillo de Tormes* of 1554 and Cervantes' *Don Quixote* of 1605 (see PICARESQUE NOVEL).

France, like Italy, produced NOVELLE. About 1450 was written the *Quinze Joies de Mariage* (anonymous) in the manner of the Italian. Antoine de La Sale's *Cent Nouvelles Nouvelles* and Bonaventure Despériers' *Nouvelles Récréations* carried on this interest. In 1535 appeared the *Gargantua* of Rabelais, which, while not a *novel*, nevertheless has sustained narrative interest. Honoré d'Urfé's *Astrée* (1610) has more definitely the qualities we demand in a *novel* today, and by the middle of the seventeenth century Mlle de Scudéry (1607–1701) was writing ROMANCES which might pass muster in the twentieth century. The romantic qualities of Scudéry called forth a realistic reaction from Scarron, who wrote *Roman Comique*. Some literary historians assign to Marguerite Pioche de la Vergne the honor of having created the first full-blown French *novels* in her *Princesse de Montpensier* (1662) and *Princesse de Clèves* (1678). Other French works important in the development of the *novel* were: La Fontaine's *Psyché* (1669), Fénelon's *Télémaque* (1669), Le Sage's *Gil Blas*

(1715, Books I–II), Marivaux's *Marianne* (1731), and Prévost's *Manon Lescaut* (1731).

English writers of the eighteenth century had as a background the experience of continental Europe. The classical literature of Greece and Rome, the CYCLES of ROMANCE, PASTORAL literature, the PICARESQUE tale of adventure, the interest in human character portrayed through the ANA—all these elements and others held in solution the material which was eventually to crystallize into the English *novel*. In addition to these beginnings from Europe, the English novelists had native parallels of their own—the Arthurian materials, the *Euphues* of Lyly (1579), the *Arcadia* of Sir Philip Sidney (1580–81), the narrative interest in Lodge's *Rosalynde* (1590), the picaresque element in Nash's *The Unfortunate Traveler* (1594), the humanitarian sympathy for the slave and the NARRATIVE chronicle of Aphra Behn's *Oroonoko* (1688), the extended NARRATIVE of moral significance in John Bunyan's *Pilgrim's Progress* (1678–1684), and the CHARACTER element present in the *Spectator* papers of Addison and Steele. Defoe, in *Robinson Crusoe* (1719) and *Moll Flanders* (1722), using very loose NARRATIVE structures, and Swift, in *Gulliver's Travels* (1726), using satiric ALLEGORY, had brought VERSIMILITUDE to the chronicling of human life, two component parts of the later *novel* form.

The Novel Matures.—With these narrative qualities already rooted in various types of English and European writing, the ground was fertile, tilled, and seeded when Samuel Richardson, in 1740, issued his *Pamela; or, Virtue Rewarded,* the first English book which practically all critics and historians are willing to call a clearly realized *novel*. Richardson's three *novels, Pamela, Clarissa Harlow* (1747–1748), and *Sir Charles Grandison* (1753) are chiefly in the EPISTOLARY form.

After Richardson's success with *Pamela*, followed rapidly other significant *novels:* Henry Fielding started his *Joseph Andrews* (1742) as a SATIRE on *Pamela*, but before going far he forgot his ironical intent and told a vigorous story of his own. In 1748 Smollett published *Roderick Random;* in 1749 came Fielding's greatest *novel, Tom Jones*, important for its development of PLOT and its realistic interpretation of English life; in 1751 both Smollett and Fielding repeated, the first with *Peregrine Pickle* and the second with *Amelia.* Defoe, Richardson, Fielding, Smollet stand at the very source of the English *novel*. The succeeding years brought other *novels* and novelists, but the first real impetus to long fiction was given by them. Sterne wrote *Tristram Shandy* (1760–1767), a work which broke, even this early, the NARRATIVE form of the *novel* and, applying Locke's psychological theories, undertook the exploration of the inner self. Horace Walpole made much of the GOTHIC mysteries in his *Castle of Otranto* (1764). Two years later Oliver Goldsmith published the *Vicar of Wakefield*. And then came such works as Fanny Burney's NOVEL OF MANNERS, *Evelina* (1778), and Ann Radcliffe's *Mysteries of Udolpho* (1794).

The nineteenth century saw the flowering of the English *novel* as an instrument portraying a middle-class society. Jane Austen produced NOVELS OF MANNERS and Scott virtually created the HISTORICAL NOVEL and carried it to a high point in the first quarter of the century. The great Victorian novelists—Dickens, Thackeray, and Trollope—created vast fictional worlds loaded with an abundance of social types and actions and arranged in complex and intricate melodramatic PLOTS. In Thomas Hardy and George Eliot the last half of the century found writers who, in differing degrees, applied the tenets of NATURALISM to the *novel*.

In the twentieth century the English *novel* has probed more and more deeply into the human mind, there to find the materials with which to work. Virginia Woolf, Dorothy Richardson, and James Joyce, writing STREAM-OF-CONSCIOUSNESS NOVELS, have greatly expanded and deepened the subject matter of the *novel* and modified the techniques of FICTION so that this new subject matter may be dealt with. This century has been marked, too, by a growing concern over critical and technical issues in FICTION.

The Novel in America.—Not for fifty years after Richardson published *Pamela* were *novels* written in America, although *Pamela* appeared in an American edition within two years of its English publication. However, before the close of the eighteenth century *The Power of Sympathy*, a moralistic TALE of seduction, by William Hill Brown (1789) appeared. With Charles Brockden Brown America produced her first important novelist. Brown, who wrote chiefly in the GOTHIC manner, was the author of four readable tales: *Arthur Mervyn* (1799), *Ormond* (1799), *Wieland* (1798), and *Edgar Huntley* (1799), as well as others less well known. Some twenty years later James Fenimore Cooper published *The Spy* (1821), *The Pioneers* (1823), *The Pilot* (1823). The Leatherstocking Series included, in addition to *The Pioneers,* already mentioned, *The Deerslayer* (1841), *The Last of the Mohicans* (1826), *The Path-*

finder (1840), and *The Prairie* (1827). By 1850, when Hawthorne's
Scarlet Letter appeared, the American *novel* had come into its full
powers, a fact made abundantly clear by the publication in 1851
of Herman Melville's *Moby-Dick*. In the last half of the nineteenth
century, REALISM, articulated as a theory by William Dean Howells
and well exemplified in his work, and made the basis of a highly self-
conscious art by Henry James, dominated the American *novel*. This
control gave way in the early years of the twentieth century to the
NATURALISM of Norris and Dreiser. After the First World War, a
group of talented young novelists introduced a number of ideas
drawn from the French realists and symbolists into American FIC-
TION and produced a new, vital, but essentially ROMANTIC *novel* with
strong naturalistic overtones. Important among them were Ernest
Hemingway and William Faulkner. Today the American *novel* is
a varied form practiced with self-conscious skill by a number of
novelists and read by large audiences more earnestly than is any
other serious literary form.

Attempts to classify the *novel* usually come to logical grief, how-
ever helpful they may be, for the terms are by no means mutually
exclusive. In this Handbook special forms of the *novel* are discussed
in separate entries, broadly classified by subject matter. They are
DETECTIVE NOVEL, PSYCHOLOGICAL NOVEL, SOCIOLOGICAL NOVEL,
SENTIMENTAL NOVEL, PROPAGANDA NOVEL, HISTORICAL NOVEL, NOVEL
OF MANNERS, NOVEL OF CHARACTER, NOVEL OF INCIDENT, NOVEL OF
THE SOIL, REGIONAL NOVEL, PICARESQUE NOVEL, GOTHIC NOVEL,
APPRENTICESHIP NOVEL, STREAM-OF-CONSCIOUSNESS NOVEL, PROBLEM
NOVEL, EPISTOLARY NOVEL, KÜNSTLERROMAN. The principal modes
in which novelists write are the general modes of their ages; such
modes are the products of STYLE, literary CONVENTION, and the au-
thor's attitude toward life. They are defined in this Handbook under
the general terms such as REALISM, ROMANTICISM, IMPRESSIONISM,
EXPRESSIONISM, NATURALISM, NEO-CLASSICISM.

Novel of Character: A NOVEL which places its major emphasis upon
the representation and development of character rather than upon
exciting EPISODE, as in the NOVEL OF INCIDENT, or unity of PLOT or
STRUCTURE. See NOVEL, CHARACTERIZATION.

Novel of Incident: A term applied to NOVELS in which action in
more or less unrelated EPISODES dominate, and PLOT and CHARACTER
are subordinate. In this type of NOVEL the PLOT structure is loose;

emphasis is on thrilling incident rather than on CHARACTERIZATION or sustained SUSPENSE. If one may call Defoe's *Robinson Crusoe* a NOVEL, then it may be used to illustrate the *novel of incident.* Here the EPISODES of the shipwreck, the meeting with Friday, the clash with visiting natives, and other incidents follow each other chronologically but they are more or less independent of each other. Dumas' *Three Musketeers* is also a *novel of incident,* though here the PLOT is more developed than in Defoe's story.

Novel of Manners: A NOVEL, among the dominant forces of which are the social customs, manners, conventions, and habits of a definite social class at a particular time and place. In the true *novel of manners* the social mores of a specific group are defined and described in detail and with great accuracy, and these mores become powerful controls over characters. The *novel of manners* is often, although by no means always, satiric; it is always realistic in manner, however. The HISTORICAL NOVEL is sometimes called the "*novel of manners* laid in the past." The NOVELS of Jane Austen, Edith Wharton, and John P. Marquand are *novels of manners.* See NOVEL, MANNERS.

Novel of Sensibility: A NOVEL in which the characters have a heightened and highly emotional response to events, actions, and sentiments. The author attempts to produce in the reader a similar heightened emotional response. Sterne's *Tristram Shandy* is a major example and Mackenzie's *Man of Feeling* unconsciously carries the idea of intensity of character response beyond the limits of reason. See SENTIMENTAL NOVEL.

Novel of the Soil, The: A special kind of REGIONALISM in the NOVEL, in which the lives of people struggling for existence in remote rural sections are starkly portrayed. Examples are Ellen Glasgow's *Barren Ground,* O. E. Rölvaag's *Giants in the Earth,* and Elizabeth Madox Roberts' *Time of Man.* It should be emphasized that the term *novel of the soil* refers primarily to a subject matter rather than to a manner; however, the term is usually restricted to portrayals of country life in the manner of REALISM or NATURALISM.

Novelette: A work of prose FICTION of intermediate length, longer than a SHORT STORY and shorter than a NOVEL. Since, however, there is little agreement on maximum length for any of these types, the

distinction that in general the *novelette* displays the customarily compact structure of the SHORT STORY with the greater development of
CHARACTER, THEME, and action of the NOVEL is perhaps useful. Melville's *Billy Budd,* Stevenson's *Dr. Jekyll and Mr. Hyde,* Henry James'
The Turn of the Screw, and Conrad's *Heart of Darkness* are examples. See SHORT NOVEL.

Novella: A TALE or SHORT STORY. The term is particularly applied
to the early TALES of Italian and French writers—such as the *Decameron* of Boccaccio and the *Heptameron* of Marguerite of Valois.
The form is of especial interest to students of English literature for
two reasons: (1) many of these early *novelle* were used by English
writers as sources for their own work, and (2) it was from this form
that the term *novel* as a designation of a form of prose FICTION developed. The *novelle* were among the significant formative influences
on the English NOVEL. (See NOVEL.) *Novella* is also a term borrowed
from the German and applied to the kind of SHORT NOVELS that developed in Germany in the nineteenth century.

Nursery Rhyme: Brief VERSES, often anonymous and traditional,
with heavy RHYTHM and frequent, heavy RHYME, written for young
children. The first important collection of *nursery rhymes* in English
was made in the eighteenth century by "Mother Goose," whose
actual identity has long been a matter of dispute. *Nursery rhymes*
include SONGS, "counting-out" games, NARRATIVES, NONSENSE VERSE,
and RHYMES that seem to have links with English political history.

O

Obiter dicta: Things said "by the way"; incidental remarks: opposed to statements based upon calculated, deliberate judgment.
Though legal in origin, the term is sometimes used in literary association, as in speaking of one author's *obiter dicta* being weightier
and wiser than another's serious, labored expressions.

Objective Correlative: A term first used by T. S. Eliot to describe
a pattern of objects, actions, or events, or a situation which can
serve effectively to awaken in the reader the emotional response
which the author desires without being a direct statement of that
emotion. It is an impersonal or objective means of communicating

feeling. Eliot calls the *objective correlative* "the only way of expressing emotion in the form of art" and defines it as "a set of objects, a situation, a chain of events which shall be the formula of that *particular* emotion, such that when the external facts, which must terminate in sensory experience, are given, the emotion is immediately evoked." The term has had wide currency in this sense among contemporary critics. It had been used by Washington Allston in a lecture on art as early as 1850 to describe the process by which the external world produces pleasurable emotion, but Eliot's usage gave it new meaning and made of it a new term. See NEGATIVE CAPABILITY, AESTHETIC DISTANCE.

Objective Theory of Art: A critical term applied by M. H. Abrams to the view which holds the literary work to be most significant as an object in itself, independent of the facts of its composition, the actuality it imitates, its author's stated intention, or the effect it produces on its audience. See CRITICISM, HISTORICAL SKETCH; AUTOTELIC; NEW CRITICISM.

Objectivity: A quality in a literary work of impersonality, of freedom from the expression of personal sentiments, attitudes, or emotions by the author. In contemporary criticism *objectivity* is a highly desirable quality in art. See AESTHETIC DISTANCE, OBJECTIVE CORRELATIVE, NEGATIVE CAPABILITY.

Obligatory Scene: An EPISODE in a play the circumstances of which are so strongly foreseen by the audience in the development of the PLOT that the playwright is obliged to write the *scene*. It is a characteristic of the WELL-MADE PLAY. *Obligatory scene* is the English equivalent of the French term SCÈNE À FAIRE.

Occasional Verse: Poetry written to grace or commemorate a social, historical, or personal event. Although the term includes VERS DE SOCIÉTÉ, it usually designates writing of more serious and more dignified purpose. POETS LAUREATE are called upon to produce *occasional verse* in the discharge of their responsibilities. Love poems of a highly personal nature and addressed to a specific person are sometimes called *occasional verse*. Among notable examples of *occasional verse* are Spenser's "Epithalamion," celebrating his marriage; Dryden's "Astraea Redux," celebrating the return to the throne of

Charles II; Marvell's "Horatian Ode upon Cromwell's Return from Ireland"; and Milton's "Lycidas," upon the death of Edward King.

Octameter: A line of VERSE consisting of eight FEET. See SCANSION.

Octastich: A group of eight lines of VERSE.

Octave: An eight-line STANZA. The chief use of the term, however, is to denote the first eight-VERSE division of the ITALIAN SONNET as separate from the last six-VERSE division, the SESTET. In this sense, it is a synonym for OCTET. In the strict SONNET usage the *octave* RHYMES *abbaabba,* and serves to state a generalization later applied or resolved in the SESTET, and comes to such a complete close at the end of the eighth line as to be marked by a full stop. An *octave* is also an eight-line, unrhymed, individual poem in IAMBIC PENTAMETER.

Octavo: A BOOK SIZE designating a book whose SIGNATURE results from sheets folded to eight leaves or sixteen pages. See BOOK SIZES.

Octet: A group of eight lines of VERSE; an OCTASTICH. Frequently used as a synonym for OCTAVE, the first eight lines of an ITALIAN SONNET.

Ode: "Any strain of enthusiastic and exalted lyrical VERSE, directed to a fixed purpose, and dealing progressively with one dignified theme." (Gosse.) The term connotes certain qualities both of manner and form. In manner, the *ode* is an elaborate LYRIC, expressed in language dignified, sincere, and imaginative and intellectual in tone. In form the *ode* is more complicated than most of the LYRIC types. Perhaps the essential distinction of form is the division into STROPHES: the STROPHE, ANTISTROPHE, and EPODE. Originally a Greek FORM used in dramatic POETRY, the *ode* was choral. Accompanied by music, the CHORUS of singers moved up one side during the STROPHE, down the other during the ANTISTROPHE, and stood in place during the EPODE. In a general way this movement emphasized the rise and fall of emotional power. In English poetry there are three types of *odes:* the PINDARIC (regular), the HORATAIN or homostrophic, and the IRREGULAR type. The PINDARIC ODE is characterized by the three-STROPHE division, the STROPHE and the ANTISTROPHE alike in form, the EPODE different from the other two. The METER and VERSE lengths may vary within any one STROPHE of the *ode*, but when the movement is repeated the metrical scheme for corresponding divisions should be similar though accompanied by new RHYMES. It is not essential that STROPHE, ANTISTROPHE, and EPODE alternate regularly, since the EPODE may be used at the end or inconsistently between the STROPHE and the ANTISTROPHE (*Ode to Liberty*, Collins). The second *ode*-form, the HORATIAN or homostrophic, consists of only one STANZA type, and that type may be almost infinitely varied within its pattern (*Ode to France*, Coleridge). The third form of the *ode*, the IRREGULAR, is credited to the poet Cowley, who seems to have thought he was writing PINDARIC ODES. Like the second type considered, freedom within the STROPHE is characteristic of this form. But here the STROPHES are rules unto themselves and all pretense at STANZA pattern may be discarded. The length of the lines may vary, the number of lines in each STROPHE may vary widely, the RHYME pattern need not be carried over from STANZA to STANZA, and the metrical MOVEMENT will quicken and slacken with the MOOD of the poet and the emotional intensity. Much more flexible than the two other forms considered, the IRREGULAR ODE affords greatest freedom of expression to the poet and, consequently, greatest license. In English poetry, these three forms are well represented in the following poems: Gray's "The Bard," an example of the strict PINDARIC ODE; Collins' "Ode to Evening," an example of the HORATIAN ODE; and Wordsworth's "Ode on Intimations of Immortality," an example of the IRREGULAR ODE. In contemporary poetry, the public nature, solemn diction, and stately gravity of the *ode* have on occasion been effectively used for ironic overtones, as in Allen Tate's "Ode on the Confederate Dead."

Oedipus Complex: In psychoanalysis a libidinal feeling that develops in a child, especially a male child, between the ages of three and six, for the parent of the opposite sex. This attachment is generally accompanied by hostility to the parent of the child's own sex. The *Oedipus complex* is usually repressed. In instances when it persists, it can work emotional havoc. The *Oedipus complex* is named for Oedipus, a Theban HERO of ancient LEGEND and of Greek TRAGEDY, who slew his father and married his mother. See ELECTRA COMPLEX, with which it is in contrast, and FREUDIANISM.

Old Comedy: Greek COMEDY of the fifth century, B.C., performed at festivals of Dionysus. *Old Comedy* was a blend of religious ceremony, SATIRE, WIT, and buffoonery. It was farcical and bawdy, and it contained much social SATIRE, laughing harshly at most religious, political, military, and intellectual aspects and issues of its day, and containing LAMPOONS of individuals. It used STOCK CHARACTERS: the ALAZON, the EIRON, the sly dissembler, the entertaining clown, and the FOIL. It used a CHORUS costumed as animals. The greatest writer of the *Old Comedy* was Aristophanes.

Old English (Language): That form of language spoken in the British Isles between the Anglo-Saxon invasions in the fifth century and the NORMAN CONQUEST in the eleventh; a Germanic dialect. See ENGLISH LANGUAGE.

Old English Period: The period in English history and literature between the invasion of England by the Teutonic tribes of Angles, Saxons, and Jutes, beginning about 428, and the establishment of the Norman rule of England around 1100, following the triumphant Conquest of England by the Norman French under William the Conqueror. Saxon monarchies were established in Sussex, Wessex, and Essex in the fifth and sixth centuries; Anglian monarchies in Northumbria, East Anglia, and Mercia in the sixth and seventh centuries. Christianity was introduced early and gradually won out over the pagan culture. It was an age of intertribal conflict and, in the ninth century, of struggles with the invading Danes. The greatest of the rulers of the period was Alfred, who, in the ninth century, effected a unification of the Teutonic groups.

Learning and culture flourished in the monasteries, with Whitby the cradle of English poetry in the North and Winchester that of English prose in the South. Although much writing throughout the period was in Latin, Christian monks began writing in the vernacular which we call OLD ENGLISH about 700. In the earliest part of the period the POETRY, written in accentual METER and linked by ALLITERATION (see OLD ENGLISH VERSIFICATION) was centered on the life of the Germanic tribes and was basically pagan, although Christian elements were incorporated early. The best of the POEMS which have survived are the great EPIC *Beowulf* (*ca.*700), "The Seafarer," "Widsith," and "Deor's Lament." Early POETRY of a more emphatically Christian nature included Caedmon's "Song," Biblical paraphrases such as *Genesis, Exodus, Daniel, Judith;* religious NARRATIVES such as the *Crist, Elene, Andreas;* and the allegorical *Phoenix* (a translation from Latin). Literature first flourished in Northumbria, but in the reign of Alfred the Great (871–899) West Saxon became

Old English Versification

the literary DIALECT. Under Alfred, much Latin literature was translated into English prose, such as Pope Gregory's *Pastoral Care,* Boethius' *Consolation of Philosophy,* and Bede's *Ecclesiastical History;* and the great *Anglo-Saxon Chronicle* was revised and expanded. A second prose revival took place in the HOMILIES of Ælfric and Wulfstan (tenth and eleventh centuries), works noted for the richness of their STYLE, reflecting Latin models. Late examples of Anglo-Saxon VERSE are the "Battle of Maldon" and the "Battle of Brunanburgh," heroic POEMS. The NORMAN CONQUEST (1066) put an end to serious literary work in the OLD ENGLISH LANGUAGE. See OLD ENGLISH (LANGUAGE), OLD ENGLISH VERSIFICATION, ENGLISH LANGUAGE, and *Outline of Literary History.*

Old English Versification: The metrical system employed by English poets in the period before 1100. It is essentially an accentual system (see METER), consisting of equal numbers of accented syllables to the line and varying numbers of unaccented syllables. The normal Old English line fell into two HEMISTICHS, each having two accented syllables and with the HEMISTICHS separated by a heavy CAESURA. The ACCENTS are grammatical; that is, they fall on syllables which would normally carry stress in that particular construction. The HEMISTICHS are bound by ALLITERATION, one or both the accented syllables of the first alliterating with the first accented syllable of the second or much more rarely with the second accented syllable. Variant lines were: the rare "short line," which contains only two stressed syllables and no CAESURA, the stressed syllables being bound by ALLITERATION; and the HYPERMETRICAL line in which three or more stressed syllables may appear in each HEMISTICH. To go beyond such a schematic outline is to enter an area of great scholarly uncertainty and controversy.

Omnibus: A volume made up of selected works, usually by one author but sometimes by several authors on one subject. The works are usually reprinted from earlier volumes.

Omniscient Point of View: A term used to describe the POINT OF VIEW in a work of FICTION in which the author is capable of knowing, seeing, and telling whatever he wishes in the story, and exercises this freedom at will. It is characterized by freedom in shifting from the exterior world to the inner selves of a number of CHARACTERS and by a freedom in movement both in time and place; but to an even

Onomatopoeia

greater extent it is characterized by the freedom of the author to comment upon the meaning of actions and to state the thematic intentions of the story whenever and wherever he desires. See POINT OF VIEW.

One-Act Play: A form of DRAMA which has attracted attention since about 1890. Before that date *one-act plays* had been used chiefly on VAUDEVILLE programs and as CURTAIN RAISERS in the LEGITIMATE THEATER. Special attention to the *one-act play* came with the LITTLE THEATER MOVEMENT and the practice of relying upon a group of such short plays for a single evening's entertainment. The fact that the FORM was adopted by playwrights of high ability (J. M. Barrie, A. W. Pinero, Gerhart Hauptmann, G. B. Shaw) furthered its development. A widening circle of authors has produced *one-act plays* in the twentieth century, both in England and America, including John Masefield, Lord Dunsany, Lady Gregory, J. M. Synge, John Galsworthy, A. A. Milne, Percy MacKaye, Eugene O'Neill, Paul Green, Thornton Wilder, Noel Coward, Tennessee Williams, Arthur Miller, and Edward Albee. The technique of the *one-act play* is highly flexible, the most important demand being for unity of EFFECT, with consequent vigor of DIALOGUE, stressing of CHARACTER, and economy of NARRATIVE materials. Its relation to the "regular" or longer DRAMA has often been likened to that of the SHORT STORY to the NOVEL.

Onomatopoeia: The use of words which in their pronunciation suggest their meaning. Some onomatopoeic words are "hiss," "slam," "buzz," "whirr," "sizzle." However, *onomatopoeia* in the hands of a poet becomes a much more subtle device than simply the use of such words when, in an effort to suit sound to sense, he creates VERSES which themselves carry their meaning in their sounds. A notable example is quoted from *The Princess* by Tennyson:

> The moan of doves in immemorial elms,
> And murmuring of innumerable bees.

The RHYTHM of the lines, the succession of sounds, the effectiveness of RHYMES, all contribute to the effect by which the POEM as a pattern of sounds echoes the sense which its words denote. Perhaps the idea, accepted by some linguists, that front vowels tend to suggest light, small, or airy things and back vowels dark, large, and heavy things operates in producing the total onomatopoeic effect of a POEM. Pope's lines in *An Essay on Criticism* may well be quoted:

Open Couplet

'Tis not enough no harshness gives offense,
The sound must seem an echo to the sense:
Soft is the strain when Zephyr gently blows,
And the smooth stream in smoother numbers flows;
But when the loud surges lash the sounding shore,
The hoarse, rough verse should like the torrent roar:
When Ajax strives some rock's vast weight to throw,
The line too labors, and the words move slow.

Open Couplet: A COUPLET in which the second line is not complete but depends on the first line of the succeeding COUPLET for completion.

Opera: Though the primary interest in *opera* is musical, it is a dramatic FORM which has exerted influence upon English STAGE history. Only its connection with English DRAMA will be noticed here. *Opera* is musical DRAMA in the sense that the DIALOGUE instead of being spoken is sung, to the accompaniment of instrumental music, now always an orchestra. A play in which incidental music is stressed may be called "operatic," but is not true *opera* if the DIALOGUE is spoken. Greek DRAMA contained DIALOGUE sung to the accompaniment of the lyre or flute and is therefore a precursor, in fact somewhat of a model, for modern *opera*, which developed in Italy about 1600 as a result of amateur efforts to recapture the quality of the musical effects of Greek TRAGEDY by means of musical recitation instrumentally accompanied. The form was at first a MONODY, as in Jacopo Peri's *Euridice* (1600), the first public production in the new style. From these beginnings developed the important form now known as grand *opera*. Italian *opera* reached England soon after 1700, but before this date certain definite advances in the direction of *opera* had taken place on the English STAGE. To some degree an outgrowth of the Renaissance MASQUE, Sir William Davenant's *Siege of Rhodes* (1656) is a precursor of the English *opera*, since it was a musical entertainment, written in RHYME and designed to be sung in recitative and aria. The attention to scenery as well as the SONGS and orchestral accompaniment were suggestive of later English *opera*. During the RESTORATION AGE operatic versions of some of Shakespeare's plays (*The Tempest, Macbeth*) were called "dramatic *operas*," but the DIALOGUE was spoken, not sung. About 1689 Henry Purcell and Nahum Tate brought out *Dido and Aeneas,* in which the DIALOGUE was in recitative. Early in the eighteenth century Italian *operas* were "translated" and sung by English singers, as *Arsinoë, Queen of Cypress* (Drury Lane, 1706), and *Camilla* (1706). Later "bilingual" *operas* appeared, in which Italian singers sang part of the DIALOGUE in Italian while English singers sang the rest in English. The first completely Italian *opera* sung in Italian in England was *Almahide* (1710), which established the success of the FORM in England. About this time George Frederick Handel came to England. He produced *Rinaldo* in 1711, and exerted a powerful influence for many years thereafter. From the first, efforts to employ Italian singers and *opera* met with disfavor, as evidenced by Addison's SATIRE and by the famous BURLESQUE *opera* by John Gay, *The Beggar's Opera* (1728). The success of *opera* and various forms of BURLESQUE *opera* at this time probably had much to do with the tendency toward lyrical and spectacular elements on the English stage which the presence of the PATENT THEATERS encouraged in the eighteenth and nineteenth centuries. See BALLAD-OPERA.

Opéra bouffe: A French term for a very light form of COMIC OPERA developed from VAUDEVILLE music and said to be the ancestor of the COMIC OPERAS of Gilbert and Sullivan.

Operetta: A COMIC OPERA, with music, SONGS, and spectacular effects but with the DIALOGUE spoken. See COMIC OPERA, OPERA.

Oration: A formal speech intended to inspire to some action. Carefully prepared and delivered in an impassioned manner, the *oration* carries its greatest power in the emotional appeal it makes. Although a major cultural interest in CLASSICAL days and even up to a few decades ago, the *oration* has lost its popular appeal and is now but rarely heard in legislative halls, the courtroom, the church. The CLASSICAL *oration* has seven parts: (1) the entrance, or EXORDIUM, to catch the audience's attention; (2) the NARRATION, to set forth the facts; (3) the EXPOSITION or DEFINITION, to define terms and open issues to be proved; (4) the proposition, to clarify the points at issue and state exactly what is to be proved; (5) the confirmation, to set forth the arguments for and against and advance proof; (6) the confutation or refutation, to refute the opponent's arguments; and (7) the conclusion or EPILOGUE, to sum up the arguments and stir the audience.

Organic Form: A concept of FORM in which the structure of a literary work is said to grow from its conception in the thought, feeling, and personality of the writer, rather than being arbitrarily shaped through mechanical force in a preconceived mold. In the theory of *organic form* the work grows like a living organism, its parts inseparable and indivisible, and the whole being greater than the sum of its parts. The concept of *organic form* was advanced by Coleridge, most vigorously in his defence of Shakespeare against the charge of formlessness. The casting aside of the established and preconceived FORMS as mechanical in favor of the concept of organic growth was not, Coleridge felt, a surrender to lawlessness or anti-intellectualism. Rather it was the acceptance of the reign of law in living nature. In the growth of a tree, Coleridge saw "a law which all the parts obey," and this law was an "essential principle" of trees. He said: "No work of true genius dare want its appropriate *form;* neither indeed is there any danger of this. As it must not, so neither can it, be lawless! For it is even this that constitutes its genius—the power of acting creatively under laws of its own origination. The true ground of the mistake [about Shakespeare's formlessness] lies in the confounding mechanical regularity with *organic form.* The form is mechanic, when on any given material we impress a predetermined form, not necessarily arising out of the properties of the material;—as when to a mass of wet clay we give whatever shape we wish it to retain when hardened. The *organic form,* on the other hand, is innate; it shapes, as it develops, itself from within, and the fulness of its development is one and the same with the perfection of its outward form. Such as the life is, such is the form." And he defines Shakespeare as "himself a nature humanized, a genial understanding directing self-consciously a power and an implicit wisdom deeper even than consciousness." This concept of the nature of the creative act and the created work of art has been pervasive for the past 150 years. The SYMBOL most frequently used for such a literary work has been that of a plant, as having a *form* and a growth uniquely true to its individual nature. Cleanth Brooks's statement that "The parts of a poem are related as are the parts of a growing plant" is a representative example.

Originality: The use of new subject matter or FORMS or STYLES by an author, rather than the employment of traditional or conventional subject matters, FORMS, or STYLES. At various periods in literary history the value placed upon *originality* by authors, readers, and critics has fluctuated greatly. See INVENTION.

Ossianic Controversy: The controversy surrounding a famous English literary deception in the eighteenth century. See FORGERIES, LITERARY.

Otiose: A term used in literary criticism to characterize a STYLE which is verbose, redundant, pleonastic. Literally it implies *leisure* and, in the special sense here employed, it designates idle, useless, inefficient writing, the use of language which is so very much at leisure that it performs no useful function.

Ottava rima: A STANZA pattern consisting of eight IAMBIC PENTAMETER lines rhyming *abababcc*. Boccaccio is credited with originating this pattern, which was much used by Tasso and Ariosto. Some of the English poets making important use of *ottava rima* are Spenser, Milton, Keats, and Byron. The illustration is from *Don Juan:*

> But words are things, and a small drop of ink
>   Falling like dew, upon a thought, produces
> That which makes thousands, perhaps millions, think;
>   'Tis strange, the shortest letter which man uses
> Instead of speech, may form a lasting link
>   Of ages; to what straits old Time reduces
> Frail man, when paper—even a rag like this,
> Survives himself, his tomb, and all that's his!

In its original Italian form *ottava rima* lines were HENDECASYLLABIC, that is, had eleven syllables.

Outride: A term Gerard Manley Hopkins applied to a SLACK SYLLABLE—that is, an unstressed syllable—added to a FOOT. An *outride* does not change the basic SCANSION of a line, for in Hopkins's system, the stressed syllables determine the SCANSION. There may be as many as three *outrides* attached to a FOOT—that is, following a stressed syllable.

Oxford Movement: Also known as "Tractarian Movement" and "Anglo-Catholic Revival." During the first third of the nineteenth century the English Church had become somewhat lax in urging the ancient doctrines, in enforcing discipline, in carrying out ritual, and in keeping up the church edifices. In 1833 a movement for reform got under way at Oxford following a sermon on "national apostasy" by John Keble. The leader was John Henry (later Cardinal) Newman, who wrote the first of the ninety papers (*Tracts for the Times,* 1833–1841) in which the ideas of the group were advocated. Other leaders were R. H. Froude, Isaac Williams, Hugh James Rose (a Cambridge man), and E. B. Pusey. The reformers aimed primarily at combating liberalism and skepticism and restoring to the Church and to church worship the dignity, beauty, purity, and zeal of earlier times. They hoped also to protect the Church from the encroachment of the State, as threatened by the Whig Reform Bill of 1832 and other measures looking toward reducing the revenues of the Church and curbing its authority.

To provide a solid foundation for their reforms, the sponsors of the movement undertook to prove the divine origin of the Church and the historical continuity connecting the early Church with the Church of England. This led them to an espousal of doctrines regarded by some as Roman Catholic, and after the publication of Newman's final tract in 1841 a storm of criticism arose, as a result of which Newman lost his position at Oxford, became a layman, and finally (1845) joined the Roman Catholic Church, later becoming a Cardinal. When Charles Kingsley attacked his sincerity, Newman replied with the famous *Apologia pro Vita Sua* (1864), a full statement of his spiritual and mental history, the candor, beauty, and force of which won for him high regard. Though some of Newman's followers also became Catholics, the main movement, led now by Pusey, continued, though in its later stages it became less controversial and theoretical and more practical, furthering the establishment of guilds, improvement of church music, revival of the ritual, building and beautifying the church buildings. The movement attracted the attention of various literary men, with Carlyle heaping disdain upon it and Arnold attacking it. Also the sponsors of the movement wrote a number of propagandist novels, like Newman's *Loss and Gain* and Charlotte M. Yonge's *The Heir of Redclyffe.* The Episcopal Church in the United States reflects much of the reform doctrine of the Tractarians.

Oxford Reformers: A term applied to a group of humanist scholars whose associations began at Oxford University in the early RENAISSANCE, particularly the three friends John Colet, Sir Thomas More, and the Dutch scholar Erasmus. Though Erasmus, who had come to Oxford to study Greek and who spent part of his life in England, was the most famous member of the group and More the best loved, Colet seems to have been the real leader. The group was interested in effecting certain reforms in Church and State based upon humanist ideas. Moral training and reform were to be accomplished through rational rather than emotional processes. Reason should dominate. Humanity should be uplifted through education and the improvement of individual character. The church should be reformed from within by purging it of corrupt practices and by improving the moral and educational standards of the clergy. The group advocated the historical method in the study of the Bible, opposed medieval scholasticism and asceticism, and advocated education as a means of improving religion, private character, and political institutions. More recorded his dream of a perfect human society and government in his *Utopia* (1516); Colet when dean of St. Paul's founded with his own funds the St. Paul's school for boys, where new methods of instruction were developed and sons of the common folk might be admitted; Erasmus outlined his ideals of state in his *Education of a Christian Prince*. Keenly interested in purging the church of the evils which Luther a few years later rebelled against, the *Oxford Reformers* were unwilling to follow either Luther or Henry VIII in breaking with Rome, and died good Catholics, though disappointed idealists.

Oxymoron: Etymologically, "pointedly foolish"; a rhetorical AN-TITHESIS bringing together two contradictory terms. Such a contrast makes for sharp emphasis. Examples are: "cheerful pessimist," "wise fool," "sad joy," "eloquent silence."

P

Pæan: A SONG of praise or joy. Originally the term was restricted to ODES sung by a Greek CHORUS in honor of Apollo; later the term was broadened to include praise sung to other deities of antiquity. In modern times, the word has come to mean simply any song of joy. Homer indicates, too, that *pæans* were frequently sung on military occasions: before an attack, after a victory, when a fleet set sail.

Pæon: In METRICS, a FOOT consisting of one long or stressed syllable and three short or unstressed syllables. *Pæons* are named in terms of the one of the four syllables which is long or stressed, a "first *pæon*" being ∕ ˘ ˘ ˘, a "second" being ˘ ∕ ˘ ˘, a "third" being

∪ ∪ ⁄ ∪, and a "fourth" being ∪ ∪ ∪ ⁄. Although not common in English VERSE, this essentially classic FOOT does occasionally appear, notably in the poetry of Gerard Manley Hopkins.

Pageant: Used in three senses: (1) a scaffold or stage on which DRAMAS were performed in the Middle Ages; (2) plays performed on such stages; (3) modern dramatic spectacles designed to celebrate some historical event, often of local interest. The medieval *pageant*, constructed on wheels for processional use, as in celebrating Corpus Christi day, was designed for the use of a particular guild for the production of a particular play and usually reflected this special purpose. Thus the *pageant* of the fisherman, designed to present the play of Noah, would be constructed and painted to represent the Ark. For a contemporary description of the medieval *pageant* and its use, see MYSTERY PLAY. Though the modern *pageant* is an outgrowth of a very ancient tradition which includes primitive religious festivals, Roman "triumphs," etc., its recent remarkable development in England and especially in America makes it essentially a twentieth-century spectacle. It is usually understood to mean an outdoor exhibition consisting of several SCENES presented with recitation (PROLOGUES, etc.) usually with DIALOGUE, with historically appropriate costumes, sometimes with musical features, the whole being designed to commemorate some event which appeals to the emotional loyalties of the populace. Sometimes the *pageant* is processional, with a series of "floats," uniformed marchers, and mounted officials, while it is sometimes presented in an outdoor theater of some sort, such as an athletic stadium. The true *pageant* is thought of as an outdoor exhibition, closely connected with the FOLK-DRAMA movement.

Palimpsest: A writing surface, whether of vellum, papyrus, or other material, which has been used twice or more for manuscript purposes. Before the invention of paper, the scarcity of writing material made such substances very valuable and the vellum surfaces were often scraped or rubbed or the papyrus surfaces washed. With material so used a second time it frequently happened that the earlier script either was not completely erased or that, with age, it showed through the new. In this way many documents of very early periods have been preserved for posterity. In one instance, for example, a Syriac text of St. Chrysostom of perhaps the tenth century was found to be superimposed on a sixth-century grammatical work in Latin, which again had covered some fifth-century Latin records. Modern chemical methods and the use of special lighting make it possible today to recover many of the original texts.

Palindrome: A word, sentence, or VERSE which reads the same from left to right and from right to left. See ANAGRAM.

Palinode: A piece of writing recanting or retracting a previous writing, particularly such a recanting, in VERSE form, of an earlier ODE.

Pamphlet: A short ESSAY or treatise, usually on a current topic, issued as a separate publication. A *pamphlet* has fewer pages than a book, is always unbound, and may or may not have paper covers. Most *pamphlets* are polemical tracts of only transitory value.

Panegyric: A formal written or oral composition lauding a person for an achievement, a EULOGY. In Roman literature *panegyrics* were usually presented in praise of a living person, thing, or achievement. In Greek literature they were often reserved for praise of the dead. This was a popular form of ORATORY among fulsome speakers who praised living emperors. Two famous *panegyrics* are those of Gorgias, the *Olympiacus,* in praise of those who established the festivals, and that of Pliny the Younger delivered when he became consul, a speech praising Trajan. The term is now often used with a derogatory connotation. See ENCOMIUM.

Panoramic Method: A term applied to POINT OF VIEW in which an author presents his material by NARRATIVE EXPOSITION rather than in SCENES, giving actions and conversations in summary rather than in detail. See SCENES (IN A NOVEL), POINT OF VIEW.

Pantheism: A philosophic-religious attitude which finds the spirit of God manifest in all things and which holds that whereas all things speak the glory of God it is equally true that the glory of God is made up of all things. Finite objects are at once both God and the manifestation of God. The term is impossible of exact definition since it is so personal a conviction as to be differently interpreted by different philosophers, but for its literary significance it is clearly enough described as an ardent faith in NATURE as both the revelation of deity and deity itself. The word was first used in

1705 by the deist John Toland who called himself a pantheist (from *pan* meaning "all" and *theos* meaning "deity"). The pantheistic attitude, however, is much older than the eighteenth century, since it pervades the primitive thought of Egypt and India, was common in Greece long before the time of Christ, was taken up by the neo-Platonists of the Middle Ages, and has played an important part in Christian and Hebraic doctrine. Spinoza is, from the philosophic point of view, the great spokesman of *pantheism,* as Goethe is the great poet of the idea. In literature *pantheism* finds frequent expression. Wordsworth in England and Emerson in America may be selected from many as giving typical expression to the pantheistic conception. The following, from Wordsworth's *Lines Composed a Few Miles above Tintern Abbey,* is a clear expression of the idea:

> . . . a sense sublime
> Of something far more deeply interfused,
> Whose dwelling is the light of setting suns,
> And the round ocean and the living air
> And the blue sky, and in the mind of man;
> A motion and a spirit, that impels
> All thinking things, all objects of all thought,
> And rolls through all things.

Pantomime: In its broad sense the term means silent acting; the form of dramatic activity in which silent motion, gesture, facial expression, and costume are relied upon to express emotional states or NARRATIVE situations. The war dances of primitive society are thus pantomimic. Partly pantomimic was the Roman MIME and completely so the English DUMB SHOW. In English stage history, *pantomime* usually means the spectacular dramatic form which flourished from the early years of the eighteenth century. Though "*pantomime* proper" (no speaking) is said to have been introduced by a dancing master in 1702 at the Drury Lane Theatre, the usual form of *pantomime,* as sponsored at Lincoln's Inn Fields theater by John Rich some years later, was more varied. There was usually a serious legendary STORY told through dancing and songs. In these STORIES moved the figures of the *commedia dell' arte,* burlesquing in silent movement the action of the TALE. A background of the most spectacular description, the lavish use of "machinery," and many changes of scene made the *pantomime* visually exciting. The *pantomime* flourished throughout the eighteenth century and until near the close of the nineteenth century. English *pantomimes* (sometimes with a girl as the "leading boy," and including dance,

SONG, and SLAPSTICK) have been common in this century and are often built around such traditional themes as Humpty-Dumpty, Dick Whittington and his cat, and Cinderella.

Pantoum: The *pantoum* may consist of an indefinite number of four-line STANZAS, but in any case the second and fourth VERSES of one STANZA must reappear as the first and third lines of the following STANZA. The STANZAS are QUATRAINS, the RHYME scheme being *abab, abab*. In the final STANZA the first and third lines of the first STANZA are repeated in reverse order, the poem thus ending with the same line with which it began. Usually considered as one of the sophisticated FRENCH FORMS though, as a matter of fact, the *pantoum* was taken over from the Malaysian by Victor Hugo and other French poets. This primitive origin is evident in the monotonous repetition of lines, a monotony possibly derived from the rhythmic beating of the Oriental tom-tom.

Parabasis: In Greek OLD COMEDY a long address to the audience by the CHORUS speaking for the author. It usually consisted of witty remarks on contemporary affairs, frequently with open personal allusions. It was not directly related to the PLOT of the COMEDY itself. See OLD COMEDY.

Parable: An illustrative story answering a question or pointing a moral or lesson. A true *parable,* however, is much more than an ANECDOTE since, implicitly at least, detail for detail in the *parable* is parallel with the situation which calls forth the *parable* for illustration. *Parables* are, in this sense, allegories (see ALLEGORY). Naturally in Christian countries the most famous *parables* are those told by Christ, such for instance as the *parable* of the sower.

Paradox: A statement which while seemingly contradictory or absurd may actually be well-founded or true. *Paradox* is a rhetorical device used to attract attention, to secure emphasis. Bentley's statement that there are "none so credulous as infidels" is an illustration. *Paradox* is a common element in epigrammatic writing, as the work of G. K. Chesterton or Oscar Wilde shows. The presence of *paradox* in POETRY has become a serious concern of some of the NEW CRITICS, notably Cleanth Brooks, who sees *paradox* as a fundamental element of poetic language.

Paragoge

Paragoge: The addition of an extra and unneeded letter, syllable, or sound at the end of a word, as in "dearie" for "dear." Such extra syllables are frequently added for the sake of the METER in NURSERY RHYMES and BALLADS, as in these lines from "The Baffled Knight":

> Quoth he, "Shall you and I, lady,
>   Among the grass lie down a?
> And I will have a special care
>   Of rumpling of your gown a."

Parallelism: A structural arrangement of parts of a sentence, sentences, paragraphs, and larger units of composition by which one element of equal importance with another is similarly developed and phrased. The principle of *parallelism* simply dictates that co-ordinate ideas should have coordinate presentation. Within a sentence, for instance, where several elements of equal importance are to be expressed, if one element is cast in a relative clause the others should be expressed in relative clauses. Conversely, of course, the principle of *parallelism* demands that unequal elements should *not* be expressed in similar constructions. Practiced writers are not likely to attempt, for example, the comparison of positive and negative statements, of inverted and uninverted constructions, of dependent and independent clauses. And, for an example of simple *parallelism,* the sentence immediately above may serve. *Parallelism* is characteristic of Oriental poetry, being notably present in the Psalms, as in

> The Heavens declare the glory of God;
> And the firmament sheweth his handywork.

It is also characteristic of the SONGS and CHANTS of the American Indians. *Parallelism* seems to be the controlling principle of the poetry of Walt Whitman. It shapes the following poem of his on almost every level from that of the word to that of the central idea:

A noiseless patient spider,
I mark'd where on a little promontory it stood isolated,
Mark'd how to explore the vacant vast surrounding,
It launch'd forth filament, filament, filament out of itself.
Ever unreeling them, ever tirelessly speeding them.

And you O my soul where you stand,
Surrounded, detached, in measureless oceans of space,
Ceaselessly musing, venturing, throwing, seeking the spheres to connect
    them.
Till the bridge you will need be form'd, till the ductile anchor hold,
Till the gossamer thread you fling catch somewhere, O my soul.

Paraphrase: A restatement of an idea in such a way as to retain the meaning while changing the DICTION and form. A *paraphrase* is often an amplification of the original for the purpose of clarity, though the term is also used for any rather general restatement of an expression or passage. Thus one might speak of a *paraphrase* from the French meaning a loose statement of the idea rather than an exact translation, or of a *paraphrase* of a poem indicating a prose explanation of a difficult passage of verse. In contemporary criticism the paraphrasing of works of literary art is frowned upon, and the followers of the NEW CRITICISM often condemn what they call the "heresy of the *paraphrase*," a term suggesting their stand that the essential nature of a POEM is incommunicable in other terms than its own. Allen Tate states it succinctly when he says, "We know the particular poem, not what it says that we can restate."

Parenthesis: An explanatory remark thrown into the body of a statement and frequently separated from it by ( ). However, any comment which is an interruption of the immediate subject is spoken of as a *parenthesis* whether it be a word, phrase, clause, sentence, or paragraph. Commas and dashes are substituted for the *parenthesis* marks when the interruption is not so abrupt as to demand the ( ). Brackets [ ] are used for parenthetical material more foreign to the subject of the sentence than *parentheses* will control and also to enclose material injected into a statement by some editorial hand. Modern novelists, interested in accurately reporting the fluid and unstable nature of thought and feeling, frequently employ *parentheses,* although often without formal punctuation. Joyce and Faulkner are noted examples. Others, anxious to qualify and define precise shades of meaning find the extensive use of parenthetical material helpful, as does Henry James.

Parnassians: A group of nineteenth-century French poets, so called from their journal *Parnasse contemporain* (1866–1876). They were influenced by Gautier's doctrine of art for art's sake, and were in reaction against the prevailing Romanticism of the first half of the century. The *Parnassians* wrote impersonal poetry with great objective clarity and precision of detail. They had a strong preoccupation with FORM, and reintroduced the FRENCH FIXED FORMS. Their leader was Leconte de Lisle; among the other *Parnassians* were Sully-Prudhomme, Albert Glatigny, François Coppée, and Théodore de Banville. In the 1870's they influenced some English poets, including

Swinburne, Dobson, Gosse, and Lang, particularly in the use of the
FRENCH FIXED FORMS.

Parnassus: The name of a mountain in Greece famed as the haunt
of Apollo and the MUSES. The word has also been used as a title for
a collection or ANTHOLOGY of poems or poetical extracts, e.g.,
England's Parnassus (1600).

Parody: A composition burlesquing or imitating another, usually
serious, piece of work. It is designed to ridicule in nonsensical
fashion, or to criticize by brilliant treatment, an original piece of
work or its author. When the *parody* is directed against an author
or his style, it is likely to fall simply into barbed witticisms, often
venting personal antagonisms of the parodist against the one parodied. When the subject matter of the original composition is parodied,
however, it may prove to be a valuable indirect criticism or it may
even imply a flattering tribute to the original writer. Often a *parody*
is more powerful in its influence on affairs of current importance—
politics, for instance—than an original composition. The *parody* is
in literature what the CARICATURE and the cartoon are in art.
Known to have been used as a potent means of SATIRE and ridicule
even as far back as Aristophanes, *parody* has made a definite place
for itself in literature and has become a popular type of literary
composition. See BURLESQUE.

Paronomasia: An old term for a PUN or play on words.

Passion Play: A DRAMA that portrays a portion of the life of a god.
The plays in the MYSTERY PLAY cycles that dealt with the life of
Christ were *Passion Plays*. The term is now customarily restricted to
plays dealing with the last days, trial, crucifixion, and resurrection
of Christ. Such a *Passion Play* has been presented every tenth year
at Oberammergau, in Upper Bavaria, since the 1630's.

Pastiche: A French word for a PARODY or literary imitation. Perhaps
for humorous or satirical purposes, perhaps as a mere literary exercise or *jeu d'espirit*, perhaps in all seriousness (as in some CLOSET
DRAMAS), a writer imitates the style or technique of some recognized
writer or work. Amy Lowell's *A Critical Fable* (1922) might be
called a *pastiche*, since it is written in the manner of James Russell
Lowell's *A Fable for Critics*. In art, a picture is called a *pastiche*
when it manages to catch something of a master's peculiar style. In

music, *pastiche* is applied to a medley or assembly of various pieces into a single work. The term is also applied to literary patchworks formed by piecing together extracts from various works by one or several authors. See CENTO, PARODY.

Pastoral: A poem treating of shepherds and rustic life, after the Latin word for shepherd, *pastor*. The *pastoral* began in the third century B.C. when the Sicilian poet Theocritus included poetic sketches of rural life in his *Idylls*. The Greek *pastorals* existed in three forms: the DIALOGUE or singing-match, usually between two shepherds, often called the ECLOGUE because of the number of singing-matches in Virgil's "Selections"; the MONOLOGUE, often the plaint of a lovesick or forlorn shepherd lover or a poem praising some personage; and the ELEGY or LAMENT for a dead friend. The *pastoral* early became a highly conventionalized form of poetry, the poet (Virgil is an example) writing of his friends and acquaintances as though they were poetic shepherds moving through rural scenes. The form is artificial and unnatural—the "shepherds" of the *pastoral* often speaking in courtly language and appearing in dress more appropriate to the drawing room than to rocky hills and swampy meadows. Between 1550 and 1750 this conventionalized *pastoral* was much written in England. In modern use the term often means any poem of rural people and setting (Untermeyer, for instance, speaks of Robert Frost as a *"pastoral"* poet). Since this classification is based on subject matter and manner rather than on FORM, we often use the term in association with other poetic types; we thus have *pastoral* LYRICS, ELEGIES, DRAMAS, or even *pastoral* EPICS. Milton's *Lycidas,* Shelley's *Adonais,* and Arnold's *Thyrsis* are examples of English *pastorals,* as is Spenser's *The Shepheardes Calender.*

Many twentieth-century critics employ a highly sophisticated concept of the *pastoral* which was advanced by William Empson. In this specialized usage, the *pastoral* is considered a device for literary INVERSION, a means of "putting the complex into the simple"—of expressing complex ideas through simple personages, for example. Empson, using this specialized definition, finds *pastoral* elements in such widely differing works as the proletarian NOVEL (whose hero undergoes an INVERSION of function) and *Alice in Wonderland.* See IDYLL, BUCOLIC, ECLOGUE, PASTORAL DRAMA, PASTORAL ELEGY.

Pastoral Drama: The PASTORAL conventions so popular at times in POETRY (as the ECLOGUE) and in the PASTORAL ROMANCE are reflected also in a form of DRAMA occasionally cultivated by English dramatists. Whether the *pastoral drama* originated in simple dramatic ECLOGUES or is more closely related to such fifteenth-century mythological plays as Politian's *Orfeo*, it is certain that the type developed in Italy in the sixteenth century and was affected by the PASTORAL ROMANCE. Tasso's *Aminta* and Guarini's *Il Pastor Fido* (1590) were models for English RENAISSANCE PASTORAL plays, by Samuel Daniel, John Fletcher, and Ben Jonson. The best is Fletcher's *The Faithful Shepherdess* (acted 1608–1609). Some of Shakespeare's ROMANTIC COMEDIES, such as *As You Like It*, were affected by the PASTORAL influences and are sometimes called PASTORAL plays. The eighteenth-century stage saw some translations and imitations of Italian *pastoral drama,* and PASTORAL conventions were utilized along with the mythological in the more spectacular forms of dramatic activity which flourished in the eighteenth and nineteenth centuries.

Pastoral Elegy: A POEM employing conventional PASTORAL IMAGERY, written in dignified, serious language, and taking as its theme the expression of grief at the loss of a friend or important person. The form represents a combining of the PASTORAL ECLOGUE and the ELEGY. The conventional divisions, as evidenced in Milton's *Lycidas,* are: the invocation of the muse, an expression of the grief felt in the loss of a friend, a procession of mourners, a digression (on the church), and, finally, a consolation in which the poet submits to the inevitable and declares that everything has turned out for the best, usually through a strengthened belief in immortality. Other conventions often present include: appearance of the poet as shepherd, praise of the dead "shepherd," the PATHETIC FALLACY, flower symbolism, invective against death, reversal of the ordinary processes of nature as result of the death, bewilderment caused by grief, declaration of belief in some form of immortality, use of a REFRAIN and of the RHETORICAL QUESTION. Moschus' lament for Bion (second century B.C.), the November ECLOGUE of Spenser's *The Shepheardes Calender,* and Shelley's *Adonais* are examples of the form. See ECLOGUE, ELEGY, PASTORAL.

Pastoral Romance: A prose NARRATIVE, usually long and complicated in PLOT, in which the characters bear PASTORAL names and in which PASTORAL conventions dominate. It often contains interspersed SONGS. Though the Greek *Daphnis and Chloë* of Longus (third century) is classed as a *pastoral romance,* the form was reborn in the RENAISSANCE with Boccaccio's *Ameto* (1342). Monte-mayor's *Diana Enamorada* (*ca.*1559) is an important Spanish *pastoral romance*. Typical English examples are Sir Philip Sidney's *Arcadia* (1580–1581) and Thomas Lodge's *Rosalynde* (1590)—the source for Shakespeare's *As You Like It*. See ECLOGUE, PASTORAL, and PASTORAL DRAMA.

Pastourelle: A medieval type of DIALOGUE POEM in which a shepherdess is wooed by a man of higher social rank. In the Latin *pastoralia* a scholar does the courting; in the French and English, a poet. The body of the poem is the DIALOGUE in which the case is argued. Sometimes the suit is successful, but often a father or brother happens along and ends the wooing. In the English forms the poet asks permission to accompany the maid to the fields; she refuses and threatens to call her mother. The *pastourelle* possibly developed from popular wooing-games and wooing-songs, though one of Theocritus' IDYLLS (no. 27) is much like the medieval *pastourelle*. The form seems to have influenced the PASTORAL dialogue-lyrics of the Elizabethans and may have figured in the development of early ROMANTIC DRAMA in England.

Patent Theaters: The removal of the ban against theatrical performances in England in 1660 resulted in much rival activity among groups seeking to operate playhouses. Before August, three independent companies were established at three old theaters, the Red Bull, the Cockpit, and Salisbury Court. At this time Sir William Davenant and Thomas Killigrew secured from Charles II a "patent" granting them the privilege of censorship of plays and the right to organize two companies and erect two theaters which should have a monopoly. Though opposed by the jealous master of the revels, Sir Henry Herbert, and by some of the independent managers, Davenant and Killigrew succeeded in enforcing their rights. Davenant's company, the "Duke of York's Company," occupied in 1661 a new theater in Lincoln's Inn Fields and later one at Dorset Garden. Killigrew's company, the "King's Company," erected the Theatre Royal, the first of a famous succession of houses on this spot, all known as Drury Lane, since 1663. The theaters used by these two favored companies are known as *"patent" theaters*. The companies united in 1682, but in 1695 Betterton led a rebellious group of actors to a second theater in Lincoln's Inn Fields. After a generation of confusion, Parliament passed a licensing act in 1737, reaffirming the patent rights and establishing the monopoly of Drury Lane and Covent Garden (erected 1732). Despite strenuous efforts of rival managers to encroach upon the privileges of the patentees, this act remained in force until 1843, when it was repealed and the patents revoked. Among the managers of Drury Lane after Killigrew are Cibber, Garrick, and Sheridan; of Covent Garden, John Rich, the elder Colman, and John P. Kemble. See PRIVATE THEATERS.

Pathetic Fallacy: A phrase coined by Ruskin to denote the tendency of poets and writers of impassioned prose to credit nature with the emotions of human beings. In a larger sense the *pathetic fallacy* is any false emotionalism in writing resulting in a too impassioned description of nature. It is the carrying over to inanimate objects of the moods and passions of a human being. This crediting of nature with human qualities is a constant device of poets. A frequently occurring expression of the IMAGINATION, it becomes a fault when it is overdone to the point of absurdity, in which case it approaches the CONCEIT. A passage from Ruskin (*Modern Paintters,* Vol. 3, Part IV, Chap. xii) in which he discusses the *pathetic fallacy* is quoted:

> They rowed her in across the rolling foam—
> The cruel, crawling foam.

The foam is not cruel, neither does it crawl. The state of mind which attributes to it these characters of a living creature is one in which the reason is unhinged by grief. All violent feelings have the same effect. They produce in us a falseness in all our impressions of external things, which I would generally characterize as the "pathetic fallacy."

Pathos: From the Greek root for suffering or deep feeling, *pathos* is the quality in art and literature which stimulates pity, tenderness, or sorrow in the reader or viewer. Although in its strict meaning it is closely associated with the pity which TRAGEDY is supposed to evoke, in common usage it describes an acquiescent or relatively helpless suffering or the sorrow occasioned by unmerited grief, as opposed to the stoic grandeur and awful justice of the tragic hero. In this distinction, Hamlet is a tragic figure and Ophelia a pathetic one; Lear's fate is tragic, Cordelia's pathetic. See BATHOS.

Pedantry: A display of learning for its own sake. The term is often used in critical reproach of an author's STYLE when that STYLE is marked by a superfluity of quotations, foreign phrases, ALLUSIONS, and such. Holofernes in Shakespeare's *Love's Labour's Lost* can hardly open his lips without giving expression to *pedantry:*

Most barbarous intimation! yet a kind of insinuation, as it were, *in via,* in way, of explication; *facere,* as it were, replication, or, rather, *ostentare,* to show, as it were, his inclination,—after his undressed, un- polished, uneducated, unpruned, untrained, or rather, unlettered, or, ratherest, unconfirmed fashion—to insert again my *haud credo* for a deer.

Pegasus: The winged horse of Grecian fable said to have sprung from Medusa's body at her death. *Pegasus* is associated with the inspiration of poetry (though in modern times in a somewhat jocular vein) because he is supposed by one blow of his hoof to have caused Hippocrene, the inspiring fountain of the MUSES, to flow from Mount Helicon. As a symbol of poetic inspiration poets have sometimes invoked the aid of *Pegasus* instead of the MUSES.

Pelagianism: A theological doctrine asserting man's original inno- cence and his capacity to achieve moral and spiritual power through his own unaided efforts. See CALVINISM, AUGUSTINIANISM.

Penny Dreadful: A cheaply produced, paperbound NOVEL or NOVELETTE of mystery, adventure, or violence in the late nineteenth and early twentieth centuries in England; a British equivalent of the American DIME NOVEL.

Pentameter: A line of VERSE consisting of five FEET. See SCANSION.

Periodical: A term applied to any publication that appears at regu- lar intervals; it includes such publications as JOURNALS, MAGAZINES, and REVIEWS, but customarily not newspapers. See MAGAZINE.

Periodical Essay: A term applied to an ESSAY written for publica- tion as the principal or only item in an issue of a PERIODICAL. The most notable *periodical essays* were written for *The Tatler* and *The Spectator,* but the form was very popular throughout most of the eighteenth century. See ESSAY.

Periodic Sentence: A sentence not grammatically complete before the end; the opposite of a LOOSE SENTENCE. The characteristic of a *periodic sentence* is that its construction is such as constantly to throw the mind forward to the idea which will complete the mean- ing. The *periodic sentence* is effective when it is desired to arouse interest and curiosity, to hold an idea in suspense before its final revelation is made. Periodicity is accomplished by the use of parallel phrases or clauses at the opening; by the use of dependent clauses preceding the independent clause, and by the use of such correlatives as *neither . . . nor, not only . . . but also,* and *both . . . and.* "Because it was raining, I went into the house" is an example of a *periodic sentence* composed of a dependent clause preceding the independent clause.

Period of Criticism and Conformity in American Literature: The year 1930 marked a decided turning point in American social and cultural history as well as the beginning of the period in literary history which lasted into the late 1960's. In October, 1929, the stock-market crash heralded the end of the prosperous twenties, and by the end of 1930 the impact of the depression was being felt in most areas of American life and thought. As the depression intensified, the social and economic revolution called the New Deal occurred, and a steadily increasing concern with sociological issues occupied the serious writer. Shortly after the depression began the expatriate group which had in Paris made a religion of art came back to America and joined the radical movements that earned the thirties the name of "The Red Decade."

Hemingway's career had been launched in the twenties, and his work in the thirties added little to his stature; but Faulkner was to produce in the first half of the decade the largest single body of his best work. Dos Passos wrote his trilogy, *U.S.A.;* and James T. Farrell, Thomas Wolfe, and John Steinbeck acquired fame and did their best work. A radical social point of view was present in most of these writers, a critical approach to American institutions. In the meantime, the poets who had in the twenties produced the *Fugitive* magazine in Nashville reacted strongly against the radical political thought and the sociological literary orientations of their world; they expressed their politico-economic reaction through the principles of AGRARIANISM and their rejection of sociological concerns in the artist through the formulation of the NEW CRITICISM. Edwin Arlington Robinson, Robert Frost, T. S. Eliot, Edna St. Vincent Millay, and Carl Sandburg continued their dominant position in poetry, and e.e. cummings, Robinson Jeffers, Archibald Macleish, and William Carlos Williams raised newer strong poetic voices. Maxwell Anderson, Eugene O'Neill, Clifford Odets, and Thornton Wilder dominated the stage.

Period of Criticism

The signing of the Russo-German pact in 1939 and the coming of the Second World War put an effective end to the radicalism of the thirties. The War and its aftermath resulted in an age of conformity and conservatism, bolstered by a burgeoning economy. American life, thought, and writing in the forties and the fifties were marked by a tendency to conformity, to traditionalism, and to reverence for artistic form and restraint; while, at the same time, the period was marked by informality in social conduct and freedom of subject matter in art.

The postwar DRAMA revealed the strong new talents of Arthur Miller, Tennessee Williams, and Edward Albee, while Thornton Wilder was doing his most mature work and Eugene O'Neill was at the end of his career dramatizing with powerful effectiveness the tragic nature of his own experience. Both poetry and criticism tended to retreat to the critical quarterlies, where each operated with a high level of technical skill and without great distinction or vitality. The major figures in the NOVEL were still Hemingway and Faulkner, both of whom received the Nobel Prize, although neither of them was producing work of the quality of that they had done in the twenties and the thirties. Of the newer novelists, Robert Penn Warren showed skill, seriousness, and virtuosity, and John P. Marquand carried the satirical NOVEL OF MANNERS to a high level of accomplishment. Ralph Ellison's *Invisible Man* made high art of the black man's situation. In James Jones, Norman Mailer, and a group of other young neo-naturalists a strong, frank, and formless kind of fiction appeared. But the remark which, perhaps, best characterizes the literature of America from the Second World War to the mid-sixties is that its major works and its major literary events were produced by writers whose careers had been firmly established in the twenties and the thirties and who had done their best work then. The chaos of a hot war and the constraint of a cold one conspired to produce either a literature of conformity or of confusion. In the last half of the sixties, the youth rebellion found expression in new LITTLE MAGAZINES, a remarkable freedom of language and subject matter, and a highly introspective kind of FICTION. The seventies began with the *conformity* of the postwar world gone but with a deep confusion about the trends, the FORMS, and the texture of the new writing. POETRY tended toward strict forms or remarkable looseness. The novelists of the sixties who gave the greatest promise of substantial work were William Styron, Saul Bellow, Bernard Malamud, and John Updike; but, significantly, none of them had by the end of the sixties established a definite MODE or staked out a clear fictional territory; like the very young, who had tremendous energy and little order, they were still experimenting. See the *Outline of Literary History*.

Periods of English and American Literary History: See ENGLISH LITERATURE, AMERICAN LITERATURE, and *Outline of Literary History*.

Peripety: The REVERSAL of fortune for the PROTAGONIST in a dramatic or fictional PLOT, whether to his fall in a TRAGEDY or to his success in a COMEDY. See DRAMATIC STRUCTURE.

Periphrasis: An indirect, abstract, roundabout method of stating ideas; the application to writing or speech of the old conviction that "the longest way 'round is the shortest way home." Used with restraint and with deliberate intent *periphrasis* may be a successful rhetorical device, but the danger is that it will be overdone and will result in mere Polonius-like verbosity. Fowler cites as an objectionable use of *periphrasis* (for "No news is good news") the periphrastic circumlocution "The absence of intelligence is an indication of satisfactory developments." Authors frequently use the form to secure humorous effects; for example, Shenstone refers to pins as "the cure of rents and separations dire, and chasms enormous."

Peroration: The conclusion of an ORATION or discourse in which the discussion is summed up, and the speaker endeavors to enforce his arguments by a pointed and rhetorical appeal to the emotions of his audience; a recapitulation of the major points of any speech.

Persiflage: Light, inconsequential chatter, written or spoken; gay, satirical banter; a trifling, flippant manner of dealing with any theme or subject matter.

Persona: Literally a mask. The term is widely used in the criticism of FICTION to refer to a "second self" created by the author and through whom the NARRATIVE is told. The *persona* may be a NARRATOR; such a *persona* exists in Huck Finn, and the debate about the freedom which the use of Huck Finn gave Mark Twain as a mask

Persuasion

through whom he could speak things he dared not utter in his own person is instructive about the function of the *persona* as teller and as mask. The *persona* can be not a CHARACTER in the STORY but "an implied author," that is, a voice not directly the author's but created by the author and through which he speaks. All FICTION is in some sense a STORY told by someone; all self-consciously artistic FICTION is told by someone created by the author and who serves, therefore, as a mask, a *persona*. The term is also used in literary BIOGRAPHY to describe the public self which some writers presented to the world and behind which they worked. In this sense "Papa Hemingway" was a *persona* behind which Ernest Hemingway hid. See NARRATOR.

Personal Essay: A kind of INFORMAL ESSAY which utilizes an intimate STYLE, some autobiographical content or interest, and an urbane conversational manner. See ESSAY.

Personification: A FIGURE OF SPEECH which endows animals, ideas, abstractions, and inanimate objects with human form, character, or sensibilities; the representing of imaginary creatures or things as having human personalities, intelligence, and emotions; an impersonation in DRAMA of one CHARACTER or person, whether real or fictitious, by another person. Keats's *personification* of the Grecian urn as the

> Sylvan historian, who canst thus express
> A flowery tale more sweetly than our rhyme:

is an obvious *personification* as are his earlier references to the urn as an "unravished bride of quietness" and as a "foster child of silence and slow time." *Personification* as a FIGURE OF SPEECH is also called PROSOPOPOEIA. See ALLEGORY.

Persuasion: That one of the major types of composition the purpose of which is to convince of the wisdom of a certain line of action. *Persuasion* is really a phase of ARGUMENTATION and resembles it in its purpose to establish the truth or falsity of a proposition, but is distinct from it in that it is calculated to arouse to some action. *Persuasion* may draw on the other types of composition—ARGUMENTATION, DESCRIPTION, EXPOSITION, and NARRATION—for support, and incorporates within itself elements of each. The most common form of *persuasion* is the ORATION.

Petrarchan Conceit

Petrarchan Conceit: The kind of CONCEIT used by the Italian poet
Petrarch in his love SONNETS and widely imitated by RENAISSANCE
English sonneteers. It rests upon elaborate and exaggerated comparisons expressing in extravagant terms the beauty, cruelty, and
charm of the beloved and the suffering and despair of the forlorn
lover. Hyperbolic analogies to ships at sea, marble tombs, wars, and
alarums are used; OXYMORON is common. Shakespeare in "Sonnet
130," which begins,

> My mistress' eyes are nothing like the sun;
> Coral is far more red than her lips' red:
> If snow be white, why then her breasts are dun;
> If hairs be wires, black wires grow on her head,

satirizes the Petrarchan conventions while giving a reasonably accurate catalog of some of the more common ones.

Petrarchan Sonnet: The ITALIAN SONNET, with OCTAVE rhyming
abbaabba and SESTET rhyming in some combination of *cde;* called
Petrarchan after Petrarch, its most successful producer.

Philippic: In modern usage, any speech or harangue bitterly invective in character; a discourse filled with denunciations and accusa-
tions. The term comes from the twelve orations of Demosthenes in
which he berated Philip II of Macedon as an enemy of Greece.

Philistinism: The worship of material and mechanical prosperity,
the disregard of culture, beauty, and spiritual things. The term was
made popular by Matthew Arnold's use of it in "Sweetness and
Light," the first chapter of *Culture and Anarchy*. Arnold wrote:

If it were not for this purging effect wrought upon our minds by culture, the whole world, the future as well as the present, would inevitably belong to the Philistines. The people who believe most that our
greatness and welfare are proved by our being very rich, and who most
give their lives and thoughts to becoming rich, are just the very people
whom we call Philistines. Culture says: "Consider these people, then,
their way of life, their habits, their manners, the very tones of their
voices; look at them attentively; observe the literature they read, the
things which give them pleasure, the words which come forth out of
their mouths, the thoughts which make the furniture of their minds;
would any amount of wealth be worth having with the condition that
one was to become just like these people by having it?"

Philology: In its general sense *philology* means the scientific study
of both language and literature. Thus there are *philological* clubs

and journals of *philology* devoted to linguistic and literary research. The late Professor A. S. Cook said: "The ideal philologist is at once antiquary, palaeographer, grammarian, lexicologist, expounder, critic, historian of literature, and, above all, lover of humanity." *Philology* was at one time used in a narrower sense to mean the scientific study of language. Today, however, the systematic study of language by scientific principles is usually called LINGUISTICS, with *philology* confined to language study whose end is literary.

Picaresque Novel, The: A CHRONICLE, usually autobiographical, presenting the life story of a rascal of low degree engaged in menial tasks and making his living more through his wits than his industry. Episodic in nature, the *picaresque novel* is, in the usual sense of the term, structureless. The *picaro,* or central figure, through the nature of his various pranks and predicaments and by virtue of his associations with people of varying degree, affords the author an opportunity for SATIRE on the social classes. Romantic in the sense of being a story of adventure, the *picaresque novel* nevertheless is strongly marked by realistic methods in its faithfulness to petty detail, its utter frankness of expression, and its drawing of incidents from low life.

From earliest times, of course, the rogue has been a favorite CHARACTER in STORY and picture. As far back as the *Satyricon,* Petronius at the court of Nero recognized the possibilities of the type. In the Middle Ages the FABLES continued the manner though they transferred roguery from man to animals. Reynard is a typical picaroon. He lives by his wits; gets into trouble and out of it, but always interests the reader. It was not until the sixteenth century that this rogue literature crystallized into a definite type. A NOVEL called *La Vida de Lazarillo de Tormes y de sus fortunas y adversidades,* probably dating from 1554, brought this about. So popular did this work become that it was one of the most-read books of the century. Cervantes took up the manner in *Don Quixote.* Soon French imitators sprang up. Of French PICARESQUE NOVELS Le Sage's *Gil Blas* (1715) was by far the most popular. So definitely was the type fixed as a Spanish form that the French writers—Le Sage among them—gave their characters Spanish names and placed their EPISODES in Spain.

The English adopted the picaresque manner. In 1594 appeared *The Unfortunate Traveller: or, The Life of Jack Wilton* by Thomas Nash—the first important *picaresque novel* in the language. With

Daniel Defoe in the eighteenth century the type became important in English literature. His *Moll Flanders* presents the life record of a female picaroon. Fielding in *Jonathan Wild* and Smollett in *Ferdinand, Count Fathom,* lent dignity to the type.

There are, perhaps, seven chief qualities distinguishing the *picaresque novel.* (1) First of all, it chronicles a part or the whole of the life of a rogue. It is likely to be done in the first person—as AUTOBIOGRAPHY—but this is by no means essential. (2) The chief figure is drawn from a low social level and is of "loose" character, according to conventional standards. The occupation of this central figure, should he tolerate employment at all, is menial in nature. (3) The NOVEL presents little PLOT. Rather is it a series of EPISODES only slightly connected. (4) There is little character interest. Progress and development of character do not take place. The central figure starts as a *picaro* and ends as a *picaro,* manifesting the same aptitudes and qualities throughout. When change occurs, as it sometimes does, it is external change brought about by the man's falling heir to a fortune or by his marrying a rich widow. Internal character development is not often a quality of the *picaresque novel.* (5) The method is realistic. While the story may be romantic in itself, it is presented with a plainness of language, a freedom in vocabulary, and a vividness of detail such as the realist only is permitted. (6) SATIRE is a prominent element. Thrown with people from every class and often from different parts of the world, the *picaro* serves them intimately in one lowly capacity or another and learns all their foibles and frailties. The *picaresque novel* may in this way be made to satirize both social castes and national or racial peculiarities. (7) The hero of the *picaresque novel* usually stops just short of being an actual criminal. The line between crime and petty rascality is a hazy one, but somehow the *picaro* always manages to draw it. Carefree, amoral perhaps, he avoids actual crime and turns from one peccadillo to disappear down the dust of the road in search of another.

Pièce bien faite: A type of French DRAMA popular in the nineteenth century. See WELL-MADE PLAY, the English equivalent term.

Pindaric Ode: The regular ODE, characterized by a division into units containing three parts—the STROPHE and ANTISTROPHE, alike in form, and the EPODE, different from the other two. See ODE.

Pirated Edition: An unauthorized EDITION of a work, usually stolen from one country and produced for sale in another. It represents an infringement of COPYRIGHT through illegal publication. The term is most often applied to the period before the establishment of modern international COPYRIGHT conventions, when the use without permission or payment of literary works copyrighted in another nation was a common practice. See COPYRIGHT.

Plagiarism: Literary theft. A writer who steals the detailed PLOT of some obscure, forgotten story and uses it as new in a story of his own is a plagiarist. *Plagiarism* is more noticeable when it involves a stealing of language than when substance only is borrowed. From flagrant exhibitions of stealing both thought and language *plagiarism* shades off into less serious things such as unconscious borrowing, borrowing of minor elements, and mere IMITATION. In fact, the critical doctrine of IMITATION, as understood in Renaissance times, often led to what would nowadays be called *plagiarism*. Thus, Spenser's free borrowings from other romantic EPICS in composing his *Faerie Queene* were by him regarded as virtues, since he was "following" a predecessor in the same type of writing. A modern dramatist could not with impunity borrow PLOTS from other DRAMAS and from old stories in the way in which Shakespeare did. With *plagiarism* compare LITERARY FORGERIES, its converse, where an author pretends that another has written what he has actually written himself.

Although the basic concept of *plagiarism* is clear—that is, that it is the use of material originated by others as one's own—the actual practice involves many shades and gradations. It is difficult to prove the borrowing of an idea and easy to demonstrate the stealing of a passage. Hence, as a legal term, *plagiarism* has very sharp limits and is considered to be a clearly demonstrable use of material plainly taken from another without credit. See GHOST-WRITER.

Plaint: VERSE expressing grief or tribulation; a chant of lamentation; a LAMENT; an expression of sorrow. See COMPLAINT.

Platonic Criticism: A term often used by contemporary critics to describe a type of criticism which finds the values of a work of art in its extrinsic rather than its intrinsic qualities, in its usefulness for non-artistic purposes. The term is currently used in opposition to ARISTOTELIAN CRITICISM, which finds the value of a work of art within the work itself. See ARISTOTELIAN CRITICISM; CRITICISM, TYPES OF.

Platonism: The idealistic philosophical doctrines of Plato, because of their concern with the aspirations of the human spirit, their tendency to exalt mind over matter, their grappling with the great problems of the universe and of man's relation to the cosmic forces, and their highly imaginative elements, have appealed strongly to certain English authors, particularly the poets of the RENAISSANCE and of the ROMANTIC PERIOD. Plato himself declined to "codify" his philosophical views and perhaps altered them much during his own life. He left expressions of them in his great DIALOGUES, in which various Greeks (such as Socrates, Alcibiades, and Aristophanes) discuss philosophical problems, particularly those involving the universe and man's relation to it, the nature of love and beauty, the constitution of the human soul, the relation of beauty to virtue. Unlike Aristotelian philosophy, which tends to be systematic, formal, scientific, logical, and critical, and which occupies itself chiefly with the visible universe, the natural world, and mankind, *Platonism* is flexible and interested in the unseen world. Plato founded his famous "Academy" in 380 B.C., where for a third of a century he taught students attracted from far and near (including Aristotle himself). Later followers now known as "neo-Platonists" modified Plato's teachings. It is difficult to distinguish the purely Platonic elements from elements added by later Platonists. Among the "neo-Platonists" there were two groups of especial importance. (1) The Alexandrian school. This group, especially Plotinus (third century), stressed the mystical elements and amalgamated them with many ideas drawn from other sources. Their neo-*Platonism* was in fact a sort of religion, which, though itself supplanted by Christianity, supplied medieval Christian thinkers (including Boethius and St. Augustine) with many ideas. (2) The neo-Platonists of the Italian RENAISSANCE. Under the leadership of Marsilio Ficino (1433–1499), who led the Platonic Academy at Florence and who translated and explained Plato, a highly complex and mystical system developed, one of the aims of which was the fusing of Platonic philosophy and Christian doctrine. It was this particular kind of neo-*Platonism* which kindled the imagination of such RENAISSANCE poets as Sidney and Spenser.

Important Platonic doctrines found in English literature include: (1) The doctrine of ideas (or "forms"). True reality is found not in the realm of sense but in the higher, spiritual realm of the ideal and the universal. Here exist the "ideas" or images or patterns of which material objects are but transitory symbols or expressions. (2) The doctrine of recollection. This implies the preexistence and immortality of the soul, which passes through a series of incarnations. Most of what the soul has seen and learned in "heaven" it forgets when imprisoned in the body of clay but it has some power of "recalling" ideas and images. Hence human knowledge. (3) The doctrine of love. There are two kinds of love and beauty, a lower and a higher. The soul or lover of beauty in its quest for perfect beauty ascends from the sensual gradually, through a process of idealization, to the spiritual, and thereby develops all the virtues both of thought and of action. Beauty and virtue become identified.

An interesting exposition of the neo-Platonic doctrines of love may be read in the fourth book of Castiglione's *The Book of the Courtier.* Representative English poems embodying Platonic ideas include: Spenser's *Hymn in Honor of Beauty,* Shelley's *Hymn to Intellectual Beauty,* and Wordsworth's *Ode on Intimations of Immortality from Recollections of Early Childhood.*

Pléiade: A term originally applied to an ancient group of seven authors (named after the constellation of the Pleiades), and to several later groups, the most important of which was the group of critics and poets which flourished in France in the second half of the sixteenth century. The leading figures were Ronsard, Du Bellay, and (later) Desportes. The poetic manifesto of the "school" is Du Bellay's *Défense et Illustration de la Langue Française* (1549). It shows an interest in developing a new vernacular literature following the types cultivated by classical writers. The popular and the medieval were to be avoided, except that certain medieval courtly pieces were to be rewritten. The native language was to be enriched by coining words, by borrowing from the Greek and Latin, and by restoring to use lost native words, so that a literary language might be produced which would make possible the creation of a new French literature comparable with classical literature. The high function of the poet and of poetry was stressed. The influence of the group was a constructive and important one upon Elizabethan poets, notably Spenser, and the more or less mythical AREOPAGUS has been regarded as an English counterpart of the *Pléiade,* since Sidney and his group were engaged in the effort to refine the English language and to create a new national literature based upon humanistic ideals.

Pleonasm: The superfluous use of words. *Pleonasm* may consist of needless repetition, or of the addition of unnecessary words in an effort to express an idea completely, or of a combination of the two. For example, in the sentence, "He walked the entire distance to the station on foot," "the entire distance" and "on foot" are pleonastic. Although *pleonasm* is a violation of correct grammatical usage, it is employed occasionally to add EMPHASIS, and in such instances its use may be considered legitimate. See TAUTOLOGY.

Plot: Although an indispensable part of all FICTION and DRAMA, whether in PROSE or VERSE, *plot* is a concept about which there has been much critical disagreement. Aristotle, who assigns it the place of chief honor in writing and calls it "the first principle, and, as it were, the soul of a TRAGEDY," formulated, in *The Poetics,* a very precise definition, which has been the basis for most discussions of *plot.* He called it "the IMITATION of an action" and also "the arrangement of the incidents." The action imitated should be "a whole"— that is, it should have a beginning, "that which does not itself follow anything by causal necessity, but after which something naturally is or comes to be"; a middle, "that which follows something as some other thing follows it"; and an end, "that which itself follows some other thing, either by necessity, or as a rule, but has nothing following it." A *plot,* Aristotle maintained, should have UNITY: it should "imitate one action and that a whole, the structural union of the parts being such that, if any one of them is displaced or removed, the whole will be disjointed and disturbed." He disliked episodic *plots,* "in which the acts succeed one another without probable or necessary sequence." His test for a sound *plot* was "whether any given event is a case of *propter hoc* or *post hoc.*" Thus, causality was a fundamental quality of a *plot* for Aristotle. The writer, he believed "should first sketch the general outline [of the plot], and then fill in the EPISODES and amplify in detail." He seems to mean that the *plot,* a general idea of a MOVEMENT, is realized by "episodizing" —that is by creating incidents to flesh it out.

E. M. Forster made a distinction between STORY and *plot* that is helpful. A STORY is "a NARRATIVE of events in their time-sequence. A *plot* is also a NARRATIVE of events, the emphasis falling on causality." A STORY arouses only curiosity; whereas a *plot* demands intelligence and memory. Thus plotting is the process of converting STORY into *plot,* of changing a sequential arrangement of incidents into a causal and inevitable arrangement. Once more, it is a functioning of some kind of intelligent overview of action that establishes principles of selection and relationship among episodes that makes a *plot*. Clearly there must be more than one EPISODE, and equally clearly the relationship among the EPISODES must be close. Out of the welter of experience, a selection of EPISODES is made that in itself constitutes a "whole" action.

Many critics, particularly in the nineteenth and twentieth centuries, have quarreled with Aristotle's assigning *plot* the chief place in a dramatic composition, and have insisted that CHARACTER and CHARACTERIZATION are more important, the *plot* being merely a mechanical means by which a structure designed to display CHARACTERS is arranged. The Neo-Aristotelian critics, largely at the University of Chicago, have attempted to extend the meaning of *plot* to make it a function of a number of elements in the work of art. Ronald S. Crane says, "The form of a given *plot* is a function of the particular correlation among . . . three variables which the completed work is calculated to establish, consistently and progressively, in our minds." These variables are "(1) the general estimate we are induced to form . . . of the moral character and deserts of the HERO . . . (2) the judgments we are led similarly to make about the nature of the events that actually befall the HERO . . . as having either painful or pleasurable consequences for him . . . permanently or temporarily; and (3) the opinions we are made to entertain concerning the degree and kind of his responsibility for what happens to him." In such a definition, although much has been added to the simple idea of a STRUCTURE of incidents, the basic view of *plot* as some large and controlling frame is still present.

Most views of *plot* have such an idea at the base of their definition. The minimal definition is "pattern." Only slightly less minimal is "pattern of events." EPISODES do not in themselves make a plot; the *plot* lies in relationships among EPISODES. Hence, we may formulate a definition like this: *Plot* is an intellectual formulation about the relationships existing among the incidents of a DRAMA or a NARRATIVE, and it is, therefore, a guiding principle for the author and an ordering control for the reader. For the author it is the chief principle for selection and arrangement; for the reader it is something perceived as STRUCTURE and UNITY. To define *plot* as an intellectual formulation is not, however, to define it as abstract idea or philosophic concept. Abstract ideas and philosophical attitudes may help in shaping the formulation, but that formulation is of incidents —CHARACTERS and ACTIONS—and how they interrelate. An ALLEGORY has *plot* not because it makes an abstract statement, but because it constructs that statement from incidents involving PERSONIFICATIONS and actions involving theme.

Since the *plot* consists of CHARACTERS performing actions in incidents that interrelate to comprise a "single, whole, and complete" action, this interrelationship involves CONFLICT, the struggle between two opposing forces (see CONFLICT for a detailed statement of the types of such struggle available to the writer). Without CONFLICT, without opposition, *plot* does not exist. We must have a Claudius flouting a Hamlet, an Iago making jealous an Othello, if we are to have *plot*. These forces may be physical (or external), or they may be spiritual (or internal); but physical or spiritual they must afford an opposition. And this opposition it is which knits one incident to another, which dictates the causal relationship, which develops the struggle. This struggle between the forces, moreover, comes to a head in some one incident—the CRISIS—which forms the turning-point of the story and which usually marks the point of greatest SUSPENSE. In this climactic EPISODE the RISING ACTION comes to a termination, the FALLING ACTION begins; and as a result of this incident some DÉNOUEMENT or CATASTROPHE is bound to follow.

Plot is, in this sense, an artificial rather than a natural ordering of events. Its function is to simplify life by imposing order upon it. It would be possible, though most tedious, to recite *all* incidents, *all* events, *all* thoughts which pass through the minds of one or more CHARACTERS during a period of, say, a week. The demands of *plot* stipulate that the author *select* from this welter of event and reflection those items which have a certain UNITY, which point to a certain end, which have a common interrelationship, which represent not more than two or three threads of interest and activity. *Plot* brings order out of life; it selects only one or two emotions out of a dozen, one or two conflicts out of hundreds, only two or three people out of thousands, and a half-dozen EPISODES from possible millions. In this sense it focuses life.

And, at least in most modern writing, it focuses with one principal idea in mind—CHARACTER. The most effective incidents are those which spring naturally from the given CHARACTERS, the most effective *plot* presents struggle such as would engage these given CHARACTERS, and the most effective emotion for the *plot* to present is that inherent in the quality of the given CHARACTERS. The function of *plot,* from this point of view, is to translate CHARACTER into action.

The use of a DEUS EX MACHINA to solve a COMPLICATION is now

pretty generally condemned as a weakness in *plot* structure since it is now generally conceded that *plot* action should spring from the innate quality of the CHARACTERS participant in the action. But *fate*, since it may be interpreted as working through character, is, with the development of the realistic method, still very popular. See DRAMATIC STRUCTURE, CHARACTERIZATION, CONFLICT.

Plurisignation: A term sometimes used by contemporary critics to describe the kind of AMBIGUITY which results from the capacity of words to stimulate several different streams of thought. See AMBIGUITY, MULTIPLE MEANINGS.

Poem: A composition characterized by the presence of IMAGINATION, emotion, truth (significant meaning), sense impressions, and concrete language; expressed rhythmically and with an orderly arrangement of parts and possessing within itself a UNITY; the whole written with the dominant purpose of giving aesthetic or emotional pleasure. A formal and final definition of POETRY is, of course, impossible; it means different things to different people at different times. See POETRY.

Poet: In the strictest sense, anyone who writes POETRY, a maker of VERSES. However, the term *poet*, in its original meaning of "maker," is applied to certain qualities held in unusual degree by a writer without reference to the particular type of his composition; these qualities include great imaginative power, flexible and effective expressiveness, a special sensitivity to experience, an ability for compressed expression, and a sense of appropriateness and grace in the use of language. By further extension, the term is sometimes used for an artist in other fields than writing whose work has the qualities of IMAGINATION, spontaneity, and lyricism, as in a phrase like "a *poet* of the violin."

Poetaster: A writer of incompetent or inferior VERSES, a pretended POET. The term is always derogatory both of the writer and of his work.

Poet Laureate: In medieval universities there arose the custom of crowning with laurel a student who was admitted to an academic degree, such as the bachelor of arts. Later the phrase *poet laureate* was used as a special degree conferred by a university in recognition of skill in Latin grammar and VERSIFICATION. There also existed in the late Middle Ages the custom of bestowing a crown of laurel on a poet for distinctive work, Petrarch being so honored in 1341. Independent of these customs and usages was the ancient practice of kings and chieftains, both in educated and barbarous nations, of maintaining "court poets," persons attached to the prince's household and maintained for the purpose of celebrating the virtues of the royal family or singing the praises of military exploits. Court poets of this type included the scop among Anglo-Saxon peoples, the skald among the Scandinavian, the filidh among the Irish, and the higher ranks of bards among the Welsh.

The modern office of *Poet Laureate* in England resulted from the application of the academic term *poet laureate* to the traditional court poet. It was established in the seventeenth century, though there were interesting anticipations earlier. Henri d'Avranches, for example, was an official *versificator regis* for Henry III. At the courts of Henry VII and Henry VIII, an academic *poet laureate* named Bernardus Andreas of Toulouse was officially recognized as a *Poet Laureate*, wrote Latin odes for his masters, and received a pension. The tradition was not carried on after the poet's death. The first officially appointed *Poet Laureate* was John Dryden, though Spenser, Daniel, Drayton, Ben Jonson, and William Davenant are often included in the list, the latter two with strong justification. Jonson received a pension, a grant of wine, and was an official writer of masques for James I and Charles I, and his contemporaries called him "the *Poet Laureate*." After Jonson's death in 1637 Davenant was hailed as Jonson's successor, and at the Restoration (1660) was informally recognized as Jonson's successor as *Poet Laureate*, though he seems not to have received any official designation as such during his lifetime. Upon Davenant's death, however, Dryden received (1670) an official appointment to the office; thus Dryden was the first whose official appointment is recorded. After the Revolution Dryden was displaced, and in 1689 Thomas Shadwell was appointed *Poet Laureate*. Successive laureates were: Nahum Tate (1692–1715), Nicholas Rowe (1715–1718), Laurence Eusden (1718–1730), Colley Cibber (1730–1757), William Whitehead (1757–1785), Thomas Warton (1785–1790), Henry James Pye (1790–1813), Robert Southey (1813–1843), William Wordsworth (1843–1850), Alfred Tennyson (1850–1892), Alfred Austin (1896–1913), Robert Bridges (1913–1930), John Masefield (1930–1967), Cecil Day-Lewis (1968–1972), Sir John Betjeman (1906–   ).

The early, primary duty of the laureate was to render professional

service to the royal family and the court. The practice of composing
ODES in celebration of royal birthdays, New Year's, and other occasions developed in the seventeenth century and became obligatory
upon the laureate in the eighteenth century. Each year such an ODE
was sung at a formal court reception held to wish the king a happy
New Year. This custom lapsed during the illness of George III and
was abolished in Southey's time. Sometimes the laureate has served
as a "poet-defender" of the king in personal and political as well as
national disputes (for example, Dryden). Later the more appropriate
custom of expecting a poem in times of national stress or strong
patriotic feeling developed, though since Southey the writing of
verse for special occasions has not been obligatory. Two of the
best-known "laureate" poems are Tennyson's "Ode" written to be
sung at the funeral of the Duke of Wellington and his "Charge of
the Light Brigade."

The perfunctory character of the laureate's duties often prevented
the appointment of the best living poets, though since Wordsworth's
time the appointment has with occasional exception been regarded as
a recognition of poetic distinction. Gray, Scott, and Samuel Rogers
declined appointments as *Poet Laureate*.

Poetic Diction: Words chosen for a supposedly inherent poetic
quality. At one time poets and critics in England sought for a special
language for POETRY which differed from the language of common
speech. Spenser sought in ARCHAISMS, for example, the materials out
of which to fashion a diction properly poetic; the poets of the
AUGUSTAN AGE subjected poetic language to the test of DECORUM
and evolved a special vocabulary for POETRY. The Romantic poets,
led by Wordsworth, denied the essential difference between the
proper language of POETRY and that of PROSE or everyday speech.
The tendency in our own time is to allow the POET the widest possible
vocabulary range, and to use a consciously *poetic diction* only for
ironic effect.

Poetic Drama: A term properly restricted to poetic plays written
to be acted. It is thus distinguished from DRAMATIC POETRY and
CLOSET DRAMA, although some writers treat *poetic drama* as synonymous with DRAMATIC POETRY, and some use *poetic drama* to designate CLOSET DRAMA.

Poetic Justice: Loosely, that ideal judgment which rewards virtue
and punishes vice among the CHARACTERS of a NARRATIVE.

Poetic License

Aristotle announced that "the mere spectacle of a virtuous man brought from prosperity to adversity moves neither pity nor fear; it merely shocks us." Suffering as an end in itself is intolerable dramatically. Hamlet dead with poison, Desdemona smothered, Juliet dead—all these placed before us on the stage unmotivated, unexplained, constitute not TRAGEDY but sheer pain. Such scenes would be exhibitions of fate over which the characters have had no control and for which they were in no sense responsible; they would be, had not Shakespeare been the artist he was, mere accidents and as such would have no claim to *poetic justice*. But, in a higher, more dramatic sense, *poetic justice* may be said to have been attained since, as Shakespeare wrote the plays, the actions moved logically, thoughtfully, consistently to some such CATASTROPHES as those which awaited these three tragic characters. *Poetic justice*, then, in this higher sense, is something greater than the mere rewarding of virtue and the punishment of vice; it is the logical and motivated outcome of the given conditions and terms of the tragic plan as presented in the earlier ACTS of the DRAMA even though, from a worldly sense, virtue meets with disaster and vice seems temporarily rewarded. With CATASTROPHES less fatal than those which visited Hamlet and Desdemona, TRAGEDY would be in danger of becoming COMEDY; DRAMA, in its purest sense, would disappear. For the reader of poetic TRAGEDY, the beauty of sorrow, the CATHARSIS which comes with the spectacle of the mysteries of life, are greater values than the knowledge that Claudius had perhaps been exiled and Iago hanged, or that Hamlet had been married to Ophelia and Othello had lived to look upon Desdemona's wrinkled cheek. In its modern sense, then, *poetic justice* may be considered as fulfilled when the outcome, however fatal to virtue, however it may reward vice, is the logical and necessary result of the action and principles of the major CHARACTERS as they have been presented by the dramatist. It should be noted that such an outcome as that described here presupposes a universe in which the author sees order and organizing principles. In the absence of such principles in the author's world view even this *poetic justice* as the motivated and logical outcome of the given conditions and terms of the narrative is impossible, as witness Kafka's *The Trial*.

Poetic License: The privilege, sometimes claimed by poets, of departing from normal order, DICTION, RHYME, or pronunciation in order that their VERSE may meet the requirements of their metrical pattern. The best poets rarely resort to *poetic license* since they take care to avoid such distortions. Readers of POETRY should not be too hasty in setting down as *license* an irregularity—such as the use of an archaic word or the departure from normal word order— which may have been deliberately planned by the poet to establish a desired poetic effect. If one applies the strict demands of PROSE to POETRY, of course most poetic expression will consist of *poetic license*. The decision is largely relative. PROSE, for instance, would state boldly: "Kubla Khan decreed that a stately palace be built in Xanadu." Coleridge, however, has it that

> In Xanadu did Kubla Khan
> A stately pleasure-dome decree . . . .

The Coleridge form includes (1) INVERSION of order (since "in Xanadu" precedes the subject and predicate), (2) the expletive use of "did" for the simple past tense form "decreed," and (3) a coined expression, "pleasure-dome," for "palace" or "pavilion." Yet all that is distorted is the normal PROSE form; as POETRY the lines are readily acceptable. The poet uses his *license* as a poet only when it is necessary to distort DICTION or grammar for the sake of form.

Poetical Miscellanies: Collections of lyric POETRY made during the RENAISSANCE. See MISCELLANIES, POETICAL.

Poetics: A system or body of theory concerning the nature of POETRY. The principles and rules of poetic composition. The term is used in two forms, *poetic* and *poetics,* with *poetics* the more common, both referring to the body of principles promulgated or exemplified by a poet or critic. The classic example, of course, is Aristotle's *Poetics* and the first paragraph of that work indicates that it is Aristotle's purpose to treat of "poetry in itself and of its various kinds, noting the essential quality of each; to inquire into the structure of the plot as requisite to a good poem; into the number and nature of the parts of which a poem is composed; and similarly into whatever else falls within the same inquiry." The term is often used today as equivalent of "aesthetic principles" governing the nature of any literary form. Thus critics sometimes speak of a "*poetics* of FICTION."

Poetry: A term applied to the many forms in which man has given a rhythmic expression to his most imaginative and intense perceptions of his world, himself, and the interrelationship of the two. Only through an examination of its origins and certain aspects of its nature can anything significant be said about *poetry*.

The origin of poetic expression is concealed in the dim past of man. No literary historian presumes to point out the beginnings of *poetry*, though the first conscious literary expression took the form of primitive VERSE. Evidence pointing to this inference comes from early tribal ceremonials; races which have no written literature employ poetic and rhythmic forms in their tribal ceremonies. The first *poetry* probably was associated with music and the dance. When a tribe or a people experienced any great event, a war, a migration, a flood, it seemed natural to chronicle and preserve these episodes in dance and song.

The following attempts to define *poetry* are noteworthy:

I would define the poetry of words as the rhythmical creation of beauty. Its sole arbiter is taste. With the intellect or with the conscience it has only collateral relations. Unless incidentally, it has no concern whatever either with duty or with truth.—*Edgar Allan Poe*

Poetry is the imaginative expression of strong feeling, usually rhythmical . . . the spontaneous overflow of powerful feelings recollected in tranquillity.—*William Wordsworth*

The proper and immediate object of Science is the acquirement or communication of truth; the proper and immediate object of Poetry is the communication of pleasure.—*Samuel Taylor Coleridge*

Poetry . . . a criticism of life under the conditions fixed for such a criticism by the laws of poetic truth and beauty.—*Matthew Arnold*

Absolute poetry is the concrete and artistic expression of the human mind in emotional and rhythmical language.—*Theodore Watts-Dunton*

Poetry is the record of the best and happiest moments of the best and happiest minds.—*Shelley*

. . . speech framed . . . to be heard for its own sake and interest even over and above its interest of meaning.—*Gerard Manley Hopkins*

An actual poem is the succession of experiences—sounds, images, thoughts, emotions—through which we pass when we are reading as poetically as we can.—*Andrew Bradley*

. . . the rhythmic, inevitably narrative, movement from an overclothed blindness to a naked vision.—*Dylan Thomas*

. . . the presentment, in musical form, to the imagination, of noble grounds for the noble emotions.—*Ruskin*

Poetry

If I read a book and it makes my whole body so cold no fire can ever warm me, I know that it is poetry. If I feel physically as if the top of my head were taken off, I know that it is poetry.—*Emily Dickinson*

Poetry is language that tells us, through a more or less emotional reaction, something that cannot be said. All poetry, great or small, does this. —*Edwin Arlington Robinson*

The art which uses words as both speech and song to reveal the realities that the senses record, the feelings salute, the mind perceives, and the shaping imagination orders.—*Babette Deutsch*

Reading over these and other similar statements, brings us certain words, certain qualities, certain ideas: *emotion, imagination, idea* (or *thought*), *truth* (or *meaning*), *sentiment, passion, power, sense impression, interpretation* ("criticism of life"), *beauty, dignity, rhythm, freshness of expression, orderly arrangement, concreteness, pleasure.* These words and phrases point the way to three qualities common to all *poetry:* (1) a particular *content,* (2) a more or less particular *form,* and (3) a particular *effect.*

The Content of Poetry.—*Poetry* deals with emotion. It presents the emotions of the poet as they are aroused by some scene, some experience, some attachment. It is often rich in sentiment and passion. (See EMOTIONAL ELEMENT IN LITERATURE.) *Poetry* is IMAGINATIVE. The poet, as someone has said, does not speak the accurate language of science, does not, for example, refer to water as H_2O but as "rippling," a "mirror," or "blue," using, not the elements which compose water but the effect which water creates in his imaginative mind and wanting the reader to respond to "water" as physical fact rather than abstract concept. It is this emotional, imaginative quality which Shakespeare had in mind in *A Midsummer Night's Dream:*

> As imagination bodies forth
> The forms of things unknown, the poet's pen
> Turns them to shapes and gives to airy nothing
> A local habitation and a name.
> Such tricks hath strong imagination,
> That, if it would but apprehend some joy,
> It comprehends some bringer of that joy.

Poetry has significance; it somehow contributes to the store of human knowledge or experience. This is what Matthew Arnold meant when he wrote of it as a "criticism of life"; what Watts-Dunton meant when he called it an "artistic expression of the human mind." This insistence on the presence of meaning was probably in E. A. Robinson's mind when he said that *poetry* tries to tell us "something that cannot be said." The existence of an idea, a significance, a meaning, an attitude, or a feeling distinguishes *poetry* from DOGGEREL. However, the fact that *poetry* is concerned with meaning does not make it DIDACTIC. Great DIDACTIC *poetry* exists, but *poetry* is not great because it is DIDACTIC.

Another key to the content of *poetry* can be found in *beauty*. All poets will agree to this element although by no means will all poets agree as to what is beautiful. To Shelley beauty meant the song of the skylark; Carl Sandburg finds it in a brickyard; Whitman in a leaf of grass. But beauty, of some degree, must be present. If it is a new, strange beauty of some familiar object so much the better. The poet, like the artist and the musician, is different from most other people because of his sensitivity to beauty in all its various forms; he is, in short, a poet chiefly because of this sensitivity. "Poetry," says Shelley, "turns all things to loveliness; it exalts the beauty of that which is most beautiful, and it adds beauty to that which is most deformed . . . ; it strips the veil of familiarity from the world, and lays bare the naked and sleeping beauty, which is the spirit of its forms," an idea which Dylan Thomas expresses as the "movement from overclothed blindness to a naked vision."

Poetry is usually dignified. In poetic composition life tends to be on parade—grand, magnificent, and marching with a fanfare. *Poetry* usually lives in Carcassonne, although the nature of Carcassonne—its language, manners, architecture, and rules of DECORUM—changes from age to age. The content of *poetry* is usually *emotional, imaginative,* compact with *meaning,* marked by *power, beauty,* and *dignity.*

The Form of Poetry.—The first characteristic of *poetry*, from the standpoint of FORM, is the presence of RHYTHM. Of course all good PROSE has a more or less conscious RHYTHM, but the RHYTHM of *poetry* is usually marked by a degree of regularity far surpassing that of PROSE (see PROSE RHYTHM). In fact, one of the chief rewards of reading *poetry* is the satisfaction which comes from finding "variety in uniformity," a shifting of RHYTHMS which, nevertheless, constantly return to the basic pattern (see RHYTHM and METER). The ear recognizes the existence of recurring ACCENTS at stated intervals and recognizes, too, variations from these RHYTHM patterns. Whatever the pattern, IAMBIC PENTAMETER, DACTYLLIC DIMETER, or any one of the many possible combinations in any of the other rhythmic systems (see METER), there is even in FREE VERSE a regularity of recurrence which is more uniform than in PROSE. Frequently RHYME affords an obvious difference by which one may distinguish the

FORM of *poetry* from that of PROSE. Another key is *arrangement, order.* The demands of the VERSE pattern—the combinations of RHYTHM and RHYME—often exact a "poetic" arrangement of the phrases and clauses. INVERSION is more justified in *poetry* than in PROSE; SYNCOPE is more common. The poet is granted a license (though modern poets hesitate to avail themselves of it) in sequence and syntax which is denied the prose-writer. Since most *poetry* is relatively short it is likely to be characterized by compactness of thought and expression, to possess an intense UNITY, to be carefully arranged in climactic order. A vital element of great *poetry* is its *concreteness. Poetry* insists on the specific, the concrete. The point may be made more obvious by quoting the following lines by Shakespeare:

> Our revels now are ended. These our actors,
> As I foretold you, were all spirits, and
> Are melted into air, into thin air:
> And, like the baseless fabric of this vision,
> The cloud-capp'd towers, the gorgeous palaces,
> The solemn temples, the great globe itself,
> Yea, all which it inherit, shall dissolve,
> And, like this insubstantial pageant faded,
> Leave not a rack behind. We are such stuff
> As dreams are made on; and our little life
> Is rounded with a sleep.

Here almost every line presents a concrete IMAGE or shows a picture-quality. The lines are alive with specific language. In a passage on the imagination Shakespeare has written imaginatively. PROSE would express the idea simply and bluntly; it might, indeed, be content with the first five words of the passage.

In addition to this concreteness, this IMAGERY already mentioned, the language of *poetry* differs further from that of PROSE. To Milton the language of *poetry* was "simple, sensuous, and impassioned." Since the function of *poetry* is to present IMAGES concretely, it is the responsibility of the poet to select language which succeeds in making his IMAGES concrete. The specific word, the word rich in connotative value, the word carrying implications of sound, color, and action—these are the especial stock of the true poet. Modern *poetry* tends to dispense with the special vocabulary which was once thought of as the language of *poetry* (see POETIC DICTION). The language of the poet is rich in the FIGURE OF SPEECH, in METONOMY, SYNECDOCHE, and METAPHOR.

The Effect or Purpose of Poetry.—With *poetry*, the chief, the ultimate purpose is *to please*. The various senses of sight, sound, and color may be appealed to, the various emotions of love, fear, and appreciation of beauty may be called forth by the poet, but whatever the immediate appeal, the ultimate effect of poetry is that of giving pleasure.

With the advance of the years from the dim past in which *poetry* found its origin, the art of poetic composition has undergone a long process of refinement. From its general or racial interest it has become intensely individualistic; from the ceremonial recounting of tribal and group movements it has become the vehicle for DRAMA, for history, for personal emotion. It is, however, still common today to classify *poetry* into three great type-divisions: the *epic,* the *dramatic,* and the *lyric.*

Forms and Types of Poetry.—These three types are, in turn, broken up into further classifications. Numerous set patterns such as the SONNET, the ODE, the ELEGY have evolved. Further subdivisions have been made on the basis of MOOD and purpose, such as the PASTORAL, and SATIRIC and DIDACTIC *poetry.* All of these types and manners are discussed in their proper position in this Handbook.

Point of Attack: A term, usually limited to DRAMA although applicable to all FICTION, which designates the moment in the work at which the main action of the PLOT begins. *Point of attack* may, but does not necessarily, coincide with the actual beginning of the STORY being told. It can come just before the CATASTROPHE with the antecedent events and situations being presented through various kinds of EXPOSITION as the PLOT marches forward to its inevitable conclusion.

Point of View: A term used in the analysis and criticism of FICTION to describe the way in which the reader is presented with the materials of the STORY, or, viewed from another angle, the vantage point from which the author presents the actions of the STORY. If the author serves as an all-knowing maker, not restricted to time, place, or character, and free to move and to comment at will, the *point of view* is usually called OMNISCIENT. At the other extreme, a CHARACTER within the STORY—major, minor, or merely a witness—may tell the story as he experienced it, saw it, heard it, and understood it. Such a character is usually called a first-person NARRATOR; if he does not comprehend the implications of what he is telling he is called a NAIVE or disingenuous NARRATOR. The author may tell the story in the third person and yet present it as it is seen and understood by a single character—major, minor, or merely witness—restricting information to what that character sees, hears, feels, and thinks; such a *point of view* is said to be limited to one character. The author may employ such a limited *point of view* and restrict the materials presented to the interior responses of the *point of view* character, resulting in the INTERIOR MONOLOGUE. The author may present his material by a process of narrative EXPOSITION, in which actions and conversations are presented in summary rather than in detail; such a method is usually called *panoramic*. On the other hand, he may present actions and conversations in detail, as they occur, and objectively—without authorial comment; such a method is usually called *scenic*. If the scenic method is carried to the point where the author never speaks in his own person and does not ostensibly intrude himself into the scenes he presents, he is said to be a SELF-EFFACING AUTHOR. In extended works of FICTION authors frequently employ combinations of several of these methods. The concern with *point of view* in current criticism and the experimentation with *point of view* by many current novelists are both very great. Since Henry James's critical essays and Prefaces, *point of view* has often been considered the technical aspect of FICTION which leads the critic most readily into the problems and the meanings of a NOVEL or a SHORT STORY. See NARRATOR and PANORAMIC METHOD.

Polemic: A vigorously argumentative work, setting forth its author's attitudes on a highly controversial subject, usually on religion, social issues, economics, or politics. John Milton's *Areopagitica* is the best known English example. *The American Crisis*, by Thomas Paine, is a series of American *polemics*.

Political Novel: A NOVEL which deals directly with significant aspects of political life and in which those aspects are essential ingredients of the work and not merely background material or secondary concerns. Works like Henry Adams's *Democracy*, Joyce Cary's Chester Nimmo trilogy, C. P. Snow's *Strangers and Brothers* series, and John Dos Passos' *District of Columbia* trilogy are *political novels*.

Polyphonic Prose: According to Amy Lowell, who made considerable use of the FORM, not really PROSE at all but VERSE. She defined the term as follows: " 'Polyphonic' means—many voiced—and the form is so called because it makes use of all the 'voices' of poetry, namely: METRE, VERS LIBRE, ASSONANCE, ALLITERATION, RHYME, and return." Printed as PROSE, this form, when read aloud reveals fleeting glimpses of the various poetic practices.

Popular Ballad: A traditional BALLAD, of unknown authorship and transmitted orally. See BALLAD.

Portmanteau Words: Words concocted by accident or for deliberate effect by telescoping two words into one, as the making of "squarson" (attributed to Bishop Wilberforce) from "squire" and "parson." *Portmanteau words* was a name given by Lewis Carroll to this type of fabrication, a type which he used in *Through the Looking Glass.* An example occurs in his famous "Jabberwocky" poem where, for instance, he made "slithy" of "lithe" and "slimy." In his "Preface" to *The Hunting of the Snark* Carroll explained the system by which such words were made: "For instance, take the two words 'fuming' and 'furious.' Make up your mind that you will say both words, but leave it unsettled which you will say first. Now open your mouth and speak. If your thoughts incline ever so little towards 'fuming' you will say 'fuming-furious'; if they turn by even a hair's breadth towards 'furious,' you will say 'furious-fuming'; but if you have that rarest of gifts, a perfectly balanced mind, you will say 'frumious.' " James Joyce in *Ulysses* and particularly in *Finnegans Wake* employs many *portmanteau words* to enrich and deepen the AMBIGUITY of his works.

Posy (Posie):   Sometimes used in the sense of "a collection of flowers" to indicate an ANTHOLOGY. The term also signifies a motto, usually in verse, inscribed on a ring. When the "mouse-trap" play begins and the PROLOGUE has been spoken Hamlet asks Ophelia: "Is this a prologue, or the posy of a ring?"

Pot-boiler: A SLANG term given to a book or an article written solely for the income derived from it. It is writing which will "keep the pot boiling" and thus supply sustenance, hopefully, for more worthy work.

Poulter's Measure: A metrical pattern, now rarely used, consisting of a COUPLET composed of a first line in IAMBIC HEXAMETER and a second line in IAMBIC HEPTAMETER. The term is said to have originated from a custom of the London poulterers of giving the customer twelve eggs to the dozen in the first dozen bought, and fourteen in the second dozen. Wyatt and Surrey, Sidney, Nicholas Grimald, and Arthur Brooke are some of the poets who have used this form. The opening lines of Arthur Brooke's *Romeus and Juliet* afford an example of *poulter's measure:*

> There is beyond the Alps, a town of ancient fame,
> Whose bright renown yet shineth clear, Verona men it name;
> Built in a happy time, built on a fertile soil,
> Maintainéd by the heavenly fates, and by the townish toil.

Poulter's measure exists today in a modified form; it is a four-line STANZA composed of IAMBIC TRIMETER verses for the first, second, and fourth lines, and an IAMBIC TETRAMETER for the third.

Practical Criticism: Criticism in which the critic's principles of art and aesthetic beliefs are applied to specific works of art; often called "applied criticism," the term is used in opposition to THEORETICAL CRITICISM, in which general principles and broad tenets are sought. See CRITICISM, TYPES OF.

Pragmatic Theory of Art: A theory of art, according to M. H. Abrams, in which the critic's major interest is in the effect that the art object produces in its audience. See CRITICISM, HISTORICAL SKETCH.

Pragmatism: A term, first used by C. S. Peirce in 1878 in an article in *Popular Science Monthly* to describe a philosophical doctrine that determines value and meaning through the test of consequences or utility. Its principal exponents have been William James and John Dewey, through whose work and influence it has made itself pervasively felt in America. The *pragmatist* insists that no questions are significant unless the results of answering them in one way rather than another have practical consequences in human affairs. In William James's words: "The 'whole meaning' of a conception expresses itself in practical consequences, consequences either in the shape of conduct to be recommended, or in that of experience to be expected, if the conception be true." John Dewey and his followers have emphasized the implications of *pragmatism* upon logical processes, insisting that logical thinking must be subordinate to practical life and that thought aims not at abstract truth but at satisfying some practical end that life demands. The world of the pragmatists is pluralistic, interested in context, relativistic in its beliefs about truth and value systems, devoid of the metaphysical concerns except as they have practical consequences. On the other hand, it places a high premium upon conduct, upon ethical concerns. In literature, *pragmatism* found its most vigorous expression in the REALISM that developed in America after 1870.

Preamble: An introductory portion of a written document. In formal sets of "resolutions" there is usually a *preamble* which sets forth the occasion for the resolutions. This *preamble* is introduced by one or more statements beginning with "Whereas" and is followed by the resolutions proper, each article of which is introduced by the word "Therefore."

Preciosity: A critical term sometimes applied to writing which is consciously "pretty," labored or affected in STYLE, fastidious in DICTION, over-refined in manner. See DANDYISM.

Précis: An ABSTRACT or EPITOME of the essential facts or statements of a work, retaining the order of the original.

Predestination: The belief that God has foreordained all things. See CALVINISM and FATALISM.

Preface: A short introductory statement printed at the beginning of a book or article—and separate from it—in which the author states his purpose in writing, makes necessary acknowledgments of assistance, points out difficulties and uncertainties in connection with the writing of the book, and, in general, informs the reader of such facts as he thinks pertinent to a reading of the text. Some writers, notably Dryden, Shaw, and Henry James, have written *prefaces* which were really extended ESSAYS.

Prelude: A short POEM, introductory in character, prefixed to a long POEM or to a section of a long POEM. Lowell's *The Vision of Sir Launfal* contains *preludes* of the latter sort. Rarely, as in the case of Wordsworth's famous *Prelude,* a poem so entitled may itself be lengthy; although Wordsworth's *Prelude* was written as an introduction to a much longer but incomplete work.

Pre-Raphaelitism: The Pre-Raphaelite movement began with the establishment in 1848 of the Pre-Raphaelite brotherhood by Dante

Gabriel Rossetti, Holman Hunt, John Everett Millais, and other artists as a protest against the conventional methods of painting then in use. The Pre-Raphaelites wished to regain the spirit of simple devotion and adherence to NATURE which they found in Italian religious art before Raphael. Ruskin asserted that *Pre-Raphaelitism* had but one principle, that of absolute uncompromising truth in all that it did, truth attained by elaborating everything, down to the most minute detail, from NATURE and from NATURE only. This meant the rejection of all conventions designed to heighten effects artificially. Several of the group were both artists and POETS, and the effect of the cult was felt in English literature. Rossetti's "Blessed Damozel," printed in 1850 in one of the four issues of *The Germ*, the organ of the group, is a narrative poem with pictorial qualities. Characteristics of Pre-Raphaelite poetry are: pictorial elements, SYMBOLISM, sensuousness, a tendency to metrical experimentation, attention to minute detail, and an interest in the medieval and the supernatural. Certain critics, who deemed sensuousness the dominant characteristic of their poetry, called the Pre-Raphaelites the "FLESHLY SCHOOL." The chief literary products of the movement were Rossetti's translation of Dante, his SONNETS, and his BALLAD-like VERSE; Christina Rossetti's LYRICS; and the poems of William Morris, such as *The Earthly Paradise* and *The Defense of Guinevere*. Morris' practical application of medieval craftsmanship to business effected a change in taste in home decoration.

Primitivism: The doctrine that primitive man, because he had remained closer to NATURE and had been less subject to the influences of society, was nobler and more nearly perfect than is civilized man. The idea flourished in eighteenth-century England and France and was an important element in the creed of the "sentimentalists" of the romantic movement. Though it is impossible to trace all the forces which aided in the development of the primitivistic doctrine, a few may be suggested. The rationalistic philosopher, the third Earl of Shaftesbury (*fl. ca.* 1710), in his effort to show that God had revealed himself completely in NATURE—and that NATURE was therefore perfect—reasoned that primitive peoples were close to God and therefore essentially moral. Man is by nature prone to do good: his evil comes from self-imposed limitations of his freedom. Romantic accounts of savage peoples by writers of travel literature added impetus to the movement, as did the linguistic researches into the origin of language by such men as Lord Monboddo (*The Origin*

Primitivism

and Progress of Language, 1773–1792), and the effort of various scholars to find the reason for Homer's greatness in his assumed primitive surroundings. Tremendous impetus from France was given the movement by the writings of Rousseau, whose slogan of "Return to Nature" was based upon his belief that man was potentially perfect and that his faults were due to the vicious effect of the type of society he had developed, one which tended progressively to restrict the freedom and hence lessen the moral goodness of man.

One of the interesting phases of *primitivism* in English literature was its doctrine that the best poetry should be natural or instinctive. There was a feverish search not only for a perfect primitive man but for a perfect "untutored" poet. Among the many savages brought by the primitivists to England in their search for the perfect natural man the enthusiasts searched for evidence of poetic genius. The "inspired peasant" was sought for, too, among the unlettered population of Great Britain, and many were fêted by high society till their fame wore out: Henry Jones, the poetical bricklayer; James Woodhouse, the poetical shoemaker; and Ann Yearsley, the poetical milk-woman of Bristol, who signed her poems "Lactilla" and was sponsored by the BLUESTOCKINGS. Gray's *The Bard* (1757) and James Beattie's *The Minstrel* (1771–1774) reflect the doctrine of primitive poetic genius. For a time the forged "Ossian" poems of James Macpherson (see LITERARY FORGERIES) seemed an answer to the romantic prayer for the discovery in Britain of the work of some primitive epic poet. When, finally, Robert Burns appeared, the doctrine of the peasant poet seemed proved, and the Scottish BARD was received with enthusiasm, especially in Edinburgh.

All England did not go primitivistic. The movement was attacked by such conservatives as Doctor Johnson and Edmund Burke. The "noble savage" idea produced the idealized American Indian, as in Cooper's novels, and American life was exploited as ideal because primitive, as in Crèvecoeur's *Letters from an American Farmer* and Gilbert Imlay's novel of pioneer life, *The Emigrants.* Elements of *primitivism,* related to the idea of natural goodness, appear throughout American writing in the nineteenth century.

A common and useful distinction is made between CULTURAL PRIMITIVISM and CHRONOLOGICAL PRIMITIVISM, CULTURAL being used for the *primitivism* that prefers the natural to the man-made, the uninhibited to the controlled, the simple and primitive to that upon which man has worked, NATURE to art; and CHRONOLOGICAL being used for the *primitivism* that looks backward to a "Golden Age" and sees man's present sad state as the product of what culture and society have done to him. If this distinction is made—and it should be recognized that the terms are not mutually exclusive—it becomes apparent that many of the political doctrines of the American founding fathers were influenced by CHRONOLOGICAL PRIMITIVISM, while CULTURAL PRIMITIVISM has been a powerful, although silent, force in American REALISM. See PROGRESS.

Printing: All the copies of a book or other publication printed at the same time; used interchangeably with IMPRESSION. See EDITION.

Printing, Introduction into American Colonies: Although the Spaniards had brought printing presses to Mexico and elsewhere much earlier, the real beginning of printing in America dates from 1639, when, according to Governor Winthrop's *Diary*, a printing house was begun by Stephen Daye. In reality, Daye was the printer, not the proprietor. The first thing printed was *The Freeman's Oath*, the next an ALMANAC, and the third the famous "Bay Psalm Book" (1640), the earliest surviving American book. William Bradford was printing in Philadelphia as early as 1683. Later he moved to New York and became the government printer. The introduction of printing into Virginia was opposed by Governor Berkeley and a printing establishment was suppressed in 1682, though printing was reintroduced not long thereafter.

Printing, Introduction into England: The circumstances surrounding the invention and development of printing in Western Europe (the Chinese and Japanese had practiced a simple form of printing centuries before) are so lost in obscurity that it is impossible to assign the invention to any country or person or exact date. Although there seems to have been some sort of forerunner of the printed book in Holland, it is fairly certain that the most important development of the art took place in Mainz, Germany, during the forties and fifties of the fifteenth century. The earliest existing book which can be dated is an "Indulgence" (Mainz, 1454); the most famous existing early book is the so-called Gutenberg Bible (Mainz, 1456). On the authority of fifteenth-century writers, John Gutenberg of Mainz is commonly given credit for the invention.

From Mainz the art spread to Italy, France, Holland, and other countries, reaching England in 1476, when William Caxton set up his famous press at Westminster. Caxton had learned printing on the Continent, and at Bruges, probably in 1475, had brought out the first book printed in English, the *Recuyell of the Historyes of Troye*. The first printed books in England were perhaps PAMPHLETS, some of them in Latin, but the first dated English book printed in England was Caxton's *Dicts or Sayings of the Philosophers* (1477). Before his death Caxton had printed about a hundred separate books. He did much to direct the public taste in reading. He specialized in translations, POETRY, and ROMANCES, two of his most important books being his edition of Chaucer's *Canterbury Tales* (1483) and his publication of Malory's *Le Morte Darthur* (1485). Other early presses in England include one at Oxford (1478) and one at St. Albans (1479), both devoted chiefly to learned works. Caxton himself was succeeded by his assistant, Wynkyn de Worde, a printer without literary talent but important because he published, during his long career, about 800 books, some of them of literary interest. An important contemporary was Richard Pynson (*fl.*1490–1530).

Private Theaters: This term seems to have arisen about 1596, when the Blackfriars theater was so described by its sponsors who were seeking privileges not granted to the PUBLIC THEATERS. The *private theaters*, though they charged a higher admission fee and attracted in general a higher class of spectators than did their "public" rivals, were open to all classes. They differed from the PUBLIC THEATERS in being indoor institutions, artificially lighted, smaller, and typically rectangular. In origin, they were connected with companies of child actors and continued to be used chiefly, but not exclusively, by such companies. These companies performed at various times at the Blackfriars, St. Paul's, the Inns of Court, and the Court. Shakespeare's company in the early seventeenth century controlled both the Blackfriars, the chief *private theater*, and the Globe, the chief PUBLIC THEATER. The *private theaters*, being indoor institutions of a somewhat aristocratic character, became of increasing importance in the seventeenth century, when the Court was fostering elaborate exhibitions (see MASQUE) and encouraging DRAMA with spectacular features, and it is from them rather than from the PUBLIC THEATERS that the playhouses of the RESTORATION and later times directly descended. See PUBLIC THEATERS.

Problem Novel: A name given to the type of PROSE FICTION which derives its chief interest from working out, through characters and incidents, some central problem. In a loose sense almost every NOVEL or PLOT presents a problem since the opposition of forces which make for PLOT and CONFLICT also should arouse some interest in the reader as to "how this is to turn out." However, the term is usually more restricted than this. It is sometimes carelessly applied to those novels which are written for deliberate purpose, a thesis, which are better called PROPAGANDA NOVELS, since they present a brief for or against one class of people, one type of living, one activity of civilization. Since human character is the subject matter surest to interest readers and since humankind is constantly confronted by the problems of life and conduct, it follows that the *problem novel*—when it is thought of as a story *with* a purpose rather than *for* a purpose—is fairly common. The REALISTIC NOVEL, centered as it is in social setting, has often employed social issues as the cruxes of its PLOTS. It is this matter of illustrating a problem by showing people confronted by it which is at the core of the *problem novel*. See PROPAGANDA NOVEL.

Problem Play: Like the PROBLEM NOVEL, its ANALOGUE in nondramatic FICTION, this term is used both in a broad sense to cover all serious drama in which problems of human life are presented as such, e.g., Shakespeare's *King Lear,* and in a more specialized sense to designate the modern "drama of ideas," as exemplified in the plays of Ibsen, Shaw, Galsworthy, and many others. Its most common usage is in the latter sense, and here it means the representation in dramatic form of a general social problem or issue, shown as it is confronted by or must be solved by the PROTAGONIST. See PROBLEM NOVEL.

Proem: A brief introduction, a PREFACE or PREAMBLE.

Profile: An ESSAY that is a combined brief biographical sketch and character study of a contemporary figure. Usually a marked point of view toward the subject of the *Profile* is taken. The type of ESSAY and the term *Profile* come from the *New Yorker Magazine,* which has been publishing such sketches and has called them "*Profiles*" for many years.

Progress: The belief that in many significant ways human history shows a pattern of improvement over the past is often called "the idea of *progress.*" In some cases, this idea is almost made into a system under which *progress*—that is, improvement of the human and social condition—is inevitable with the passage of time. In its naive statements it can be a childishly optimistic doctrine. When held by serious and thoughtful men, as it often has been, the idea of *progress* is a strong antidote to the doctrine of CHRONOLOGICAL PRIMITIVISM. It has often been said that American ROMANTICISM in the nineteenth century rested upon the doctrine of natural goodness (CULTURAL PRIMITIVISM) and the idea of *progress*. See PRIMITIVISM.

Prolegomenon: A foreword or PREFACE. The heading *prolegomena* (the plural form) may be given to the introductory section of a book containing observations on the subject of the book itself.

Prolepsis: An anticipating; the type of ANACHRONISM in which an event is pictured as taking place before it could have done so, the treating of a future event as if past. Rhetorically, the word may be applied to a preliminary statement or summary which is to be followed by a detailed treatment. In ARGUMENTATION *prolepsis* may mean the device of anticipating and answering an opponent's argument before the opponent has an opportunity to introduce it, thus detracting from its effectiveness if later employed.

Prologue: A PREFACE or INTRODUCTION most frequently associated with DRAMA and especially common in England in the plays of the RESTORATION and the eighteenth century. In the plays of ancient Greece a speaker announced, before the beginning of the play proper, such salient facts as the audience should know to understand the play itself. In Latin DRAMA the same custom prevailed, Plautus having left some of the most mature *prologues* in dramatic literature. European dramatists in both France and England followed the classical tradition, from the time of the MIRACLE and MYSTERY PLAYS (which may be said to have used *prologues* of a "moral" nature) well into modern times. *Prologues* were frequently written by the author of a play and delivered by one of the chief actors; it was, however, in the eighteenth century, common practice for writers of established reputations, such as Pope, Doctor Johnson, and Garrick, to write *prologues* for plays by their friends and acquaintances. Sometimes, as in the play within the play in *Hamlet,* the actor who spoke the *prologue* was himself called "the prologue." The first part of Shakespeare's *King Henry IV* opens with an explanatory speech, not formally a *prologue,* which serves the function of a real *prologue.* Part two of the same play opens with a *prologue* called an INDUCTION. See INDUCTION and EPILOGUE.

Propaganda Novel: A NOVEL dealing with a special social, political, economic, or moral issue or problem and strongly advocating a doctrinaire solution. See PROBLEM NOVEL.

Proscenium: Properly used, the term now designates that part of the stage in a modern theater which lies between the orchestra and the curtain. In the ancient theater the *proscenium* extended from the orchestra to the background, and the term is not infrequently used, even nowadays, merely as a synonym for the stage itself. The arch over the front of the stage from which the CURTAIN hangs and which, together with the CURTAIN, separates the stage from the audience is called the *proscenium* arch. In a BOX SET it forms the FOURTH WALL of the stage-as-room.

Prose: In its broadest sense, the term is applied to all forms of written or spoken expression which do not have a regular rhythmic pattern (see METER). *Prose* is most often meant to designate a conscious, cultivated writing, not merely a bringing together of vocabularies, a listing of ideas, a catalog of objects. And, while *prose* is like VERSE in that good *prose* has a RHYTHM, it is unlike VERSE in that this RHYTHM is not to be scanned by any of the normal metrical schemes or marked by such devices of reiteration as FREE-VERSE uses. But a clear line between *prose* and POETRY is difficult to draw. Some of the qualities of *prose* are: (1) it is without sustained rhythmic regularity; (2) it has some logical, grammatical order, and its ideas are connectedly stated rather than merely listed; (3) it is characterized by STYLE, though the STYLE will vary from writer to writer; (4) it will secure variety of expression through DICTION and through sentence structure.

Prose in all literatures has developed more slowly than VERSE. English *prose* is usually said to find its beginnings in the work of Alfred, whose *Handbook* (887) is sometimes cited as the earliest specimen of finished English *prose.* Other names significant in the development of English *prose* are Thomas Usk, John Wycliffe, Malory, Caxton, Roger Ascham, Holinshed, Lyly, Raleigh, Donne, Jeremy Taylor, Milton, Dryden, Addison, and Hemingway. For many centuries English *prose* had to compete with Latin for recognition, and for many more years Latin forms and syntax shaped its STYLE. The single book which did most to mold present English *prose* STYLE was the King James version of the BIBLE.

Prose Poetry: A form of PROSE with marked (although preferably not too regular) CADENCE and frequently with extensive use of FIGURATIVE LANGUAGE and IMAGERY. If *prose poetry* is to be distinguished from POLYPHONIC PROSE, the distinction is that POLYPHONIC PROSE is usually reserved for a kind of writing which has marked VERSE characteristics in PROSE form, whereas *prose poetry* is predominantly PROSE but borrows enriching characteristics from the RHYTHMS and IMAGERY of POETRY. See POLYPHONIC PROSE, PROSE RHYTHM.

Prose Rhythm: The recurrence of STRESS and EMPHASIS at regular or, much more usually, irregular intervals which gives to some PROSE a pleasurable rise and fall of MOVEMENT. *Prose rhythm* is distinguished from the RHYTHM of VERSE in that it never for long falls into a recognizable pattern, for if it does it becomes VERSE rather than PROSE. RHYTHM in PROSE is essentially an aspect of STYLE. The greater freedom of *prose rhythm,* as compared with the RHYTHM of VERSE, springs from its wider choice in the placing of STRESS. There is no necessity to force a line to a certain rhythmic pattern. The normal ACCENT of words first determines the rhythmic EMPHASIS. But this is augmented by the secondary ACCENTS (in such words as ob″-ser-va′-tion and el″-e-men′-ta-ry) and increased again by the tendency of the reader to emphasize certain words importantly placed or rendered significant because of their meaning. (See RHETORICAL ACCENT and ACCENT.) Attempts have been made from time to time to evolve a system of SCANSION for PROSE, but none of them has proved satisfactory.

Prosody: The theory and principles of VERSIFICATION, particularly as they refer to RHYTHM, ACCENT, and STANZA. See METER, SCANSION, VERSIFICATION.

Prosopopoeia: A term sometimes used for PERSONIFICATION.

Protagonist: The chief character in a play or story. The word *protagonist* was originally applied to the first actor in early Greek DRAMA. The actor was added to the CHORUS and was its leader; hence the continuing meaning of *protagonist* as the "first" or chief player in a DRAMA. In Greek DRAMA an AGON is a contest. The *protagonist,* the chief CHARACTER, and the ANTAGONIST, the second most important CHARACTER, are the contenders in the AGON. The *protagonist* is the leading figure both in terms of his importance in the play and in terms of his ability to enlist our interest and sympathy, whether his cause is heroic or ignoble. The term *protagonist* is used in a similar sense for the leading CHARACTER in any work of FICTION. In Shakespeare's *Hamlet,* Hamlet is himself the *protagonist,* as his fortunes are the chief interest in the play. King Claudius and Laertes are his ANTAGONISTS. The sentence "The protagonists of Christopher Marlowe's tragedies are usually the super-personality type" illustrates a usual use of the word. *Protagonist* is sometimes used in the looser sense of champion or chief advocate of a cause or movement, as when Bryan is called the *protagonist* of the free-silver movement in 1896.

Protasis: The term applied by the classical critics to the introductory ACT or the EXPOSITION of a DRAMA. See DRAMATIC STRUCTURE.

Prothesis: The addition of a letter or a syllable at the beginning of a word for EMPHASIS, effect, or to meet metrical needs, as in Keats's line, "The owl for all his feathers was a-cold."

Prototype: A first form or original instance of a thing, or model or pattern for later forms or examples. Thus the PERIODICAL ESSAY of the eighteenth century as written by Addison or Steele may be called the *prototype* of the FAMILIAR ESSAY as written by Lamb or Stevenson, the later form being developed from the earlier. Or the "Vice" of the MORALITY PLAYS may be regarded as the *prototype* of the clown of ELIZABETHAN DRAMA.

Proverb: A sentence or phrase which briefly and strikingly expresses some recognized truth or shrewd observation about practical life and which has been preserved by oral tradition, though it may be preserved and transmitted in written literature as well. So far as FORM goes, *proverbs* may owe their appeal to the use of a METAPHOR ("Still waters run deep"); ANTITHESIS ("Man proposes, God disposes"), a play on words ("Forewarned, forearmed"); RHYME ("A friend in need is a friend indeed"); or ALLITERATION or PARALLELISM. Some are epigrammatic. Since the true *proverb* is old, its language is sometimes archaic. Words or meanings or idioms or grammatical constructions not now common may be used. A misunderstanding of the original meaning may result. Thus in "Time and tide wait for no man" *tide* is probably the old word for "season." The range of interest of the *proverb* is wide: the weather, remedies for illness, legal shifts, superstitions, agriculture, efficiency in practical life, SATIRE on other races or on rival countries or localities. *Proverbs* pass freely from language to language.

Provincialism: A word, phrase, or manner of expression peculiar to a special region and not commonly used outside that region, therefore, not fashionable or sophisticated. The term is applied not only to language but to customs, dress, and other characteristics of a special region.

Psalm: A lyrical composition of praise. Most frequently the term is applied to the sacred and devout LYRICS in the Book of Psalms ascribed to David.

Pseudonym: A fictitious name sometimes assumed by writers and others. See NOM DE PLUME, PUTATIVE AUTHOR, ALLONYM.

Pseudo-Shakespearean Plays: Plays attributed to Shakespeare at one time or another but not accepted as his by the best authorities. Some non-Shakespearean plays, such as *Locrine,* were printed during Shakespeare's lifetime with his initials or name on the title page; others, such as *The Birth of Merlin,* were so printed after Shakespeare's death. Another group, including *Mucedorus,* consists of plays labeled as Shakespeare's in the copies of them found in the library of Charles II. Many others, including *Sir Thomas More* (the manuscript copy of which is thought by some experts to be partly in Shakespeare's handwriting) and *Arden of Feversham,* have been assigned to Shakespeare by editors, booksellers, or critics chiefly on the basis of their literary or technical qualities. A collection of *pseudo-Shakespearean plays* has been printed by Tucker Brooke in his *Shakespeare Apocrypha.* Some of the plays dubiously assigned to Shakespeare, such as *Cardenio,* have not survived.

Psychic Distance: The necessary DISTANCE between a work of art and a member of its audience. The reader or viewer needs, aestheticians say, to maintain a separation between his personal needs

Psychological Novel

and feelings and the situation and emotion represented in a work of
art, so that the work—DRAMA, POEM, NOVEL, painting, sculpture—
may be viewed objectively and not in terms of the individual situations or feelings of the reader or viewer. See DISTANCE.

Psychological Novel: PROSE FICTION which places more than the
usual amount of emphasis on interior CHARACTERIZATION, and on
the motives, circumstances, and internal action which springs from,
and develops, external action. The *psychological novel* is not content to state what happens but goes on to explain the *why* of this
action. In this type of writing CHARACTERIZATION is more than usually important. In one sense the psychological story is as old as the
first DRAMA, TALE, or BALLAD which accounted for external action
by recounting the qualities of the CHARACTER of the PROTAGONIST.
Chaucer's *Troilus and Criseyde* is a *psychological novel* in VERSE.
Hamlet is a psychological DRAMA; but so are most of Shakespeare's
better plays. The *psychological novel* is, as one critic has said, an
interpretation of "the invisible life." The term was first importantly
applied to a group of novelists in the middle of the nineteenth
century, a group of which Mrs. Gaskell, George Eliot, and George
Meredith were the chief writers. Mrs. Gaskell, writing about the
middle of the nineteenth century, stated that "all deeds however
hidden and long passed by have their external consequences"—thus
giving expression to an attitude long realized and felt if not always
deliberately expressed. Thackeray and Dickens, too, were interested
enough in motives and details to be classified, in a looser sense,
with the forerunners of the *psychological novel*. Hardy and Conrad
were also interested in the picturing of interior motive and psychological effect. Henry James, with his intense concern for the psychological life of his characters and with his development of a novelistic
technique that centered itself in the representation of the effect
produced in the inner self by external events, may be said to have
created the modern *psychological novel*. In the twentieth century,
with the advance of psychology as a science, the term has come
into popular use. FREUDIANISM particularly gave impetus to the type.
The modern *psychological novel* may at one extreme record the
inner experience of characters as reported by an author, as James
tends to do, or at the other extreme utilize the INTERIOR MONOLOGUE
to recount the non-verbalized and subconscious life of a character,
as in some of the work of James Joyce and William Faulkner. See
NOVEL, STREAM-OF-CONSCIOUSNESS NOVEL, INTERIOR MONOLOGUE.

Public Theaters: The English playhouse developed in the ELIZA-
BETHAN AGE as a natural accompaniment of the increased interest
in the DRAMA. In earlier times plays had been produced on PAGEANTS
and in indoor rooms such as guild halls and the halls of great houses,
schools, INNS OF COURT, and inn-yards, which were square or rectangular courts enclosed by the inner porches or balconies of the
inn building. In one end would be erected a temporary stage connected with rooms of the inn. The spectators might stand in the
open court ("groundlings") or get seats on the surrounding balconies.
Meantime the need for a place for bear- or bull-baiting spectacles
and acrobatic performances had been met in the development of a
sort of ring or amphitheater. Out of the physical features of the
inn-yard (surrounding galleries or boxes, open central space or pit,
stage extending into pit) and the bear garden (circular form of
building) the plan of the first *public theater* was evolved. The
front stage was open to the sky, the rear stage covered by a ceiling.
Above this ceiling was a room for the machinery needed in lowering
persons and objects to the stage below, or raising them from it.
There was an "inner" stage at the rear, provided with a curtain and
connected with a balcony above, also curtained. The rear stage was
used chiefly for special settings such as a forest or bedroom, while
the bare outer stage was used for street scenes, battles, and the like.
The scenery and the costumes of the actors were largely conventional and symbolic, though certainly very realistic at times.

The first *public theater* in London was the Theatre, built in
1576 by James Burbage in Shoreditch. It was followed in 1577 by
the Curtain in the same neighborhood. About ten years later Henslowe built the Rose on the Bankside, and in this locality appeared
also the Swan (1594). In 1599 the Theatre was torn down and re-
erected on the Bankside as the Globe, the most important one of
the *public theaters*. The Globe was used and controlled by the company to which Shakespeare belonged. Henslowe built the Fortune
in 1600, the Red Bull appeared soon after in St. John's Street, and
the Hope in 1614 near the Rose and the new Globe. For distinction
between "public" and "private" theaters see PRIVATE THEATERS.

Pulitzer Prizes: Annual prizes for journalism, literature, and music,
awarded annually since 1917 by the School of Journalism and the
Board of Trustees of Columbia University. The prizes are supported
by a bequest from Joseph Pulitzer. An Advisory Board of the Pulitzer
Prizes selects distinguished work published or produced in the

Purist

United States during the preceding year and recommends recipients to the Board of Trustees, who make the awards. Eight prizes are awarded for various kinds of meritorious service rendered by newspapers. One prize is awarded for a musical composition. Six awards are given in literature: for the most distinguished novel, preferably dealing with American life; for the American play best showing the power and educational value of the theater; for the finest book on American history; for the best biography or autobiography, teaching patriotic and unselfish services to people; for the most distinguished volume of verse; and for the best book of general nonfiction not fitting into any of these categories. There has been much debate over the recipients of the awards in literature and drama. A listing of the Pulitzer Prizes in fiction, poetry, and drama is given in the APPENDIX.

Pulp Magazines: MAGAZINES printed on rough pulp paper, cheaply produced, with lurid illustrations and gaudy covers, and filled with melodramatic TALES of love, crime, and the West. Popular in the first half of the twentieth century, particularly in the 1920's and 1930's, the *pulp magazines* were the successors to the DIME NOVELS.

Pun: A play on words based on the similarity of sound between two words with different meanings. An example is Thomas Hood's: "They went and told the sexton and the sexton tolled the bell." See EQUIVOQUE.

Pure Poetry: A term applied to POETRY which is free from conceptualized statement, instructive content, or moral preachment; or those portions of a poem which remain after such materials as can be paraphrased adequately in PROSE are removed. The term was first used by Baudelaire in an essay on Edgar Allan Poe. For many critics Poe's theory and practice of POETRY are archetypically pure; as George Moore said of Poe's poems when including them in an anthology of *pure poetry,* they "are almost free from thought." Wallace Stevens is often cited as a contemporary poet who practiced an art close to that of *pure poetry.*

Purist: One who habitually stresses, or overstresses, correctness or "purity" in language, particularly in minor or "fine" points of grammar, DICTION, pronunciation, and rhetorical STYLE. The term is commonly used in a spirit of deprecation or mild reproach, but it must be remembered that it is difficult to draw the line between the *purist* and the person who takes a commendable interest in achieving that accuracy and precision in language which are important.

A related though different use of the word is its application to a person who feels that the "purity" of a language can be preserved by the exclusion of foreign words and of words not used by the best stylists. Thus the so-called CICERONIANS of the RENAISSANCE, a group of Latin stylists who would not use any Latin word that could not be found in Cicero's writings, have been called *purists*, as have the English scholars of the sixteenth century and later who insisted upon a "pure" English diction "unmixed and unmangled with borrowing of other tongues." The famous schoolmasters Sir John Cheke and Roger Ascham and the rhetorician Thomas Wilson were leaders in this movement. In the main they were not absolute *purists*, however, since they recognized that English might legitimately be enriched by the use of some foreign words; and they opposed strongly the pedantic tendency of the time which threatened to make literary English a mere Latin *patois*. The struggle between these *purists* and their INKHORNIST opponents is sometimes referred to as the "purist-improver" controversy.

Later movements toward purism included: the unsuccessful effort in the seventeenth century to establish (on the model of the French Academy) a British Academy to regulate language; eighteenth-century efforts at standardization through the establishment of some definite linguistic authority (opposed by Doctor Johnson); and efforts to stress the Anglo-Saxon elements in the vocabulary and to check the importation of foreign words (noteworthy is Edna St. Vincent Millay's attempt to write a long poem, *The King's Henchman*, employing only words of Anglo-Saxon derivation).

Puritanism: A religious-political movement which developed in England about the middle of the sixteenth century and later spread its influence into the New England colonies in America. While politically it died with the return of Charles the Second to London in 1660, *Puritanism* left its impress and many of its attitudes on the habits and thought of the people, especially of America today. As a term, *Puritan* was, in Elizabeth's reign, applied in derision to those who wished to "purify" the Church of England. The spirit which prompted *Puritanism* was an outgrowth of CALVINISM which had spread from Geneva to England.

In principle the Puritans objected to certain forms of the Established Church. They objected, for instance, to the wearing of the surplice, and to government by the prelates, and they demanded the right to partake of the communion in a sitting posture. The Millenary Petition (1603) of the Puritans requested a reform of the church courts, a doing away with "superstitious" customs, a discarding of the use of APOCRYPHAL books of the BIBLE, a serious observance of the Sabbath, and various ecclesiastical reforms. While at first *Puritanism* in England was not directly affiliated with Presbyterianism, it later on allied itself, largely for political reasons, very definitely with the Presbyterian movement. Thomas Cartwright, the first important spokesman of *Puritanism,* hated most emphatically the Church of England.

The conception of the Puritans popularly held today, however, is very unfair to the general tone and temper of the early sponsors of the movement. These early English Puritans were not long-faced reformers, teetotalers, or haters of art and music. They were often patrons of art and lovers of music, fencing, and dancing. They were intelligent, self-controlled, plainly dressed citizens who held to simplicity and to democratic principles. But under the persecution of Charles and the double-dealing of Laud they were harried into bitterness.

Puritanism was a natural aftermath of the RENAISSANCE, the REFORMATION, the establishment. of the Church of England, and the growth of Presbyterianism. Through all of these great movements one sees emerging the right of the individual to political and religious independence. The reading of the Bible had become general. The Catholic Church had lost its pristine power in England, but there were still thousands of Catholics who wanted their old power restored. The people were always suspicious that their rulers, a James I or a Charles I, might swing back to the faith of Spain and Italy. Political power for the commoners lay with Presbyterianism, a religious movement based on the political control of presbyters drawn from the people. Catholicism and even the Church of England were far too reminiscent of autocracy and of divine right to rule. Whitgift and Laud wished to stamp out *Puritanism;* James I had promised that if necessary he would "harry the Puritans out of the land." Charles I and Laud fought popular rights and suppressed Parliament. The Church of England took little note of the handwriting on the wall. Milton at this time wrote his famous digression in *Lycidas* to condemn the Church and the clergy: "Blind mouths! that scarce themselves know how to hold a sheephook." From 1642 to 1646 civil war was waged in England, a civil war from which rose to power a new Puritan leader, Oliver Cromwell. In 1649 Charles was beheaded. The Puritan Commonwealth was established. And on May 25, 1660, Charles II landed at Dover.

Some of the "Brownists," a group of Puritans who had left England for seclusion in Holland, came to America in the *Mayflower*. They wished to set up a new theocracy in which the Puritan ideas of religion and government were to go hand in hand. "I shall call that my country where I may most glorify God and enjoy the presence of my dearest friends," said young Winthrop. In one year as many as three thousand rebels left England for the Colonies; in ten years there were twenty thousand English in America. Many of these new-comers were men of education, intelligence, family position, and culture. Those who settled in and around Massachusetts were bent on forming a new government, a theocracy, with God and Christ at the head, and with their own chosen rulers to interpret God's will for them. What now seems, as we look back at it all, a gesture toward conservatism, a threat against freedom of speech, art, and individualism, was at that time essentially a radical movement.

From the Puritans in England two great writers emerge to tower over all others of the century, John Bunyan and John Milton.

In America, a dozen or two writers have attained positions in American literature largely because they happened to stand at the source of the stream. Such theologians as John Cotton, Thomas Hooker, John Eliot, Cotton Mather; such historians as William Bradford, John Winthrop, Thomas Hutchinson, and Samuel Sewall; and such poets as Nathaniel Ward, Anne Bradstreet, Michael Wigglesworth, and Edward Taylor derive importance from their historical position. *The Bay Psalm Book* (1640) became almost the book of a people.

With the Scotch-Irish settlements of the Middle Atlantic and Southern colonies came another and a strong strain of *Puritanism*, that of the Scotch Presbyterians. And as the restless and the discontented, North and South, moved westward into the beckoning frontier they carried with them the Bible, a simple and fundamentally Puritan faith, and the stern impulse to independence and freedom. Across the pages of American literature *Puritanism* is written large. It may almost be considered the ethical mode of American thought. See CALVINISM.

"Purple Patch": A piece of "fine writing." Now and then authors in a strongly emotional passage will give free play to most of the stylistic tricks in their bag. They will write PROSE which is intensely colorful, more than usually rhythmic, marked by an involved PARALLELISM, full of IMAGERY and FIGURES OF SPEECH, characterized by a POETIC DICTION. When there is an unusual piling up of these devices in such a way as to evidence a self-conscious literary effort, the section is spoken of as a *purple patch*—a colorful passage standing out from the writing around it. Although frequently used in a non-evaluative, descriptive sense, the term is more often employed in a derogatory sense, to suggest overstraining.

Puseyism: The later OXFORD MOVEMENT, particularly at the time of the debates over ritualism in the Church of England; so-called for one of the leaders, Edward B. Pusey. See OXFORD MOVEMENT and ERASTIANISM.

Putative Author: The fictional author of a work, supposedly written by someone other than its actual author. Lemuel Gulliver is the *putative author* of his *Travels,* not Jonathan Swift; Tristram Shandy is the *putative author* of his *Life and Opinions,* not Laurence Sterne. When an author uses a NOM DE PLUME, he merely hides his identity behind an assumed name, but when he uses a *putative author,* he creates a character who writes the book. Washington Irving merely hid his name when he signed the *Sketch Book* as "Geoffrey Crayon," but he created a *putative author* who wrote and signed Diedrich Knickerbocker's *History of New York.* See POINT OF VIEW, NARRATOR, and PERSONA.

Pyrrhic: A FOOT of two unaccented syllables (˘ ˘); the opposite of SPONDEE (´ ´). Common in CLASSICAL POETRY, the *pyrrhic* is unusual in English VERSIFICATION and is not accepted as a FOOT at all by some prosodists since it contains no accented syllable. Fowler states that the English *pyrrhic* is represented chiefly by double ANACRUSIS, as *O my* in

$$\breve{O} \ \widrecheck{my} \mid \acute{M}ar\widehat{i} \mid \acute{on}'s \ \breve{a} \mid \acute{bonny} \mid \acute{lass}.$$

Q

Quadrivium: In the medieval university curriculum, the four subjects leading to the M. A. degree: arithmetic, music, geometry, and astronomy. See SEVEN LIBERAL ARTS, THE.

Quantitative Verse: Verse whose basic RHYTHM is determined by QUANTITY, that is, duration of sound in utterance. CLASSICAL POETRY was *quantitative,* as English poetry has been ACCENTUAL-SYLLABIC. However, a number of English poets have experimented with *quantitative verse* forms, among them Campion, Sidney, Spenser, Coleridge, Tennyson, Longfellow, and Lanier. A few of the CLASSICAL *quantitative* forms occasionally are used in English, among them ALCAICS, CHORIAMBICS, ELEGIACS, HENDECASYLLABICS, SAPPHICS. See METER.

Quantity: In classical PROSODY, the fundamental rhythmic unit, *quantity* is the relative length of time required to utter a syllable. In Greek and Latin VERSIFICATION a syllable was considered long if it contained a long vowel or a short vowel followed by two consonants; otherwise, it was considered short, except for a few vowels and syllables which varied in duration between these limits and were called common. A long syllable was roughly the equivalent of two short syllables in duration; or a long syllable may be thought of as equivalent to a quarter note in music and a short syllable to an eighth. While duration is unquestionably a quality in English VERSIFICATION, the distinguishing and determining rhythmic pattern of English appears to be ACCENTUAL-SYLLABIC, so that the RHYTHMS which a skillful poet gains from the control of *quantity* or duration are merely subsidiary or complimentary to the fundamental RHYTHMS of regularly recurring ACCENT. See METER, ACCENT, ACCENTUAL-SYLLABIC VERSE, STRESS.

Quarterly Review, The: A British Tory critical JOURNAL founded in 1809. See EDINBURGH REVIEW.

Quarto: A BOOK SIZE designating a book whose SIGNATURES result from sheets folded to four leaves or eight pages. See BOOK SIZES.

Quaternion: A literary work with a set or sets of fours forming a basic part of its STRUCTURE. *Quaternion* usually implies several interlocking sets of fours. Floyd Stovall, for example, calls "The Bells," by Poe, a *quaternion,* because it consists of four parts, describes four bells, made of four metals, and represents four stages in a man's life.

Quatorzain: A STANZA or POEM of fourteen lines. The term, however is not now specifically applied to the SONNET (though of course the SONNET is a fourteen-line form) but is usually reserved for poems which do not otherwise conform to one or another of the SONNET patterns.

Quatrain: A STANZA consisting of four VERSES. In its narrow meaning, the term is restricted to a complete poem consisting of four lines only, but in its broader sense it signifies any one of many four-VERSE STANZA forms. The possible RHYME-SCHEMES within the STANZA vary from an unrhymed *quatrain* to almost any arrangement of one-RHYME, two-RHYME, or three-RHYME lines. Perhaps the most common form is the *abab* sequence; other popular RHYME patterns are *aabb; abba; aaba; abcb.* A *quatrain* of this last pattern is quoted from Robert Burns:

> Ye flowery banks o' bonnie Doon
> How can ye blume sae fair?
> How can ye chant, ye little birds,
> And I sae fu' o' care?

Quibble: A PUN or play upon words, or especially a verbal device for evading the point at issue, as when debaters engage in *quibbles* over the interpretation of a question or term.

Quintain or **Quintet:** A STANZA consisting of five VERSES in any METER and with any RHYME-SCHEME.

Quip: A retort or sarcastic jest; hence any witty saying, especially a PUN or QUIBBLE.

R

Raisonneur: A CHARACTER in a DRAMA who is the level-headed, calm personification of reason and logical action. He is usually not closely connected to the central action, and he is in the play for one or more of three reasons: (1) to serve as a standard against which the actions of other CHARACTERS may be measured, (2) to articulate the questions in the audience's mind, as the CHORUS did in Greek DRAMA, and (3) to utter judgments on the CHARACTERS and their actions, thus serving as an author-SURROGATE. The *raison-*

neur was a very common character in the WELL-MADE PLAY of the nineteenth century. He plays a role somewhat like that of the CONFIDANT in a NOVEL.

Ratiocination: A systematic process of reasoning which proceeds from the examination of data to the formulation of conclusions. The term was given literary significance by Poe, who wrote several tales which he called "ratiocinative," among them "The Murders in the Rue Morgue," "The Gold Bug," "The Purloined Letter," "The Mystery of Marie Rogêt," and "Thou Art the Man." The introductory paragraphs of "The Murders in the Rue Morgue" manifest Poe's high respect for the type of mind which works in this way. In general, then, *ratiocination*, as a literary or critical term, signifies a type of writing which solves, through the application of logical processes, some sort of enigma. It was once commonly applied to the DETECTIVE STORY.

Rationalism: This term embraces related "systems" of thought (philosophical, scientific, religious) which rest upon the authority of reason rather than sense-perceptions, revelation, or traditional authority. In England the rationalist attitude, especially in the eighteenth century, profoundly affected religion and literature. The early humanists (see OXFORD REFORMERS) had insisted upon the control of reason, but their teachings had little effect upon prevailing religious thought until reinforced by the scientific thinking of the seventeenth century (Newton), although as early as 1624 Lord Herbert of Cherbury had drawn up certain general principles which he thought all existing religious factions could accept. By the end of the century the theologians were generally agreed that the most vital religious doctrines were deducible from reason or NATURE. The more conservative ones ("supernatural rationalists") insisted also upon the importance of revelation in addition, while the more radical "deists" (see DEISM) rejected revelation. The former group included Newton himself and the great philosopher John Locke. The "natural religion" arising from *rationalism* stressed reason as a guide and good conduct as an effect. Its three propositions were: (1) there is an omnipotent God, (2) he demands virtuous living in obedience to his will, (3) there is a future life where the good will be rewarded and the wicked punished. This creed was accepted both by radicals and conservatives. The stressing of reason made *rationalism* an ally of NEO-CLASSICISM, while the stressing of the potential power and good in human nature, as by Shaftesbury, led toward ROMANTICISM. For notices of some of the effects of *rationalism* upon literature, see DEISM, PRIMITIVISM, ROMANTICISM, SENTIMENTALISM, NEO-CLASSICISM, HUMANISM. See also CALVINISM, PURITANISM, and MYSTICISM for opposing attitudes.

Rationalize: A verb used to indicate a rather specious form of *ex parte* reasoning. An author is said "to *rationalize*" when, once having accepted a position, a belief, through some intuitive process or through some prejudice, he tries to justify his stand by some process of the mind. That is, writing is said to *rationalize* when the author reasons insincerely and with intellectual sophistry to justify a position prompted by his emotions rather than by his reason.

Realism: *Realism* is, in the broadest sense, simply fidelity to actuality in its representation in literature; a term loosely synonymous with VERISIMILITUDE; and in this sense it has been a significant element in almost every school of writing in human history. In order to give it more precise definition, however, one needs to limit it to the movement which arose in the nineteenth century, at least partially in reaction against ROMANTICISM, which was centered in the NOVEL, and which was dominant in France, England, and America from roughly mid-century to the closing decade, when it was replaced by NATURALISM. In this latter sense, *realism* defines a literary method, a philosophical and political attitude, and a particular kind of subject matter.

Realism has been defined as "the truthful treatment of material" by one of its most vigorous advocates, William Dean Howells, but the statement means little until the realist's concept of truth and his selection of materials are designated. Generally, the realist is a believer in PRAGMATISM, and the truth he seeks to find and express is a relativistic truth, associated with discernible consequences and verifiable by experience. Generally, too, the realist is a believer in democracy, and the materials he elects to describe are the common, the average, the everyday. Furthermore, *realism* can be thought of as the ultimate of middle-class art, and it finds its subjects in bourgeois life and manners. Where the romanticist transcends the immediate to find the ideal, and the naturalist plumbs the actual to find the scientific laws which control its actions, the realist centers his attention to a remarkable degree on the immediate, the here and now, the specific action, and the verifiable consequence. (See

NATURALISM for a further discussion of the distinctions among these three terms.)

The realist espouses what is essentially a MIMETIC THEORY OF ART, centering his attention in the thing imitated and asking for something close to a one-to-one correspondence between the representation and the subject. He usually has, however, a powerful interest in the audience to whom his work is addressed, feeling it to be his obligation to deal with it with absolute truthfulness. Furthermore, the realist is unusually interested in the effect his work has on the audience and its life (in this respect he tends toward a PRAGMATIC THEORY OF ART); George Eliot, in Chapter XVII of *Adam Bede* (a classic statement of the intention of the realist), expresses her desire that her pictures of common life and average experience should knit more tightly the bonds of human sympathy among her readers. Howells, concerned with his audience of young ladies, felt so strongly the obligation not to do them moral injury that he shut the doors of his own works to most of the aspects of life connected with passion and sex.

The realist eschews the traditional patterns of the NOVEL. In part the rise of *realism* came as a protest against the falseness and sentimentality which the realist thought he saw in romantic FICTION. Life, he felt, lacked symmetry and PLOT; FICTION which truthfully reflected life should, therefore, avoid symmetry and PLOT. Simple, clear, direct prose was the desirable vehicle, and objectivity on the part of the novelist the proper attitude. The central issues of life tend to be ethical—that is, issues of conduct. FICTION should, therefore, concern itself with such issues, and—since selection is a necessary part of any art—select with a view to presenting these issues accurately as they affect men and women in actual situations. Furthermore, the democratic attitudes of the realist tended to make him value the individual very highly and to praise CHARACTERIZATION as the center of the NOVEL. Hence, he had a great concern for the effect of action upon character, and a tendency to explore the psychology of the actors in his stories. In Henry James, perhaps the greatest of the realists, this tendency to explore the inner selves of characters confronted with complex ethical choices earned for him not only the title of "father of the PSYCHOLOGICAL NOVEL" but also "biographer of fine consciences."

The surface details, the common actions, and the minor catastrophes of a middle-class society constituted the chief subject matter of the movement. Most of the realists avoided situations with tragic or cataclysmic implications. Their tone was often comic, frequently satiric, seldom grim or somber. Their general attitude was broadly optimistic, although James is a great exception.

Although aspects of *realism* appeared almost with the beginnings of the English NOVEL, for they are certainly present in Defoe, Richardson, Fielding, Smollett, Jane Austen, Trollope, Thackeray, and Dickens, the realistic movement found its effective origins in France with Balzac, in England with George Eliot, and in America with Howells and Mark Twain. Writers like Arnold Bennett, John Galsworthy, and H. G. Wells in England; and Henry James, Edith Wharton, Ellen Glasgow, Sinclair Lewis, John O'Hara, John P. Marquand, and Louis Auchincloss in America kept and are keeping the realistic tradition alive in the contemporary NOVEL.

It should be emphasized, however, that no single realistic NOVEL exemplifies all the characteristics that are listed in this article. In general, though, the realistic NOVEL tends toward the directions here indicated. See NATURALISM, ROMANTICISM.

Realistic Comedy: Any COMEDY employing the methods of REAL-ISM, but particularly the COMEDY developed by Jonson, Chapman, Middleton, and other Elizabethan and Jacobean dramatists. It is opposed to the ROMANTIC COMEDY; in fact it appeared more or less as a protest against the ROMANTIC COMEDY of the Elizabethans. It reflects the general reaction in the late 1590's against Elizabethan ROMANTICISM and extravagance as well as an effort to produce an English COMEDY after the manner of classical COMEDY. This *realistic comedy* deals with London life, is strongly satirical and sometimes cynical in tone, is interested in both individuals and types of character, and rests upon an observation of contemporary life. The appeal is intellectual and the tone coarse. This COMEDY is sometimes treated as COMEDY OF MANNERS, various subclasses being distinguishable in Jacobean plays. It became especially popular in the reign of James I. The COMEDY OF HUMOURS was a special form representing the first stage of the development of important *realistic comedy*. Jonson's *The Alchemist* and Middleton's *A Trick to Catch the Old One* are typical Jacobean *realistic comedies*. Though in the main Shakespeare represents the tradition of ROMANTIC COMEDY, some of his plays, including the comic SUBPLOT of the *King Henry IV* plays, are realistic in technique. The RESTORATION COMEDY OF

MANNERS, though chiefly a new growth, owes something to this earlier form, and one RESTORATION dramatist (Shadwell) actually wrote COMEDY of the Jonsonian type.

Realistic Novel: A type of NOVEL that places a strong emphasis on the truthful representation of the actual in FICTION. See REALISM.

Realistic Period in American Literature, 1865–1900:   In the period between the end of the Civil War in 1865 and the dawn of the twentieth century, modern America was born and grew to a lusty although not always happy or attractive adolescence. The Civil War had been, at least in part, a struggle between the concept of agrarian democracy and that of industrial and capitalistic democracy, and the result of the Northern victory was the triumphant emergence of industrialism. This industrialism was to bring great mechanical and material advances for the nation but it was also to bring great difficulties in the form of severe labor disputes, economic depression, and strikes that erupted in violence; its capitalistic aspect was to produce a group of powerful and ruthless moneyed men who have gone down in history as the "robber barons"; its application to politics, particularly in the rapidly developing great cities, was to produce "bossism" and a form of political corruption known by Lincoln Steffens' phrase, "the shame of cities." The impact of invention and industrial development was tremendous. The greatest advances were made in communications; the Atlantic cable was laid in 1866, the transcontinental railroad completed in 1869, the telephone invented in 1876, the automobile with the internal-combustion engine being manufactured by the 1890's. By the last two decades of the century many thoughtful men had begun to march under various banners declaring that somewhere and somehow the promise of the American dream had been lost—they often said "betrayed"—and that drastic changes needed to be made in order to recapture it. The Populist Party, the Grange, Henry George's "single tax," and the socialism of the American intellectual were all reflections of a disillusionment with American life never before widespread in the nation.

Intellectually, too, the average American was living in a new world, although he did not always realize it. The impact of Darwin, Marx, Comte, Spencer, and others advancing a scientific view of man sharply at variance with the older religious view was cutting from beneath the thoughtful American—even while he vehemently denied it—his old certainty about his perfectibility and about the inevitability of progress. The passing by 1890 of the physical frontier removed from his society a natural safety valve that had acted to protect him against the malcontents and the restless in his world; now he must absorb them and adjust to the fact of their presence; no longer could they seek virgin land on which to build their notions of a world. The rapid growth of education and the rise of the mass-circulation MAGAZINE, paying its way by advertising, created a mass audience for his authors, and the passage in 1891 of the International Copyright Act protected foreign authors from piracy in America and by the same token protected the native literary product from being undercut by PIRATED EDITIONS of foreign works.

In poetry the field appeared to be held by a group of sweetly singing but sentimental imitators of the English Romantics—Stedman, Stoddard, Hovey, Aldrich—but, in fact, three new and authentic poetic voices were raised in the period: Walt Whitman's in his democratic chant cast in experimental rhythmic poetry; Sidney Lanier's in his moral statements couched in experimental musical poetry; and Emily Dickinson's in her gnomic utterances cast in witty variations on traditional forms. Toward the close of the century Stephen Crane raised a haunting but strident voice in sparse experimental VERSE that was close to that of the IMAGISTS of the twentieth century, and Edwin Arlington Robinson published his first volume.

On the stage the older melodramatic habits held and the "star system" subordinating play and players to a "name" actor continued to fill the American theater with spectacle but little meaning. American DRAMA saw little that was new and felt only slight impacts of the new European PROBLEM PLAYS before the end of the century. James A. Herne's *Margaret Fleming* demonstrated a realistic promise that was largely unrealized. *Uncle Tom's Cabin* and *Rip Van Winkle* continued to dominate the American boards.

In FICTION, however, the new turbulence, the growing skepticism and disillusionment found an effective voice. The developing mass audience was served by LOCAL-COLOR WRITING, which filled the popular MAGAZINES, and by the HISTORICAL NOVEL, which had a great upsurge of popularity as the century drew toward a close. But in the work of Mark Twain, of William Dean Howells, and of Henry James the greatest contributions of the age were made. In the works of these men and of lesser writers—largely from the Middle West—REALISM was formulated as a literary doctrine and practiced as an art form which came to dominate the American literary scene. William James's PRAGMATISM not only expressed the mood of the *Realistic Period*, it also shaped its literary expression, an expression that became increasingly critical of American life as the century drew toward its end.

By the 1890's a cynical application of Darwinism to social structures, together with an acceptance of Nietzsche's doctrine of the superman and of Emile Zola's concept of the experimental NOVEL, resulted in a NATURALISM markedly different from anything America had previously known. The publication of Theodore Dreiser's *Sister Carrie* in 1900 told, perhaps more clearly than any historical document could have, that a new America had grown from the travail of the post-Civil War period. See REALISM, *Outline of Literary History*.

Realistic Period in English Literature, 1870–1914: In the latter portion of the reign of Queen Victoria and during the reign of Edward, the reaction to ROMANTICISM, which had had its beginnings fairly early in Victoria's reign, reached its peak in full-fledged REALISM and by the beginning of the First World War had itself begun to come under attack. This fact brings into question the customary division of the literature of England in the nineteenth century, a division in which ROMANTICISM is considered to dominate until 1832, after which time VICTORIAN literature holds sway until the end of the century. The early portion of Victoria's reign saw a continuance and a gradual weakening of ROMANTICISM (see EARLY VICTORIAN AGE); whereas the LATE VICTORIAN AGE witnessed the arrival of a literary movement that was to reach its fruition and pass into the early years of its decline in the EDWARDIAN AGE.

The last three decades of the nineteenth century saw the great parliamentary contests between Gladstone and Disraeli, the rise of the concept of British imperialism, and a growth in British sophistication and cosmopolitanism. Intellectually, the serious Englishman began to feel the impact of the scientific revolution which distinguished nineteenth-century thought. Newton's mechanics, Darwin's evolution, Marx's view of history, Comte's view of society, Taine's view of literature—each in its way chipped away at the complacency and the optimism that had characterized the early years of the Victorian rule. Foreign writers began to be widely read—Zola, Balzac, Flaubert, Maupassant, Sudermann, Ibsen, Tolstoi, Chekhov, Turgenev. By the turn of the century a reaction to Victorian life and to complacent earnestness was being expressed, notably in the

Rebuttal

work of DECADENTS like Oscar Wilde, Ernest Dowson, and Aubrey Beardsley. A full-fledged revolt against the mores and standards of the Victorian world marked the early years of the twentieth century. Politically, the protest of writers like Carlyle and Ruskin gave way to a full embracing of Fabian socialism in writers like William Morris and the young George Bernard Shaw. The imperial adventure of the Boer War (1899–1902) was hailed by many as a proper extension of the empire and at the same time it raised grave doubts.

In POETRY, the voices of the great Victorians, Tennyson and Browning, were still heard, but a new poetry, interested in FRENCH FORMS and lacking in "moral earnestness," was present in Swinburne and the DECADENTS. Hardy, Kipling, Yeats, and Bridges were to do distinguished work before the beginning of the First World War, but of the group only Kipling would have felt at home in the England of Victoria's early reign.

In DRAMA, the French stage and Ibsen combined to offer examples of REALISM. The LITTLE THEATER MOVEMENT got under way in England in the 1890's, about the same time that the CELTIC RENAISSANCE was enlivening the Irish stage. The PROBLEM PLAY established itself as a serious and respectable form in the works of A. W. Pinero, H. A. Jones, and John Galsworthy. In the last decades of the century Wilde's wit and the LIGHT OPERAS of Gilbert and Sullivan brightened the English theater, while the witty wisdom of G. B. Shaw's plays enlightened most of the period. Under the impact of REALISM the British stage abandoned Shakespeare for a life of its own.

In the serious ESSAY Arnold, Huxley, Spencer, and Pater explored a variety of topics with earnestness and force, but it was the NOVEL in which the age found its fullest expression. A few writers like Kipling and Stevenson continued a romantic vein, but George Eliot, Thomas Hardy, George Meredith, George Gissing, Joseph Conrad, John Galsworthy, Arnold Bennett, H. G. Wells, and Samuel Butler established a realistic mode for the NOVEL strong enough to make it the point against which the SYMBOLISTS of the next age launched their attacks. See REALISM, EDWARDIAN AGE, LATE VICTORIAN AGE, and *Outline of Literary History*.

Rebuttal: A term borrowed from debating procedure and signifying a rejoinder or reply to an argument; particularly it is a final summing up of answers to the arguments of the opposition.

Recantation

Recantation: A PALINODE, a formal repudiation of something done or written earlier. *The Canterbury Tales* ends with a *recantation* of Chaucer's "enditynges of worldly vanitees . . . [and tales] that sownen into synne."

Recension: A copy of a text which incorporates the most plausible readings taken by critical editing from several sources. The word literally means "survey," and a *recension* is a critical text established through a survey of all surviving sources for such a text. It has been most often applied to texts of materials existing in manuscript sources, such as Biblical texts. In this sense *The New English Bible* may be called a *recension*.

Recognition Plot (or **Scene**): A *recognition plot* is one in which the principal REVERSAL or PERIPETY results from the acquisition by one of the characters of knowledge which was previously withheld (either by the CHARACTERS in the play or STORY or by the author in constructing the PLOT) and which, now known, results in a decisive change of course for the character. In *Oedipus Rex,* considered by Aristotle the finest example of a *recognition plot,* the King, seeking the one whose crime has brought on the national calamity in order to banish him, at last discovers that he has killed his father and married his mother. In James's *The Ambassadors* Lambert Strether discovers the true nature of the liaison between Chad and Madame de Vionnet, with the result that his whole course of action is changed. A *recognition plot* may result in either TRAGEDY or COMEDY. A DETECTIVE STORY, for instance, is sometimes said to have a *recognition plot* used as an end in itself, in that the entire purpose of the PLOT is to have the PROTAGONIST (the detective) come into knowledge ("whodunit") which he did not possess at the beginning of the story. The SCENE in a DRAMA, a NOVEL, or a SHORT STORY in which the recognition occurs is called a *recognition scene*. See DRAMATIC STRUCTURE.

Redaction: A revision or editing of a MANUSCRIPT. The purpose of *redaction* is to express appropriately writing inappropriately phrased or stated in a wrong form. Sometimes, too, the term implies simply a digest of a longer piece of work, or a new version or edition of an older piece of writing. Malory's *Le Morte Darthur* is a *redaction* of many of the Arthurian stories.

Reductio ad absurdum: A "reducing to absurdity" to show the falsity of an ARGUMENT or position. As a method of ARGUMENT or PERSUASION this is a process which carries to its extreme, but logical, conclusion some general statement. One might say, for instance, that the more sleep one takes the more healthy one is, and then, by the logical *reductio ad absurdum* process, someone would be sure to point out that, on such a premise, he who has sleeping sickness and sleeps for months on end is really in the best of health.

Redundant: Characterized by the use of superfluous words. As a critical term *redundant* is applied to a literary STYLE marked by verbiage, an excess of REPETITION, pleonastic expression. (See PLEONASM, TAUTOLOGY.) The use of REPETITION and PLEONASM may, on occasion, be justified by a desire to secure EMPHASIS, but redundancy differs from these rhetorical devices in that it is usually applied to the superfluous, the unjustified REPETITION which springs from carelessness or ignorance. Old Polonius is made the doddering old man he is largely through the redundancies of his expression:

> Madam, I swear I use no art at all.
> That he is mad, 'tis true; 'tis true 'tis pity;
> And pity 'tis 'tis true; a foolish figure;
> But farewell it, for I will use no art.
> Mad let us grant him, then; and now remains
> That we find out the cause of this effect,
> Or rather say, the cause of this defect,
> For this effect defective comes by cause;
> Thus it remains and the remainder thus.

Reform Bill of 1832: This important liberal enactment of the English Parliament was proposed in 1830 and passed in 1832 with the support of King William IV and the Whig Party under Earl Grey over the strong opposition of Wellington. The measure denied Parliamentary representation to 56 "rotten" boroughs, provided representation for 156 new communities, and extended the voting power to include large numbers of the middle classes hitherto denied the ballot; it did not, however, give the franchise to the laborers. It was the beginning of a series of reform measures which followed during the next decade, including the suppression of slavery in the British colonies (1833); the curbing of commercial monopoly; a lessening of pauperism; a liberalization of the marriage laws; and great expansion and extension of public educational facilities. These events stimulated the idealism of many of the authors of the time,

Refrain

some of whom were active agitators for reform, and affected profoundly the spirit of literature in the Victorian period. Carlyle and Ruskin in their lectures and ESSAYS; Dickens, Disraeli, Mrs. Gaskell, Kingsley, and George Eliot in their NOVELS; and Hood, Tennyson, and Mrs. Browning in their POEMS reflect the new aspirations aroused by these humanitarian movements and the subsequent efforts for further reforms in social, political, and educational realism. The Reform Bill of 1867, passed by the Conservatives under pressures from the Liberals, further extended the franchise. Democratic representation was carried still further by the Reform Bill of 1884, extending suffrage to nearly all men. In 1918 suffrage was extended to all men and to women over thirty, and in 1928 to all persons over twenty-one. See CHARTISM, INDUSTRIAL REVOLUTION.

Refrain: A group of words forming a phrase or sentence and consisting of one or more lines repeated at intervals in a poem, usually at the end of a STANZA.

Refrains are of various types. First and most regular is the use of the same line at the close of each STANZA (as is common in the BALLAD). Another, less regular form, is that in which the *refrain* line (or lines) recurs somewhat erratically throughout the STANZA —sometimes in one place, sometimes in another. Again a *refrain* may be used with a slight variation in wording at each recurrence, though here it approaches the REPETEND. Still another variety of the *refrain* is the use of some rather meaningless phrase which, by its mere repetition at the close of STANZAS presenting different ideas and different moods, seems to take on a different significance upon each appearance—as in Poe's "Nevermore" and William Morris's "Two red roses across the moon." Poets have made so much of the *refrain*, have wrought so many variations in FORM and manner, as to have greatly enriched English verse.

Regionalism: A quality in literature which is the product of its fidelity to a particular geographical section, accurately representing its habits, speech, manners, history, folklore, or beliefs. In one sense, the test of *regionalism* is that the action and personages of a NOVEL, a SHORT STORY, or a DRAMA that is called regional cannot be moved, without major loss or distortion, to any other geographical setting. Thomas Hardy in his portrayal of life in Wessex wrote regional NOVELS. The LOCAL-COLOR WRITING in America in the last third of the nineteenth century was a form of *regionalism*. Arnold

Bennett's novels of the Five Towns are markedly regional. The literature of the recent American South has been regional in large part. In this century a concept of *regionalism* much more complex and philosophically deeper than that of nineteenth-century *regionalism*, has developed, partly as the result of the work of cultural anthropologists and sociologists (notably Howard W. Odum), and has expressed itself in literature through the conscious seeking out in the local and the particular of those aspects of the human character and of the human dilemma common to all men in all ages and places. In this respect the work of Willa Cather, Ellen Glasgow, William Faulkner, and Robert Penn Warren has gained great distinction. See LOCAL-COLOR WRITING.

Relief Scene: A SCENE in a TRAGEDY, usually as a part of the FALLING ACTION, whose purpose is to provide emotional relaxation for the audience. See DRAMATIC STRUCTURE.

Religious Drama: A term applied to the DRAMA of the Middle Ages, when its relations to the church and to religious subject matter was very great. See MEDIEVAL DRAMA, MYSTERY PLAY, MIRACLE PLAY, MORALITY PLAY.

Relique: An old spelling for "relic," something which survives. The famous use of the term in literature is in the title of Bishop Percy's printed collection of old ballads: *Reliques of Ancient English Poetry* (1765).

Renaissance: This word, meaning "rebirth," is commonly applied to the movement or period which marks the transition from the medieval to the modern world in Western Europe. Special students of the movement are inclined to trace the impulse back to the earlier *Renaissance* of the twelfth and thirteenth centuries and to date the full realization or effects of *Renaissance* forces as late as the eighteenth century. In the usual sense of the word, however, *Renaissance* suggests especially the fourteenth, fifteenth, sixteenth, and early seventeenth centuries, the dates differing for different countries (the English *Renaissance,* for example, being a full century behind the Italian *Renaissance* in its flowering). The break from medievalism was gradual, some *Renaissance* attitudes going back into the heart of the medieval period and some medieval traits persisting well into or even through the *Renaissance.* Yet the fact that a break *was* effected is the essential thing about the *Renaissance,* and the change when completed was so radical a one that "medieval" on the one hand and *Renaissance* or "modern" on the other imply a sharp contrast.

It is best to regard the *Renaissance* as the result of a new emphasis upon and a new combination of tendencies and attitudes already existing, stimulated by a series of historical events. It resulted from new forces arising within the old order, with attempts to effect some kind of adjustment between traditional allegiances and modern demands. So it was an age of compromise, a chief aspect of which was a noble but difficult and confusing endeavor to harmonize a newly interpreted Christian tradition with an ardently admired and in part a newly discovered tradition of pagan CLASSICAL culture.

The new humanistic learning (see HUMANISM) which resulted from the rediscovery of CLASSICAL literature is frequently taken as the beginning of the *Renaissance* on its conscious, intellectual side, since it was to the treasures of classical culture and to the authority of classical writers that the man of the *Renaissance* turned for inspiration. Here the break with medievalism was inescapable. In medieval society, man's interests as an individual were subordinated to his function as an element in a social unit (see FEUDALISM); in medieval theology man's relation to the world about him was largely reduced to a problem of adapting or avoiding the circumstances of earthly life in an effort to prepare his soul for a future life. But the *Renaissance* man had caught from his glimpses of CLASSICAL culture a vision of human life quite at odds with these attitudes. The Hellenistic spirit (see HEBRAISM) had taught him that man, far from being a groveling worm, was a glorious creature, capable of infinite individual development in the direction of perfection, and set in a world it was his not to despise but to interrogate, explore, and enjoy.

The individualism implied in this view of life exerted a strong influence upon English *Renaissance* life and literature, as did many other facts and forces; such as: the Protestant Reformation, itself in part an aspect of the *Renaissance* in Germany; the introduction of printing (see PRINTING, INTRODUCTION INTO ENGLAND), leading to a commercial market for literature; the great economic and political changes leading to the rise of democracy, the spirit of nationalism, an ambitious commercialism, opportunities for individuals to rise above their birth economically and politically; the revitalized university life; the courtly encouragement of literature; the new geography (discovery of America); the new astronomy (Copernicus, Galileo); and the growing "new science" which made man and nature the results of natural and demonstrable law rather than a mysterious group of entities subject to occult powers.

The period in English literature generally called the *Renaissance* is usually considered to have begun a little before 1500 and to have lasted until the COMMONWEALTH INTERREGNUM. It consisted of the EARLY TUDOR AGE (*ca.*1500–1557), the ELIZABETHAN AGE (1558–1603), the JACOBEAN AGE (1603–1625), the CAROLINE AGE (1625–1642). In the early period, English authors felt the impact of CLASSICAL learning and of foreign literatures, together with the sudden, although painful, release from the authority of the church. The new world lying to the west was transforming England into a trading nation no longer at the periphery of the world but at its very crossroads. During the reign of Elizabeth England reached status as a world power; its DRAMA and its POETRY attained great heights in the work of men like Spenser, Sidney, and Shakespeare. By the time that James came to the throne, a reaction was beginning to set in, expressed through a growing cynicism, a CLASSICAL dissatisfaction with the extravagance and unbounded enthusiasm of the sixteenth century, a tendency toward melancholy and DECADENCE. As the conflict of PURITAN and CAVALIER grew in intensity, these elements grew also. And by the time Charles lost his head, the PURITANISM which was itself a major outgrowth of the intense individualism of the *Renaissance* had spelled an end to most of its literary greatness. Yet Cromwell had as Latin Secretary the last of the great English *Renaissance* men, John Milton, who was to produce his greatest work in the hostile world of the NEO-CLASSICAL RESTORATION. For details about the *Renaissance* in England, see EARLY TUDOR AGE, ELIZABETHAN AGE, JACOBEAN AGE, CAROLINE AGE, HUMANISM, ELIZABETHAN DRAMA, and the *Outline of Literary History*.

Repartee: A quick, ingenious response or rejoinder; a retort aptly twisted; conversation made up of brilliant witticisms, or, more loosely, any clever reply; also anyone's facility and aptness in such ready wit. The term is borrowed from fencing terminology. Sydney Smith, Charles Lamb, and Oscar Wilde are figures important in literature famous for their command of *repartee*. An instance of *repartee* may be cited from an Oxford account of the meeting of "Beau" Nash and John Wesley. According to this tradition the two met on a narrow pavement. Nash was brusque. "I never make way for a fool," he said insolently. "Don't you? I always do," responded Wesley, stepping to one side.

Repetend: A poetical device marked by a REPETITION or partial REPETITION of a word, phrase, or clause more or less frequently throughout a STANZA or POEM. *Repetend* differs from REFRAIN in that the REFRAIN usually appears at predetermined places within the poem whereas the chief poetic merit of the *repetend* is the element of pleasant surprise it is supposed to bring to the reader through its irregular appearance. A further difference from the REFRAIN lies in the fact that the *repetend* only partially repeats whereas the REFRAIN usually repeats in its entirety a whole line or combination of lines. Both Coleridge and Poe make frequent use of the *repetend*. An example from Poe's *Ulalume* is quoted, with some of the *repetends* italicized:

> The skies *they were* ashen *and* sober:
> *The leaves they were* crisped *and sere—*
> *The leaves they were* withering *and sere;*
> *It was* night in the lonesome October
> Of my most immemorial year;
> *It was* hard *by the* dim lake *of Auber,*
> *In the* misty mid region *of Weir—*
> *It was* down *by the* dank tarn *of Auber,*
> *In the* ghoul-haunted woodland *of Weir.*

Repetition: A rhetorical device reiterating a word or phrase, or rewording the same idea, to secure EMPHASIS. *Repetition* used carelessly (see TAUTOLOGY, PLEONASM) is unpleasantly noticeable. Employed by deliberate design, it adds force and clarity to a statement. Particularly effective in PERSUASION, *repetition* is a favorite form with orators. The use of the REPETEND or REFRAIN in verse, a use essentially based on *repetition*, makes this rhetorical method more obvious than is usual in prose. One of the most notable examples is, of course, Poe's "The Bells." *Repetition* as a stylistic and poetic device gives pleasure by arousing, by satisfying, or by producing surprise by failing to satisfy a sense of expectancy. In the broadest sense, *repetition* is present in RHYME of all kinds, in METER, and in STANZA forms. It appears to be an inescapable element of POETRY. Whitman, for example, who eschews *repetition* in the form of RHYME, METER, or STANZA, employs it widely in his elaborate verbal and grammatical PARALLELISMS. See REFRAIN, REPETEND, ANAPHORA, PLEONASM.

Requiem: A CHANT embodying a prayer for the repose of the dead; a DIRGE; a solemn mass beginning as in *Requiem aeternam dona eis, Domine* ("Give eternal rest to them, O Lord"). The following lines are an example from Matthew Arnold's *Requiescat:*

> Strew on her roses, roses
> And never a spray of yew!
> In quiet she reposes;
> Ah, would that I did too!

Resolution: The events which follow the CLIMAX in a PLOT. See FALLING ACTION, for which it is a synonym, and PLOT and DRAMATIC STRUCTURE.

Resolved Stress: A term used interchangeably with HOVERING STRESS and DISTRIBUTED STRESS. See DISTRIBUTED STRESS.

Restoration Age: The restoration of the Stuarts in the person of Charles II in 1660 has given a name to a period of literary history embracing the latter part of the seventeenth century. The fashionable literature of the time reflects the reaction against PURITANISM, the receptiveness to French influence, and the dominance of the CLASSICAL point of view in criticism and original compositions. The revival of the DRAMA, under new influences and theories, is an especially interesting feature of the *Restoration Age*. The COMEDY OF MANNERS was developed by such writers as Etherege, Wycherly, and Congreve; the HEROIC DRAMA by such writers as Dryden, Howard, and Otway. Dryden was the greatest poet of the period, although no one equaled Milton, whose greatest works came in the 1660's and 1670's. John Locke, Sir William Temple, and Samuel Pepys were, in their differing ways, the major prose writers after John Bunyan. See NEO-CLASSIC PERIOD and *Outline of Literary History.*

Restraint: A critical term applied to writing which holds in decent check the emotional elements of a given situation. Great literature, FICTION and POETRY especially, makes frequent use of emotion, but distinguishes itself from tawdry writing in that the emotional qualities of the situation are held in reserve. Psychologically it is true that mankind attributes greater strength and force of character to the person who gives the impression of holding something back than to the person who pours forth all his feelings and sensibilities—or to an outburst in spite of previously demonstrated restraint, as with Lear on the heath. In fact, it is often *restraint* in emotional situations which marks the work of great artists.

Revenge Tragedy: A form of TRAGEDY made popular on the Elizabethan stage by Thomas Kyd, whose *Spanish Tragedy* is an early example of the type. It is largely SENECAN in its inspiration and technique. The theme is the revenge of a father for a son or *vice versa*, the revenge being directed by the ghost of the murdered man, as in *Hamlet*. Other traits often found in the *revenge tragedies* include the hesitation of the hero, the use of either real or pretended insanity, suicide, intrigue, an able scheming villain, philosophic soliloquies, and the sensational use of horrors (murders on the stage, exhibition of dead bodies, etc.). Examples of the type are Shakespeare's *Titus Andronicus,* Marston's *Antonio's Revenge,* Shakespeare's *Hamlet, Hoffman* (author not certain, but attributed to Henry Chettle), and Tourneur's *Atheist's Tragedy.* See SENECAN TRAGEDY, TRAGEDY OF BLOOD.

Reversal: The change in fortune for the PROTAGONIST in a dramatic or fictional PLOT; the PERIPETY. See PERIPETY, DRAMATIC STRUCTURE.

Review: A notice of a current book or play, published in a PERIODICAL. It is important to distinguish between a *review* and a piece of serious CRITICISM. The *review* announces a work, describes its subject, discusses its method and its technical qualities, and examines its merit when it is compared with other similar works; its function is to give its reader an accurate idea of the book under consideration, in order that he may decide whether he wishes to read it or not. The CRITIC, on the other hand, usually writes about works which have some standing and which are not brand new, judging them by critical standards which are either consciously formulated or implied in the critical article. The boundary line between the two forms is very uncertain in actual practice, however. For example, Poe's *review* of Hawthorne's *Twice-Told Tales* fits almost perfectly the description here given and yet it is one of the major critical documents in American literary history. On the other hand, the critical quarterlies often carry pieces that are ostentatiously CRITICISM and yet remain at the core merely journalistic *reviews*.

Review is also used in the titles of PERIODICALS to indicate the presence in the journal both of critical ARTICLES and of ARTICLES on current affairs; for example, the *North American Review*, the *Saturday Review*, the *Edinburgh Review*, the *Kenyon Review*. See CRITICISM, TYPES OF.

Revolutionary Age in American Literature, 1765–1790: In the period between the Stamp Act in 1765 and the formation of the Federal Government in 1789, American writers were, by and large, engaged in nonbelletristic pursuits. Poetry was largely NEO-CLASSICAL, with the influence of Pope dominating, although strains of early ROMANTICISM, notably those associated with the GRAVEYARD SCHOOL and with a renewed appreciation of wild NATURE, were felt. Trumbull, Freneau, Hopkinson, Dwight, and Barlow sang a patriotic strain in varied FORMS, often burlesque and satiric. The first play written by an American and acted in America, Godfrey's *The Prince of Parthia*, was performed in 1767, and the stage grew to be an increasing influence on American art outside of New England. In Philadelphia and New York it was particularly important and, after 1773, it was a significant aspect of Southern life through the theater at Charleston. Much of the prose writing of the age was polemical, like that of Thomas Paine, Samuel Adams, and Hamilton and Madison (*The Federalist* papers). The first American novel, *The Power of Sympathy*, by William Hill Brown, was published in 1789. But the two major prose writers of the period were Franklin, with his *Autobiography*, and Thomas Jefferson, whose *Declaration of Independence* has certainly proved to be one of the most influential pieces of writing in human history. See REVOLUTIONARY AND EARLY NATIONAL PERIOD IN AMERICAN LITERATURE and *Outline of Literary History*.

Revolutionary and Early National Period in American Literature, 1765–1830: The period in American history between the Stamp Act and the triumph of the "second revolution" represented by the ascendancy of Jacksonian democracy was the time of the establishment of the new nation. A time of beginnings, it saw the first strong reaction to British rule in the response to the Stamp Act in 1765, the First Continental Congress in 1774, the beginnings of armed rebellion in 1775, the *Declaration of Independence* in 1776, the surrender of Cornwallis in 1781, the Constitutional Convention in 1787, the establishment of a Federal Government in 1789, the founding of the Library of Congress in 1800, and in 1812–1814 a second successful war with England. In 1820 the Missouri Compromise, following by twelve years the abolition of the importing of slaves, established a pattern of political compromise over the issue of slavery; in 1823 America asserted its dominance in the New World through the Monroe Doctrine. In 1829 Andrew Jackson, as seventh president of the nation, brought backwoods egalitarianism into triumph over the conservative Federalism which for a while had dominated the early life of the young land.

It was a time of literary beginnings as well. It fell into two relatively distinct ages, that of the Revolution, 1765–1790, and that of the Federalists, 1790–1830. During this time the faint and imitative voices of the Revolutionary poets—Brackenridge, Freneau, and Hopkinson—and the HARTFORD WITS gave way before the calm strength of Bryant's verses. By 1827, Poe had published *Tamerlane*. In 1767 Thomas Godfrey's *Prince of Parthia*, the first American play to be acted, was performed, and American playwriting was established, although it was to be highly imitative of English DRAMA and largely lacking in literary value throughout the period. In 1789 the first American novel, *The Power of Sympathy*, by William Hill Brown, was published. Charles Brockden Brown, the first American novelist of marked ability, flourished briefly between 1798 and 1801; his *Wieland* (1798) was a distinguished piece of American GOTHIC. Before 1830 the career of James Fenimore Cooper, America's first major novelist, was well launched; his first significant novel, *The Spy*, appeared in 1821, and the first of the "Leatherstocking Tales" in 1823. Washington Irving, writing with urbane wit and Addisonian grace, became the first truly successful American prose writer, gaining international fame, particularly for his *Knickerbocker's History* (1809) and his *Sketch Book* (1820). The first major American magazine that was to have a long history was established in 1815, *The North American Review*.

In 1830 America was a young nation, fully established, rawboned and robust and self-confident, but possessed of a great internal problem, slavery, which was just beginning to put the Federal Union to a serious test. Those who were to produce the important literary works of the nation's first major artistic period had already been born and many were already at work. See FEDERALIST AGE IN AMERICAN LITERATURE, REVOLUTIONARY AGE IN AMERICAN LITERATURE, and *Outline of Literary History*.

Revue: A light musical entertainment without connected PLOT and consisting of a variety of SONGS, dances, CHORUSES, and SKITS. Satiric comment on contemporary personalities and events forms a characteristic element as does the effort to impress by a spectacular display of magnificence in setting and scenery.

Rhetoric: The body of principles and theory having to do with the presentation of facts and ideas in clear, convincing, and attractive language. *Rhetoric* as an art has had a long career in the curricula of ancient and modern schools. Along with grammar and logic it made up the basic TRIVIUM of medieval academic study. Before this, such ancients as Aristotle, who wrote a *rhetoric* about 320 B.C.; Quintilian, whose *Institutio Oratoria* (about A.D. 90) long served as the background for study even in the more modern days of Oxford and Cambridge; Longinus, who wrote an *Art of Rhetoric* (about A.D. 260), and Aphthonius (about A.D. 380) gave the subject a code and organization which have persisted throughout the centuries. The actual founder of *rhetoric* is said to be Corax of Syracuse, who in the fifth century B.C. stipulated certain fundamental principles for public argument and laid down five divisions for a speech: PROEM, NARRATIVE, ARGUMENT, remarks, and PERORATION or conclusion. For a period the sophists emphasized the importance of *rhetoric* for its own sake—deftness, skill, and cleverness in performance being rated above soundness and truth of argument.

To the ancients the aim of *rhetoric* was to give effectiveness to public speech, to ORATORY. According to the Aristotelian conception *rhetoric* was a manner of effectively organizing material for the presentation of truth, for an appeal to the intellect through speech, and was distinct from POETICS, a manner of composition presenting ideas emotionally and imaginatively. At one time the sophists and others so exalted *rhetoric* that it threatened to become little more than a system of public discussion whereby, rightly or wrongly, by fair means or foul, a point was carried. It was, as Isocrates once noted, "the art of making great matters small, and small things great." This tendency has given to modern ears the suggestion of oratorical emptiness which we so often associate with the word "rhetorical."

During the Middle Ages *rhetoric* was continued as a serious study through its place in the TRIVIUM, and the intricate rhetorical systems kept alive an interest in the forms of expression.

In England the RENAISSANCE brought little that was new to *rhetoric* though such books as Sir Thomas Wilson's *The Arte of Rhetorique* (1553) and George (or Richard) Puttenham's *Arte of English Poesie* (1589) did much to popularize the best practice of the early CLASSICAL writers on the subject. In modern education *rhetoric* as a subject by itself has largely disappeared though, of course, it still is respected as a phase of study in "English" courses and persists in debating and oratorical contests. The great number of rhetorical terms included in this Handbook shows, perhaps as clearly as any other testimony, the basic importance of rhetorical principles in their relation to literature.

Rhetorical Accent: The ACCENT resulting from the placement of STRESS as determined by the meaning or intention of the sentence; used in METRICS in opposition to METRICAL ACCENT, in which the prosodic pattern of the line determines the placement of STRESS. See ACCENT.

Rhetorical Figures of Speech: FIGURES OF SPEECH which are departures from customary or standard uses of language to achieve special effects without changing the basic meaning of the words. Compare with TROPE; see FIGURES OF SPEECH.

Rhetorical Question: A question propounded for its rhetorical effect and not requiring a reply or intended to induce a reply. The *rhetorical question* is most used in PERSUASION and in ORATORY, the principle supporting the use of the *rhetorical question* being that since its answer is obvious and usually the only one possible, a deeper impression will be made on the hearer by raising the question than by the speaker's making a direct statement. The too frequent use of this device imparts a tone of artificiality and insincerity to discourse. Pope's lines from "The Rape of the Lock" illustrate the use of *rhetorical questions* for MOCK HEROIC effect:

> Was it for this you took such constant care
> The bodkin, comb, and essence to prepare?
> For this your locks in paper durance bound?
> For this with tort'ring iron wreath'd around?
> For this with fillets strain'd your tender head,
> And bravely bore the double loads of lead!
> Gods! shall the ravisher display your hair,
> While the fops envy, and the ladies stare?

Rhyme: Similarity or identity of sound existing between accented syllables occupying corresponding positions within two or more lines of VERSE. The correspondence of sound is based on the *vowels and succeeding consonants* of the accented syllables, which must, for a perfect *rhyme*, be preceded by different consonants. That is, "fan" and "ran" constitute perfect *rhymes* because the vowel and succeeding consonant sounds are identical and the preceding consonants ("f" and "r") are different. *Rhyme*, in that it is based on this correspondence of sounds, is related to ASSONANCE and ALLITERATION, but is unlike these two forms both in construction and in the fact that it is commonly used at stipulated intervals, whereas ASSONANCE and ALLITERATION are likely to range with relative freedom through various positions.

Rhyme is more than a mere ornament or device of VERSIFICATION. It performs valuable functions. It affords pleasure through the sense impression it makes. The ear of the reader recognizes a sound already echoing in his consciousness and the accord the two similar sounds set up is likely, if the poet has deftly rhymed, to bring the reader a sensuous gratification. The recurrence of *rhyme* at regular intervals helps to establish the form of the STANZA. *Rhyme* serves to unify and distinguish divisions of the POEM since it is likely that the *rhyme* sounds followed in one STANZA—the Spenserian for instance—will be changed when the next STANZA is started. This principle at once gives UNITY to the one STANZA and marks it off as separate from the next, affording a sense of MOVEMENT to the poem as a whole. The fact that these qualities as well as others reside in *rhyme* will be granted when we recall how commonly folklore and the play of children—to take only two instances—resort to *rhyme* to make memorizing easy.

The types of *rhyme* are classified according to two schemes: (1) as to the position of the rhymed syllables in the line, and (2) as to the number of syllables in which the identity of sound occurs.

On the basis of the position of the *rhyme*, we have: (1) END RHYME, much the most common type, which occurs at the end of the VERSE; (2) INTERNAL RHYME (sometimes called LEONINE RHYME), which occurs at some place after the beginning and before the closing syllables; (3) BEGINNING RHYME, which occurs in the first syllable (or syllables) of the VERSE.

On the basis of the number of syllables presenting similarity of sound, we have: (1) MASCULINE RHYME, where the correspondence of sound is restricted to the final accented syllable as "fan" and "ran." This type of *rhyme* is generally more forceful, more vigorous than those following. (2) FEMININE RHYME, where the correspondence of sound lies in *two* consecutive syllables, the second of which is unstressed, as in "lighting" and "fighting." This is sometimes called *double rhyme.* FEMININE RHYME is used for lightness and delicacy in movement. (3) TRIPLE RHYME, where the correspondence of sound lies in *three* consecutive syllables, as in "glorious" and "victorious." TRIPLE RHYME has been used for serious work—such as Thomas Hood's "Bridge of Sighs"—but much more frequently it is reserved for humorous, satirical verse, for the sort of use Byron makes of it in his satiric poems, and Ogden Nash in his comic ones.

While at one time or another most poets have been responsible for poor *rhymes*, have violated consciously one or another of the rhyming customs, still these CONVENTIONS persist. Some of them may be mentioned here:

1. Syllables which are spelled differently but which have the same pronunciation (such as "rite" and "right") do not make acceptable *rhymes.*

2. A true *rhyme* is based on the correspondence of sound in *accented* syllables as opposed to unaccented syllables. "Stating" and "mating" thus make a good *rhyme,* and for the same reason, "rating" and "forming" make a bad *rhyme* since the correspondence is between unaccented syllables.

3. For a true *rhyme* all syllables *following* the accented syllable must *rhyme,* as is the case, for instance, with "fascinate" and "deracinate." According to this rule "fascinate" and "deracinating" would not be true *rhyme* because of the difference between the last syllables.

4. It is well to avoid repetition of the same vowel sounds in different *rhymes* which occur near each other. For instance "stone" and "bone" are good rhymes as are also "home" and "tome" but a QUATRAIN composed of those four *rhymes* would usually be condemned as weak because of the repetition of the long *o* throughout. Of course, like all rules, this may be violated when there is a special reason for doing so.

5. Conversely to 4 above, it should be noted that there should not be too great a separation between *rhyme*-sounds since such separation will result in a loss of effect. A *rhyme* occurring in the first line and the sixth line, for instance, is a strain on the reader's attention.

6. It is permissible, when not done too frequently, to allow a *rhyme* to fall on an unaccented syllable. There is a certain variety coming from the rhyming of "free" and "prosperity," for instance, which justifies its use occasionally.

Rhyme and the importance it enjoys in modern VERSIFICATION are comparatively modern developments. The ancient Greek and Latin poetry was not rhymed; our earliest English verse (*Beowulf* is an example) was not based on *rhyme*. Historians of the subject generally credit the development of *rhyme* to ceremonials within the Catholic Church and suggest that the priests made use of *rhyme* as a device to aid the worshipers in their singing and memorizing of the ritualistic procedure. *Dies Irae* is an example of one of the earliest rhymed SONGS of the Church.

Among contemporary poets a tendency to use imperfect *rhymes*, substituting ASSONANCE, CONSONANCE, and DISSONANCE for true *rhymes*, is widespread; and most present-day poets take interesting liberties with the traditional "rules" for *rhyme* cited in this article. See ASSONANCE, DISSONANCE, CONSONANCE, SLANT RHYME.

Rhyme Royal: A seven-line IAMBIC PENTAMETER STANZA rhyming *ababbcc*. The name has been said to derive from its employment by the Scottish King James I; but since Chaucer and other predecessors of James had used *rhyme royal* extensively it must be attributed to James, if at all, as an honor in recognition of the fact that a king wrote VERSE rather than that he originated the pattern. Chaucer used *rhyme royal* in the *Parlement of Foules*, the *Man of Law's Tale*, the *Clerk's Tale*, and *Troilus and Criseyde*, and found the form adapted to his best descriptive, NARRATIVE, and reflective manners. Some other poets who have written in *rhyme royal* are Lydgate, Hoccleve, Dunbar, Skelton, Wyatt, Shakespeare, and Morris. In recent times the poet who has used it with most success has perhaps been John Masefield, who wrote both *The Widow in the Bye Street* and *Dauber* in *rhyme royal*. The last stanza of Shakespeare's *Rape of Lucrece* is a good example:

> When they had sworn to this advised doom,
> They did conclude to bear dead Lucrece thence;
> To show her bleeding body thorough Rome,
> And so to publish Tarquin's foul offence:
> Which being done with speedy diligence,
>   The Romans plausibly did give consent
>   To Tarquin's everlasting banishment.

Rhyme-scheme: The pattern, or sequence, in which the RHYME sounds occur in a STANZA or POEM. *Rhyme-schemes*, for the purpose of analysis, are usually presented by the assignment to each similar sound in a STANZA of the same letter of the alphabet. Thus, the pattern of the SPENSERIAN STANZA is *ababbcbcc*. An example of another RHYME pattern follows:

Rhythm

The time I've lost in wooing,	*a*
In watching and pursuing	*a*
The light that lies	*b*
In woman's eyes,	*b*
Has been my heart's undoing.	*a*
Tho' wisdom oft has sought me,	*c*
I scorned the lore she brought me,	*c*
My only books	*d*
Were woman's looks,	*d*
And folly's all they've taught me.	*c*

—Thomas Moore

Here *wooing, pursuing, undoing* all have the same RHYME and are arbitrarily marked with the symbol *a; lies, eyes* are alike and assigned the symbol *b; sought me, brought me, taught me* are all alike and given the symbol *c; books* and *looks* are alike and are set down as symbol *d.* Thus finally the *rhyme-scheme* of the stanza is *aabbaccddc.*

Rhythm: The passage of regular or approximately equivalent time intervals between definite events or the recurrence of specific sounds or kinds of sounds or the recurrence of stressed and unstressed syllables is called *rhythm.* Man has a seemingly basic need for such regularity of recurrence, or for the effect produced by it, as laboratory experiments in psychology have demonstrated and as one can see for himself by watching a crew of men digging a deep ditch or hammering a long stake or by listening to CHANTEYS and work SONGS.

In both PROSE and POETRY the presence of rhythmic patterns lends both pleasure and heightened emotional response to the listener or reader, for it establishes for him a pattern of expectations and rewards him with the pleasure of a series of fulfillments or gratifications of expectation. In POETRY three different elements may function in a pattern of seemingly regular temporal occurrence: QUANTITY, ACCENT, and number of syllables (see METER). In English poetry, the rhythmic pattern is most often established by a combination of ACCENT and number of syllables. This pattern of a fairly regular number of syllables with a relatively fixed sequence of stressed and unstressed syllables lends itself to certain kinds of basic rhythmic analysis in English VERSIFICATION. The *rhythm* may be "marching" or DUPLE—that is, involve one stressed and one unstressed syllable, as in IAMBS and TROCHEES. Or it may be "dancing" or TRIPLE—that is, involve one stressed and two unstressed syllables, as in DACTYLS and ANAPESTS. It may be RISING—that is, beginning with unstressed and ending with stressed syllables, as in IAMBS and ANAPESTS. Or it may be FALLING—that is, beginning with stressed and ending with unstressed syllables, as in TROCHEES and DACTYLS. Other kinds of *rhythm* than these are, of course, possible (and even common) in English verse, as witness SPRUNG RHYTHM and FREE VERSE, as well as the *rhythm* used in OLD ENGLISH VERSIFICATION or that used by Walt Whitman.

In PROSE, despite the absence of the formal regularity of pattern here described for VERSE, CADENCE is usually present and in impassioned PROSE it often establishes definite patterns of rhythmic recurrence. See PROSE RHYTHMS, QUANTITY, ACCENT, METER, SCANSION.

Riddle: The modern *riddle* has its more dignified ancestor in the *riddles* of medieval literature. Based on Latin prototypes, *riddles* became an important "type" of the vernacular literatures of Western Europe, including Old English. The *riddles* of Aldhelm (seventh century), though written in Latin, are English in tone, and the Exeter Book (eleventh century) contains an interesting collection of nearly a hundred *riddles* in Old English. They are of unknown authorship (formerly ascribed to Cynewulf). The interpretation of the *riddles* is sometimes obvious, sometimes obscure; but the descriptive power of the POETRY is often high, and the IMAGERY is fresh and picturesque. The new moon is a young viking sailing the skies; the falcon wears the bloom of trees upon her breast; the swan is a wandering spirit wearing a "noiseless robe." The swan, the falcon, the helmet, the horn, the hen, the onion, beer, the Bible manuscript, the storm-spirit, and many other objects connected with war, seamanship, nature, religion, and everyday life, describe themselves by descriptive EPITHET, characteristic act, apt METAPHOR, and end with a "Tell me what I'm called." These *riddles* contain some of the best existing evidence of the use of external nature in the period and have been termed the most secular of all existing Old English literature.

Rime Couée: A TAIL-RHYME STANZA, one in which two lines, usually in TETRAMETER, are followed by a short line, usually in TRIMETER, two successive short lines rhyming—as, for example, *aabccb*, where the *a* and *c* lines are TETRAMETER and the *b* lines are TRIMETER. See TAIL-RHYME STANZA.

Rising Action: The part of a dramatic PLOT which has to do with the COMPLICATION of the action. It begins with the EXCITING FORCE,

gains in interest and power as the opposing groups come into CON-
FLICT (the HERO usually being in the ascendancy), and proceeds to
the CLIMAX or turning point. See DRAMATIC STRUCTURE.

Rising Rhythm: In METRICS, a FOOT in which the last syllable is
accented; thus, in English either the IAMBUS or the ANAPEST.
Coleridge illustrates *rising rhythm* in these lines:

> Iámbics márch from shórt to lóng.
>
> With a léap and a bóund the swíft Ánapests thróng.

Rocking Rhythm: In METRICS, a FOOT in which a stressed syllable
falls between two unstressed syllables, an AMPHIBRACH. *Rocking
rhythm* is illustrated in this line from Swinburne:

> The séarch, and | the sóught, and | the séeker, | —the sóul and |
> the bódy | that ís.

Rococo: In the history of European architecture the *rococo* period
follows the BAROQUE and precedes the NEO-CLASSIC, embracing in
time most of the eighteenth century. The style arose in France,
flourished on the Continent, but made little headway in England.
It was marked by a wealth of decorative detail suggestive of grace,
intimacy, playfulness. The fashion spread to furniture. It avoided
the grandiose, the serious, the "logical" effects. Since the style was
often regarded in England as a decadent phase of the RENAISSANCE
or BAROQUE styles, the term *rococo* has frequently been employed
in a derogatory sense to suggest the overdecorative or "impudently
audacious," and is not infrequently confused with the BAROQUE
(also unfavorably interpreted). In its older sense Swinburne uses
the term as the title of one of his love lyrics—one in which the
lover implores his three-day mistress not to forget their ardent but
brief love. A more discriminating reference to the earlier meaning
is found in Professor Friedrich Brie's phrase the *rococo* EPIC, as
applied to such pieces as Pope's *Rape of the Lock* and Gay's *Fan,*
in which the small luxuries of life, particularly of fashionable women,
are prominent sources of interest. See BAROQUE.

Rodomontade: Ostentatious bragging or blustering. Falstaff's famous description of his bold fight with the highwaymen is an example of *rodomontade,* as is his boastful, "There live not three good

men unhanged in England, and one of them is fat and grows old. . . ." So called after the braggart Moorish king Rodomonte in Ariosto's *Orlando Furioso*.

Roman à Clef: A NOVEL in which actual persons and events are presented under the guise of FICTION. Notable examples of the GENRE have been Aldous Huxley's *Point Counter-Point* and Ernest Hemingway's *The Sun Also Rises*. See FICTION.

Romance: This word was first used for Old French as a language *derived* from Latin or "Roman" to distinguish it from Latin itself (this meaning has now been extended so that any of the languages derived from Latin, such as Spanish or Italian, is called a Romance language). Later *romance* was applied to any work written in French, and as STORIES of knights and their deeds were the dominant form of Old French literature, the word *romance* was narrowed to mean such STORIES. The first Old French *romances* were translated from Latin and may have helped to fix the name *romance* upon them. For a further account of these early *romances*, see MEDIEVAL ROMANCE. Special modern uses of the word *romance* may be noted from the account in the *New English Dictionary:* "romantic FICTION"; "an extravagant FICTION"; a "fictitious NARRATIVE in PROSE of which the scene and incidents are very remote from those of ordinary life, especially of the class prevalent in the sixteenth and seventeenth centuries, in which the story is overlaid with digressions." In RENAISSANCE criticism the ROMANTIC EPIC was called simply *romance*. *Romance* is now frequently used as a term to designate a kind of FICTION that differs from the NOVEL in being more freely the product of the author's imagination than the product of an effort to represent the actual world with VERISIMILITUDE. In American literature, in particular, it has become fashionable to speak of the "tradition of the American novel" as being that of the *romance*, following distinctions between the two made by William Gilmore Simms, in *The Yemassee* (1835), and Hawthorne, in the prefaces to his novels, particularly *The House of the Seven Gables* (1851). See NOVEL, ROMANTIC NOVEL, ROMANTICISM, MEDIEVAL ROMANCE, METRICAL ROMANCE, ARTHURIAN LEGEND.

Romanesque: A term sometimes used to characterize writing which is fanciful or fabulous. It is more rarely used simply to denote the presence of a ROMANCE quality in a work.

Romantic Comedy: A COMEDY in which serious love is the chief concern and source of interest, especially the type of COMEDY developed on the early Elizabethan stage by such writers as Robert Greene and Shakespeare. Greene's *James the Fourth* represents the *romantic comedy* as Shakespeare found it and is supposed to have influenced Shakespeare in his *Two Gentlemen of Verona*. A few years later Shakespeare perfected the type in such plays as *The Merchant of Venice* and *As You Like It*. Characteristics commonly found include: love as chief motive; much out-of-door action; an idealized HEROINE (who usually masks as a man); love subjected to great difficulties; POETIC JUSTICE often violated; balancing of characters; easy reconciliations; happy ending. Shakespeare's last group of plays, the TRAGI-COMEDIES or "serene romances" (such as *Winter's Tale* and *Cymbeline*), are in some sense a modification of the earlier *romantic comedy*.

Romantic Criticism: A term sometimes used for the body of critical ideas which developed late in the eighteenth and early in the nineteenth century as a part of the triumph of ROMANTICISM over NEO-CLASSICISM. It accompanied and to some extent guided the revolt against the CLASSICAL attitudes of the eighteenth century, and was inspired in part by the necessity of "answering" conservative critics such as Francis Jeffrey, Sydney Smith, and William Gifford. The "artificial" character of Pope's poetic IMAGERY was attacked by W. L. Bowles, who in turn was "answered" by Lord Byron and others. New theories about the genius of Shakespeare were espoused by Coleridge and others: instead of being regarded as a "wild, irregular genius," who succeeded in spite of his violation of the "laws" of dramatic composition, his art was studied on the assumption that it succeeded because it followed laws of its own organism, which were more authentic than man-made "formal" rules. (See ORGANIC FORM.) This view harmonized with the new critical ideas as to the nature of the poetic IMAGINATION. The *romantic criticism* of Shakespeare thus led to the view that Shakespeare, like Nature, was infallible. "If we do not understand him, it is our fault or the fault of copyists or typographers" (Coleridge). Much extravagant Shakespeare "idolatry" followed in the wake of this attitude. Another aspect of *romantic criticism* was Wordsworth's theory of poetry as calling for simple themes drawn from humble life expressed in the language of ordinary life—a sharp reaction from the conventions of NEO-CLASSIC POETRY. In general the romantic critic saw art as an expression of the artist (the EXPRESSIVE THEORY OF ART), valued it as a living organism, sought its highest expressions among simple people, primitive cultures, and aspects of the world unsullied by artifice or by commerce with human society. See PRIMITIVISM; CULTURAL PRIMITIVISM; ROMANTICISM; CRITICISM, TYPES OF; and ORGANIC FORM.

Romantic Epic: A type of long NARRATIVE POEM developed by Italian RENAISSANCE poets (late fifteenth and sixteenth centuries) by combining the materials and something of the method of the MEDIEVAL ROMANCE with the manner and technique of the CLASSICAL EPIC. Such poets as Pulci, Boiardo, and Ariosto produced *romantic epics* which were like MEDIEVAL ROMANCES in stressing the love element, in their complicated and loose STRUCTURE, in the multiplicity of CHARACTERS and EPISODES, and in freedom of VERSE FORM. Yet they were like the Virgilian EPIC in their use of a formal INVOCATION, statement of theme, set speeches, formal descriptions, use of EPIC SIMILES, supernatural machinery, division into books, etc. Later, Tasso (*Jerusalem Delivered*, 1581) infused a strong tone of moral instruction and religious propaganda into the type. The method of ALLEGORY was also employed in the Italian *romantic epics*. The literary critics of the time were divided in their attitudes toward the new type of EPIC, the conservatives strongly opposing it because of its departure from CLASSICAL standards. The form proved generally popular with readers, however, and when Edmund Spenser came to write his ambitious English EPIC, he actually modeled his poem largely upon the *romantic epics* of Ariosto (*Orlando Furioso*, 1516) and Tasso. Thus *The Faerie Queene*, EPIC in its high patriotic purpose and in much of its technique, romantic in its chivalric atmosphere and Arthurian setting, became, by following the general method of Ariosto and Tasso, the great example in English literature of a *romantic epic*.

Romantic Novel: A type of NOVEL marked by strong interest in action and presenting EPISODES often based on love, adventure, and combat. The term ROMANTIC owes its origin to the early type of STORY embraced by the ROMANCE of medieval times, but with the march of time other elements have been added. The FABLIAU and the NOVELLA particularly have contributed qualities. A ROMANCE, in its modern meaning, signifies that type of NOVEL which is more concerned with action than with character, which is more properly

fictional than legendary since it is woven so largely from the IMAGI-
NATION of the author, which is read more as a means of escape from
existence than of familiarity with the actualities of life. The writers
of modern ROMANCE are too numerous to mention: Sir Walter Scott's
name may be allowed to represent the long list of romancers in English and American literature. In another sense *romantic novel* is
used interchangeably with ROMANCE, as a form relatively free of the
demands of the actual and thus able to reflect the imaginative truth
which its author perceives. See ROMANCE.

Romantic Period in American Literature, 1830–1865:   The period
between the "second revolution" of the Jacksonian Era and the
close of the Civil War in America saw the testing of the American
nation and its development by ordeal. It was an age of great westward expansion, of the increasing gravity of the slavery question,
of an intensification of the spirit of embattled sectionalism in the
South, of a powerful impulse to reform in the North. Its culminating
act was the trial by arms of the opposing views of the two sections
in a Civil War, whose conclusion certified the fact of a united nation dedicated to the concepts of industry and capitalism and philosophically committed to the doctrine of absolute egalitarianism. In
a sense it may be said that the three decades following the inaugura-
tion of Andrew Jackson as president in 1829 put to the test his
views of democracy and saw emerge from the test a secure union
committed to essentially Jacksonian principles.

   In literature it was America's first great creative period, a full
flowering of the romantic impulse on American soil. Surviving from
the FEDERALIST AGE were its three major literary figures: Bryant,
Irving, and Cooper. Emerging as new writers of strength and creative power were the novelists Hawthorne, Simms, Melville, and
Mrs. Stowe; the poets Poe, Whittier, Longfellow, Lowell, and
Whitman; the essayists and poets Thoreau, Emerson, Holmes; the
critics Poe, Lowell, and Simms. The South, moving toward a concept of Southern independence, advanced three distinguished
PERIODICALS, the *Southern Review,* the *Southern Literary Messenger,* and the *Southern Quarterly Review.* In the North the *Knickerbocker Magazine* and the *Democratic Review* joined the continuing
arbiter of Northern taste, the *North American Review,* and then were
followed by *Harper's Magazine* (1850) and the *Atlantic Monthly*
(1857). Between 1830 and 1855 the GIFT BOOKS and ANNUALS
proved to be remunerative markets for ESSAYS and TALES.

Romantic Period in American Literature

The POETRY of the period was predominantly romantic in spirit and form. Moral qualities were significantly present in the VERSE of Emerson, Bryant, Longfellow, Whittier, Lowell, and Thoreau. The sectional issues were debated in POETRY by Whittier and Lowell speaking for abolition, and Timrod, Hayne, and Simms speaking for the South. Poe formulated his Aristotelian theory of POETRY and in some fifty LYRICS practiced a symbolist VERSE that was to be, despite the charge of triviality by such contemporaries as Emerson, the strongest single poetic influence emerging from pre-Civil War America, particularly in its impact on European POETRY. Lowell wrote satiric VERSE in DIALECT. Whitman, beginning with the 1855 edition of *Leaves of Grass* was the ultimate expression in America of a POETRY organic in form and romantic in spirit, united to a concept of democracy that was pervasively egalitarian.

In the ESSAY and on the lecture platform the New England transcendentalists—Emerson, Thoreau, Margaret Fuller, and Alcott—carried the literary expression of philosophic and religious ideas to a high level. In critical ESSAYS, Lowell wrote with distinction, Simms with skill, and Poe with genius. Until 1850 the NOVEL continued to follow the path of Scott, with Cooper and Simms as its major producers. In the 1850's, however, emerged the powerful symbolic NOVELS of Hawthorne and Melville, and the effective PROPAGANDA NOVEL of Mrs. Stowe. Poe, Hawthorne, and Simms practiced the writing of SHORT STORIES throughout the period, taking up where Irving had left off in the development of the form. Humorous writing by A. B. Longstreet, George W. Harris, Artemus Ward, Josh Billings, and the early Mark Twain was establishing a basis for a realistic literature in the language of the common man, but it failed in this period to receive the critical attention it was later to have.

In the DRAMA the "star" system, the imitation of English "spectacle" DRAMA, and ROMANTIC TRAGEDY modeled on Shakespeare were dominant. Although N. P. Willis and R. M. Bird were successful dramatists, only George Henry Boker, with his *Francesca da Rimini*, displayed any distinctive literary talent in the theater. *Uncle Tom's Cabin* and *Rip Van Winkle* began stage careers that were to be phenomenally successful.

At the end of the Civil War a new nation had been born in the ordeal of war, and it was to demand and receive a new literature less idealistic and more practical, less exalted and more earthy, less consciously artistic and more direct than that produced in the age

463

when the American dream had glowed with greatest intensity and American writers had made a great literary period by capturing on their pages the enthusiasm and the optimism of that dream. See *Outline of Literary History.*

Romantic Period in English Literature, 1798–1870: In the period between the publication of *Lyrical Ballads* (1798) and the death of Dickens, English literature was dominated by the spirit of ROMANTICISM. One commonly used way for designating literary periods in English history is to call the AGE OF THE ROMANTIC TRIUMPH (1798–1832) the *Romantic Period* and to lump together the time between the death of Scott in 1832 and the end of the century as the VICTORIAN AGE, since Queen Victoria reigned through much of it. However, the romantic impulse which flowered with such spectacular force in 1798 remained the dominant literary impulse well into the 1860's; hence the divisions employed in this Handbook. (See REALISTIC PERIOD IN ENGLISH LITERATURE.)

The *Romantic Period* came into being during the Napoleonic Wars, and flourished during the painful economic dislocations which were their aftermath. It saw union with Ireland; it witnessed the suffering which was attendant upon the INDUSTRIAL REVOLUTION; it was torn by CHARTISM and the great debates centering around the REFORM BILL; it developed a sensitive humanitarianism out of witnessing the suffering of the masses; it both espoused and despised the doctrine of UTILITARIANISM. An industrial England was being born in pain and suffering. The throes of developing democracy, the ugliness of the sudden growth of cities, the prevalence of human pain, the blatant presence of the "profit motive"—all helped to characterize what was in many respects "the best of times . . . the worst of times."

In the first half of the period, during the AGE OF THE ROMANTIC TRIUMPH, a philosophical ROMANTICISM based on value in the individual, on the romantic view of NATURE, and on an organic concept of art dominated the English literary mind. Optimism was the spirit of the times, although it was often an optimism closely associated with the impulse to revolt and with radical political reform. In the second half of the period, the EARLY VICTORIAN AGE, the impact of the INDUSTRIAL REVOLUTION was more immediately felt and the implications of the new science upon philosophy and religious belief began to be obvious. The romantic philosophy still held, and the spirit of ROMANTICISM permeated literature and much

Romanticism

of life, but it found itself seriously in conflict with much of the world it saw around it, and out of that conflict came a literature of doubt and questioning. If, for example, the attitudes of Coleridge and Shelley are compared with those of Carlyle—all three clearly romantics—the extent to which the ROMANTICISM of the earlier period was being qualified by the conditions of industrial England and was being used to test those conditions becomes obvious.

In POETRY the *Romantic Period* was a "golden age," rich with the sonorous voices of Wordsworth, Coleridge, Shelley, Keats, Byron, Tennyson, Arnold, and the Pre-Raphaelites, and enlivened by the harsher tones of Browning. It was a great age for the NOVEL, producing Godwin, Scott, Austen, the Brontës, Thackeray, Dickens, Trollope, and the early George Eliot. A period of serious critical and social debate in the ESSAY, it produced Carlyle, Ruskin, Macaulay, Arnold, and Newman. In the INFORMAL ESSAY, it produced Lamb, Hazlitt, Hunt, and De Quincey. Only in the DRAMA, bound by the PATENT THEATERS and a blind idolatry of Shakespeare and hampered by the "star" system, did the *Romantic Period* fail to produce work of true distinction; it was the weakest period in the English stage since Elizabeth I ascended the throne.

For the literary history of the period, see AGE OF THE ROMANTIC TRIUMPH, EARLY VICTORIAN AGE, and *Outline of Literary History*. See, also, ROMANTICISM.

Romantic Tragedy: Non-classical TRAGEDY. The term is used for such modern TRAGEDY as does not conform to the traditions or aims of CLASSICAL TRAGEDY. It differs from the latter in its greater freedom of technique, its wider scope of theme and treatment, its greater emphasis on CHARACTER (as compared with emphasis on PLOT), its looser STRUCTURE, its freer employment of IMAGINATION, its greater variety of STYLE, and its readiness to admit humorous and even GROTESQUE elements. ELIZABETHAN TRAGEDY is largely romantic, e.g., Shakespeare's. See CLASSICAL TRAGEDY; TRAGEDY; and CRITICISM, HISTORICAL SKETCH.

Romanticism: A MOVEMENT of the eighteenth and nineteenth centuries which marked the reaction in literature, philosophy, art, religion, and politics from the NEO-CLASSICISM and formal orthodoxy of the preceding period. *Romanticism* arose so gradually and exhibited so many phases that a satisfactory definition is not possible. The aspect most stressed in France is reflected in Victor Hugo's phrase "liberalism in literature," meaning especially the freeing of the artist and writer from the restraints and rules of the classicists and suggesting that phase of individualism marked by the encouragement of revolutionary political ideas. The poet Heine noted the chief aspect of German *romanticism* in calling it the revival of medievalism in art, letters, and life. A late nineteenth-century English critic, Walter Pater, thought the addition of strangeness to beauty (the neo-classicists having insisted upon order in beauty) constituted the romantic temper. An American transcendentalist, Dr. F. H. Hedge, thought the essence of *romanticism* was aspiration, having its origin in wonder and mystery. An interesting schematic explanation calls *romanticism* the predominance of IMAGINATION over reason and formal rules (CLASSICISM) and over the sense of fact or the actual (REALISM), a formula which recalls Hazlitt's statement (1816) that the CLASSIC beauty of a Greek temple resided chiefly in its actual form and its obvious connotations, while the "romantic" beauty of a GOTHIC building or ruin arose from associated ideas which the IMAGINATION was stimulated to conjure up. The term is used in many senses, a favorite recent one being that which sees in the romantic mood a psychological desire to escape from unpleasant realities.

Perhaps more useful to the student than definitions will be a list of romantic characteristics or "earmarks," though *romanticism* was not a clearly conceived system. Among the aspects of the "romantic" movement in England may be listed: SENSIBILITY; PRIMITIVISM; love of NATURE; sympathetic interest in the past, especially the medieval (see GOTHIC); MYSTICISM; individualism; ROMANTIC CRITICISM; and a reaction against whatever characterized NEO-CLASSICISM. Among the specific characteristics embraced by these general attitudes are: the abandonment of the HEROIC COUPLET in favor of BLANK VERSE, the SONNET, the SPENSERIAN STANZA, and many experimental VERSE FORMS; the dropping of the conventional POETIC DICTION in favor of fresher language and bolder figures; the idealization of rural life (Goldsmith); enthusiasm for the wild, irregular, or GROTESQUE in NATURE and art; unrestrained IMAGINATION; enthusiasm for the uncivilized or "natural"; interest in human rights (Burns, Byron); sympathy with animal life (Cowper); sentimental melancholy (Gray); emotional psychology in FICTION (Richardson); collection and imitation of popular BALLADS (Percy, Scott); interest in ancient Celtic and Scandinavian mythology and literature (see CELTIC REVIVAL); renewed interest in Spenser, Shakespeare, and Milton. Typical literary forms of the romantic writers include the LYRIC, especially the love LYRIC, the reflective LYRIC, the nature LYRIC (see NATURE), and the LYRIC of morbid melancholy (see GRAVEYARD SCHOOL); the SENTIMENTAL NOVEL; the METRICAL RO-MANCE; SENTIMENTAL COMEDY; the BALLAD; the PROBLEM NOVEL; the HISTORICAL NOVEL; the GOTHIC ROMANCE; the SONNET; and the CRITICAL ESSAY (see ROMANTIC CRITICISM).

Although the romantic movement in English literature had its beginnings or anticipations in the earlier eighteenth century (Shaftesbury, Thomson, Dyer, Lady Winchilsea), it was not till the middle of the century that its characteristics became prominent and self-conscious (Blair, Akenside, Joseph and Thomas Warton, Gray, Richardson, Sterne, Walpole, Goldsmith, and somewhat later Cowper, Burns, and Blake), while its complete triumph was reserved for the early years of the nineteenth century (Wordsworth, Coleridge, Scott, Southey, Byron, Shelley, Keats). A little later in the nineteenth century came the great romantic period in American literature (Bryant, Emerson, Lowell, Thoreau, Whittier, Hawthorne, Melville).

The last third of the nineteenth century witnessed the substitution of a soberer mood than prevailed earlier in the century, and although the late nineteenth century and the early twentieth century, both in England and America, have been marked by a sharp reaction against the romantic, especially the sentimental, spirit in literature, it is to be remembered that much late VICTORIAN literature was romantic and that the vitality of *romanticism* is evidenced by the great volume of romantic writing being produced in the twentieth century.

By way of caution it may be said that such descriptions of *romanticism* as this one probably overstress the distinction between *romanticism* and CLASSICISM or NEO-CLASSICISM, and cannot hope to resolve that confusion over what "romantic" means which Professor A. O. Lovejoy asserts has "for a century been the scandal" of literary history and criticism. As early as 1824 an effort to discover what the authorities meant by the term proved disappointing, and the succeeding century has increased the number of divergent, often contradictory, senses in which the term is employed. Some writers, like Professor Walter Raleigh and Sir Arthur Quiller-Couch, have even urged the desirability of abandoning the terms "romantic" and "classic," pointing out that their use adds to the critical confusion and tends to distort the facts of literary history and divert attention away from the natural processes of literary composition. Several have noted that Homer's *Odyssey*, for example, is cited by some as the very essence of the romantic, by others as a true exemplar of CLASSICISM. Professor Lovejoy, noting that the "romantic" movement has meant different things in different countries and that even in a single country "romantic" is often used in conflicting senses, proposes that the term be employed in the plural only, as a recognition of the various *romanticisms*. Even if the term "romantic" were always employed in the same sense and its characteristics could be safely and comprehensively enumerated, it would still be true that one could not use a single characteristic, like the love of wild scenery or the use of BLANK VERSE, as a "key" for classifying as romantic any single poem or poet.

Yet, viewed in philosophical terms, *romanticism* does have a fairly definite meaning for the student of literature. The term designates a literary and philosophical theory which tends to see the individual at the very center of all life and all experience, and it places him, therefore, at the center of art, making literature most valuable as an expression of his unique feelings and particular attitudes (the EXPRESSIVE THEORY OF ART) and valuing its accuracy in portraying his experiences, however fragmentary and incomplete, more than it values its adherence to completeness, UNITY, or the demands of GENRE. It places a high premium upon the creative function of the IMAGINATION, seeing art as a formulation of intuitive imaginative perceptions that tend to speak a nobler truth than that of fact, logic, or the here and now. It sees in NATURE a revelation of Truth, the "living garment of God," and often, pantheistically, a sensate portion of deity itself, and certainly a more suitable subject for true art than those aspects of the world sullied by man's artifice (CULTURAL PRIMITIVISM). It differs significantly from the literary movements which were to follow it, REALISM and NATURALISM, in where it finds its values. Employing the commonplace, the natural, the simple as its materials, it seeks always to find the Absolute, the Ideal, by transcending the actual, whereas REALISM finds its values in the actual and NATURALISM in the scientific laws which undergird the actual (see NATURALISM).

Ultimately, it must be admitted that the conflict of ideas and attitudes which occurred in the eighteenth century and which saw the triumph of *romanticism* over CLASSICISM, however much exaggerated in standard literary histories, did go a very long way toward the establishment of our modern democratic world, and where REALISM

Rondel

and NATURALISM are significantly different from *romanticism*, they are closer to it than they are to the CLASSICISM with which it broke. Wherever faith in the individual and in his freedom from rules, systems, or even from RATIONALISM appear, there one aspect of *romanticism* speaks. Contradictory as its attributes are and however true Professor Lovejoy's assertion that it should be spoken of always in the plural, *romanticisms* shape the controlling attitudes of the democratic world. See NATURALISM, REALISM, NEO-CLASSICISM, CLASSICISM, PRIMITIVISM, GOTHIC, ROMANTIC CRITICISM, ROMANTIC PERIOD IN ENGLISH LITERATURE, ROMANTIC PERIOD IN AMERICAN LITERATURE.

Romany: The language of the gypsies. It is a DIALECT form of the Indian branch of the Indo-Iranian languages, blended with many words and phrases from various European languages and spoken in many DIALECTS. A gypsy; or a descriptive way of designating anything pertaining to the gypsies. *Romany* ways and manners have been much written about by George Borrow.

Rondeau: A set French VERSE pattern, artificial but very popular with many English poets. Generally used for light and fanciful expression. The *rondeau* pattern consists characteristically of fifteen lines, the ninth and fifteenth being short lines—a REFRAIN. Only two RHYMES (exclusive of the REFRAIN) are allowed, the RHYME-SCHEME running *aabba aabc aabbac*. The *c*-RHYME here represents the REFRAIN, a group of words, usually the first half of the line, selected from the opening VERSE. The form divides itself into three STANZAS with the REFRAIN at the end of the second and third STANZAS. The VERSES most frequently consist of eight syllables. There is also a form of the *rondeau* which consists of twelve lines, ten using two RHYMES plus REFRAINS, rhyming *abba abc abbac*. Another, known as the *rondeau redoublé,* consists of six QUATRAINS rhyming *abab*, with the first four lines forming in succession the last lines of the second, third, fourth, and fifth QUATRAINS.

Rondel: A French VERSE FORM, a variant of the RONDEAU, to which it is related historically. It consists of fourteen or thirteen lines (depending on whether the two-line REFRAIN is kept at the close or simply one line). The RHYME-SCHEME most usual is *ab*baabab-abba*ab* (the italicized RHYMES here representing VERSES used as a REFRAIN and repeated in their entirety). As in the other French forms repetition of RHYME-words is not allowed. The *rondel* differs from the RONDEAU in two chief respects: the number of lines, and the use of complete (rather than partial) lines for the REFRAIN.

Round Character: A term used by E. M. Forster to designate a CHARACTER drawn with sufficient complexity to be able to surprise the reader without losing its credibility. A *round character*, Forster says, "has the incalculability of life about it." See CHARACTERIZATION, FLAT CHARACTER.

Roundel: A variation of the French RONDEAU pattern, generally attributed to Swinburne who wrote "A Century of Roundels" and gave the form its popularity. The *roundel* is characterized by its eleven-line form and the presence, in the fourth and eleventh lines, of a REFRAIN taken, as in the RONDEAU, from the first part of the first line. The RHYME-SCHEME (using *c* to indicate the refrain) is *abacbababac*. *Roundel* is also the Chaucerian spelling for RONDEL.

Roundelay: A modification of the RONDEL, a French LYRIC VERSE FORM. The *roundelay* is a simple POEM or SONG of about fourteen lines in which part of one line frequently recurs as a REFRAIN. The term may also mean the musical setting of a RONDEAU so that it may be sung or chanted as an accompaniment for a folk-dance.

Roundheads: During the English Civil War, the members of the Puritan or Parliamentarian party. See CAVALIER LYRISTS.

Rubáiyát: The plural of the Arabic word for QUATRAIN, hence a collection of four-line STANZAS. The best-known use of the word in English is in Edward FitzGerald's translation of *The Rubáiyát of Omar Khayyám*.

Rubáiyát Stanza: The STANZA that FitzGerald used for his translation of *The Rubáiyát of Omar Khayyám*. It is a QUATRAIN of IAMBIC PENTAMETER lines, rhyming *aaba*.

Rune: A character in a sort of alphabet developed about the second or third century by the Germanic tribes in Europe. A *boc* (modern "book") was a runic tablet of "beech" wood. Later, *runes* were carved upon stones, drinking horns, weapons, and ornaments. In very early times *rune* developed the special meaning of a character or sign or written formula which had magical power. *Runes* were used for charms, healing formulas, incantations, etc. The Norse god Odin is said to have been driven to insanity by the power of a *rune* sent to him by a certain maiden who was declining his love. Likewise, a *rune* came to mean any secret means of communication. Thus the Anglo-Saxon poet Cynewulf signed some of his poems by placing in runic characters in these poems a sequence of words the first letters of which spelled his name. Runic writing was very common in Anglo-Saxon England until gradually crowded out by the Latin alphabet used by the Christian missionaries. *Rune* may also mean a Finnish poem and (less accurately) an old Scandinavian poem. Emerson even used the word in the sense of "any SONG, POEM, or VERSE."

Run-on Lines: The carrying over of sense and grammatic structure from one VERSE to a succeeding one for completion. The opposite of END-STOPPED LINES. See ENJAMBEMENT.

S

Saga: In its strictest sense, applied to Icelandic or other Scandinavian stories of the medieval period recording the legendary and historical accounts of heroic adventure, especially of members of certain important families. The earlier Icelandic *sagas*, like the early Irish EPICS and ROMANCES, were in PROSE. There were also "mythological" *sagas*. The term came to be used for an historical legend developed by oral tradition till it was popularly accepted as true— a FORM lying between authentic history and intentional FICTION. This meaning is not confined to Scandinavian pieces, and the commonest meaning now for *saga* is a NARRATIVE having the characteristics of the Icelandic *sagas;* hence any traditional tale of heroic achievement or extraordinary or marvelous adventure. The best example of the true *saga* is that of Grettir the Strong, suggestive of the story of Beowulf. Others are included in the famous *Heimskringla,* from which Longfellow drew material for his *Saga of King Olaf.* John Galsworthy has used the term in the title of his story of the Forsytes, a series of novels called *The Forsyte Saga.*

Saints' Lives: Highly eulogistic accounts of the miraculous experiences of the saints; a kind of religious ROMANCE extremely popular in the medieval world. Chaucer's "Man of Law's Tale" in *The Canterbury Tales* is typical in everything except its literary excellence. See BIOGRAPHY.

Saint's Play: A medieval play based on the legend of some saint. See MIRACLE PLAY.

Sapphic: A stanzaic pattern deriving its name from the Greek poetess, Sappho, who wrote love LYRICS of great beauty about 600 B.C. The pattern consists of three VERSES of eleven syllables each (⌣ | ⌣ | ⌣ ⌣ | ⌣ | ⌣) called HENDECASYLLABICS and a fourth VERSE of five syllables (⌣ ⌣ | ⌣). The pattern has been frequently tried in English, but the demand for three SPONDEES in each STANZA results too often in distortion. Swinburne and Ezra Pound are generally conceded to have been the most successful modern writers of *sapphics*. A stanza from Swinburne is quoted:

> Then to | me so | lying a | wake a | vision
> Came with | out sleep | over the | seas and | touched me,
> Softly | touched mine | eyelids and | lips; and | I too,
>   Full of the | vision.

Sarcasm: A form of verbal IRONY, in which, under the guise of praise a caustic and bitter expression of strong and personal disapproval is given. *Sarcasm* is personal, jeering, intended to hurt, and is intended as a sneering taunt. See IRONY.

Satanic School: A phrase used by Southey in the "Preface" to his *Vision of Judgment* (1821) to designate the members of the literary group made up of Byron, Shelley, Hunt, and their associates, whose irregular lives and radical ideas—defiantly flaunted in their writings—suggested the term. They were not infrequently contrasted with the "pious" group of the LAKE SCHOOL—Wordsworth, Coleridge, and Southey. By a natural extension in the use of the term writers of more recent times who have attacked conventional moral standards sometimes have been spoken of as belonging to the *Satanic School* of literature.

Satanism: The worship of Satan, probably a survival of heathen fertility cults. In the twelfth century it gained strength through a secret rebellion against the Church. At its center is the Black Mass, an ugly and blasphemous PARODY of the Christian mass, with a nude woman on the altar with the Host sometimes being the ashes and blood of murdered children. It was revived during the reign of Louis XIV in France, and was again revived in the 1890's, when it attracted some literary attention. Interest in *Satanism,* or at least its literary expression, seems to be increasing. It is closely connected with witchcraft.

Satire: A literary manner which blends a critical attitude with HUMOR and WIT to the end that human institutions or humanity may be improved. The true satirist is conscious of the frailty of institutions of man's devising and attempts through laughter not so much to tear them down as to inspire a remodeling. If the critic simply abuses he is writing INVECTIVE; if he is personal and splenetic he is writing SARCASM; if he is sad and morose over the state of society he is writing IRONY or a JEREMIAD. As a rule modern *satire* spares the individual and follows Addison's self-imposed rule: to "pass over a single foe to charge whole armies."

Satire existed in the literature of Greece and Rome. Aristophanes, Juvenal, Horace, Martial, and Petronius are indicative of the rich satiric vein in CLASSICAL literature. Through the Middle Ages *satire* persisted in the FABLIAU and BEAST-EPIC. In Spain the PICARESQUE NOVEL developed a strong element of *satire*; in France Molière and Le Sage handled the manner deftly, and somewhat later Voltaire established himself as the arch-satirist of literature. In England, from the time of Gascoigne (*Steel Glass,* 1576) and Lodge (*Fig for Momus,* 1595) writers condemned the vices and follies of the age in VERSE and PROSE (Hall, Nash, Donne, Jonson). By the time of Charles I, however, interest in *satire* had declined, only to revive with the struggle between Cavaliers and Puritans. At the hands of Dryden the HEROIC COUPLET, already the favorite form with most English satirists, developed into the finest satiric VERSE FORM. The eighteenth century in England became a period of *satire;* POETRY, DRAMA, ESSAYS, CRITICISM, all took on the satirical manner at the hands of such men as Dryden, Swift, Addison, Steele, Pope, and Fielding. In the nineteenth century Byron and Thackeray were fine satirists.

Early American *satire* naturally followed English in STYLE. Before the Revolution, American *satire* dealt chiefly with the political struggle. Of the HARTFORD WITS Trumbull produced *M'Fingal,* a Hudibrastic *satire* on Tories. Hopkinson amusingly attacked the British in his *Battle of the Kegs* (1778). Freneau (*The British Prison Ship*) wrote the strongest Revolutionary *satire*. Shortly after the Revolution, the *Anarchiad* (VERSE) by Trumbull, Barlow, Humphreys, and Hopkins, and *Modern Chivalry* (FICTION) by Brackenridge, attacked domestic political difficulties and the crudities of our frontier. Irving's good-humored *satire* in *The Sketch Book* and *Knickerbocker's History*, Holmes' SOCIETY VERSE, Lowell's DIALECT poems (*Biglow Papers*), and Mark Twain's prose represent the general trend of American *satire* up to the twentieth century.

In the twentieth century English writers like G. B. Shaw, Noel Coward, Evelyn Waugh, and Aldous Huxley have maintained the satiric spirit in the face of the gravity of NATURALISM and the earnestness of SYMBOLISM. In America, Eugene O'Neill (on occasion), Edith Wharton, Sinclair Lewis, Kaufman and Hart, John P. Marquand, and Joseph Heller have commented critically upon man and his institutions.

Satire is fundamentally of two types, named for their most distinguished classical practitioners: *Horatian satire* is gentle, urbane, smiling; it aims to correct by gentle and broadly sympathetic laughter; *Juvenalian satire* is biting, bitter, angry; it points with contempt and moral indignation to the corruption and evil of men and institutions. Addison is a *Horatian* satirist, Swift a *Juvenalian* one.

For centuries the word *satire*, which literally means "a dish filled with mixed fruits," was reserved for long poems, such as the pseudo-Homeric *Battle of the Frogs and Mice*, the poems of Juvenal and Horace, *The Vision of Piers Plowman*, Chaucer's "Nun's Priest's Tale," Butler's *Hudibras*, Pope's *The Rape of the Lock*, Lowell's *A Fable for Critics*. Almost from its origins, however, the DRAMA has been suited to the satiric spirit, and from Aristophanes to Shaw and Noel Coward, it has commented with penetrating IRONY on human foibles. There was a notable concentration of its attention on Horatian *satire* in the COMEDY OF MANNERS of the RESTORATION AGE. But it has been in the fictional NARRATIVE, particularly the NOVEL, that *satire* has found its chief vehicle in the modern world. Cervantes, Rabelais, Voltaire, Swift, Fielding, Jane Austen, Thackeray, Mark Twain, Edith Wharton, Sinclair Lewis, Aldous Huxley, Evelyn Waugh, John P. Marquand, Joseph Heller, all have made extended fictional NARRATIVES the vehicles for a wide-ranging and powerfully effective satiric treatment of man and his institutions.

Scansion

In England, since 1841 *Punch* has maintained a high level of comic *satire*. In America, the *New Yorker* has demonstrated since 1925 the continuing appeal of sophisticated Horatian *satire*. The motion pictures, the plastic and graphic arts, and the newspaper comic strip and political cartoon have all been instruments of telling, satiric comment on human affairs.

For satiric methods, see IRONY, BURLESQUE, PARODY, SARCASM, INVECTIVE, INNUENDO.

Satiric Poetry: Verse treating its subject with IRONY or ridicule. (See SATIRE above.) The term is a loose one, since it characterizes method of treatment rather than content or FORM. Thus we may have a satiric EPIC (Pope's *Dunciad*) or a satiric LYRIC (Stephen Crane's *War Is Kind*). Perhaps the greatest masters of SATIRE in English poetry are Dryden, Pope, and Byron. In America, Lowell with his *Biglow Papers* and *A Fable for Critics* holds first place although both Emily Dickinson and Stephen Crane have written fine ironic VERSES.

Saturday Club: A club of literary and scientific people in and around Cambridge and Boston in the mid-nineteenth century, the members of which came together chiefly for social intercourse and good conversation, at irregular intervals. There were no bylaws. Some of the more famous members were: Emerson, Longfellow, Agassiz, Prescott, Whittier, and Holmes; among the frequent visitors were Hawthorne, Motley, and Sumner. Holmes paid tribute to the organization in verse (*At the Saturday Club*) and Dr. E. W. Emerson wrote an official history of the Club.

Satyr Play: The fourth and final play in the bill of TRAGEDIES in Greek DRAMA: so called because the CHORUS was made up of horse-tailed goat-men, called satyrs. The *satyr play* was intended to bring comic relief after the three TRAGEDIES which preceded it. It had the STRUCTURE of a TRAGEDY, subject matter from serious mythology, but was grotesquely comic in manner. Euripides' *Cyclops* is the only surviving *satyr play*.

Scald: Variant spelling for SKALD, an early Scandinavian POET. See SKALD.

Scansion: The dividing of VERSE into FEET by indicating ACCENTS and counting syllables to determine the METER of a poem. *Scansion*

is a means of studying the mechanical elements by which the POET
has established his rhythmical effects. The METER, once the scanning has been performed, is named according to the type and
number of FEET employed in a VERSE. The major types of METER,
explained elsewhere, are IAMBUS ($\smile$ $\diagup$), TROCHEE ($\diagup$ $\smile$), ANAPEST
($\smile$ $\smile$ $\diagup$), DACTYL ($\diagup$ $\smile$ $\smile$), SPONDEE ($\diagup$ $\diagup$), and PYRRHIC ($\smile$ $\smile$). A
verse of one foot (of any type) is called MONOMETER; of two feet,
DIMETER; of three feet, TRIMETER; of four feet, TETRAMETER; of five
feet, PENTAMETER; of six feet, HEXAMETER; of seven feet, HEP-
TAMETER; of eight feet, OCTAMETER. Thus a verse consisting of two
trochaic feet is called TROCHAIC DIMETER; of five iambic feet, IAMBIC
PENTAMETER; of six dactylic feet, DACTYLIC HEXAMETER, and so on.

Applied to a single STANZA of *The Eve of St. Agnes*, a scanning
would show (if we are pretty mechanical and are content to resort
to singsong for the sake of EMPHASIS and clearness) the following
ACCENTS and divisions into FEET:

> And still | she slept | an az | ure-lid | ded sleep |
>
> In blanch | ed lin | en, smooth | and lav | endered, |
>
> While he | from forth | the clos | et brought | a heap |
>
> Of can | died ap | ple, quince, | and plum, | and gourd; |
>
> With jel | lies sooth | er than | the cream | y curd, |
>
> And lu | cent syr | ops, tinct | with cin | namon; |
>
> Manna | and dates, | in ar | gosy | transferred |
>
> From Fez; | and spic | ed dain | ties, ev | ery one |
>
> From silk | en Sam | ar cand | to ce | dared Leb | a non. |

Such a mechanical marking of ACCENTS and dividing into FEET
discloses that the METER of the STANZA is predominantly composed
of one unaccented syllable followed by an accented syllable, and
this we have called above the IAMBIC FOOT. We next discover that
characteristically there are five of these FEET to the line, and a
five-foot line we have called PENTAMETER. We are now, as the
result of our scanning, prepared to state that the METER of *The
Eve of St. Agnes* is IAMBIC PENTAMETER. As the STANZA is scanned
above, there are only two obvious exceptions to this pattern:
(1) the first FOOT of the seventh VERSE consists of an accented
syllable preceding an unaccented (and is thus a TROCHEE) and,

(2) the ninth VERSE consists of six IAMBIC FEET instead of five (and is thus an HEXAMETER or an ALEXANDRINE). So, finally, we have found that our STANZA consists of eight IAMBIC PENTAMETER VERSES with a ninth VERSE which is an ALEXANDRINE—a pattern called the SPENSERIAN STANZA. *Scansion* is often considered to include the RHYME-SCHEME as well as the VERSE analysis. In that case we would say of the above STANZA that it rhymes *ababbcbcc*.

It should be noted that this mechanical system of *scansion*, which is almost universally employed in the analysis of English poetry, was borrowed entire from classical QUANTITATIVE VERSE, and does not always fit readily on the English ACCENTUAL-SYLLABIC rhythmic pattern. It obviously cannot be applied to SPRUNG RHYTHM or to FREE VERSE. An additional caveat is in order: the failure of a VERSE or a STANZA of English poetry to fit readily into a regular *scansion* pattern does not necessarily indicate ineptness on the part of the POET; it may indicate that he is constructing his POEM upon rhythmic patterns that do not readily lend themselves to such mechanical analysis. See METER, ACCENT, RHYTHM, ELISION, ANACRUSIS, TRUNCATION, CATALEXSIS, STRESS, SECONDARY STRESS.

Scenario: A skeleton outline of a DRAMA, which gives the sequence of actions that make up the PLOT and the successive appearances of the principal CHARACTERS. The PLOT of a DRAMA is itself sometimes called the *scenario*. A play written in a form ready for filming as a motion picture DRAMA is also called a *scenario*.

Scène à faire: A SCENE in a play so thoroughly prepared for that the author is obliged to write it. See OBLIGATORY SCENE, which is the English equivalent term.

Scenes (in a Novel): In the NOVEL which is dramatic, that is, presents its actions as they are imagined to occur rather than summarizes them in NARRATIVE EXPOSITION, there is a tendency for the author to construct his story in a sequence of self-explanatory *scenes,* similar in many respects to those of the DRAMA. This tendency in NOVELS using the SELF-EFFACING AUTHOR is sufficiently marked to result in the dramatic technique of the NOVEL being called the "scenic method." The construction of a typical chapter of a Henry James novel illustrates the "scenic method": such a chapter (it may be selected almost at random from *The Portrait of a Lady*) will usually open with a detailed description of SETTING and of the interior state of the CHARACTER through whom the action is being presented (Isabel Archer, in *The Portrait*); then, when everything has been well prepared for, the action and conversation are presented directly and in great detail, the action rising to a CLIMAX upon which the CURTAIN figuratively falls, such a CURTAIN being represented by the abrupt ending of the chapter. See SCENES (OF A DRAMA).

Scenes (of a Drama): The division of the ACT of a DRAMA into *scenes* is less logical or scientifically systematic even than the division of the play itself into ACTS. This is partly due to the lack of agreement as to what should constitute a *scene*. Sometimes the entrances and exits of important personages determine the beginning and ending of *scenes*, as in French DRAMA. In some plays a *scene* is a logical unit in the development of the action. Many English dramatists regard the clearing of the stage as the sign of a change of *scene*. Some authorities, however, think that not all stage-clearings or entrances and exits really indicate a new *scene*. Thus Sir Edmund Chambers (*Elizabethan Stage*) uses *scene* as "a continuous section of action in an unchanged locality." Theoretically, a well-managed *scene* should have a structure comparable to that of a play itself, with the five logical parts (see DRAMATIC STRUCTURE). The plays of Shakespeare, of course, do not conform to this requirement, though some of the *scenes* can be analyzed successfully on this basis. The most important principle in scene-construction, perhaps, is that of climactic arrangement. *Scenes* have been loosely classified on such varying principles as length, structural function, internal technique, external background. Thus there may be long *scenes* and short *scenes;* transitional *scenes,* expository *scenes,* development *scenes,* climactic *scenes,* relief *scenes,* and the like; messenger *scenes,* MONOLOGUE *scenes,* DIALOGUE *scenes,* ensemble *scenes,* forest *scenes,* battle *scenes,* balcony *scenes,* street *scenes,* garden or orchard *scenes,* court *scenes,* banquet-hall *scenes,* and chamber *scenes.*

Scheme: In RHETORIC an unusual arrangement or rearrangement of words in which the literal sense of the words is not modified by the arrangement. It is thus a pattern of words in which sound rather than sense is changed. Hence it is a RHETORICAL FIGURE OF SPEECH. See TROPE.

Scholasticism: The name is said to have come from the title *doctor scholasticus* applied to a teacher in the religious "schools" established

School of Night

in the ninth and tenth centuries. Although such doctors were supposed to teach the SEVEN ARTS, they became chiefly professors of logic. As developed a century or so later, *scholasticism* became a complicated system which relied upon logical methods in an effort to reconcile the tenets of Christianity with the demands of reason. The logical method of Aristotle was employed. It has been said that no problem was so difficult that the Schoolmen would not confidently attempt to solve it by syllogistic reasoning. Such speculative problems as the relations to one another of the persons of the Holy Trinity, the nature and attributes of God, and the relation of the finite to the infinite were treated.

Scholastic reasoning as applied by different men led to diverging views. The "first era" of *scholasticism* (twelfth century) marked the break from the freer reasoning of the earlier ("patristic") theologians, and includes Abelard, Bernard of Clairvaux, and Anselm, "father of scholasticism." The second era (thirteenth century) was the flourishing period, marked by the dominance of Aristotelian influence, and includes the two great Schoolmen Thomas Aquinas and Duns Scotus, heads of opposing groups known as "Thomists" and "Scotists." The third era (especially fifteenth century) marked the decline of *scholasticism,* when it became largely occupied with trivialities. This lost vitality made it an easy victim to the fresh and vigorous intellectualism of the RENAISSANCE, and *scholasticism* had lost its dominance by the early sixteenth century. Indeed, the great Erasmus, typical of Renaissance HUMANISM, at first an adherent of scholastic method, is said to have been persuaded to forsake it by the English scholar, John Colet. *Scholasticism* employed the deductive method of reasoning, and its overthrow prepared the way for the inductive method, advocated by Francis Bacon, which has led to the achievements of modern science. The positive effect of scholastic thinking upon all medieval literature and thinking was incalculable in extent, and its insistence upon rigid, accurate reasoning has had a wholesome effect upon succeeding thought and writing.

Scholiast: One who wrote *scholia* or marginal comments explaining the grammar or meaning of passages in medieval MANUSCRIPTS, particularly copies of Greek and Latin texts.

School of Night: A group of Elizabethan DRAMATISTS, POETS, and scholars, with, perhaps, some of the nobility. Its leader was Sir Walter Raleigh, and its members included Christopher Marlowe, George

479

Chapman, and the mathematician Thomas Herriot. They studied the natural sciences, philosophy, and religion, and were suspected of being atheists. Shakespeare seems to condemn them in *Love's Labour's Lost* in the lines:

> . . . Black is the badge of hell,
> The hue of dungeons and the School of Night.

School of Spenser: A name given to a group of seventeenth-century poets who showed the influence of Edmund Spenser. The chief poets of the school were Giles and Phineas Fletcher, William Browne, George Wither, William Drummond of Hawthornden, Sir John Davies, and the Scottish Sir William Alexander. The school is marked by such characteristics as sensuousness, melody, PERSONIFICATIONS, pictorial quality, interest in NARRATIVE, medievalism (especially in use of ALLEGORY), ARCHAISMS, modified or genuine SPENSERIAN STANZA, pastoralism, moral earnestness. The art and outlook of the school led in the direction of Milton, whom they influenced. They thus form a link between Spenser and Milton, the two great Puritan poets of the English RENAISSANCE.

School Plays: One of the most important traditions contributing to the development of ELIZABETHAN DRAMA was the practice of writing and performing plays at schools. Little is known of the history, extent, or character of dramatic activities in universities before the RENAISSANCE, though there is some evidence that student plays existed throughout the late Middle Ages. Records of *school plays* from the fifteenth century possibly refer to such medieval forms as DISGUISINGS (see MASQUE). The interest in Latin DRAMA aroused by the Italian RENAISSANCE (Petrarch wrote a Terentian comedy about 1331) led to translations and imitations of Plautus and Terence in other countries, such as Germany and Holland (where *school plays* of the "Prodigal Son" formula flourished), and eventually England (early sixteenth century). Boys in grammar schools (St. Paul's, Eton) acted both CLASSICAL and original plays in the 1520's. By 1560 both Latin and English plays were produced at Eton, and in Spenser's time (1560's) Richard Mulcaster's boys at the Merchant Taylors' School performed plays annually before the queen. Nicholas Udall's *Ralph Roister Doister*, probably written before 1553 for performance by the boys of Westminster School, is regarded as the first regular English COMEDY.

However important the production of plays in the grammar

schools may have been, of greater significance in the development of the DRAMA was the practice, common in the sixteenth century, of writing and performing plays at the universities. Plays of Terence were acted by undergraduates in Cambridge as early as 1510. In 1546 at Trinity College, Cambridge, refusal of a student to take part in a play was punishable by expulsion. Though the primary purpose of the plays was educational, entertainment for its own sake was more and more recognized, and the use of English became more and more common. When Queen Elizabeth visited Cambridge in 1564 and Oxford in 1566 she was entertained with series of plays of various types, foreshadowing later FORMS on the Elizabethan stage. The earliest extant university play in English is *Gammer Gurton's Needle* (written *ca.*1560). Some university pieces were connected with later Elizabethan plays, such as Thomas Legge's SENECAN TRAGEDY on Richard III, which may have contributed features to Shakespeare's play.

The UNIVERSITY WITS left the universities at a time when academic plays were flourishing and went to London to play important roles during the formative period of ELIZABETHAN DRAMA. In the main the academic DRAMA transmitted to the professional DRAMA the CLASSICAL FORMS represented by Seneca in TRAGEDY and by Plautus and Terence in COMEDY, though Italian sources were also employed. The plays were most commonly performed at night in the college hall before a restricted audience. The actors were costumed.

Schoolmen: Medieval philosophers who followed the method of SCHOLASTICISM in their "disputations." Called "hair-splitters" by Francis Bacon. See SCHOLASTICISM.

Science Fiction: A form of FANTASY in which scientific facts, assumptions, or hypotheses form the basis, by logical extrapolation, of adventures in the future, on other planets, in other dimensions in time, or under new variants of scientific law. See FANTASY.

Scop: A sort of Anglo-Saxon court poet. Though the *scop* probably traveled about from court to court like the GLEEMAN, he occupied a position of importance and permanence in the king's retinue comparable to that of the Welsh BARD (see WELSH LITERATURE) and the Irish FILIDH (see IRISH LITERATURE). He was a composer as well as a reciter, and his themes were drawn chiefly from the heroic traditions of the early Germanic peoples, though later he employed Biblical themes, and he no doubt was expected to eulogize the family which employed him. He has been called a precursor of the modern POET LAUREATE.

Scottish Chaucerians: POETS of fifteenth- and sixteenth-century Scotland who wrote in imitation of Chaucer's STYLE and FORMS. They included Robert Henryson (*The Testament of Cresseid*), William Dunbar (*Thrissil and the Rois, Goldyn Targe*), Gavin Douglas, translator of *The Aeneid,* and James I (*The Kingis Quair*).

Scottish Literature: The main stream of the literature of Scotland is rightly regarded as a part of English literary history. The fact of political independence in early times and the use of the Scots language or Scottish DIALECT of English by many writers, however, warrants special notice of *Scottish literature.* John Barbour's *Bruce* (1375), a sort of Scottish national EPIC (in twenty books), is often taken as the beginning of *Scottish literature.* In the fifteenth and sixteenth centuries there flourished a school of SCOTTISH CHAUCERIANS. Somewhat later appeared Sir David Lyndsay's *Satire of the Three Estates,* an ambitious MORALITY play said to have been acted in 1540. Early Scotland is noted, too, for her popular BALLADS, some of which probably belong to the fifteenth and sixteenth centuries, though most of the existing ones seem to have been composed a century or more later. The controversial PROSE, on religious and historical or political topics, of the famous John Knox (sixteenth century) aided a tendency toward the use of English by Scottish writers. Among the poets Alexander Montgomerie (*ca.*1545–*ca.*1610) is sometimes called the last of the native Scottish "makers." By the seventeenth century the Scots DIALECT as a literary vehicle was rare.

A migration of Scottish professional and business men to London in the seventeenth and eighteenth centuries makes increasingly difficult a separation of Scottish and English literature. In poetry the works of James Thomson (*The Seasons*) and Robert Blair (*The Grave*) are noteworthy in English literary history, as are such PROSE pieces as Adam Smith's *Wealth of Nations* and David Hume's *Enquiry Concerning Human Understanding.* At the very end of the century appeared Robert Burns, whose use of native DIALECT (following a tradition set by Allan Ramsay and others) found an immediate response in the literary circles of Edinburgh.

Though much conscious feeling for native tradition appears in some nineteenth-century Scottish writers (like Sir Walter Scott) and though the native DIALECTS have been employed by such writers of regional literature as J. M. Barrie (see KAILYARD SCHOOL), in general literary men of Scottish birth (e.g., Carlyle, Stevenson) have been regarded, since 1800, as "English." One notable achievement in English literary history was the establishment in Scotland in the early nineteenth century of literary and critical MAGAZINES, e.g., *The Edinburgh Review* (1802).

Scriblerus Club: A club of writers organized in London in 1714 by Jonathan Swift with the object of satirizing literary incompetence. Among its members were Pope, Arbuthnot, Bolingbroke, Gay, and Congreve. It expressed its opinions of the false taste of the age, particularly in learning, through the satiric fragment, *The Memoirs of the Extraordinary Life, Works, and Discoveries of Martinus Scriblerus,* written in large part by Dr. Arbuthnot.

Scriptural Drama: Plays based upon the Old and New Testaments, produced first by churches and then by town GUILDS in the Middle Ages. See MYSTERY PLAY.

Secondary Stress: A STRESS put upon a syllable that is medial in its weight (or force) between a full (primary) STRESS and an unstressed syllable. It usually occurs in polysyllabic words, but sometimes is the result of the CADENCE and sense of the line. In the word elementary the third syllable carries a STRESS, indicated by the mark ⟍, lighter than that on the first syllable. However, in the SCANSION of English VERSE, the metrical pattern is formed of stressed and unstressed syllables, and those with *secondary stress* are resolved into one or the other. In actual practice, however, *secondary stress* creates effective variations within basically regular lines.

Self-Effacing Author: When, in the NOVEL or the SHORT STORY, OBJECTIVITY is so used in the narrative POINT OF VIEW that the author ostensibly ceases to exist and seems to become merely an impersonal and nonevaluating medium through whom the actions and actors of the story are seen, he is said to be *self-effacing.* The *self-effacing author* is a typical device in the "scenic method." See SCENE (IN A NOVEL), NARRATOR, POINT OF VIEW, OBJECTIVITY.

Senecan Style: The anti-Ciceronian STYLE of the late sixteenth and seventeenth centuries. It is curt, abrupt, and uneven, giving the

Senecan Tragedy

effect of unadorned factual statement. Its chief characteristic is the so-called exploded period, a series of independent statements set down in simple sentences or clauses, and tied together, if at all, by coordinating conjunctions. It tends to be jagged and excited or to flow in unevaluated directness. It is sometimes called ATTIC. See CICERONIAN STYLE.

Senecan Tragedy: The Latin TRAGEDIES attributed to the Stoic philosopher Seneca (first century). They were modeled largely upon the Greek TRAGEDIES of Euripides (but written to be recited rather than acted) and exerted a great influence upon RENAISSANCE playwrights, who thought them intended for actual performance. In general the nine plays are marked by: (1) conventional five-ACT division; (2) the use of a CHORUS (for comment rather than participation in the action) and such STOCK CHARACTERS as a ghost, a cruel tyrant, the faithful male servant, and the female CONFIDANTE; (3) the presentation of much of the action (especially the horrors) through long NARRATIVE reports recited by messengers as a substitute for stage-action; (4) the employment of sensational themes drawn from Greek mythology, involving much use of "blood and lust" material connected with unnatural crimes (adultery, incest, infanticide, etc.) and often motivated by revenge and leading to retribution; (5) a highly rhetorical style marked by hyperbolic expressions, detailed descriptions, exaggerated comparisons, APHORISMS, EPIGRAMS, and the sharp line-for-line DIALOGUE known as STICHOMYTHIA; (6) lack of careful CHARACTER delineation but much use of introspection and SOLILOQUY.

Renaissance HUMANISM stimulated interest in the *Senecan tragedies* and they were translated and imitated in early academic and court DRAMA in Italy, France, and England. The first English TRAGEDY, Sackville and Norton's *Gorboduc* (acted 1562), was an imitation of Seneca as were such later INNS-OF-COURT plays as *Jocasta* (acted 1566), *Tancred and Gismund* (acted 1568), and *The Misfortunes of Arthur* (1588), some of which were influenced by Italian Senecan plays rather than by the Latin plays themselves. After 1588 two groups of English *Senecan tragedies* are to be distinguished. The Countess of Pembroke and playwrights under her influence produced "true" Senecan plays modeled upon the French *Senecan tragedies* of Robert Garnier. In this group are Kyd's translation of Garnier's *Cornélie*, Daniel's *The Tragedy of Cleopatra* and

Sensibility

his *Philotas* (1605), and Fulke Greville's original plays based on Senecan models, e.g., *Mustapha.*

The second and far more important group begins with the plays produced by Marlowe and Kyd for the popular stage. These plays combined native English tragic tradition with a modified Senecan technique and led directly toward the typical ELIZABETHAN TRAG-EDY. Kyd's *Spanish Tragedy,* for example, though reflecting such Senecan traits as sensationalism, bombastic rhetoric, the use of the CHORUS and the ghost, departed from the Senecan method in that it placed the murders and horrors upon the stage, in response to popular Elizabethan taste and in defiance of Horace's dictum that good taste demanded leaving such matters for off-stage action. The fashion so inaugurated led to a long line of ELIZABETHAN TRAGEDIES, the greatest of which is Shakespeare's *Hamlet.* The importance of the Latin Senecan plays in the evolution of English TRAGEDY is very great. In Professor A. H. Thorndike's words, they called attention to DRAMA "not as an EXPOSITION of events or as an ALLEGORY of life, but as a field for the study of human emotion. Their brilliant if bombastic RHETORIC aroused enthusiasm for the DRAMA as literature and POETRY; and their reflective and aphoristic STYLE encouraged an effort to elevate TRAGEDY above its too familiar converse with COMEDY into the realm of austere philosophy." See REVENGE TRAGEDY, TRAGEDY OF BLOOD.

Sensibility: A term used to indicate emotionalism as opposed to RATIONALISM; a reliance upon the feelings as guides to truth and conduct as opposed to reason and law as regulations both in human and metaphysical relations. It is connected with such eighteenth-century attitudes as PRIMITIVISM, SENTIMENTALISM, the nature movement (see NATURE), and other aspects of ROMANTICISM. Joseph Warton in *The Enthusiast* (1744) reflects many of the attitudes of the "School of Sensibility": "on the one hand, he expressed the contempt for cities, formal gardens, conventional society, business, law-courts, and Augustan style; on the other, the love of the simple life, solitude, mountains, stormy oceans, instinctively noble savages, untutored poets who 'warbled wildly,' and tragedies of terror" (Bernbaum). The high value that the eighteenth century put upon *sensibility* was a reaction against the STOICISM of the seventeenth century and the theories advanced by Hobbes and others that man was motivated primarily by self-interest. Benevolence, resting upon the

485

ability to sympathize to a marked degree with the joys and the sorrows of one's fellows, was asserted by many, notably the Earl of Shaftesbury, as an innate human characteristic. From this position to the idea of the virtue of the sympathetic tear was a short distance soon traveled. This extreme *sensibility* expressed itself in the DRAMA in SENTIMENTAL COMEDY, in FICTION in the SENTIMENTAL NOVEL.

In the twentieth century, the term *sensibility* is used in a radically different sense, to designate the innate sensitivity of the poet (and his reader) to sensory experience, out of which he fashions his art. It is most common in T. S. Eliot's phrase "DISSOCIATION OF SENSIBILITY," by which he means the disunion of feeling and thought which, he thinks, occurred in English poetry with Dryden and Milton. Only when thought and feeling have been re-united can English poetry again establish its true mode, he thinks. See META-PHYSICAL POETRY, SENTIMENTALISM, SENTIMENTAL COMEDY, SENTIMENTAL NOVEL, DISSOCIATION OF SENSIBILITY.

Sensual and Sensuous: *Sensuous* is a critical term characterizing writing which plays fully upon the various *senses* of the reader. The term is not to be confused with *sensual* which is now generally used in an unfavorable sense and implies writing which is fleshly or carnal, in which the author displays the voluptuous and abandons his work to the presentation of a single sense impression. *Sensuous,* then, denotes writing that makes a restrained use of the various senses; *sensual* denotes writing that approaches unrestrained abandonment to one sense—the passion of physical love. Through the careful use of pictures and IMAGES which appeal to the senses, such a use as Keats makes in *The Eve of St. Agnes,* writing may be said to be made *sensuous,* a quality which Milton stipulated as characterizing good POETRY in his famous estimate of POETRY as "simple, sensuous, and passionate." The writing of Ernest Hemingway, with its use of physical IMAGES and its attempt to "rub the fact on the exposed nerve end," is markedly *sensuous,* although it is only occasionally *sensual.* In a quite different style, Thomas Wolfe's writing, evoking sharp sensory response, is also *sensuous.*

Sentence: A rhetorical term formerly in use in the sense of APO-THEGM or MAXIM (Lat. *sententia*), usually applied to quoted "wise sayings." In old writings, too, the student may come upon the use of *sentence* for *sense, gist,* or *theme,* as when Chanticleer in Chaucer's *Nun's Priest's Tale* tells Pertelot (trickily) that the *sentence* of the

Sentimental Comedy

Latin phrase is such and such. In modern grammatical usage, of course, *sentence* is restricted to a group of words having a subject and predicate and expressing a complete thought.

Sententia: A Latin term for a short, pithy statement of general truth. See APHORISM, MAXIM, SENTENCE.

Sentimental Comedy: Just as the COMEDY OF MANNERS reflected in its immorality the reaction of the RESTORATION from the severity of the Puritan code of the Commonwealth period, so the COMEDY which displaced it, known as *sentimental comedy*, or "reformed comedy," sprang up in the early years of the eighteenth century in response to a growing reaction against the tone of RESTORATION plays. Signs of this reaction appeared soon after the dethronement of James II (1688) and found influential expression in Jeremy Collier's famous *Short View of the Immorality and Profaneness of the English Stage* (1698), which charged that plays as a whole "rewarded debauchery," "ridiculed virtue and learning," and were "disserviceable to probity and religion." Although Colley Cibber's *Love's Last Shift* (1696) shows transitional anticipations of the new reformed COMEDY, Richard Steele is generally regarded as the founder of the type. His *The Funeral* (1701), *The Lying Lover* (1703), and *The Tender Husband* (1705) reflect the development of the form, while his *The Conscious Lovers* (1722) is the CLASSIC example of the fully developed type.

Through the violence of its reaction *sentimental comedy* became a very weak thing dramatically, lacking humor, reality, spice, and lightness of touch. The CHARACTERS were either so good or so bad that they became mere CARICATURES, and PLOTS were violently handled so that virtue would triumph. The dramatists resorted shamelessly to sentimental emotion in their effort to interest and move the spectators. The HERO in *The Conscious Lovers* ("conscious" in the sense of "conscientious") is perfectly moral; he has no bad habits; he is indifferent to "sordid lucre"; he is good to inferiors from principle, even thanking servants for paid services; he is guided by a sense of honor and is superior to all ordinary passions. His conversations with the HEROINE Indiana, whom he loves but who agrees with him that he must marry Lucinda to please his parents, are veritable TRAVESTIES upon the art of love-making. Where the COMEDY OF MANNERS of the preceding age had sacrificed moral tone in its effort to amuse, the *sentimental comedy* sacrificed dramatic

487

reality in its effort to instruct through an appeal to the heart. The domestic trials of middle-class couples are usually portrayed: their "private woes" are exhibited with much emotional stress intended to arouse the spectator's pity and suspense in advance of the approaching melodramatic happy ending.

This COMEDY held the boards on the English stage for more than a half century. Hugh Kelly's *False Delicacy* (1768), first acted shortly before the appearance of Goldsmith's *Good Natured Man* (brought out in protest against *sentimental comedies*), and Richard Cumberland's *The West Indian* (1771) illustrate the complete development of the type. Though weakened by the attacks and dramatic creations of Goldsmith and Sheridan, who revived in a somewhat chastened FORM the old COMEDY OF MANNERS, plays of the sentimental type lived on till after the middle of the nineteenth century, though no longer dominant. The DOMESTIC TRAGEDY of a sentimental sort developed by Nicholas Rowe (1674–1718) and George Lillo (1693–1739) shows much the same characteristics as the COMEDY with which it coexisted. Both forms are based upon the same fundamentals as those of MELODRAMA.

Sentimental Novel: The SENTIMENTALISM of the eighteenth century was reflected not only in the SENTIMENTAL COMEDY and in the DOMESTIC TRAGEDY, but in the early NOVELS as well. Richardson's *Pamela, or Virtue Rewarded* (1740) was the beginning of the vogue, and although the rival REALISTIC NOVEL sprang up in protest (e.g., Fielding's *Tom Jones*) the *sentimental novel* (also called NOVEL OF SENSIBILITY) continued popular for many years. One of the best of the type is Goldsmith's *The Vicar of Wakefield* (1766) and one of the most extravagant is Henry Mackenzie's *Man of Feeling* (1771). Laurence Sterne's *Tristram Shandy* (1760–1767) is another example of the type. See NOVEL, SENTIMENTALISM.

Sentimentalism: The term is used in two senses important in the study of literature: (1) an overindulgence in emotion, especially the conscious effort to induce emotion in order to analyze or enjoy it; also the failure to restrain or evaluate emotion through the exercise of the judgment; (2) an optimistic overemphasis of the goodness of humanity (SENSIBILITY), representing in part a reaction against orthodox Calvinistic theology, which regarded human nature as depraved. It is connected with the development of PRIMITIVISM. In the first sense given above *sentimentalism* is found in MELO-

DRAMA, in the fainting heroines of sentimental fiction, in the melancholic verse of the GRAVEYARD SCHOOL, in humanitarian literature, and in such modern phenomena as moving pictures and legal and political oratory. In the second sense it appears in SENTIMENTAL COMEDY, sentimental fiction, and primitivistic poetry. Both types of sentimentality figured largely in the literature of the romantic movement. Writers reflecting eighteenth-century *sentimentalism* include Richard Steele (*The Conscious Lovers*); Joseph Warton (*The Enthusiast*); the poems of William Collins and Thomas Gray; Laurence Sterne (*A Sentimental Journey*); Oliver Goldsmith (*The Deserted Village*); Henry Mackenzie (*The Man of Feeling*). The neo-classicists themselves, though opposed fundamentally to *sentimentalism*, sometimes exhibit it, as when Addison avers that he resorts to Westminster Abbey for the purpose of enjoying the emotions called up by the sombre surroundings. In its broadest sense *sentimentalism* may be said to result whenever a reader or an audience is asked to experience an emotional response in excess of that merited by the occasion or one that has not been adequately prepared for. See SENSIBILITY.

Sentimentality: The effort to induce an emotional response disproportionate to the situation, and thus to substitute heightened and generally unthinking feeling for normal ethical and intellectual judgment. It is a particularly pernicious form of anti-intellectualism. See SENTIMENTALISM.

Septenary: A seven-stress VERSE often employed in medieval and RENAISSANCE poetry. See FOURTEENERS.

Septet: A STANZA of seven lines. One of the few in English VERSE is the RHYME ROYAL.

Septuagint: A Greek version of the Old Testament begun in the third century before Christ. It is still in use in the Greek Church and is the version from which New Testament writers quote. It takes its name from an old but discredited story that it was prepared by seventy-two Jewish scholars at the request of Ptolemy Philadelphus (309–246 B.C.).

Serenade: A sentimental composition, written as though intended to be sung out of doors at night under a lady's window and in praise of a loved one. Bayard Taylor's "Bedouin Song," the last stanza of which is quoted, is a *serenade* which once was very popular:

> My steps are nightly driven,
>   By the fever in my breast,
> To hear from thy lattice breathed
>   The word that shall give me rest.
> Open the door of thy heart,
>   And open thy chamber door,
> And my kisses shall teach thy lips
>   The love that shall fade no more
> *Till the sun grows cold,*
> *And the stars are old,*
> *And the leaves of the Judgment Book unfold!*

Sestet: The second, SIX-VERSE division of an ITALIAN SONNET. Following the eight-VERSE division (see OCTAVE) the *sestet* usually makes specific a general statement which has been presented in the OCTAVE or indicates the personal emotion of the author in a situation which the OCTAVE has developed. The most authentic RHYME-SCHEME is the *cdecde* (following the *abbaabba* of the OCTAVE), but sonneteers have tried so many rearrangements of the SONNET RHYME pattern as to make almost any sequence now acceptable. Strictly speaking, any six-line POEM or STANZA is a *sestet*.

Sestina: One of the most difficult and complex of the various FRENCH FORMS. The *sestina* is a poem consisting of six six-line STANZAS and a three-line ENVOY. It makes no use of the REFRAIN. This form is usually unrhymed, the effect of RHYME being taken over by a fixed pattern of end-words which demands that these end-words in each STANZA be the same, though arranged in a different sequence each time. If we take 1–2–3–4–5–6 to represent the end-words of the first STANZA, then the first line of the second STANZA must end with 6 (the last end-word used in the preceding STANZA), the second with 1, the third with 5, the fourth with 2, the fifth with 4, the sixth with 3—and so to the next STANZA. The order of the first three STANZAS, for instance, would be: 1–2–3–4–5–6; 6–1–5–2–4–3; 3–6–4–1–2–5. The conclusion, or ENVOY, of three lines must use as end-words 5–3–1, these being the final end-words, in the same sequence, of the sixth STANZA. But the poet must exercise even greater ingenuity than all this, since buried in each line of the ENVOY must appear the other three end-words, 2–4–6. Thus so highly artificial a pattern affords a FORM which, for most poets, can never prove anything more than a poetic exercise. Yet it has been practiced with success in English by Swinburne, Kipling, and Auden.

Setting: The physical, and sometimes spiritual, background against which the action of a NARRATIVE (NOVEL, DRAMA, SHORT STORY, POEM) takes place. The elements which go to make up a *setting* are: (1) the actual geographical location, its topography, scenery, and such physical arrangements as the location of the windows and doors in a room; (2) the occupations and daily manner of living of the characters; (3) the time or period in which the action takes place, e.g., epoch in history, season of the year, etc.; (4) the general environment of the characters, e.g., religious, mental, moral, social, and emotional conditions through which the people in the NARRATIVE move. From one point of view most fiction can be broken up into four elements: *setting*, INCIDENT (or PLOT), CHARACTERIZATION, and EFFECT. When *setting* dominates, or when a piece of FICTION is written largely to present the manners and customs of a locality, the writing is often called LOCAL COLOR WRITING or REGIONALISM. The term is also often applied to the stage *setting* of a play. See MISE EN SCÈNE.

Seven Cardinal Virtues, The: In medieval theology, the *seven cardinal virtues* were faith, hope, and love (drawn from Biblical teaching) and the four natural virtues: prudence, justice, fortitude, and temperance (adapted from the four cardinal virtues of the Greeks). Seven was, of course, a mystic number. There are the SEVEN DEADLY SINS, the SEVEN LIBERAL ARTS, the seven ages of the world, the seven sacraments, the seven words on the cross, the seven ages of man, and an endless number of other "sevens."

Seven Deadly Sins, The: The seven cardinal sins which, according to medieval theology, entailed spiritual death and could be atoned for only by perfect penitence: pride, envy, wrath, sloth, avarice, gluttony, and lust. Dante treats all seven as arising from imperfect love—pride, envy, and wrath resulting from perverted love; sloth from defective love; avarice, gluttony, and lust from excessive love. Pride was the most heinous of the sins, because it led to treachery and disloyalty, as in the case of Satan. Innumerable didactic and theological works on the *seven deadly sins* appeared in the Middle Ages and thousands of sermons were based upon them. The conception of the *seven deadly sins* was so widespread that it permeated the literature of medieval and RENAISSANCE times, its influence appearing not only in the ideas implicit in many literary works but often controlling the very structure, as in the "visions" built around a framework of the seven sins. A few examples of the idea in English literature are: Chaucer's "Parson's Tale" in the *Canterbury Tales; The Vision of Piers the Plowman,* Gower's *Confessio Amantis,* and Spenser's *The Fairie Queene* (Book 1, Canto iv).

Seven Liberal Arts, The: The seven subjects studied in the medieval university. The three studies pursued during the four-year course leading to the A.B. degree were known as the TRIVIUM. They were grammar (Latin), logic, and RHETORIC (especially public speaking). The four branches followed in the three-year course leading to the M.A. degree were arithmetic, music, geometry, astronomy. These were called the QUADRIVIUM.

Shakespeare, Early Editors of: About half of Shakespeare's plays were printed separately during his lifetime in QUARTO editions, presumably without the author's consent in most cases. Shakespeare was a shareholder in the company which acted his plays, and companies owning acting rights often objected to efforts to sell their plays to the public in printed form while the plays were in their current repertoire. Though there may have been an imperfect effort in 1619, three years after the dramatist's death, to get together a collection of Shakespeare's plays (involving the false dating of certain QUARTOS), the first edition is the famous First Folio (1623) prepared by Shakespeare's friends, the actors John Heminge and Henry Condell. For several reasons the texts of the plays in the First Folio vary greatly in accuracy. Some of them follow QUARTO texts closely, others vary both in length and readings, and there are a good many mistakes—e.g., the printing of one word for another word similar in sound or spelling—so that in many passages we cannot be sure what Shakespeare wrote. There is also reason for thinking that the FOLIO both omits plays which Shakespeare wrote, at least in part (as *Pericles*), and includes some which he possibly had little to do with (see PSEUDO-SHAKESPEAREAN PLAYS). This situation has created a series of problems which have greatly concerned later editors and critics eager to find out as nearly as possible just what Shakespeare wrote. The Second Folio appeared in 1632 and a third in 1663, the third being reissued in 1664 with *Pericles* and six "spurious" plays added. The fourth FOLIO was printed in 1685. These late FOLIOS were only slightly edited.

The first real editor of Shakespeare was Nicholas Rowe, POET LAUREATE. In his editions (1709 and 1714) Rowe made some corrections in the text, modernized the punctuation and spelling, supplied lists of CHARACTERS and made ACT and SCENE divisions for most of the plays (this had been partly done in the FOLIOS), and added stage directions. In 1725 Alexander Pope undertook to make an "authoritative" edition. In fact, however, he did much mischievous tampering with Rowe's text. He "corrected" the METER, emended (by guess largely) difficult passages, placed "degrading" passages at the foot of the page, and placed marks of approval on what he thought to be fine passages. He omitted the seven plays not in the First Folio. Pope's work was followed by a careful edition by Lewis Theobald (1733), who had before exposed some of Pope's mistakes and made some ingenious emendations. In retaliation Pope made him the chief dunce in the revised edition of his *Dunciad*. In 1744 Sir Thomas Hanmer printed an elegant edition, which followed Pope. William Warburton's edition (1747) was of little value, but in 1765 appeared the famous edition of Samuel Johnson, whose "Preface" and notes have high critical value.

Edward Capell (1768) made the first serious effort to prepare a scientific text based on all the early editions, including QUARTOS. In 1773 appeared the Johnson-Steevens VARIORUM EDITION; this reappeared in 1785 with revisions by Isaac Reed. In 1790 was printed an edition by the important scholar Edward Malone, whose still more extensive "third variorum" edition, published after Malone's death by James Boswell (the younger), came in 1821. Many editions have appeared after 1800. Most of the plays have been edited separately in the *New Variorum Shakespeare* (beginning in 1871), by Henry Howard Furness (father and son), which undertakes to give a complete abstract of all earlier efforts to establish a text and of all important Shakespearean criticism.

Shakespearean Sonnet: The ENGLISH SONNET, consisting of three QUATRAINS rhyming *abab cdcd efef* and a COUPLET rhyming *gg*. It is called the *Shakespearean sonnet* because Shakespeare was its most distinguished practitioner. See SONNET.

Shanty: A sailor's working SONG. See CHANTEY.

493

Shaped Verse

Shaped Verse: A POEM so constructed that its printed version takes a form that suggests its subject matter. See CARMEN FIGURATUM.

Short Couplet: An octasyllabic COUPLET; two lines of either IAMBIC TETRAMETER or TROCHAIC TETRAMETER that rhyme.

Short Measure (or **Meter**): A STANZA widely used for HYMNS, consisting of four VERSES, rhyming either *abab* or *abcb*. It usually has the first and third lines in IAMBIC TETRAMETER and the second and fourth in IAMBIC TRIMETER; although occasionally the first, second, and fourth lines are IAMBIC TRIMETER and the third is IAMBIC TETRAMETER. When *short measure* is $a_4b_3c_4b_3$ it is, in fact, a COUPLET in POULTER'S MEASURE.

Short Novel: A work of FICTION which falls in an intermediate length between the SHORT STORY and the NOVEL. If described strictly in terms of length, it is generally considered to be between 15,000 and 50,000 words. It is more often defined, however, in terms of a group of characteristics relative to the SHORT STORY and the NOVEL. Where the SHORT STORY is usually content to reveal a CHARACTER through an action, to be what Joyce called an EPIPHANY, the *short novel* is concerned with CHARACTER development. Where the NOVEL in its concern with CHARACTER development employs a broad canvas, a number of CHARACTERS, and frequently a broad time span, the *short novel* concentrates on a limited cast of CHARACTERS, a relatively short time span, and one connected chain of events. Thus it is an artistic attempt to combine the compression of the SHORT STORY with the CHARACTER development of the NOVEL. However, such definitions are extremely relative. No one has ever formulated a truly satisfactory definition of the *short novel*, but it has had a distinctive history. Henry James, who did distinguished work in the form, called it "our ideal, the beautiful and blest *nouvelle*." Other writers who have found it an attractive form in which to work include: Thomas Mann, Laurence Sterne, Tolstoi, Kafka, Camus, Gide, Moravia, Melville, Conrad, Edith Wharton, Wolfe, Steinbeck, Faulkner, Virginia Woolf, Willa Cather, and Thornton Wilder. See NOVEL, SHORT STORY, NOUVELLE, NOVELETTE.

Short-Short Story: A brief SHORT STORY, usually between 500 and 2,000 words in length, with a "twist" or surprise ending. Its best-known practitioner was O. Henry.

494

Short Story

Short Story, The: Stories, in one form or another, have existed throughout all history. Egyptian papyri, dating from 3000 to 4000 B.C., reveal how the sons of Cheops regaled their father with NARRATIVE. Some three hundred years before the birth of Christ, we had such Old Testament stories as those of Jonah and of Ruth. Christ spoke in PARABLES. The Greeks and Romans left us EPISODES and INCIDENTS in their early classics. In the Middle Ages the impulse to story-telling manifested itself in FABLES and EPICS about beasts, and in the MEDIEVAL ROMANCE. In England, about 1250, some two hundred well-known TALES were collected in the *Gesta Romanorum.* In the middle of the fourteenth century, Boccaccio assembled a hundred TALES in a book called *The Decameron.* In the same century Chaucer wrote his frame-work collection, *The Canterbury Tales.* In the fifteenth century Malory, in *Le Morte Darthur,* gathered a series of long NARRATIVES recounting the exploits of ancient knighthood. In the eighteenth century came the NOVEL, growing out of the PICARESQUE NOVEL of the sixteenth and seventeenth centuries, both continuing tributes to man's love of NARRATIVE and both factors in the development of a formal kind of story-telling. The eighteenth century also saw the development of the INFORMAL ESSAY, which frequently derived some of its interest from such EPISODES and SKETCHES as Addison uses in the "Sir Roger de Coverley papers" or in "The Vision of Mirzah." In the nineteenth century came Sir Walter Scott, Washington Irving, Nathaniel Hawthorne, Edgar Allan Poe, Mérimée and Balzac, Gautier and Musset, Maupassant, Chekhov, and E. T. A. Hoffman. With these writers the *short story* as a distinct literary GENRE came into being.

In view of this long development it seems foolish to name one man as the founder of the *short story* or to credit one nation with its development. A form which comes to us from the ancient past and was known in both the Orient and the Occident, which drew its first breath from oral tradition, and which has existed as a portion of much of man's literary expression in all ages can ultimately be said to have no origin more specific than the inherent creative spirit of man satisfying his desire to tell and to hear stories. Yet in the nineteenth century a group of writers did consciously formulate the *short story* as an art form, notable among them being Hawthorne and Poe in America, Mérimée and Balzac in France, and E. T. A. Hoffman in Germany. This development flowered with such speed and force in America that the modern *short story* is often called an American art form, with only minor exaggeration.

495

Short Story

In the early nineteenth century, under the impulse of Poe's persuasive statement in his 1842 review of Hawthorne's *Twice-Told Tales*, critics formulated a definite structure and technique for the *short story*. To this was added around the end of the century the tightly constructed "surprise-ending story" of O. Henry, and the *short story* came to be thought of as corresponding to a "formula," a pattern which was repeated in endless retellings of its limited variations in the popular *short story*. Around the turn of the century, however, the impact of REALISM and the advent of NATURALISM joined with the example of Chekhov's "slice of life" stories to force the "formula" open for the serious writer, and such masters of the form as Somerset Maugham and Katherine Mansfield in England and Sherwood Anderson and Ernest Hemingway in America began producing *short stories* of great integrity which reflected the complex formlessness of life itself.

A practical definition of the *short story*, must be broad enough to include the "surprise-ending" STORY of Maupassant and O. Henry, the TALE of unified effect of Poe, the "slice of life" STORY of Chekhov, Katherine Mansfield, and Sherwood Anderson, and the symbolic and mythic STORIES that are extremely popular in the LITTLE MAGAZINES today. At the same time, within the breadth which such a statement must have, there should be distinguishing characteristics that set the *short story* off from other PROSE FICTION forms.

A *short story* is a relatively brief fictional NARRATIVE in PROSE. It may range in length from the SHORT-SHORT STORY of 500 words up to the "long-short story" of 12,000 to 15,000 words. It may be distinguished from the SKETCH and the TALE in that it has a definite formal development, a firmness in construction; however, it finds its UNITY in many things other than PLOT, although it often finds it there—in effect, in theme, in CHARACTER, in TONE, in MOOD, even, on occasion, in STYLE. It may be distinguished from the NOVEL in that it tends to reveal character through a series of actions or under stress, the purpose of the story being accomplished when the reader comes to know what the true nature of a character (or sometimes a SITUATION) is (James Joyce called a *short story* an EPIPHANY, because of this quality of "revelation"); whereas, the NOVEL tends to show CHARACTER developing as a result of actions and under the impact of events. This generalization, like every generalization about the *short story* and the NOVEL, grossly overstates its case; yet in a broad sense, it does define a basic difference between the two GENRES.

However natural and formless the *short story* may sometimes give the impression of being, however much it may appear to be the simple setting down of an overheard oral NARRATION, as in Ring Lardner's or Somerset Maugham's stories, or the unadorned report of an action, as in Hemingway's or John O'Hara's, a distinguishing characteristic of the GENRE is that it is consciously *made*, that it reveals itself, upon careful analysis, to be the result of conscious craftsmanship and artistic skill. Furthermore, however slight the *short story* may appear, it consists of more than a mere record of an INCIDENT or an ANECDOTE. It has a beginning, a middle, and an end; it possesses the rudiments of PLOT, with the conscious STRUCTURE that PLOT implies.

To be more specific as to form about so protean a GENRE would be to invite error. Although it differs from DRAMA, even from the ONE-ACT PLAY, in not being prepared for dramatic presentation but for reading and from the NOVEL in the attitude it takes toward CHARACTERIZATION, the comments on the nature of DRAMATIC STRUCTURE, of TRAGEDY, of the NOVEL, of CHARACTERIZATION, and of PLOT made elsewhere in this Handbook, apply to the *short story*.

Sigmatism: The marked use of the letters *s, z, j* and such related combinations of letters as *sh, zh,* and *ch.* Too great profusion of such *sibilant* sounds constitutes a fault which good writers avoid. On the other hand, for certain effects they have been much used in poetry. Poe, in the "Valley of Unrest," has twenty-seven lines each with its *sibilants*, the whole somehow planned to give an effect of unease:

> Now each visitor shall confess
> The sad valley's restlessness.
> Nothing there is motionless—
> Nothing save the airs that brood
> Over the magic solitude.

Tennyson tried to avoid the too frequent use of *sibilants* and is credited with calling his efforts to rid his verse of them "kicking the geese out of the boat."

Signature (in printing): A letter or figure placed at the foot of the first page of each GATHERING or section of a book, such a GATHERING consisting of the pages resulting from a sheet folded to page size and cut; hence the term *signature* is also applied to the GATHERING itself, or to the sheet after it is folded and ready to be GATHERED. In early printing the *signature* was often placed on the first, third,

Silver-Fork School

fifth, and seventh pages of an OCTAVO GATHERING (sixteen pages).
See BOOK SIZE.

Silver-Fork School, The: A name applied in derision to a group of
nineteenth-century English novelists who placed a great emphasis
upon gentility and matters of etiquette. Among the members of the
Silver-Fork School were Frances Trollope, Theodore Hook, Lady
Blessington, Lady Caroline Lamb, and Benjamin Disraeli.

Simile: A FIGURE OF SPEECH in which a similarity between two
objects is directly expressed, as in Milton's

> A *dungeon horrible,* on all sides round,
> As *one great furnace flamed;*

Here the comparison between the dungeon (Hell) and the great
furnace is directly expressed in the *as* which labels the comparison
a *simile.* Most *similes* are introduced by *as* or *like.* In the illustration
above, the similarity between Hell (the dungeon) and the furnace
is based on the great heat of the two. So it is generally with this
FIGURE OF SPEECH: the comparison of two things essentially unlike,
on the basis of a resemblance in one aspect, forms a *simile.* It is,
however, no *simile* to say, "My house is like your house," although,
of course, comparison does exist. Another way of expressing it is to
say that in a *simile* both TENOR and VEHICLE are clearly expressed
and are joined by an indicator of resemblance, "like" or "as." See
METAPHOR, EPIC SIMILE.

Sincerity: A term used in criticism in two distinct senses. In one it
reflects the correspondence of the work produced by an author to
the ideas and beliefs of the author and thus examines the work in
the light of biographical data (see BELIEF, PROBLEM OF). In the
other sense, it refers to the integrity with which the work adheres
to its own demands, assumptions, and attitudes; if a work has
sincerity, it restricts the emotions it calls for to those demanded by
its actions and actors (see SENTIMENTALITY); it avoids the use of
unmotivated actions (see MELODRAMA); it avoids the use of POETIC
JUSTICE when the universe it depicts does not contain an order
which justifies such a concept. An author may construct the micro-
cosmic universe of his story or poem according to any principle he
chooses, but, if his work is to meet the test of *sincerity,* having
chosen, he must act consistently with that choice.

Skeltonic Verse

Situation: A term used in the discussion of PLOT to denote (1) a given group of circumstances in which a CHARACTER finds himself, or (2) the given conditions under which a STORY opens before the action of the PLOT proper actually begins. Thus, to use *Hamlet* for illustration, the question might be asked, in the first sense, what the proper line of action was for Hamlet when he found himself in the *situation* brought about by the fact that Laertes had challenged him to a duel. In the second, and more technical sense, the *situation* consists of those events which had taken place before the play opens: the murder of Hamlet's father, the incestuous acts of his mother, the general down-at-the-heel condition of the state. In its primary relation to PLOT, then, the *situation* is the group of circumstances in which the CHARACTER or CHARACTERS find themselves at the beginning of the dramatic action.

Skald (Scald): An ancient Scandinavian POET, especially of the Viking period, corresponding roughly with the Anglo-Saxon SCOP.

Skeltonic Verse ("Skeltonics" or "Skeltoniads"): A rollicking form of VERSE employed by the English POET John Skelton (*ca.*1460–1529) consisting of short lines rhymed in groups of varying length, intentionally designed to give the effects of unconventionality and lack of dignity which Skelton felt to be a fitting vehicle for his "poetry of revolt." *Skeltonic verse* is, especially for a modern reader, closely akin to DOGGEREL. Something of its spirit and characteristics, though not its full variety, may be found in the following brief passage from *The Tunnynge of Elynoure Rummynge:*

> But to make up my tale,
> She brueth noppy ale,
> And maketh thereof sale
> To travellers, to tinkers,
> To sweaters, to swinkers,
> And all good ale-drinkers,
> That will nothing spare
> But dryncke till they stare
> And bring themselves bare,
> With now away the mare
> And let us slay Care,
> As wise as an hare.

Much of Skelton's poetry is satirical, and Skelton himself was at outs with the humanists of his day. In his desire to shock, to be novel, and to write in a VERSE FORM as defiant as was his SATIRE, he plays with this peculiar VERSE in a fashion that was apparently intentionally irritating to his more formal and orthodox contemporaries. *Skeltonic verse* has its analogues in French and in Italian, and derives from a form of medieval Latin VERSE which was associated with the unruly side of university life and which was particularly distasteful to Skelton's humanistic, learned contemporaries. *Skeltonic verse* is also called TUMBLING VERSE.

Sketch: A brief composition simply constructed and usually most unified in that it presents a single scene, a single CHARACTER, a single incident. It lacks developed PLOT or very great CHARACTERIZATION. Originally used in the sense of an artist's *sketch* as preliminary groundwork for more developed work, it is now often employed for a finished product of simple proportions, as a CHARACTER *sketch*, a VAUDEVILLE *sketch*, a descriptive *sketch*. See SHORT STORY.

Skit: A short dramatic SKETCH or a brief, self-contained comic or BURLESQUE SCENE, usually presented as a part of a REVUE or on a television or radio program.

Slack Syllable: In METRICS, an unstressed syllable.

Slang: A vernacular speech, not accepted as suitable for formal usage, though much used in conversation and colloquial expression. The purpose behind the origin of all *slang* is that of stating an idea vividly and freshly, though sometimes the expressions themselves are not obvious enough to reveal how this purpose is accomplished. The aptness of *slang* is usually based on its HUMOR, its exaggeration, its onomatopoeic effect, or on a combination of these qualities. Frequently, too, *slang* develops as a short cut, an abbreviated form of expression. There are, as well, the special terms developing in professions or trades, in sports, in localities, among groups possessing any common interest, and in the underworld.

Collections of *slang* date from the sixteenth century, but there are plenty of instances to show that *slang* expressions developed much earlier than this. François Villon, for instance, introduced much rogue's *argot* in his VERSES of the fifteenth century. *Slang* terms ultimately pass in one of three directions: (1) they die out and are lost unless their vividness is such that (2) they continue as *slang* over a long period and (3) they frequently become accepted good usage. "Skidoo" in the sense of "go away" is an instance of the first; "guy" meaning "a man" is an instance of the second; and "banter" in the sense of "ridicule" is an example of the third. See JARGON.

Slant Rhyme: Approximate or near RHYME; usually the substitution of ASSONANCE or CONSONANCE for true RHYME. Although *slant rhyme* is a common device in contemporary POETRY, the reader should always be certain that he is dealing with something intended to be an imperfect RHYME rather than a mere change in pronunciation with the passage of time or change from one region to another before he assigns the term *slant rhyme* to what seems to him to be an imperfect RHYME.

Slapstick: LOW COMEDY involving physical action, practical jokes, and such actions as pie-throwing and pratfalls. The name is taken from a paddle consisting of two flat pieces of wood so attached to a handle that it makes a loud sound when a painless blow is struck with it.

Slave Narratives: In the period between 1830 and 1860, as a part of the abolition movement in America, a number of autobiographical accounts of slavery by escaped slaves were published. They are known as *slave narratives*. The best of them was *A Narrative of the Life of Frederick Douglass: An American Slave* (1845).

Slice of Life: A term used to describe the unselective and non-evaluative presentation of a segment of life in its unordered totality, which was considered one of the objectives of the naturalists. *Slice of life* is the English translation of the French phrase *tranche de vie*, which was applied to the work of Zola and the French naturalists.

Slick Magazine: A MAGAZINE printed on coated—"slick"—paper, illustrated lavishly, and carrying extensive advertising. The term was applied in the 1920's, 1930's, and 1940's to general circulation MAGAZINES with broad popular appeal, such as the *Saturday Evening Post* and the *American Magazine*. Although the name is taken from the kind of paper on which the MAGAZINE is printed, its use is restricted to general-purpose, mass-circulation publications. Many MAGAZINES printed on coated paper but addressed to specialized audiences are anything but *slick magazines*, as the *New Yorker*, *House Beautiful*, and the *National Geographic* illustrate.

Society Verse

Society Verse: Light, sophisticated VERSE. See VERS DE SOCIÉTÉ, OCCASIONAL VERSE, and LIGHT VERSE.

Sociological Novel: A form of the PROBLEM NOVEL which centers its principal attention on the nature, function, and effect of the society in which the characters live and on the social forces playing upon them. Usually the *sociological novel* presents a thesis and argues for it as a resolution to a social problem, but it is by no means always a PROPAGANDA NOVEL. The serious examination of social issues became an important element of FICTION with the INDUSTRIAL REVOLUTION, which centered attention on the condition of the laborer and his family and resulted in such NOVELS as Dickens' *Hard Times*, Kingsley's *Yeast*, and Mrs. Gaskell's *Mary Barton*. George Eliot in *Middlemarch* subjected an entire provincial town to sociological examination. American novelists have always had a serious interest in social issues. Mrs. Stowe's *Uncle Tom's Cabin* explored the conditions and the social status of the Negro, a theme that was to prove of enduring interest as a social problem through such works as G. W. Cable's *The Grandissimes,* and the NOVELS of Richard Wright and Ralph Ellison. The MUCKRAKERS at the turn of the century produced a number of *sociological novels,* the most successful being Upton Sinclair's *The Jungle.* John Steinbeck, John Dos Passos, Erskine Caldwell, and James T. Farrell have all written NOVELS whose central issues were sociological in implication. See PROBLEM NOVEL.

Sock: The low-heeled slipper conventionally worn by the comic actor on the ancient stage, hence (figuratively) COMEDY itself. See BUSKIN.

Socratic: The "*Socratic* method" in argument or explanation is the use of the question-and-answer formula employed by Socrates in Plato's *Dialogues.* Socrates would feign ignorance of the subject under discussion and then proceed to develop his point by the question-and-answer device. The method of assuming ignorance for the sake of taking advantage of an opponent in debate is known as "*Socratic* IRONY." This pretense of ignorance on the part of Socrates, who was really regarded as the most intelligent of the group, was referred to as his IRONY by his companions.

Solecism: A violation of grammatical structure or IDIOM in speech or writing. "He don't" and "between you and I" are *solecisms.*

502

Loosely any error in DICTION or grammar or propriety is called a *solecism*. Strictly interpreted, however, the term *solecism* is reserved for errors in grammar and idiom and is distinguished from "impropriety," which is employed to indicate the false use of one part of speech for another (as "to suicide" for "to commit suicide"), and from BARBARISM, which is used to indicate words coined from analogies falsely made with other words in good standing (as "preventative" for "preventive").

Soliloquy: A speech of a CHARACTER in a play or other composition delivered while the speaker is alone (*solus*) and calculated to inform the audience or reader of what is passing in the character's mind or to give information concerning other participants in the action which it is essential for the reader to know. Hamlet's famous *soliloquy*, "To be, or not to be," is an obvious example.

Solution: A term sometimes employed in place of CATASTROPHE or DÉNOUEMENT to indicate the outcome of a piece of FICTION. It is used in the sense that a *solution* is presented for the COMPLICATION which was developed in the PLOT. See PLOT, DRAMATIC STRUCTURE.

Song: A LYRIC POEM adapted to musical expression. *Song* LYRICS are usually short, simple, sensuous, emotional—perhaps the most spontaneous LYRIC form. Since civilized and barbaric man has always sought emotional outlet through *songs*, either communal or individual, the record of the form extends back into the dim past. *Songs* have been of every type and subject; no satisfactory classification for the various types can be devised. There have been, for instance, a variety of working songs, dance songs, love songs, war songs, play songs, drinking songs, and songs for festivals, church gatherings, and political meetings, as well as a host of others. Perhaps the period in English literature richest in *songs* was the ELIZABETHAN, when Shakespeare gave us such *song* POEMS as "Who is Sylvia?" and Jonson, "Drink to Me Only with Thine Eyes."

Sonnet: A LYRIC POEM of fourteen lines, highly arbitrary in form, and following one or another of several set RHYME-SCHEMES. Critics of the *sonnet* have recognized varying classifications, but to all essential purposes two types only need be discussed if the student will understand that each of these two, in turn, has undergone

Sonnet

various modifications by experimenters. The two characteristic *sonnet* types are the ITALIAN (PETRARCHAN) and the ENGLISH (SHAKESPEAREAN). The first, the ITALIAN form, is distinguished by its bipartite division into the OCTAVE and the SESTET: the OCTAVE consisting of a first division of eight lines rhyming *abbaabba* and the SESTET, or second division, consisting of six lines rhyming *cdecde, cdccdc,* or *cdedce*. On this twofold division of the ITALIAN *sonnet* Charles Gayley notes: "The octave bears the burden; a doubt, a problem, a reflection, a query, an historical statement, a cry of indignation or desire, a vision of the ideal. The sestet eases the load, resolves the problem or doubt, answers the query, solaces the yearning, realizes the vision." Again it might be said that the OCTAVE presents the NARRATIVE, states the proposition or raises a question; the SESTET drives home the NARRATIVE by making an abstract comment, applies the proposition, or solves the problem. So much for the strict interpretation of the ITALIAN form; as a matter of fact English poets have varied these items greatly. The OCTAVE and SESTET division is not always kept; the RHYME-SCHEME is often varied, but within limits—no ITALIAN *sonnet* properly allowing more than five RHYMES. IAMBIC PENTAMETER is essentially the METER, but here again certain poets have experimented with HEXAMETER and other METERS.

The ENGLISH (SHAKESPEAREAN) *sonnet*, on the other hand, is so different from the ITALIAN (though it grew from that form) as to permit of a separate classification. Instead of the OCTAVE and SESTET divisions, this *sonnet* characteristically embodies four divisions: three QUATRAINS (each with a RHYME-SCHEME of its own) and a rhymed COUPLET. Thus the typical RHYME-SCHEME for the ENGLISH *sonnet* is *abab cdcd efef gg*. The COUPLET at the end is usually a commentary on the foregoing, an epigrammatic close. The SPENSERIAN *sonnet* combines the ITALIAN and the SHAKESPEAREAN forms, using three QUATRAINS and a COUPLET but employing linking RHYMES between the QUATRAINS, thus *abab bcbc cdcd ee*.

Certain qualities common to the *sonnet* as a FORM should be noted. Its definite restrictions make it a challenge to the artistry of the poet and call for all the technical skill at the poet's command. The more or less set RHYME patterns occurring regularly within the short space of fourteen lines afford a pleasant effect on the ear of the reader, and can create truly musical effects. The rigidity of the FORM precludes a too great economy or too great prodigality of words. Emphasis is placed on exactness and perfection of expression.

The brevity of the FORM favors concentrated expression of idea or passion.

The *sonnet* as a FORM developed in Italy probably in the thirteenth century. Petrarch, in the fourteenth century, raised the *sonnet* to its greatest Italian perfection and so gave it, for English readers, his own name. The form was introduced into England by Thomas Wyatt, who translated PETRARCHAN *sonnets* and left over thirty examples of his own in English. Surrey, an associate, shares with Wyatt the credit for introducing the FORM to England and is important as an early modifier of the ITALIAN FORM. Gradually the ITALIAN *sonnet* pattern was changed and since Shakespeare attained fame for the greatest poems of this modified type his name has often been given to the English form. Among the most famous sonneteers in England have been Shakespeare, Milton, Wordsworth, and D. G. Rossetti. Longfellow, Jones Very, G. H. Boker, and E. A. Robinson are generally credited with writing some of the best *sonnets* in America. With the interest in this poetic FORM, certain POETS following the example of Petrarch have written a series of *sonnets* linked one to the other and dealing with some unified subject. Such series are called SONNET SEQUENCES. Some of the most famous SONNET SEQUENCES in English literature are those by Shakespeare (154 in the group), Sidney's *Astrophel and Stella,* Spenser's *Amoretti,* Rossetti's *House of Life,* and Mrs. Browning's *Sonnets from the Portuguese.* William Ellery Leonard, Elinor Wylie, Edna St. Vincent Millay, and W. H. Auden have done distinguished work in the *sonnet* and the SONNET SEQUENCE in this century.

Sonnet Sequence: A connected group of SONNETS. See SONNET.

Source: The person, manuscript, or book from which information is derived. If such a person, manuscript, or book represents a direct and immediate acquaintance with the information—a person with firsthand experience, a book which is itself the subject of the discussion, a manuscript written at the time or on the scene—the *source* is called a "primary" *source.* If the person, book, or manuscript represents an indirect acquaintance with the information— the person recounting experience at second or third hand, the book being about the book under discussion, the manuscript being a copy or a summary of primary material—the *source* is called a "secondary" *source.* The term *source* is also used to designate the origin of literary works, philosophical ideas, or artistic forms. In this sense, Lodge's *Rosalynde* is a *source* for Shakespeare's *As You Like It*, since the dramatist took his PLOT in part from the prose IDYLL.

Spasmodic School: A phrase applied by W. E. Aytoun in 1854 to a group of English poets who wrote in the 1840's and 1850's. The spirit of the VERSE (influenced by Shelley and Byron) reflected discontent and unrest, while its style was marked by jerkiness and forced or strained EMPHASIS. In his poem "America" (1855) Sydney Dobell in addressing "Columbia" alludes to the typical early English progenitor of Americans as "thy satchelled ancestor." Belonging to the group, besides Dobell, were Alexander Smith, P. J. Bailey, George Gilfillan, and other minor writers. The general *spasmodic* tendency is said also to appear in the early verse of Robert Browning and Elizabeth Barrett Browning, and in Tennyson's *Maud*.

Spenserian Sonnet: A SONNET of the ENGLISH type in that it has three QUATRAINS and a COUPLET, but is modified in the direction of the ITALIAN SONNET by having the QUATRAINS joined by the use of linking RHYMES. The RHYME-SCHEME is *abab bcbc cdcd ee*. It was used by Spenser in his SONNET SEQUENCE, *Amoretti*. See SONNET, LINKED RHYME.

Spenserian Stanza: A stanzaic pattern consisting of nine VERSES, the first eight being IAMBIC PENTAMETER, and the ninth an IAMBIC HEXAMETER. The RHYME-SCHEME is *ababbcbcc*. (See SCANSION.) The form derives its name from Edmund Spenser, who created the pattern for *The Faerie Queene*, from which the first stanza of Canto I is cited as an example:

> A Gentle Knight was pricking on the plaine,
> Y-cladd in mightie armes and silver shielde,
> Wherein old dints of deepe wounds did remaine,
> The cruell markes of many' a bloudy fielde;
> Yet armes till that time did he never wield:
> His angry steede did chide his foming bitt,
> As much disdayning to the curbe to yield:
> Full jolly knight he seemd, and faire did sitt,
> As one for knightly giusts and fierce encounters fitt.

This stanzaic FORM is notable for two qualities: the method of "tying-in" the three RHYMES promotes unity of effect and tightness of thought; the ALEXANDRINE at the close adds dignity to the sweep of the FORM and, at the same time, affords an opportunity for summary and epigrammatic expression which permits the line to knit up the thought of the whole STANZA. Other poets than Spenser have made notable use of the form. Burns used the *Spenserian stanza* in *The Cotter's Saturday Night*, Shelley in *The Revolt of Islam* and in *Adonais*; Keats used it in *The Eve of St. Agnes*, and Byron in *Childe Harold*.

Spondee: A FOOT composed of two accented syllables (⁄ ⁄). The form is rare in English VERSE, since most of our polysyllabic words carry a primary ACCENT. *Spondees* in our poetry are usually composed of two monosyllabic words as *all joy!* Poe in writing of the subject found only three or four instances (one of which was *football*) in English where real *spondees* occurred in a single word. Untermeyer finds a longer list (really compounds composed of monosyllabic words) and cites *heartbreak, childhood, bright-eyed, bookcase, wineglass,* and *Mayday.* In Milton's line:

> Silence, ye troubled waves, and thou deep, peace!

"deep, peace" is a perfect spondaic FOOT.

Spoonerism: An accidental interchange of sounds, usually the initial ones, in two or more words, such as *bl*ushing *cr*ow for *cr*ushing *bl*ow or well-*b*oiled icicle for well-oiled *b*icycle. The term owes its name to Dr. W. A. Spooner, of New College, Oxford, who was inordinately guilty of such transpositions.

Sprung Rhythm: A term coined by Gerard Manley Hopkins to designate the METER of POETRY whose RHYTHM is based on the number of stressed syllables in a VERSE without regard to the number of unstressed syllables. Put another way, *sprung rhythm* may be said to designate the METER of a VERSE which contains FEET of varying numbers of syllables, with the first syllable accented in each case. The FEET possible are the monosyllabic (a single stressed syllable), the TROCHEE, the DACTYL, and the first PÆON: ⁄ | ⁄ ⌣ | ⁄ ⌣ ⌣ | ⁄ ⌣ ⌣ ⌣. The obvious result of a line composed of combinations of such varying FEET is extreme metrical irregularity. The SCANSION of such poetry is, as W. B. Yeats noted, difficult because "it may not be certain at first glance where the stress falls." The following lines from Hopkins' "The Starlight Night" indicate both the effect of *sprung rhythm* and the difficulty of scanning it:

Stanza

Lóok ăt thĕ | stárs! | loŏk, | loŏk ŭp ăt thĕ | skíes!

Ŏ | loŏk ăt aĬl thĕ | fíre-fólk | sitting ĭn thĕ | aír!

Thĕ | bríght | bŏrŏŭgh, thĕ | círcle | cítădels | thĕre! |

Dówn ĭn | dĭm woŏds thĕ | díamŏnd | délves! thĕ | élves'-eyĕs!

(Note that a FOOT may continue to the beginning of the next line.) This passage, the opening lines of a SONNET, is clearly PENTAMETER, but of an indeterminable type of FOOT.

Hopkins said that he used *sprung rhythm* because "it is nearest to the rhythm of prose, that is the native and natural rhythm of speech," and he cited as earlier users the author of *Piers Plowman,* the CHORUS in Milton's *Samson Agonistes,* and old nursery RHYMES. See PROSE RHYTHM, ACCENT, METER, OLD ENGLISH VERSIFICATION.

Stanza: A recurrent grouping of two or more lines of a POEM in terms of length, metrical form, and, often, RHYME-SCHEME. However, the division into *stanzas* is sometimes made according to *thought* as well as form, in which case the *stanza* is a unit not unlike a paragraph of PROSE. STROPHE is another term used for *stanza,* but one should avoid VERSE in this sense, since VERSE is properly reserved to indicate a single line of poetry. Some of the more common stanzaic FORMS are COUPLET, TERCET, QUATRAIN, RHYME ROYAL, OTTAVA RIMA, and the SPENSERIAN STANZA, all of which are discussed in their proper places.

Static Character: A CHARACTER in a NOVEL, a SHORT STORY, or a DRAMA who changes little if at all in the progress of the action. Things happen to *static characters* without modifying their interior selves; the pattern of action reveals CHARACTERS as they are without showing them in the process of development. See CHARACTERIZATION.

Stave: A STANZA, particularly of a poem intended to be sung.

Stereotype: The metal duplication of a printing surface, cast from a mold made of the surface, usually by wet paper pulp. A *stereotype* plate enables the original surface to be exactly duplicated many times. By extension, *stereotype* has come to mean anything that repeats or duplicates something else without variation; hence something that lacks individualizing characteristics. The term is applied to commonly-held and oversimplified mental pictures or judgments of a person, a race, an issue, a kind of art, or anything.

-stich: A stem word meaning "line," as in HEMISTICH, a half line, or in DISTICH, a COUPLET.

Stichomythia: A form of REPARTEE developed in CLASSICAL DRAMA and often employed by Elizabethan writers, especially in plays which imitated the SENECAN TRAGEDIES. It is a sort of line-for-line "verbal fencing match" in which the principals in the DIALOGUE retort sharply to each other in lines which echo the opponent's words and FIGURES OF SPEECH. ANTITHESIS is freely used. The thought is often sententious. A few lines quoted from Hamlet's interview with his mother in the scene where Polonius is killed will serve as an instance of *stichomythia*:

> *Hamlet:* Now, mother, what's the matter?
> *Queen:* Hamlet, thou hast thy father much offended.
> *Hamlet:* Mother, you have my father much offended.
> *Queen:* Come, come, you answer with an idle tongue.
> *Hamlet:* Go, go, you question with a wicked tongue.

A more sustained example is found in the interview between King Richard and the Queen in *King Richard III* (IV, iv, 343 ff.).

Stock Characters: Conventional CHARACTER types belonging by custom to given FORMS of literature. Thus a boisterous CHARACTER known as the Vice came to be expected in a MORALITY play. The Elizabethan REVENGE TRAGEDY commonly employed, among other *stock characters*, a high-thinking vengeance-seeking HERO (Hamlet), the ghost of a murdered father or son, and a scheming murderer-villain (Claudius). In Elizabethan dramatic tradition in general one may expect such stock figures as a disguised romantic HEROINE (Portia), a melancholy man (Jaques), a loquacious old counsellor (Polonius), a female servant-CONFIDANTE (Nerissa), a court fool (Feste), a witty clownish servant (Launcelot Gobbo). In fairy tales the cruel stepmother and prince charming are examples. In the SENTIMENTAL NOVEL one expects a fainting HEROINE. So every type of fictional literature—NOVELS, ROMANCES, DETECTIVE TALES, moving pictures, the various kinds of COMEDIES and TRAGEDIES, METRICAL ROMANCES—tends to develop *stock characters* whose conventional nature a reader does well to recognize so that he can distinguish between the individual, personal characteristics of a given CHARACTER and the conventional traits drawn from the tradition of the *stock character* represented. See further under various types of literature, such as COMEDY OF HUMOURS, PICARESQUE NOVEL.

Stock Response: The traditional, conventional response to literature or art; poor artists and writers, like the preparers of advertising copy, call for *stock responses* by the use of STOCK CHARACTERS, STOCK SITUATIONS, and traditional SYMBOLS and standardized attitudes, such as the flag, mother love, and peace. Such materials have a "built-in" response for the unsophisticated reader. The serious artists and writers, however, attempt to provide sound grounds for the desired responses within the work itself. See SINCERITY.

Stock Situation: A SITUATION recurring frequently in a literary form, whether it be a general PLOT SITUATION, such as boy-meets-girl or rags-to-riches, or a recurrent detail, such as mixed identity or birthmarks that betray kinship. Note, however, that certain fundamental SITUATIONS, such as the search for a father, death and rebirth, the Oedipus attachment, and the loss of Paradise are more nearly archetypal patterns than *stock situations,* since they seem to echo recurrent human views of our life and its meaning. See ARCHETYPE.

Stoicism: The philosophical doctrine of the Stoics, a group of Greek philosophers, founded by Zeno late in the fourth century B.C. *Stoicism* exalts the ideals of virtue, endurance, and self-sufficiency. Virtue consists in living in conformity to the laws of nature; "to live consistently with nature" was one of the Stoics' most common admonitions. Endurance lies in the recognition that what is experienced is experienced by necessity and therefore must be endured. Self-sufficiency resides in extreme self-control, which holds in restraint all feelings, whether pleasurable or painful. *Stoicism* was the most attractive of the Greek philosophies to the Roman world, and its great influence in English literature comes through three Roman writers: Cicero, Epictetus, and Marcus Aurelius. There have been notable instances of the use of Stoic philosophy in English literature from "The Knight's Tale" in *The Canterbury Tales* to Addison's TRAGEDY, *Cato*—perhaps the most complete statement of the Stoic position in our language—to Ernest Hemingway's ideal of "grace under pressure."

Storm and Stress: An eighteenth-century German literary MOVE-MENT. See STURM UND DRANG.

Story: In its broadest sense any account, written, oral or in the mind, true or imaginary, of actions in a time sequence; any NARRA-TIVE of events in a sequential arrangement. The one merit of *story*, as *story*, is its ability to make us want to know what happened next; if other merits are to be gained they must be gained through what is done to *story* and not through *story* alone. In this broad sense, it is time and time only that is the determinant of selection—this happened, and then this, and then this, and now what?—other and higher concerns do not enter *story* as *story*.

Story is thus the basis of all literary GENRES that are NARRATIVE or DRAMATIC, for in each instance of each of them *story* is the collection of things that happen in the work. It is thus a common ele-ment—E. M. Forster would insist the only common element—among NOVELS, ROMANCES, SHORT STORIES, DRAMAS, EPIC POEMS, NARRATIVE POEMS, ALLEGORIES, PARABLES, SKETCHES, and all other FORMS with any basis in a sequence of events. *Story* may be looked upon as the raw material for all these FORMS, and they differ sig-nificantly in how and for what purposes they use *story* in the shaping of the work. *Story*, in this sense, is not PLOT but is an ingredient of PLOT. PLOT takes a *story*, selects its materials in terms not of time but of causality, gives it a beginning, a middle, and an end, makes it serve to elucidate or develop CHARACTER, embody a theme, ex-press an idea, incite to an action, or express an abstract concept. See PLOT.

Stream of Consciousness: The total range of awareness and emo-tive-mental response of an individual, from the lowest pre-speech level to the highest fully articulated level of rational thought. The assumption is that in the mind of an individual at a given moment his *stream of consciousness* (the phrase originated in this sense with William James) is a mixture of all the levels of awareness, an unend-ing flow of sensations, thoughts, memories, associations, and reflec-tions; if the exact content of the mind ("consciousness") is to be described at any moment, then these varied, disjointed, and illogical

Stream-of-Consciousness Novel

elements must find expression in a flow of words, images, and ideas similar to the unorganized flow of the mind.

Stream-of-Consciousness Novel, The: The type of PSYCHOLOGICAL NOVEL which takes as its subject matter the uninterrupted, uneven, and endless flow of the STREAM OF CONSCIOUSNESS of one or more of its characters. The *stream-of-consciousness novel* uses varied techniques to represent this consciousness adequately. In general, most PSYCHOLOGICAL NOVELS report the flow of conscious and ordered intelligence, as in Henry James, or the flow of memory recalled by association, as in Marcel Proust; but the *stream-of-consciousness novel* tends to concentrate its attention chiefly on the pre-speech, nonverbalized level, where the IMAGE must express the unarticulated response and where the logic of grammar belongs to another world. However differing the techniques employed, the writers of the *stream-of-consciousness novel* seem to share certain common assumptions: (1) that the significant existence of man is to be found in his mental-emotional processes and not in the outside world, (2) that this mental-emotional life is disjointed, illogical, and (3) that a pattern of free psychological association rather than of logical relationship determines the shifting sequence of thought and feeling.

Attempts to concentrate the subject matter of FICTION on the inner consciousness are not new by any means. The earliest impressive example seems to be Laurence Sterne's *Tristram Shandy* (1759–1767), with its motto from Epictetus: "It is not actions, but opinions about actions, which disturb men," and with its application of Locke's psychological theories of association and duration to the functioning of the human mind. Yet Sterne, although he freed the sequence of thought from the rigors of logical organization, did not get beneath the speech level in his portrait of Tristram's consciousness. Henry James, in his PSYCHOLOGICAL NOVELS, too, remained on a consciously articulated level. In a major sense, the present-day *stream-of-consciousness novel* is a product of Freudian psychology with its structure of psychological levels, although it first appeared in *Les lauriers sont coupés*, by Edouard Dujardin, in 1888, where the INTERIOR MONOLOGUE was used for the first time in the modern sense. Other important users of the INTERIOR MONOLOGUE to create reports on the *stream-of-consciousness* have been Dorothy Richardson, Virginia Woolf, James Joyce, William Faulkner. The tendency today is to see the *stream-of-consciousness* subject matter and the INTERIOR MONOLOGUE technique as tools to be used in the presentation of CHARACTER in depth, but not as the exclusive subjects or methods of whole NOVELS. See PSYCHOLOGICAL NOVEL, INTERIOR MONOLOGUE, STREAM OF CONSCIOUSNESS.

Stress: The vocal EMPHASIS given a syllable in the SCANSION of VERSE. There is debate by prosodists as to whether *stress* is the equivalent of ACCENT or whether *stress* should be used for metrical EMPHASIS and ACCENT be reserved for EMPHASIS that is determined by the meaning of the sentence (see RHETORICAL ACCENT). There is no agreement among prosodists on this matter, and in this Handbook *stress* and ACCENT have both been used to designate the vocal EMPHASIS placed on a syllable. See ACCENT, FOOT, METER, ARSIS, ICTUS, SCANSION.

Strong Curtain: A dramatically powerful conclusion to an ACT or to a play. See CURTAIN.

Strophe: A STANZA. In the PINDARIC ODE (see ODE) the *strophe* signifies particularly the first STANZA, and every subsequent third STANZA—i.e., the fourth, seventh, etc.

Structure: The planned framework of a piece of literature. Though such external matters as kind of language used (French or English, PROSE or VERSE, or kind of VERSE, or type of sentence) are sometimes referred to as "structural" features, the term usually is applied to the general plan or outline. Thus the scheme of topics (as revealed in a topical outline) determines the *structure* of a FORMAL ESSAY. The logical division of the action of a DRAMA (see DRAMATIC STRUCTURE) and also the mechanical division into ACTS and SCENES are matters of *structure*. In a narrative the PLOT itself is the structural element. Groups of stories may be set in a larger structural plan (see FRAMEWORK STORY) such as the pilgrimage in Chaucer's *Canterbury Tales*. The *structure* of an ITALIAN SONNET suggests first its division into OCTAVE and SESTET, and more minutely the internal plan of each of these two parts. A PINDARIC ODE follows a special structural plan which determines not only the development of the theme but the sequence of stanzaic forms. Often the author advertises his *structure* as a means of securing clarity (as in some college textbooks), while at other times the artistic purpose of the author leads him to conceal his *structure* (as in NARRATIVES) or subordinate it altogether (as in some INFORMAL ESSAYS). In the

NOVEL, the SHORT STORY, and the DRAMA, the *structure* is generally regarded today as the most reliable as well as the most revealing key to the meaning of the work. In the contemporary criticism of poetry, too, *structure* is used to define not only VERSE FORM and formal arrangement but also the sequence of IMAGES and ideas which unite to convey the meaning of the poem.

Sturm und Drang (**Storm and Stress**):   A literary MOVEMENT in Germany during the last quarter of the eighteenth century. The MOVEMENT derives its name from the title of a DRAMA, *Sturm und Drang* (1776) by Klinger, although Goethe's *Götz von Berlichingen* was probably the most significant literary production of the group. Goethe's *The Sorrows of Young Werther* (a NOVEL) reflects the *Sturm und Drang* attitude as does Schiller's *Die Räuber* (1781). The real founder and pioneer of the movement was Herder (1744–1803). Other leaders were Lenz, Klinger, and Friedrich Müller. The DRAMA was much used as a medium of expression and the dramatists were greatly influenced by Shakespeare and his freedom from classical standards. The *Sturm und Drang* MOVEMENT was a revolt from classical conventions and the tenets of French CLASSICISM. The writing was imbued with a strong nationalistic and folk element, was characterized by fervor and enthusiasm, a restless turbulency of spirit, the portrayal of great passion, a reliance upon emotional experiences and spiritual struggles and was intensely personal.

Style: The arrangement of words in a manner which at once best expresses the individuality of the author and the idea and intent in his mind. The best *style*, for any given purpose, is that which most nearly approximates a perfect adaptation of one's language to one's ideas. *Style* is a combination of two elements: the idea to be expressed, and the individuality of the author. It is, as Lowell said, "the establishment of a perfect mutual understanding between the worker and his material." From this point of view it is impossible to change the DICTION or to alter the phrasing of a statement and thus to say exactly the same thing; for what the reader receives from a statement is not alone what is said, but also certain CONNOTATIONS which affect his consciousness from the manner in which the statement is made. And from this it follows that, just as no two personalities are alike, no two *styles* are actually alike.

There are, in fact, many *styles*. The critic is fond of categories and fixes a label to a Milton, a Pope, a Hemingway; gives a name to

Subjective

a *style* and calls it ornamental, forceful, poetic, or what-not, in the
conviction perhaps that he has described the *style* of a writer when
all he has done has been to place him in a group with others who
have written ornate or forceful or poetic PROSE. A mere recital of
some of these categories may, however, be suggestive of the infinite
range of manners the one word *style* covers. We speak, for instance,
of journalistic, scientific, or literary *styles;* we call the manners of
other writers ABSTRACT or CONCRETE, rhythmic or pedestrian, sincere
or artificial, dignified or comic, original or imitative, dull or vivid, as
though each of these was somehow a final category of its own. But,
if we are actually to estimate a *style,* we need more delicate tests than
these; we need terms which will be so final in their sensitiveness as
ultimately to distinguish the work of each writer from that of all
other writers, since, as has been said, in the last analysis no two
styles are exactly comparable.

A study of *styles* for the purpose of analysis will include, in
addition to the infinity of personal detail suggested above, such general qualities as: DICTION, sentence structure and variety, IMAGERY,
RHYTHM, REPETITION, COHERENCE, EMPHASIS, and arrangement of
ideas. There is a growing interest in the study of *style* and language
in FICTION.

Subject Bibliography: A list of books, articles, manuscripts, or other
forms of writing, either complete or selected on any of various
principles, on one specific subject. See BIBLIOGRAPHY.

Subjective: A term frequently used in criticism to denote writing
which is expressive in an intensely personal manner of the inner
convictions, beliefs, dreams, or ideals of the author. *Subjective* writing is, of course, opposed to objective writing, which is impersonal,
CONCRETE, and concerned largely with NARRATIVE, analysis, or the
DESCRIPTION of externalities. One might, for instance, speak of the
subjective element in Shakespeare's SONNETS and the objective qualities of *The Rape of Lucrece;* the first tells of Shakespeare's reflective spirit; the second retells an old Roman story.

Another way of seeing the distinction between *subjective* and
objective is to associate *subjective* with the seer of an object or
the reporter of it and objective with the object seen or reported.
If the emphasis is upon the response of the reporter, the work is
subjective; if it is upon the object reported, the work is objective.
It should be noted that *subjective* may be used in two distinct senses,

just as the PERSONA has two possible distinct relationships with the author. *Subjective,* in one sense, may refer to the presence in the work of events and emotions that are autobiographical (the PERSONA speaks the author's personal responses, as the character Eugene Gant speaks Thomas Wolfe's). In the other sense, *subjective* may refer to the recounting of an emotional response by a PERSONA who is a dramatically realized CHARACTER, assumed to be feeling emotions peculiar to the dramatic situation and not necessarily those of the author, as the NARRATOR Ishmael speaks dramatically rather than autobiographically in Melville's *Moby-Dick.* By present-day critical standards the first kind of subjectivity is suspect, the second admirable. See OBJECTIVITY, NEGATIVE CAPABILITY, OBJECTIVE CORRELATIVE, AESTHETIC DISTANCE.

Sublime: Characterized by nobility and grandeur, impressive, exalted, raised above ordinary human qualities—these were asserted to be the essential qualities of great art in the aesthetic treatise, *On the Sublime,* by "Longinus" (50 A.D.). "Longinus" regarded the *sublime* as a thing of spirit, a spark leaping from writer to reader, rather than a product of technique. He lists five sources of the *sublime,* the first two of which—great thoughts and noble feelings—are gifts of nature, and the last three of which—lofty FIGURES OF SPEECH, DICTION, and arrangement—are products of art. Edmund Burke in 1756 wrote *A Philosophical Inquiry into the Origin of our Ideas of the Sublime and the Beautiful.* Kant followed Burke's line of thinking, in his *Critique of Judgment* (1790), where he linked beauty with the finite and the *sublime* with the infinite.

Subplot: A subordinate or minor COMPLICATION running through a piece of FICTION. This secondary PLOT interest, if skillfully handled, has a direct relationship to the main PLOT, contributing to it in interest and in COMPLICATION and struggle. (See PLOT.) Some writers have carried the intricacies and surprises of PLOT relationships so far as to create not only one, but sometimes three, four, or more *subplots.* The characteristic difference, it has been observed, between the FICTION of France, Italy—the romance countries in general—and the FICTION of the Anglo-Saxons is that the romance authors are generally satisfied with simple, unified PLOT relationships, whereas northern writers are more given to an intricate series of *subplots* supporting and complicating the major PLOT. There are said to be seventy-five characters in Dickens' *Our Mutual*

Friend and sixty in Thackeray's *Vanity Fair*. When so many people are introduced into a work of FICTION it is obvious that their relationship to the chief characters of the main PLOT must shade off into very subordinate *subplots*. As instances of *subplots* in Shakespeare may be cited from *Hamlet* the Laertes-Hamlet struggle (as subordinate to the Claudius-Hamlet major PLOT). It may be observed that writers use *subplots* of at least two different degrees: first, those which are directly related to, and which give impetus and action to, the main PLOT; and second, those which are more or less extraneous to the chief PLOT interest and which are introduced frankly as a secondary story to give zest and EMPHASIS, or relief, to the main PLOT.

Substitution: In PROSODY, a term used to describe the use of one kind of FOOT in place of the one normally demanded by the METER of a VERSE, as a TROCHEE for an IAMB or a DACTYL or ANAPEST for a TROCHEE or IAMB. See COMPENSATION.

Surrealism: A MOVEMENT in art and literature emphasizing the expression of the IMAGINATION as realized in dreams and presented without conscious control. It developed in France under the leadership of André Breton, whose *Manifeste du surréalisme* appeared in 1924. *Surrealism* is often regarded as an outgrowth of DADA, although it has discernible roots reaching back to Baudelaire and Rimbaud, and it demonstrates the marked influence of Freud. As a literary MOVEMENT it has been confined almost entirely to France, but as a MOVEMENT in modern art it has had many followers, among them Dali, Miró, Duchamp, and Max Ernst. See DADA.

Surrogate: A person or a thing that is substituted for or speaks for another. In FICTION, if an author creates a CHARACTER—such as the RAISONNEUR of the WELL-MADE PLAY—who embodies the ideals of the author or who utters speeches which are the expression of the author's opinions and judgments, such a CHARACTER is said to be an author-SURROGATE.

Suspense: The poised anticipation of the reader or audience as to the outcome of the events of a SHORT STORY, a NOVEL, or a DRAMA, particularly as these events affect a CHARACTER in the work for whom the reader or audience has formed a sympathetic attachment. *Suspense* is a major device for the securing and maintaining of interest in all FORMS of FICTION. It may be either of two major types: in one, the outcome is uncertain and the *suspense* resides in the question of who or what or how; in the other, the outcome is inevitable from the events which have gone before (see DRAMATIC IRONY) and the *suspense* resides in the audience's frightened anticipation, in the question of when.

"Sweetness and Light": A phrase given great popularity by Matthew Arnold, who used it as the title for the first chapter of *Culture and Anarchy* (1869). Arnold did not create the term but borrowed it from Swift's *The Battle of the Books*, where Swift, in recounting the APOLOGUE of the Spider and the Bee, summarized the argument relating to the superiority of ancient over modern authors (see ANCIENTS AND MODERNS, QUARREL OF) in these words: "Instead of dirt and poison we have rather chosen to fill our hives with honey and wax, thus furnishing mankind with the two noblest of things, which are sweetness and light." These two "noblest of things," as Arnold uses the term, are *beauty* and *intelligence*—and it is to these two qualities that "sweetness and light" refers.

Syllabic Verse: VERSE in which the measure of the line is determined by the number of syllables in the line regardless of the stressed or unstressed syllables. The naming of lines in *syllabic verse* is by the use of numerical prefixes added to *syllabic*, as *monosyllabic* for one syllable, *trisyllabic* for three syllables, *decasyllabic* for ten syllables, *duodecasyllabic* for twelve syllables, etc. *Syllabic verse* is not common in English, but it is the standard METER for POETRY in most of the Romance languages, as it is in Japanese POETRY (see HAIKU).

Syllabus: An outline or abstract containing the major heads of a book, a course of lectures, an ARGUMENT, program of study. A DIGEST of the chief "points" of a larger work.

Syllepsis: A grammatically correct construction in which one word is placed in the same grammatical relationship to two words but in quite different senses, as *stain* is linked in different senses to *honor* and *brocade* in Pope's line, "Or stain her honor, or her new brocade." But see ZEUGMA.

Syllogism: A formula for presenting an argument logically. The *syllogism* affords a method of demonstrating the logic of an argument through analysis. In its simplest form, it consists of three divisions, a major premise, a minor premise, and a conclusion.

Major premise: All public libraries should serve the people.
Minor premise: This is a public library.
Conclusion: Therefore this library should serve the people.

There are, it is to be noticed, three terms as well as three divisions to the *syllogism*. In the major premise "should serve the people" is the "major term"; in the minor premise "this (library)" is the "minor term"; and the term appearing in both the major and the minor premise, "public library," is called the "middle term."

Symbol: On the most literal level, a *symbol* is something which is itself and yet stands for or suggests or means something else; as the letters *a p p l e* form a word which stands for a particular objective reality; or as a flag is a piece of colored cloth which stands for a nation. All language is symbolic in this sense, and many of the objects which we commonly use in daily life are.

In a literary sense, a *symbol* is a TROPE which combines a literal and sensuous quality with an abstract or suggestive aspect, a definition which also applies to the function of the flag as *symbol*. However, in criticism it is necessary to distinguish *symbol* from IMAGE, ALLEGORY, and METAPHOR. If we consider an IMAGE to have a concrete referent in the objective world and to function as IMAGE when it powerfully evokes that referent, then a *symbol* is like an IMAGE in doing the same thing but different from it in going beyond the evoking of the objective referent by making that referent suggest to the reader or audience a meaning beyond itself; in other words, a *symbol* is an IMAGE which evokes an objective, concrete reality and has that reality suggest another level of meaning. However, the *symbol* does not "stand for" the meaning; it evokes an object which suggests the meaning. As Coleridge said, "It partakes of the reality which it renders intelligible." *Symbol* differs from ALLEGORY in that in ALLEGORY the objective referent evoked is without value until it is translated into the fixed meaning that it has in its own particular structure of ideas (see ALLEGORY), whereas a *symbol* includes permanent objective value, independent of the meanings which it may suggest. It differs from METAPHOR in that a METAPHOR evokes an object in order to illustrate an idea or demonstrate a quality, whereas a *symbol* embodies the idea or the quality. As W. M. Urban said, "The metaphor becomes a symbol when by means of it we embody an ideal content not otherwise expressible."

Symbolism

Literary *symbols* are of two broad types: one includes those which embody within themselves universal suggestions of meaning, as the land and ocean suggest time and eternity, the voyage suggests life, and phallic *symbols* are universally recognized. Such *symbols* are used widely (and sometimes unconsciously) in the world's literature. The other type of *symbol* secures its suggestiveness not from qualities inherent in itself but from the way in which it is used in a given work. Thus in *Moby-Dick* the voyage, the land, the ocean—these objects are pregnant with meanings that seem almost independent of Melville's use of them in his story; on the other hand, the white whale is invested with meaning—and differing meanings for different crew members—through the handling of materials in the novel. Similarly, in Hemingway's *A Farewell to Arms,* rain, which is merely a physical fact in the opening chapter, is converted into a *symbol* of death through the uses to which it is put in the book. See ALLEGORY, IMAGE, IMAGERY, METAPHOR, SIMILE, TROPE.

Symbolism: In its broad sense, *symbolism* is the use of one object to represent or suggest another; or, in literature, the use of SYMBOLS in writing, particularly the serious and extensive use of such SYMBOLS.

Symbolism is also the name given to a literary MOVEMENT which originated in France in the last half of the nineteenth century, strongly influenced Irish and British writing around the turn of the century, and has been a dominant force in much British and American POETRY in the twentieth century. This *symbolism* represents one of the romantic reactions to REALISM. It sees the immediate, unique, and personal emotional response as the proper subject of art, and its full expression as the ultimate aim of art. Since the emotions experienced by a poet in a given moment are unique to that person and that moment and are finally both fleeting and incommunicable, the POET is reduced to the use of a complex and highly private kind of symbolization in an effort to give expression to his ineffable feeling. The result is a kind of writing consisting of what Edmund Wilson has called "a medley of metaphor" in which SYMBOLS lacking apparent logical relation are put together in a pattern, one of whose characteristics is an indefiniteness as great as the indefiniteness of the experience itself and another of whose characteristics is the conscious effort to use words for their musical effect, without very much attention to precise meaning.

As Baudelaire, one of the principal forerunners of the movement, said, man lives in a "forest of symbols" which results from the fact that the materiality and individuality of the physical world dissolves into the "dark and confused unity" of the unseen world. In this process SYNAESTHESIA takes place. Baudelaire and the later symbolists, particularly Mallarmé and Valéry, were greatly influenced by the theory and poetic practice of Edgar Allan Poe. Other important French writers in the movement were Rimbaud, Verlaine, Leforgue, Rémy de Gourmont, and Claudel, and Maeterlinck in the DRAMA and Huysman in the NOVEL. The Irish writers of this century, particularly Yeats in POETRY, Synge in the DRAMA, and Joyce in the NOVEL, have been notably responsive to the movement. In Germany Rilke and Stefan George have functioned as symbolist poets. In America the IMAGIST poets reflected the movement, as did Eugene O'Neill in the DRAMA. Through its pervasive influence on T. S. Eliot, *symbolism* has affected much of the best British and American poetry in our time.

In America in the middle of the nineteenth century *symbolism* of the sort typical of ROMANTICISM was the dominant literary mode. In this symbolist MOVEMENT the details of the natural world and the actions of people were used to suggest philosophical ideas and themes. Romantic *symbolism* was the fundamental practice of the Transcendentalists (see TRANSCENDENTALISM). Emerson, the chief spokesman for the MOVEMENT, declared that "Particular natural facts are symbols of particular spiritual facts" and that "Nature is the symbol of spirit," and Henry David Thoreau made life itself a symbolic action in *Walden*. The symbolic method was present in the POETRY of these men and also in that of Walt Whitman. *Symbolism* was a distinctive feature of the NOVELS of Hawthorne—notably *The Scarlet Letter* and *The Marble Faun*—and of Melville, whose *Moby-Dick* is probably the most original work of symbolic art in American literature. See SYMBOL.

Symposium: A Greek word meaning "a drinking together" or banquet. As such convivial meetings were characterized by free conversation, the word later came to mean discussion by different persons of a single topic, or a collection of speeches or ESSAYS on a given subject. One of Plato's best known DIALOGUES is *The Symposium* and later literary uses of the word are much under its influence.

Synaesthesia

Synaesthesia: The concurrent response of two or more of the senses to the stimulation of one. The term is applied in literature to the description of one kind of sensation in terms of another—that is, the description of sounds in terms of colors, as a "blue note," of colors in terms of temperature, as a "cool green," etc. Poe employed *synaesthesia* often; Baudelaire gave it wide currency through his practice and particularly his sonnet, *"Correspondances."* It is one of the most distinctive characteristics of the poetry of the SYMBOLISM movement. Dame Edith Sitwell employs it as a major poetic device.

Syncopation: A term used in music to describe the effect produced by a temporary displacing or shifting of the regular metrical accent. In PROSODY it is used to describe the effect produced by SUBSTITUTION and also the effect produced when the METRICAL ACCENT and the RHETORICAL ACCENT differ sufficiently in a VERSE to create the effect of two different metrical patterns existing concurrently in the line.

Syncope: A cutting short of words through the omission of a letter or a syllable. *Syncope* is distinguished from ELISION in that it is usually confined to omissions of letters (usually vowels) within the word, whereas ELISION usually runs two words together by the omission of a final or initial letter. *Ev'ry* for *every* is an example of *syncope*. Naturally the greatest use for this omission of sounds is in VERSE where a desired metrical effect is sought. However, *syncope* has taken place frequently in English simply to shorten words, as *pacificist* has become *pacifist*.

Synecdoche: A form of METAPHOR which in mentioning a part signifies the whole or the whole signifies the part. In order to be clear, a good *synecdoche* must be based on an *important* part of the whole and not a minor part and, usually, the part selected to stand for the whole must be the part most directly associated with the subject under discussion. Thus under the first restriction we say *motor* for automobile (rather than *tire*), and under the second we speak of infantry on the march as *foot* rather than as *hands* just as we use *hands* rather than *foot* for men who are at work at manual labor.

Synonyms: Words in the same language with the same or similar meanings. Rarely in English are two words exact *synonyms* although it may happen that in a single sentence any one of two or three words may serve the desired purpose. Conventional usage has given most of our words certain associations and CONNOTATIONS, certain idiomatic connections, which make impossible a free substituting of one for another. As one commentator has pointed out *humble* and *lowly* may appear synonymous, but no one yet has ever signed a letter "your *lowly* servant." The presence of so many Romance words in English has enriched the language by offering choice between Old English and Romance forms—*help* and *assist* for example.

Synopsis: A summary, a résumé of the main points of a composition or argument so made as to show the relationship of each part to the whole. An ABSTRACT. A *synopsis* is usually more connected than an outline since it is likely to be given in complete sentences.

Syzygy: In classical PROSODY, a term used to designate two coupled feet serving as a unit. As used by Sidney Lanier and later prosodists, it refers to the use of consonant sounds at the end of one word and at the beginning of another that can be spoken together easily and harmoniously. Both Poe and Lanier were greatly concerned with *syzygy*.

T

Tableau: An interlude during a SCENE of a play in which the actors freeze in position and then resume action as before or hold their positions until the CURTAIN falls. In the nineteenth century many plays ended their ACTS with *tableaux,* and frequently the play ended with a *tableau.* For the costumed representation of well-known scenes, pictures, or personages, the term *tableau vivant* (living picture) was used. Such *tableaux* are often presented in PAGEANTS or on floats. The identification of the figure represented in a *tableau vivant* was once a social game; an instance is described in *The House of Mirth* by Edith Wharton.

Tail-rhyme Romance: A term applied to METRICAL ROMANCES employing the TAIL-RHYME STANZA, especially the large group, including *Amis and Amiloun, Athelston, Horn Childe* (and some twenty others), which employed a TAIL-RHYME STANZA of twelve lines made up of four groups or parts, each with a short "tail" line, such as aa*b* aa*b* cc*b* dd*b*. There existed a "school" of minstrels writing *tail-rhyme romances* in East Anglia in the fourteenth century.

Tail-rhyme Stanza: A STANZA of VERSE containing among longer lines two or more short lines which RHYME with each other and serve as "tails" to the divisions or parts of the STANZA. The form developed in medieval times and is known in French as RIME COUÉE. Chaucer's "Rime of Sir Thopas" in the *Canterbury Tales* is written in *tail-rhyme stanza*.

Tale: A simple NARRATIVE in PROSE or VERSE without complicated PLOT. Formerly no very real distinction was made between the *tale* and the SHORT STORY; the two terms were used interchangeably. *Tale,* however, has always been a more general term than SHORT STORY since the latter has been reserved for NARRATIVE following a fairly technical routine and the former has been loosely used to denote any short NARRATIVE, either true or fictitious.

Tall Tale: A kind of humorous TALE common on the American frontier, which uses realistic detail, a literal manner, and common speech to recount extravagantly impossible happenings, usually resulting from the superhuman abilities of a CHARACTER. The TALES about Paul Bunyan, Mike Fink, and Davy Crockett are typical frontier *tall tales*. The German *Adventures of Baron Munchausen* is, perhaps, the best known literary use of the *tall tale*.

Tanka: A type of Japanese poetry similar to the HAIKU. It consists of thirty-one syllables, arranged in five lines, each of seven syllables, except the first and third, which are each of five. See HAIKU.

Taste: A term used in criticism to designate the basis for the personal acceptance or rejection of a work of art as producing pleasure or pain in its reader, hearer, or viewer. Perhaps no critical term remains, despite all efforts at analysis, more purely subjective than does *taste*. However, as it is commonly used, it does have two distinct meanings: it may refer to the mere condition of liking or disliking an object, in which case it may be deplored but not debated ("There is no accounting for taste." "Each to his own taste." "*De gustibus non est disputandum.*"); on the other hand, it may refer to the ability to discern the beautiful and to appreciate it, in which case *taste* is capable of being educated and is subject to examination in terms of its operating principles. T. S. Eliot had such a view of *taste* when he saw one of the functions of criticism to be "the correction of taste," and so had Addison when he said that *taste* "discerns the Beauties of an Author with Pleasure, and the Imperfections with Dislike." *Taste* in the first sense is used to describe a purely impressionistic response, as in the criticism of Croce; in the second sense it designates a kind of aesthetic judgment, as it does with Eliot. In the latter case, *taste* becomes a sense of what is harmonious, appropriate, or beautiful, a kind of critical tact, and as such it designates a quality essential to the artist, the critic, and the serious student.

Tautology: The use of superfluous, repetitious words. "He wrote an autobiography of his life" might much better be stated "He wrote an autobiography." *Tautology* differs from the kinds of REPETITION used for clarity, EMPHASIS, or effect, in that it repeats the idea without the addition of forcefulness or clearness to the expression.

Telestich: An ACROSTIC in which the final letters form a word. See ACROSTIC.

Tenor and **Vehicle:**   Terms used by I. A. Richards for the two essential elements of a METAPHOR. The *tenor* is the discourse or subject which the *vehicle* illustrates or illuminates; or, stated another way, the *vehicle* is the figure that carries the weight of the comparison, while the *tenor* is the subject to which the *vehicle* refers. According to Richards' definition, a METAPHOR always involves two ideas—*tenor* and *vehicle*. If it is impossible to distinguish them, we are dealing with a literal statement; if we can distinguish them, even slightly, we are dealing with a metaphoric expression. Hamlet's question, "What should such fellows as I do crawling between earth and heaven?" is metaphoric. While Hamlet may literally crawl, there is, as Richards points out, "an unmistakable reference to other things that crawl . . . and this reference is the *vehicle* as Hamlet . . . is the *tenor*." See METAPHOR.

Tension: A term introduced into contemporary criticism by Allen Tate, by which he means the integral UNITY of a poem, a UNITY which results from the successful resolution in the work of the conflicts of abstraction and concreteness, of general and particular, of DENOTATION and CONNOTATION. The term results from removing

Tercet

the prefixes from two terms in logic: *intension,* which refers to the abstract attributes of objects which can properly be named by a word; and *extension,* which refers to the specific object named by the word. Good poetry, Tate asserts, is the "full, organized body of all the extension and intension that we can find in it." This concept has been widely used by the New Critics, particularly in their examination of poetry as a pattern of PARADOX or as a form of IRONY. See CONCRETE UNIVERSAL.

Tercet: A STANZA of three lines, a TRIPLET, in which each line ends with the same RHYME. The term is also used to denote either of the two three-line groups forming the SESTET of the Italian SONNET. A *tercet* of the type first mentioned is quoted from Herrick:

> Whenas in silks my Julia goes,
> Then, then, methinks, how sweetly flows
> That liquefaction of her clothes.

The term is also applied to the TERZA RIMA STANZA.

Terza rima: A three-line STANZA form borrowed from the Italian POETS. The RHYME-SCHEME is *aba, bcb, cdc, ded,* etc. In other words one RHYME-sound is used for the first and third line of each STANZA and a new RHYME introduced for the second line, this new RHYME, in turn, being used for the first and third lines of the subsequent STANZA. Usually the METER is IAMBIC PENTAMETER. The opening of Shelley's *Ode to the West Wind,* which is written in *terza rima,* illustrates it:

O wild West Wind, thou breath of Autumn's being,	a
Thou, from whose unseen presence the leaves dead	b
Are driven, like ghosts from an enchanter fleeing	a
Yellow, and black, and pale, and hectic red.	b
Pestilence-stricken multitudes: O thou,	c
Who chariotest to their dark wintry bed ...	b

The *terza rima* has been popular with English poets, being used by Milton, Shelley, and Byron, among many others. With variations in METER and the use of imperfect RHYMES, it has been widely used by contemporary POETS, particularly MacLeish, Auden, and Eliot.

Testament: As a literary form the term has two distinct meanings. It may be a literary "last will and testament" or it may be a piece of literature which "bears witness to" or "makes a covenant with" in the Biblical sense. The former sort of *testament* originated with the Romans of the decadent period and was developed by the French in the late medieval and early RENAISSANCE periods. It was especially popular in the fifteenth century and was often characterized by HUMOR, ribaldry, and SATIRE, as in the half-serious, half-ribald *Grand Testament* and *Petit Testament* of François Villon, perhaps the greatest examples of this type. In the popular literature of the first half of the sixteenth century in England there were many wills and *testaments* of the humorous and satiric sort, such as *Jyl of Breynt-ford's Testament, Colin Blowbol's Testament,* and Humphrey Powell's popular *Wyll of the Devil* (*ca.*1550). Some literary *testaments,* however, were more serious; for example, the *Testament of Cresseid* by the Scotch poet Robert Henryson (1430–1506), a continuation of Chaucer's *Troilus and Criseyde,* in which Cressida is pictured as thoroughly degraded in character and suffering from leprosy. In her poverty-stricken last days she bequeaths her scant belongings to her fellow-sufferers. Another serious *testament* is the love COMPLAINT, "The Testament of the Hawthorne" in *Tottel's Miscellany* (1557).

The second type of *testament,* that which "bears witness to," was also developed in the late medieval period. Its best representative in English is perhaps *The Testament of Love* by Thomas Usk (?), written about 1384. This is a long prose treatise in which Divine Love appears in a role similar to that of Philosophy in Boethius' *Consolation of Philosophy,* to which it is somewhat akin. A modern representative is Robert Bridges' *The Testament of Beauty* (1929).

Tetralogy: Four works, usually DRAMAS or NOVELS, that constitute a group. Thus Shakespeare's CHRONICLE PLAYS *Richard II, Henry IV,* Parts One and Two, and *Henry V* constitute a *tetralogy.* Greek DRAMA was presented in *tetralogies,* consisting of three TRAGEDIES followed by a SATYR PLAY.

Tetrameter: A line of VERSE consisting of four FEET. See SCANSION.

Textual Criticism: A scholarly activity which attempts by all available means to reconstruct the original manuscript or the authoritative text of a work. According to Fredson Bowers, the four basic functions of the textual critic are (1) to analyze the characteristics of an extant manuscript, (2) to recover the characteristics of the lost manuscript that served as copy for a printed text, (3) to study the transmission of a printed text, and (4) to present an established and edited text to the public. See CRITICISM, TYPES OF.

Texture: A term applied to the elements which remain in a work of literary art after a PARAPHRASE of its ARGUMENT has been made. Among such elements are details of SITUATION, METAPHOR, METER, IMAGERY, TONE COLOR, RHYME—in fact, all elements that are not considered to be a part of the STRUCTURE of the work. The separation of TEXTURE and STRUCTURE is a strategy often employed by the NEW CRITICS.

Theater-in-the-Round: The presentation of plays on a stage surrounded by the audience. See ARENA STAGE.

Theater of Cruelty: DRAMA which subordinates words to action, gesture, and sound in an effort to overwhelm the spectator and liberate his instinctual preoccupations with crime, cruelty, and eroticism. See CRUELTY, THEATER OF.

Theater of the Absurd: An AVANT-GARDE kind of DRAMA that represents the absurdity of the human condition by abandoning rational devices and realistic FORM. See ABSURD, THEATER OF THE.

Theme: The central or dominating idea in a literary work. In non-FICTION PROSE it may be thought of as the general topic of discussion, the subject of the discourse, the THESIS. In POETRY, FICTION, and DRAMA it is the abstract concept which is made concrete through its representation in person, action, and IMAGE in the work.

Theoretical Criticism: A kind of criticism that attempts to arrive at the general principles of art and to formulate inclusive and enduring aesthetic and critical tenets. See CRITICISM, TYPES OF.

Thesis: An attitude or position on a problem taken by a writer or speaker with the purpose of proving or supporting it. The term is also used for the paper which is written to support the *thesis*. That is, *thesis* is used both for the problem to be established and for the ESSAY which, presumably, establishes it. In college and university circles the word has the special connotation of a paper expounding some special problem and written as a requirement for a bachelor's or master's degree. See DISSERTATION. *Thesis* as a term in PROSODY, was used by the Greeks to refer to stressed syllables; however, later Latin usage applied ARSIS to the stressed and *thesis* to the unstressed syllables. The terms are rarely used today, but when they are, the later Latin usage is almost always intended. See ARSIS, ACCENT.

Thesis Novel: A NOVEL that deals with some social, economic, political, or religious problem in such a way that it suggests a *thesis,* usually in the form of a solution to the problem. Among the types of NOVELS that are called *thesis novels* are SOCIOLOGICAL NOVELS, POLITICAL NOVELS, PROBLEM NOVELS, and PROPAGANDA NOVELS. The French term *roman à thèse* is sometimes used instead of *thesis novel.*

Thesis Play: A DRAMA which presents a social problem and proposes a solution. It is sometimes known by the French term *pièce à thèse.* See PROBLEM PLAY, for which *thesis play* is an equivalent term.

Threnody: A SONG of death, a DIRGE, a lamentation.

Title: The distinguishing name attached to any written production, a book, a section of a book, a chapter, a SHORT STORY, a POEM, etc. Although modern *titles* are usually brief, an older practice produced *titles* that sometimes filled a closely printed page. For bibliographical purposes, the entire *title* page, including the author's name and the publication facts, is considered the *title,* and when it is copied, the actual typography and lineation are usually indicated.

Tone (Tone Color): *Tone* is used in contemporary criticism, following I. A. Richards' example, as a term designating the attitudes toward the subject and toward the audience implied in a literary work. In such a usage, a work may have a *tone* that is formal, informal, intimate, solemn, sombre, playful, serious, ironic, condescending, or any of many other possible attitudes. Clearly, *tone* in this sense contributes in a major way to the effect and the effectiveness of a literary work.

In another sense, *tone* is used to designate the MOOD of the work itself and the various devices that are used to create that MOOD. In this sense, *tone* results from combinations and variations of such things as METER, RHYME, ALLITERATION, ASSONANCE, CONSONANCE, DICTION, SENTENCE STRUCTURE, REPETITION, IMAGERY, SYMBOLISM, etc.

Tone or *tone color* is sometimes used to designate a musical quality in language which Sidney Lanier discussed in *The Science of English Verse*, where he asserts that the sounds of words have qualities equivalent to timbre in music. "When the ear exactly coordinates a series of sounds with primary reference to their tone-color, the result is a conception of (in music, flute-tone as distinct from violin-tone, and the like; in verse, rhyme as opposed to rhyme, vowel varied with vowel, phonetic syzygy, and the like), in general . . . *tone-color*."

Topographical Poetry: A GENRE established in English POETRY by John Denham's *Cooper's Hill* (1642), *topographical poetry* is VERSE in which, according to Samuel Johnson's definition, "the fundamental subject is some particular landscape." It was immensely popular in the seventeenth and eighteenth centuries. Among its practitioners were Thomson, Dyer, and Crabbe. During its ascendancy critics recognized nine categories of *topographical poetry*, such as hills, towns, rivers, caves, and buildings.

Touchstone: A term used metaphorically as a critical standard by Matthew Arnold in "The Study of Poetry." A *touchstone* is literally a hard black stone once used to test the quality of gold or silver by comparing the streak left on the stone by one of these metals with that made by a standard alloy of the metal. *Touchstones* for Arnold were "lines and expressions of the great masters," which the critic should hold always in his mind and apply "as a *touchstone* to other POETRY." They form, he believed, an infallible way of "detecting the presence or absence of high poetic quality . . . in all other poetry which we may place beside them." Most of Arnold's *touchstones* met his expressed standard that great POETRY should have "high seriousness."

Tour de force: Actually any feat of strength and virtuosity. *Tour de force* is used in literary criticism to refer to works which make outstanding demonstrations of the author's skill. Although some works so called have great literary merit, such as Joyce's *Ulysses*, James's *The Turn of the Screw*, and Faulkner's *The Sound and the Fury*, *tour de force* more often implies technical virtuosity than literary strength.

Tract: A PAMPHLET, usually an argumentative document on some religious or political topic, often distributed free for propaganda

purposes. For a classic example of the use of the term, see Oxford
Movement.

Tractarianism: The religious attitudes and principles of the founders of the Oxford Movement, as set forth in the ninety pamphlets
called *Tracts for the Times* (1833–1841). See Oxford Movement.

Tradition: A body of beliefs, customs, sayings, or skills handed
down from age to age or from generation to generation. Thus ballads and folk literature in general as well as superstitions and popular proverbs are passed on by oral *tradition*. A set idea may be
called a *tradition*, like the idea which prevailed throughout the
Middle Ages that Homer's account of the Trojan War was to be discredited in favor of certain forged accounts claiming to be written
by participants in the war. The *tradition* of pastoral literature
means the underlying conceptions and technique of pastoral literature carried down, with modifications, from Theocritus (third century b.c.) to Pope. A *traditional* element in literature suggests something which the author has inherited from the past rather than
something of his own invention. In another sense, *tradition* may be
thought of as the inheritance from the past of a body of literary
conventions that are still alive in the present, as opposed to conventions of the past which died with their peculiar age and circumstance.

Tragedy: A drama, in prose or verse, which recounts an important and causally related series of events in the life of a person of
significance, such events culminating in an unhappy catastrophe,
the whole treated with great dignity and seriousness. According to
Aristotle, whose definition in the *Poetics* is an inductive description
of the Greek *tragedies*, the purpose of a *tragedy* is to arouse the
emotions of pity and fear and thus to produce in the audience a
catharsis of these emotions. Such a definition as this is broad enough
to admit almost any drama that is serious and that ends with an
unhappy catastrophe, although its various formulations have been
interpreted from time to time in terms of the attitudes and conventions of the age in which the formulations have been made. The
question of the nature of the significance of the tragic hero is answered in each age by the concept of significance that is held by that
age. In a period of monarchy, Shakespeare's protagonists were

kings and rulers; in other ages they have been and will be other kinds of men. In a democratic nation, founded on an egalitarian concept of man, a tragic HERO can be the archetypal common man —a shoe salesman, a policeman, a gangster, a New England farmer, a Negro servant. From time to time the basis of UNITY has been debated. With the classical writers of the RENAISSANCE and in the NEO-CLASSIC PERIOD, the UNITIES were observed with rigor. Yet ages which find UNITY in other aspects of DRAMA than its technique, may wed the serious and the comic, may take liberties with time and place, may use multiple PLOTS, and still achieve a unified effect as the non-classic RENAISSANCE writers did. What constitutes dignity and seriousness in presentation is also subject to the interpretation of the age in which the play is produced. In its own way Arthur Miller's *The Death of a Salesman* is fully as serious and as dignified for our world as *Hamlet* was for Elizabethan England, although it is a lesser play. CLASSICAL TRAGEDY and ROMANTIC TRAGEDY both emphasize the significance of a choice made by the PROTAGONIST but dictated by his "flaw," his HAMARTIA; yet to insist that *tragedy* be confined to this particular view of man and life is to limit it in indefensible ways. Clearly *tragedy* defies specific definition, each age producing works that speak in the conventions and beliefs of that age the enduring sense that man seems to have of the tragic nature of his existence and of the grandeur of the human spirit in facing it.

In the Middle Ages the term *tragedy* did not refer to a DRAMA but to any NARRATIVE which recounted how a person of high rank, through ill fortune or his own vice or error, fell from high estate to low. The *tragedies* recounted in Chaucer's "Monk's Tale," in Lydgate's *Fall of Princes*, and in the RENAISSANCE collection, *The Mirror for Magistrates*, are of this sort. In the sixteenth century the influence of CLASSICAL TRAGEDY, particularly of SENECAN TRAGEDY, combined with notable elements of the MEDIEVAL DRAMA to produce English *tragedy*. In 1559 came the first translation of a SENE-CAN TRAGEDY, and in 1562 was acted Sackville and Norton's *Gorboduc,* "the first regular English *tragedy*." The genius for the stage which characterized the ELIZABETHAN AGE worked upon this FORM to produce the greatest flowering in the DRAMA that England has known. Yet the *tragedy* which emerged was not the CLASSICAL TRAGEDY of Aristotle's definition, despite the efforts of men like Ben Jonson to school it into being so, but plays of a heterogeneous character known as ROMANTIC TRAGEDY—plays which tended to ignore the UNITIES, which followed medieval tradition in mixing sadness and mirth, and which strove at any cost—including SUBPLOTS and comic RELIEF SCENES—to satisfy the spectators with vigorous action and gripping spectacle. Shakespeare worked in the forms of the REVENGE TRAGEDY, the DOMESTIC TRAGEDY, and the CHRONICLE PLAY.

The seventeenth century saw the ELIZABETHAN TRAGEDY continued with a growing emphasis on violence and shock during its first half, to be replaced with the HEROIC DRAMA, with its stylized conflict of love and honor, during its second half. The eighteenth century saw the development of a DRAMA around middle-class figures, known as DOMESTIC TRAGEDY, which was serious in intent but superficial in importance. With the emergence of Ibsen in the late nineteenth century came the concept of middle-class *tragedy* growing out of social problems and issues. In the twentieth century, middle-class and laboring-class characters are often portrayed in their circumstances as the victims of social, hereditary, and environmental forces. When, as often happens, they receive their fate with a self-pitying whimper, they can hardly be said to have tragic dimensions. But when, as also happens in much modern serious DRAMA, they face their destiny, however evil and unmerited, with courage and dignity, they are probably as truly tragic, *mutatis mutandis,* as Oedipus was to Sophocles' Athenians or Hamlet was to Shakespeare's Englishmen.

If a generalization can be made about so protean a subject as TRAGEDY, it is probably that TRAGEDY treats man in terms of his godlike potential, of his transcendent ideals, of the part of himself that is in rebellion against not only the implacable universe but the frailty of his own flesh and will. In this sense TRAGEDY as the record of man's strivings and aspirations is in contrast to COMEDY, which is the amusing spectacle of man's limitations and frailties. See DRAMATIC STRUCTURE, CATHARSIS, DRAMA, COMEDY.

Tragedy of Blood: An intensified FORM of the REVENGE TRAGEDY popular on the Elizabethan stage. It works out the theme of revenge and retribution (borrowed from Seneca) through murder, assassination, mutilation, and carnage. The horrors which in the Latin Senecan plays had been merely described were placed upon the stage to satisfy the craving for morbid excitement displayed by an Elizabethan audience brought up on bear-baiting spectacles and public executions (hangings, mutilations, burnings). Besides including such revenge plays as Kyd's *Spanish Tragedy,* Shakespeare's *Titus Andronicus,* and *Hamlet,* the *tragedy of blood* led to such later "horror" TRAGEDIES as Webster's *The Duchess of Malfi* and *The White Devil*. See REVENGE TRAGEDY, SENECAN TRAGEDY.

Tragic Flaw: The flaw, error, or defect in the tragic HERO which leads to his downfall. See HAMARTIA, for which *tragic flaw* is a synonym.

Tragic Force: The event or force which starts the FALLING ACTION in a TRAGEDY. It is either a separate event following closely upon the CLIMAX or is identified with the CLIMAX itself. The escape of Fleance is the *tragic force* in *Macbeth,* marking as it does the beginning of Macbeth's misfortunes and leading to the overthrow of the HERO in the resulting CATASTROPHE. See DRAMATIC STRUCTURE.

Tragic Irony: That form of DRAMATIC IRONY in which a character in a TRAGEDY uses words which mean one thing to him and another to those better acquainted with his real situation, especially when he is about to become a victim of Fate. Othello's allusion to the VILLAIN who is about to deceive him as "honest Iago" is an example.

Tragi-comedy: A play which employs a PLOT suitable to TRAGEDY but which ends happily like a COMEDY. The action, serious in THEME and subject matter and sometimes in TONE also, seems to be leading to a tragic CATASTROPHE until an unexpected turn in events, often in the form of a DEUS EX MACHINA, brings about the happy DÉNOUEMENT. In this sense Shakespeare's *The Merchant of Venice* is a *tragi-comedy*, though it is also a ROMANTIC COMEDY. If the "trick" about the shedding of blood were omitted and Shylock allowed to "have his bond," the play might easily be made into a TRAGEDY; conversely Shakespeare's *King Lear,* a pure TRAGEDY, was made into a COMEDY by Nahum Tate for the RESTORATION stage. In English dramatic history the term *tragi-comedy* is usually employed to designate the particular kind of play developed by Beaumont and Fletcher about 1610, a type of which *Philaster* is perhaps most typical. Fletcher's own definition may be quoted: "A tragi-comedy is not so called in respect of mirth and killing, but in respect it wants deaths, which is enough to make it no tragedy, yet brings some near it, which is enough to make it no comedy, which must be a representation of familiar people, with such kind of trouble as no life be question'd; so that a god is as lawful in this [tragi-comedy] as in a tragedy, and mean people as in a comedy" (from

Transcendentalism

"To the Reader," *The Faithful Shepherdess*). Some of the characteristics are: improbable PLOT; unnatural SITUATIONS; actors of high social class, usually of the nobility; love as the central interest, pure love and gross love often being contrasted; highly complicated PLOT; rapid action; contrast of deep villainy and exalted virtue; saving of HERO and HEROINE in the nick of time; penitent VILLAIN (as Iachimo in *Cymbeline*); disguises; surprises; jealousy; treachery; intrigue; enveloping action of war or rebellion. Shakespeare's *Cymbeline* and *The Winter's Tale* are examples of the GENRE. Fletcher's *The Faithful Shepherdess* is a PASTORAL *tragi-comedy*. Later seventeenth-century *tragi-comedies* are Killigrew's *The Prisoner*, Davenant's *Fair Favorite*, Shadwell's *Royal Shepherdess*, and Dryden's *Secret Love* and *Love Triumphant*. Such plays as these tended to approach the HEROIC DRAMA. The type practically disappeared in the early eighteenth century, although a number of its characteristics reappear in the MELODRAMA of the nineteenth and twentieth centuries.

Transcendental Club: An informal organization of leading transcendentalists living in or near Boston. The group came together for their first meeting, September 19, 1836, at the home of George Ripley. Thereafter, they met occasionally at Emerson's home in Concord and elsewhere for seven or eight years, calling themselves "The Symposium" and "The Hedge Club." Their chief interests were the new developments in theology, philosophy, and literature, and the purpose of their coming together was to discuss the "new thought" of the day. The movement was closely associated with the growth of the Unitarian spirit in New England. The leading members of the Club were such figures as Ralph Waldo Emerson, Convers Francis, Frederick Henry Hedge, Amos Bronson Alcott, George Ripley, Margaret Fuller, Nathaniel Hawthorne, Henry D. Thoreau, and William Ellery Channing. See TRANSCENDENTALISM.

Transcendentalism: A reliance on the intuition and the conscience, a form of idealism; a philosophical ROMANTICISM reaching America a generation or two after it developed in Europe. *Transcendentalism,* though based on doctrines of ancient and modern European philosophers (particularly Kant) and sponsored in America chiefly by Emerson after he had absorbed it from Carlyle, Coleridge, Goethe, and others, took on especial significance in the United States, where it so largely dominated the New England authors as to become a literary movement as well as a philosophic conception.

Transcendentalism

The movement gained its impetus in America in part from meetings of a small group which came together to discuss the "new thought" of the time. While holding different opinions about many things, the group seemed in general harmony in their conviction that within the nature of man there was a something which transcended human experience—an intuitive and personal revelation. Variously called the Symposium Club and the HEDGE CLUB, the group was soon known as the TRANSCENDENTAL CLUB because of the ideas advanced by its members.

As the "movement" developed, it sponsored two important activities: the publication of THE DIAL from 1840–1844 and BROOK FARM. Some of the various doctrines which one or another of the American transcendentalists promulgated and which have somehow been accepted as "transcendental" may be restated here. They believed in living close to nature (Thoreau) and taught the dignity of manual labor (Thoreau). They strongly felt the need of intellectual companionships and interests (BROOK FARM) and placed great emphasis on the importance of spiritual living. Man's relationship to God was a personal matter and was to be established directly by the individual himself (UNITARIANISM) rather than through the intermediation of the ritualistic church. They held firmly that man was divine in his own right, an opinion opposed to the doctrines held by the Puritan Calvinists in New England, and they urged strongly the essential divinity of man and one great brotherhood. Self-trust and self-reliance were to be practiced at all times and on all occasions, since to trust self was really to trust the voice of God speaking intuitively within us (Emerson). The transcendentalists felt called upon to resist the "vulgar prosperity of the barbarian," believed firmly in democracy, and insisted on an intense individualism. Some of the extremists in their number went so far as to evolve a system of dietetics and to rule out coffee, wine, and tobacco—all on the basis that the body was the temple of the soul and that for the tenant's sake it was well to keep the dwelling undefiled. And most of the transcendentalists were by nature reformers, though Emerson—the most vocal interpreter of the group —refused to go so far in this direction as, for instance, Bronson Alcott. Emerson's position here is that it is man's responsibility to be "a brave and upright man, who must find or cut a straight path to everything excellent in the earth, and not only go honorably himself, but make it easier for all who follow him to go in honor and with benefit." In this way most of the reforms were attempts to awaken and regenerate the human spirit rather than to prescribe particular and concrete movements which were to be fostered. The transcendentalists were, for instance, among the early advocates of the enfranchisement of women.

Ultimately, despite these practical manifestations, *transcendentalism* was an epistemology, a way of knowing, and the ultimate characteristics that tied together the frequently contradictory attitudes of the loosely formed group called "The Transcendentalists" was the belief that man can intuitively transcend the limits of the senses and of logic and receive directly higher truths and greater knowledge denied to these mundane methods of knowing.

Among the most famous of the transcendental leaders, in addition to Emerson, Thoreau, and Bronson Alcott, were Margaret Fuller, George Ripley, F. H. Hedge, James Freeman Clark, Elizabeth Peabody, Theodore Parker, Jones Very, and W. H. Channing. But the arch-advocates in literature of most that the transcendentalists stood for were Emerson and Thoreau; and the two documents which most definitely give literary expression to their views are Emerson's *Nature* (1836) and Thoreau's *Walden* (1854).

Transferred Epithet: An adjective used to limit a noun which it cannot logically modify. See EPITHET.

Translation: The rendering of a literary work, originally produced in one language, into another. At one extreme of *translation* stands the literal rendering of the work into the other language, word for word, without concern for the primary differences in IDIOM and IMAGERY between the two languages. At the other extreme is the ADAPTATION of the work into the other language, an attempt to comprehend and communicate the spirit and meaning of the work by adapting it to the conventions and idioms of the language into which it is being rendered. Each translator must strike some kind of balance between these extremes—which Croce called "faithful ugliness or faithless beauty." Some *translations* have great literary merit in themselves; notably, the King James Version of the Holy BIBLE, Amyot's Plutarch, Schlegel's Shakespeare, Baudelaire's and Mallarmé's Poe, Putnam's Cervantes.

Travesty: Writing which by its incongruity of STYLE or treatment ridicules a subject inherently noble or dignified. The derivation of the word, from *trans* (over or across) and *vestire* (to clothe or dress) clearly suggests the meaning of presenting a subject in a dress intended for another type of subject. *Travesty* may be thought of as the opposite of the MOCK EPIC since the latter treats a frivolous subject seriously and the *travesty* usually presents a serious subject frivolously. *Don Quixote* is, in a very real sense, a *travesty* on the MEDIEVAL ROMANCE. See BURLESQUE.

"Tribe of Ben":   A contemporary nickname for the young poets and dramatists of the seventeenth century who acknowledged "rare Ben Jonson" as their master. The chief of the "tribe" was Robert Herrick, and the group included the CAVALIER LYRISTS and other of the younger poets and dramatists of Jacobean times. Jonson's influence upon his followers was in the direction of classical polish and sense of FORM, study and imitation of classical writers and literary types (as the ODE, the EPIGRAM, SATIRE), and classical ideals of criticism. The attitude represented a revolt from the PURITANISM and Italian ROMANTICISM represented in Spenser. The poets strove to make the LYRIC graceful, and in general the group followed the creed: "Live merrily and write good verses."

Tribrach: A metrical FOOT of three short or unstressed syllables. It rarely occurs in English VERSE, and many prosodists regard an English FOOT without a stressed syllable as impossible.

Trilogy: A literary composition more usually a NOVEL or a play, written in three parts, each of which is in itself a complete unit. Shakespeare's *King Henry VI* is an example. The *trilogy* usually is written against a large background which may be historical, philosophical, or social in its interests.

Trimeter: A line of VERSE consisting of three FEET. See SCANSION.

Triolet: One of the simpler French VERSE FORMS. It consists of eight lines, the first two being repeated as the last two lines and the first recurring also as the fourth line. There are only two RHYMES, and their arrangement is: *ab*aa*ab*. (Italics indicate repetition of whole lines.) Certain skillful poets have given different meanings to the REFRAIN lines from that which they carried at the opening of the poem as in this example by Austin Dobson:

Trochee

A KISS

Rose kissed me today,
   Will she kiss me tomorrow?
Let it be as it may,
Rose kissed me today.
But the pleasure gives way
   To a savor of sorrow;—
Rose kissed me today,—
   Will she kiss me tomorrow?

Triple Meter: In METRICS a line consisting of FEET of three sylla-bles, that is, of ANAPESTS or DACTYLS. Often called *triple rhythm*.

Triple Rhyme: RHYME in which the correspondence of sounds lies in three consecutive syllables. See RHYME.

Triplet: A sequence of three rhyming VERSES, often introduced as a variation in the HEROIC COUPLET. See TERCET.

Tristich: A STANZA of three lines of VERSE. See TERCET, TRIPLET.

Tritagonist: The actor taking the part third in importance in a Greek DRAMA. Sophocles added this third actor to the PROTAGONIST and DEUTERAGONIST in the Greek plays through Aeschylus. By analogy, the term is sometimes applied to the CHARACTER of third ranking importance in a play. See PROTAGONIST, DEUTERAGONIST.

Trite Expression: A CLICHÉ.

Trivium: The three studies leading to the bachelor's degree in the medieval universities: grammar, logic, and RHETORIC. See SEVEN LIBERAL ARTS.

Trochee: A poetic FOOT consisting of an accented and an unac-cented syllable, as in the word *háppy*. Trochaics are generally unpopular with poets for sustained writing since they so soon degen-erate into rocking-horse RHYTHM, a fact which makes them popular with children. The ease and frequency with which Longfellow's *Hiawatha* has been parodied ("Sweet trochaic milk and water") bears evidence to this quality of the trochaic measure. On the other hand, for short songs and lyrics the *trochee* has been very popular. It is often used as the meter of the supernatural as in Shakespeare's

Trope

Dŏublĕ, dŏublĕ, tóil aňd trŏublĕ,
Fíre bŭrn aňd cáuldrŏn búbblĕ.

Trope: In RHETORIC a *trope* is a FIGURE OF SPEECH involving a "turn" or change of sense—the use of a word in a sense other than its proper or literal one; in this sense figures of comparison (see METAPHOR, SIMILE) as well as ironical expressions are *tropes* or FIGURES OF SPEECH.

Another use of the word is important to students of the origin of MEDIEVAL DRAMA. As early as the eighth or ninth centuries, certain musical additions to the Gregorian antiphons in the liturgy of the Catholic Church were permitted as pleasurable elaborations of the service. At first they were merely prolongations of the melody on a vowel sound, giving rise to *jubila,* the manuscript notation for a *jubilum* being known as a *neuma,* which looked somewhat like shorthand notes. Later, words were added to old *jubila* and new compositions of both words and music added, the texts of which were called *tropes.* These *tropes,* or "amplifications of the liturgical texts," were sometimes in PROSE, sometimes in VERSE; sometimes purely musical, sometimes requiring DIALOGUE, presented antiphonally by the two parts of the choir. From this DIALOGUE form of the *trope* developed the LITURGICAL DRAMA. See MEDIEVAL DRAMA.

Troubadour: A name given to the aristocratic LYRIC poets of Provence (Southern France) in the twelfth and thirteenth centuries. The name is derived from a word meaning "to find," suggesting that the *troubadour* was regarded as an inventor and experimenter in poetic technique. *Troubadours* were essentially LYRIC poets, occupied with themes of love and chivalry. The conventional themes arose from the social conditions, the *troubadour* usually addressing his VERSE to a married lady, whose patronage he courted. *Troubadour* poetry figured importantly in the development of COURTLY LOVE, and influenced the TROUVÈRE of Northern France. The earliest *troubadour* of record is William, Count of Poitiers (1071–1127), other famous *troubadours* being Bernard de Ventadour, Arnaut de Mareuil, Bertran de Born, and Arnaut Daniel. Some of the forms invented by the *troubadours* are: the CANSO (love song), *ballada* (dance song), *tenson* (dialogue), PASTOURELLE (pastoral wooing song), and the ALBA (dawn song). Much use was made of RHYME, and varied stanzaic forms were developed, including the SESTINA used later by Dante and others. The SONNET form itself probably developed from *troubadour* stanzaic inventions. The poetry was intended to be sung, sometimes by the *troubadour* himself, sometimes by an assistant or apprentice or professional entertainer, as the JONGLEUR.

Trouvère: A term applied to a group or school of poets who flourished in Northern France in the twelfth and thirteenth centuries. The *trouvères* were much influenced by the art of the TROUBADOURS of Southern France, and concerned themselves largely with LYRICS of love, though they produced also CHANSONS DE GESTE and CHIVALRIC ROMANCES. Indeed, to the activity of one of them, the famous Chrétien de Troyes (twelfth century), we owe some of the earliest and best of the Arthurian romances. See ARTHURIAN LEGEND.

Truncation: In METRICS the omission of a syllable or syllables at the beginning or end of a line. See CATALEXSIS.

Tudor: The royal house that ruled England from 1485 to 1603. The rulers were Henry VII (1485–1509), Henry VIII (1509–1547), Edward VI (1547–1553), Mary (1553–1558), and Elizabeth (1558–1603).

Tumbling Verse: A rough, heavily stressed POETRY. See SKELTONIC VERSE, for which it is another name.

Type: A group of persons or things that have in common certain characteristics that distinguish them as being members of a definite group or class. In literary criticism the term *type* has two distinct usages. In one it refers to a literary GENRE, a KIND, with definable distinguishing characteristics. In the other it is applied to a CHARACTER who is a representative of a class or kind of person. Henry James uses it in this sense in "The Art of Fiction" when he says, "She had got her direct personal impression, and she turned out her *type*. She knew what youth was, and what Protestantism; she also had the advantage of having seen what it was to be French, so that she converted these ideas into a concrete image and produced a reality [of French Protestant youth]." A *type* CHARACTER in this sense differs sharply from a STOCK CHARACTER. The *type* CHARACTER need not have any qualities borrowed from literary traditions and may be sharply individualized; he is a *type* CHARACTER because he embodies a substantial number of significant distinguishing characteristics of his group or class. A STOCK CHARACTER, on the other hand, is a STEREOTYPE, a CHARACTER modeled on other and frequently used CHARACTERS, but often is representative of no actual group but simply of similar STOCK CHARACTERS. *Type* is also sometimes used as a synonym for SYMBOL, particularly in the religious sense of standing for something that is to come, as in the statement, "The Old Testament sacrificial lamb was a *type* of Christ."

U

Ubi sunt Formula: A CONVENTION much used in VERSE, especially in the FRENCH FORMS, which asks "where are" (*ubi sunt*) these things, and these, and these, the poetic impression on the reader being largely effected by the EMPHASIS the FORMULA places on the transitory qualities of life. The most famous example in English is probably Dante Gabriel Rossetti's "The Ballade of Dead Ladies," a poetic TRANSLATION of François Villon's BALLADE:

> But where are the snows of yester-year?

In Justin H. McCarthy's poem, "I Wonder in What Isle of Bliss," successive STANZAS close with "Where are the Gods of Yesterday?" "Where are the Dreams of Yesterday?" "Where are the Girls of Yesterday?" "Where are the Snows of Yesterday?" In Edmund Gosse's "The Ballad of Dead Cities," the three STANZAS begin with "Where are the Cities of the plain?" "Where now is Karnak, that great fane . . . ?" "And where is white Shushan, again . . . ?" Each of the STANZAS in this poem closes with "Where are the cities of old time?" These examples illustrate the tendency to place the *ubi sunt* query in the opening line of a STANZA or to use it as a REFRAIN or REPETEND.

Ultima Thule: The farthest possible place. Used often in the sense of a remote goal, an ideal and mysterious country. To the ancients *Thule* was one of the northern lands of Europe, most likely one of the Shetland Islands, although Iceland and Norway have been suggested. From the Latin reference to the region as the *ultima* (farthest) *Thule*, the expression has taken on the literary significance given it above.

Unities

Underground Press: Beginning in the mid-1960's there have been a large number of *underground* publications by numerous groups, some of them clandestine but many associated with universities. Many of these publications have been newspapers, but a number have been MAGAZINES publishing ESSAYS, POETRY, and FICTION, usually of an experimental, AVANT-GARDE, or politically radical type. The term *underground* is now applied to any AVANT-GARDE art that is privately produced and concerned with artistic and social experiment. There are *underground* films, *underground* art, as well as the *underground press*. Much of the work produced by the *underground press* is in the form of LITTLE MAGAZINES, of which there are now thousands with very limited—and in most cases very local—circulation. See LITTLE MAGAZINES.

Understatement: A form of IRONY in which something is intentionally represented as less than in fact it is. See MEIOSIS.

Unitarianism: The creed of a sect coming into importance in America about 1820, a sect which discarded the earlier faith in the existence of a Trinity and held for the unity of God, accepting Christ as divine in the same sense that man is, but not as a member of a divine Trinity. In its more evolved form this new *Unitarianism* stood for "the fatherhood of God, the brotherhood of man, the leadership of Jesus, salvation by character, and the progress of mankind onward and upward forever."

Unities: The principles of DRAMATIC STRUCTURE involving *action, time,* and *place.* The most important *unity* and the only one enjoined by Aristotle is that of action. He called a TRAGEDY "an imitation of an action that is complete, and whole, and of a certain magnitude"; a whole should have beginning, middle, and end, with a causal relationship in the different parts of the play. Inevitability and concentration result from adherence to the *unity of action.* This *unity,* Aristotle warned, was not necessarily obtained simply by making one man the subject. Later critics declared that a SUBPLOT tends to destroy the *unity* of any serious play and that tragic and comic elements should not be mixed. Thus the legitimacy of TRAGI-COMEDY was for a long time a matter of dispute; Sidney opposed it and Doctor Johnson vindicated it.

The *unity of time* was developed from Aristotle's simple and undogmatic statement concerning tragic usage: "Tragedy endeavors,

543

as far as possible, to confine itself to a single revolution of the sun, or but slightly to exceed this limit." The Italian critics of the sixteenth century formulated the doctrine that the action should be limited to one day; many French and English critics of the seventeenth and eighteenth centuries accepted this *unity,* and many dramatists used it. There were different interpretations of the *unity of time*—some favored the natural day of twenty-four hours, others the artificial day of twelve hours, and others the several hours that correspond to the actual time of theatrical representation.

The *unity of place,* limiting the action to one place, was the last to emerge and was not mentioned by Aristotle. It followed, quite naturally, the requirement of limiting the action to a particular time; as the RENAISSANCE critics of Italy developed their theories of VERISIMILITUDE, of making the action of a play approximate that of stage representation, the *unity of place* completed the trilogy. Some critics were content to have the action confined merely to the same town or city. The *unity of place* was closely allied to that of time in the theory and practice of neo-classic writers.

The dramatic *unities* have had a long and extremely complicated history. For more than two centuries in England the three *unities* were denounced and defended and (as in Dryden's *Essay of Dramatic Poesy*) debated. When NEO-CLASSICISM gave way to ROMANTICISM, they lost their importance.

Many great English plays violate all three *unities. Unity of action,* however, is commonly recognized as an important requirement in serious DRAMA, and Shakespeare's greatest TRAGEDIES, such as *Hamlet* and *Othello,* show the effects of such *unity.* In two plays, the *Comedy of Errors* and *The Tempest,* Shakespeare observed all three of the *unities.* The theory of the *unities* has been, in truth, a matter of more concern to critics than to dramatists. Yet the concentration and strength that result from efforts at attaining *unity of action, time, and place* may be regarded as dramatic virtues.

Modern dramatists are less interested in traditional formulae than in the *unity of impression,* the singleness of emotional EFFECT, which is related to the *unity of action.* Moreover, in recent years effective experiments with the minor *unities of time and place* have been made in stage and screen plays. See CRITICISM, HISTORICAL SKETCH.

Unity: The concept that a literary work shall have in it some organizing principle to which all its parts are related so that, viewed in the light of that principle, the work is an organic whole. A work which has *unity* is cohesive in its parts, complete, self-contained, and integrated; it possesses one-ness. The concept of *unity* in the DRAMA has often been mechanically applied (see UNITIES). In other literary forms, it is often considered to reside in a unified action or PLOT or in CHARACTERIZATION. A work may, however, be unified by FORM, by intent, by THEME, by SYMBOLISM— in fact, by any means which can so integrate and organize its elements that they have a necessary relationship to each other and an essential relationship to the whole of which they are parts.

Universality: A critical term frequently employed to indicate the presence in a piece of writing of an appeal to all readers of all time. When writing presents the great human emotions common to all peoples of all civilizations—jealousy, love, pride, courage, etc.—in literary FORM and through CHARACTERS and actions that remain meaningful to other ages, it may be said to have *universality*. Of all qualities which make for *universality* in literature, the successful portrayal of human CHARACTER is the most important, but only slightly more so than fidelity to the unchanging physical facts of the natural world. See CONCRETE UNIVERSAL.

University Plays: Plays produced by undergraduates at Oxford and Cambridge during the ELIZABETHAN AGE. See SCHOOL PLAYS.

University Wits: A name used for certain young University men who came to London in the late 1580's and undertook careers as professional men of letters. They played an important part in the development of the great literature, especially the DRAMA, that characterized the latter part of Elizabeth's reign. The most important one was Christopher Marlowe. Others included are Robert Greene, George Peele, Thomas Lodge, Thomas Nash, and Thomas Kyd. Some authorities include John Lyly, though Lyly was an older man and perhaps not personally associated with the others. They lived irregular lives, Greene and Marlowe being particularly known as Bohemians. Their literary work, while uneven in quality, much of it being hack work, was varied and influential. They were largely instrumental in freeing TRAGEDY from the artificial restrictions imposed by classical authority, and their cultivation of BLANK VERSE, especially the "mighty line" of Marlowe, paved the way for Shakespeare's masterful use of this form. They devised or developed types of plays later perfected by Shakespeare: the REVENGE TRAGEDY or

Unreliable Narrator

TRAGEDY OF BLOOD (Kyd), the TRAGEDY built around a great personality (Marlowe), ROMANTIC COMEDY (Greene and Peele), CHRONICLE PLAY (Marlowe and others), and the COURT COMEDY (Lyly). Lodge and Greene cultivated the PASTORAL ROMANCE and Nash wrote the first PICARESQUE NOVEL in English. The group was especially active between 1585 and 1595.

Unreliable Narrator: A NARRATOR or viewpoint CHARACTER who may be in error in his understanding or report of things and who thus leaves the reader without the guides essential to his making judgments about the CHARACTER and the actions with any confidence that his conclusions are those intended by the author. The *unreliable narrator* is most frequently found in works by a SELF-EFFACING AUTHOR. For example, Lambert Strether, the viewpoint CHARACTER in Henry James' *The Ambassadors,* is often wrong in his conclusions about things, but we must await the outcome of events in order to find out when he is. In James' *The Turn of the Screw* the debate over what actually happens in the STORY is really over the reliability of the Governess's NARRATIVE. Huck Finn, in Mark Twain's *Adventures of Huckleberry Finn,* is often uncomprehending about the situations he describes, as most NAIVE NARRATORS are; hence, he is *unreliable*. See NARRATOR, NAIVE NARRATOR.

Usage: The standard which sets the speech of a people. Good *usage* is established by the forms of language used by educated people and by intelligent writers, but this does not mean at all that *usage* is *fixed.* It is, in fact, constantly shifting, old forms becoming obsolescent and obsolete, new forms entering by way of SLANG, passing through the colloquial stage, and sometimes finally arriving at recognition as "good *usage.*" Dictionaries and grammars properly *follow usage* rather than *set* it, though, of course, both do much toward standardization and stabilization.

Utilitarianism: A theory of ethics formulated in England in the eighteenth century by Jeremy Bentham, who believed that the test of ethical concerns was their usefulness to society and who defined utility as "the greatest happiness for the greatest number." The theory was advanced and modified in the nineteenth century by James Mill and his son John Stuart Mill, both of whom wanted to define "happiness" in qualitative rather than quantitative terms, whereas Bentham had equated it with pleasure. It is a significant movement in nineteenth-century thought not only because of the excellence with which John Stuart Mill expounded it but also because it was a central issue for a number of writers, among them Thomas Carlyle and Charles Dickens, both of whom attacked the system. It is sometimes called "Benthamism" after its originator.

Utopia: A word meaning "nowhere" coined by Thomas More to represent the seat of his ideal republic as pictured in his *Utopia* (1516). The idea of presenting plans for ideal commonwealths has interested many philosophers and writers. Plato's *Republic,* of course, is the best known. Some others are Campanella's *Civitas Solis* (1623), Bacon's *New Atlantis* (1627), Harrington's *Oceana* (1656), Samuel Butler's *Erewhon* (1872), Bellamy's *Looking Backward* (1888), William Morris' *News from Nowhere* (1891), H. G. Wells' *A Modern Utopia* (1905), and Aldous Huxley's satiric *Brave New World* (1932).

V

Vade mecum: An article which one keeps constantly with him. By association the term has come to mean any book much used, as a *handbook,* a *thesaurus.*

Vapours: A word commonly used in eighteenth-century literature to account for the eccentric action of people. *Vapours* were exhalations which were presumably given off by the stomach or other organs of the body and rose to the head causing depression, melancholy, hysteria, etc. In 1541 Sir Thomas Elyot wrote that "of humours some are more grosse and cold, some are subtyl and hot and are called vapours." HEROINES of eighteenth-century fiction were particularly subject to attacks of this malady. Young, in 1728, gave us these lines:

> Sometimes, thro' pride the sexes change their airs;
> My lord has vapours, and my lady swears.

See HUMOURS.

Variorum Edition: An edition of an author's work presenting complete variant readings of the possible texts and full notes of critical comments and interpretation passed upon the text by major writers. The term is an abbreviation of the Latin phrase *cum notis vari-*

orum ("with notes of various persons"). In the field of English litera-
ture, the most conspicuous successes in this type of editing are the
"New Variorum Shakespeare" edited by Furness, and the "Variorum
Spenser," edited by Edwin Greenlaw.

Vatic: From the earliest times it was believed that some POETS or
BARDS were divinely inspired and were thus seers who spoke prophetic truth; such POETS were called *vates,* of which Sybil was the
most famous. Hence the term *vatic* in reference to a POET or a POEM
means that it is regarded as divinely inspired, prophetic, or oracular.
Blake and Whitman have been called *vatic* poets.

Vaudeville: An entertainment consisting of successive performances of unrelated SONGS, dances, dramatic SKETCHES, acrobatic
feats, juggling, PANTOMIME, puppet-shows, and varied "stunts." The
word is derived from *Vau-de-Vire,* a village in Normandy, where a
famous composer of lively, satirical SONGS lived in the eighteenth
century. From these SONGS, modified later by PANTOMIME, developed
the "variety" shows now known as *vaudeville.* The elements of
vaudeville are old (see LOW COMEDY, BURLESQUE, FARCE), but the
modern *vaudeville* type of variety show developed in the eighteenth
and nineteenth centuries. Under the direction of John Rich these
shows became very popular in eighteenth-century England, continued so through the nineteenth century, and have continued so in
the twentieth century. The name *vaudeville* seems to have become
finally attached to the variety show as a result of its development
in America, especially in the early years of the twentieth century,
when *vaudeville* actors were organized into "circuits" by B. F.
Keith and others and when elaborate theaters were devoted to their
use. The popularity of *vaudeville* decreased after the advent of the
talking moving pictures, radio, and television.

Vehicle: The immediate subject, as opposed to the ultimate or ul-
terior intentional subject of a METAPHOR. See TENOR.

Verisimilitude: The appearance or semblance of truth and actuality. The term has been used in criticism to indicate the degree to
which a writer faithfully creates the semblance of the truth. In his
Life of Swift, Scott writes: "Swift possessed the art of verisimilitude."
The word was a favorite one with Poe who used it in the sense of
presenting details, howsoever far-fetched, in such a way as to give

them the *semblance* of truth. In *The Facts in the Case of M. Valdemar*, for instance, Poe gives way to the wildest kind of romancing, but the items are so marshaled as to sweep the reader into at least a momentary acceptance of them, and the story may, therefore, be said to respect Poe's own demands for *verisimilitude*.

Vers de société: Brief lyrical VERSE written in genial, sportive mood and sophisticated both in subject and treatment. Sometimes called LIGHT VERSE. Its characteristics are polish, *savoir faire*, grace, and ease of expression. It usually presents aspects of conventional social relationships. Locker-Lampson in a much-quoted introduction to his collection of *vers de société, Lyra Elegantiarum*, states: "OCCASIONAL VERSE should be short, graceful, refined, and fanciful, not seldom distinguished by chastened sentiment, and often playful. The TONE should not be pitched high; it should be terse and idiomatic, and rather in the conversational key. The RHYTHM should be crisp and sparkling, the RHYME frequent and never forced, while the entire POEM should be marked by tasteful moderation, high finish and completeness." Though gaining in favor in recent centuries, LIGHT VERSE was popular in classical literature. The seventeenth and eighteenth centuries in England saw a high development of the type. See LIGHT VERSE, OCCASIONAL VERSE.

Verse: Is used in two senses: (1) as a unit of POETRY, in which case it has the same significance as *line;* and (2) as a name given generally to metrical composition. In the second sense, *verse* is simply a generic term applied to rhythmical and, most frequently, metrical and rhymed composition, in which case it implies little as to the merit of the composition, the term POETRY or POEM being reserved especially to indicate *verse* of high merit. An inherent suggestion that *verse* is of a lower order than POETRY lies in the fact that *verse* is used in association with such terms as *society verse, occasional verse*, etc., which, it is generally conceded, are rarely applied to great POETRY. The use of *verse* to indicate a STANZA, while common, is not justified.

Verse Paragraph: A non-stanzaic, continuous VERSE FORM, in which the lines are grouped together not through a STANZA pattern but in unequal blocks of thought, meaning, logic, or content. The beginning of a *verse paragraph* is indicated by indentation, as in PROSE. The VERSE FORM for POETRY written in *paragraphs* rather than STANZAS is

usually either BLANK VERSE or FREE VERSE. Milton's *Paradise Lost* is
in BLANK VERSE *paragraphs;* much of Whitman's *Leaves of Grass* is
in FREE VERSE *paragraphs.*

Versification: The art and practice of writing VERSE. Like PROSODY
the term is an inclusive one, being generally used to connote all
the mechanical elements going to make up poetic composition:
ACCENT, RHYTHM, the FOOT, METER, RHYME, STANZA FORM, DICTION,
and such aids as ASSONANCE, ONOMATOPOEIA, and ALLITERATION.
In a narrower sense *versification* signifies simply the *structural* FORM
of a VERSE or STANZA such as is revealed by careful SCANSION.

Vers libre: A nineteenth-century French poetic movement to free
POETRY from the shackles of strict rules of VERSIFICATION resulted
in cadenced and rhythmic POETRY called *vers libre.* The term, which
literally means *free verse,* has been used as a synonym for FREE
VERSE in English. See FREE VERSE.

Victorian: A term used (1) to designate broadly the literature
written during the reign of Queen Victoria (1837–1901) or its
characteristic qualities and attitudes; and (2) more narrowly, to
suggest a certain complacency or hypocrisy or squeamishness more
or less justly assumed to be traceable to or similar to prevailing
Victorian attitudes. Pride in the growing power of England,
optimism born of the new science, the dominance of Puritan ideals
tenaciously held by the rising middle class, and the example of a
royal court scrupulous in its adherence to high standards of
"decency" and respectability combined to produce a spirit of
moral earnestness linked with self-satisfaction which was protested
against at the time and in the generations immediately to follow
as hypocritical, false, complacent, and narrow. The cautious manner in which "mid-Victorian" writers in particular were prone to
treat such matters as profanity and sex has been especially responsible for the common use of the term *Victorian* or "mid-
Victorian," to indicate false modesty, empty respectability, or callous
complacency. Though justified in part, this use of *Victorian* rests in
some degree upon exaggeration, and at best fails to take into consideration the fact that even in the heart of the *Victorian* period a
very large part of the literature either did not exhibit such traits or
set itself flatly in protest against them. As a matter of fact, *Victorian*
literature is many-sided and complex, and reflects both romantically

and realistically the great changes that were going on in life and thought. The religious and philosophical doubts and hopes raised by the new science, the social problems arising from the new industrial conditions, the conscious resort of literary men to foreign sources of inspiration, the rise of a new middle-class audience and new media of publication (the MAGAZINES) are among the forces which colored literature during Victoria's reign. Since there are marked differences between the literature written in the early years of Victoria's reign and that written in the later years, this Handbook treats the early years as a part of the ROMANTIC PERIOD and the later years as a part of the REALISTIC PERIOD. See EARLY VICTORIAN AGE, LATE VICTORIAN AGE, ROMANTIC PERIOD IN ENGLISH LITERATURE, REALISTIC PERIOD IN ENGLISH LITERATURE, and the *Outline of Literary History*.

Vignette: A SKETCH or ESSAY or brief NARRATIVE characterized by great precision and delicate accuracy of composition. The term is borrowed from that used for unbordered but delicate decorative designs for a book, and it implies writing with comparable grace and economy. It may be a separate whole or a portion of a larger work. The term is also applied to very brief SHORT-SHORT STORIES, less than five hundred words in length.

Villain: An evil CHARACTER, guilty of, or at the least thoroughly capable of, serious crimes and who acts in opposition to the HERO. He is the ANTAGONIST in a DRAMA.

Villanelle: A French VERSE form calculated, through its complexity and artificiality, to give an impression of simplicity and spontaneity. The *villanelle* was originally chiefly PASTORAL and an element of formal lightness is still uppermost since it is frequently used for poetic expression which is idyllic, delicate, simple, and slight. The two REFRAIN lines, however, can be repeated in such a way that they can be made thunderingly forceful and the POEM can have an elementary gravity and power, as it has in Dylan Thomas's villanelle, "Do Not Go Gentle Into That Good Night." In form the *villanelle* is characterized by nineteen lines divided into five TERCETS and a final four-line STANZA, and it uses only two RHYMES. The division of VERSES is, then: *aba aba aba aba aba abaa*. Line 1 is repeated entirely to form lines 6, 12, and 18, and line 3 is repeated entirely to form lines 9, 15, and 19: thus eight of the nineteen lines are REFRAIN.

Virelay: A French VERSE FORM (related to LAI) of which the number of STANZAS and the number of lines to the STANZA are unlimited. Each STANZA is made up of an indefinite number of TERCETS rhyming *aab* for the first STANZA, *bbc* for the second, *ccd* for the third, etc. The *virelay* has never become popular among English POETS, probably because of the monotony of the RHYME-SCHEME.

Virgin Play: A medieval non-Scriptural play based on SAINTS' LIVES, in which the Virgin Mary takes an active role in performing miracles. See MIRACLE PLAY.

Virgule: A slanting or an upright line used in PROSODY to mark off metrical FEET, as in the following example from Shelley:

> The sun | is warm, | the sky | is clear,
> The waves | are dan | cing fast | and bright.

Volta: The turn in thought—from question to answer, from instance to application, from problem to solution—that occurs at the end of the OCTAVE in the ITALIAN SONNET. The *volta* sometimes occurs in the SHAKESPEAREAN SONNET between the twelfth and the thirteenth lines. The distinctive thing about the MILTONIC SONNET is the absence of the *volta* in a fixed position, although the FORM is Italian in RHYME-SCHEME.

Vulgate: The word comes from Latin *vulgus,* "crowd" and means "common" or commonly used. Note two chief uses: (1) the *Vulgate* Bible is the Latin version made by Saint Jerome in the fourth century and is the authorized Bible of the Catholic Church; (2) the "*Vulgate* ROMANCES" are the versions of various CYCLES of Arthurian ROMANCE which were written in Old French prose (common or colloquial speech) in the thirteenth century and were the most widely used forms of these stories, forming the basis of Malory's *Le Morte Darthur* and other later treatments. See ARTHURIAN ROMANCE.

W

Wardour-Street English: A style strongly marked by ARCHAISMS; an insincere, artificial expression. Wardour Street, in London, is a street housing many antique dealers selling genuine and imitation antiques. *Wardour-Street English* is a term coined on the ANALOGY of imitation ARCHAISMS in writing and imitation antiques in furniture. It was, for instance, applied to William Morris's translation of the *Odyssey*.

War of the Theaters: A complicated series of quarrels among certain Elizabethan dramatists in the years 1598–1602. Ben Jonson and John Marston were the chief opponents, though many other dramatists, including Dekker certainly and Shakespeare possibly, were concerned. Among the causes of the quarrel were the personal and professional jealousies among some of the playwrights and the keen competition among the rival theaters and their companies of actors. Particularly important was the struggle for supremacy between the stock companies of professionals (see PUBLIC THEATERS) and the companies of boy actors, the "Children of the Chapel"— acting at the Blackfriars—and the "Children of Paul's." The child actors were becoming very popular and were threatening to supersede the "common stages," as Shakespeare himself termed his fellows and himself in his allusion to the situation in *Hamlet* (Act II, Scene ii). The details of the affair have not been very completely recovered by modern students. Some of the plays concerned are: Jonson's *Every Man in his Humour* (1598), Marston's *Histriomastix* (1599) and *Jack Drum's Entertainment* (1600), Dekker and others' *Patient Grissel* (1600), Jonson's *Cynthia's Revels* (1600), Dekker's *Satiromastix* (1601). Shakespeare's connection with the quarrel is inferred from the statement in the university play *The Return from Parnasus* (1601–1602) that Shakespeare had bested Jonson, and from the theory that *Troilus and Cressida* reflects the "war." There is a clear allusion to the rivalry of the boy actors and the "common stages" in *Hamlet* (Act II, Scene ii). See SCHOOL PLAYS.

Weak Ending: A syllable at the end of a VERSE which carries METRICAL ACCENT but would not normally carry RHETORICAL ACCENT. These lines from Shakespeare's *Antony and Cleopatra* illustrate *weak ending*, in that "shall" as an auxiliary would not normally be stressed and yet is placed where the METER calls for STRESS:

> Your scutcheons and your signs of conquest shall
> Hang in what place you please.

Well-Made Novel: A NOVEL with a tightly constructed PLOT, a freedom from extraneous INCIDENTS or SUBPLOTS, a clear MOTIVATION for the several actions of its CHARACTERS, and a sense of economy and inevitability in its development. In a *well-made novel* all the parts are necessary to the STORY and are in a strict causal relationship to each other. Despite the fact that such requirements sound mechanical, great NOVELS have been produced that are justifiably called *well-made*. Jane Austen was remarkably successful with the *well-made novel*, and Hawthorne's *The Scarlet Letter* is an excellent example. The qualities of the *well-made novel*, however, more frequently appear in the SHORT NOVEL than in the full-length NOVEL.

Well-Made Play: A term applied to PROBLEM PLAYS, COMEDIES OF MANNERS, and FARCES in the nineteenth century, particularly in France, where the equivalent term was PIÈCE BIEN FAITE, but also in England and America. The term *well-made* refers to the very tight and logical construction of these plays, with their apparent logical inevitability. They usually contained these CONVENTIONS in their STRUCTURE: (1) a PLOT based on a withheld secret that, being revealed at the CLIMAX, produces a favorable REVERSAL for the HERO; (2) a steadily mounting SUSPENSE depending on rising action, exactly timed entrances, mistaken identity, withholding of information from CHARACTERS, misplaced letters and documents, and a battle of wits between HERO and VILLAIN; (3) a CLIMAX culminating in an OBLIGATORY SCENE (SCÈNE À FAIRE) in which the withheld secret is revealed and the REVERSAL of the HERO's fortunes achieved; and (4) a logical DÉNOUEMENT. Often this pattern was followed in each of the ACTS as well as in the total play. The chief creator of the *well-made play* was the French dramatist Eugène Scribe; after Scribe the best of the *well-made plays* were by Victorien Sardou. Almost all French DRAMA of the nineteenth century was influenced by Scribe and Sardou, and their plays were translated and performed with great success in England and America. The popular British playwrights Bulwer-Lytton, Tom Taylor, and T. W. Robertson wrote *well-made plays,* and Henrik Ibsen directed more than twenty Scribe plays in Norway before he launched his own powerfully influential DRAMAS, which incorporate in their STRUCTURE some of the tightly knit characteristics of the *well-made play*.

Welsh Literature: Though records are scanty it is probable that there was much literary activity in Wales in the early Middle Ages (sixth to ninth centuries). In eastern and central Wales there developed the *englyn,* a form of epigrammatic VERSE possibly derived from Latin literature. The northern district produced the most famous of early Welsh poets, Taliessin and Aneurin (sixth century?), who sang of early Welsh warriors, including heroes traditionally associated with King Arthur. This literature is probably related to the Irish. The western CYCLE deals with very early material, such as MYTHS of the gods. Chiefly from this Western literature come the best known stories of early Welsh authorship, those now collected in the famous MABINOGION. The tales were probably collected and written down in the eleventh and twelfth centuries, though the manuscripts of the MABINOGION date from a few centuries later. The stories in the MABINOGION fall into five classes. The first is the MABINOGION proper, or the "four branches." It includes four STORIES which are the written versions of spoken TALES belonging to the repertory of the lower orders of Welsh BARDS, and which preserve primitive tradition. The titles are *Pwyll Prince of Dyved, Branwen daughter of Llyr, Manawyddan son of Llyr,* and *Math son of Mathonwy.* The second group includes two TALES based on legendary British historical tradition: *Dream of Macsen Wledig, Llud and Llefelys.* The third class, old Arthurian folk-TALES current in southwest Wales retold by eleventh- or twelfth-century writers with some admixture of other matter, partly Irish, is represented by *Culhwh and Olwen.* This story is of great interest to students of Arthurian ROMANCE as it may reflect a very early stage of the development of Arthurian stories, before magic and grotesqueness had not been displaced by chivalric manners. The fourth class consists of Arthurian stories paralleled in courtly French versions of the twelfth century (some and perhaps all based partly at least upon the French versions): *Peredur, Gereint, The Lady of the Fountain* (or *Owein*). The fifth class (imaginary, sophisticated literary TALES) is represented by *The Dream of Rhonabwy.*

Under Gruffydd ab Cynan (1054–1137) there was a renaissance of Welsh poetry with courtly patronage—the bardic system was now flourishing. These court POETS followed a traditional poetic technique, employing ancient CONVENTIONS and archaic words to such an extent that a contemporary could hardly understand the verse. With the English conquest (1282) the old POETRY declined, and in the fourteenth and fifteenth centuries, known as a "golden age," under the leadership of the poet Dafydd ap Gwilym, a contemporary of Chaucer, the basis of modern Welsh POETRY was laid. The language actually spoken was employed, and love and nature were exploited as poetic THEMES. Under the TUDORS the aggressive

English influence depressed native Welsh POETRY, though the BARDS remained active till mid-seventeenth century. In the seventeenth century a new school of POETS who utilized native folk materials arose and in the eighteenth century came the classical revival under the influence of the English AUGUSTANS. Poetry in the nineteenth century was largely religious.

The development of PROSE in Wales, as in England, in the sixteenth and seventeenth centuries was fostered by the availability of the printing press and by the vogue of controversial writings, especially those connected with the religious movements of early Protestant times. In the late eighteenth and early nineteenth centuries the liberal movement in politics stimulated further activity in PROSE, and thereafter Welsh literature, both PROSE and POETRY, has been inclined to follow general European movements, as has criticism. Coincident with other phases of the CELTIC RENAISSANCE there was a distinct revival of literary activity in the late nineteenth and early twentieth centuries.

Westerns: SHORT STORIES and NOVELS laid in the Western United States and dealing with the adventurous lives of frontiersmen, Indian fighters, scouts, and cowboys. Western material has been a major source for American ROMANCE since early in the nineteenth century. Cooper's *The Prairie* (1827) has many of the characteristics of the *Western*. *Westerns* were staple fare in the DIME NOVELS and the PULP MAGAZINES and through these popular media passed into the consciousness of the mass American public. *Westerns* are usually written to a very simple FORMULA, in which the hero, with gun and horse, defends justice against the threat of the VILLAIN. Within that FORMULA the CHARACTERS are conventionalized and the actions so stylized that they often seem like movements in an intricate dance. A few novelists, like Owen Wister (*The Virginian*, 1902) and Walter van Tilburg Clark (*The Ox-Bow Incident*, 1940), have produced FICTION of substantial literary worth, using these materials, but most *Westerns* have been written by prolific writers such as Zane Grey, Max Brand, Ernest Haycox, W. M. Raine, C. E. Mulford, and B. M. Bower. The *Western* became a stock PLOT for low-budget motion pictures, and since the advent of television, these STEREOTYPE stories have been the most common fictional fare of the average American. If out of the American experience there has come a representative action that has the characteristics of a MYTH and expresses in PLOT and CHARACTER the average American's view of the cosmos, it appears to be the *Western*.

Whimsical: A critical term characterizing writing which is fanciful, odd, eccentric. Whimsy, in a sense now obsolete, was used as "a whimsy in the head, or in the blood," implying a sort of vertigo. *Whimsical* writing, then, is writing inspired by a fantastic or fanciful mood. Lamb's ESSAYS are often *whimsical* in this sense.

Widow: In printing, a short line ending a paragraph and appearing at the top of a page or a column. *Widows* traditionally should be avoided in printing.

Wit and Humor: Although neither of these words originally was concerned with the laughable, both now find their chief uses in this connection. At present the distinction between the two terms, though generally recognized to exist, is difficult to draw, although there have been numerous attempts at definition. One great "wit" in fact made a witticism out of his observation that any person who attempted to distinguish between *wit* and *humor* thereby demonstrated that he himself possessed neither *wit* (in the sense of superior mental powers) nor *humor* (which implies a sense of proportion and self-evaluation that would show him the difficulty of attempting a cold analysis of so fugitive a thing as *humor*).

Humor is the American spelling of HUMOUR, originally a physiological term which because of its psychological implications came to carry the meaning of "eccentric": from this meaning developed the modern implications of the term. *Wit*, meaning originally knowledge, came in the late Middle Ages to signify "intellect," "the seat of consciousness," the "inner" senses as contrasted with the five "outer" senses. In RENAISSANCE times, though used in various senses, *wit* usually meant "wisdom" or "mental activity." An important critical use developed in the seventeenth century when the term, as applied for example to the metaphysical poets (see METAPHYSICAL VERSE), meant "fancy," in the sense of inspiration, ORIGINALITY, or creative IMAGINATION—this being the literary virtue particularly prized at the time. With the coming of NEO-CLASSICISM, however, the term took on new meanings to reflect new critical attitudes, and for a hundred years many philosophers (including Hobbes, Locke, and Hume) and critics (including Dryden, Addison, Pope,

Wit and Humor

and Johnson) wrestled with efforts to define *wit*. Hobbes asserted that fancy without judgment or reason could not constitute *wit*, though judgment without fancy could. Pope used the word in both of the contrasting senses of fancy and judgment. Dryden had called *wit* "propriety of thought and words," and Locke thought of it as an agreeable and prompt assemblage of ideas, ability to see comparisons. Hume stressed the idea that *wit* is that which pleases ("good TASTE" being the criterion). Amid the confusing variety of eighteenth-century uses of the word, this notion of *wit* as a social grace which gave pleasure led to its comparison with *humor*, and before 1800 both words came to be associated with the laughable, though the older, serious meaning of *wit* did not die out, as the earlier meanings of *humor* (both the medical meaning of one of the four liquids of the human body and the derived meaning of "individual disposition" or "eccentricity") had done. Modern definitions of *wit* reflect both the original and the late eighteenth-century conceptions: "that quality of speech or writing which consists in the apt association of thought and expression, calculated to surprise and delight by its unexpectedness; later always with reference to the utterance of brilliant or sparkling things in an amusing way" (*New English Dictionary*).

It is for the most part agreed that *wit* is primarily intellectual, the perception of similarities in seemingly dissimilar things—the "swift play and flash of mind,"—and is expressed in skillful phraseology, plays upon words, surprising contrasts, PARADOXES, EPIGRAMS, comparisons, etc., while *humor* implies a sympathetic recognition of human values and deals with the foibles and incongruities of human nature, good-naturedly exhibited. A few quotations from writers who have made serious attempts to distinguish between the two terms may help further to clarify the conceptions. *Humor* "deals with incongruities of character and circumstance, as *Wit* does in those of arbitrary ideas" (Hunt). "*Wit* is intensive or incisive, while *humor* is expansive. *Wit* is rapid, *humor* is slow. *Wit* is sharp, *humor* is gentle. . . . *Wit* is subjective while *humor* is objective. . . . *Wit* is art, *humor* is nature" (Carolyn Wells). "*Wit* apart from *Humor*, generally speaking, is but an element for professors to sport with. In combination with *Humor* it runs into the richest utility, and helps to humanize the world" (Hunt). "*Humor* always laughs, however earnestly it feels, and sometimes chuckles; but it never sniggers" (Saintsbury).

Wrenched Accent

Falstaff in Shakespeare's *Henry IV*, Part I, is an example of a subtle interweaving of *wit* and *humor*. The verbal fencing, the punning, and particularly the sophistical maneuvering whereby Falstaff invariably extricates himself from difficult situations with an apparent saving of his face, rest upon his *wit*. On the other hand, the easy recognition on the part of the reader not only that Falstaff is bluffing and is cutting a highly ludicrous figure but also that the old rascal is inwardly laughing at himself, that he sees clearly the incongruities of his situation and behavior and realizes that his lies will be recognized as such by the Prince, is an element of *humor*. See HUMOURS, COMEDY, SATIRE.

Women as Actors: Although they appeared on the Italian and French stages during the RENAISSANCE, women were not countenanced on the professional stage in England, where boys were specially trained to act women's parts. There were sporadic cases of the appearance of women on the stage in England, as in the case of the French actresses in London in 1629, but they were unfavorably received. The part of Ianthe in Davenant's *Siege of Rhodes* (1656) was played by Mrs. Coleman, and the tradition of English actresses is usually dated from this event. However, this piece was more musical and spectacular than dramatic, and Mrs. Coleman's appearance may have been regarded as justified by the custom of having women (not professional actresses) take parts in MASQUES. With the sudden revival of dramatic activity in 1660, actresses became a permanent feature of the English stage. The influence of the French theater and the lack of a supply of trained boy-actors were perhaps chiefly responsible. Boy-actors were by no means unknown in feminine roles on the RESTORATION stage, however. Some women who early gained fame as actresses were: Mrs. Barry, Mrs. Betterton, Mrs. Bracegirdle (seventeenth century); and Mrs. Susannah Cibber, Mrs. Oldfield, Mrs. Prichard, and Mrs. Siddons (eighteenth century).

Word Accent: The normal or accepted placement of STRESS on the syllables of a word. See ACCENT, RHETORICAL ACCENT.

Wrenched Accent: An alteration in the customary pronunciation of a word—that is, a shift in WORD ACCENT—to accommodate the demands of METRICAL ACCENT in a line of VERSE. See ACCENT.

Z

Zeugma: A term usually applied in America to any construction in which one word is placed in the same grammatical relationship to two other words with which it can be yoked only in different senses, as *cultivate* is linked in different senses with *matrimony* and *estate* in Goldsmith's sentence, "I had fancied you were gone down to cultivate matrimony and your estate in the country." Strictly speaking, if the linkage is grammatically correct, as the above example is, the yoking is called SYLLEPSIS rather than *zeugma*, with *zeugma* restricted to yokings that are grammatically incorrect, as in "With *weeping* eyes and hearts" or "The orange *was* eaten but the grapes neglected." The distinction, however, is rarely made and *zeugma* is commonly used to include both *zeugma* and SYLLEPSIS.

OUTLINE OF
Literary History
English and American

Both English and American literary history have been divided into relatively arbitrary *periods*, and historical subdivisions within these periods are designated as *ages*. Although this outline gives a few historical facts and general statements about the characteristics of *periods* and *ages*, the fuller treatment of such historical units is reserved for the Handbook, where brief essays on the *periods* and shorter comments on the *ages* are given at the proper places in the alphabetic listings.

Beginning with the year 1607 American items appear in a separate column which runs parallel with the English.

Titles are often abbreviated or modernized to forms commonly encountered by the student. Translated titles appear in quotation marks in the early periods.

Dates for titles of printed books are ordinarily the dates of first publication. Dates for works written before the era of printing are dates of composition, often approximate.

Abbreviations and Symbols
  ? —questionable date or statement of fact.
  * —non-English item.
  w —written.
  a —acted.
  ca. —about: dating is approximate.
  fl. —flourishing, or flourished.
  Lat. —Latin.
  A.S. —Anglo-Saxon.

? B.C.–A.D. 428 CELTIC AND ROMAN BRITAIN

? B.C.–A.D. 82	Celtic Britain.
55, 54 B.C.	Julius Caesar invades Britain.
43–410	Roman-Celtic period in Britain: government Roman, population largely Celtic. No literature extant.
43	Invasion of Claudius.

*ca.*85	Roman power established in Britain.
98	°Tacitus, *Germania* (Lat.): early account of Teutonic ancestors of English.
313	°Christianity established at Rome by Constantine.
410	°Rome sacked by Alaric. Roman legions leave Britain.

428–1100 OLD ENGLISH (ANGLO-SAXON) PERIOD

*ca.*428	Germanic tribes begin invasion of Britain.
449	Traditional date (from Gildas and Bede) for Germanic invasion of Britain under Hengist and Horsa.
*ca.*450–*ca.*700	Probable period of composition of Old English poems reflecting Continental life: *Beowulf,* epic; *Waldhere,* fragmentary epic of Theodoric saga; *Finnsburg,* fragmentary, related to *Beowulf* background; *Widsith,* lyric, adventures of a wandering poet; *Deor's Lament,* lyric account of poet's troubles; *The Wanderer,* reflective poem on cruelty of fate; *The Seafarer,* reflective, descriptive lyric on sailor's lot in life; *The Wife's Complaint, The Husband's Message:* love poems notable for romantic treatment of nature; *Charms,* miscellaneous incantations reflecting early superstitions, ceremonies, and remedies; formulistic.
*ca.*500–*ca.*700	°Christian culture flourishes in Ireland after being almost obliterated on Continent by Teutonic invasion; activity of Irish missionaries in Scotland, Iceland, France, Germany, Switzerland, and Italy aids in rechristianizing Western Europe.
*ca.*524	°Boëthius, "Consolation of Philosophy" (Lat.): one of greatest books of early Middle Ages; translated into English, successively, by King Alfred, Chaucer, and Queen Elizabeth.
563	St. Columba (Irish Monk) establishes monastery at Iona, thus preparing for spread of Celtic Christianity in Scotland and Northern England.
597	Saint Augustine (the missionary) places Roman Christianity on firm basis in Southern England.
600–700	Establishment of powerful Anglo-Saxon kingdoms.
*ca.*600–*ca.*800	°Irish saga literature assumes written form.
*ca.*633	°The Koran; texts recorded; canonical version, 651–52.
640?–709	Aldhelm: famous scholar of Canterbury school—Latin works survive; English poems (probably ballads) lost.

664	Synod of Whitby: triumph of Roman over Celtic Christianity in Britain.
ca.670	Caedmon, *Hymns*, etc.: first English poet known by name.
ca.690	Adamnan, *Life of St. Columba* (Lat.): first biography in Britain.
ca.700	"School of Caedmon" *fl.*: Genesis, Exodus, Daniel—Biblical paraphrases; Judith, apocryphal.
	Beowulf composed in present form: great A.S. epic.
731	Bede (Bæda), The Venerable, "Ecclesiastical History" (Lat.): first history of English people.

750

ca.750–ca.800	Flourishing period of Christian poetry in Northumbria (preserved in later West Saxon versions).
	Cynewulf and his "school": *Crist,* narrative; *Elene, Juliana, Fates of the Apostles, Andreas,* saints' legends. *The Phoenix,* myth interpreted as Christian allegory.
787	First Danish invasion.
ca.800	Nennius (a Welshman), "History of the Britons" (Lat.): first mention of Arthur.
827–1017	Anglo-Saxon kings (Egbert to Edmund Ironside).

850

ca.850	Danish conquest of England.
871–899	Reign of Alfred the Great. Alfred's translations of Pope Gregory's *Pastoral Care,* Boëthius, Orosius, Bede; *Anglo-Saxon Chronicle* revised and continued to 892; West Saxon *Martyrology;* sermons; saints' lives.
ca.875–900	°Probable beginnings of medieval drama. Dramatization of liturgy. First known text an Easter trope, *Quem Quaeritis,* from Swiss monastery of St. Gall.
878	Peace of Wedmore; partial Danish evacuation.
893	Asser, *Life of Alfred the Great:* "first life-record of a layman."
901–1066	Later Old English Period. *Chronicle* continued; poetry, sermons, Biblical translations and paraphrases, saints' lives, lyrics.
ca.937	*Battle of Brunanburh:* heroic poem.
950–1000	Monastic revival under Dunstan, Aethelwold, and Aelfric.

Outline of Literary History

*ca.*950	*Junius* MS written: contains "School of Caedmon" poems.
971	*Blickling Homilies:* colloquial tendencies.
*ca.*975	St. Aethelwold's *Regularis Concordia:* earliest evidence of dramatic activity in England.
979–1016	Second period of Danish invasions.
*ca.*991	*Battle of Maldon:* heroic poem.

1000

1000–1200	Transition period, English to Norman French. Decline of A.S. heroic verse; reduced literary activity in English.
*ca.*1000	A.S. *Gospels* written. Aelfric, *Sermons.*
	Beowulf MS written.
*ca.*1000–1025	The *Exeter Book:* A.S. MS containing Cynewulf poems.
*ca.*1000–1100	*Vercelli Book:* A.S. MS containing *Andreas,* etc.
	°Probable period of full development of Christmas and Easter cycles of plays in Western Europe.
1017–1042	Danish kings (Canute to Hardicanute).
1042–1066	Saxon kings restored (Edward the Confessor to Harold II).
1066	Battle of Senlac (Hastings). Norman conquest.
1066–1154	Norman kings (William I to Stephen).
1086	*Domesday Book:* important English census.
1087–1100	William II: centralization of kingdom.
1096–1099	The First Crusade.

1100–1350 ANGLO-NORMAN PERIOD

1100–1200	°French literature dominating Western Europe.
1100–1135	Reign of Henry I ("Beauclerc").
*ca.*1100–1250	°Icelandic sagas written: *Grettirsaga, Volsungsaga,* etc.
*ca.*1100	"Play of St. Catherine" (*a.* at Dunstable): first recorded "miracle" or saint's play in England.
	°Earlier tales in Welsh *Mabinogion* (*w*).
	°Great period of French poetry begins. *Chanson de Roland:* French epic.
*ca.*1124	Eadmer, *Life of Anselm:* human element in biography.

Outline of Literary History

*ca.*1125–1300	Latin chronicles *fl.*
*ca.*1125	Henry of Huntingdon and William of Malmesbury: chronicles.
1135–1154	Reign of Stephen.
*ca.*1136	Geoffrey of Monmouth, "History of the Kings of Britain" (Lat. chronicle). First elaborate account of Arthurian court.

1150

1154–1399	Plantagenet kings (Henry II to Richard II).
1154–1189	Reign of Henry II: his court a center of literature and learning—historians, philosophers, theologians, poets.
1154	End of entries in *A.S. Chronicle* (Peterborough).
*ca.*1170	*Poema Morale.*
*ca.*1185–1190	°Giraldus Cambrensis, "Itinerary": description of Wales.
1189–1199	Reign of Richard I ("The Lion-hearted").
*ca.*1190	Nigel Wireker, *Speculum stultorum* (Lat.), "The Fool's Looking-glass."
1199–1216	Reign of John.

1200

*ca.*1200–1250	*King Horn, Beves of Hampton* (earliest form): English metrical romances using English themes.
*ca.*1200–1225	°The Vulgate Romances (expansion of Arthurian romance material in French prose).
*ca.*1200	Walter Map *fl.*: court satirist.
	Orm, *Ormulum:* Scriptural poem.
*ca.*1205	Layamon, *Brut.*
1215	*Magna Charta.*
1216–1272	Reign of Henry III.
*ca.*1225	°St. Thomas Aquinas born. Died 1274.
*ca.*1230,*ca.*1270	°*Roman de la Rose* by Guillaume de Lorris and Jean de Meun.

1250

*ca.*1250–1300	*Sir Tristrem, Floris and Blanchefleur* (romances).
*ca.*1250	Nicholas of Guilford, *The Owl and the Nightingale.* The "Cuckoo Song" (*Sumer is Icumen in*).

*ca.*1250	°*Gesta Romanorum.*
1258	Henry III uses English as well as French in proclamation.
1265	°Dante born. Died 1321.
1272–1307	Reign of Edward I.
*ca.*1294	°Dante, *Vita Nuova.*

1300

1300–1400	English displaces French in speech of upper classes, and in schools and law pleadings. Mystery plays now in hands of guilds: more actors, more spectators, outdoor stages, comic elements, "cyclic" development (York plays probably oldest existing cycle).
*ca.*1307–1321	°Dante's *Divina Commedia.*
*ca.*1300–1350	*Guy of Warwick, Havelok the Dane, Richard Lionheart, Amis and Amiloun:* romances.
*ca.*1300	°Marco Polo, "Travels." *Cursor Mundi.*
1304	°Petrarch born. Died 1374.
1307–1327	Reign of Edward II.
1311	Feast of Corpus Christi, established in 1264, was made operative, leading to popularization of cyclic plays at this summer festival and perhaps to use of movable stages or "pageants."
1313	°Boccaccio born. Died 1375.
1314	Battle of Bannockburn.
1327–1377	Reign of Edward III.
1328(?)	Chester cycle of plays composed.
1337–1453	The Hundred Years' War.
*ca.*1340	Geoffrey Chaucer born. Died 1400. *The Prick of Conscience.*
1342	°Boccaccio, *Ameto:* "first pastoral romance."
1346	Battle of Crécy.
1348–1350	The Black Death in England.

1350–1500 MIDDLE ENGLISH PERIOD

1350–1400	*Sir Eglamour, Morte Arthure, Sir Gawayne and the Green Knight, Athelston, William of Palerne, Sir Ferumbras, Sir Isumbras,* and other romances.

*ca.*1350	*Petrarch, eclogues (Lat.), printed 1504. "Sonnets to Laura" partly written.
	*Boccaccio, *Decameron.*
1356 (?)	"Sir John Mandeville," *Voyage and Travels.*
*ca.*1360	*The Pearl.*
1362	English language used in court pleadings and in opening Parliament.
*ca.*1362 *et seq.*	*Piers Plowman.*
*ca.*1370	Chaucer, *The Book of the Duchess.*
*ca.*1375	Barbour, *Bruce.*
	"Paternoster" and "Creed" plays (*a*): forerunners of morality plays.
1377–1399	Richard II.
*ca.*1379	Chaucer, *House of Fame.*
*ca.*1380	Wycliffe and others, translation of Bible into English.
1381	Wat Tyler's rebellion.
*ca.*1383	Chaucer, *Troilus and Criseyde.*
*ca.*1385	English replaces French as language of the schools. Chaucer, *Legend of Good Women.*
*ca.*1387	Chaucer, "Prologue" to *Canterbury Tales* (tales themselves written, some earlier, some later).
*ca.*1388	Usk, *The Testament of Love.*
*ca.*1390	Gower, *Confessio Amantis.*
1399–1461	House of Lancaster (Henry IV to Henry VI).
1399–1413	Reign of Henry IV.
1400	Death of Chaucer.

1400

1400–1450	Later romances in prose and verse.
1400–1425	Wakefield cycle of plays (MS, *ca.*1450).
	The Pride of Life (fragmentary): earliest extant morality play.
1400	*Froissart, *Chronicles.*
*ca.*1405	*Castle of Perseverance;* first complete morality play.
*ca.*1412	Hoccleve, *The Regiment of Princes* (*w*).
1413–1422	Reign of Henry V.
1415	Battle of Agincourt.

*ca.*1415	Lydgate, *Troy Book.*
1422–1509	The *Paston Letters:* family correspondence reflecting social conditions.
1422–1461	Reign of Henry VI.
*ca.*1425	Humanists active under patronage of Humphrey, Duke of Gloucester: Lydgate, Pecock, etc.
1440	Galfridus Grammaticus, *Promptorium Parvulorum:* English-Latin word-list, beginning of English lexicography.

1450

1450	Jack Cade's rebellion.
*ca.*1450	"Tiptoft" School of humanists active.
	°Gutenberg press: beginning of modern printing.
	Beginning of Lowland Scotch as northern literary dialect.
*ca.*1450–1525	Scottish poets of Chaucerian school: Henryson, Dunbar, Douglas, and probably King James I of Scotland.
1453	°Fall of Constantinople: end of Eastern Empire.
1455–1485	Wars of the Roses: depressing effect on literary activity.
1456	°The Gutenberg Bible.
*ca.*1460	John Skelton born. Died 1529.
1461–1485	House of York (Edward IV to Richard III).
1461–1483	Reign of Edward IV.
1469	Sir Thomas Malory completes composition of *Le Morte Darthur* (pub. 1485).
*ca.*1474	Caxton prints (at Bruges) the *Recuyell of the Histories of Troy:* first book printed in English.
*ca.*1477	Caxton's press set up at Westminster: first printing press in England. *Dictes and Sayings of the Philosophers,* the first dated book (1477) printed in England.
1478	Sir Thomas More born. Died 1535.
1483	Reign of Edward V.
1483–1485	Reign of Richard III.
1485–1603	House of Tudor (Henry VII to Elizabeth).
1485–1509	Reign of Henry VII.
1485	Caxton publishes Malory's *Le Morte Darthur.*
1490–1520	"Oxford Reformers" (Linacre, Grocyn, Colet, Erasmus, More) active.
1491	Greek taught at Oxford.

1492	*Discovery of America by Columbus.
ca.1497	Medwall, *Fulgens and Lucres* (*a*).
1499	Erasmus in England.

1500–1660 THE RENAISSANCE

1500–1557 EARLY TUDOR AGE

1500–1550	Romances.—*Valentine and Orson*, Lord Berners' *Arthur of Little Britain, Huon of Bordeaux*, etc.
ca.1500	*Everyman.*
1503 (?)	Sir Thomas Wyatt born. Died 1542.
ca.1508	Skelton, *Philip Sparrow*.
1509–1547	Reign of Henry VIII.
1509	Barclay, *Ship of Fools*.
	Hawes, *Pastime of Pleasure*.
	*Erasmus, "The Praise of Folly" (Lat.) (*w*), social satire.
1510	Acting of Terence's comedies an established practice at Oxford and Cambridge.
1515	Roger Ascham born. Died 1568.
1516	More, *Utopia* (Lat.).
ca.1516	*Ariosto, *Orlando Furioso*.
	Skelton, *Magnificence*.
ca.1517	Henry Howard, Earl of Surrey born. Died 1547.
1517	*Luther posts his theses in Wittenberg; leads to Protestant Revolution, 1520 *et seq*.
1519	Rastell, *The Four Elements:* first published interlude. Advocates adequacy of English for literary purposes.
	*Cortez conquers Mexico.
1520–1530	Latin plays acted in grammar schools.
ca.1520	Skelton's poetical satires (*Colin Clout, Why Come Ye Not to Court*, etc.).
1523	Lord Berners' trans. of Froissart's *Chronicles*.

1525

1525	Tyndale, *New Testament:* printed at Worms; first printed English translation of any part of Bible.

Outline of Literary History

1528	*Castiglione, *The Courtier.*
1529	Simon Fish, *Supplication for the Beggars.*
	Fall of Wolsey.
ca.1530–1540	Heywood's "Interludes": realistic farce.
ca.1530	The "New Poetry" movement under way.
1531	Elyot, *The Boke Named the Governour.*
1532	*Machiavelli, *The Prince* (*w* 1513).
	*Rabelais, *Pantagruel.*
1533	Separation of English church from Rome.
	John Leland made "King's Antiquary."
1534	Act of Supremacy: Henry VIII head of Church of England.
1535	Execution of More.
	Coverdale's first complete English Bible.
1536	Execution of Tyndale.
	*Calvin, *Institutes of Christian Religion* (Lat.).
1538	Sir Thomas Elyot, *Dictionarie.*
1539	English Bible (the "Great Bible") published.
1540	Lyndsay, *Satyre of the Three Estaits.*
1542	Death of Wyatt.
	Hall's *Chronicle.*
1542 (?)	George Gascoigne born. Died 1577.
1545	Ascham, *Toxophilus.*
	*Council of Trent.
1547-1553	Reign of Edward VI.
1547	Execution of Surrey.
1549–1552	*Book of Common Prayer.*

1550

ca.1552	Edmund Spenser born. Died 1599.
	Sir Walter Raleigh born. Died 1618.
	Udall, *Ralph Roister Doister* (*w*): first "regular" English comedy.
1553–1558	Reign of Mary.
1553	Wilson, *Arte of Rhetorique.*
1554	Sir Philip Sidney born. Died 1586.

ca.1555	Roper, *Life of Sir Thomas More* (*w*).
	Cavendish, *Life of Cardinal Wolsey* (*w*).
1557	*Songs and Sonnets* ("Tottel's Miscellany"), containing Surrey's trans. of two books of the *Aeneid* in blank verse.
	North's trans. of Guevara's *Dial of Princes*.
	Stationers' Company incorporated.

1558–1603 ELIZABETHAN AGE

1558–1603	Reign of Elizabeth.
1558–1575	Translations numerous, classics often translated into English through French versions. Much interest in lyrics.
1558	John Knox, *First Blast of the Trumpet against the Monstrous Regiment of Women.*
1559	Elizabethan Prayer-book.
	The Mirror for Magistrates.
	°Amyot, Plutarch's *Lives* translated into French: basis of North's English version of Plutarch.
	°Minturno, *De Poeta:* Italian critical work.
1559 (?)	George Chapman born. Died 1634.
ca.1560	*Gammer Gurton's Needle* (*w*).
1561	Hoby's translation of Castiglione's *The Courtier.*
	Francis Bacon born. Died 1626.
	°Scaliger, *Poetics:* Italian critical work.
1562	Sackville and Norton, *Gorboduc* (*a*): first English tragedy.
	Samuel Daniel born. Died 1619.
1563	Foxe, *Book of Martyrs:* (Lat. original, 1559).
	Sackville's "Induction" (to portion of *Mirror for Magistrates*).
	Michael Drayton born. Died 1631.
ca.1563	Sir Humphrey Gilbert, *Queen Elizabeth's Academy.*
1564	Preston, *Cambises* (*a*).
	Christopher Marlowe born. Died 1593.
	William Shakespeare born. Died 1616.
	°Galileo born. Died 1642.
1565–1567	Golding's translation of Ovid's *Metamorphoses.*

1566	Gascoigne's *Supposes* (*a*) and *Jocasta* (*a*).
1566–1567	Painter, *Palace of Pleasure.*
1567	Turberville, *Epitaphs, Epigrams, Songes, and Sonets.*
1570	Ascham, *Schoolmaster.*
*ca.*1573	John Donne born. Died 1631.
	Ben Jonson born. Died 1637.

1575

1575	Gascoigne, *The Posies:* poems with first English treatise on versification appended.
	Mystery plays still being acted at Chester.
1576–1580	Spenser's early poetry (*w*).
1576	*Paradise of Dainty Devices.*
	The Theatre (first London playhouse) built.
	Gascoigne, *The Steel Glass.*
	George Pettie, *A Petite Palace of Pettie his Pleasure.*
1577	Holinshed, *Chronicles.*
	A Gorgeous Gallery of Gallant Inventions: poetical miscellany.
1577–1580	Drake circumnavigates globe.
1579	Lyly, *Euphues, the Anatomy of Wit.*
	Spenser, *The Shepheardes Calender* (pub. anonymously).
	Gosson, *School of Abuse:* attack on poetry and the stage.
	North, trans. of Plutarch's *Lives.*
	John Fletcher born. Died 1625.
1580–1600	Elizabethan "novels" popular: Lyly, Greene, Lodge, Sidney, Nash, Deloney. Pastoral poetry popular.
1580	°Montaigne, *Essays:* beginning of modern "personal" essay.
*ca.*1581	Peele, *Arraignment of Paris* (*a*).
	Sidney, *Defence of Poesie* (*w*) (pub. 1595).
1582–1600	Hakluyt publishes various collections of "voyages"—Renaissance and medieval, notably *Principal Navigations* (1st ed. 1589).
1582	Stanyhurst, trans. of Virgil's *Æneid* (i–iv) in quantitative verse.
1583	P. Stubbs, *Anatomie of Abuses.*

*ca.*1583	Lyly, *Alexander and Campaspe* (*a*).
1584	Scot, *Discovery of Witchcraft.*
	Handful of Pleasant Delights: ballad miscellany.
1585–1586	Raleigh fails in effort to colonize Virginia.
1586	Kyd, *The Spanish Tragedy* (*a*).
	Warner, *Albion's England.*
	Camden, *Britannia* (Lat.).
	Death of Sidney.
1586 (?)	Shakespeare comes to London.
1587	Marlowe, *Tamburlaine* (*a*).
	Execution of Mary Queen of Scots.
1588–1589	"Martin Marprelate" papers.
1588	Defeat of Spanish Armada.
*ca.*1588	Marlowe, *Doctor Faustus* (*a*).
1589	Greene, *Menaphon.*
	Puttenham (?), *The Arte of English Poesie.*

1590

1590	Lodge, *Rosalynde.*
	Sidney, *Arcadia* (*w ca.*1581).
	Spenser, *Faerie Queene,* Books I–III.
*ca.*1590	Greene (?), *James IV* (*a*).
	Shakespeare begins career as playwright, with *The Comedy of Errors.*
1591–1596	Sonnet cycles: Sidney, Daniel, Drayton, Lodge, Spenser, and others.
1591	Spenser, *Complaints:* includes *Mother Hubberds Tale.*
	Harrington, trans. of Ariosto's *Orlando Furioso.*
	Sidney, *Astrophel and Stella.*
	Robert Herrick born. Died 1674.
1592–1593	Shakespeare, *Richard III* (*a*).
1593	Shakespeare, *Venus and Adonis.*
	Phoenix Nest: poetical miscellany.
	Death of Marlowe.
	Izaak Walton born. Died 1683.

	George Herbert born. Died 1633.
1594	Hooker, *Ecclesiastical Polity,* Books I–IV.
	Shakespeare, *Rape of Lucrece.*
	Nash, *The Unfortunate Traveler:* picaresque romance.
1595	Spenser, *Amoretti; Epithalamion.*
	Sidney, *Defence of Poesie* (*w ca.*1581).
	Daniel, *Civil Wars.*
	Lodge, *A Fig for Momus.*
	Donne's poetry circulating in manuscript.
	Shakespeare, *Midsummer Night's Dream* (*a*).
1596	Raleigh, *Discovery of Guiana* (*w*) (pub. 1606).
	Shakespeare, *Romeo and Juliet* (*a*).
	Spenser, *Faerie Queene,* Books IV–VI.
1597–1600	Shakespeare's Falstaff plays (*a*): *Henry IV,* 1, 2; *Henry V; Merry Wives of Windsor.*
1597	Shakespeare, *Merchant of Venice* (*a*).
	Drayton, *Heroical Epistles.*
	Bacon, *Essays* (1st ed.).
	Hall, *Virgidemiarum.* Vol. I.
	King James (of Scotland), *Demonology:* answers Scot and defends reality of witchcraft.
1598	Shakespeare, *Julius Caesar* (*a*).
	Meres, *Palladis Tamia,* "Wit's Treasury."
	Ben Jonson begins career as playwright—*Everyman in His Humour* (*a*).
	Chapman, translation of *Iliad* (seven books in "fourteeners").
*ca.*1598	Deloney, *The Gentle Craft.*
1598–1600	Shakespeare's "joyous comedies": *Much Ado about Nothing; As You Like It; Twelfth Night.*
1599	*The Passionate Pilgrim:* miscellany containing some of Shakespeare's poems.
	Globe theater built: used by Shakespeare's company.
	Death of Spenser.

1600

| 1600 | *England's Helicon:* poetical miscellany. |

Outline of Literary History

1601	Shakespeare, *Hamlet* (*a*).
1602	Campion, *Observations in the Art of English Poesie.*
	Founding of the Bodleian Library (Oxford).
*ca.*1602	Daniel, *Defence of Ryme.*
1602–1604	Shakespeare, the "bitter comedies": *Troilus and Cressida, All's Well That Ends Well, Measure for Measure* (*a*).

1603–1625 JACOBEAN AGE

1603–1688	The Stuarts.
1603–1625	Reign of James I—union of English and Scottish crowns.
1603	T. Heywood, *A Woman Killed with Kindness* (*a*).
	Jonson, *Sejanus* (*a*).
	Florio, translation of Montaigne.
1604	Shakespeare, *Othello* (*a*).
1605	Bacon, *Advancement of Learning.*
	Gunpowder Plot.
	*Cervantes, *Don Quixote*, Part I.
	Sir Thomas Browne born. Died 1682.
	Shakespeare, *Macbeth* (*a*), *King Lear* (*a*).
1606	Jonson, *Volpone* (*a*).
	Sir William Davenant born. Died 1668.

ENGLISH

AMERICAN

1607–1765 COLONIAL PERIOD

	ENGLISH		AMERICAN
1607	Shakespeare, *Antony and Cleopatra* (*a*).	1607	Settlement at Jamestown, Virginia.
	Beaumont and Fletcher, *Knight of the Burning Pestle* (*a*).		
1608	John Milton born. Died 1674.	1608	Capt. John Smith, *True Relation:* early experiences in Virginia.
	Joseph Hall, *Characters of Virtues and Vices.*		

Outline of Literary History

ENGLISH

AMERICAN

1609 Shakespeare, *Sonnets* (*w.* earlier).

Beaumont and Fletcher, *Philaster* (*a*).

Dekker, *Gull's Hornbook.*

1609 Champlain discovers Lake Champlain.

Henry Hudson explores Hudson River.

1610

1609–1611 Shakespeare, tragi-comedies: *Cymbeline, Winter's Tale, Tempest* (*a*).

1610 Jonson, *Alchemist* (*a*).

1610 Strachey, *True Repertory.*

1611 King James translation of the Bible.

*ca.*1611 Shakespeare returns to Stratford.

1612 Bacon, *Essays* (2nd ed.).

Donne, First and Second *Anniversaries.*

Samuel Butler born. Died 1680.

1612 Capt. John Smith, *A Map of Virginia.*

1613 *Purchas His Pilgrimage:* travel literature.

Wither, *Abuses Stript and Whipt.*

1614 Overbury, *Characters.*

Raleigh, *History of the World.*

Webster, *Duchess of Malfi* (*a*).

1614–1616 Chapman, *Odyssey* translated.

1615 Harrington, *Epigrams.*

1616 Death of Shakespeare and of °Cervantes.

1616 Capt. John Smith, *A Description of New England.*

1618 Raleigh executed.

Harvey discovers circulation of the blood.

Abraham Cowley born. Died 1667.

576

ENGLISH		AMERICAN	
1619	Drayton, *Collected Poems.* Death of Daniel.	1619	First American legislative assembly, at Jamestown. Negro slavery introduced into Virginia.

1620

1620	Bacon, *Novum Organum* (Lat.).	1620	Pilgrims land at Plymouth. *Mayflower Compact* (*w*).
1621	Burton, *Anatomy of Melancholy.*		
1622	Donne, *Sermon on Judges xx.15* (other sermons published in 1623, 1624, 1625, 1626, 1627, and later).	1622	George Sandys completes translation of Ovid's *Metamorphoses.* Mourts' *Relation* by Bradford and others: journal.
1623	First Folio edition of Shakespeare's *Plays.*		
		1624	Capt. John Smith, *General History of Virginia.* Edward Winslow, *Good News out of New England.*

1625–1649 CAROLINE AGE

1625

1625–1649	Reign of Charles I.		
1625	Bacon, *Essays,* final edition.	1625	Morrell, *Nova Anglia.*
1626	Death of Bacon.	1626	Minuit founds New Amsterdam.
1627	Bacon, *New Atlantis* (Lat.): fragmentary "utopia." Drayton, *Battle of Agincourt.*	1627	Thomas Morton sets up Maypole at Merrymount: reflects opposition to Puritans.
1628	John Bunyan born. Died 1688.		

Outline of Literary History

1629   Ford, *The Broken Heart* (*a*).

         Milton, *Ode on the Morning of Christ's Nativity* (*w*).

1630

                                1630–1647   Bradford, *History of the Plymouth Plantation* (*w*).

                                1630–1649   Winthrop, *History of New England* (*w*).

1630   Milton, *On Shakespeare* (*w*).   1630   Massachusetts Bay Colony established at Salem.

1631   Deaths of Drayton and Donne.

         John Dryden born. Died 1700.

1632   Second Folio edition of Shakespeare.   1632   Thomas Hooker, *The Soul's Preparation.*

1633   Herbert, *The Temple.*

         Donne, *Poems* (first collected edition).

         Phineas Fletcher, *The Purple Island.*

1633(?)   Milton's *L'Allegro* and *Il Penseroso* written.

         Samuel Pepys born. Died 1703.

1634   Milton, *Comus* (*a*).   1634   Maryland settled by English.

         Davenant, *The Temple of Love:* French Platonic love.   Connecticut Valley settled.

         Death of George Chapman

1635   Quarles, *Emblems.*

1636   *Corneille, *The Cid.*   1636   Roger Williams founds Providence; all sects tolerated.

                                  Harvard College founded.

1637   Death of Jonson.   1637   Pequot War.

         *Descartes, *Discours sur la Méthode.*   Thomas Morton, *New English Canaan.*

Outline of Literary History

1638   Milton, *Lycidas.*

                                             1639   First printing press in America set up at Cambridge.

                                                       Increase Mather born. Died 1723.

1640

1640   Jonson, *Timber, or Discoveries Made upon Men and Matter.*

        Izaak Walton, *Life of Donne.*

                                             1640   *Bay Psalm Book:* first book printed in America.

                                             1641   Shepard, *The Sincere Convert.*

1642   Fuller, *Holy State.*

        Denham, *Cooper's Hill.*

        Sir Thomas Browne, *Religio Medici.*

        Sir Isaac Newton born. Died 1727.

        Civil War. Theaters closed.

1644   Milton, *Areopagitica.*

        Milton, *Tractate on Education* and divorce pamphlets.

                                             1644   Roger Williams, *Bloody Tenent of Persecution.*

                                                      Roger Williams visits Milton; teaches him Dutch.

1645   Howell, *Familiar Letters.*

        Waller, *Poems.*

        Founding of Philosophical Society.

                                             *ca.*1645   Edward Taylor born. Died 1729. *Poems,* posthumously pub. 1939.

1646   Vaughan, *Poems.*

                                             1647   Nathaniel Ward, *Simple Cobbler of Aggawam.*

1648   Herrick, *Hesperides.*

ENGLISH · AMERICAN

1649–1660 COMMON-
WEALTH INTERREGNUM

1649 Execution of Charles I.

Lovelace, *Lucasta.*

1650

1650–1728 Flourishing of the
"Mather Dynasty."

1650 Davenant, *Gondibert.*

Taylor, *Holy Living.*

*ca.*1650 Many French romances
and novels translated into
English.

1650 Anne Bradstreet, *The
Tenth Muse, Lately Sprung
up in America.*

1651 Milton, *Defence of the English People* (Lat.).

Hobbes, *Leviathan.*

1651 *Cambridge Platform* passed
by General Court.

1652 "Quaker" Movement culminating.

1653 Walton, *The Compleat Angler.*

1654 Boyle, *Parthenissa.*

1654 Capt. Edward Johnson,
*Wonder-Working Provi-
dence.*

1656 Cowley, *Poems, Davideis,
Pindaric Odes.*

Davenant, *Siege of Rhodes*
(*a*).

1656 Hammond, *Leah and Ra-
chel,* or *The Two Fruitful
Sisters, Virginia and Maryland.*

Quakers arrive in Massachusetts.

1658 Dryden, *Stanzas on the
Death of Cromwell.*

1659 John Eliot, *The Christian
Commonwealth.*

ENGLISH   AMERICAN

1660–1798 NEO-CLASSICAL
PERIOD

1660–1700 RESTORATION
AGE

1660–1714 Stuarts restored
(Charles II to Anne).

1660–1685   Reign of Charles II.

1660–1669   Pepys's *Diary* (*w*)
(pub 1825).

1660   Dryden, *Astraea Redux:*
welcomes Charles II.

*ca.*1660   Daniel Defoe born. Died
1731.

1662   Fuller, *Worthies of En-*
gland.

The Royal Society founded
as reorganization of the
Philosophical Society.

1663   Butler, *Hudibras,* Part I.

Drury Lane Theatre (first
called Theatre Royal) built.

1664   Dryden and Howard, *The*
Indian Queen (*a*).

1665   Dryden, *The Indian Em-*
peror.

Head, *The English Rogue.*

1666   Bunyan, *Grace Abounding.*

1667   Jonathan Swift born. Died
1745.

Sprat, *History of the Royal*
Society.

Milton, *Paradise Lost.*

1668   Sprat, *Life of Cowley:* starts
tradition of "discreet" biography.

Dryden, *Essay of Dramatic*
Poesy.

1660–1700   Verse elegies popular.

1662   Wigglesworth, *Day of*
Doom.

"Half-Way Covenant": low-
ers requirements for church
membership in Massachu-
setts.

1663   Eliot translates Bible into
Indian language.

Cotton Mather born. Died
1728.

1665   Baptist Church established
in Boston.

1666   George Alsop, *A Character*
of the Province of Maryland.

581

Outline of Literary History

1670

1670 Dryden, *Conquest of Granada* (*a*). Dryden made Poet Laureate.	1670 Denton, *Brief Description of New York*. Mason, *Pequot War* (*w*) (pub. 1736).
1671 Milton, *Paradise Regained* and *Samson Agonistes*. Villiers (Buckingham) and others, *The Rehearsal* (*a*).	1671 Eliot, *Progress of the Gospel Among the Indians in New England*.
1672 Joseph Addison born. Died 1719. Sir Richard Steele born. Died 1729.	1672 Eliot, *The Logick Primer*: "for the use of praying Indians."
	1673 Increase Mather, *Woe to Drunkards*.
	1674–1729 Samuel Sewall, *Diary* (*w*).
1674 Wycherley, *The Plain-Dealer* (*a*). Death of Milton and Herrick.	
1676 Etherege, *The Man of Mode*.	
	1677 Urian Oakes, *Elegy on Thomas Shepard*.
1678 Bunyan, *Pilgrim's Progress*, Part I. Dryden, *All for Love*. Popish Plot.	

1680

	1680 *The Burwell Papers* (*w*).
1681 Dryden, *Absalom and Achitophel*.	
1682 Otway, *Venice Preserved*. Dryden, *MacFlecknoe*.	1682 Penn settles Pennsylvania. La Salle explores Mississippi.

Outline of Literary History

			Mary Rowlandson, *Narrative of the Captivity* (*w*): life among the Indians.
		1683	Increase Mather, *Discourse Concerning Comets.*
		1684	Increase Mather, *Illustrious Providences.*
1685–1688	Reign of James II.		
		1685	Cotton Mather, *Memorable Providences.*
1687	Sir Isaac Newton, *Principia* (Lat.).	1687	Church of England worship established in Boston.
	Dryden, *The Hind and the Panther.*		
1688	The "Bloodless Revolution."		
	Death of Bunyan.		
	Alexander Pope born. Died 1744.		
	Mrs. Behn, *Oroonoko.*		
1689–1702	Reign of William and Mary.		
1689	Samuel Richardson born. Died 1761.		

1690

1690	Locke, *Essay Concerning the Human Understanding.*		
1691	Dunton, *Athenian Gazette.*	1691	(or earlier) *New England Primer.*
1692	Sir William Temple, *Essays.*	1692	Salem witchcraft executions.
		1693	William and Mary College founded.
			Cotton Mather, *Wonders of the Invisible World.*
1694	Wotton, *Reflections upon Ancient and Modern Learning.*		

ENGLISH	AMERICAN
1696 Toland, *Christianity not Mysterious*.	
1697 Dryden, *Alexander's Feast*.	
1698 Congreve, *Love for Love*.	
Jeremy Collier, *Short View of the Immorality and Profaneness of the English stage*.	
	1699 Jonathan Dickinson, *God's Protecting Providence*.

1700

1700–1750 AUGUSTAN AGE

1700 Death of Dryden.	1700 Samuel Sewall, *The Selling of Joseph*.
1701 Steele, *The Christian Hero; The Funeral*.	1701 Cotton Mather, *Death Made Easy and Happy*.
	Yale University founded.
1702 *The Daily Courant:* first daily newspaper.	1702 Cotton Mather, *Magnalia Christi Americana*.
Defoe, *The Shortest Way with the Dissenters*.	Increase Mather, *Ichabod*.
1702–1714 Reign of Anne.	
1703 John Wesley (founder of Methodist Church) born. Died 1791.	1703 Jonathan Edwards born. Died 1758.
Rowe, *The Fair Penitent*.	
1704–1713 Defoe, *The Review*.	
1704 Swift, *Battle of the Books* (*w. ca.*1697); *Tale of a Tub*.	1704 First American newspaper, *Boston News Letter*.
	Sarah K. Knight, *Journal of a Journey* (*w*).
1705 Steele, *The Tender Husband*.	1705 Anon., *Questions and Proposals*.
	1706 Benjamin Franklin born. Died 1790.
1707 Henry Fielding born. Died 1754.	

Outline of Literary History

1708   Ebenezer Cook, *Sot-Weed Factor.*

Cotton Mather, *Consequences of the Prevailing Abuse of Rum.*

1709–1711   Steele (and Addison), *The Tatler.*

1709   Pope, *Pastorals.*

Rowe's edition of Shakespeare.

Samuel Johnson born. Died 1784.

1710

1710–1713   Swift, *Journal to Stella* (*w*).

1710   Berkeley, *Principles of Human Knowledge.*

1710   Cotton Mather, *Essays to Do Good.*

First complete performance of Italian opera in England (*Almahide*).

John Wise, *The Churches' Quarrel Espoused.*

Handel comes to England.

1711–1712   Addison, Steele, etc. *The Spectator.*

1711   Pope, *Essay on Criticism.*

Shaftesbury, *Characteristics of Men.*

1712, 1714 Pope, *Rape of the Lock.*

1713   Pope, *Windsor Forest.*

Addison, *Cato.*

1713   Increase Mather, *A Plain Discourse Showing Who Shall and Who Shall not Enter Heaven.*

1714–1901   House of Hanover (George I to Victoria).

1714–1727   George I.

1714   Mandeville, *Fable of the Bees.*

Spectator revived.

1715   Pope, trans. *Iliad,* i–iv.

Outline of Literary History

ENGLISH	AMERICAN

Jacobite Revolt.

1716 Thomas Gray born. Died 1771.

1717 Horace Walpole born. Died 1797.

David Garrick born. Died 1779.

1719 Watts, *Psalms and Hymns.*

Defoe, *Robinson Crusoe.*

Death of Addison.

1717 William Southeby, *An Anti-Slavery Tract.*

1719 Establishment of *Boston Gazette* and the *American Weekly Mercury* (Phila.).

1720

1720 "South Sea Bubble."

1722 Defoe, *Journal of the Plague Year; Moll Flanders.*

Steele, *The Conscious Lovers* (*a*).

Parnell, *Night-Piece on Death.*

1724 Swift, *Drapier's Letters.*

Ramsay, *The Evergreen:* collection of old Scotch poetry.

1725 Pope's edition of Shakespeare.

1726 Thomson, *Winter.*

Swift, *Gulliver's Travels.*

Dyer, *Grongar Hill.*

1720 Wadsworth, *The Lord's Day Proved to be the Christian Sabbath.*

1721 James Franklin establishes the *New England Courant.*

1722 Benjamin Franklin, *Silence Dogood* papers.

1723 Death of Increase Mather.

1725–1775 Nathaniel Ames, *Astronomical Diary and Almanac.*

1725 Josiah Dwight, *Essay to Silence the Outcry . . . against Regular Singing.*

New York Gazette estab.

1726 Anon., *Hoop Petticoats Arraigned and Condemned by the Light of Nature and the Law of God.*

Outline of Literary History

ENGLISH   AMERICAN

ENGLISH	AMERICAN
1727–1760 George II.	1727 Byles, *Poem on Death of King George I.*
1728 Pope, *Dunciad.* Gay, *Beggar's Opera.* Oliver Goldsmith born. Died 1774.	1728 First newspaper in Maryland estab. Death of Cotton Mather.
1729 Swift, *A Modest Proposal.* Death of Steele. Edmund Burke born. Died 1797.	1729 Byrd, *History of the Dividing Line* (*w*). Death of Edward Taylor.

1730

1730 Methodist Society at Oxford. Tindal, *Christianity as Old as the Creation.*	1730 Seccomb, *Father Abbey's Will.* Printing press set up in Charleston, S. C.
1731 *Gentleman's Magazine* est. Lillo, *The London Merchant.* Death of Defoe. William Cowper born. Died 1800.	
	1732–1757 Franklin, *Poor Richard's Almanac.*
1732 Covent Garden Theatre built.	1732 Byles, *Sermon on the Vileness of the Body.*
1733 Pope, *Essay on Man.* Theobald's edition of Shakespeare.	1733 William Byrd, *Journal of Journey to the Land of Eden* (North Carolina) (*w*). Georgia settled by Oglethorpe. J. P. Zenger begins publication of *New York Weekly Journal.*
	1734 Edwards conducts his first great revival meetings at Northampton.
1735 Pope, *Epistle to Dr. Arbuthnot.*	1735 John and Charles Wesley visit America.

ENGLISH		AMERICAN	
			Zenger found not guilty in libel suit over *Journal;* first important "freedom of the press" suit.
1736	Joseph Butler, *The Analogy of Religion.*	1736	First newspaper in Virginia.
1737–1742	Shenstone, *Schoolmistress.*		
1737	Edward Gibbon born. Died 1794.		
	Theatre Licensing Act.		
1738	Johnson, *London.*	1738	Whitefield's first preaching tour in America.
	Wesley, *Psalms and Hymns.*		
	Bolingbroke, *Letters on the Study of History.*		

1740

ENGLISH		AMERICAN	
		1740–1745	The "Great Awakening" (religious revival).
1740	Cibber, *Apology for the Life of Colley Cibber.*		
	Richardson, *Pamela.*		
		1741	Edwards, *Sinners in the Hands of An Angry God.*
1742	Fielding, *Joseph Andrews.*		
	Young, *Night Thoughts.*		
1742–44	Roger North, *Lives of the Norths.*		
1743	Blair, *The Grave.*	1743	Thomas Jefferson born. Died 1826.
1744	Joseph Warton, *The Enthusiast.*		
	Dr. Johnson, *Life of Richard Savage.*		
	Death of Pope.		
1745	Death of Swift.		
	Jacobite Rebellion.		
1747	Collins, *Odes.*	1747	Stith, *First Discovery and Settlement of Virginia.*

ENGLISH	AMERICAN
1748 Thomson, *Castle of Indolence.*	
Richardson, *Clarissa Harlowe.*	
Smollett, *Roderick Random.*	
Hume, *Inquiry Concerning Human Understanding.*	
1749 Fielding, *Tom Jones.*	1749 University of Pennsylvania founded.
Johnson, *The Vanity of Human Wishes.*	

1750–1798 AGE OF JOHNSON

ENGLISH	AMERICAN
1750–1752 Johnson, *The Rambler:* periodical essays.	
1751 Gray, *Elegy Written in a Country Churchyard.*	1751 Bartram, *Observations on American Plants.*
	Franklin, *Experiments and Observations in Electricity.*
1752 Gregorian Calendar adopted.	1752 Philip Freneau born. Died 1832.
1753 British Museum founded.	
1754 T. Warton, *Observations on the Fairy Queen of Spenser.*	1754 Edwards, *Freedom of the Will.*
	1755–1772 Woolman, *Journal* (*w*) (pub. 1774).
1755 Johnson, *Dictionary.*	
1756 J. Warton, *Essay on Pope.*	
Home, *Douglas.*	
1757 Gray, *The Bard* and *The Progress of Poesy.*	1757 Witherspoon, *Serious Inquiry into the Nature and Effects of the Stage.*
William Blake born. Died 1827.	
1758–1760 Johnson, The "Idler" papers.	1758 Edwards, *The Great Christian Doctrine of Original Sin Defended.*
	Death of Edwards.

1759 Johnson, *Rasselas.*

Annual Register established.
Robert Burns born. Died
1796.

1759 Winthrop, *Lectures on the Comets.*

1760

1760–1820 George III.

1760–1767 Sterne, *Tristram Shandy.*

1760–1761 Goldsmith, *Letters from a Citizen of the World.*

1760 MacPherson publishes his Ossianic *Fragments.*

1761 Churchill, *The Rosciad.*

1761 Otis, Speeches.

1762 MacPherson, *Fingal.*

Leland, *Longsword.*

1762 Printing press set up in Georgia.

1764–1770 The Chatterton poems (*w*) (pub. 1777).

1764 Walpole, *Castle of Otranto.*

Literary Club established in London (Doctor Samuel Johnson and others).

1764 Otis, *Rights of British Colonies.*

1765–1830 REVOLUTIONARY AND EARLY NATIONAL PERIOD

1765–1790 REVOLUTIONARY AGE

1765 Percy, *Reliques of Ancient English Poetry.*

Invention of steam engine by Watt.

1765 The Stamp Act.

1766–1770 Brooke, *The Fool of Quality.*

1766 Goldsmith, *The Vicar of Wakefield.*

1766 Franklin, *Examination before the House of Commons.*

Outline of Literary History

1767–1768   Dickinson, *Letters of a Farmer in Pennsylvania.*

1767   Godfrey, *Prince of Parthia* (*a*): tragedy, first American play to be acted.

1768   Kelly, *False Delicacy* (*a*).

Goldsmith, *Good-Natured Man* (*a*).

Gray, *Poems.*

Sterne, *Sentimental Journey.*

Spinning machine invented.

1769–1772   *Letters of Junius.*

1769   Samuel Adams (and others), *Appeal to the World.*

1770

1770   Goldsmith, *Deserted Village.*

Burke, *Thoughts on the Present Discontent.*

William Wordsworth born. Died 1850.

1771, 1784, and later, Franklin, *Autobiography* (*w*).

1771   Beattie, *The Minstrel,* Bk. I.

Smollet, *Expedition of Humphrey Clinker.*

Sir Walter Scott born. Died 1832.

1771   Charles Brockden Brown born. Died 1810.

1772   Samuel Taylor Coleridge born. Died 1834.

1772   Trumbull, *Progress of Dullness,* Part I.

Freneau, *Rising Glories of America.*

1773   Goldsmith, *She Stoops to Conquer.*

Steevens' edition of Shakespeare.

Lord Monboddo, *Origin and Progress of Language.*

1773   Phillis Wheatley (Peters), *Poems:* poetry written by a young slave girl.

First theater in Charleston, S. C.

Outline of Literary History

ENGLISH	AMERICAN
1774 T. Warton, *History of English Poetry*, Vol. I. Chesterfield, *Letters to His Son.* Death of Goldsmith. Robert Southey born. Died 1843.	1774 Jefferson, *Summary View of Rights of British America.* Rush, *Natural History of Medicine Among Indians of North America.* First Continental Congress.
1775–1783 War with American colonies.	1775–1783 Revolutionary War.
1775 Sheridan, *The Rivals.* Burke, *Speech on Conciliation.* Mason, *Memoirs of the Life and Writings of Thomas Gray.* Charles Lamb born. Died 1834. Walter Savage Landor born. Died 1864. Jane Austen born. Died 1817.	1775 Trumbull, *M'Fingal,* Canto I. Mrs. Warren, *The Group.* Battles of Lexington and Bunker Hill.
	1776–1783 Thomas Paine, *The Crisis.*
1776 Gibbon, *Decline and Fall of the Roman Empire.* Adam Smith, *Wealth of Nations.*	1776 Paine, *Common Sense.* Brackenridge, *Battle of Bunkers Hill.* Jefferson, *Declaration of Independence.*
1777 Sheridan, *School for Scandal* (*a*). Burke, *Letter to the Sheriffs of Bristol.*	1777 *Articles of Confederation.* Surrender of Burgoyne.
1778 Frances Burney, *Evelina.* William Hazlitt born. Died 1830.	1778 Franklin, *Ephemera.* Freneau, *American Independence.* Carver, *Travels.* Hopkinson, *Battle of the Kegs.*
1779 Johnson, *Lives of the Poets.*	1779 Odell, *The Conflagration.*

ENGLISH

AMERICAN

Rev. John Newton and William Cowper, *Olney Hymns.*

Hume, *Natural History of Religion.*

Ethan Allen, *Narrative of the Captivity.*

Paul Jones' naval victories.

1780

1781   Macklin, *Man of the World.*

1781   Surrender of Cornwallis at Yorktown.

Articles of Confederation ratified.

1782   Cowper, *Table Talk.*

1782   Crèvecoeur, *Letters from an American Farmer.*

Paine, *Letter to the Abbé Raynal.*

1783–1785   Noah Webster, *Grammatical Institute of the English Language* (speller, grammar, reader).

1783   Crabbe, *The Village.*

Blair, *Rhetoric.*

Ritson, *Collection of English Songs.*

1783   Washington Irving born. Died 1859.

England acknowledges American independence.

1784   Death of Samuel Johnson.

Leigh Hunt born. Died 1859.

1784   Franklin, *Information for Those Who Would Remove to America.*

1785   Cowper, *The Task.*

Thomas De Quincey born. Died 1859.

1785   Dwight, *Conquest of Canaan:* epic.

1786–1787   Trumbull and others, *The Anarchiad.*

1786   Burns, *Poems.*

Beckford, *Vathek.*

1786   Freneau, *Poems.*

1787–1788   Hamilton (and others), *The Federalist.*

1787   Barlow, *Vision of Columbus:* epic.

Tyler, *The Contrast (a):* first American comedy acted by professionals.

Constitutional Convention.

Outline of Literary History

ENGLISH	AMERICAN
1788 George Gordon, Lord Byron, born. Died 1824.	1788 Markoe, *The Times.* Constitution ratified by eleven states.
1789 Blake, *Songs of Innocence.* Bowles, *Fourteen Sonnets.* *French Revolution begins.	1789 William Hill Brown, *The Power of Sympathy:* first American novel. Washington, *First Inaugural.* James Fenimore Cooper born. Died 1851. Federal government established.

1790–1830 FEDERALIST AGE

1790 Burke, *Reflections on the Revolution in France.* Malone's edition of Shakespeare.	1790 Death of Franklin.
1791 Boswell, *Life of Johnson.* Erasmus Darwin, *The Botanic Garden.* Mrs. Susanna Rowson, *Charlotte Temple.*	1791 William Bartram, *Travels through North and South Carolina.* 1791–1792 Paine, *Rights of Man.* 1792–1815 Brackenridge, *Modern Chivalry.*
1792 Wollstonecraft, *Rights of Woman.* Percy Bysshe Shelley born. Died 1822.	
1793 Wordsworth, *Descriptive Sketches.* Godwin, *Political Justice.* War with France.	1793 Barlow, *Hasty Pudding (w).* Imlay, *Emigrants.*
	1794–1796 Paine, *Age of Reason.*
1794 Blake, *Songs of Experience.* Radcliffe, *Mysteries of Udolpho.* Godwin, *Caleb Williams.*	1794 Dwight, *Greenfield Hill.* Dunlap, *Leicester: "The Fatal Legacy" (a).* William Cullen Bryant born. Died 1878.

Outline of Literary History

ENGLISH	AMERICAN
1795 John Keats born. Died 1821. Thomas Carlyle born. Died 1881.	1795 Murray, *English Grammar*.
1796 Coleridge, *The Watchman*. Southey, *Joan of Arc*. Colman, *Iron Chest (a)*. Lewis, *The Monk*. Death of Burns.	1796 Washington, *Farewell Address*. Dennie, *Lay Preacher*.
1797–1798 *The Anti-Jacobin*.	
1797 Wordsworth, *The Borderers* (*w*) (pub. 1842).	1797 Tyler, *Algerian Captive*.

1798–1870 ROMANTIC PERIOD

1798–1832 AGE OF THE TRIUMPH OF ROMANTICISM

1798 Wordsworth and Coleridge, *Lyrical Ballads*. Landor, *Gebir*. Malthus, *Essay on Population*.	1798 C. B. Brown, *Alcuin: a Dialogue on The Rights of Women; Wieland*.
1799 Campbell, *Pleasures of Hope*.	1799 Brown, *Ormond; Arthur Mervyn*, Part I; *Edgar Huntly*.

1800

1800 Coleridge, trans. of Schiller's *Wallenstein*. Maria Edgeworth, *Castle Rackrent*. Wordsworth and Coleridge, *Lyrical Ballads*, 2d ed., with famous *Preface*. Thomas Babington Macaulay born. Died 1859.	1800 Weems, *Life of Washington*. Brown, *Arthur Mervyn*, Part II. Library of Congress founded.

595

Outline of Literary History

1801   Southey, *Thalaba.*

John Henry Newman born. Died 1890.

1802   Scott, *Minstrelsy of the Scottish Border.*

Edinburgh Review founded.

1803   Jane Porter, *Thaddeus of Warsaw.*

Bulwer-Lytton born. Died 1873.

1804   Benjamin Disraeli, Earl of Beaconsfield born. Died 1881.

1805   Wordsworth, *Prelude* (*w*) (pub. 1850).

Scott, *Lay of the Last Minstrel.*

1806   Elizabeth Barrett (Browning) born. Died 1861.

John Stuart Mill born. Died 1873.

1807   Byron, *Hours of Idleness.*

C. and M. Lamb, *Tales from Shakespeare.*

Abolition of slave trade.

1808   Hunt, *The Examiner.*

Scott, *Marmion.*

Lamb, *Specimens of English Dramatic Poets.*

1809   Byron, *English Bards and Scotch Reviewers.*

Charles Darwin born. Died 1882.

Alfred, Lord Tennyson born. Died 1892.

1801   Brown, *Clara Howard, Jane Talbot.*

1803   Wirt, *Letters of a British Spy.*

Louisiana Purchase.

Ralph Waldo Emerson born. Died 1882.

1804   J. Q. Adams, *Letters.*

Nathaniel Hawthorne born. Died 1864.

1806   Noah Webster, *Compendious Dictionary of the English Language.*

William Gilmore Simms born. Died 1870.

1807   Barlow, *Columbiad.*

Irving and Paulding, *Salmagundi Papers.*

John Greenleaf Whittier born. Died 1892.

Henry Wadsworth Longfellow born. Died 1882.

1808   Bryant, *The Embargo.*

1809   Irving, *Knickerbocker's History.*

Edgar Allan Poe born. Died 1849.

Oliver Wendell Holmes born. Died 1894.

ENGLISH	AMERICAN
William E. Gladstone born. Died 1898.	Abraham Lincoln born. Died 1865.
First issue of *Quarterly Review*.	

1810

	ENGLISH		AMERICAN
1810	Scott, *Lady of the Lake*.		
	Porter, *Scottish Chiefs*.		
	Crabbe, *The Borough*.		
	Southey, *Curse of Kehama*.		
1811	Austen, *Sense and Sensibility*.		
	William Makepeace Thackeray born. Died 1863.		
		1812–1815	War with England.
1812	Byron, *Childe Harold*, Cantos I, II.		
	Charles Dickens born. Died 1870.		
	Robert Browning born. Died 1889.		
1813	Byron, *Bride of Abydos*.	1813	Allston, *Sylphs of the Seasons*.
	Shelley, *Queen Mab*.		
	Austen, *Pride and Prejudice*.		
	Southey made Poet Laureate.		
1814	Scott, *Waverley:* begins vogue of historical novel.		
	Wordsworth, *Excursion*.		
1815	Scott, *Guy Mannering*.	1815	Freneau, *Poems on American Affairs*.
	Battle of Waterloo.		
	Anthony Trollope born. Died 1882.		*North American Review* established.
1816	Coleridge, *Christabel* (*w* 1797–98 and 1800).	1816	Pickering, *Vocabulary of Americanisms*.
	Byron, *Prisoner of Chillon*.		
	Shelley, *Alastor*.		
	Peacock, *Headlong Hall*.		

ENGLISH	AMERICAN
1817 Mary Shelley, *Frankenstein.*	1817 Bryant, *Thanatopsis* (*w.* 1811).
Moore, *Lalla Rookh.*	
Byron, *Manfred.*	Henry David Thoreau born. Died 1862.
Coleridge, *Biographia Literaria.*	
Keats, *Poems.*	
Blackwood's Magazine established.	
1818 Keats, *Endymion.*	1818 Payne, *Brutus* (*a.* London).
Scott, *Heart of Midlothian.*	
Shelley, *Revolt of Islam.*	
Austen, *Northanger Abbey* (*w. ca.*1800).	
1819 Byron, *Don Juan,* I, II.	1819 Halleck, *Fanny.*
Shelley, *The Cenci:* tragedy.	Drake, *The Culprit Fay* (*w*).
Mary Ann Evans ("George Eliot") born. Died 1880.	James Russell Lowell born. Died 1891.
John Ruskin born. Died 1900.	Herman Melville born. Died 1891.
Charles Kingsley born. Died 1875.	Walt Whitman born. Died 1892.

1820

1820–1830 George IV.	
1820–1823 Lamb, *Essays of Elia.*	
1820 Scott, *Ivanhoe.*	1820 Missouri Compromise.
Shelley, *Prometheus Unbound.*	Irving, *Sketch Book.*
Keats, *Lamia . . . and other Poems.*	
Maturin, *Melmoth the Wanderer.*	
Herbert Spencer born. Died 1903.	
1821 Scott, *Kenilworth.*	1821 Bryant, *Poems.*
Southey, *Vision of Judgment.*	Cooper, *The Spy.*

Outline of Literary History

Shelley, *Adonais.*

De Quincy, *Confessions of an English Opium-Eater.*

Byron, *Cain.*

Death of Keats.

ENGLISH		AMERICAN	
1822	Byron, *Vision of Judgment.* Matthew Arnold born. Died 1888. Death of Shelley.	1822	Irving, *Bracebridge Hall.*
1823	Scott, *Quentin Durward.* Carlyle, *Life of Schiller.*	1823	Cooper, *Pioneers:* first of Leatherstocking series. Francis Parkman born. Died 1893.
1824	Landor, *Imaginary Conversations,* Vol. I. Death of Byron.	1824	Irving, *Tales of a Traveler.* E. Everett, *Progress of Literature in America.*
1825	Macaulay, *Essay on Milton.* Hazlitt, *Spirit of the Age.* Thomas Henry Huxley born. Died 1895.	1825	Halleck, *Marco Bozzaris.* Italian opera introduced into America.
1826	Scott, *Woodstock.* Disraeli, *Vivian Gray.*	1826	Cooper, *Last of the Mohicans.* Payne, *Richelieu* (*a*). *The Atlantic Souvenir:* annual "gift book."
		1827	Cooper, *The Prairie.* Poe, *Tamerlane.* Simms, *Lyrical and Other Poems.* Willis, *Sketches:* poems.
1828–1830	Taylor, *Historic Survey of German Poetry.*	1827–1838	Audubon, *Birds of America.*
1828	Catholic Emancipation Act. Dante Gabriel Rossetti born. Died 1882. George Meredith born. Died 1909.	1828	Hawthorne, *Fanshawe.* Irving, *Columbus.* Webster, *An American Dictionary.* Hall, *Letters from the West.*

ENGLISH	AMERICAN
1829 Jerrold, *Black-ey'd Susan.*	1829 Irving, *Conquest of Granada.*
	Henry D. Timrod born. Died 1867.

1830–1865 ROMANTIC PERIOD

1830–1837 William IV.	
1830–1833 Lyell, *Principles of Geology.*	
1830 Tennyson, *Poems Chiefly Lyrical.*	1830 Holmes, *Old Ironsides.*
Moore, *Letters and Journals of Lord Byron.*	*Godey's Lady's Book* founded.
Scott, *Letters on Demonology and Witchcraft.*	Emily Dickinson born. Died 1886.
1831 Scott, *Castle Dangerous.*	1831 Poe, *Poems.*
Disraeli, *The Young Duke.*	Whittier, *Legends of New England.*
	Garrison founds the *Liberator.*
	New England Anti-Slavery Society founded.

1832–1870 VICTORIAN AGE

1832 Reform Bill.	1832 Poe: five tales appear in *Philadelphia Saturday Courier.*
"Lewis Carroll" (C. L. Dodgson) born. Died 1898.	
Death of Scott and *Goethe.	Bryant, *Poems* (2d ed.).
	Simms, *Atalantis.*
	Whittier, *Moll Pitcher.*
	Irving, *The Alhambra.*
	Dunlap, *History of the American Theatre.*

Outline of Literary History

1833–1834 Carlyle, *Sartor Resartus.*

1833–1841 The Oxford Movement (Tractarians).

1833 Lamb, *Last Essays of Elia.*

Browning, *Pauline.*

Newman, *Tracts for the Times* (begun).

Surtees, *Jorrock's Jaunts and Jollities.*

1833 Longfellow, *Outre-Mer* (first numbers).

Poe, *Manuscript Found in a Bottle.*

1834 Bulwer-Lytton, *Last Days of Pompeii.*

William Morris born. Died 1896.

Death of Coleridge and Lamb.

1834 Bancroft, *History of the United States,* Vol. I.

Crockett, *Autobiography.*

Southern Literary Messenger established.

1835 Browning, *Paracelsus.*

Samuel Butler born. Died 1902.

Alfred Austin born. Died 1913.

1835 Simms, *The Partisan; The Yemassee.*

Longstreet, *Georgia Scenes.*

"Mark Twain" born. Died 1910.

1836 Dickens, *Pickwick Papers.*

Marryat, *Mr. Midshipman Easy.*

1836 Emerson, *Nature.*

Holmes, *Poems.*

Irving, *Astoria.*

Bret Harte born. Died 1902.

1837–1901 Victoria.

1837 Dickens, *Oliver Twist.*

Browning, *Strafford.*

Carlyle, *French Revolution.*

Lockhart, *Life of Scott.*

Algernon Charles Swinburne born. Died 1909.

1837 Hawthorne, *Twice-Told Tales.*

Whittier, *Poems.*

Emerson, *The American Scholar.*

William Dean Howells born. Died 1920.

1838–1849 The Chartist Movement for extending the franchise.

1838 Ocean steamships connect England and United States.

1838 Morse demonstrates telegraph apparatus before President Van Buren.

ENGLISH	AMERICAN
1839 Bulwer-Lytton, *Cardinal Richelieu.* Carlyle, *Chartism.* Walter Pater born. Died 1894.	1839 Longfellow, *Hyperion; Voices of the Night.*

1840

ENGLISH	AMERICAN
1840 Browning, *Sordello.* Dickens, *Old Curiosity Shop.* Thomas Hardy born. Died 1928.	1840 Cooper, *Pathfinder.* Dana, *Two Years before the Mast.* Poe, *Tales of the Grotesque and Arabesque.* Brook Farm established *The Dial* established (discontinued 1844).
1841 Browning, *Pippa Passes.* Carlyle, *Heroes and Hero-Worship.* Macaulay, *Warren Hastings.* Boucicault, *London Assurance* (*a*).	1841 Cooper, *The Deerslayer.* Emerson, *Essays.* Longfellow, *Ballads and Other Poems.*
1842 Browning, *Dramatic Lyrics.* Tennyson, *Poems.* Dickens, *American Notes.* Macaulay, *Lays of Ancient Rome.* Newman, *Essay on Miracles.*	1842 Longfellow, *Poems on Slavery.* Griswold, *Poets and Poetry of America.* Sidney Lanier born. Died 1881.
1843 Carlyle, *Past and Present.* Dickens, *Christmas Carol.* Ruskin, *Modern Painters,* Vol. I. Hood, *Song of the Shirt.* Wordsworth made Poet Laureate. Repeal of Licensing Act of 1737: end of monopoly of the "patent" theaters in London.	1843 Prescott, *Conquest of Mexico.* Whittier, *Lays of My Home and Other Poems.* Henry James born. Died 1916.

Outline of Literary History

	ENGLISH		AMERICAN
1844	Thackeray, *Barry Lyndon.*	1844	Emerson, *Essays* (2d ser.).
	Elizabeth Barrett (Browning), *Poems.*		
	Disraeli, *Coningsby.*		
	Robert Bridges born. Died 1930.		
1845	Dickens, *Cricket on the Hearth.*	1845	Poe, *The Raven.*
	Repeal of Corn Laws.		Margaret Fuller (Ossoli), *Woman in the Nineteenth Century.*
1846	Brontë sisters, *Poems.*	1846	Hawthorne, *Mosses from an Old Manse.*
			Holmes, *Poems.*
			Melville, *Typee.*
1847–1848	Thackeray, *Vanity Fair.*		
1847	E. Brontë, *Wuthering Heights.*	1847	Emerson, *Poems.*
	C. Brontë, *Jane Eyre.*		Longfellow, *Evangeline.*
	Tennyson, *The Princess.*		Prescott, *Conquest of Peru.*
	Hunt, *Men, Women, and Books.*		Agassiz, *Introduction to Natural History.*
			Melville, *Omoo.*
1848	Mill, *Political Economy.*	1848	Lowell, *A Fable for Critics; Biglow Papers.*
	Macaulay, *History of England,* Vols. I, II.		Bartlett, *Dictionary of Americanisms.*
	Pre-Raphaelite Brotherhood founded by Rossetti.		
1849–1850	Dickens, *David Copperfield.*	1849	Whittier, *Voices of Freedom.*
1849	Ruskin, *Seven Lamps of Architecture.*		Parkman, *Oregon Trail.*
	Bulwer-Lytton, *The Caxtons.*		Thoreau, *Week on the Concord and Merrimac Rivers.*
			Melville, *Mardi.*
			Death of Poe.

1850

1850	Mrs. Browning, *Sonnets from the Portuguese.*	1850	Emerson, *Representative Men.*

	ENGLISH		AMERICAN
	Thackeray, *Pendennis*.		Hawthorne, *Scarlet Letter*.
	Tennyson, *In Memoriam*.		Irving, *Mahomet*.
	Hunt, *Autobiography; Table Talk*.		Whittier, *Songs of Labor*.
	Kingsley, *Alton Locke*.		Poe, *Poetic Principle*.
	Death of Wordsworth.		*Harper's Magazine* established.
	Tennyson made Poet Laureate.		
	Robert Louis Stevenson born. Died 1894.		
1851	Ruskin, *Stones of Venice*.	1851	Hawthorne, *House of the Seven Gables*.
	Borrow, *Lavengro*.		Melville, *Moby-Dick*.
1852	Thackeray, *Henry Esmond*.	1852	Hawthorne, *Blithedale Romance*.
	Tennyson, *Ode on the Death of the Duke of Wellington*.		Mrs. Stowe, *Uncle Tom's Cabin*.
1853	Thackeray, *English Humorists*.		
	Dickens, *Bleak House*.		
	Mrs. Gaskell, *Cranford*.		
	Kingsley, *Hypatia*.		
	Arnold, *Poems*.		
	C. Brontë, *Villette*.		
1854	Dickens, *Hard Times*.	1854	Thoreau, *Walden*.
	The Crimean War.		
1855	Browning, *Men and Women*.	1855	Whitman, *Leaves of Grass*.
	Tennyson, *Maud*.		Longfellow, *Hiawatha*.
	Thackeray, *The Newcomes*.		Irving, *Life of Washington* (begun, completed 1859).
	Trollope, *The Warden*.		Hayne, *Poems*.
	Kingsley, *Westward Ho*.		Boker, *Francesca da Rimini*.
1856	Mrs. Browning, *Aurora Leigh*.	1856	Emerson, *English Traits*.
	James Anthony Froude, *History of England*, Vols. I, II.		Motley, *Rise of the Dutch Republic*.
	Oscar Wilde born. Died 1900.		Woodrow Wilson born. Died 1924.

ENGLISH	AMERICAN
George Bernard Shaw born. Died 1950.	
1857 Trollope, *Barchester Towers.*	**1857** Child, ed., *English and Scottish Popular Ballads.*
Dickens, *Little Dorrit.*	
Joseph Conrad born. Died 1924.	*Atlantic Monthly* established.
	Dred Scott decision.
1858 "George Eliot," *Scenes of Clerical Life.*	**1858** Holmes, *Autocrat of the Breakfast Table.*
Carlyle, *Frederick II*, Vols. I, II.	Longfellow, *Courtship of Miles Standish.*
Morris, *Defence of Guinevere.*	Theodore Roosevelt born. Died 1919.
1859 Tennyson, *Idylls of the King.*	**1859** Margaret Fuller (Ossoli), *Life Without and Life Within.*
Dickens, *Tale of Two Cities.*	
Thackeray, *The Virginians.*	Joseph Jefferson, *Rip Van Winkle* (a).
Eliot, *Adam Bede.*	
Meredith, *Ordeal of Richard Feverel.*	
Fitzgerald, trans. *Rubaiyat of Omar Khayyam.*	
Darwin, *Origin of Species.*	
John Stuart Mill, *On Liberty.*	
Deaths of Macaulay, Hunt, DeQuincey.	
Alfred E. Housman born. Died 1936.	
Arthur Conan Doyle born. Died 1930.	
Francis Thompson born. Died 1907.	

1860

1860–1863 Thackeray, *Roundabout Papers.*	
1860 Eliot, *Mill on the Floss.*	**1860** Emerson, *Conduct of Life.*
"Owen Meredith," *Lucile.*	Hawthorne, *Marble Faun.*

Outline of Literary History

ENGLISH

AMERICAN

1865–1900 REALISTIC PERIOD

1866   Swinburne, *Poems and Ballads.*

Ruskin, *Crown of Wild Olive.*

Kingsley, *Hereward the Wake.*

H. G. Wells born. Died 1946.

1867   Bagehot, *English Constitution.*

Darwin, *Animals and Plants under Domestication.*

*Karl Marx, *Das Kapital.*

Arnold Bennett born. Died 1931.

John Galsworthy born. Died 1933.

1868   Collins, *The Moonstone.*

Morris, *Earthly Paradise,* Vols. I, II.

1869   Trollope, *Phineas Finn.*

Blackmore, *Lorna Doone.*

Ruskin, *Queen of the Air.*

Arnold, *Culture and Anarchy.*

Browning, *The Ring and the Book.*

Suez Canal opened.

1866   Shaw, *Josh Billings: His Sayings.*

Whittier, *Snow-Bound.*

Howells, *Venetian Life.*

Atlantic cable completed.

1867   Mark Twain, *The Celebrated Jumping Frog of Calaveras County.*

Holmes, *Guardian Angel.*

Lanier, *Tiger Lilies.*

Longfellow, translation of Dante.

Lowell, *Biglow Papers* (2d ser.).

1868   Alcott, *Little Women.*

Hawthorne, *American Notebooks.*

1869   Mark Twain, *The Innocents Abroad.*

Whittier, *Among the Hills.*

Transcontinental railroad completed.

Edwin Arlington Robinson born. Died 1935.

William Vaughn Moody born. Died 1910.

1870–1914 REALISTIC PERIOD

1870–1901 LATE VICTORIAN AGE

	ENGLISH		AMERICAN
1870	Rossetti, *Poems.* Huxley, *Lay Sermons.* Death of Dickens.	1870	Lowell, *Among My Books* (1st ser.). Harte, *Luck of Roaring Camp.* Bryant, translation of the *Iliad.*
1871	Darwin, *Descent of Man.* John Millington Synge born. Died 1909.	1871	Eggleston, *Hoosier Schoolmaster.* Whitman, *Democratic Vistas.* Howells, *Their Wedding Journey.* Bryant, translation of the *Odyssey.* Lowell, *My Study Windows.*
1872	Butler, *Erewhon.* Hardy, *Under the Greenwood Tree.* Eliot, *Middlemarch.*	1872	Mark Twain, *Roughing It.*
1873	Arnold, *Literature and Dogma.* Pater, *Studies in the Renaissance.* Newman, *The Idea of a University.*	1873	Aldrich, *Marjorie Daw.*
1874	Hardy, *Far from the Madding Crowd.* John Stuart Mill, *Autobiography.*	1874	Amy Lowell born. Died 1925.
1875	Arnold, *God and the Bible.*	1875	Howells, *A Foregone Conclusion.*
1876	Eliot, *Daniel Deronda.* Morris, *Sigurd the Volsung.* Tennyson, *Queen Mary* (a).	1876	Mark Twain, *Tom Sawyer.* Henry James, *Roderick Hudson.*

Outline of Literary History

ENGLISH	AMERICAN
Trevelyan, *Life of Macaulay*.	Lowell, *Among My Books* (2d ser.).
	Invention of telephone.
	1877 James, *The American*.
	Lanier, *Poems*.
1878 Stevenson, *An Inland Voyage*.	
Hardy, *Return of the Native*.	
1879 Meredith, *The Egoist*.	1879 Howells, *The Lady of the Aroostook*.
Spencer, *Data of Ethics*, Part I of his *Principles of Ethics*.	Cable, *Old Creole Days*.
Browning, *Dramatic Idylls* (1st ser.).	Henry George, *Progress and Poverty*.
Bagehot, *Literary Studies*.	James, *Daisy Miller*.
*Ibsen, *The Doll's House*.	

1880

ENGLISH	AMERICAN
1880 Gissing. *Workers in the Dawn*.	1880 Longfellow, *Ultima Thule*.
	Harris, *Uncle Remus*.
	Cable, *The Grandissimes*.
	Lanier, *Science of English Verse*.
1881 Stevenson, *Virginibus Puerisque*.	1881 James, *Portrait of a Lady; Washington Square*.
Rossetti, *Ballads and Sonnets*.	Cable, *Madame Delphine*.
Swinburne, *Mary Stuart*.	
Death of Carlyle.	
1882 Swinburne, *Tristram of Lyonesse*.	1882 Mark Twain, *The Prince and the Pauper*.
Stevenson, *Familiar Studies, New Arabian Nights*.	Howells, *A Modern Instance*.
Froude, *Life of Carlyle*.	Whitman, *Specimen Days*.
Deaths of Darwin, Rossetti, Trollope.	

Outline of Literary History

AMERICAN

1883 Schreiner, *The Story of an African Farm.*

Stevenson, *Treasure Island.*

1884 Tennyson, *Becket.*

Jones, *Saints and Sinners* (*a*).

1885 Hudson, *The Purple Land.*

Gilbert and Sullivan, *The Mikado* (*a*).

Meredith, *Diana of the Crossways.*

Ruskin, *Praeterita.*

Pater, *Marius the Epicurean.*

1886 Hardy, *Mayor of Casterbridge.*

Stevenson, *Doctor Jekyll and Mr. Hyde; Kidnapped.*

Tennyson, *Locksley Hall Sixty Years After.*

Kipling, *Departmental Ditties.*

1887 Lang, *Myth, Ritual, and Religion.*

1888 Kipling, *Plain Tales from the Hills.*

Ward, *Robert Elsmere.*

Death of Arnold.

1889 Browning, *Asolando.*

Stevenson, *Master of Ballantrae.*

Pater, *Appreciations.*

1883 Mark Twain, *Life on the Mississippi.*

Howe, *Story of a Country Town.*

1884 Mark Twain, *Huckleberry Finn.*

Jewett, *A Country Doctor.*

"Charles Egbert Craddock," *In the Tennessee Mountains.*

1885 Howells, *Rise of Silas Lapham.*

1886 Howells, *Indian Summer.*

James, *The Bostonians; Princess Casamassima.*

1887 Page, *In Ole Virginia.*

Freeman, *A Humble Romance.*

Lowell, *Democracy.*

1888 James, *Partial Portraits; Aspern Papers.*

Lowell, *Political Essays.*

Bellamy, *Looking Backward.*

Howard, *Shenandoah* (*a*).

1889 Mark Twain, *A Connecticut Yankee at King Arthur's Court.*

Barrie, *A Window in Thrums.*

Death of Browning.

1890

ENGLISH		AMERICAN
1890	Watson, *Wordsworth's Grave.*	1890
	Bridges, *Shorter Poems.*	

1890	Dickinson, *Poems.*	
	James, *Tragic Muse.*	
	William James, *Principles of Psychology.*	

1891   Hardy, *Tess of the D'Urber-villes.*

Doyle, *Adventures of Sherlock Holmes.*

Kipling, *The Light that Failed.*

Barrie, *The Little Minister.*

Gissing, *New Grub Street.*

Independent Theater opens: start of "Little Theater" movement in England.

1891   Garland, *Main-Travelled Roads.*

Bierce, *Tales of Soldiers and Civilians.*

Freeman, *A New England Nun.*

Howells, *Criticism and Fiction.*

International Copyright Act: protecting rights of foreign authors and publishers.

1892   Kipling, *Barrack-Room Ballads.*

Zangwill, *Children of the Ghetto.*

Wilde, *Lady Windermere's Fan*(*a*).

Death of Tennyson.

1892   Page, *The Old South.*

Howard, *Aristocracy* (*a*).

1893   Thompson, *Poems.*

Shaw, *Mrs. Warren's Profession* (*w,* acted 1902).

Pinero, *The Second Mrs. Tanqueray* (*a*).

1893   James, *The Real Thing and Other Tales.*

Crane, *Maggie: A Girl of the Streets.*

1894   Yeats, *Land of Heart's Desire.*

Moore, *Esther Waters.*

Kipling, *Jungle Book.*

Death of Stevenson.

1894   Howells, *A Traveler from Altruria.*

Hearn, *Glimpses of Unfamiliar Japan.*

Mark Twain, *Pudd'nhead Wilson.*

	ENGLISH		AMERICAN
1895	Wilde, *The Importance of Being Earnest* (*a*).	1895	Crane, *The Red Badge of Courage.*
	Wells, *The Time Machine.*		
	Conrad, *Almayer's Folly.*		
	Kipling, "The Brushwood Boy."		
1896	Housman, *A Shropshire Lad.*	1896	Robinson, *The Torrent and the Night Before.*
	Barrie, *Sentimental Tommy.*		Jewett, *Country of the Pointed Firs.*
	Hardy, *Jude the Obscure.*		Frederic, *The Damnation of Theron Ware.*
	Alfred Austin made Poet Laureate.		
1897	Conrad, *The Nigger of the Narcissus.*	1897	Allen, *The Choir Invisible.*
	Kipling, *Captains Courageous.*		James, *What Maisie Knew; Spoils of Poynton.*
1898	Hardy, *Wessex Poems.*	1898	Page, *Red Rock.*
	Shaw, *Plays Pleasant and Unpleasant.*		Dunne, *Mr. Dooley in Peace and War.*
	Wilde, *Ballad of Reading Gaol.*		
	Moore, *Evelyn Innes.*		
	Wells, *The War of the Worlds.*		
1899	Irish Literary Theatre founded in Dublin.	1899	Churchill, *Richard Carvel.*
			Crane, *War is Kind.*
			James, *The Awkward Age.*
			Markham, *The Man with the Hoe.*
			Ade, *Fables in Slang.*

1900–1930 NATURALISTIC AND SYMBOLISTIC PERIOD

1900	Conrad, *Lord Jim.*	1900	Bacheller, *Eben Holden.*
	Hudson, *Nature in Downland.*		Crane, *Wounds in the Rain.*
			Dreiser, *Sister Carrie.*

Outline of Literary History

*Edmond Rostand, *L'Aiglon.*

Death of Ruskin.

Dunne, *Mr. Dooley's Philosophy.*

London, *The Son of the Wolf.*

Tarkington, *Monsieur Beaucaire.*

1901 Barrie, *Quality Street.*

Kipling, *Kim.*

Binyon, *Odes.*

Death of Victoria.

1901 Churchill, *The Crisis.*

Moody, *Poems.*

Norris, *The Octopus.*

Washington, *Up From Slavery.*

James, *The Sacred Fount.*

1901–1914
EDWARDIAN AGE

1901–1910   Reign of Edward VII.

1902 Bennett, *Anna of the Five Towns.*

Conrad, *Youth.*

Masefield, *Saltwater Ballads.*

Yeats, *Cathleen ni Houlihan.*

Death of Samuel Butler.

1902 Glasgow, *The Battle-Ground.*

James, *The Wings of the Dove.*

Wister, *The Virginian.*

Death of Bret Harte.

1903 Conrad, *Typhoon and Other Stories.*

Butler, *The Way of All Flesh.*

Kipling, *The Five Nations.*

Shaw, *Man and Superman.*

1903 James, *The Ambassadors.*

London, *The Call of the Wild.*

Norris, *The Pit.*

1904 Barrie, *Peter Pan.*

Conrad, *Nostromo.*

Hardy, *The Dynasts* (first part).

Hudson, *Green Mansions.*

Kipling, *Traffics and Discoveries.*

Synge, *Riders to the Sea.*

1904 Churchill, *The Crossing.*

O. Henry, *Cabbages and Kings.*

James, *The Golden Bowl.*

London, *The Sea-Wolf.*

Moody, *The Fire-Bringer.*

Steffens, *The Shame of Cities.*

Outline of Literary History

	1905 Wharton, *The House of Mirth.*
1906 Conrad, *Mirror of the Sea.* Kipling, *Puck of Pook's Hill.* Watson, *Collected Poems.*	1906 O. Henry, *The Four Million.* Sinclair, *The Jungle.* Beginning of "Little Theater" movement in America.
1907 Russell (A. E.), *Deirdre.* Synge, *The Playboy of the Western World.* Yeats, *Deirdre.*	1907 Fitch, *The Truth.* Adams, *The Education of Henry Adams.* William James, *Pragmatism.*
1908 Barrie, *What Every Woman Knows.* Bennett, *The Old Wives' Tale.* Wells, *New Worlds for Old.*	1908 O. Henry, *The Voice of the City.* Herrick, *Together.*
1909 Galsworthy, *Plays.* Kipling, *Actions and Reactions.* Pinero, *Mid-Channel.* Wells, *Ann Veronica; Tono-Bungay.* Deaths of Meredith and Swinburne.	1909 London, *Martin Eden.* Moody, *The Great Divide.* Pound, *Personae.* Reese, *A Wayside Lute.* Stein, *Three Lives.*
1910 Bennett, *Clayhanger.* Lord Dunsany, *A Dreamer's Tales.* Galsworthy, *Justice.* Kipling, *Rewards and Fairies.* Noyes, *Collected Poems.*	1910 Robinson, *The Town Down the River.* Sheldon, *The Nigger.* Deaths of William Vaughn Moody, Mark Twain.
1910–1936 Reign of George V.	
1911 Beerbohm, *Zuleika Dobson.* Bennett, *Hilda Lessways.* Masefield, *The Everlasting Mercy.*	1911 Belasco, *The Return of Peter Grimm.* Dreiser, *Jennie Gerhardt.* Wharton, *Ethan Frome.*
1912 Bridges, *Poetical Works.* Galsworthy, *The Pigeon.*	1912 Dreiser, *The Financier.* *Poetry: A Magazine of Verse* founded.

Monro (ed.), *Georgian Poetry.*

Shaw, *Pygmalion.*

Stephens, *The Crock of Gold.*

Tomlinson, *The Sea and the Jungle.*

1913 D. H. Lawrence, *Sons and Lovers.*

Masefield, *Dauber.*

Death of Alfred Austin.

Robert Bridges made Poet Laureate.

Millay, *Renascence.*

1913 Cather, *O Pioneers!*

Glasgow, *Virginia.*

Lindsay, *General William Booth Enters Heaven.*

Frost, *A Boy's Will.*

1914– CONTEMPORARY PERIOD

1914 Sinclair, *The Three Sisters.*

1915 Conrad, *Victory.*

Brooke, *Collected Poems.*

Galsworthy, *The Freelands.*

Maugham, *Of Human Bondage.*

D. Richardson, *Pointed Roofs.*

1916 W. H. Davies, *Collected Poems.*

Lord Dunsany, *Tales of Wonder.*

Joyce, *Portrait of the Artist as a Young Man.*

Moore, *The Brook Kerith.*

Wells, *Mr. Britling Sees It Through.*

1914 Frost, *North of Boston.*

Lindsay, *The Congo.*

Amy Lowell, *Sword Blades and Poppy Seeds.*

Stein, *Tender Buttons.*

1915 Brooks, *America's Coming of Age.*

Cabell, *The Rivet in Grandfather's Neck.*

Masters, *Spoon River Anthology.*

1916 Frost, *Mountain Interval.*

Amy Lowell, *Men, Women, and Ghosts.*

Robinson, *Man Against the Sky.*

Sandburg, *Chicago Poems.*

Mark Twain, *The Mysterious Stranger.*

Outline of Literary History

Deaths of Henry James, Jack London.

1917 Douglas, *South Wind.*

Shaw, *Heartbreak House.*

Hodgson, *Poems.*

Barrie, *Dear Brutus.*

Swinnerton, *Nocturne.*

1917 Garland, *A Son of the Middle Border.*

Eliot, *Prufrock.*

1918 D. H. Lawrence, *New Poems.*

Hopkins, *Poems* (first published).

Strachey, *Eminent Victorians.*

1918 Cather, *My Ántonia.*

Sandburg, *Cornhuskers.*

O'Neill, *Moon of the Caribees.*

Theatre Guild established.

1919 Conrad, *The Arrow of Gold.*

Maugham, *The Moon and Sixpence.*

Hardy, *Collected Poems.*

Masefield, *Reynard the Fox.*

1919 S. Anderson, *Winesburg, Ohio.*

Cabell, *Jurgen.*

Amy Lowell, *Pictures of the Floating World.*

Pound, First *Cantos* (magazine publication).

1920 De la Mare, *Collected Poems.*

Mansfield, *Bliss.*

Wells, *The Outline of History.*

1920 Eliot, *Poems.*

Fitzgerald, *This Side of Paradise.*

Lewis, *Main Street.*

Millay, *A Few Figs from Thistles.*

O'Neill, *Beyond the Horizon; The Emperor Jones.*

Robinson, *Lancelot.*

Wharton, *The Age of Innocence.*

1921 De la Mare, *Memoirs of a Midget.*

Strachey, *Queen Victoria.*

Huxley, *Crome Yellow.*

D. H. Lawrence, *Women in Love.*

Moore, *Héloise and Abelard.*

1921 S. Anderson, *The Triumph of the Egg.*

Dos Passos, *Three Soldiers.*

O'Neill, *Anna Christie.*

Tarkington, *Alice Adams.*

Wylie, *Nets to Catch the Wind.*

Outline of Literary History

1922   Galsworthy, *The Forsyte Saga* (1906–1922).

Housman, *Last Poems*.

Joyce, *Ulysses*.

Mansfield, *The Garden Party*.

Woolf, *Jacob's Room*.

1923   Coppard, *The Black Dog*.

Hardy, *Collected Poems*.

Huxley, *Antic Hay*.

Macaulay, *Told by an Idiot*.

D. H. Lawrence, *Studies in Classic American Literature*.

Shaw, *Saint Joan*

1924   Ford, *Some Do Not*.

Forster, *A Passage to India*.

Masefield, *Sard Harker*.

Death of Conrad.

1925   Galsworthy, *Caravan*.

Woolf, *Mrs. Dalloway*.

°Gide, *The Counterfeiters*.

°Kafka, *The Trial*.

Nobel Prize awarded to Shaw.

1922   Cummings, *The Enormous Room*.

Eliot, *The Waste Land*.

Lewis, *Babbitt*.

O'Neill, *The Hairy Ape*.

1923   Cather, *A Lost Lady*.

Frost, *New Hampshire*.

Rice, *The Adding Machine*.

Santayana, *Poems*.

Stevens, *Harmonium*.

1924   Ade, *The County Chairman*.

M. Anderson (with L. Stalling), *What Price Glory*.

Hemingway, *in our time*.

Jeffers, *Tamar and Other Poems*.

Melville, *Billy Budd* (first published).

Ransom, *Chills and Fever*.

1925   Cather, *The Professor's House*.

Cummings, *XLI Poems*.

Dos Passos, *Manhattan Transfer*.

Dreiser, *An American Tragedy*.

Fitzgerald, *The Great Gatsby*.

Glasgow, *Barren Ground*.

Lewis, *Arrowsmith*.

O'Neill, *Desire Under the Elms*.

Death of Amy Lowell.

ENGLISH	AMERICAN
1926 Kipling, *Debits and Credits.*	1926 Glasgow, *The Romantic Comedians.*
D. H. Lawrence, *The Plumed Serpent.*	Hemingway, *The Sun Also Rises.*
T. E. Lawrence, *The Seven Pillars of Wisdom.*	O'Neill, *The Great God Brown.*
Stephens, *Collected Poems.*	Roberts, *The Time of Man.*
1927 Chesterton, *Collected Poems.*	1927 Cather, *Death Comes for the Archbishop.*
T. E. Lawrence, *Revolt in the Desert.*	Jeffers, *The Women at Point Sur.*
Tomlinson, *Gallions Reach.*	O'Neill, *Marco Millions.*
Woolf, *To the Lighthouse.*	Robinson, *Tristram.*
	Wilder, *The Bridge of San Luis Rey.*
1928 Huxley, *Point Counter Point.*	1928 Benét, *John Brown's Body.*
D. H. Lawrence, *Lady Chatterley's Lover.*	Frost, *West-Running Brook.*
Death of Thomas Hardy.	MacLeish, *The Hamlet of A. MacLeish.*
	Tate, *Mr. Pope and Other Poems.*
1929 Aldington, *Death of a Hero.*	1929 Connelly, *Green Pastures.*
Bridges, *The Testament of Beauty.*	Faulkner, *The Sound and the Fury.*
Galsworthy, *A Modern Comedy.*	Glasgow, *They Stooped to Folly.*
Graves, *Goodbye to All That.*	Hemingway, *A Farewell to Arms.*
Woolf, *A Room of One's Own.*	Lewis, *Dodsworth.*
	Wolfe, *Look Homeward, Angel.*

1930– PERIOD OF CONFORMITY AND CRITICISM

1930 Maugham, *Cakes and Ale.*	1930 Eliot, *Ash Wednesday.*
Coward, *Private Lives.*	M. Anderson, *Elizabeth the Queen.*
Edith Sitwell, *Collected Poems.*	H. Crane, *The Bridge.*

ENGLISH	AMERICAN
Waugh, *Vile Bodies.*	Dos Passos, *The 42nd Parallel.*
Death of Bridges.	
Masefield made Poet Laureate.	Porter, *Flowering Judas.*
	Roberts, *The Great Meadow.*
	Lewis awarded the Nobel Prize.
1931 Binyon, *Collected Poems.*	**1931** Buck, *The Good Earth.*
Galsworthy, *Maid in Waiting.*	Cather, *Shadows on the Rock.*
D. H. Lawrence, *The Man Who Died.*	Faulkner, *Sanctuary.*
Woolf, *The Waves.*	O'Neill, *Mourning Becomes Electra.*
1932 Auden, *The Orators.*	**1932** Caldwell, *Tobacco Road.*
Huxley, *Brave New World.*	Farrell, *Young Lonigan.*
Masefield, *Tale of Troy.*	Faulkner, *Light in August.*
Shaw, *Pen Portraits.*	Dos Passos, *1919.*
Nobel Prize awarded Galsworthy.	Glasgow, *The Sheltered Life.*
	Jeffers, *Thurso's Landing.*
	MacLeish, *Conquistador.*
1933 Auden, *Dance of Death.*	**1933** Caldwell, *God's Little Acre.*
Spender, *Poems.*	Cozzens, *The Last Adam.*
Woolf, *Flush, a Biography.*	MacLeish, *Frescoes for Mr. Rockefeller's City.*
Yeats, *Collected Poems.*	Stein, *The Autobiography of Alice B. Toklas.*
1934 Graves, *I, Claudius.*	**1934** Farrell, *The Young Manhood of Studs Lonigan.*
Swinnerton, *Elizabeth.*	
Waugh, *A Handful of Dust.*	Fitzgerald, *Tender is the Night.*
	Millay, *Wine from These Grapes.*
	O'Hara, *Appointment in Samarra.*
1935 C. D. Lewis, *A Time to Dance.*	**1935** M. Anderson, *Winterset.*
MacNeice, *Poems.*	Eliot, *Murder in the Cathedral.*

·

Spender, *The Destructive Element.*

Farrell, *Judgment Day* (completes the "Studs Lonigan Trilogy").

Steinbeck, *Tortilla Flat.*

Stevens, *Ideas of Order.*

Wolfe, *Of Time and the River.*

1936 Auden, *Look, Stranger.*

Housman, *More Poems.*

Huxley, *Eyeless in Gaza.*

Thomas, *25 Poems.*

Edward VIII, 1936.

George VI, 1936–1952.

1936 Frost, *A Further Range.*

Faulkner, *Absalom, Absalom!*

Cozzens, *Men and Brethren.*

Dos Passos, *The Big Money* (completes the "U.S.A. Trilogy").

Mitchell, *Gone with the Wind.*

Sandburg, *The People, Yes.*

O'Neill awarded the Nobel Prize.

1937 Maugham, *Theatre.*

Woolf, *The Years.*

1937 Hemingway, *To Have and Have Not.*

Marquand, *The Late George Apley.*

Millay, *Conversations at Midnight.*

Steinbeck, *Of Mice and Men; The Red Pony.*

Stevens, *The Man with the Blue Guitar.*

1938 Graves, *Collected Poems 1914–1926.*

Hughes, *In Hazard.*

Richardson, *Pilgrimage* (16 novel sequence completed).

C. D. Lewis, *Overtures to Death.*

1938 Hemingway, *The Fifth Column and the First Forty-Nine Stories.*

Faulkner, *The Unvanquished.*

Sherwood, *Abe Lincoln in Illinois.*

Wilder, *Our Town.*

Pearl Buck awarded the Nobel Prize.

Death of Wolfe.

Outline of Literary History

1939 Joyce, *Finnegans Wake.*

C. D. Lewis, *A Hope for Poetry.*

Thomas, *The World I Breathe.*

Death of Yeats.

1940 Auden, *Selected Poems.*

Snow, *Strangers and Brothers* (begun; completed in 11 novels; 1970).

Yeats, *Last Poems and Plays.*

1941 Barker, *Selected Poems.*

Cary, *Herself Surprised.*

De la Mare, *Bells and Grass.*

Huxley, *Grey Eminence.*

Spender, *Ruins and Visions.*

Deaths of Joyce, Virginia Woolf, Walpole.

1942 Cary, *To Be a Pilgrim.*

Coward, *Blithe Spirit.*

Waugh, *Put Out More Flags.*

1943 Coward, *This Happy Breed.*

H. Green, *Caught.*

1944 Barker, *Eros in Dogma.*

1939 Taylor, *Poetical Works* (first published).

Marquand, *Wickford Point.*

Porter, *Pale Horse, Pale Rider.*

Steinbeck, *The Grapes of Wrath.*

Wolfe, *The Web and the Rock.*

1940 Cozzens, *Ask Me Tomorrow.*

Faulkner, *The Hamlet.*

Hemingway, *For Whom the Bell Tolls.*

Pound, *Cantos.*

Wolfe, *You Can't Go Home Again.*

Wright, *Native Son.*

1941 Fitzgerald, *The Last Tycoon.*

Glasgow, *In This Our Life.*

Jeffers, *Be Angry at the Sun.*

Marquand, *H. M. Pulham, Esquire.*

Welty, *A Curtain of Green.*

1942 Aiken, *Brownstone Eclogues.*

Cozzens, *The Just and the Unjust.*

Faulkner, *Go Down, Moses.*

Jarrell, *Blood for a Stranger.*

Wilder, *Skin of Our Teeth.*

1943 Benét, *Western Star.*

Dos Passos, *Number One.*

Eliot, *Four Quartets.*

Warren, *At Heaven's Gate; Selected Poems.*

1944 Hersey, *A Bell for Adano.*

ENGLISH	AMERICAN
Cary, *The Horse's Mouth*.	R. Lowell, *Land of Unlikeness*.
Connolly, *The Unquiet Grave*.	Porter, *The Leaning Tower*.
Huxley, *Time Must Have a Stop*.	Shapiro, *V-Letter*.
1945 Connolly, *The Condemned Playground*.	**1945** Frost, *A Masque of Reason*.
H. Green, *Loving*.	Jarrell, *Little Friend, Little Friend*.
Isherwood, *Prater Violet*.	Ransom, *Selected Poems*.
C. D. Lewis, *Short Is The Time*.	T. Williams, *The Glass Menagerie*.
Waugh, *Brideshead Revisited*.	Wright, *Black Boy*.
1946 H. Green, *Back*.	**1946** Dreiser, *The Bulwark*.
Orwell, *Animal Farm*.	Jeffers, *Medea*.
Spender, *European Witness*.	O'Neill, *The Iceman Cometh*.
Thomas, *Deaths and Entrances*.	Warren, *All the King's Men*.
	Welty, *Delta Wedding*.
	W. C. Williams, *Paterson, I*.
1947 Auden, *The Age of Anxiety*.	**1947** Dreiser, *The Stoic*.
Barker, *Love Poems*.	Frost, *A Masque of Mercy*.
Spender, *Poems of Dedication*.	Stevens, *Transport to Summer*.
	T. Williams, *A Streetcar Named Desire*.
1948 Fry, *The Lady's Not for Burning*.	**1948** Cozzens, *Guard of Honor*.
H. Green, *Concluding*.	Faulkner, *Intruder in the Dust*.
G. Greene, *The Heart of the Matter*.	Jarrell, *Losses*.
Huxley, *Ape and Essence*.	Jeffers, *The Double Axe*.
Waugh, *The Loved One*.	Mailer, *The Naked and the Dead*.
	Pound, *Pisan Cantos*.
1949 Cary, *A Fearful Joy*.	**1949** Dos Passos, *The Grand Design* (completes "District of Columbia Trilogy").
Orwell, *Nineteen Eighty-Four*.	

Outline of Literary History

Spender, *The Edge of Being.*

Faulkner, *Knight's Gambit.*

Marquand, *Point of No Return.*

Miller, *Death of a Salesman.*

Welty, *The Golden Apples.*

1950 Auden, *The Enchafèd Flood.*

Barker, *The Dead Seagull.*

De la Mare, *Inward Companion.*

H. Green, *Nothing.*

Thomas, *Twenty-six Poems.*

Death of Shaw.

1950 Cummings, *XAIPE: seventy-one poems.*

Eliot, *The Cocktail Party.*

Hemingway, *Across the River and Into the Trees.*

Stevens, *Auroras of Autumn.*

Faulkner awarded the Nobel Prize for 1949.

1951 Auden, *Nones.*

Fry, *A Sleep of Prisoners.*

G. Greene, *The End of the Affair.*

Spender, *World Within World.*

Beckett, *Molloy.*

1951 Faulkner, *Requiem for a Nun.*

Jarrell, *Seven-League Crutches.*

Jones, *From Here to Eternity.*

R. Lowell, *Mills of the Kavanaughs.*

Salinger, *Catcher in the Rye.*

Death of Sinclair Lewis.

1952 Betjeman, *First and Last Loves.*

Beckett, *Waiting for Godot.*

Cary, *Prisoner of Grace.*

H. Green, *Dying.*

Thomas, *In Country Sleep.*

Elizabeth II, 1952—.

1952 Davis, *Wings of Morning.*

Hemingway, *The Old Man and the Sea.*

Steinbeck, *East of Eden.*

1953 Cary, *Except the Lord.*

Waugh, *Love Among the Ruins.*

Churchill awarded the Nobel Prize.

1953 Roethke, *The Waking.*

Warren, *Brother to Dragons.*

T. Williams, *Camino Real.*

Death of O'Neill.

1954 Barker, *A Vision of Beasts and Gods.*

Betjeman, *A Few Late Chrysanthemums.*

1954 Eliot, *The Confidential Clerk.*

Faulkner, *A Fable.*

Outline of Literary History

MacNeice, *Autumn Sequel.*

Thomas, *Under Milk Wood.*

Amis, *Lucky Jim.*

Glasgow, *The Woman Within.*

Jeffers, *Hungerfield and Other Poems.*

Hemingway awarded the Nobel Prize.

1955 Auden, *The Shield of Achilles.*

Cary, *Not Honour More.*

Thomas, *Adventures in the Skin Trade.*

1955 E. Bishop, *North and South —A Cold Spring.*

Marquand, *Sincerely, Willis Wayde.*

T. Williams, *Cat on a Hot Tin Roof.*

Death of Wallace Stevens.

1956 O'Casey, *Mirror in My House.*

Osborne, *Look Back in Anger.*

1956 Moore, *Like a Bulwark.*

O'Neill, *A Long Day's Journey into Night.*

Pound, *Section: Rock Drill.*

Wolfe, *Letters.*

Wilbur, *Things of This World.*

1957 Edith Sitwell, *Collected Poems.*

Hartley, *The Hireling.*

Joyce, *Letters.*

Osborne, *The Entertainer.*

Waugh, *The Ordeal of Gilbert Pinford.*

1957 Agee, *A Death in the Family.*

Cozzens, *By Love Possessed.*

Faulkner, *The Town.*

O'Neill, *A Touch of the Poet.*

Warren, *Promises.*

1958 Beckett, *Endgame.*

C. D. Lewis, *Pegasus and Other Poems.*

White, *The Once and Future King.*

1958 Cummings, *95 Poems.*

MacLeish, *J. B.*

Marquand, *Women and Thomas Harrow.*

Pound, *Pavannes and Divagations.*

W. T. Scott, *The Dark Sister.*

1959 Cary, *The Captive and the Free.*

Golding, *Free Fall.*

1959 Eliot, *The Elder Statesman.*

Faulkner, *The Mansion.*

R. Lowell, *Life Studies.*

Outline of Literary History

ENGLISH	AMERICAN
Sacheverell Sitwell, *Journey to the Ends of Time*, Vol. I.	Snodgrass, *Heart's Needle*.

1960	Durrell, *Alexandria Quartet* (completed). Powell, *Casanova's Chinese Restaurant*. Redgrove, *The Collector*.	1960	Hellman, *Toys in the Attic*. Jarrell, *The Woman at the Washington Zoo*. Pound, *Thrones*. O'Connor, *The Violent Bear It Away*.
1961	Hughes, *The Fox in the Attic*. MacNeice, *Solstices*. Murdock, *A Severed Head*. Osborne, *Luther*. Wain, *Weep Before God*.	1961	Dos Passos, *Midcentury*. Heller, *Catch-22*. Salinger, *Franny and Zooey*. Steinbeck, *The Winter of Our Discontent*. Wilbur, *Advice to a Prophet*. Death of Hemingway.
1962	Graves, *New Poems 1962*. C. D. Lewis, *The Gate*. Powell, *The Kindly Ones*. Edith Sitwell, *The Outcasts*. Ustinov, *Photo Finish*.	1962	Albee, *Who's Afraid of Virginia Woolf?* Baldwin, *Another Country*. Faulkner, *The Reivers*. Frost, *In the Clearing*. Porter, *Ship of Fools*. T. Williams, *The Night of the Iguana*. Deaths of Cummings, Faulkner, Jeffers. Steinbeck awarded the Nobel Prize.
1963	Fowles, *The Collector*. G. Greene, *A Sense of Reality*. MacBeth, *The Broken Places*.	1963	Cummings, *73 Poems*. Jeffers, *The Beginning and the End*. Salinger, *Raise High the Roof Beam, Carpenters*. W. C. Williams, *Pictures from Brueghel*. Deaths of Frost, Roethke, W. C. Williams.
1964	Larkin, *The Whitsun Weddings*.	1964	Bellow, *Herzog*.

Outline of Literary History

Outline of Literary History

APPENDICES

National Book Awards:
Fiction, Poetry, Arts and Letters

Nobel Prizes for Literature

Pulitzer Prizes:
Fiction, Poetry, and Drama

NATIONAL BOOK AWARDS

1950

Fiction	Nelson Algren, for *The Man With the Golden Arm*
Poetry	William Carlos Williams, for *Paterson*
Nonfiction	Ralph L. Rusk, for *The Life of Ralph Waldo Emerson*

1951

Fiction	William Faulkner, for *The Collected Stories of William Faulkner*
Poetry	Wallace Stevens, for *The Auroras of Autumn*
Nonfiction	Newton Arvin, for *Herman Melville*

1952

Fiction	James Jones, for *From Here to Eternity*
Poetry	Marianne Moore, for *Collected Poems*
Nonfiction	Rachel L. Carson, for *The Sea Around Us*

1953

Fiction	Ralph Ellison, for *Invisible Man*
Poetry	Archibald MacLeish, for *Collected Poems: 1917–1952*
Nonfiction	Bernard De Voto, for *The Course of Empire*

1954

Fiction	Saul Bellow, for *The Adventures of Augie March*
Poetry	Conrad Aiken, for *Collected Poems*
Nonfiction	Bruce Catton, for *A Stillness at Appomattox*

National Book Awards

1955

Fiction	William Faulkner, for *A Fable*
Poetry	Wallace Stevens, for *Collected Poems*
	Special citation to E. E. Cummings, for *Poems 1923–1954*
Nonfiction	Joseph Wood Krutch, for *The Measure of Man*

1956

Fiction	John O'Hara, for *Ten North Frederick*
Poetry	W. H. Auden, for *The Shield of Achilles*
Nonfiction	Herbert Kubly, for *American in Italy*

1957

Fiction	Wright Morris, for *The Field of Vision*
Poetry	Richard Wilbur, for *Things of This World*
Nonfiction	George F. Kennan, for *Russia Leaves the War*

1958

Fiction	John Cheever, for *The Wapshot Chronicle*
Poetry	Robert Penn Warren, for *Promises: Poems 1954–1956*
Nonfiction	Catherine Drinker Bowen, for *The Lion and the Throne*

1959

Fiction	Bernard Malamud, for *The Magic Barrel*
Poetry	Theodore Roethke, for *Words for the Wind*
Nonfiction	J. Christopher Herold, for *Mistress to an Age*

1960

Fiction	Philip Roth, for *Goodbye, Columbus*

National Book Awards

Poetry	Robert Lowell, for *Life Studies*
Nonfiction	Richard Ellmann, for *James Joyce*

1961

Fiction	Conrad Richter, for *The Waters of Kronos*
Poetry	Randall Jarrell, for *The Woman at the Washington Zoo*
Nonfiction	William L. Shirer, for *The Rise and Fall of the Third Reich*

1962

Fiction	Walker Percy, for *The Moviegoer*
Poetry	Alan Dugan, for *Poems*
Nonfiction	Lewis Mumford, for *The City in History*

1963

Fiction	J. F. Powers, for *Morte D'Urban*
Poetry	William Edgar Stafford, for *Travelling Through the Dark*
Nonfiction	Leon Edel, for *Henry James: The Conquest of London* and *Henry James: The Middle Years*.

1964

Fiction	John Updike, for *The Centaur*
Poetry	John Crowe Ransom, for *Selected Poems*
Arts & Letters	Aileen Ward, for *John Keats: The Making of a Poet*

1965

Fiction	Saul Bellow, for *Herzog*
Poetry	Theodore Roethke (posthumously), for *The Far Field*

Arts & Letters Eleanor Clark, for *The Oysters of Locmariaquer*

1966

Fiction Katherine Anne Porter, for *The Collected Stories of Katherine Anne Porter*

Poetry James Dickey, for *Buckdancer's Choice*

Arts & Letters Janet Flanner (Genêt), for *Paris Journal of 1944–1965*

1967

Fiction Bernard Malamud, for *The Fixer*

Poetry James Merrill, for *Nights and Days*

Arts & Letters Justin Kaplan, for *Mr. Clemens and Mark Twain*

1968

Fiction Thornton Wilder, for *The Eighth Day*

Poetry Robert Bly, for *The Light Around the Body*

Arts & Letters William Troy, for *Selected Essays*

1969

Fiction Jerzy Kosinski, for *Steps*

Poetry John Berryman, for *His Toy, His Dream, His Rest*

Arts & Letters Norman Mailer, for *Armies of the Night*

1970

Fiction Joyce Carol Oates, for *Them*

Poetry Elizabeth Bishop, for *The Complete Poems*

Arts & Letters Lillian Hellman, for *An Unfinished Woman*

1971

Fiction	Saul Bellow, for *Mr. Sammler's Planet*
Poetry	Mona Van Duyn, for *To See, To Take*
Arts & Letters	Francis Steegmuller, for *Cocteau*

1972

Fiction	Flannery O'Connor, for *The Complete Stories*
Poetry	Howard Moss, for *Selected Poems* Frank O'Hare, for *Collected Poems*
Arts & Letters	Charles Rosen, for *The Classical Style*

NOBEL PRIZE FOR LITERATURE

1901	René F. A. Sully-Prudhomme (1839–1907), French
1902	Theodor Mommsen (1817–1903), German
1903	Björnstjerne Björnson (1832–1910), Norwegian
1904	Frédéric Mistral (1830–1914), French
	José Echegaray (1832–1916), Spanish
1905	Henryk Sienkiewicz (1846–1916), Polish
1906	Giosuè Carducci (1835–1907), Italian
1907	Rudyard Kipling (1856–1936), British
1908	Rudolf C. Eucken (1846–1926), German
1909	Selma Lagerlöf (1858–1940), Swedish
1910	Paul J. L. Heyse (1830–1914), German
1911	Maurice Maeterlinck (1862–1949), Belgian
1912	Gerhart Hauptmann (1862–1946), German
1913	Rabindranath Tagore (1861–1941), Indian
1914	No award
1915	Romain Rolland (1866–1944), French
1916	Verner von Heidenstam (1859–1940), Swedish
1917	Karl A. Gjellerup (1857–1919), Danish
	Henrik Pontoppidan (1857–1943), Danish
1918	No award
1919	Carl F. G. Spitteler (1845–1924), Swiss
1920	Knut Hamsun (1859–1952), Norwegian
1921	Anatole France (1844–1924), French
1922	Jacinto Benavente y Martinez (1866–1954), Spanish
1923	William Butler Yeats (1865–1939), Irish
1924	Ladislaus S. Reymont (c. 1867–1925), Polish
1925	George Bernard Shaw (1856–1950), British (b. Ireland)
1926	Grazia Deledda (1875–1936), Italian

Nobel Prize for Literature

1927   Henri Bergson (1859–1941), French

1928   Sigrid Undset (1882–1949), Norwegian (*b.* Denmark)

1929   Thomas Mann (1875–1955), German

1930   Sinclair Lewis (1885–1951), American

1931   Erik A. Karlfeldt (1864–1931), Swedish (awarded posthumously)

1932   John Galsworthy (1867–1933), English

1933   Ivan A. Bunin (1870–1953), French (*b.* Russia)

1934   Luigi Pirandello (1867–1936), Italian

1935   No award

1936   Eugene O'Neill (1888–1953), American

1937   Roger Martin du Gard (1881–1958), French

1938   Pearl S. Buck (1892–   ), American

1939   Frans E. Sillanpää (1888–1964), Finnish

1940   No award

1941   No award

1942   No award

1943   No award

1944   Johannes V. Jensen (1873–1950), Danish

1945   Gabriela Mistral (1889–1957), Chilean

1946   Hermann Hesse (1877–1962), Swiss (*b.* Germany)

1947   André Gide (1869–1951), French

1948   T. S. Eliot (1888–1965), British (*b.* United States)

1949   William Faulkner (1897–1962), American

1950   Bertrand A. W. Russell (1872–1970), British

1951   Pär F. Lagerkvist (1891–   ), Swedish

1952   François Mauriac (1885–   ), French

1953   Sir Winston Churchill (1874–1965), British

1954   Ernest Hemingway (1899–1961), American

1955   Halldór K. Laxness (1902–   ), Icelandic

Nobel Prize for Literature

1956	Juan Ramón Jiménez (1881–1958), Spanish
1957	Albert Camus (1913–1960), French
1958	Boris L. Pasternak (1890–1960), Russian (prize declined)
1959	Salvatore Quasimodo (1901–1968), Italian
1960	Saint-John Perse (1887–), French
1961	Ivo Andríc (1892–), Yugoslav
1962	John Steinbeck (1902–1968), American
1963	Giorgos Seferis (1900–), Greek
1964	Jean-Paul Sartre (1905–), French (award declined)
1965	Mikhail A. Sholokov (1905–), Russian
1966	Samuel J. Agnon (1888–), Israeli (*b*. Poland)
	Nelly Sachs (1891–), Swedish (*b*. Germany)
1967	Miguel Angel Asturias (1899–), Guatemalan
1968	Yasunari Kawabata (1899–), Japanese
1969	Samuel Beckett (1906–), Anglo-French (*b*. Ireland)
1970	Alexander I. Solzhenitsyn (1919–), Russian
1971	Pablo Neruda (1904–), Chilean
1972	Heinrich Böll (1917–), German

PULITZER PRIZES FOR FICTION

1917   No award

1918   *His Family*, by Ernest Poole

1919   *The Magnificent Ambersons*, by Booth Tarkington

1920   No award

1921   *The Age of Innocence*, by Edith Wharton

1922   *Alice Adams*, by Booth Tarkington

1923   *One of Ours*, by Willa Cather

1924   *The Able McLaughlins*, by Margaret Wilson

1925   *So Big*, by Edna Ferber

1926   *Arrowsmith*, by Sinclair Lewis (prize declined)

1927   *Early Autumn*, by Louis Bromfield

1928   *The Bridge of San Luis Rey*, by Thornton Wilder

1929   *Scarlet Sister Mary*, by Julia Peterkin

1930   *Laughing Boy*, by Oliver LaFarge

1931   *Years of Grace*, by Margaret Ayer Barnes

1932   *The Good Earth*, by Pearl S. Buck

1933   *The Store*, by T. S. Stribling

1934   *Lamb in His Bosom*, by Caroline Miller

1935   *Now in November*, by Josephine Winslow Johnson

1936   *Honey in the Horn*, by Harold L. Davis

1937   *Gone With the Wind*, by Margaret Mitchell

1938   *The Late George Apley*, by John Phillips Marquand

1939   *The Yearling*, by Marjorie Kinnan Rawlings

1940   *The Grapes of Wrath*, by John Steinbeck

1941   No award

1942   *In This Our Life*, by Ellen Glasgow

1943   *Dragon's Teeth*, by Upton Sinclair

1944   *Journey in the Dark*, by Martin Flavin

Pulitzer Prizes for Fiction

1945	*A Bell for Adano,* by John Hersey
1946	No award
1947	*All the King's Men,* by Robert Penn Warren
1948	*Tales of the South Pacific,* by James A. Michener
1949	*Guard of Honor,* by James Gould Cozzens
1950	*The Way West,* by A. B. Guthrie, Jr.
1951	*The Town,* by Conrad Richter
1952	*The Caine Mutiny,* by Herman Wouk
1953	*The Old Man and the Sea,* by Ernest Hemingway
1954	No award
1955	*A Fable,* by William Faulkner
1956	*Andersonville,* by MacKinlay Kantor
1957	No award
1958	*A Death in the Family,* by James Agee
1959	*The Travels of Jaimie McPheeters,* by Robert Lewis Taylor
1960	*Advise and Consent,* by Allen Drury
1961	*To Kill a Mockingbird,* by Harper Lee
1962	*The Edge of Sadness,* by Edwin O'Connor
1963	*The Reivers,* by William Faulkner
1964	No award
1965	*The Keepers of the House,* by Shirley Ann Grau
1966	*Collected Short Stories,* by Katherine Anne Porter
1967	*The Fixer,* by Bernard Malamud
1968	*The Confessions of Nat Turner,* by William Styron
1969	*House Made of Dawn,* by M. Scott Momaday
1970	*Collected Stories,* by Jean Stafford
1971	No award
1972	*Angle of Repose,* by Wallace Stegner

PULITZER PRIZES FOR POETRY

Previous to the establishment of this prize in 1922, the following awards had been made from gifts provided by the Poetry Society:

1918   *Love Song*, by Sara Teasdale

1919   *Old Road to Paradise*, by Margaret Widdemer

1919   *Corn Huskers*, by Carl Sandburg

The Pulitzer Poetry Prizes follow:

1922   *Collected Poems*, by Edwin Arlington Robinson

1923   *The Ballad of the Harp-Weaver; A Few Figs From Thistles;* eight sonnets in *American Poetry, 1922, A Miscellany;* by Edna St. Vincent Millay

1924   *New Hampshire: A Poem With Notes and Grace Notes*, by Robert Frost

1925   *The Man Who Died Twice*, by Edwin Arlington Robinson

1926   *What's O'Clock*, by Amy Lowell

1927   *Fiddler's Farewell*, by Leonora Speyer

1928   *Tristram*, by Edwin Arlington Robinson

1929   *John Brown's Body*, by Stephen Vincent Benét

1930   *Selected Poems*, by Conrad Aiken

1931   *Collected Poems*, by Robert Frost

1932   *The Flowering Stone*, by George Dillon

1933   *Conquistador*, by Archibald MacLeish

1934   *Collected Verse*, by Robert Hillyer

1935   *Bright Ambush*, by Audrey Wurdemann

1936   *Strange Holiness*, by Robert P. Tristram Coffin

1937   *A Further Range*, by Robert Frost

1938   *Cold Morning Sky*, by Marya Zaturenska

1939   *Selected Poems*, by John Gould Fletcher

1940   *Collected Poems*, by Mark Van Doren

Pulitzer Prizes for Poetry

1941	*Sunderland Capture*, by Leonard Bacon
1942	*The Dust Which Is God*, by William Rose Benét
1943	*A Witness Tree*, by Robert Frost
1944	*Western Star*, by Stephen Vincent Benét
1945	*V-Letter and Other Poems*, by Karl Shapiro
1946	No award
1947	*Lord Weary's Castle*, by Robert Lowell
1948	*The Age of Anxiety*, by W. H. Auden
1949	*Terror and Decorum*, by Peter Viereck
1950	*Annie Allen*, by Gwendolyn Brooks
1951	*Complete Poems*, by Carl Sandburg
1952	*Collected Poems*, by Marianne Moore
1953	*Collected Poems 1917–1952*, by Archibald MacLeish
1954	*The Waking*, by Theodore Roethke
1955	*Collected Poems*, by Wallace Stevens
1956	*Poems—North & South*, by Elizabeth Bishop
1957	*Things of This World*, by Richard Wilbur
1958	*Promises: Poems 1954–1956*, by Robert Penn Warren
1959	*Selected Poems 1928–1958*, by Stanley Kunitz
1960	*Heart's Needle*, by W. D. Snodgrass
1961	*Times Three: Selected Verse from Three Decades*, by Phyllis McGinley
1962	*Poems*, by Alan Dugan
1963	*Pictures from Brueghel*, by William Carlos Williams
1964	*At the End of the Open Road*, by Louis Simpson
1965	*77 Dream Songs*, by John Berryman
1966	*Selected Poems*, by Richard Eberhart
1967	*Live or Die*, by Anne Sexton
1968	*The Hard Hours*, by Anthony Hecht
1969	*Of Being Numerous*, by George Oppen

Pulitzer Prizes for Poetry

1970   *Untitled Subjects,* by Richard Howard

1971   *The Carrier of Ladders,* by W. S. Merwin

1972   *Collected Poems,* by James Wright

PULITZER PRIZES FOR DRAMA

1917   No award

1918   *Why Marry?*, by Jesse Lynch Williams

1919   No award

1920   *Beyond the Horizon,* by Eugene O'Neill

1921   *Miss Lulu Bett,* by Zona Gale

1922   *Anna Christie,* by Eugene O'Neill

1923   *Icebound,* by Owen Davis

1924   *Hell-Bent fer Heaven,* by Hatcher Hughes

1925   *They Knew What They Wanted,* by Sidney Howard

1926   *Craig's Wife,* by George Kelly

1927   *In Abraham's Bosom,* by Paul Green

1928   *Strange Interlude,* by Eugene O'Neill

1929   *Street Scene,* by Elmer L. Rice

1930   *The Green Pastures,* by Marc Connelly

1931   *Alison's House,* by Susan Glaspell

1932   *Of Thee I Sing,* by George S. Kaufman, Morrie Ryskind, and Ira Gershwin (with music by George Gershwin)

1933   *Both Your Houses,* by Maxwell Anderson

1934   *Men in White,* by Sidney Kingsley

1935   *The Old Maid,* by Zoë Akins

1936   *Idiot's Delight,* by Robert E. Sherwood

1937   *You Can't Take It with You,* by Moss Hart and George S. Kaufman

1938   *Our Town,* by Thornton Wilder

1939   *Abe Lincoln in Illinois,* by Robert E. Sherwood

1940   *The Time of Your Life,* by William Saroyan (declined)

1941   *There Shall Be No Night,* by Robert E. Sherwood

1942   No award

Pulitzer Prizes for Drama

1943   *The Skin of Our Teeth,* by Thornton Wilder

1944   No award

1945   *Harvey,* by Mary Chase

1946   *State of the Union,* by Russel Crouse and Howard Lindsay

1947   No award

1948   *A Streetcar Named Desire,* by Tennessee Williams

1949   *Death of a Salesman,* by Arthur Miller

1950   *South Pacific,* by Richard Rodgers, Oscar Hammerstein II, and Joshua Logan

1951   No award

1952   *The Shrike,* by Joseph Kramm

1953   *Picnic,* by William Inge

1954   *The Teahouse of the August Moon,* by John Patrick

1955   *Cat on a Hot Tin Roof,* by Tennessee Williams

1956   *The Diary of Anne Frank,* by Albert Hackett and Frances Goodrich

1957   *Long Day's Journey into Night,* by Eugene O'Neill

1958   *Look Homeward, Angel,* by Ketti Frings

1959   *J. B.,* by Archibald MacLeish

1960   *Fiorello!,* book by Jerome Weidman and George Abbott, music by Jerry Bock, and lyrics by Sheldon Harnick

1961   *All the Way Home,* by Tad Mosel

1962   *How To Succeed in Business Without Really Trying,* by Frank Loesser and Abe Burrows

1963   No award

1964   No award

1965   *The Subject Was Roses,* by Frank D. Gilroy

1966   No award

1967   *A Delicate Balance,* by Edward Albee

1968   No award

1969   *The Great White Hope,* by Howard Sackler

Pulitzer Prizes for Drama

1970   *No Place to Be Somebody,* by Charles Gordone

1971   *The Effect of Gamma Rays on Man-in-the-Moon Marigolds,* by Paul Zindel

1972   No Award